Lecture Notes in Artificial Intelligence   1137

Subseries of Lecture Notes in Computer Science
Edited by J. G. Carbonell and J. Siekmann

Lecture Notes in Computer Science

Edited by G. Goos, J. Hartmanis and J. van Leeuwen

Springer
Berlin
Heidelberg
New York
Barcelona
Budapest
Hong Kong
London
Milan
Paris
Santa Clara
Singapore
Tokyo

Günther Görz   Steffen Hölldobler (Eds.)

KI-96: Advances in Artificial Intelligence

20th Annual German Conference
on Artificial Intelligence
Dresden, Germany, September 17-19, 1996
Proceedings

 Springer

Series Editors
Jaime G. Carbonell, Carnegie Mellon University, Pittsburgh, PA, USA
Jörg Siekmann, University of Saarland, Saarbrücken, Germany

Volume Editors

Günther Görz
University of Erlangen-Nürnberg, IMMD 8 - KI (Computer Science)
Am Weichselgarten 9, D-91058 Erlangen, Germany
E-mail: goerz@informatik.uni-erlangen.de

Steffen Hölldobler
Technical University of Dresden
Institute of Artificial Intelligence and Computer Science
D-01062 Dresden, Germany
E-mail: sh@inf.tu-dresden.de

Cataloging-in-Publication Data applied for

Die Deutsche Bibliothek - CIP-Einheitsaufnahme

Advances in artificial intelligence : proceedings / KI-96, 20th
Annual German Conference on Artificial Intelligence,
Dresden, Germany, September 17 - 19, 1996 / Günther Görz ;
Steffen Hölldobler (ed.). - Berlin ; Heidelberg ; New York ;
Barcelona ; Budapest ; Hong Kong ; London ; Milan ; Paris ;
Santa Clara ; Singapore ; Tokyo : Springer, 1996
  (Lecture notes in computer science ; Vol. 1137 : Lecture notes in
  artificial intelligence)
  ISBN 3-540-61708-6
NE: Görz, Günther [Hrsg.]; KI <20, 1996, Dresden>; GT

CR Subject Classification (1991): I.2

ISBN 3-540-61708-6 Springer-Verlag Berlin Heidelberg New York

© Springer-Verlag Berlin Heidelberg 1996
Printed in Germany

Typesetting: Camera ready by author
SPIN 10513657   06/3142 – 5 4 3 2 1 0   Printed on acid-free paper

Preface

This Lecture Notes volume contains three invited contributions, 23 research papers, nine posters, and four system demonstration summaries that were accepted for presentation and publication in the scientific program of the 20th Annual German Conference on Artificial Intelligence KI-96 in Dresden.

The invited talks by Christopher Habel, Stuart Russell, and Henning Scheich consider a fundamental issue of Artificial Intelligence, *Representation*, from different perspectives — cognitive science, rational multiagent systems, and neuroscience, in order to emphasize its interdisciplinary character.

We received a large number of excellent contributions of which a considerable part had been submitted from abroad. The program committee had to be very restrictive in selecting the best papers. Although the call for papers was open for contributions from all fields of Artificial Intelligence, to our surprise most of the papers are about new developments in theorem proving, knowledge representation, and reasoning. The quality of its contributions is the primary measure for the success of a conference, and we are happy to say that our expectations were considerably exceeded. Many thanks to all authors!

We have the pleasure of thanking our colleagues of the program committee cordially for their hard and excellent work. In addition, many thanks to the many reviewers who were very helpful in completing this task successfully. Last but not least, we are very grateful to the local organizers in Dresden, to our conference secretary Mrs. Christine Harms, and to our local secretaries in Dresden and Erlangen for the excellent preparation of this conference.

In addition to the scientific program, KI-96 also offers an applications track, organized by our colleague Heinz Schwärtzel, which is documented in a separate volume, issued by the Computer Science Department of the Technical University of Dresden.

July 1996
Erlangen–Nürnberg
Dresden

Günther Görz
Steffen Hölldobler

Organization

KI-96 is organized by the FB1 KI of the Gesellschaft für Informatik e.V.

Conference Chair: Günther Görz (University Erlangen–Nbg., Germany)
Program Chair: Steffen Hölldobler (TU Dresden, Germany)
Application Chair: Heinz G. Schwärtzel (FAST e.V.,München, Germany)
Workshop Organization: Michael Thielscher (ICSI, Berkeley, Germany)
Program Committee:

>Hassan Aït-Kaci (Simon Fraser University, Vancouver, Canada)
>Franz Baader (RWTH Aachen, Germany)
>Gerhard Barth (Daimler Benz, Ulm, Germany)
>Peter Bosch (IBM Heidelberg, Germany)
>Georg Dorffner (University of Vienna, Austria)
>Randy Göbel (University of Alberta, Canada)
>Andreas Günter (University of Bremen, Germany)
>Barbara Hemforth (University of Freiburg, Germany)
>Heinrich Niemann (University Erlangen-Nürnberg, Germany)
>Michael Rusinowitch (INRIA, Nancy, France)
>Kerstin Schill (LMU München, Germany)
>Michael Thielscher (ICSI, Berkeley, USA)
>Sebastian Thrun (CMU, Pittsburgh, USA)
>Ipke Wachsmuth (University of Bielefeld, Germany)
>Stefan Wrobel (GMD Bonn, Germany)

Local Organization Committee:

>Sven–Erik Bornscheuer (TU Dresden, Germany),
>Yvonne Kalinke (TU Dresden, Germany),
>Stephanie Rinkel (TU Dresden, Germany),
>Eckhard Koch (TU Dresden, Germany)

Conference Secretary:

>Christine Harms (GMD Sankt Augustin, Germany)

Additional Referees

Peter Alshuth
Grigoris Antoniou
Alessandro Armando
Thomas Augustin
Chitta Baral
Peter Baumgartner
Gérard Becher
Chris Beck
Michael Beetz
Siegfried Bell
Francoise Bellegarde
Ralph Bergmann
Susanne Biundo
Uta Bohnebeck
Toni Bollinger
Maria Paola Bonacina
Sven-Erik Bornscheuer
Thierry Boy De La Tour
Gerd Brewka
Peter Brockhausen
Norbert Bröker
Hans-Jürgen Bürckert
Wolfram Burgard
Ricardo Caferra
Jürgen Denzler
Jürgen Dix
Saso Dzeroski
Uwe Egly
Andreas Eisenkolb
Werner Emde
Luis Farinas del Cerro
Enrico Franconi
Bernd Freisleben
Bertram Fronhöfer
Siegfried Fuchs
Uli Furbach
Ulrich Geske
Aditya Ghose
Carsten Günther
Hans Guesgen
Helmar Gust

Reiner Hähnle
Jochen Heinsohn
Christoph Herrmann
Joachim Hertzberg
Katsumi Inoue
Manfred Jäger
Dietmar Janetzko
Bernhard Jung
Gerd Kamp
Alex Kean
Margit Kinder
Christoph Klauck
Volker Klingspor
Willi Klösgen
Thomas Kolbe
Gerhard Kraetzschmar
Franz Kurfess
Jean Lieber
Thomas Linke
Denis Lugiez
Christopher Lynch
Bernard Malfon
Jean-Yves Marion
Laura Martignon
Frank Maurer
Franz Mechsner
Stephan Mehl
Josef Meyer-Fujara
Knut Möller
Eric Monfroy
Jürgen Müller
Detlef Nauck
Abaya Nayak
Peter Neuhaus
Ilkka Niemela
Lin Padgham
Harold Paredes-Frigolett
Pavlos Peppas
Christoph Perleth
Uwe Petersohn
Stefan Posch

Katalin Prasser
Erich Prem
Joachim Quantz
Thomas Rath
Antoine Rauzy
Michael Richter
Martin Riedmiller
Claus-Rainer Rollinger
Gernot Salzer
Enno Sandner
Ulrike Sattler
Ulrich Schade
Stephanie Schäffer
Torsten Schaub
Christoph Scheepers
Josef Schneeberger
Johann Schumann
Camilla Schwind
Dietmar Seipel
Joachim Selbig
Lokendra Shastri
Alan Smaill
Bruce Spencer
Volker Sperschneider
Benno Stein
Patrick Sturt
George Tsiknis
Elisabeth Umkehrer
Laurent Vigneron
Andrei Voronkov
Toby Walsh
Thomas Waschulzik
Peter Weierich
Stefan Wermter
Dietrich Wettschereck
Emil Weydert
Andreas Zell
Chengqi Zhang
Qi Zhao

Contents

Rational Models of Normal Logic Programs*

Sven-Erik Bornscheuer

KI, Informatik, TU Dresden, 01062 Dresden

seb@inf.tu-dresden.de

Abstract. In general, the application of the meaning function $T_\mathcal{P}$ to a normal logic program $\mathcal{P}$ results in infinite expressions and, hence, is infeasible in practice. On the other hand, the iteration of $T_\mathcal{P}$ is of interest for several fields in AI. Therefore, we introduce a new representation of interpretations and adopt $T_\mathcal{P}$ to this. The resulting function always results in finite expressions of tractable length and overcomes some limitations of usual model generating systems.

1 Motivation

Model generation is of interest for several fields in AI. For example, the computation of the extensions of a default logic [7] is a generation of models, and P. N. Johnson–Laird assumes that the human way of reasoning corresponds to the generation of models [3].

Wrt. logic programming, the iteration of the meaning function $T_\mathcal{P}$ corresponding to a logic program $\mathcal{P}$ is the basic method of model generation[2]. In general, the application of the meaning function $T_\mathcal{P}$ corresponding to a normal logic program $\mathcal{P}$ results in infinite interpretations of $\mathcal{P}$ and is, hence, infeasible in practice. For this reason, model generating systems like SATCHMO [5] can be applied only to range restricted programs[3]: $T_\mathcal{P}(I)$ is finite if I is a finite interpretation and $\mathcal{P}$ is a range restricted program. As stated in [5], every program can easily be transformed into a range restricted program. But, however, $T_{\mathcal{P}'}$ does not reach a fixed point in finite time if $\mathcal{P}'$ results from such a transformation of a not range restricted program $\mathcal{P}$, even if $T_\mathcal{P}$ reaches a fixed point in finite time. Hence, model generating systems like SATCHMO can not compute complete minimal models of not range restricted programs in finite time.

We therefore introduce a new representation of interpretations, viz. so–called rational interpretations, and adopt $T_\mathcal{P}$ to this. The resulting function $S_\mathcal{P}$ always yields finite expressions of tractable length. By this, we overcome the problem mentioned above: By the iteration of $S_\mathcal{P}$ a finite representation of a complete minimal model of $\mathcal{P}$ is computed in finite time if $T_\mathcal{P}$ reaches a fixed point in finite number of steps. In the full paper [1] we introduce a distributed architecture performing a distributed computation of $S_\mathcal{P}$.

---

* This paper is an extended abstract of the work presented in [1]

[2] The reader is assumed to be familiar with the notions and notations concerning logic programs (cf. [4]).

[3] A program $\mathcal{P}$ is called *range restricted* if each variable occurring in a clause C of $\mathcal{P}$ occurs in a negative literal of C.

2 Rational Interpretations

As mentioned in the introduction we will use finite representations of interpretations. To this end, we use non–ground atoms to represent the set of all their ground instances. A function $\mathcal{G}$ is used for mapping atoms to the set of ground atoms they represent.

Definition 1. If A is an atom, then $\mathcal{G}(A)$ is the set of all ground instances of A.

For example, $\mathcal{G}(pX) = \{pa, pfa), \ldots\}$ if a is the only constant and f is the only function symbol in the considered program. Using sets of non–ground atoms interpreted in this way is sufficient for finitely representing interpretations resulting from the application of $T_{\mathcal{P}}$.[4] However, such representations may be unnecessary extensive.

Example: Consider the program $\mathcal{P}$ consisting of the clause $\neg qX \rightarrow pfX$ and the interpretation $I = \{qffa\}$. $T_{\mathcal{P}}(I)$ contains all ground instances of pX, *except* the ground atom $\{pfffa\}$, i.e.

$$T_{\mathcal{P}}(I) = \{pa, pfa, pffa\} \cup \mathcal{G}(pfffX).$$

$\square$

In general, the length of a representation of a relative complement by non–ground atoms is linear in the number of arguments of the considered atom, the depth of the terms occurring in this atom, and the number of constants and function symbols occurring in the considered program [1]. Therefore, we use a more sophisticated representation, which reflects the application of $T_{\mathcal{P}}$. We represent interpretations by *rational interpretations* $\tilde{I}$, which are are finite sets of so–called restricted atoms. A *restricted atom* $A\Sigma$ consists of an (possibly non–ground) atom A and a finite set of substitutions Σ, and represents all ground instances of the atom A *except* the ground instances of all $A\sigma$ where $\sigma \in \Sigma$.[5] The intended meaning of rational interpretations is formalized by extending the function $\mathcal{G}$:

Definition 2. Consider a rational interpretation $\tilde{I}$. Then

$$\mathcal{G}(\tilde{I}) \;=\; \bigcup_{A\Sigma \in \tilde{I}} \mathcal{G}(A\Sigma)\,, \text{ where}$$

$$\mathcal{G}(A\Sigma) \;=\; \mathcal{G}(A) \setminus \bigcup_{\sigma \in \Sigma} \mathcal{G}(A\sigma)$$

Example: Consider the program $\mathcal{P}$ consisting of the clause $\neg qX \rightarrow pfX$ and the interpretation $I = \{qffa\}$. Then

$$T_{\mathcal{P}}(I) = \mathcal{G}(\{pX\{X \setminus fffa\}\})\,.$$

$\square$

---

[4] a corresponding approach is presented in [2]
[5] the use of non–ground substitutions for representing sets of substitutions is similar to the use of *substitution trees* in [6]

Of course, there are interpretations which cannot be represented by a rational interpretation. The crucial point is, that the interpretations resulting from an application of $T_{\mathcal{P}}$ can be finitely represented. In [1] we give the following theorem:

Theorem 3. *Consider a normal logic program $\mathcal{P}$ and an interpretation I. If there is a rational interpretation $\tilde{I}_1$ such that $\mathcal{G}(\tilde{I}_1) = I$, then a rational interpretation $\tilde{I}_2$ exists such that $\mathcal{G}(\tilde{I}_2) = T_{\mathcal{P}}(I)$.*

Since every finite interpretation can be represented by a rational interpretation, this theorem yields the following corollary:

Corollary 4. *For each normal logic program $\mathcal{P}$ and $n \in \mathbb{N}$ there exists a rational interpretation $\tilde{I}$ such that $\mathcal{G}(\tilde{I}) = T_{\mathcal{P}}{}^n(\emptyset)$.*

In other words, every interpretation resulting during the generation of models of normal logic programs can be finitely represented by a rational interpretation.

3 $S_{\mathcal{P}}$

In the previous section, we introduced a finite representation of the results of $T_{\mathcal{P}}$. The remaining question is, how to compute these representations. The crucial demand on such a computation is not only to result in the wanted finite representation, but also to avoid the occurrence of infinite constructs during computation. In [1] we introduce a function $S_{\mathcal{P}}$ (and its computation) which meets these conditions. Due to the lack of space and since the definition of $S_{\mathcal{P}}$ is quite complex, we do not present this definition in this paper, but summarize the fundamental properties of $S_{\mathcal{P}}$ by the following theorem (c.f. [1]).

Theorem 5. *Consider a normal logic program $\mathcal{P}$ and a rational interpretation $\tilde{I}$. Then*

$$\mathcal{G}(S_{\mathcal{P}}(\tilde{I})) = T_{\mathcal{P}}(\mathcal{G}(\tilde{I})).$$

$S_{\mathcal{P}}(\tilde{I})$ *can be computed in finite time and by processing finite constructs, only.*

Since $\mathcal{G}(\emptyset) = \emptyset$, this theorem yields the following corollary:

Corollary 6. *For every normal logic program $\mathcal{P}$ and $n \in \mathbb{N}$,*

$$\mathcal{G}(S_{\mathcal{P}}{}^n(\emptyset)) = T_{\mathcal{P}}{}^n(\emptyset).$$

$S_{\mathcal{P}}{}^n(\emptyset)$ *can be computed in finite time and by processing finite constructs, only.*

In other words, the models[6] of every normal logic program $\mathcal{P}$ can be generated in finite time by finite computers, iff the iteration of $T_{\mathcal{P}}$ reaches a fixed point after a finite number of steps.

---

[6] i.e. rational models which represent them

4 Summary

By defining a new representation of interpretations, i.e. rational interpretations, and adapting T_P to this representation by constructing the function S_P, we enable for iterating the meaning function T_P wrt. normal logic programs by only using finite expressions of tractable length. This allows to compute finite representations of minimal models (i.e. rational models) of programs in finite time, if T_P converges to a fixed point after a finite number of steps. This is in favorable contrast to the iteration of T_P and model generating systems like SATCHMO, which can compute minimal models of range restricted programs, only. We strongly assume, that the time complexity of the computation of S_P wrt. a normal program $\mathcal{P}$ is linear in the time complexity of the computation of T_P wrt. $\mathcal{P}$ after deleting negations (if T_P can be computed). In [1] we also give a connectionist system performing a distributed computation of S_P.

Acknowledgements
The author acknowledges support from the German Research Community (DFG) within project MPS under grant no. Ho1294/3-3. Special thanks are addressed to Yvonne Kalinke for valuable discussions on a previous version of this paper.

References

1. S.-E. Bornscheuer. Distributed generation of rational models. Technical report, TUD, 1996. (to appear).
2. M Falaschi, G. Levi, M. Martelli, and C. Palamidessi. A new declarative semantics for logic languages. In *Proceedings of the International Conference and Symposium on Logic Programming*, 1988.
3. P. N. Johnson-Laird and R. M. J. Byrne. *Deduction*. Lawrence Erlbaum Associates, Hove and London (UK), 1991.
4. J. W. Lloyd. *Foundations of Logic Programming*. Springer, 1987.
5. R. Manthey and F. Bry. Satchmo: a theorem prover implemented in prolog. In *Proc. 9th Int. Conf. on Automated Deduction (CADE)*, pages 68–77, Springer, LNCS 310, 1988.
6. H. J. Ohlbach. Abstraction tree indexing for terms. In L. C. Aiello, editor, *Proceedings of the European Conference on Artificial Intelligence*, pages 479–484, 1990.
7. R. Reiter. A logic for default reasoning. *Artificial Intelligence*, 13:81 – 132, 1980.

Massively Parallel Reasoning about Actions*

Sven-Erik Bornscheuer   Torsten Seiler

KI, Informatik, TU Dresden, D–01062 Dresden (Germany)

Abstract. In [2] C. Baral and M. Gelfond present the language $\mathcal{A}_C$ for representing concurrent actions in dynamic systems, and give a sound but incomplete encoding of this language in terms of extended logic programming. Using their program, the time the computation of the transition from one situation to another takes increases quadraticly with the size of the considered domain. In this paper, we present a mapping of domain descriptions in $\mathcal{A}_C$ into neural networks of linear size. These networks take only four steps for the sound and complete computation of the transition of situations. This allows for reasoning about concurrent actions wrt. extensive real-time domains.

1   Introduction

In a lively, never resting world the concept of change is central to the representation of knowledge. An intelligent, free agent in a dynamic system acts according to its knowledge about the effects of its actions on the system he is a part of. Hence, automated reasoning about actions and their effects on the world is an important topic of Artificial Intelligence.

Since J. McCarthy and P. J. Hayes introduced their well-known *situation calculus* [18], numerous approaches to this field were presented (e.g. [1, 8, 14, 16, 9, 17, 20, 12]). Some years ago, several publications (e.g. [15, 16, 19, 21]) demanded a more methodical way of representing actions and change, since the approaches to more and more complex domains became quite unreadable. Therefore, recent work usually introduced pure semantics of action descriptions, and, additionally, translations of these semantics and descriptions to formalisms usable for automated inference, namely first order logic resp. logic programs.

While even the more expressive languages used for describing dynamic systems use more or less simple concepts for representing actions and their effects on the considered domain, their encodings make use of full first order logic resp. logic programs[2]. This disproportion leads to inadequate effort for computing the effects of actions.

As a typical example, we use the language $\mathcal{A}_C$ introduced by C. Baral and M. Gelfond. $\mathcal{A}_C$ allows the description of concurrent actions and was developed

---

* The authors were supported by the Deutsche Forschungsgemeinschaft (DFG) within project MPS under grant no. Ho 1294/3-3.

[2] Actually, various kinds of logic programs are used, e.g. *Extended Logic Programming* [8], abductive logic programs [7, 6] and *Equational Logic Programming* [24]

in [2] as an extension of the *Action Description Language* $\mathcal{A}$ [8] which was introduced in 1992 and became very popular. Both $\mathcal{A}$ and $\mathcal{A}_C$ attract by the simple, elegant, and natural way in which the effects of actions are described. The execution of actions adds or removes elements from a particular set of facts representing some situation in the world; all non-affected facts continue to hold in the resulting situation due to the common assumption of persistence. Since most complex dynamic systems include some kind of concurrency, the description of simultaneous actions is of central interest in the field of action and change. In [5] $\mathcal{A}_C$ was compared to other work [9, 17] and was found to be one of the most expressive approaches to the representation of concurrent actions.

In [8], the notion of causality underlying $\mathcal{A}_C$ is formalized by defining a *transition function* which maps a current situation and an action to a resulting situation. This transition function is encoded in rules of an Extended Logic Program. The effects of actions are then computed by applying these rules to each combination of partial action descriptions wrt. each fact describing a part of the world. The resulting complexity of $O(n^2)$ disables for reasoning about extensive real-time domains and is a general problem of encodings closely following the situation calculus [13]. Moreover, this first encoding was incomplete.[3]

In this paper, we present a mapping of domain descriptions in $\mathcal{A}_C$ into neural networks of linear size. These networks take only four steps for the sound and complete computation of the transition of situations. This allows for an actual use of reasoning about concurrent actions wrt. extensive real-time domains, e.g. the control of complex plants.

The speedup wrt. encodings into logic programs is achieved by a) inferring the change of all facts from all partial descriptions concurrently, and b) using the network to encode the sophisticated relations between the partial action descriptions in its own connectivity. This precomputation initializes the network and takes three complex steps for each effect proposition[4] in a considered domain description.

By means of a specialized application, our work is related to the various approaches to the encoding of logic formulae resp. logic programs to connectionist networks (e.g. [23, 10]). The most corresponding general approach is the one of Hölldobler and Kalinke [11], which is a connectionistic computation of the meaning function T_P determined by a propositional logic program $\mathcal{P}$. By constructing a network which implements the structure of a given domain more clearly than a general approach, we enable for easily changing this underlying structure corresponding to the special needs of the considered application, i.e. in this case the incorporation of the above mentioned relation between the partial action descriptions.

The paper is organized as follows. The language $\mathcal{A}_C$ is introduced in Section 2. In Section 3 we give the construction of the neural network computing the transition function defined by a domain description in $\mathcal{A}_C$. In Section 4 we

---

[3] In [5] a sound and complete translation of $\mathcal{A}_C$ in terms of Equational Logic Programming was given. The time complexity of this approach is in $O(n)$ [3].

[4] effect propositions are certain parts of domain descriptions in $\mathcal{A}_C$

summarize and discuss our work. In [4] we also give a formal definition of our networks.

2 $\mathcal{A}_C$

We briefly review the concepts underlying the language $\mathcal{A}_C$ as defined in [2].

A *domain description* D in $\mathcal{A}_C$ consists of two disjoint sets of symbols, namely a set F_D of *fluent names* and a set A_D of *unit action names*, along with a set of *value propositions* (v-propositions) — each denoting the value of a single fluent in a particular situation — and a set E_D of *effect propositions* (e-propositions) denoting the effects of *actions*. A (compound) *action* is a non-empty subset of A_D with the intended meaning that all of its elements are executed concurrently. A v-proposition is of the form

$$f \text{ after } [a_1, \ldots, a_m] \tag{1}$$

where $a_1, \ldots, a_m$ ($m \geq 0$) are (compound) actions and f is a *fluent literal*, i.e. a fluent name possibly preceded by $\neg$. Such a v-proposition should be interpreted as: f has been observed to hold after having executed the sequence of actions $[a_1, \ldots, a_m]$. In case $m = 0$, (1) is written as $\text{initially } f$.

An e-proposition is of the form

$$a \text{ causes } f \text{ if } c_1, \ldots, c_n \tag{2}$$

where a is an action and f as well as $c_1, \ldots, c_n$ ($n \geq 0$) are fluent literals. (2) should be read as: Executing action a causes f to hold in the resulting situation provided the conditions $c_1, \ldots, c_n$ hold in the actual situation.

Example. You can open a door by running into it if at the same time you activate the electric door opener; otherwise, you will hurt yourself by doing this. The dog sleeping beside the door will wake up when the door opener is activated. You can close the door by pulling it. To formalize this scenario in $\mathcal{A}_C$, consider the two sets $A_{D_1} = \{activate,\ pull, run\_into\}$ and $F_{D_1} = \{open, sleeps, hurt\}$. The initial situation is partially described by the v-proposition $\text{initially } sleeps$, and the effects of the actions can be described by the e-propositions

$\{activate\}$	causes	$\neg sleeps$
$\{run\_into\}$	causes	$hurt$ if $\neg open$
$\{pull\}$	causes	$\neg open$
$\{activate, run\_into\}$	causes	$open$
$\{activate, run\_into\}$	causes	$\neg hurt$ if $\neg hurt$

Informally, the last e-proposition is needed to restrict the application of the second one (which we call to *overrule* an e-proposition). Let D_1 denote the domain description given by these propositions.

Given a domain description D, a *situation* σ is simply a subset of the set of fluent names F_D. For any $f \in F_D$, if $f \in \sigma$ then f is said to *hold* in σ, otherwise $\neg f$ holds. For instance, *sleeps* and $\neg$*open* hold in $\{sleeps, hurt\}$. A *structure* M is a pair (σ_0, Φ) where σ_0 is a situation — called the *initial situation* — and Φ is a partially defined mapping — called a *transition function* — from pairs consisting of an action and a situation into the set of situations. If $\Phi(a, \sigma)$ is defined then its value is interpreted as the result of executing a in σ.

Let $M^{(a_1,\ldots,a_k)}$ be an abbreviation of $\Phi(a_k, \Phi(a_{k-1}, \ldots, \Phi(a_1, \sigma_0) \ldots))$ where $M = (\sigma_0, \Phi)$, then a v-proposition like (1) is *true* in M iff

$$\forall 1 \leq k \leq m \,.\, M^{(a_1 \cdots a_k)} \text{ is defined and}$$
$$f \text{ holds in } M^{(a_1,\ldots,a_m)}.$$

The given set of e-propositions determines how a transition function should be designed which is suitable for a domain description. If a is an action, f a fluent literal, and σ a situation then we say (executing) a *causes* f *in* σ iff there is an action b such that a causes f by b in σ. We say that a causes f by b in σ iff

1. $b \subseteq a$,
2. there is an e-proposition b **causes** f **if** $c_1, \ldots, c_n$ such that each $c_1, \ldots, c_n$ holds in σ.   (3)
3. there is no action c such that $b \subset c \subseteq a$ and a causes $\neg f$ by c in σ.

If 3. does not hold then action b is called to be *overruled* (by action c). An e-proposition b **causes** f **if** $c_1, \ldots, c_n$ is said to be *applicable* wrt. an action a and a situation σ iff $b \subseteq a$, $\{c_1, \ldots, c_n\} \subseteq \sigma$ and b is not overruled.

Using the two sets

$$B_f(a, \sigma) := \{f \in F_D \,|\, a \text{ causes } f \text{ in } \sigma\}$$
$$\overline{B_f}(a, \sigma) := \{f \in F_D \,|\, a \text{ causes } \neg f \text{ in } \sigma\},$$ (4)

a structure $M = (\sigma_0, \Phi)$ is called a *model* of a domain description iff

1. every v-proposition is true in M and
2. for every action a and every situation σ, $\Phi(a, \sigma)$ is only defined in case   (5)
   $$B_f(a, \sigma) \cap \overline{B_f}(a, \sigma) = \{\}.$$
   If it is defined then $\Phi(a, \sigma) = \sigma \cup B_f(a, \sigma) \setminus \overline{B_f}(a, \sigma)$.

A domain description admitting at least one model is said to be *consistent*. A v-proposition ν like (1) is *entailed* by a domain description D, written $D \models \nu$, if ν is true in every model of D.

Example (continued). The transition function determined by the e-propositions in our domain description D_1 is defined as follows. Let σ be an arbitrary situation then

$$\Phi(\{\}, \sigma) = \sigma$$
$$\Phi(\{run\_into\}, \sigma \cup \{open\}) = \sigma \cup \{open\}$$
$$\Phi(\{run\_into\}, \sigma \setminus \{open\}) = \sigma \setminus \{open\} \cup \{hurt\}$$
$$\Phi(\{pull\}, \sigma) = \sigma \setminus \{open\}$$
$$\Phi(\{activate\}, \sigma) = \sigma \setminus \{sleeps\}$$
$$\Phi(\{activate, pull\}, \sigma) = \sigma \setminus \{sleeps, open\}$$
$$\Phi(\{run\_into, pull\}, \sigma \cup \{open\}) = \sigma \setminus \{open\}$$

$$\Phi(\{run\_into, pull\}, \sigma \setminus \{open\}) = \sigma \setminus \{open\} \cup \{hurt\}$$
$$\Phi(\{activate, run\_into\}, \sigma) = \sigma \cup \{open\}$$
$$\Phi(\{activate, run\_into, pull\}, \sigma) \quad \text{is undefined}$$

D_1 has four models, viz.

$$(\{sleeps\}, \Phi) \qquad (\{open, sleeps\}, \Phi)$$
$$(\{sleeps, hurt\}, \Phi) \quad (\{open, sleeps, hurt\}, \Phi) \tag{6}$$

If, for instance, the v-proposition $\neg hurt$ **after** $\{run\_into\}$ is added to D_1 (expressing that, actually, an agent was observed not to be hurt after running into the door) then the only remaining model is $(\{open, sleeps\}, \Phi)$ since for all other structures in (6) we find that $hurt \in \Phi(\{run\_into\}, \sigma_0)$: it follows from the observation formalized by this additional v-proposition that the v-proposition **initially** $open$, say, is entailed by this extended domain.

3   A Neural Network computing Φ

In this section, we give the construction of a neural network $\mathcal{N}_D$ which computes the transition function Φ_D according to some domain description D in $\mathcal{A}_C$ within four steps. The necessary initializing prescription of the network takes three complex steps for each e-proposition in D.

In $\mathcal{A}_C$, the considered concepts are represented by subsets of the sets a domain description consists of, e.g. actions by subsets of A_D, situations and caused effects (B_f resp. $\overline{B_f}$) by subsets of F_D. The relation between these subsets is, actually, given by independent relations between their elements.

Therefore, the idea underlying our work is to represent the sets of fluents, actions, and e-propositions[5] by corresponding sets of units of a neural network, the currently considered subsets of them by activation patterns, and the relation between them by the connections of the resulting network.

This section is organized as follows: In subsection 3.1, we explain the construction of the network and the computation it performs and illustrate this by

---

[5]   v-propositions are not considered since they are not involved in the definition of the transition function, but used as query language

example of the domain description D_1 introduced in section 2. The corresponding formal definitions are given in [4]. In subsection 3.2 we will introduce how the network encodes the overrule-relations, which are not explicitly given by a domain description in $\mathcal{A}_C$.

3.1 Constructing $\mathcal{N}_D$ from a domain description D

We will first introduce the units we use and what they represent wrt. $\mathcal{A}_C$. Then we will give the connections of these units encoding the relations between the concepts represented by the units, and illustrate the computation the network performs. The network $\mathcal{N}_{D_1}$ corresponding to our example domain description D_1 is depicted in Figure 1.

The Units Let D be a domain description in $\mathcal{A}_C$.

- For each fluent in D, $\mathcal{N}_D$ includes a so called *fluent unit*. The output of all fluent units represents a current situation. The output of one fluent unit is 1 iff the corresponding fluent is true in the current situation, and -1 otherwise. [6]

- For each action in D, $\mathcal{N}_D$ includes a so called *action unit*. The activation of these action units represents the currently considered compound action. The output of an action unit is 1 iff the corresponding action is part of the considered compound action and 0 otherwise.[7]

- For each e-proposition in D, $\mathcal{N}_D$ includes a so called *e-prop unit*. The output of an e-prop unit is[8] 1 if the corresponding e-proposition is applicable wrt. the action represented by the output of the action units and the situation represented by the output of the fluent units. Otherwise, its output is 0.

For each fluent in D, $\mathcal{N}_D$ includes four so called *vote-units*, which compute the resulting situation from the current situation and the applicable e-prop units.

- The *vote-d units* represent the persistence assumption. Their output corresponds to the output of the corresponding fluent unit, iff the considered action does not cause an effect concerning the corresponding fluent. Otherwise, their output is 0.

---

[6] This output is caused by an external input or by the recurrent output of this network (for computing the effect of a sequence of actions, the output units (see below) of the network are connected with the corresponding fluent units)

[7] This output is set by an external input (except for the training period (Subsection 3.2))

[8] We use the term "is" as a short form of "is, by the construction of our network, determined to be ... after ... steps"; during the precomputation performed by the net, this output is caused by an external input.

- The *vote–a units* represent the union of B_f and $\overline{B_f}$: Their output is 1 iff the corresponding fluent is in one of these sets, i.e. iff the considered action causes an effect concerning this fluent. Otherwise, their output is 0 .

- The *vote–b units* represent the effects proposed by the applicable e-propositions: Their output is 1 (−1) iff the corresponding fluent is *only* in B_f ($\overline{B_f}$), and 0 otherwise.

- The *vote–o units* represent the resulting situation in analogy to the fluent units. If a fluent is proposed both to be true and false, i.e. if the transition function determined by $\mathcal{A}_C$ is not defined wrt. the currently considered situation and action, the output of the corresponding vote–o unit is 0 .

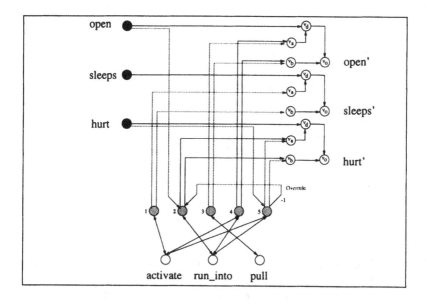

Fig. 1. The neural network $\mathcal{N}_{D_1}$ corresponding to our example domain description D_1 consists of three action units representing the actions *activate*, *run_into*, and *pull*, five e–prop units (marked by the number of the e–proposition they represent wrt. the list on fluents *open*, *sleeps*, and *hurt*, each of them corresponding to four vote units which compute if the respective fluent holds in the resulting situation (represented by the output of the vote–o units (v_o)). The connection from the fifth to the second e-prop-unit inhibits the activation of the second e-prop-unit and represents the corresponding overruled–relation. (Inhibitory connections are depicted dashed.)

The Connections We now introduce the connections encoding the relations between the concepts represented by the units of our network. First, we introduce the connections which represent general rules of persistence and causality and do not depend on the description of actions given by a domain description.

First of all, the vote–o units are connected with the corresponding vote–d and vote–b units. According to our previous descriptions, corresponding vote–d and vote–b units cannot be active simultaneously. If a vote–d unit is active, the corresponding vote–o unit forwards its output, thereby following the assumption of persistence. If a vote–b unit is active, the corresponding vote–o unit forwards its output, i.e. an effect caused by the considered action. If the output of two corresponding vote–d and vote–b units is 0, then the corresponding fluent is in B_f and $\overline{B_f}$, the transition function is not defined and the output of the corresponding vote–o is 0.

The vote–d units are connected with the corresponding vote–a and fluent units. If a vote–a unit is active, i.e. an effect is caused concerning the corresponding fluent, the corresponding vote–d unit is inactivated. Otherwise, this vote–d unit forwards the output of the corresponding fluent unit.

The output of the vote–a and the vote–b units we determined in their description, is an analysis of the sets B_f and $\overline{B_f}$. Their input (i.e. the elements of B_f and $\overline{B_f}$) is computed by the e–prop units. Each e–prop unit forwards its output to the vote–a and vote–b units corresponding to its effect. If this effect is a negated fluent, these inputs are negated by the weights of the connections.

An active e–prop unit represents the applicability of the corresponding e–proposition. A e–proposition b **causes** f **if** $c_1, \ldots, c_n$ is applicable wrt. an action a and a situation σ iff $b \subseteq a$, $\{c_1, \ldots, c_n\} \subseteq \sigma$ and b is not overruled, where a is the considered action and σ the current situation (s. Def. 3). Hence, an e–prop unit representing an e–proposition b **causes** f **if** $c_1, \ldots, c_n$ is connected to all action units (fluent units) representing an action (fluent) in b ($\{c_1, \ldots, c_n\}$). Wrt. the first two conditions, the e–prop unit becomes active only if all of these action and fluent units are active.

For encoding the last condition, we have to augment the net by connections representing the overruled relation. Consider an e–proposition (represented by an unit e_1) that overrules another e–proposition (represented by an unit e_2) wrt. some action and situation. Then the network is augmented by a connection which inhibits the activation of e_2 if e_1 is active. In our example network we have to add one connection of this kind.

Since the overruled relations are not explicitly given by a domain description D in $\mathcal{A}_C$, we use the network $\mathcal{N}_D$ for computing them in linear time. This computation is presented in Section 3.2.

The Computation After describing the construction of a neural network $\mathcal{N}_D$ corresponding to a given domain description D in $\mathcal{A}_C$, we now show that $\mathcal{N}_D$ computes the transition function Φ_D.

The input units of $\mathcal{N}_D$ are the fluent units and the action units. For representing the current situation and the considered action, each fluent unit is

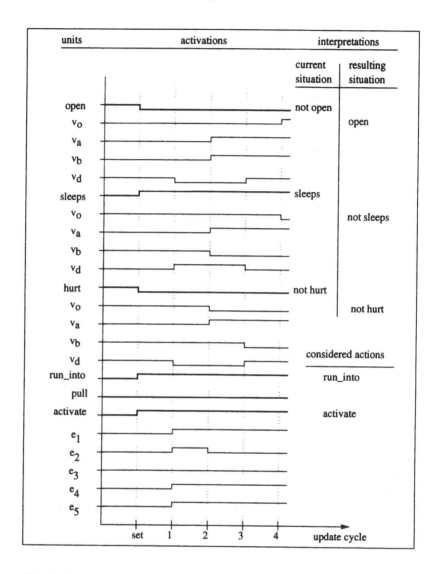

Fig. 2. Pattern of activation during computation.

clamped to 1 (if the corresponding fluent is an element of the current situation) or to −1 (else); each action unit is clamped to 1 (if the corresponding unit action is an element of the considered compound action) or 0 (otherwise).

In the first step, each e-prop unit is activated iff the action it describes is a subset of the considered action and the conditions it describes hold in the current situation. Since the fluent and action units are clamped, all e-prop units stay inactive during the rest of computation if they are not activated in this first step.

In the second step, overruled e–prop units are deactivated. If a unit, say a, is deactivated that deactivates another unit, say b, b might become active again in further steps. This can only happen if b describes the same effect than a third unit that is not overruled; otherwise, it is overruled by a non-overruled unit[9]. Hence, the sets B_f and $\overline{B_f}$ defined by the effects of the active e–prop units will not change during the rest of computation. Each vote–a unit is activated iff a effect is caused concerning the corresponding fluent. The vote–a units keep their activity (resp. inactivity) during the rest of computation; if an e–prop unit is deactivated later on, there must be some non–overruled e–prop unit corresponding to the same fluent.

In the third step, each vote–d unit is inactivated by the input of the corresponding vote–a unit, iff an effect is caused concerning the corresponding fluent; otherwise, the vote–d unit proceeds forwarding the current situation. Each vote–b unit is inactivated iff the corresponding fluent occurs resp. does not occur in both B_f and $\overline{B_f}$; otherwise, its output is 1 if this fluent is in B_f and -1, if it is in $\overline{B_f}$. Hence, corresponding vote–d and vote–b units are both inactive iff the corresponding fluent occurs in both B_f and $\overline{B_f}$; otherwise, either the vote–d or the vote–b unit is active. No vote–d ore vote–b unit will change its output during the rest of computation.

In the fourth step, each vote–o unit is inactivated iff the corresponding fluent occurs in both B_f and $\overline{B_f}$; otherwise, its output becomes 1 if the corresponding fluent holds in Φ_D and -1, if this fluent does not hold in Φ_D. The vote–o unit will then not change its output later on.

Hence, iff Φ_D is not defined wrt. the current situation and the considered action, at least one of the vote–o units is inactive after four computational steps. Otherwise, i.e. if Φ_D is defined, the output of the vote–o units represents the situation resulting from the execution of the considered action a in the current state σ, i.e. $\Phi_D(a, \sigma)$.

For the full formal proof of soundness and completeness see [22].

For example, the computation of the effects of executing $\{run\_into, activate\}$ in the situation $\{sleeps\}$ performed by the network $\mathcal{N}_{D1}$ are depicted in figure 2.

3.2 Encoding the overruled relation

Since the overruled relation is not explicitly given by a domain description D in $\mathcal{A}_C$, we use the network defined in subsection 3.2, but without the connections representing the overruled relation, for computing and adding these connections in linear time.

Consider two e–propositions e_1 and e_2 describing the actions a_1 resp. a_2 and effects f_1 resp. f_2. There is an action and a situation such that e_1 overrules e_2, iff $a_2 \subset a_1$ and $f_1 = \neg f_2$. These conditions can be checked by our

---

[9] The proof of this proposition is by induction over all sequences of e–propositions starting with b, where each element overrules its predecessor.

network. If an e–prop unit is activated, the set of units representing the compound action the corresponding e–proposition describes are activated in the next step of computation. After one more step, all e–propositions describing a subset of this set of actions are activated. Further, this e–prop unit activates the vote–b unit corresponding to its effect in a first step. This vote–b unit is also connected to the other e–prop units describing this effect, but the connection is from the e–prop units to the vote–b units. We therefore augment the network by con-

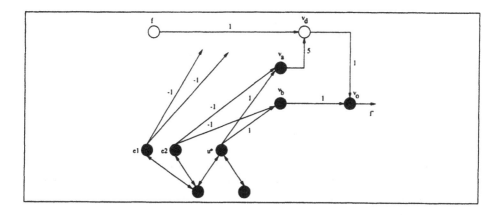

Fig. 3. A part of the network $\mathcal{N}_{D_1}$ modified for learning the overruled relation, where the e–prop unit 5 is currently chosen as u^*. After activating u^*, the action units representing *activate* and *run_into* as well as the vote–b unit corresponding to *hurt* are activated. In the following step e–prop unit 2 will be activated and establish an inhibitory connection from u^* to e–prop unit 2 representing that e–prop unit 5 overrules e–prop unit 2, if e–prop unit 5 is active.

nections from the vote–b units to the e–prop units describing a corresponding effect, and increase the threshold of the e–prop units by 1. Of course, these modifications must be reset after learning the overruled relations.

If in the so modified network a e–prop unit is activated, the corresponding action units and the corresponding vote–b unit are activated in the next step. These units then activate the e–prop units which are overruled by the e–prop which was activated initially and have to be connected to this by an inhibitory link. After executing this procedure for every e–prop unit, all connections needed to represent the overruled relation are established.

So far, this procedure does not distinguish the relations $\subset$ and $\subseteq$. This means that inhibitory connections are added linking pairs of e–propositions like a causes f if C_1 and a causes $\neg f$ if C_2, where C_1 and C_2 are sets of fluent literals; but by the semantics of $\mathcal{A}_C$ these propositions do not overrule each other, since $a \not\subset a$. By the semantics of $\mathcal{A}_C$, the application of such propositions is not defined. Hence, it seems not to be a strong restriction to forbid the occurrence of such tuples. However, in [4] we present are more sophisticated solution overcoming this problem.

4 Summary and Discussion

We introduced a mapping of domain descriptions in $\mathcal{A}_C$ into neural networks, and a algorithm for initializing these networks by their own use in linear time. After this training, the networks compute the transition function defined by the corresponding domain description in constant time, i.e. in four steps.

For using these networks to compute the effects of a sequence of actions, the output layer (i.e. the vote–o units) have to be recurred to the corresponding units of the input layer (i.e. the corresponding fluent units). Since a change of input activation results in a change of output faster then the correct result is computed, this recurrent input has to be buffered. Therefore, a cycle of computation then takes six steps. The network is then initialized by activating the fluent units corresponding to an initial situation, and the elements of the considered sequence of actions determine the sequential input to the action units. By this, the truth of v–propositions can be computed in accordance to $\mathcal{A}_C$ and corresponding to the way of reasoning described in [2, 5].

Whereas reasoning about incomplete situations is not possible by the use of $\mathcal{A}_C$, it can be performed by our network in accordance, e.g, to [12], since the representation of fluents by activations of corresponding units we defined uses three possible states ($1, -1$, and 0) instead of two (in the set describing a situation or not) like in $\mathcal{A}_C$. Instead of interpreting the state 0 as impossible like the semantics of $\mathcal{A}_C$ do, they could also be interpreted as unknown. The occurrence of a conflict wrt. the proposed effects then has to be inferred from the vote–a and vote–b units.

References

1. A. B. Baker. Nonmonotonic reasoning in the framework of situation calculus. *Artificial Intelligence Journal*, 49:5–23, 1991.
2. Chitta Baral and Michael Gelfond. Representing Concurrent Actions in Extended Logic Programming. In R. Bajcsy, editor, *Proceedings of the International Joint Conference on Artificial Intelligence (IJCAI)*, pages 866–871, Chambéry, France, August 1993. Morgan Kaufmann.
3. S.-E. Bornscheuer. Gleichzeitige Aktionen im ELP-basierten Planungsansatz. Diplomarbeit, THD, 1994.
4. S.-E. Bornscheuer and T. Seiler. Massively Parallel Reasoning about Actions. Technical report, TUD, 1996. (to appear).
5. S.-E. Bornscheuer and M. Thielscher. Representing Concurrent Actions and Solving Conflicts. *Journal of the IGPL*, Special Issue 'Mechanising Deduction in the Logics of Practical Reasoning', 1996. (to appear).
6. M. Denecker and D. de Schreye. Representing Incomplete Knowledge in Abductive Logic Programming. In D. Miller, editor, *Proceedings of the International Logic Programming Symposium (ILPS)*, pages 147–163, Vancouver, October 1993. MIT Press.

7. P. M. Dung. Representing Actions in Logic Programming and its Applications in Database Updates. In D. S. Warren, editor, *Proceedings of the International Conference on Logic Programming (ICLP)*, pages 222–238, Budapest, June 1993. MIT Press.

8. Michael Gelfond and Vladimir Lifschitz. Representing Action and Change by Logic Programs. *Journal of Logic Programming*, 17:301–321, 1993.

9. Gerd Große. State-Event Logic. Technical Report AIDA-93-08, FG Intellektik, TH Darmstadt, 1993.

10. S. Hölldobler. Automated inferencing and connectionist models. Technical Report AIDA-93-06, Intellektik, Informatik, TH Darmstadt, 1993. (Postdoctoral Thesis).

11. S. Hölldobler and Y. Kalinke. Towards a Massively Parallel Computational Model for Logic programming. In *Proceedings of the ECAI94 Workshop on Combining Symbolic and Connectionist Processing*, pages 68–77. ECCAI, 1994.

12. S. Hölldobler and J. Schneeberger. A New Deductive Approach to Planning. *New Generation Computing*, 8:225–244, 1990.

13. S. Hölldobler and M. Thielscher. Properties vs. resources — Solving simple frame problems. Technical Report AIDA-94-15, Intellektik, Informatik, TH Darmstadt, 1994.

14. G. N. Kartha. Soundness and Completeness Theorems for Three Formalizations of Actions. In R. Bajcsy, editor, *Proceedings of the International Joint Conference on Artificial Intelligence (IJCAI)*, pages 724–729, Chambéry, France, August 1993. Morgan Kaufmann.

15. V. Lifschitz. Towards a metatheory of action. In J. Allen, R. Fikes, and E. Sandewall, editors, *Proceedings of the International Conference on Principles of Knowledge Representation an Reasoning (KR)*, pages 376–386, 1994.

16. F. Lin and Y. Shoham. Provably correct theories of actions. In *AAAI*, pages 349–354, South Lake Tahoe, California, 1991.

17. Fangzhen Lin and Yoav Shoham. Concurrent Actions in the Situation Calculus. In *Proceedings of the AAAI National Conference on Artificial Intelligence*, pages 590–595, San Jose, California, 1992. MIT Press.

18. John McCarthy and Patrick J. Hayes. Some Philosophical Problems from the Standpoint of Artificial Intelligence. *Machine Intelligence*, 4:463–502, 1969.

19. E. Pednault. ADL: Exploring the middle ground between STRIPS and the situation calculus. In R. Brachman, H. J. Levesque, and R. Reiter, editors, *Proceedings of the International Conference on Principles of Knowledge Representation and Reasoning (KR)*, pages 324–332, Toronto, 1989. Morgan Kaufmann.

20. Erik Sandewall. The range of applicability of nonmonotonic logics for the inertia problem. In R. Bajcsy, editor, *Proceedings of the International Joint Conference on Artificial Intelligence (IJCAI)*, pages 738–743, Chambéry, France, August 1993. Morgan Kaufmann.

21. Erik Sandewall. *Features and Fluents.* Oxford University Press, 1994.

22. Torsten Seiler. Konstruktion eines massiv parallelen Planers – Transformation von Systembeschreibungen in $\mathcal{A}_C$ in neuronale Netze, Dezember 1995. Grosser Beleg, TU-Dresden 1995, Germany.

23. L. Shastri and V. Ajjanagadde. From associations to systematic reasoning: A connectionist representation of rules, variables and dynamic bindings using temporal synchrony. *Behavioural and Brain Sciences*, 16(3):417–494, September 1993.

24. Michael Thielscher. Representing Actions in Equational Logic Programming. pages 207–224, Santa Margherita Ligure, Italy, June 1994. MIT Press.

DisLoP: A Disjunctive Logic Programming System Based on PROTEIN Theorem Prover

Chandrabose Aravindan*

Fachbereich Informatik
Universität Koblenz-Landau
Rheinau 1, D-56075 Koblenz, Germany.
<arvind@informatik.uni-koblenz.de>

Abstract. In this paper, we describe a disjunctive logic programming system, referred to as DisLoP, based on PROTEIN theorem prover. PRO-TEIN supports certain theorem proving calculi, such as restart model elimination and hyper tableaux, that are suitable for working with positive disjunctive logic programs. In particular, restart model elimination calculus is answer complete for postive queries. The DisLoP project started at this point with the aim of extending this further to minimal model reasoning and query processing wrt normal disjunctive logic programming too. The first phase of the project is complete and DisLoP can now perform minimal model reasoning with positive disjunctive logic programs, using both bottom-up and top-down strategies.

1 Introduction

Disjunctive logic programs have been intensively studied in the recent past as an extension of logic programming that provides more expressivity, especially in expressing incomplete information. Various semantics have been developed to capture the intended meaning of a given disjunctive logic program. Though there is no general consensus on any specific semantics for programs with non-monotonic negation in the body, minimal model semantics is an accepted standard for positive programs. Moreover, all well-known semantics for normal programs are conservative extensions of minimal model semantics.

While there is a lot of research work on semantics of programs, there is relatively little work on realising a disjunctive logic programming system. The aim of our project is to develop necessary implementation strategies to obtain a disjunctive logic programming system, referred to as DisLoP, which is similar to Prolog for conventional logic programming. As stressed above, any such system must be capable of performing minimal model reasoning, and we addressed this issue in the first phase of DisLoP development.

We have identified the PROTEIN theorem prover [3] as a starting point for the intended disjunctive logic programming system DisLoP. This is not an

---

* the author is not the only one involved in this project and is just reporting the work done by all members of DisLoP project. More information on this project can be obtained from the web site <http://www.uni-koblenz.de/ag-ki/DLP/>

arbitrary choice and PROTEIN supports certain theorem proving calculi, such as restart model elimination [4] and hyper tableaux [5], that are well suited for disjunctive logic programming. Hyper tableaux calculus can generate models of a given program and can be tuned to generate minimal models. Restart model elimination calculus does not require contrapositives of given clauses and thus allows for their procedural reading. Further, it has been shown that it is answer complete for positive queries wrt positive disjunctive logic programs [6].

In this paper, we describe the first phase of DisLoP which extends PROTEIN to include minimal model reasoning wrt generalised and weak generalised closed world assumptions [11, for example]. This minimal model reasoning can be carried out in both bottom-up and top-down manners and we describe these strategies in separate sections. The bottom-up method is based on a novel test strategy that checks the minimality of a model without any reference to other models. The top-down method is based on abductive reasoning. In the next phase of development, we plan to extend DisLoP to handle D-WFS [8] and STATIC [14, 10] semantics.

2 Minimal Model Reasoning With Model Generation Calculus

One way of performing minimal model reasoning wrt the given program D and goal G is to generate all necessary models of D in which G holds and check if they are minimal or not. We have developed efficient optimisation techniques to generate only necessary models one by one without any repetition. And the important part of this method is a test strategy, that can check the minimality of one given model without any reference to other models. These two steps are explained briefly below.

For generating models, we have developed a specific tableau calculus, referred to as hyper tableaux [5], which seems to have some favourable properties for minimal model reasoning. In particular, when generating counter-models hyper tableaux prefer minimal models. The hyper tableaux idea can be further optimised towards minimal model reasoning by introducing, e.g., cut rules.

To check the minimality of a generated model, we have developed a characterisation of minimal models which makes it possible to determine whether a model is a minimal one independently of other models using one theorem prover call. Given a program D and a model M of it, this test checks if every atom in M is a logical consequence of $D \cup \overline{M}$, where $\overline{M}$ stands for negation of all atoms not present in M. This leads to a method for minimal model reasoning where counter-models can be generated one at a time and a low space complexity is achieved. Further details, experimental results and comparison to previous approaches can be found in [12, 13].

Example 1. Consider a disjunctive logic program with clauses: $m(X) \vee f(X) \leftarrow p(X)$, $p(a)$, $p(b)$, and $m(b)$, where m, f, and p stand for male, female, and person respectively. a and b are two known persons and it is also known that b is a male. Consider the query $\neg f(b)$. Our bottom-up procedure, tries to generate all potential minimal models of D in which $f(b)$ holds, as shown in the figure. First a potential minimal model $\{p(a), p(b), m(b), f(b), m(a)\}$ is generated. Then the minimality test is carried out. Since $f(b)$ is not a logical consequence of $D \cup \{\neg f(a)\}$, this is discarded as non-minimal. The next generated model is also discarded on a similar basis.

There are no more potential models to be generated and the procedure concludes that $f(b)$ does not hold in any minimal model and declares it to be false.

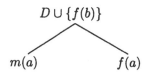

$$D \cup \{f(b)\}$$

$$m(a) \qquad f(a)$$

3 Minimal Model Reasoning With Model Elimination Calculus

In [1], we have developed an abductive framework that captures the minimal model reasoning wrt both GCWA and WGCWA. Given a program D and a goal G, an abductive explanation Δ for G consists only of negative literals s.t. $D \cup \Delta \models G$ and $D \cup \Delta$ is consistent. We have introduced an inference rule, referred to as *negation by failure to explain*, that allows us to infer negation of an atom A if there is no abductive explanation for A wrt D. It is also shown that negation by failure to explain is equivalent to negation by GCWA.

To generate abductive explanations of G wrt D, we have modified the restart model elimination calculus of [4]. The modified calculus is used to generate all necessary potential candidates Δ s.t. $D \cup \Delta \models G$, and consistency checks are then carried out to verify if $D \cup \Delta$ is consistent or not. If no abductive explanation for G is found, then G is declared to be false under GCWA.

Reasoning wrt WGCWA is relatively easier and requires no consistency check. Given a program D and a goal G, the same modified calculus is used to check if there exists a Δ, referred to as a potential candidate, s.t. $D \cup \Delta \vdash G$. G is declared to be false under WGCWA if there exists no potential candidate (possibly empty) to explain it.

Example 2. Consider the same program D as in Example 1 and a goal $\neg f(a)$. We try to generate all abductive explanations for $f(a)$ using a modified restart model elimination calculus as shown in the figure. When a potential candidate $\Delta = \{\neg m(a)\}$ is generated, consistency check is carried out for $D \cup \Delta$. In this case, it is consistent and so Δ is an abductive explanation for $f(a)$.

Hence we conclude that $f(a)$ is not false wrt GCWA. Further, since $\emptyset$ is not an abductive explanation, we also conclude that $f(a)$ is not true either. It is not difficult to see that $f(b)$ does not have any abductive explanation and hence our procedure will conclude $f(b)$ to be false wrt GCWA.

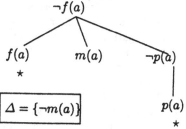

4 Concluding Remarks

We have developed a disjunctive logic programming system DisLoP, that can currently perform minimal model reasoning wrt GCWA and WGCWA, for positive disjunctive logic programs. DisLoP is an extension of the PROTEIN theorem prover, which is capable for computing answers for positive goals wrt positive disjunctive logic programs. We expect DisLoP to be available for public distribution soon.

The minimal model reasoning of DisLoP can be carried out in both bottom-up and top-down strategies. The bottom-up strategy is based on a novel test that can verify the minimality of a given model without any reference to other models. The top-down strategy is based on abductive reasoning, which tries to generate abductive explanations for given goal wrt the given program. Both these strategies have their own advantages and disadvantages, and we are currently carrying out experiments to compare these two methods.

Minimal model reasoning with positive disjunctive logic programs is an important problem, since any semantics for normal disjunctive logic programs is a conservative extension of minimal model reasoning. Thus, DisLoP can be extended to implement any non-monotonic semantics for normal disjunctive logic programs. Currently, we are working on extending DisLoP to handle D-WFS semantics [8, 9] and STATIC semantics [14, 10]. We already have an experimental Prolog program to handle D-WFS semantics based on both bottom-up partial evaluation and a confluent calculus presented in [9]. Another line of development of DisLoP will be to exploit the constraint solving [7] and theory reasoning [2] capabilities of PROTEIN in the context of disjunctive logic programming.

Acknowledgements

We thank all members of the Artificial Intelligence Research Group at the University of Koblenz, Germany, for useful discussions and comments on this paper. Special thanks are due to Peter Baumgartner and Ilkka Niemelä, who made significant contributions to this paper. This project on disjunctive logic programming is sponsored by DFG under the grant number Fu 263/3-1.

References

1. Aravindan, C.: An abductive framework for negation in disjunctive logic programming. Technical Report 9–96, Universität Koblenz-Landau, Koblenz, Germany, 1996. (to appear in proc. of JELIA'96)
2. Baumgartner, P.: Refinements of theory model elimination and a variant without contrapositives. In: A.G. Cohn (ed.), Proc. of ECAI '94, Wiley, 1994.
3. Baumgartner, P., Furbach, U.: PROTEIN: A PROver with a Theory Extension/INterface. In: A. Bundy (ed.), Proc. of CADE-12, LNAI 814, Springer-Verlag, 1994, pp. 769–773.
4. Baumgartner, P., Furbach, U.: Model elimination without contrapositives and its application to PTTP. Journal of automated reasoning, 13:339–359, 1994.

5. Baumgartner, P., Furbach, U., Niemelä, I.: Hyper Tableau. Technical Report 8–96, Universität Koblenz-Landau, Koblenz, Germany, 1996. (to appear in proc. of JELIA'96)

6. Baumgartner, P., Furbach, U., Stolzenburg, F.: Model elimination, Logic programming, and Computing answers. In: Proc. of IJCAI '95, Vol. 1, 1995. (to appear in Artificial Intelligence)

7. Baumgartner, P., Stolzenburg, F.: Constraint model elimination and a PTTP implementation. In: Proc. of the 4th workshop on theorem proving with analytic tableaux and related methods, LNAI 918, Springer-Verlag, 1995, pp. 201–216.

8. Brass, S., Dix, J.: Disjunctive semantics based upon partial and bottom-up evaluation. In: Proc. of the 12th int. conf. on logic programming, MIT Press, 1995, pp. 199–213.

9. Brass, S., Dix, J.: Characterizing D-WFS: Confluence and iterated GCWA. To appear in proc. of JELIA'96.

10. Brass, S., Dix, J., Przymusinski, T.: Characterizations and implementation of static semantics of disjunctive programs. Technical report 4–96, Universität Koblenz-Landau, Koblenz, Germany, 1996.

11. Lobo, J., Minker, J., Rajasekar, A.: Foundations of disjunctive logic programming. MIT Press, 1992.

12. Niemelä, I.: A tableau calculus for minimal model reasoning. In: Proc. of the 5th workshop on theorem proving with analytic tableaux and related methods, LNAI 1071, Springer-Verlag, 1996, pp. 278–294.

13. Niemelä, I.: Implementing circumscription using a tableau calculus. Technical report 6–96, Universität Koblenz-Landau, Koblenz, Germany, 1996. (to appear in proc. of ECAI '96)

14. Przymusinski, T.: Static semantics for normal and disjunctive logic programs. Annals of mathematics and artificial intelligence, Special issue on disjunctive programs, 1995.

15. Smullyan, R. M.: First-Order Logic. Springer-Verlag, 1968.

Abstraction as a Heuristic to Guide Planning

Michael Contzen, Knut Möller

Bonn University
Dept. of Computer Science I
Römerstr. 164
D-53117 Bonn, FRG
{contzen,moeller}@cs.uni-bonn.de

Abstract. In this paper we propose a novel way how to incorporate abstraction into planning. The approach is robust and complete, i.e. if a solution exists it will be found by our search method. Design criteria for a suitable abstraction function can be derived from formal analysis. Furthermore our approach allows the integration of heuristics formulated at different abstraction levels, thus providing a powerful and convenient tool for problem solving.

1 Introduction

Planning as a method to solve difficult problems is usually described within the state space search paradigm [FN71, Her89]. Although the underlying assumptions (e.g. discrete representations without explicit reference to time, no uncertain or incomplete information) are extreme simplifications of reality this commonly used approach suffers from combinatorial explosion. Early in the seventies this was recognized and heuristics as well as abstraction introduced to overcome this problem[Pea84, Sac74, Wil88]. While heuristics are used to restrict the explored state space by rules of thumb, abstraction reduces search by collapsing sets of states into abstract ones (situation abstraction). But the approaches of abstract planning (e.g. [Sac74, Wil88, Kno94, AKP$^+$91]) are characterized by a restricted use of abstraction. First, those abstractions are pure information loss approaches[1], second, abstraction is used rather inflexible. If abstraction is inadequate for a problem, it will not succeed. It may be misleading and may even prevent a planner from finding a solution. Bad abstraction may even increase complexity by an exponential factor.

2 Planning with abstraction

In the following abstraction is considered to be a transformation of a planning system into a more abstract one. At each level a planning system $_i\Sigma$ is defined, which – among others[2] – consists of a state space $_iS$, and a set of operator

---

[1] Abstraction is usually associated with information loss, i.e. details are suppressed at abstract levels. This is just one side of abstraction. On the other side it may be viewed as a recognition process which discovers structures and relations not visible on more concrete levels [Chr94]. For example consider a number of *bricks* that altogether might form a *house*. Houses have completely different properties and features not deducible from bricks alone. This information should be utilized for problem solving.

[2] A complete, exact description of abstract planning is not subject of this paper.

schemata $_iOP$. A function $\mathbb{AB}$ ($_i\mathbb{AB}$: $_iS \longmapsto {}_{i+1}S$) is defined that maps state descriptions from one abstraction level to the next higher one. Usually the inverse $_i\mathbb{AB}^{-1}$: $_{i+1}S \longmapsto {}_iS^*$ is not well defined, as it is a desired property of abstractions that multiple states are merged into one. A plan (of the i-th level planning system $_i\Sigma$) $_ipl_iS =< {}_iop_1, ..., {}_iop_k >$ consists of a sequence of admissible operators $_iop_j \in {}_iOP_\phi{}^3$, $(1 \leq j \leq k)$ at level i starting at state $_iS$. Such abstract operations lead to a sequence of abstract states, each of which may be refined to the next lower level by potentially a number of different states.

To get some intuition about abstract planning a simple example is given in fig.1) without explicit reference to operators. Start ($_0S_0$) and goal state ($_0S_g$) are abstracted to $_1S_0$ and $_1S_g$ respectively. An abstract plan is found at level 1 that has two intermediate states ($_1S_1$ and $_1S_2$). $_1S_1$ and $_1S_2$ are refined to a sequence of sets $_0H =< \{_0S_{11}, {}_0S_{12}, {}_0S_{13}\}, \{_0S_{21}, {}_0S_{22}, {}_0S_{23}\} >$ (dashed arrows), that in the sequel will be called *hint sets*.

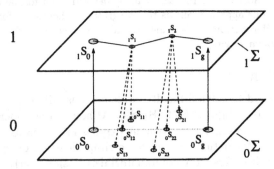

Fig. 1. A two layered planning task

3 Abstraction as a search heuristic

Consider that (by $_i\mathbb{AB}^{-1}$ [4]) intermediate abstract states $_{i+1}S$ can be refined to sets of subgoals. As mentioned above the resulting sequence of sets is called *hints* $_iH$, for the next lower level i. Instead of just searching from subgoal to subgoal as is usually done with plan refinement, we start a *heuristic* search from the i-th level start state $_iS_0$ to a goal state $_iS_g$. During planning the heuristic (evaluation) function provides a value estimating the distance to a goal state. If the search front traverses an element of the hint sets, the evaluation function at this state returns a reduced value. Paths including states of the hint sets are thus preferred for future expansion.

3.1 The heuristic function

To construct a suitable heuristic function we assume that a certain minimal refinement length $rlng(_{i+1}op)$ is required to achieve – at level i – the effects of any operator at level $i+1$. This assumption is justified by the fact that abstraction is applied to reduce search space. Any state transition in an abstract state

---

[3] OP_ϕ is the set of ground instantiated operator schemata (operators).

[4] This is just possible with *some* restricted abstraction functions. Our approach does not rely on the existence of such a computable refinement operators.

space should be equivalent to a number of transitions in more concrete spaces independent of the applied abstraction.

The *minimal refinement length* $rlng(_{i+1}op)$ is the length of the shortest plan $_ipl$ at level i which reaches a state $_iS$ whose abstraction is equal to the state at level $i + 1$ resulting from the application of operator $_{i+1}op$. To get a more rigorous and handy description in the following we always refer to the minimum over the minimal refinement lengths of the complete operator set at level $i + 1$. In principle this simplification is not necessary, but description and analysis of the approach is clarified. $(minrlng(_{i+1}OP) := \min_{_{i+1}op \in _{i+1}OP} rlng(_{i+1}op))$ Given $minrlng(_{i+1}OP)$ it is easy to estimate the minimal length of a solution path at level i that passes via the hints. Remember, that the sequence of hint sets H is created by the abstract planning process. $|H|$ denotes the number of hint sets in H. Thus any path via the hint sets will at least consist of $(|H| + 1)$ times the minimal number of refinement steps (operator applications) at level i. $_iplng_{iH,i+1}OP := (|_iH| + 1)minrlng(_{i+1}OP)$

To define the heuristic function a counter $lastvisited$[5] is needed for proper estimation of the remaining path length. To assure that the correct value of the distance to a goal state (h^*) is underestimated (i.e. the search algorithm is admissible) the last part of the solution path is assumed to have zero length. Given a characteristic function $notgoal$ [6] the heuristic can be written:

$$_ih_{,H,,i+1}OP(_iS, _ipl) := minrlng(_{i+1}OP)(|_iH| - lastvisited(pl, S, _iH)) \, notgoal(S, S_g) \tag{1}$$

4 A short analytical view

Under the assumptions, that the mean branching factor $B = _iB$ is almost equal for all levels, and that there is a constant reductions factor[7] the number of explored states W_{all} can be derived depending on the number of abstraction levels n in the hierarchy:

$$W_{all} = \left(\sum_{i=0}^{n-1} \frac{_0l}{\gamma^i} B^\gamma \right) + B^{\frac{_0l}{\gamma^n}} = {}_0l \, \frac{1 - \gamma^{-(n+1)}}{1 - \gamma^{-1}} B^\gamma + B^{\frac{_0l}{\gamma^n}} \tag{2}$$

Fig.2 depicts the relation between planning effort W_{all} and "problem size" $_0l$. For small l the linear part of equation 2 is dominant. With increasing l the exponential part of the sum (right term) overtakes and leads to the fast growing effort. Thus an estimate of the mean problem size of a domain can be used to extract information how to construct the abstraction hierarchy. Other criteria and a more elaborate analysis can be found (among other results) in [Con96].

5 Conclusion

In this paper we introduce a robust technique how to integrate abstraction into planning. As shown by analysis [Con96] under certain assumptions a considerable

---

[5] $lastvisited(pl, S)$ is a function that returns the index of the last hint set in H a member of which occured in pl. If no hint was reached yet, its return value is zero.

[6] $notgoal(S, S_g)$ returns 0 if $S \subseteq S_g$ else it returns value 1

[7] Given a problem, the plan lengths $_il$ of the respective solutions decrease with growing abstraction. It is assumed, that this reduction can be captured by a factor γ, i.e. $_il = \gamma \, _{i+1}l$.

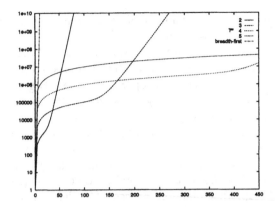

Fig. 2. The explored state space W_{all} in dependence of "problem size" $_0l$: $n=3$, $B=10$

(exponential) speed up is achieved. Furthermore the analysis gives some *guidance how to design an abstraction function*. Heuristics formulated at *different abstraction levels* can be efficiently combined.

The presented approach does not rely on any specific search technique. Just to simplify the description forward breadth first search was chosen in this paper.

The approach is currently integrated into our multi-robot control system [FMR+96], which is a hierarchically structured architecture providing access to the robots at different levels of abstraction. Planning using abstraction will be used as a high level user interface.

References

[AKP+91] J. F. Allen, H. A. Kautz, R. N. Pelavin and J. D. Tenenberg. Reasoning about Plans. Morgan Kaufmann Publishers, 1991 .

[Con96] M. Contzen. Hierarchisches Planen. PhD Thesis, to appear, Dept. of Computer Science, Bonn Univ.,1996.

[Chr94] L. Chrisman. Reasoning about Probabilistic Actions at Multiple Levels of Granularity. Working Notes AAAI Spring Symposium Series, Stanford University, 1994.

[FMR+96] J. Frings, K. Möller, C. Reiner and M. Contzen. MARC: Eine Implementierungsplattform für Robotersysteme. in C. Cap (ed.) SIWORK'96, vdf, Zürich.

[FN71] R. E. Fikes and N. J. Nilsson. STRIPS: a new approch to the application of theorem proving to problem solving. *Artificial Intelligence* 2(3/4): 189–208.

[Her89] J. Hertzberg. Planen: Einführung in die Planerstellungsmethoden der Künstlichen Intelligenz. BI-Verlag, 1989.

[Kno94] C. A. Knoblock. Automatically generating abstractions for planning. *Artificial Intelligence* 68(2): 243–302, 1994.

[Pea84] J. Pearl. Heuristics. *Addison-Wesley*, 1984.

[Sac74] E. D. Sacerdoti. Planning in a hierarchy of abstraction spaces. *Artificial Intelligence* 5(2): 115-135, 1974.

[Wil88] D. E. Wilkins. Practical Planning: Extending the Classical AI Planning Paradigm. *Morgan Kaufmann Publishers*, 1988.

Equational Theorem Proving Using Taxonomic Constraints

Jörg Denzinger

FB Informatik, Universität Kaiserslautern
Postfach 3049, 67653 Kaiserslautern
E-mail: denzinge@informatik.uni-kl.de

Abstract. We present an approach to prove several theorems in slightly different axiom systems simultaneously. We represent the different problems as a taxonomy, i.e. a tree in which each node inherits all knowledge of its predecessors, and solve the problems using inference steps on rules and equations with simple constraints, i.e. words identifying nodes in the taxonomy. We demonstrate that a substantial gain can be achieved by using taxonomic constraints, not only by avoiding the repetition of inference steps but also by achieving run times that are much shorter than the accumulated run times when proving each problem separately.

1 Introduction

If one takes a look at the scenarios in which automated theorem provers are intended to be used, then one can observe that typically there is not one single proof problem to solve, but several or even many of them. Also those problems are connected with each other, typically by sharing of axioms. Examples for such scenarios are retrieval of formally specified software components to fulfill an also specified request (for each component several proof problems have to be solved, all connected to the request) or proof assistants for which the user divides a hard problem into several connected subproblems that have to be proved. In order to prove these connected problems with a prover each problem requires its own proof run without any connection to the proof runs of the other problems. Obviously, if the problems share many axioms this results in repeating many inference steps (involving the shared axioms) many times.

We will present a concept to avoid this repetition by simultaneously solving the connected proof problems represented in form of a so-called *taxonomy* T. A taxonomy is a tree in which with each node a set of facts is associated, initially the axioms, that are inherited by all successors of the node and a set of theorems to prove. Taxonomies and the inheritance aspect play also an important role in KL-ONE based knowledge representation formalisms (see [BS85]).

In order to incorporate the taxonomy information into an inference rule system we added to a fact a taxonomic constraint w describing the path from the root of T to the node N that contains the fact. In a similar way taxonomic constraints are added to the theorems to prove. Inferences between axioms and/or theorems are only allowed if their nodes are on a common path. This can be tested easily by determining whether one of the corresponding constraints is a prefix of the other one. The result of an inference step is stored in the deeper one of the two nodes involved.

Our concept of a constraint is quite different from the common concept of constraints used in deduction processes (see [Bü90] or [KKR90]). Normally, constraints are added to some derived fact F to describe the validity of F. In other words, a constraint C assigned to a fact F (a clause, an equation, a formula) is a logical formula. Then $\sigma(F)$ is valid for those substitutions σ only that satisfy C. In this context the problem arises how to handle the constraints, especially when and how to solve them. These problems do not appear in our context.

The concept of taxonomic constraints can be easily incorporated in existing theorem provers and it allows one to simultaneously solve sets of problems with less inference steps. Since the constraint handling is extremely simple this results directly in faster proofs. In this report we will demonstrate the usefulness of our concept for the case of equational deduction by (unfailing) completion.

2 Basic Definitions

Equational theorem proving deals with solving the following problem:

> **Input:** E, a set of equations over a fixed signature sig;
> $s = t$, a goal equation over sig
> **Question:** Does $s = t$ hold in every model of E ?

In this paper we will deal with the following modification of this problem, which in fact means dealing with several instances of the original problem simultaneously.

> **Input:** $\{E^i | 1 \leq i \leq k\}$, all E^i sets of equations over a fixed signature sig;
> k goal equations $s_i = t_i$ over sig
> **Question:** Does for all i $s_i = t_i$ hold in every model of E^i ?

Let us first take a closer look at the first problem. Provers based on rewriting and completion techniques developed by Knuth and Bendix ([KB70]), improved to unfailing completion ([HR87], [BDP89]), have proven to be quite successful in solving this first problem. We assume the reader to be familiar with rewriting and completion techniques (see [DJ90]).

A signature $sig = (S, F, \tau)$ consists of a set S of sorts, a set F of operators and a function $\tau : F \rightarrow S^+$ that fixes the input and output sorts of the operators. Let $T(F, V)$ denote the set of terms over F and a set V of variables. By t/p we denote the subterm of t at position p and by t[p←s] the replacement of t/p in t by s. By $T(F) = T(F, \emptyset)$ we denote a set of *ground terms* over F. Let K be a set of new constants. A *reduction ordering* $\succ$ is a well-founded ordering on $T(F \cup K, V)$ that is compatible with substitutions and the term structure, i.e. $t_1 \succ t_2$ implies $\sigma(t_1) \succ \sigma(t_2)$ and $t[p \leftarrow t_1] \succ t[p \leftarrow t_2]$.

A *rule* is an oriented equation, written as $l \rightarrow r$, such that $Var(r) \subseteq Var(l)$. A set R of rules is *compatible* with $\succ$ if $l \succ r$ for every $l \rightarrow r$ in R. If E is a set of equations then $R_E = \{\sigma(u) \rightarrow \sigma(v) \mid u \doteq v$ in E, σ a substitution,

$\sigma(u) \succ \sigma(v)\}$ is the set of orientable instances of equations in E. (We use $u \doteq v$ to denote $u = v$ or $v = u$.) Finally, we have $R(E) = R \cup R_E$. If $l \rightarrow r \in R(E)$ and $\sigma(l) \equiv t/p$ and $t[p \leftarrow \sigma(r)] \equiv s$, then t is called *reducible* to s and we write t $\Rightarrow$ s. If a term t is not reducible with any element of $R(E)$, then it is in *normal form*. Let $u \doteq v$ and $s \doteq t$ be equations in $E \cup R$. Let u/p be a non-variable subterm of u that is unifiable with s, say with most general unifier $\sigma = mgu(u/p, s)$. Then $\sigma(u)[p \leftarrow \sigma(t)] = \sigma(v)$ is valid in $R \cup E$. If $\sigma(u)[p \leftarrow \sigma(t)]) \not\succeq \sigma(u)$ and $\sigma(v) \not\succeq \sigma(u)$, then $\sigma(u)[p \leftarrow \sigma(t)] = \sigma(v)$ is a *critical pair* of R, E.

Since we will base our inference system for unfailing completion with taxonomic constraints on the inference system $\mathcal{U}$ presented in [AD93], we need also another ordering on terms, namely the encompassment ordering $\triangleright$. It is the strict part of the quasi-ordering $\trianglerighteq$ defined by $s \trianglerighteq t$ iff $\sigma(t) \equiv s/p$ for some substitution σ and some position p.

In general, a proof procedure for equational theorem proving using unfailing completion works as follows: Input is the set E and g, a ground equation over $F \cup K$ (the skolemized goal $s = t$) and a reduction ordering $\succ$. The procedure uses sets R,E and CP. The input equations are put into CP (therefore $E = \emptyset$). Then the following loop is repeated until the normal forms of the terms of g are the same or subsumed by an equation of E or until the set CP is empty: Select an equation s'=t' out of CP. Let s" and t" be normal forms of s' and t' with respect to R(E). If neither s"=t" is subsumed by an equation in E nor s" $\equiv$ t", then all critical pairs between s"=t" and E and R are added to CP (resp. their normal forms). If s" and t" are comparable with respect to $\succ$, then the appropriate rule is added to R, else s"=t" is added to E. All elements of E and R that can be reduced with the new rule or equation are removed from R or E and their normal forms are added to CP.

For simultaneous theorem proving, as defined above, we will use taxonomic constraints. Therefore we have to define what a taxonomy is.

Definition 1 : Taxonomy.

A tree T in which each node N is assigned a set E_N of equations, a set R_N of rules and a set G_N of goal equations over a fixed signature *sig* is called a *taxonomy*. If a node N has n successors $N_1, ..., N_n$, then these successors are ordered and the i-th node in this ordering is assigned the number i. Therefore each node N can be described by the path from the root to it, represented by a word w_N in $\mathbb{N}_+^*$: $w_N = \epsilon$ if N is the root and $w_N = w_M i$, if N is the i-th successor of node M.

The accumulated sets of equations E^N and rules R^N are defined recursively. If N is the root, then $E^N = E_N$ and $R^N = R_N$. If N is a successor of node M, then $E^N = E_N \cup E^M$, $R^N = R_N \cup R^M$.

The equality relation $=_N$ to a node N of T is naturally the equality induced by its accumulated equations and rules, i.e. $=_N = =_{E^N \cup R^N}$.

Note that for our purposes it is sufficient to define a taxonomy as a tree. Some readers may find it useful to use directed acyclic graphs, as can be the case in some taxonomy definitions that are used in knowledge representation.

3 Unfailing Completion and Theorem Proving with Taxonomic Constraints

3.1 The inference system

Before we present our inference system, we have to define the form of the taxonomic constraints and their semantics, we have to transfer our set of problems into a taxonomy and we have to transfer the taxonomy back into starting sets for our completion inference system.

Definition 2 : Taxonomic constraint, constrained equation/rule/goal.

Let T be a taxonomy and N a node of T. The word w_N to N is called the *taxonomic constraint* to N. If w is a taxonomic constraint, s=t an equation, $l \rightarrow r$ a rule and u=v a goal equation, then s=t|w is a *constrained equation*, $l \rightarrow r|w$ a *constrained rule* and u=v|w a *constrained goal*.

As already stated, we want to solve several proof problems $s_i =_{E^i} t_i$ simultaneously by means of transforming them into a taxonomy and then performing completion with constrained rules, equations and goals obtained from the taxonomy. It is our goal to change standard unfailing completion as little as possible to accomplish this task. Since the constraints of the rules, equations and goals are sufficient to represent the taxonomy T from which they were obtained we will identify in the following a node N of T and its constraint w_N.

As a result of performing completion we have to expect that the sets E_N, R_N and G_N of a node N of a taxonomy change if an appropriate inference rule is applied. But we will prove that $=_N$ remains the same during the whole completion process for each node N of the taxonomy.

Standard unfailing completion works on sets of equations and rules. In order to solve our problem we will also need sets of goals. Initially, these sets have to be obtained from a taxonomy T. Therefore we have to construct such a taxonomy out of our proof problems $s_i =_{E^i} t_i$. Since there are several ways to construct a taxonomy out of these problems this task has to be done by the user of our system $\mathcal{TAX}$. However, the following construction can be used to obtain an initial taxonomy T to the proof problems. The root node N_0 of T is defined by
$$E_{N_0} = \bigcap_{i=1,...,n} E^i, \; R_{N_0} = \emptyset \text{ and } G_{N_0} = \{s_i = t_i | E^i = E_{N_0}\}.$$
Then we partition the set $M = \{E^i | E^i \neq E_{N_0}\}$ into several sets M_1 to M_m, such that $M_i \cap M_j = \emptyset$ for all $i \neq j$, $\bigcup_{j=1,...,m} M_j = M$ and $\bigcap_{F \in M_j} F \neq \emptyset$ for all j. For each M_j a node N_j as successor of the last node is constructed by
$$E_{N_j} = \bigcap_{F \in M_j} F \setminus E_{N_0}, \; R_{N_j} = \emptyset \text{ and } G_{N_j} = \{s_i = t_i | E^i = E^{N_j}\}.$$
Then for each M_j this construction is repeated on and on until for all $i = 1,...,n$ $s_i = t_i \in \bigcup_{N \in T_0} G_N$.

Note that there may be several partitions of a set M into M_1 to M_m and one of these partitions (preferably with small m and big sets E_{N_j}) has to be selected.

Definition 3 : Inference system $\mathcal{TAX}$.

Let T be a taxonomy. The inference system $\mathcal{TAX}$ works on triples
(E,R,G), where E is a set of constrained equations, R a set of constrained
rules and G a set of constrained goals. The initial set (E_0, R_0, G_0) to T
is defined by

$E_0 = \{s\dot{=}t|w \mid s\dot{=}t \in E_N$ for some $N \in T$ and w the constraint to $N\}$
$R_0 = \emptyset$
$G_0 = \{s\dot{=}t|w \mid s\dot{=}t \in G_N$ for some $N \in T$ and w the constraint to $N\}$.

The inference rules of $\mathcal{TAX}$ are as follows:

1. Orient: $(E \cup \{s \dot{=} t|w\}, R, G) \vdash_{\mathcal{TAX}} (E, R \cup \{s \rightarrow t|w\}, G)$
   if $s \succ t$.

2. Generate: $(E, R, G) \vdash_{\mathcal{TAX}} (E \cup \{s \dot{=} t|w\}, R, G)$
   if $l_1 = r_1|w_1, l_2 = r_2|w_2 \in R \cup E$, s=t critical pair to $l_1 \rightarrow r_1$
   and $l_2 \rightarrow r_2$ with mgu σ, $\sigma(l_1) \not\geq \sigma(r_1)$ and $\sigma(l_2) \not\geq \sigma(r_2)$, $w_2=w_1u$
   and $w=w_2$ or $w_1=w_2u$ and $w=w_1$.

3. Simplify equation: $(E \cup \{s \dot{=} t|v\}, R, G) \vdash_{\mathcal{TAX}} (E \cup \{u \dot{=} t|v\}, R, G)$
   if $s \Rightarrow u$ with $l \rightarrow r|w \in R(E)$, $v = wv'$, $s \rhd l$.

4. Simplify right side of rule: $(E, R \cup \{l_1 \rightarrow r_1|w_1\}, G) \vdash_{\mathcal{TAX}}$
   $\qquad\qquad\qquad\qquad\qquad\qquad (E, R \cup \{l_1 \rightarrow s|w_1\}, G)$
   if $r_1 \Rightarrow s$ with $l_2 \rightarrow r_2|w_2 \in R(E)$, $w_1 = w_2v$.

5. Simplify left side of rule: $(E, R \cup \{l_1 \rightarrow r_1|w_1\}, G) \vdash_{\mathcal{TAX}}$
   $\qquad\qquad\qquad\qquad\qquad\qquad (E \cup \{s \dot{=} r_1|w_1\}, R, G)$
   if $l_1 \Rightarrow s$ with $l_2 \rightarrow r_2|w_2 \in R(E)$, $w_1 = w_2v$, $l_1 \rhd l_2$.

6. Subsume equation: $(E \cup \{s_1 \dot{=} t_1|w_1, s_2 \dot{=} t_2|w_2\}, R, G) \vdash_{\mathcal{TAX}}$
   $\qquad\qquad\qquad\qquad\qquad\qquad (E \cup \{s_2 \dot{=} t_2|w_2\}, R, G)$
   if $s_1/p \equiv \sigma(s_2)$, $t_1 \equiv s_1[p \leftarrow \sigma(t_2)]$, $s_1 \rhd s_2$, $w_1 = w_2v$.

7. Simplify goal: $(E, R, G \cup \{s \dot{=} t|w\}) \vdash_{\mathcal{TAX}} (E, R, G \cup \{u \dot{=} t|w\})$
   if $s \Rightarrow u$ with $l \rightarrow r|v \in R(E)$, $w=vv'$.

8. Subsume goal: $(E \cup \{s_1 \dot{=} t_1|w_1\}, R, G \cup \{s_2 \dot{=} t_2|w_2\}) \vdash_{\mathcal{TAX}}$
   $\qquad\qquad\qquad\qquad\qquad\qquad (E \cup \{s_1 \dot{=} t_1|w_1\}, R, G)$
   if $s_2/p \equiv \sigma(s_1)$, $s_2[p \leftarrow \sigma(t_1)] \equiv t_2$, $w_2 = w_1v$.

9. Delete goal: $(E, R, G \cup \{s \dot{=} t|w\}) \vdash_{\mathcal{TAX}} (E, R, G)$
   if $s \equiv t$.

10. Success: $(E, R, \{s \dot{=} t|w\}) \vdash_{\mathcal{TAX}} Success$
    if $s \equiv t$.

So, $\mathcal{TAX}$ deals with facts that are associated with paths in a taxonomy.
For manipulating a fact of a given level of the path only facts with the same
or higher level, representing more general knowledge, can be used. The results
of inferences involving facts of different levels will always belong to the deeper,
more specialized level.

Note that there are some differences between $\mathcal{TAX}$ and the very general
method of constraint theorem proving described in [KKR90]. Each equation has
only one constraint and no merging of constraints due to applications of inference
rules is necessary. Especially, we do not allow the reduction of a constrained rule,
equation or goal with a rule or equation with more specialized constraint. As we

will see in section 4 these reductions are not very important for efficiency. We also do not need a concept for solving constraints, which is the reason for major problems of other constraint completion approaches.

3.2 Theoretical aspects

Since the inference rules of $\mathcal{TAX}$ are essentially the same rules as those in [AD93], the necessary additional definitions and the proofs to establish correctness and completeness of [BDP89] can be taken over with very minor modifications. For more details we refer to [De95]. Thus we have

Theorem 4 : Correctness of $\mathcal{TAX}$.

> *Let (E,R,G) be the constrained equations, rules and goals of a taxonomy T. Let further (E',R',G') be the result of applying one of the rules of $\mathcal{TAX}$ to (E,R,G). Then for all nodes N of $T =_{E^N \cup R^N} == _{E'^N \cup R'^N}$ holds.*

An important property of an algorithm based on an inference rule system is a fair selection of applications of the inference rules. As already stated, for completion only a fair selection of critical pairs is required. Again, the definition of fairness of [BDP89] can be extended to constrained critical pairs straightforward.

Definition 5 : Fairness.

> *A derivation $(E_i, R_i, G_i)_{i \in \mathbb{N}}$, where $(E_{i+1}, R_{i+1}, G_{i+1})$ is derived from (E_i, R_i, G_i) by application of a rule of $\mathcal{TAX}$, is called fair, if for each critical pair u = v|w of E^∞, R^∞ there is an i such that u =v|w $\in E_i$. Here, $E^\infty = \bigcup_{i \geq 0} \bigcap_{j \geq i} E_j$ and $R^\infty = \bigcup_{i \geq 0} \bigcap_{j \geq i} R_j$.*

So, if we omit the constraint w, this would be the usual definition of fairness. Now we have

Theorem 6 : Completeness of $\mathcal{TAX}$.

> *Let T be a taxonomy to the input problems $s_i =_{E^i} t_i$ and let $\succ$ be a ground reduction ordering and $(E_j, R_j, G_j)_{j \in \mathbb{N}}$ an derivation that is fair with E_0, R_0 and G_0 as defined before. Then for each pair of ground terms (s,t) with $s =_{E^i} t$ for an $i \in 1,...,n$, there is an $j \in \mathbb{N}$ such that the normal forms of s and t with respect to $R_j(E_j)$ are identical.*

3.3 Practical aspects

The problem we have to face is how to guarantee derivations to be fair. An obvious solution is to use the FIFO-strategy for selecting the critical pairs, but it is well known that FIFO performs very badly. Therefore more intelligent strategies are needed. One way would be to extend a known (intelligent) strategy for unfailing completion to deal also with the constraints. Fortunately, this is not necessary. A very often used selection strategy, the smallest-component strategy

of [Hu80] (we call it AddWeight, see [AD93]), produces fair derivations also for
$\mathcal{TAX}$ without the need of considering the constraints.

AddWeight always selects a critical pair with the smallest term weight, which
(in our system) is computed by counting a function symbol as 2 and a variable
as 1. The term weight of each term of a critical pair is added to get the weight of
a pair (hence the name *Add*Weight). Since there is only a limited number of term
pairs that have a lower term weight than a given critical pair and since there is
also only a limited number of term pairs with the same weight, AddWeight is
a fair selection strategy with respect to the fairness defined in [BDP89]. Since
the number of nodes in T is also limited, each term pair can only occur with a
limited number of different constraints. Therefore there is only a limited number
of term pairs with constraints that have a lower weight than a given constrained
critical pair and this means that AddWeight is indeed fair.

Another aspect when looking for a selection strategy (or heuristic) for critical
pairs that is often criticized is the absence of any goal orientation. The same
criticism may also be directed towards our system $\mathcal{TAX}$. But, as in the case of
standard unfailing completion, goal oriented selection heuristics, as defined in
[DF94], can be used. If we use a list of critical pairs for each node N of T, choose
in turn a pair from each list, but use for each list different heuristics, then lists
to nodes that contain only one goal can employ goal oriented heuristics. But, so
far using only AddWeight was sufficient (see section 4).

4 Experimental Results

Equational theorem proving with taxonomic constraints is intended for situations
in which from several slightly different sets of equations several goals have to be
proved. Typically, such situations occur when one wants to prove the validity of
several conditional equations in a theory consisting of unconditional equations.

For our experiments we have chosen two such theories, namely *lattice ordered
groups* and an equational axiomatization of the *propositional calculus*, and for
each theory we have chosen several conditional equations of which we generated
several problem sets we solved using our implementation of $\mathcal{TAX}$. We will compare run times, numbers of rules and equations generated, numbers of critical
pairs computed and numbers of reduction steps made of our implementation using constraints and the accumulated results obtained with our implementation
when proving each conditional equation alone.

All experiments were performed on a SUN Sparc 20 and the times are given
in seconds. Our implementation is in C (based on DISCOUNT, see [ADF95]),
but does not use indexing techniques or realizing lists of critical pairs as heaps.

4.1 Lattice ordered groups

The theory of lattice ordered groups is given by the following set of equations:

$$f(f(x,y),z) = f(x,f(y,z)), \qquad f(1,x) = x, \qquad f(i(x),x) = 1$$

$$l(l(x,y),z) = l(x,l(y,z)), \qquad l(x,y) = l(y,x), \quad l(x,x) = x$$
$$u(u(x,y),z) = u(x,u(y,z)), \qquad u(x,y) = u(y,x), \quad u(x,x) = x$$
$$f(x,l(y,z)) = l(f(x,y),f(x,z)), \quad u(x,l(x,y)) = x, \quad f(l(x,y),z) = l(f(x,z),f(y,z))$$
$$f(x,u(y,z)) = u(f(x,y),f(x,z)), \quad l(x,u(x,y)) = x, \quad f(u(x,y),z) = u(f(x,z),f(y,z))$$

In literature (see [KK74]) lattice ordered groups are characterized as the combination of two mathematical structures, namely lattices and groups. Above can be seen the group operator f, its neutral element 1 and the inverse operator i. A lattice is based on a partial ordering $\leq$ and two binary functions l and u, the greatest lower bound and the least upper bound of two elements. l and u can be used to get rid of the partial ordering $\leq$ with the help of the definition $x \leq y$ *iff* $l(x,y) = x$ or $x \leq y$ *iff* $u(x,y) = y$ that was already used in the axiomatization above. Since there are two ways for eliminating $\leq$, there are several possible formulations of a given problem. This is indicated in the following by the last letter of the names of the examples. So, lat2a und lat2b are two different formulations for the same problem. We present the conditional theorems already skolemized and in the form "additional axioms $\Rightarrow$ goal to prove".

ax_mono1a:	$u(a,b) = b$	$\Rightarrow u(f(a,c),f(b,c)) = f(b,c)$
ax_mono1b:	$l(a,b) = a$	$\Rightarrow l(f(a,c),f(b,c)) = f(a,c)$
ax_mono1c:	$u(a,b) = b$	$\Rightarrow l(f(a,c),f(b,c)) = f(a,c)$
ax_mono2a:	$u(a,b) = b$	$\Rightarrow u(f(c,a),f(c,b)) = f(c,b)$
ax_mono2b:	$l(a,b) = a$	$\Rightarrow l(f(c,a),f(c,b)) = f(c,a)$
ax_mono2c:	$l(a,b) = a$	$\Rightarrow u(f(c,a),f(c,b)) = f(c,b)$
lat1a:	$u(a,1) = a$	$\Rightarrow u(a,f(a,a)) = f(a,a)$
lat2a:	$u(a,1) = a,\ u(b,1) = b$	$\Rightarrow u(a,f(a,b)) = f(a,b)$
lat2b:	$l(a,1) = 1,\ l(b,1) = 1$	$\Rightarrow l(a,f(a,b)) = a$
lat3a:	$u(a,1) = a,\ u(b,1) = b$	$\Rightarrow u(a,f(b,a)) = f(b,a)$
lat3b:	$l(a,1) = 1,\ l(b,1) = 1$	$\Rightarrow l(a,f(b,a)) = a$
p04a:	$u(1,a) = a,\ u(1,b) = b$	$\Rightarrow u(1,f(a,b)) = f(a,b)$
p04b:	$l(1,a) = 1,\ l(1,b) = 1$	$\Rightarrow l(1,f(a,b)) = 1$
p04c:	$u(1,a) = a,\ u(1,b) = b$	$\Rightarrow l(1,f(a,b)) = 1$
p04d:	$l(1,a) = 1,\ l(1,b) = 1$	$\Rightarrow u(1,f(a,b)) = f(a,b)$
p05a:	$u(1,a) = 1,\ u(1,i(a)) = 1$	$\Rightarrow 1 = a$
p05b:	$l(1,a) = 1,\ l(1,i(a)) = 1$	$\Rightarrow 1 = a$
p39a:	$u(a,b) = a$	$\Rightarrow u(i(a),i(b)) = i(b)$
p39b:	$l(a,b) = b$	$\Rightarrow l(i(a),i(b)) = i(a)$
p39c:	$u(a,b) = a$	$\Rightarrow l(i(a),i(b)) = i(a)$
p39d:	$l(a,b) = b$	$\Rightarrow u(i(a),i(b)) = i(b)$

Using the LPO with precedence $i > f > l > u > 1 > a > b > c$ we get the results reported in Table 1 when proving each example separately.

We generated from these examples the following experiments.

LOGExp1 :

Partition at first level: {ax_mono1a,ax_mono1c,ax_mono2a}, {ax_mono1b, ax_mono2b,ax_mono2c}, {lat1a,lat2a,lat3a}, {lat2b,lat3b}, {p04a,p04c}, {p04b,p04d}, {p05a}, {p05b}, {p39a,p39c}, {p39b,p39d}

Second level: {lat2a}, {lat3a}

Ex.	Run Time	Rules	crit. Pairs	Reductions
ax_mono1a	21.59	118	8806	13610
ax_mono1b	21.99	122	9037	13976
ax_mono1c	22.50	122	9037	13976
ax_mono2a	21.30	108	8270	12819
ax_mono2b	21.48	114	8584	13282
ax_mono2c	21.17	108	8270	12819
lat1a	2.88	61	2230	2570
lat2a	4.00	90	3484	3921
lat2b	4.42	91	3521	3954
lat3a	27.56	293	20125	22079
lat3b	29.04	294	20204	22178
p04a	15.46	212	12338	12869
p04b	4.14	96	3670	4115
p04c	4.24	96	3670	4115
p04d	16.53	212	12338	12869
p05a	3.44	75	2819	3276
p05b	3.53	75	2816	3236
p39a	20.32	112	8492	13137
p39b	20.20	113	8535	13192
p39c	21.00	113	8535	13192
p39d	21.59	112	8492	13137

Table 1 : Lattice ordered groups: statistics for runs of one example only

LOGExp2 :
Partition at first level: {ax_mono1a,ax_mono1c,ax_mono2a}, {ax_mono1b, ax_mono2b,ax_mono2c}, {lat1a,lat2a,lat3a}, {lat2b,lat3b}, {p04a,p04c}, {p04b,p04d}, {p05a}, {p05b}
Second level: {lat2a}, {lat3a}
LOGExp3 :
Partition at first level: {ax_mono1a,ax_mono1c,ax_mono2a}, {lat1a,lat2a,lat3a}, {p04a,p04c}, {p05a}, {p39a,p39c}
Second level: {lat2a}, {lat3a}
LOGExp4 :
Partition at first level: {ax_mono1b,ax_mono2b,ax_mono2c}, {lat2b,lat3b}, {p04b,p04d}, {p05b}, {p39b,p39d}
LOGExp5 :
Partition at first level: {lat3a}, {lat3b}

4.2 Propositional calculus

An equational axiomatization of the propositional calculus is given by

$$C(T,x) = x \qquad C(C(p,C(q,r)),C(C(p,q),C(p,r))) = T$$
$$C(p,C(q,p)) = T \quad C(C(p,C(q,r)),C(q,C(p,r))) = T$$

$$C(N(N(p)),p) = T \quad C(C(p,q),C(N(q),N(p))) = T \quad C(p,N(N(p))) = T$$

This axiomatization is inspired by [Ta56]. The function C represents the logical implication, N the negation and T true. We selected out of [KW76] (pages 181, 182) the following conditional equations. The numbers are the numbers of [KW76] (the examples not appearing here either used additional connectives or were too easy, meaning that they were solved in under one second).

9: $C(A,B) = T, C(A,N(B)) = T \Rightarrow N(A) = T$
26: $C(A,B) = T, C(B,D) = T \quad \Rightarrow C(A,D) = T$
27: $C(A,B) = T \quad\quad\quad\quad\quad \Rightarrow C(C(B,D),C(A,D)) = T$
28: $C(A,B) = T \quad\quad\quad\quad\quad \Rightarrow C(C(D,A),C(D,B)) = T$
29: $C(C(A,B),D) = T \quad\quad\quad \Rightarrow C(A,C(B,D)) = T$
36: $C(A,N(A)) = T \quad\quad\quad\quad \Rightarrow N(A) = T$
37: $C(N(A),A) = T \quad\quad\quad\quad \Rightarrow A = T$
39: $N(A) = T \quad\quad\quad\quad\quad\quad \Rightarrow C(A,B) = T$
40: $A = T \quad\quad\quad\quad\quad\quad\quad\; \Rightarrow C(N(A),B) = T$
44: $C(N(B),N(A)) = T \quad\quad\quad \Rightarrow C(A,B) = T$
45: $C(A,N(B)) = T \quad\quad\quad\quad \Rightarrow C(B,N(A)) = T$
46: $C(N(A),B) = T \quad\quad\quad\quad \Rightarrow C(N(B),A) = T$
55: $C(A,B) = T, C(N(A),B) = T \Rightarrow B = T$

Using the LPO with precedence $C > N > A > B > D > T$ we get the results of Table 2 when proving these examples without taxonomic constaints.

Ex.	Run Time	Rules	crit. Pairs	Reductions
9	8.12	142	15275	25469
26	3.70	103	7840	13281
27	8.98	149	18044	30769
28	2.90	84	6380	10895
29	7.60	119	14273	24623
36	6.00	110	11950	20123
37	4.49	100	9878	16161
39	4.24	96	9067	16032
40	2.76	74	6292	10936
44	10.61	148	20335	33656
45	11.80	154	21674	35662
46	4.20	85	7461	12851
55	7.35	147	15017	24876

Table 2: Propositional calculus: statistics for runs of one example only

Out of these examples we generated the following experiments.
PCExp1 :
Partition at first level: $\{9,26,27,28,55\}, \{29\}, \{36\}, \{37\}, \{39\}, \{40\}, \{44\}, \{45\}, \{46\}$
Second level: $\{9\}, \{26\}, \{55\}$

PCExp2 :
Partition at first level: {9,45}, {26,27,28}, {46,55}, {36}, {37}, {39}, {40}, {44}
Second level: {9}, {26}, {55}
PCExp3 :
Partition at first level: {9,26,27,28}, {44}, {45}
Second level: {9}, {26}
PCExp4 :
Partition at first level: {9,26,27,28,55}, {44}, {45}
Second level: {9}, {26}, {55}
PCExp5 :
Partition at first level: {28}, {29}, {36}, {37}, {39}, {40}, {44}, {45}, {46}
PCExp6 :
Partition at first level: {29}, {36}, {37}, {39}, {40}, {44}
PCExp7 :
Partition at first level: {9,45}, {46,55}, {26,27,28}
Second level: {9}, {55}, {26}
PCExp8 :
Partition at first level: {9,45}, {46,55}, {40}, {44}
Second level: {9}, {55}

4.3   Discussion of the results

The first, obvious and most important result of our experiments (see Table 3) is that not only the number of inferences done by $\mathcal{TAX}$ is substantially smaller than the accumulated sum of the runs of single examples, but also the run times. This proves our claim that taxonomic constraints are easy and efficient to handle. But typically, the ratios of $\sum$ (the accumulated sum) to $\mathcal{TAX}$ for rules, critical pairs and reductions are slightly higher than for the run time.

If we compare the two example domains, the number of equations that are shared by all examples is for lattice ordered groups twice the number of that for propositional calculus. Concerning the experiments in which all examples were included (LOGExp1, PCExp1, PCExp2) we have more theorems to prove for lattice ordered groups than for propositional calculus. Therefore one would expect that the ratio of $\sum$ to $\mathcal{TAX}$ would be much better in all statistics for lattice ordered groups than for propositional calculus. But this is not true.

To explain this phenomenon we comment on the search heuristic AddWeight and on the structure of the two domains. The additional axioms of the theorems of both domains are quite short. This means that they produce many critical pairs that are also short and therefore will be selected by AddWeight prior to most of the critical pairs between elements of the axioms of the domain. So, in both domains the number of axioms is not so important for the statistics.

If we take a closer look at the examples of the domain lattice ordered groups we can observe that the additional axioms either use the operators l or u (due to the two translations of $\leq$). Therefore some proofs do not have many proof steps in common, although the number of steps is quite similar. This is illustrated by the examples lat3a and lat3b. LOGExp5 solves them together and it can be seen that here $\mathcal{TAX}$ needs nearly the same number of rules, critical pairs and reductions as the accumulated sum of the separated runs. Therefore the examples of the domain lattice ordered groups have to be divided into two groups, those using the u- and those using the l-translation. If we look at the results of $\mathcal{TAX}$ when given only the examples of one group (experiments LOGExp3 and LOGExp4), then the ratio of $\sum$ to $\mathcal{TAX}$ is better in all statistics than for LOGExp1.

Exp.	Run times		Rules		crit. Pairs		Reduktions	
	$\sum$	$\mathcal{TAX}$	$\sum$	$\mathcal{TAX}$	$\sum$	$\mathcal{TAX}$	$\sum$	$\mathcal{TAX}$
LOGExp1	328.38	157.99	2737	1114	173273	80201	228332	95217
LOGExp2	245.27	136.90	2287	1046	139219	73764	175674	85423
LOGExp3	164.29	71.66	1400	596	87806	42706	115564	51589
LOGExp4	164.09	71.29	1337	597	85467	42782	112768	51647
LOGExp5	56.60	54.89	587	539	40329	38689	44257	42477
PCExp1	82.75	36.31	1511	407	163086	54023	275334	89557
PCExp2	82.75	29.48	1511	419	163086	50867	275334	85054
PCExp3	46.11	23.81	780	267	89548	38443	149735	62570
PCExp4	53.46	23.67	927	300	104565	41756	174611	67913
PCExp5	54.60	21.58	970	279	106910	35225	180939	59227
PCExp6	35.70	14.44	647	227	71395	29485	121531	50197
PCExp7	47.05	21.09	864	306	91691	37679	153803	61885
PCExp8	44.84	21.72	750	282	86053	35149	143450	57616
CombExp1	40.84	40.93	448	448	41878	41878	57840	57978
CombExp2	101.71	79.59	1367	806	129877	77132	193992	105238
CombExp3	411.13	192.17	4248	1533	336359	131068	503666	180408

Table 3: Statistics of runs using taxonomic constraints

Another expectation one may have is that adding more examples from a given domain –that do not require totally different proofs– will not increase the statistics of $\mathcal{TAX}$ as much as the statistics of $\sum$. This is indeed the case as proven by experiments LOGExp2 and LOGExp1, PCExp3 and PCExp4, PCExp7 and PCExp2 or PCExp6 and PCExp5. For all these pairs of experiments the increase of $\mathcal{TAX}$ is less than that of $\sum$ for all statistics of Table 3.

Some of the experiments in the domain propositional calculus demonstrate the effects of different partitions of the examples (i.e. PCExp1, PCExp2, PCExp4 and PCExp7). In general one can say that our results do not allow to favor a certain partition heuristic. This is because all the examples to prove, not only those that allow different partitions, determine the statistics of a run.

Another question is how $\mathcal{TAX}$ behaves when proving examples that are totally different, i.e. with no equations in common. To answer this question we combined examples from both domains in single experiments. The results are also given in Table 3. The experiment CombExp1 includes one example from each domain, namely lat3b and 45. In experiment CombExp2 we added to the examples of LOGExp5 the examples of PCExp3. In CombExp3 we solved the examples of LOGExp1 and PCExp2 together. For experiments CombExp2 and

CombExp3 the interesting times for answering the question are the sums of the basic experiments, i.e. the sum of the results of LOGExp5 and PCExp3 : 78.7 sec, resp. LOGExp1 and PCExp2: 187.47 sec. As can be seen, the overhead produced is neglectable. So, the gains provided by the constraints are not disturbed by adding other unrelated examples.

Finally, there is the question whether our restriction of the interreduction (no simplification of term pairs that are higher up in the taxonomy than the applied rule) causes any problems. The answer to this question is negative. The ratio of $\sum$ to $\mathcal{TAX}$ for the number of rules or the number of critical pairs is in all our experiments comparable to this ratio for the number of reductions.

5 Dynamic taxonomies and some applications

So far, taxonomies did not change during completion. In the following we will discuss situations in which a certain change of the taxonomy used, namely a dynamic extension, is required. We speak of a *dynamic taxonomy*, if during the proof task new successors to nodes of the taxonomy may be added. Of course, these new successors must inherit the equations and rules of their ancestors, which is easily achieved by $\mathcal{TAX}$. As long as the taxonomy remains finite, this dynamic change does not influence the correctness and completeness results.

There are several situations where dynamic taxonomies in combination with $\mathcal{TAX}$ are useful. We will sketch two. The first situation is trying to complete a set of equations without knowing the right reduction ordering. One way to deal with this problem is to use several reduction orderings in parallel (see [KKO95]). Unfortunatly this method lacks the dynamic addition of further orderings, so that one has, for example, to start with all possible permutations of the precedence ordering to an LPO or RPO. But many comparisons between function symbols may never be necessary due to the form of the equations, which suggests to use incremental extension of orderings. So, one can modify $\mathcal{TAX}$ in such a way that the nodes of the taxonomy represent reduction orderings. Then successor nodes N of M represent different extensions of the ordering M and so can be added on demand.

The other situation stems from using completion theorem provers in interactive proof environments that are used as proof assistants. Such an environment is the ILF-System [Da+94] in which the DISCOUNT-System is used for solving pure equational problems. Often a user of such a system is interested in checking the consequences of some manipulations of parts of the axioms for proving a goal. This means that some equations may be withdrawn while others are added. Instead of doing a new proof run after each such action one can start $\mathcal{TAX}$ with a degenerated taxonomy that has only one path in which the candidates for withdrawal all have their own nodes (they have to be arranged with respect to the possibility that they are withdrawn). If such a candidate is withdrawn, then a new successor to the predecessor of the respective node is added with the new equations. So, assuming a careful planning of the experiments, many results of prior experiments can be used for new ones. This improves the acceptance by the user of the whole proof assistant.

6   Conclusion and Future Work

We have presented taxonomic constraints as a way to reduce the repetition of many inferences when one wants to prove theorems in slightly different axiom systems for the case of equational deduction by unfailing completion. By transforming all proof tasks into a taxonomy and then transforming this taxonomy back into sets of constrained equations, rules and goals we were able to develop a theorem prover that performes not only much less inference steps than those that were needed to prove each of the examples separately but also needs less time. We also sketched several situations in which a theorem prover using taxonomic constraints may be very useful.

Future work should center on exploiting the use of dynamic taxonomies, on the development of more selection heuristics for constrained critical pairs and on the implementation and experimental evaluation of the idea presented in section 3.3 to use goal oriented selection heuristics. Also the use of taxonomic constraints in other theorem provers may be of interest.

References

[AD93]   Avenhaus, J. ; Denzinger, J.: *Distributing equational theorem proving*, Proc. 5th RTA, Montreal, LNCS 690, 1993, pp. 62-76.

[ADF95]   Avenhaus, J. ; Denzinger, J. ; Fuchs, M.: *DISCOUNT: A system for distributed equational deduction*, Proc. 6th RTA, Kaiserslautern, LNCS 914, 1995, pp. 397-402.

[BDP89]   Bachmair, L. ; Dershowitz, N. ; Plaisted, D.A.: *Completion without Failure*, Coll. on the Resolution of Equations in Algebraic Structures, Austin (1987), Academic Press, 1989.

[BS85]   Brachman, R.J.; Schmolze, J.G.: *On Overview of the KL-ONE Knowledge Representation System*, Cognitive Science 9(2), 1985, pp. 171-216.

[Bü90]   Bürckert, H.-J.: *A Resolution Principle for Clauses with Constraints*, Proc. 10th CADE, Kaiserslautern, Springer, LNAI 449, 1990, pp. 178-192.

[Da+94]   Dahn, B.I. ; Gehne, J. ; Honigmann, T. ; Walther, L. ; Wolf, A.: *Integrating Logical Functions with ILF*, Internal report, Humbold-University, Berlin, 1994.

[De95]   Denzinger, J.: *Completion and Equational Theorem Proving using Taxonomic Constraints*, SEKI-Report SR-95-11, University of Kaiserslautern, 1995.

[DF94]   Denzinger, J. ; Fuchs, M.: *Goal oriented equational theorem proving using teamwork*, Proc. 18th KI-94, Saarbrücken, LNAI 861, 1994, pp. 343-354.

[DJ90]   Dershowitz, N. ; Jouannaud, J.P.: *Rewriting systems*, in J. van Leeuwen (Ed.): Handbook of theoretical computer science, Vol. B., Elsevier, 1990, pp. 241-320.

[HR87]   Hsiang, J. ; Rusinowitch, M.: *On word problems in equational theories*, Proc. 14th ICALP, Karlsruhe, LNCS 267, 1987, pp. 54-71.

[Hu80]   Huet, G.: *Confluent Reductions: Abstract Properties and Applications to Term Rewriting Systems*, Journal of ACM, Vol. 27, No. 4, 1980, pp. 798-821.

[KB70]   Knuth, D.E. ; Bendix, P.B.: *Simple Word Problems in Universal Algebra*, Computational Algebra, J. Leech, Pergamon Press, 1970, pp. 263-297.

[KK74]   Kokorin, A.I. ; Kopytov, V.M.: *Fully ordered groups*, Halsted Press, 1974.

[KKO95]   Kurihara, M. ; Kondo, H. ; Ohuchi, A.: *Completion for Multiple Reduction Orderings*, Proc. 6th RTA, Kaiserslautern, LNCS 914, 1995, pp. 71-85.

[KKR90]   Kirchner, C. ; Kirchner, H. ; Rusinowitch, M.: *Deduction with symbolic constraints*, Revue d'Intelligence Artificielle 4(3), 1990, pp. 9-52.

[KW76]   Kleinknecht, R. ; Wüst, E.: *Lehrbuch der elementaren Logik, Bd. 1: Aussagenlogik*, DTV-Verlag, 1976.

[Ta56]   Tarski, A.: *Logic, Semantics, Metamathematics*, Oxford University Press, 1956.

Planning for Distributed Theorem Proving: The Teamwork Approach

Jörg Denzinger, Martin Kronenburg
Department of Computer Science
University of Kaiserslautern
Postfach 3049, 67653 Kaiserslautern
E-mail: {denzinge, kronburg}@informatik.uni-kl.de

Abstract. We present a new way to use planning in automated theorem proving by means of distribution. To overcome the problem that often subtasks of a problem cannot be detected a priori (which prevents the use of known planning and distribution techniques) we use the teamwork approach: A team of experts independently works on the problem with different heuristics. After a certain amount of time referees judge their results using the impact of the results on the behaviour of the experts. Then a supervisor combines the selected results to a new starting point. The supervisor also selects the experts that will work on the problem in the next round. This selection is a reactive planning task. We outline which information the supervisor can use to fulfill this task and how this information is processed to result in a plan or in revising a plan. Experimental results show that this planning approach for the assignment of experts to a team enables the system to solve many different examples in an acceptable time with the same start configuration and without any intervention by the user.

Keywords: Theorem proving, reactive planning, distributed problem solving

1 Introduction

A major problem of automated theorem proving is the immense search space that even for small problems a theorem prover has to deal with. Research for solutions to this problem centers on two directions, the use of distributed provers and the use of knowledge to guide the prover through the search space. Although this guidance has been used quite some time in provers by means of heuristics, only in the last few years better concepts of guidance, namely planning, have found their way into proving systems. Both, distributed provers and provers using planning have to deal with the same problem: the difficulty, almost inability, of finding a priori appropriate subtasks of a proof problem. Such subtasks can only be determined, if very much about a proof problem is known. But what should be done when the knowledge about the proof problem (besides the input) is vague?

To deal with this problem we developed the teamwork method (see [AD93], [De95]). This method allows the distribution of search processes where the descriptions of the processes show no obvious ways for distribution. The general idea of teamwork is to let a team of several so-called experts (which are computational agents) work independently on the proof problem. They differ in the heuristics they use to determine the next step to do. After a given amount of time the experts stop their work and for each expert a referee assesses the work of the expert and reports a general assessment and a few good results to a supervisor. This supervisor collects the reports, generates – based on these reports – as a new starting point for the experts a new set of equations, and selects experts and referees for the next working round. We call the phase when the referees and the supervisor are working a team meeting.

Structure and behaviour of our teams lead to a system that uses both, competition and cooperation between its components (mainly the experts) to solve given problems. The experts compete with each other in order to stay in the team. But with the help of the referees they also cooperate, because their best results are used to form a new starting point for the work of the team.

In [AD93] we concentrated on the general aspects of this approach and showed that for many examples there exist teams that allow enormous speed-ups. In [DF94] we designed powerful experts and demonstrated that we are able to solve examples using teamwork that could not be solved by any of our experts working alone. But the question remains how to choose *automatically* good teams for an example, so that a lot of different examples can be solved in an acceptable time without any intervention by the user. The solution to this problem is the supervisor. During the team meetings it selects the members of the next team.

We see this process of creating a new team in each team meeting as a kind of *reactive planning*. The supervisor uses a long-term memory (general knowledge about experts, referees and their relationships, dependencies and incompatibilities) in combination with a short-term memory (the results of the experts on the given problem so far) to determine the team members. It not only selects the team members of the next round, but also can make assignments for further rounds provided that the selected team comes up with the expected results. Otherwise the behaviour of the selected team is used to find better suited experts. This is a kind of replanning or plan revision which we call *maintenance* of a plan.

For planning a team in this way it is not necessary to find subtasks of a proof problem. If subtasks can be detected, they can be assigned to experts that are capable to prove them. If no subtasks can be found, the supervisor tests several experts and adjusts the whole system more and more to the given problem.

Using reactive planning by the supervisor we were able to solve automatically most of the examples of [DF94] and [AD93] without any intervention by the user: no team selection, no parameter adjustment by the user was necessary, just planning using general but vague knowledge was enough (see section 5). The knowledge-based reactive planning approach used by the supervisor of a team presented in this paper allows for a much easier extension of the system to new domains than the auto mode of Otter (see [Mc94]) does. There the code must be changed in order to deal with new domains. This auto mode was, like teamwork, designed to provide a fully automatic theorem prover to users who do not want to learn all about the tricks of a prover in order to use it successfully.

2 Automated Theorem Proving and Completion

Since this paper is aiming to analyze and describe the planning aspect of team-work, we only give a very brief introduction into automated theorem proving, equational theorem proving and the completion method for equational proving. For more details we refer to [CL73], [HR87], [BDP89] and [AD93].

Theorem proving means solving the following problem:

     Given: A set A of axioms and a theorem T to prove.

     Question: Is T a logical consequence of A?

In equational theorem proving $A = \{s_i = t_i \mid i = 1, \ldots, n\}$ is a set of (universally quantified) equations and T is an equation u = v, too.

All successful methods for automated theorem proving, if equality is involved, are based on two kinds of inference rules: generation rules and contraction rules. The generation inference rules add new facts to the data base. These facts are derived either from the axioms alone (as in the case of equational theorem proving by completion, i.e. the critical pair generation) or from both the axioms and the theorem T (as in the case of resolution and paramodulation). The contraction inference rules change or delete facts from the data base. A well known contraction inference is the reduction (or demodulation) that uses an equation l = r as a rule l → r in order to exchange instances of l in a fact by the appropriate (smaller) instance of r. A fact is in normal form, if no reduction with any equation of the data base is possible.

From a theoretical point of view we need for a theorem prover, besides the inference rules, fairness criteria for the use of these rules. These criteria guarantee that each application of an inference rule, that is enabled infinitely often, will finally be executed. But, for challenging examples there are many possible inferences and a systematic application results both in enormous run times and the need of much (memory) space. For such examples the prover very often has an agenda of 50,000, 100,000 or even more inference rule applications.

Therefore, implementations of automated theorem provers use strategies and heuristics to select the next inference rule to apply and the facts these rules should work on. A strategy guarantees theoretical completeness whereas for heuristics it is possible that the prover will not find a proof even if there is one and enough time and space are provided. Many theorem provers allow the user to choose between various strategies and heuristics. But two problems remain. First, for a given problem there may be no appropriate strategy or heuristic implemented in the system. Second, even if there is a good one implemented, how does the user know which one is good? We tackled both problems with our teamwork method as we will demonstrate in the next section.

3 The Teamwork Method

The teamwork method is inspired by project teams in business companies. Due to their temporary existence they allow an exact tuning to the problem they have to solve. This tuning is achieved by the supervisor of the team who always chooses the team he thinks is best suited for the current status of the solution of the given problem.

So, one major task of the supervisor is a planned selection of the team members. This planning must also allow a fast reaction to problems concerning the selected teams or when unexpected breakthroughs occur. We will discuss this task of the supervisor in more detail in the next section. In this section we will look briefly at the other components of a team, the experts and referees, and their tasks and how they compete and cooperate to solve a given problem.

Experts are those components that work on the problem solution by generating new facts. Each expert has to work on an own processor. Usually there are more experts than processors. Therefore the experts have to compete with each other to get a processor for the next working period. Each expert uses other methods to gain new data. In automated theorem proving the experts differ in the selection methods for the next inference step. There are many criteria that can be used to get different heuristics. For example, one can focus on parts of the set of known facts, focus on statistical properties of the facts (for example the number of symbols), or focus on the goal to prove (see [AD93], [DF94]).

Experts compete for processors, but another characteristic of a project team is that the members of the team cooperate with each other. As a result of this cooperation, problems can be solved much faster than by a single team member alone, even if we consider as the time for finding the solution the sum of the times needed by all members. So, cooperation leads to *synergetic* effects.

The teamwork method achieves cooperation between the experts by using referees and team meetings. After certain periods of time during which the experts work independently on the problem, a team meeting takes place. Before the meeting each expert and its work is evaluated by a referee. The tasks of the referees are to compute a measure for the success of their experts and to select good results of the experts. The measure of an expert is used by the supervisor to determine the team members of the next round. The selected results are used to generate a new data base of facts that is the starting point for the next round.

The main problem in designing referees is how to compute measures for the overall behaviour of an expert on a problem and for the usefulness of generated results. For both measures there are statistical criteria that have proven to be quite successful in our application, namely automated theorem proving, and which can be computed efficiently. Our referees use a weighted sum containing, besides others, the following numbers: the size of the data base, the number of contraction inferences that were performed, and the number of potential inferences, which are the critical pairs in our case (again, see [AD93]). Referees differ in the weights they use to compute the weighted sum.

In order to select good results we use similar statistical criteria, but compute them for each fact, for example the number of contractions performed with this fact. Moreover, we give the referees a maximal number of facts that can be selected and a minimal measure that each selected fact must achieve. Thus we avoid blowing up the search space with unnecessary results.

The supervisor constructs the new starting data base by using the data base of the best assessed expert as basis. This guarantees completeness of our prover. Then it adds the selected results of the other experts to this basis. This combination leads to a significant speed-up in most examples.

4 Planning by the Supervisor

As in the case of human project teams, systems based on the teamwork method rely on a good use of the given resources, i.e. the processors. The supervisor is responsible for the assignment of these resources. In order to find such an assignment it has to use planning. The main problem one has to face if one wants to use planning in theorem proving is a *general vagueness of all information* one can use. In contrast to planning in the blocks world or even the navigation of robots, there are no operators with fixed pre- and postconditions that can be put together in order to obtain an executable plan. In theorem proving the only candidates for such operators are the inference rules themselves and using them would lead back to the initial proof problem.

Therefore one has to do the planning on an abstract level. But this can lead to two new problems. On the one hand it may be possible that – due to the abstraction – there is not enough information to generate a plan on the abstract level at all. On the other hand it could be possible that the next step of a generated abstract plan cannot be executed on the concrete level of the inference rules, because prior steps did not deliver the expected results. In both cases one can say that a reliable plan can be constructed more frequently if more knowledge about the current problem is available. This is the way the known planning approaches for theorem proving, for example [Bu88] (see section 6), deal with this problem. They require a lot of very concrete, even specialized knowledge – for example detected subproblems – to be able to operate.

The abstraction level provided by the experts and referees in the teamwork method is even higher. This means that our planning approach uses very vague information and that it especially does not rely on the detection of subproblems. The consequences of planning on such a high level are: Firstly, we always have to expect that generated plans are vague and that they may be wrong. Secondly, at no time we can plan the complete proof, because the more future steps we plan the more vague is the information about the outcome of these steps.

Since we use the teamwork method to handle the problem of vagueness we have to deal with a second problem: the supervisor which is responsible for the planning is the *bottleneck of our distributed system*. Therefore we have to limit the time the supervisor has for planning to a certain period of time, which must be adapted to the current state of the plan and the proof and which must be small with regard to the length of a working period.

Our solutions to these problems are based on three concepts. The fundamental concept is *teamwork* itself. Since the experts make it possible to follow several promising directions at once some vagueness can be compensated. The referees enable the system to find the most promising direction (expert) and good results of other experts. The reports of the referees also help the supervisor to decide whether a plan must be changed or not. This leads to our second concept, the general planning approach, which is based on the ideas of *reactive planning* (see [Mc90], [Be91]). The main idea is to combine a long-term memory with knowledge about earlier proof attempts and a short-term memory containing all the information about the experts and referees concerning the actual problem. By combining these two kinds of knowledge the supervisor can easily react to unsuccessful plans and perform replanning. The third concept solves the "bottleneck problem". We implemented the planning of the supervisor as an *anytime algorithm*, which means that the planning can be stopped at any time and a plan will be available. We hope that a plan is improved if the planning time increases but due to the vagueness of the underlying knowledge this cannot be guaranteed.

The following two subsections describe these three concepts and the planning process in more detail. In 4.1 we introduce the notion of a *domain* and show how a domain can support the planning process. Subsection 4.2 deals with the *maintenance* of the plan performed by the supervisor during the team meetings.

4.1 Domains

A domain is – as in other proof planning systems – a collection of information about a set of proof examples one is (or was) interested in. In our system a domain consists of facts defining the domain, consequences of these facts, methods suitable to the domain and further informations. The information about a domain is represented in a frame. The following example shows the description of the domain ring. Such domain frames and the expert frames, which are introduced in the following section, are constructed (at the moment) manually by exploiting the experience made by several experiments.

domainname:	ring
signature:	$+:2; 0:0; -:1; *:2$
equations:	$x+0 = x; x+(-x) = 0; (x+y)+z = x+(y+z)$
	$x+y = y+x; (x*y)+(z*y) = (x+z)*y$
	$(x*y)*z = x*(y*z); (x*y)+(x*z) = x*(y+z)$
consequences:	$0+x = x; (-x)+x = 0$
starting team:	Add-Weight; Add-RWeight
middle team:	Add-Weight; Add-RWeight
end team:	Add-Weight; Goal-in-CP
superior domain:	group
specialized domains:	boolean ring
similar domains:	non-associative ring

Detection of a Domain. Before the supervisor can use any information about a domain for its planning the domain must be detected in the current proof problem. This detection process is performed by an expert, a so-called *domain detection specialist*. This specialist is always a member of the first team. Note, that by using an expert for this task we avoid consuming the time of the supervisor, our bottleneck. Moreover, parallel to the detection process, other experts can already be trying to solve the example. The specialist checks many domain descriptions and reports to the supervisor those domains for which the detection process was successful. In general, several domains are found. It may also report the equations of the slot **consequences** (or a referee's selection of them).

There are several possibilities to determine whether an example belongs to a domain or not. They differ in the amount of deduction used and therefore in the chances that a domain is detected. They all have in common that they try to find a match Σ from the signature of the domain (slot **signature**) to the signature of the example and then perform tests with the facts listed under **equations**, instantiated by Σ. If the tests are successful, the domain is detected.

The first possibility is to simply test, if all instantiated equations are among the facts of the example (up to renaming of variables). In practice this method cannot deal with situations in which equations from the example can reduce other equations that are needed for the detection. In such situations the domain is not detected although the example belongs to the domain.

The second possibility is the other extreme: for all facts s=t in **equations**, it is tested, if $\Sigma(s) = \Sigma(t)$ can be proved as consequence of the set E defining the example. In this case we have to show many equations instead of one with a process that may not terminate, if an equation is not a consequence.

The possibility we have chosen lies between these extremes. For each equation s=t in **equations** we check, if the normal forms of $\Sigma(s)$ and $\Sigma(t)$ are identical or if $\Sigma(s) = \Sigma(t)$ is subsumed by an equation of the example. This overcomes the problem of the first possibility while still being a decidable (and fast) test.

Determination of a First Plan. In the first team meeting the supervisor begins with the planning of the team. Because the short-term memory consists only of the referee reports of one working period, the composition of the next team is determined by the information provided by the long-term memory. A central part is played by the *plan skeleton* of the "best" detected domain. A plan skeleton (to a domain) is represented by the contents of the slots **starting team, middle team** and **end team** of a domain. The experts in these slots have proven to be useful for many examples of the domain in the three phases we have observed in many proofs. If the supervisor determines that a proof attempt has reached the middle or the end phase, then the experts mentioned in those slots should be used in the next team. Note that there are powerful experts that have been designed for the use in the end phase of a proof (see [DF94]).

With the selection of the "best" domain of an example we have the core of the next team. For determining this domain, the supervisor uses the hierarchical information that is given in the slots **superior domain, specialized domains** and **similar domains** of the domain description. By eliminating all those detected domains that are superior domains to another detected one or that are similar to a domain which is superior to a detected domain we can obtain a hopefully small set of candidates or even a single one. Since in the first team meeting the supervisor has no information about these remaining domains with regard to the actual proof problem a random candidate is chosen as the domain the supervisor will concentrate on (for the moment).

If there are more processors available than there are experts in the starting team of the chosen domain, then the domain detection specialist can be incorporated in the team again with the task to look especially at those domains that are specialized versions of the chosen one. Additionally, experts that are mentioned in the starting teams of other detected domains can be used to complete the team.

4.2 Maintenance of the Plan

As already stated, one can never be sure that a plan or a plan skeleton succeeds in finding a proof of a given problem. In most cases adjustments of the plan have to be made, ranging from small changes up to generating a totally new plan. This *maintenance* of the plan is the task of the supervisor and is performed in four steps during a team meeting: restricting the time for planning, determining proof phase and domain changes, selecting the next team, and computing the next cycle length.

Determination of the Time Available for Planning. As already stated, the periods of time in which the supervisor is active have to be very short. Therefore we allow the supervisor to use 1% of the length of the last working period.

Change of the Proof Phase and Selection of a new Domain. We define the start of a new proof phase as the team meeting in which most members of the suggested team of the prior phase either are not members of the actual team anymore or have a measure that is below a predefined percentage of the best expert's. If the start of the next proof phase is detected, then the members in the appropriate slot of the chosen domain will be members of the next team.

There are two reasons for changing the chosen domain and consequently the plan skeleton that is used. The first reason is that the specialist detects a new domain which is a specialization of the already used one. Then the supervisor immediately switches to the plan skeleton of this new domain. If a new domain is detected that is superior to the chosen domain, then no modification of the plan is necessary. The second reason is that the experts of the chosen plan skeleton are much worse rated by their referees than the best experts of the last team (and a change of the proof phase does not alter this fact).

If this second reason occurs all domains that have been detected so far are rated as follows: For each domain the supervisor sums up the measures of the experts which are mentioned in the plan skeleton of the domains. Each measure of an expert is weighted by 1 divided by the number of working periods since the measure was given. In this way older information gets less credit. The domain with the best sum is selected, if a certain threshold is reached. Otherwise the supervisor uses no domain information to choose experts. If an expert has never been member of a team during the proof attempt, it gets a measure of 0.

Selection of the Members of the next Team. Since the competition aspect is an important feature of teamwork, the supervisor always selects the best expert of the last working period as member of the next team. Also those experts that are suggested by the plan skeleton and have not performed much worse than the best expert get a place in the next team. The remaining places in the team are filled according to the following routine.

If the plan skeleton of a new domain has been selected or the proof phase has changed the experts mentioned in the corresponding slot of the actual plan skeleton get places in the next team, provided they did not perform unsatisfactorally in the last team. If there remain open places, then some computation is necessary to decide which experts should take these places. This computation is designed and implemented as an anytime algorithm, which – as already stated – means that the algorithm can be stopped at any time and the open places can be filled as good as possible with regard to the time used for this computation. To achieve this we want to examine at each time only a few experts and this examination is done in several rounds taking more and more criteria into account. In order to have always only a few experts under consideration we group the experts into five classes which are in order of importance:

- the experts of the last team,
- the experts that work well together with the best expert of the last period,
- the experts that work well together with the experts of the current phase of the plan skeleton,
- the experts that are suggested by other detected domains,
- all other experts.

For doing this classification and also for the examination and evaluation of the experts we need further information about experts. Like the domains we represent the knowledge about an expert in a frame. The following is an example.

expertname:	Add-Weight
robustness:	0.8
knowledge involved:	0.1
proof phase:	start: 0.6; middle: 0.5; end: 0.5
referees:	start: Statistic-1; middle: Statistic-4; end: Statistic-6
domains:	all
similar experts:	Add-FWeight-1; Add-RWeight
cooperative experts:	Goal-in-CP; CP-in-Goal
impossible experts:	none

The experts of the slot **cooperative experts** form the group of experts that work well together with the expert described in the frame (in our example Add-Weight). The other information is needed to determine a weight for this expert.

For each expert of the actual group the computation of this weight is done several times, each time taking more criteria into account. These criteria are:

- How good was the expert in the last phase?
- How good is the rating the expert received with respect to the detected domains and the phase of the proof?
- How good were the results of the expert in earlier phases of this proof?
- How well does the expert cooperate with the already chosen team members?
- How specialized is the expert?
- How good is the robustness of the expert?

Each criterion will lead to a measure between -1 (bad) and 1 (good) and the weight of the expert is a weighted sum of these measures. For each time the weight is computed, adjusted weights for the measures have to be used in order to compare experts of groups that were fully evaluated with experts of a group for which only weights using part of the criteria could be computed (due to lack of time). For comparisons always the weight using the most criteria is used. Also for experts that never have been team members or that have not been members of the last team adjusted weights have to be used.

If we have n free processors, the supervisor will choose the n experts with the highest weight. Note that the more time the supervisor has the more experts can be examined and the more knowledge can be used to come to a decision. But, because of the vagueness of the information we use, there is no guarantee that this decision will really improve over the time. Let us now take a closer look at the criteria we use to examine and evaluate experts.

The rating of the suitability of an expert for a domain takes into account, whether the expert is member of the team of the plan skeleton of the domain for the current phase and whether the domain is in the **domain** slot of the expert. If this is the case for all detected domains we would get a measure of 1. Note that experts that are not members of a plan skeleton of a domain may have the domain in their **domain** slot.

The measure that represents the history of the expert on the current proof attempt is computed as the mean value of the comparisons of the expert with the best experts of the working phases when the expert was member of the team. We get the comparison by dividing the result of the expert by the result of the best expert.

The measure for cooperation uses the slots **similar experts, cooperative experts** and **impossible experts**. For each already chosen expert we add 1, if the chosen expert is in **cooperative experts**, we add -1, if the chosen expert is in **impossible experts** and we add -0.1, if the chosen expert is similar to the expert we check at the moment. We add a small negative number, because this way the more similar experts we have in a team the more unlikely it would be to add another similar one. Then the sum is divided by the number of chosen experts that are mentioned in the three slots.

If at least one domain was detected, we use the value of **knowledge involved** as indication for the specialization of the expert. Finally, we multiply **robustness** with the appropriate value of **proof phase** to get a measure of the robustness of the expert.

Determination of the Length of the next Working Period. It is quite obvious that the length of the next period has to take into account the members of the new team and especially the differences between new and old team. Therefore, if the plan has been successful so far, meaning that the experts of the chosen plan skeleton or all experts of the last round have had good measures, then the lengths of the working periods increase linearly. When most of the experts did not have the time to perform more than 10 inference steps, the supervisor will use an exponential growing length.

If most of the experts of the next team are new, then it is difficult to tell whether the team will be good or bad. Therefore the length of the next working period will be shorter. How short depends on the number of facts that constitute the current problem description. The reason for this is that the more facts there are the more time is needed to perform an inference step and that, in order to get useful measures from the referees, the experts have to perform several inference steps in the working period. If the team was successful, then it will get more time the next round, else other experts will be tried.

5 Experiences

In the last section we described how the supervisor plans a proof attempt and reacts to the reports that it gets from the referees. In this section we will demonstrate that this planning enhances the performance of the whole system.

Information about the implementation of the system can be found in [AD93]. For a description of the strategies and heuristics of the experts see [DF94].

In [AD93] and [DF94] we showed by experiments that teamwork, without planning by the supervisor, can reduce the run-time of a system on a proof problem dramatically compared to the run times of the used experts when working alone. But these results have a drawback: we selected the team members of the teams. And these teams changed from example to example.

It is well known that all automated theorem provers have many parameters that can (and must) be adjusted to a given proof problem. Our important parameter was the composition of the team. But this requires that the user of a theorem prover has much knowledge about the prover and its parameters, so that he can plan his proof attempts. But we want a system which can solve many, very different examples in an acceptable time without any help of the user.

We demonstrate that teamwork with planning enables us to build such a system by reporting results obtained with examples from four domains: propositional calculus (cal1 to cal4), lattice ordered groups (p1a to p10), boolean rings (bool5b) and rings (lusk6). For the descriptions of these examples see [DF94] and [AD93]. We added the last two examples to make the detection of domains more difficult. The four domains provide a wide range of equational problems.

Table 1 documents our results. Besides the run-times of a team using planning we give the run-times of the best team consisting of two experts we were able to find, the two experts that form this best team and the run-time of the best expert working alone on the problem. We have chosen to use only two processors because with small resources a good use of them is important. In order to allow a better comparison we also restricted the best user selected teams to two processors.

The team runs using planning were always started with the same starting team and the same system configuration. Besides the input equations, a reduction ordering, the goal of an example and the start command, no interaction between system and user took place. The alterations in the composition of the team were only effected by the actions described in section 4. The system configuration specially includes some basic data for computing the lengths of the working periods which play an important part in the run of a proof. Note that for the times of the best teams the lengths of the several periods have also been adapted by the user to the specific examples.

The main observation in Table 1 is that the team with planning needs more time than the best team for most of the examples but still can also solve those

example	team with planning	best team	best team members	best sequential expert
cal1 (luka1)	29.91	35.07	MaxWeight, CP-in-Goal	40.99
cal2 (luka2)	50.18	14.21	AddFWeight, GTWeight	45.02
cal3 (luka3)	84.86	96.47	Goal-in-CP, CP-in-Goal	—
cal4 (luka4)	202.89	72.19	Goal-in-CP, AddRWeight	297.16
p1a	0.71	0.28	Occnest, MaxWeight	0.27
p1b	0.68	0.47	Occnest, AddWeight	0.28
p2a	2.46	5.41	AddRWeight, Occnest	79.52
p3a	3.04	4.23	Occnest, AddWeight	4.14
p3b	2.94	2.62	GTWeight, Occnest	2.55
p4a	2.02	2.46	GTWeight, Occnest	1.84
p4b	1.93	2.06	Occnest, AddWeight	1.71
p6a	0.84	0.40	Occnest, MaxWeight	0.39
p6b	0.58	0.16	Occnest, MaxWeight	0.16
p8b	93.54	56.84	MaxRWeight, Goal-in-CP	—
p9a	22.58	8.66	Occnest, AddWeight	19.57
p9b	23.95	8.44	AddWeight, Occnest	50.95
p10	37.94	25.20	MaxRWeight, Goal-in-CP	—
bool5b	50.11	58.86	Goal-in-CP, AddWeight	—
lusk6	500.08	307.96	AddWeight, AddRWeight	3019.00

Table 1: comparison team with planning vs best team and best expert (in sec)

examples that no single expert can solve. It is clear that using planning we have to expect a certain overhead. Our analysis of the runs using our proof extraction and analysis tool (see [DS96]) showed that not the time for doing the planning is responsible for the longer run times but the need to try out experts and the replanning that is involved when adjusting the team to a problem.

If we take a look at the experts of the best teams, it is quite obvious that even in one domain very different teams were needed. Especially in the domain propositional calculus for each example a different team was best. Therefore it cannot be expected that the first plan to a domain always succeeds. Instead the reactive part of the system must detect and exchange bad experts.

Interestingly, there are some examples (cal1, cal3, bool5b, p2a, p3a, p4a, p4b) for which the team with planning needs less time than the best two-expert team. While the run times for the lattice examples are so short that this would not be significant, the other three examples proved to be interesting. Our analysis (and later experiments) showed that the better run times of the team with planning were due to the fact that experts that were not members of the best team – but chosen by the supervisor in the run using planning – provided results necessary for the proof a little earlier than the members of the best team. But they were not able to produce enough results to form a better two-expert team with one of the members of the best team. Using a team with three experts we were able to obtain a better run time than the team with planning. For these examples planning allows us a better use of the resources. But in general we have to expect that a change of the initial plan is necessary for many examples and that in some working periods some experts do not contribute to a proof.

If we compare the team using planning with the best sequential experts for an example we can observe that for small, easy examples the best sequential expert finds a proof faster. But for harder examples the team with planning clearly outperforms the best sequential expert and it still finds proofs when no sequential expert can. If we would compare our team using planning with a fixed sequential expert there would be much more examples for which this expert would find no proof. So the synergetic effect of teamwork can also be observed when the team uses planning.

Finally we have to point out that in section 4 two ways of using a detected domain have been described: for adding known consequences and for planning purposes of the supervisor. In all the examples listed in Table 1 a domain was only used in the second way, in order to emphasize the planning aspect of a domain.

6 Related Work

The work presented here is related to three areas of artificial intelligence, namely automated theorem proving, planning and distributed artificial intelligence. The first work that is related to the first two areas is due to A. Bundy (see [Bu88]), who coined the term *proof planning*. He concentrated on inductive theorem proving and used a STRIPS-like (see [FHN81]) planning approach. He invented so-called tactics that are similar to the operators that can be defined in STRIPS. A proof attempt consists of two phases, a planning phase, where on a meta-level a plan is constructed using the tactics, and a proof phase, where the selected tactics are evaluated on the level of inference rules.

The problem of this approach is that the domains of the proof problems have to be understood very well, so that it will be possible to find appropriate subproblems to a proof problem. In equational or first-order theorem proving this is not the case as we stated in the introduction. The information about domains we have access to is much too vague to allow the use of Bundy's approach.

In the area of planning we were inspired by the works of McDermott and Beetz on planning reactive behaviour (see [Mc90], [Be91]). Here planning was intended to help a robot navigate through an area and perform certain tasks with limited planning time. This limitation is also an important point of our approach. Although robot control and automated theorem proving are very different areas, both, as stated before, have to deal with vague information. By the use of several experts we have the possibility to choose the situation we want to continue on, which is not possible for only one robot.

In the areas of planning and distributed AI the research mainly concentrates on planning for autonomous agents, i.e. systems without a central control (see for example [DL87]), or on central planning of tasks that require coordination, because there are dependencies between the actions of the agents (for example plans for several robots, see [Ro82]). As the supervisor is the central control of the team and theorem proving using teamwork is a task where no dependencies occur, we have easy solutions to most of the problems addressed in these papers.

7 Conclusion and Future Work

We have presented a distributed theorem proving method where planning of the assignment of agents to the processors allows us to improve significantly the number of theorems that can be proved without the user fiddling with parameters of the prover. Although the run times of the version of our prover using planning are slower than the run times of the best known teams for the problems we were able to prove examples from different domains to which none of our sequential provers could find a solution thus still showing synergetic effects. Further, reactive planning enables us to prove examples from one domain where the best known teams differ from example to example.

Our approach to proof planning allows us to deal with knowledge about domains that is vague, unstructured and possibly contradictory. This is due to the competition of the experts in the teams. All other approaches to proof planning require exact and often total knowledge about a domain of interest in order to achieve satisfactory results. Furthermore, the addition of new domains to our system is easy because of the explicit representation of the knowledge by frames.

The detection of subproblems and the use of special methods to solve them – which are characteristic for other approaches – can also be integrated in our approach without losing the ability to deal with vague information. This is one direction into which we want to investigate. Other topics of future research are to automate the generation of domain information by learning from examples and the improvement of planning by not only selecting known experts but also by generating new experts using parameter adjustments of generic experts.

References

[AD93]   **Avenhaus, J.; Denzinger, J.**: *Distributing equational theorem proving*, Proc. 5th RTA, Montreal, LNCS 690, 1993, pp. 62-76.

[BD88]   **Boddy, M.; Dean, T.**: *An Analysis of Time-Dependent Planning*, Proc. 7. National Conf. on AI, Minneapolis, 1988, pp. 49-54.

[BDP89]   **Bachmair, L.; Dershowitz, N.; Plaisted, D.A.**: *Completion without Failure*, Coll. on the Resolution of Equations in Algebraic Structures, Austin (1987), Academic Press, 1989.

[Be91]   **Beetz, M.**: *Decision-theoretic Transformational Planning*, Internal report, Yale University, 1991.

[Bu88]   **Bundy, A.**: *The use of explicit plans to guide inductive proofs*, Proc. 9th CADE, 1988.

[CL73]   **Chang, C.L.; Lee, R.C.**: *Symbolic Logic and Mechanical Theorem Proving*, Academic Press, 1973.

[De95]   **Denzinger, J.**: *Knowledge-Based Distributed Search Using Teamwork*, Proc. ICMAS-95, San Francisco, AAAI-Press, 1995, pp. 81-88.

[DF94]   **Denzinger, J.; Fuchs, M.**: *Goal oriented equational theorem proving using teamwork*, Proc. KI-94, Saarbrücken, LNAI 861, 1994, pp. 343-354.

[DL87]   **Durfee, E.H.; Lesser, V.R.**: *Using Partial Global Plans to Coordinate Distributed Problem Solvers*, Proc. IJCAI-87, 1987, pp.875-883.

[DS96]   **Denzinger, J.; Schulz, S.**: *Recording and Analyzing Knowledge-Based Distributed Deduction Processes*, to appear in Journal of Symbolic Computation, 1996.

[FHN81]   **Fikes, R.E.; Hart, P.E.; Nilsson, N.J.**: *Learning and executing generalized robot plans*, in Webber, Nilsson (eds.) Readings in AI, 1981, pp.231-249.

[HR87]   **Hsiang, J.; Rusinowitch, M.**: *On word problems in equational theories*, Proc. 14th ICALP, Karlsruhe, LNCS 267, 1987, pp. 54-71.

[Mc94]   **McCune, W.W.**: *OTTER 3.0 Reference manual and Guide*, Tech. Rep. ANL-94/6, Argonne National Laboratory, 1994.

[Mc90]   **Mc Dermott, D.**: *Planning reactive behaviour: A progress report*, in J. Allen, J.Handler, A. Tate: Innovative Approaches to Planning, Scheduling and Control, Kaufmann, 1990, pp.450-458.

[Ro82]   **Rosenschein, J.S.**: *Synchronization of Multi-Agent Plans*, Proc. AAAI-82, 1982, pp.115-119.

A Revision of Dependency-Directed Backtracking for JTMS

Truong Quoc Dung

IRIDIA
UNIVERSITE LIBRE DE BRUXELLES

50 Av. F. Roosevelt, CP 194/6 - 1050 Brussels (Belgium)

Abstract. Current algorithms for Dependency-Directed Backtracking (DDB) suffer from several limitations. The added justifications produced by Doyle's DDB are sufficient but are neither safe nor complete. Petrie's DDB solves this problem, but it can lead to cases where odd loops are introduced *later* into JTMS network by new justifications, and so can sometimes miss legitimate admissible labelings. Moreover, Petrie's DDB cannot resolve an inconsistency if all possible added justifications produce an odd loop, although a solution may exist. We propose a revised method based on elective sets and premise sets of contradiction foundations that allows to use the premises as added justifications. Our revised DDB allows to resolve more inconsistencies than Petrie's DDB. Moreover, a preference ordering over the assumption justifications can be integrated; this order gives the problem solver some control over the choice of electives.

1. Introduction

Doyle [Doyle 79] was the first to present an algorithm to remove the inconsistency by Dependency-Directed Backtracking (DDB) in a Justification-based Truth Maintenance System (JTMS). DDB is required whenever a node which has been declared to be a *contradiction* is found to have a valid justification. An *added justification* is constructed by DDB. The validity of this new justification will mean that the justification for the contradiction is no longer valid. Unfortunately, the added justifications produced by Doyle's DDB are sufficient but neither safe nor complete. Petrie [Petrie 87] proposed a revised DDB algorithm whose added justifications are sufficient, safe and complete. However, Petrie's DDB still has some drawbacks. Petrie's DDB prevents the introduction of odd loops into JTMS network to ensure the non-existence of unsatisfiable loops produced by the added justifications. This is overdoing, because the presence of odd loops does not necessarily lead to the existence of unsatisfiable loops. Moreover, the odd loop test process is based only on the topology of JTMS network, i.e., this process is performed separately from the labeling propagation process. Worse, Petrie's DDB can lead to cases where the odd loops could be introduced *later* into JTMS network by the new justifications, and so can sometimes eliminate legitimate admissible labelings. Finally, if all possible added justifications produce an odd loop, the inconsistency *can not* be resolved by Petrie's DDB, although a solution may exist.

Motivated by these considerations, we propose a revised method based on *elective sets* and *premise sets* of contradiction foundations that allows to use the premises as added justifications. These premises never introduce unsatisfiable loops into a JTMS network. All steps of our revised DDB are performed simultaneously with the labeling propagation process. We also propose a local criterion for elective choice based on a preference order between the assumption justifications. This order can possibly be provided by the problem solver, thus giving the problem solver some control over the labeling process.

2 Revision of added justifications

Petrie's DDB is performed without taking into consideration any relation between the nodes of elective set into consideration. However, the following theorem shows the important role played by this set in the contradiction resolution process.

Theorem 2.1

Let F(C) be a contradiction foundation of a contradiction node C, E(C) its elective set and P(C) its premise set. If all the nodes belonging to P(C) are labeled IN and all the nodes belonging to E(C) is labeled OUT then the contradiction node C is necessarily labeled IN.

JTMSs are typically used incrementally: the justifications passed by problem solver are never removed. Thus, the only way to remove an inconsistency is to label IN one of the nodes belonging to the elective set. We propose a revised method based on *elective sets* and *premise sets* of contradiction foundations that allows to use *the premises* as added justifications — i.e., for each contradiction foundation, a premise $\left(\langle\{\ \},\{\ \}\rangle : e\right)$ will be added to remove this inconsistency, where e belongs to the elective set of the contradiction foundation.

3 Revision of DDB

We use the following rules to construct our revision of DDB [Dung 95].

R1: Before calling DDB to remove the inconsistencies from an admissible and inconsistent labeling, the following procedure must be performed:

For every contradiction foundation F(C) with $j \equiv \left(\langle\{\ \},\{\ \}\rangle : i\right)$ its added premise Do
For every node d belonging to the elective set E(C) Do
Update the supporting nodes of the nodes belonging to the ancestor of d such that j is a supporting justification used to construct the ancestor of d iff there exists not another possibility.

R2: Because the added premises can belong to the premise set of the foundation for a contradiction node C, the elective set E(C) of this contradiction foundation must be computed by E(C) := Elective_Set(C).

FUNCTION Elective_Set(i)
Let $j \equiv \left(\langle In(I), Out(O)\rangle : i\right)$ be the supporting justification for i.
If $(I = \varnothing)$ and $(O = \varnothing)$
Then If j is an added premise of a contradiction foundation F(C)

<u>Then</u> Return $(E(C)-\{i\})$ <u>Else</u> Return $(\varnothing)$

$$\underline{\text{Else}}\ \text{Return}\left(\left\{o \mid o \in (O-CN)\right\} \cup \left(\bigcup_{t\in I} \text{Elective\_Set(t)}\right)\right)$$

Where CN is the set of contradiction nodes.

R3: The completeness of the added premises is ensured as follows: for every contradiction foundation F(C) with an added premise $j \equiv \left(\langle\{\ \},\{\ \}\rangle : i\right)$, if there is another node e labeled IN belonging to the elective set E(C) such that j is not a supporting justification used to construct the ancestor of e, (in other words, e can be labeled IN independently of the added premise j), then j must be removed.

R4: The sufficiency of added premises is ensured as follows: for every contradiction foundation F(C) with an elective set E(C), if all the nodes belonging to E(C) are labeled OUT then an added premise for one of the nodes belonging to the elective set must be inserted or reinserted.

R5: The unwanted labeling problem is resolved as follows: for every contradiction foundation F(C) with an added premise $j \equiv \left(\langle\{\ \},\{\ \}\rangle : i\right)$, if there is a node e labeled OUT belonging to the elective set E(C) such that j is a supporting justification used to construct the ancestor of e, (in other words, e can be labeled IN if j is removed), then j must be removed.

R6: The inconsistency is unresolved if there is a contradiction foundation F(C) whose elective set E(C) is empty.

Theorem 3.1

If an inconsistency can be removed by Petrie's DDB with an added justification $j \equiv \left(\langle\text{In}(I), \text{Out}(O)\rangle : i\right)$, then this inconsistency can be also removed by our DDB with the added premise $j' \equiv \left(\langle\{\ \},\{\ \}\rangle : i\right)$. Moreover, if later j is invalidated by Petrie's DDB then j' must be removed by our DDB.

Interestingly, there are the cases where the inconsistency can not be removed by Petrie's DDB, while it can be removed by our DDB. Moreover, our DDB sometimes finds legitimate admissible and consistent labelings which can not be found by Petrie's DDB. Finally, all steps of our DDB are performed simultaneously with the labeling propagation process.

4 Elective Choice

We finally address the issue of how to choose the elective from the elective set of a contradiction foundation. It is commonly required that the changes performed to remove the inconsistencies should be "minimal" in some reasonable sense. Doyle [Doyle 83] investigated a possible definition of minimality where the symetric difference between the believed nodes of two belief sets is used to characterize the closeness of these sets. He also remarks that it is difficult to ensure this minimality. This notion of minimality demands a global consideration of all the possible labelings of a JTMS— clearly a hard task, as a JTMS is a single context system. Thus, using a local minimality criterion may seem more appropriate. We propose a local criterion for elective choice based on a given preference order between assumption justifications. This ordering can be effectively used by our DDB algorithm to select the assumption justification which must be invalidated. The ordering can possibly be provided by the problem solver, based on domain-specific knowledge. This gives some control over the labeling process.

5 Conclusion

We have discussed a revision of the Dependency-Directed backtracking used in a JTMS. This revised DDB allows to use the premise as added justification The sufficient and safe properties are automatically guaranteed by these added premises. However some operations must be performed to ensure the completeness of the added premises. Moreover, this revised DDB allows to eliminate the unwanted admissible labelings.

An interesting advantage of our revised DDB algorithm is its ability to integrate a preference ordering over the assumption justifications; this order gives some control over the choice of assumption justifications which may be invalidated.

References

[[Doyle 79] Doyle, J., A Truth Maintenance System, Artificial Intelligence 12, pp. 259-279, 1979.

[Doyle 83] Doyle, J., The Ins and Outs of Reason Maintenance, Proc. IJCAI 83, Karlsruhe Germany, pp. 349-351, 1983.

[Dung 95] Dung, T. Q., A Revision of Dependency-Directed Backtracking for JTMS, Technical Report, IRIDIA - ULB (Belgium), 1995.

[Petrie 87] Petrie, C. J., Revised Dependency-Directed Backtracking for default reasoning, Proc. AAAI 87, Seattle, Washington, pp. 167-172, 1987.

A Compiler-Interpreter-System for Decoding the User's Intention Within a Speech Understanding Application

Michael Ebersberger, Johannes Müller, Holger Stahl

Institute for Human-Machine-Communication, Munich University of Technology
Arcisstraße 21, D-80290 Munich
email: {ebe,mue,sta}@mmk.e-technik.tu-muenchen.de

Abstract: For a speech understanding graphic editor, a compiler-interpreter-system is introduced to process a semantic structure, a special form for representing the semantic content of a spoken utterance. After a semantic structure has been converted to database queries by the compiler, the interpreter processes all these queries and updates the corresponding database, i.e. in our case the graphics data base containing the features of all objects on the screen. The system has been tested with 1843 semantic structures of spoken utterances within the 'graphic editor' domain. The rate for correct database queries is 97.3%. Storage of the whole domain-specific knowledge in external and editable files enables easy portability to other domains.

1 Introduction

To demonstrate a speech understanding system, we implemented a speech understanding graphic editor, which allows the user to create, modify or delete three-dimensional objects such as cones, cuboids, cylinders or spheres only by spoken commands. The system reacts upon a spoken input by a graphic output on the screen and synthetic speech. The speech signal is recorded and preprocessed to an observation sequence O.

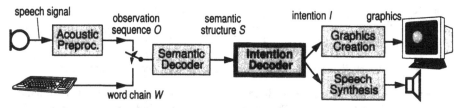

Fig. 1: Block diagram of the application ‚speech understanding graphic editor'

By maximizing the conditional probability $P(S|O)$ [7][8], the semantic decoder computes the most probable semantic structure S, which is used to find the user's intention I. Subsequently, operations on a graphic database are performed. The data of all objects shown on the screen are saved in this database and used to generate a pixel sequence, which is displayed on the screen. Furthermore, the database provides the possibility to pass textual information, which is given out by synthetic speech.

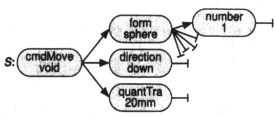

Fig. 2: Semantic structure S of an utterance

The semantic structure as semantic representation of a spoken or written utterance forms the input of the intention decoder. The user's utterance *"move the sphere two centimetres downwards"* is transformed by the semantic decoder into the semantic structure S, which is depicted in figure 2. In general, a semantic structure has the following characteristics [3]:

- The semantic structure S is a tree consisting of a finite number N of semantic units (simply called *semuns*) s_n: $S = \{s_1, s_2, ..., s_n, ..., s_N\}$
- Each semun s_n has a type $t[s_n]$ and a value $v[s_n]$. It can be drawn as $\boxed{\begin{smallmatrix} t[s_n] \\ v[s_n] \end{smallmatrix}}$.
- Each semun s_n refers to a certain number $X \geq 1$ (depending on $t[s_n]$) of successor semuns $q_1[s_n], ..., q_X[s_n] \in \{s_2, ..., s_N, \text{blk}\} \setminus \{s_n\}$, connected by edges "$\longrightarrow$".
- The blank-semun 'blk' forms an exception. It represents a leaf of the tree, drawn as "$\longrightarrow\!\!\mid$". It has the type $t[\text{blk}] = \text{blk}$, no value and no successor.

2 General Approach for the Intention Decoder

For decoding the user's intention, i.e. the execution of the desired actions, a combination of compiler and interpreter is suggested. The preprocessed semantic structure forms the source language P_Q for the compiler. It represents the intention of the user to manipulate graphic objects. The result of the compiler is a program in the intermediate language P_I, which has especially been designed for that purpose. This intermediate language provides commands for arithmetic operations, control of data flow and database operations. The interpreter executes the instructions of the intermediate language by loading object data from the database, modifying these data and storing data of new objects into the database.

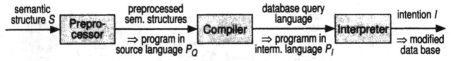

Fig. 3: Block diagram of the intention decoder as compiler-interpreter-system

Before using this system, a system administrator describes each semun with commands of the intermediate language P_I. The semun and the commands represent the same information. Additional semuns can be easily integrated at a later stage. (The use of a database language like SQL [5] is possible, too. For that reason, this article describes neither the structure of the intermediate language nor the functioning of the interpreter).

3 Preprocessor

Before a semantic structure is executed by the compiler-interpreter-system, it is possibly simplified or split by a relational preprocessor [1]. To keep the intermediate language simple, to minimize the compilation time and to reduce the instruction complexity, the preprocessor can split a semantic structure at special places, which represent for example the combination of two attributes or actions. The semantic structure of *"create a sphere and a cube"* is divided into two semantic structures corresponding to *"create a sphere"* and *"create a cube"*. The semun representing the *"and"* was eliminated.

4 Compiler

The input program of the compiler (in source language P_Q) consists of one or more semantic structures. These semantic structures can only be transformed in database actions, if the context sensitivity of natural language has been eliminated.

4.1 Contextual Sensitivity

The following two word chains may introduce the problem of context sensitiveness.
- W_1: *"move a sphere above the cone to the right"*
  The system has to find a sphere in the database, which should be moved.
- W_2: *"paint a sphere"*
  The sphere is an attribute of a new object. The system must not search for that sphere.

In both cases, *"sphere"* is represented by the same semun. Only the context of the word gives some advice about the meaning. For that reason, the *status model* and the *status transition model* are established to describe the context of a semun.

4.2 Status Model

For each semun s_n, a status $z[s_n]$ is introduced. The number of all possible states is described in a status model. Within the 'graphic editor' domain, we defined five different states:

- The **cmd**-status is the command status of a semantic structure.
- The **new**-status collects attributes for a new object.
- The **what**-status searches for objects in the database.
- The **how**-status integrates new attributes for already existing objects.
- The **how-much**-status collects quantitative information.

4.3 Status Transition Model and Status Analysis

Each semun is understood as a status transition machine, which switches to a following status considering the type, the status and the successors of that semun. The sequence of states is described in the *status transition model* for all combinations of any type and any status. If the semun with the type "cmdMove" has got the status "cmd", its first successor-semun gets the status "what" (objects are searched by the system), its second successor-semun gets the status "how" (how are the objects manipulated), and the third successor gets the status "how-much" (which quantity of objects are manipulated).

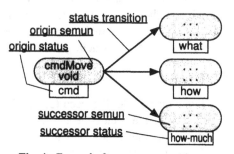

Fig. 4: Example for a status transition

During the status analysis, the status of each semun s_n within S has to be examined. For that purpose, the status transition model is used. The whole semantic structure is processed and the actual status for each semun is extracted. The actual semun status represents the actual context of this semun.

4.4 Production of Intermediate Code

The knowledge of each semun about its context is used to receive a new representation of the semantic structure. With the parameters type $t[s_n]$, value $v[s_n]$ and status $z[s_n]$, each semun s_n is transformed into certain commands, which are stored in a command model. In this model, each semun is linked with a series of commands, called basic commands, which can be processed by the interpreter. The semantic structure is transformed into a *basic command tree*, which has to be linearized before being processed by the interpreter. The execution of the commands modifies the actual knowledge of the system, which consists of a number of variables.

Fig. 5: Determination of the basic commands by the command model

4.5 System Knowledge

Whereas the compiler uses the system knowledge for common operations, the interpreter modifies the system knowledge by executing basic commands. The system knowledge is actualized until the whole basic command tree is processed. The system knowledge consists of two types of variables:

- **Internal variables** cannot be defined by the user. The system itself manages the handling of theses variables. For example, the result of searching operations is stored in internal variables.
- **External variables** can be defined by the user and are needed for the calculations. For example, the utterance *"move the cylinder to the right"* does not mention how far the cylinder has to be moved, thus the system uses external variables as defaults.

4.6 Linearizing the basic command tree by a "top-up" approach

The basic command tree has to be linearized for the interpreter. To determine the status $z[s_n]$ of each semun s_n, the basic instruction tree has to be processed "top-down" using the status transition model. However, commands can only be generated "bottom-up" [2], since basic commands in lower levels of the tree include some information, which is used in higher levels. Therefore a combination of both methods is used "top-up". Note in fig. 6 the three main steps 'DESCEND' for descending the semantic structure, 'CONSTRUCT' for constructing the linearized commands and 'FINISH' for terminating.

5 Results

The intention decoder has been tested with 1843 semantic structures of spoken utterances, which have been collected from 33 subjects during a Wizard-of-Oz simulation within the 'graphic editor' domain [4]. For the corresponding semantic structures, the rate for correct database queries amounts to 97.3%. It is impossible to reach 100%, since the execution of a language representation becomes more complex, the closer to natural language that representation is located [6]. In fact, the semantic structure claims to be close to the word level [3]. Due to the universality of the interpreter commands and the status analysis, as well as the storage of domain-specific knowledge in external files, the portability of the intention decoder to other domains is easily possible.

65

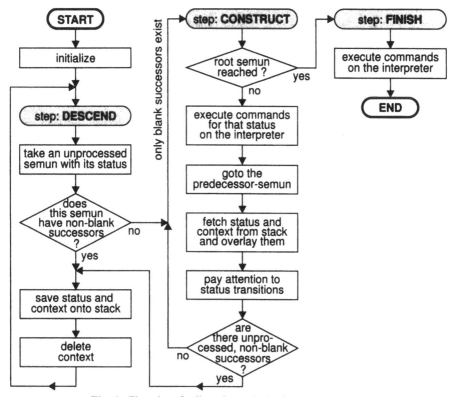

Fig. 6: Flowchart for linearizing the basic command tree

6 Acknowledgement

An online 'graphic editor' including the described intention decoder for German text input is running on WWW. If you try it, please be aware of out-of-vocabulary errors. The internet-address is: http://www.mmk.e-technik.tu-muenchen.de/~mue/nasgra/

References

[1] A. Aho, R. Sethi, J.D. Ullmann: *Compilerbau*, Addison Wesley, 1988

[2] L. Goldschlager, A. Lister: *Informatik: Eine moderne Einführung*, Hanser, 1990

[3] J. Müller, H. Stahl: *Die semantische Gliederung als adäquate semantische Repräsentationsebene für einen sprachgesteuerten ‚Grafikeditor‘*, in L. Hitzenberger (ed.): Angewandte Computerlinguistik, „Sprache und Computer" (No. 15), Georg Olms, 1995, pp. 211-225

[4] J. Müller, H. Stahl: *Collecting and Analyzing Spoken Utterances for a Speech Controlled Application*, Proc. Eurospeech 1995 (Madrid, Spain), pp. 1437-1440

[5] D. Petkovic: *SQL die Datenbanksprache*, McGraw-Hill, 1990

[6] R. Pieraccini, E. Levin, E. Vidal: *Learning how to Understand Language*, Proc. Eurospeech 1993 (Berlin, Germany), pp. 1407-1412

[7] H. Stahl, J. Müller: *A Stochastic Grammar for Isolated Representation of Syntactic and Semantic Knowledge*, Proc. Eurospeech 1995 (Madrid, Spain), pp. 551-554

[8] H. Stahl, J. Müller, M. Lang: *An Efficient Top-Down Parsing Algorithm for Understanding Speech by Using Stochastic Syntactic and Semantic Models*, Proc. ICASSP 1996 (Atlanta, USA), pp. 397-400

Cyclic Rules in
Linear Connection Proofs

Bertram Fronhöfer

Fac. des Sciences, Dep. d'Inform., Université d'Angers, F–49045 Angers Cedex 01
on leave from: Institut für Informatik, TU München, D – 80290 München
fronhoef@informatik.tu-muenchen.de

Abstract

In this paper we discuss the role of certain cyclic rules—and in particular their ressemblance to Frame Axioms—which show up in a backward proof procedure for Linear Connection Proofs (see [4]). Trying to avoid these cyclic rules in proof search leads to an improved search procedure of which we give the basic idea as well as the results of an experimental evaluation.

1   Introduction: Linear Connection Proofs

In 1986 W. Bibel proposed *Linear Connection Proofs* as a new logic-based approach to plan generation (see [1]). Since in contrast to other logics proposed so far, this approach worked without Frame Axioms —at least no Frame Axioms were explicitly specified—it offered a realistic possibility for plan generation via theorem proving.

For working with Linear Connection Proofs a plan generation problem $(\mathbf{I}, \mathbf{A}, \mathbf{G})$ must be given as follows:

- $\mathbf{I}$ is a finite set $\{F_1, \ldots, F_n\}$ of ground facts (*initial situation*).
- $\mathbf{A}$ is a finite set $\{R_1, \ldots, R_k\}$ of *actions* where each R_i is a universally closed formula of the form $A_{i1} \wedge \ldots \wedge A_{ig} \longrightarrow C_{i1} \wedge \ldots \wedge C_{ih}$
  with facts $A_{i1}, \ldots, A_{ig}, C_{i1}, \ldots, C_{ih}$.
- $\mathbf{G}$ is a finite set $\{G_1, \ldots, G_m\}$ of ground facts (*goal*).

The plan generation problem $(\mathbf{I}, \mathbf{A}, \mathbf{G})$ is *solvable* iff there is a Linear Connection Proof for the *specification theorem* $T_{(\mathbf{I},\mathbf{A},\mathbf{G})}$:

$$F_1 \wedge \ldots \wedge F_n \wedge R_1 \wedge \ldots \wedge R_k \longrightarrow G_1 \wedge \ldots \wedge G_m$$

In addition, the following requirements about the intended meaning of the implications which specify the actions must be observed: The *antecedent* shall comprise all facts of the existing situation which are involved in the action—either as being necessary conditions for the action's application or as being facts which shall no longer be valid after the action has been carried out. The *consequent* shall comprise all facts which are either newly created by the action or which is involved in the action as preconditions, but are not affected by it. This convention about the specification of actions entails that all those facts of a situation, which are not included in the antecedent shall survive the application of the action. Intuitively spoken, with Linear Connection Proofs the action-implications work like replacement rules on the set of facts which is initialized by $\mathbf{I}$.

In [2] and [4]—to which we refer for details—we presented a backward proof search algorithm for Linear Connection Proofs which we called *Linear Backward Chaining* (**LBC**). It is a kind of tableau calculus which searches for a Linear Connection Proof of a specification theorem $T_{(I,A,G)}$. This proof search algorithm has much resemblance to a Horn clause interpreter. One big difference is that the replacement character of our action-implications compels us to assure that no literal/fact is used twice, for which reason instead of the usual set of unit clauses we have to maintain an alternating pool of currently unconnected literals, which is initialized by the facts from **I**. Moreover, we transform every action-implication a from **A** (of the form $A_1 \wedge \ldots \wedge A_g \longrightarrow C_1 \wedge \ldots \wedge C_h$) into h *rules* which we write down in a PROLOG-like notation:

$$
\begin{aligned}
C_1 \quad &:- \quad A_1, \ldots, A_g, \mathsf{NF}(C_2), \ldots, \mathsf{NF}(C_h). \\
C_2 \quad &:- \quad A_1, \ldots, A_g, \mathsf{NF}(C_1), \mathsf{NF}(C_3), \ldots, \mathsf{NF}(C_h). \\
&\quad\vdots \\
C_{h-1} \quad &:- \quad A_1, \ldots, A_g, \mathsf{NF}(C_1), \ldots, \mathsf{NF}(C_{h-2}), \mathsf{NF}(C_h). \\
C_h \quad &:- \quad A_1, \ldots, A_g, \mathsf{NF}(C_1), \ldots, \mathsf{NF}(C_{h-1}).
\end{aligned}
$$

The evaluation of a literal $\mathsf{NF}(C)$ adds C to the pool of facts. The facts from **G** yield a goal clause, from which we start an ordinary backward chaining process, the main difference to Horn clause reasoning is that a literal/fact A is removed from the pool when it unifies with a subgoal A in a tableau extension step. ∎

2 Frame Axioms and Cyclic Rules

If one of the literals in the consequent, say C_i, occurs also in the antecedent, e.g. $C_i = A_j$, then we get the cyclic rule

$C_i :- A_1, \ldots, A_{j-1}, C_i, A_{j+1}, \ldots, A_g \ldots, \mathsf{NF}(C_1), \ldots, \mathsf{NF}(C_{i-1}), \mathsf{NF}(C_{i+1}), \ldots, \mathsf{NF}(C_h)$

which, unfortunately, is indispensable for the completeness of the LBC-algorithm (A respective example is presented in [3]).

Being quite unpleasant for proof search, these cyclic rules are of theoretical interest due to their ressemblance to Frame Axioms, of which we will discuss the pros and cons.

1.Argument: The rule above is cyclic in the literal C_i. Intuitively, the cyclic rule given above, says '*if C_i is valid in a certain situation and if all $A_{k \neq j}$ are valid in this situation as well, then C_i will also be valid in the situation resulting from the application of action a* '; or in other words, '*C_i survives under action a, provided that all $A_{k \neq j}$* '. Without any doubt, this looks like a typical Frame Axiom.

Objection: However, the fact C_i is not an arbitrary fact, but an indispensable precondition of the action **a**. (Otherwise, C_i could be dropped from the antecedent and the consequent of the action **a**.) Consequently, we may object, that the fact C_i belongs to the action a proper and not to the frame, and therefore the cyclic rule should not be called a Frame Axiom. ∎

2.Argument: If n actions have C_i as a surviving precondition, then we will get n cyclic rules with head C_i, which entails a search space explosion for subgoal C_i with branching factor n due to these cyclic rules alone; quite similar to the space explosion caused by usual frame axioms (see [4] for a detailed discussion of these problems). ∎

Objection: Usually with traditional Frame Axioms the number n is usually quite close to the number of all actions, since in general there will be only few actions which destroy C_i. On the other hand, the number of actions which have C_i as a precondition is usually rather small, thus resulting in a huge difference of the branching factor. ■

3.Argument: Similar to Frame Axioms cyclic rules sometimes act as place holders for yet unspecified actions. This analogy becomes apparent when we try to solve the well-known *Sussman Anomaly* both with the LBC-algorithm and with Situational Calculus (we refer again to [3] where we show how the interlacing of two plans is achieved by introducing a cyclic rule at the right moment).

Objection: Although the cyclic rule does duty as a Frame Axiom as place holder for a yet unknown action, traditional Frame Axioms play this role to a far greater extent: For instance, if with Situational Calculus we have to prove conjunctive goals like: $\exists z : A(z) \wedge B(z)$, where z will refer to a plan (encoded as a term) which leads to a situation in which both A and B hold. If we solve $A(z)$ with a plan p, but $B(p)$ is not accidentally true as well, we enter a huge backtracking process, where by means of Frame Axioms for A we *guess without any guidance* a sequence of action place holders, i.e. a plan, for extending plan p such that B holds as well. Since this kind of backtracking will not occur when searching for Linear Connection Proofs due to the absence of such (shared) variables like z —we just backtrack if p cannot be extended to a plan for (A and) B —and therefore the role of cyclic rules as place holders for nearly unspecified actions is much more limited than in the case of general Frame Axioms. ■

Whichever stand we might eventually take about hidden Frame Axioms—a completely impartial judgement seems to be unattainable—we will try to get rid of these cyclic rules for the evident interest in speeding up proof search.

3 The LIP Proof Search Procedure

To get rid of these cyclic rules we do the following: If we come across a subgoal K^k in the antecedent of action k, which is rementioned in this action's consequent, then instead of solving it via an extension step, we may look for a connection $(\overline{K^i}, K^j)$ which we cut, i.e. which we replace it by the two connections $(\overline{K^i}, K^k)$ and $(\overline{K^k}, K^j)$ as is shown in Figure 1.

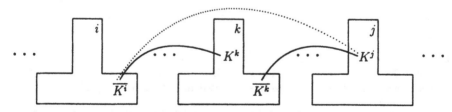

(Fig. 1): Cutting a connection

Adding this possibility to insert actions into a plan by cutting connections to the LBC-algorithm we obtained the LIP-algorithm (Linear Insertion Planning). (For a detailed presentation of this algorithm and a proof of its correctness and completeness we refer to [3].)

To get a feeling for the comparative performance of the LIP- and the LBC-algorithm, we ran both on a set of benchmark problems from the blocks world. These examples

Problem	LBC		LIP			Problem	LBC		LIP		
RBW-6-1	13.66	[108]	1.90	[366]	+	RBW-7-1	124.18	[141]	119.74	[517]	+
RBW-6-2	8.84	[104]	4.87	[363]	+	RBW-7-2	2.01	[108]	1.93	[374]	+
RBW-6-3	0.15	[76]	0.04	[218]	+	RBW-7-3	91.88	[117]	9.22	[376]	+
RBW-6-4	0.87	[83]	0.11	[252]	+	RBW-7-4	11.46	[126]	6.46	[382]	+
RBW-6-5	0.08	[85]	0.07	[255]	+	RBW-7-5	19550.99	[128]	10205.84	[590]	+
RBW-6-6	3.01	[109]	1.54	[321]	+	RBW-7-6	0.02	[100]	0.03	[244]	−
RBW-6-7	4.73	[103]	2.57	[361]	+	RBW-7-7	1976.05	[120]	224.29	[440]	+
RBW-6-8	16.60	[108]	2.60	[364]	+	RBW-7-8	0.21	[105]	0.19	[282]	+
RBW-6-9	2.00	[108]	1.84	[374]	+	RBW-7-9	159.33	[134]	134.91	[510]	+
RBW-6-10	0.95	[88]	0.10	[252]	+	RBW-7-10	8.72	[120]	8.73	[442]	−
RBW-6-11	3.41	[119]	3.90	[428]	−						
RBW-6-12	0.25	[95]	0.26	[311]	−						

(Fig. 2): Problems with 6 and 7 blocks (runtimes [proof sizes] speed up [+/−])

were generated by a random generator which is delivered with UCPOP, a partial order planner developed at the University of Washington, Seattle[1]. In [4] we showed with the same benchmarks that the LBC-algorithm performs quite well with respect to UCPOP. The problems are enumerated in the order of their random generation, and the number in the middle of the problems' names indicates how many blocks are involved in the problem: E.g. RBW-6-5 refers to the 5th generated problem with 6 blocks.

The runtimes—for LBC and LIP—are displayed in Figure 2. Both algorithms were implemented on top of the SETHEO[2] theorem prover (version 3.2 extended by some special built-ins) and were run on a HP 735/99.

Acknowledgements: We want to thank Johann Schumann for providing some useful built-ins in SETHEO which helped to speed up the LIP-algorithm.

References

[1] W. Bibel. A Deductive Solution for Plan Generation. *New Generation Computing*, 6:115–132, 1986.

[2] B. Fronhöfer. *The Action-as-Implication Paradigm: Formal Systems and Application.* CSpress, München, 1996.

[3] B. Fronhöfer. Cutting Connections in Linear Connection Proofs. Technical Report AR-96-01, Technische Universität München, 1996. available from ftp://ftp.informatik.tu-muenchen.de/local/lehrstuhl/jessen/Automated_Reasoning/Reports/AR-96-01.ps.gz.

[4] B. Fronhöfer. Situational Calculus, Linear Connection Proofs and STRIPS-like Planning: An Experimental Comparison. In P. Miglioli, U. Moscato, D. Mundici, and M. Ornaghi, editors, *5th Workshop on Theorem Proving with Analytic Tableaux and Related Methods*, pages 193–209. Terrasini, Palermo, Springer, LNAI 1071, May 1996.

---

[1]the UCPOP system is available via anonymous ftp from ~ftp/pub/ai/ at cs.washington.edu.

[2]SETHEO is a theorem prover for classical full 1-order logic, based on connection tableau (model elimination). It can be obtained via ftp. For further information see http://wwwjessen.informatik.tu-muenchen.de/forschung/reasoning/setheo.html .

Optimized Nearest-Neighbor Classifiers Using Generated Instances

Matthias Fuchs[1] and Andreas Abecker[2]

[1] Center for Learning Systems and Applications
Computer Science Dept., University of Kaiserslautern
P.O. 3049, D-67653 Kaiserslautern, Germany
e-mail: fuchs@informatik.uni-kl.de
[2] German Research Center for Artificial Intelligence
DFKI GmbH, Kaiserslautern
P.O. 2080, D-67608 Kaiserslautern, Germany
e-mail: aabecker@dfki.uni-kl.de

Abstract. We present a novel approach to classification, based on a
tight coupling of instance-based learning and a genetic algorithm. In
contrast to the usual instance-based learning setting, we do not rely on
(parts of) the given training set as the basis of a nearest-neighbor classifier, but we try to employ artificially generated instances as concept
prototypes. The extremely hard problem of finding an appropriate set
of concept prototypes is tackled by a genetic search procedure with the
classification accuracy on the given training set as evaluation criterion
for the genetic fitness measure. Experiments show that—due to the ability to find concise and accurate concept descriptions that contain few,
but typical instances—this classification approach is considerably robust
against noise, untypical training instances and irrelevant attributes.

1 Introduction

Memory-based approaches to classification have shown their usefulness in many
applications. In domains with weak or intractable background theory, when
searching for goal concepts consisting of many small disjuncts or when being
faced with poor predictive power of attributes or with imprecise and polymor-
phous concepts [3, 2, 16], methods like nearest-neighbor algorithms (k-NN) or
instance-based learning (IBL) often produce good classification results. These
results are achieved by easily understandable and implementable algorithms: In
the learning phase, they simply record the given training examples (instances)
together with their classifications. The training instances are attribute-value representations describing points in the attribute space (or, instance space) that are
example instances of concepts. Concepts are understood as sets of points in the
attribute space. Subsequently presented unseen examples are classified by searching the k most similar stored instances and determining the most frequent class
in this set of nearest neighbors. Thus, a memory-based classifier consists of a set
of stored training instances (the *concept description*) plus the k-NN classification

rule [4] for some specific k. However, when storing *all* presented examples, large storage requirements and high classification costs become a serious problem.

Thus, approaches like IB3 [2] or TIBL [24] store only a *subset* of the presented instances that is expected to be sufficient for a good characterisation of the goal concept. This is achieved in IB3 by considering the instances' classification performance on subsequently presented training examples in order to discriminate good classifying instances from noisy ones. While IB3 hence evaluates the "usefulness" of instances indirectly via their classification behavior, TIBL employs an *explicit* measurement of "typicality" of instances based on inter-concept and intra-concept similarity. Despite their different motivation and technical approach both algorithms obtain smaller concept descriptions and better classification accuracy (esp., in noisy domains) by concentrating on central points in clusters of instances with the same class.

However, in real-world domains the presented examples will often contain a more or less random selection of somehow biased and noisy instances that highlight only certain aspects of the goal concept. Consequently, approaches that preserve the idea of using only *presented* instances for a concept description impose unnecessary limitations on themselves when considering these instances as a starting point for constructing a concept description.

If we want to liberate us from the *direct* use of the training set, we have to face an extremely hard search problem: The search space contains all possible concept descriptions, i.e. all sets of arbitrary points in the attribute space and there is no heuristic knowledge for guiding the search and no known structure of this search space. Furthermore, since the training set is the *only* information available (provided that there is no background knowledge used), we must nonetheless finally rely on this data. Thus we propose to use it to evaluate a (partial) solution candidate by measuring its classification accuracy on this example set. So we have an indirect use as in IB3, but we are free to construct arbitrary concept descriptions not restricted by the example instances.

Genetic Algorithms (GA) have demonstrated their power under such conditions: huge, unstructured search spaces and the only available knowledge given as an a posteriori evaluation of a solution candidate's quality. This led us to the idea of our algorithm GIGA: Generate Instances for concept descriptions using a Genetic Algorithm. GIGA employs genetic search to find optimal concept descriptions (to be used by a k-NN classifier). Since these concept descriptions are artificially generated and are not restricted to the use of presented instances, they can contain arbitrary instances and have thus the chance of finding *"ideal"* concept descriptions with better performance w.r.t. both classification accuracy and storage requirements. Moreover, because our candidate evaluation always regards all information available, it is not as exposed to the danger of being trapped in local optima as incremental instance-based approaches can be.

This paper is organized as follows: In section 2, we give a more detailed description of GIGA followed by a discussion of interesting properties of our approach (section 3). Some artificial datasets demonstrate GIGA's ability to find concise concept descriptions (containing few, but typical instances) and to handle untypical training data, and its robustness against noisy examples and irrelevant attributes. In section 4, we report promising experimental results on well-known publicly available datasets. In section 5, we sketch related work, strengths and limitations of our approach, and some possible future improvements.

2 GIGA: The Basic Algorithm

Section 1 outlined the motivation for generating instances for concept descriptions instead of using (a subset of) given training instances. Generating a concept description essentially amounts to a search. The search space is the set of all concept descriptions, i.e., the set of all sets of instances. In practice, we limit the number of instances of a concept description to some fixed $n_I \in \mathbb{N}$. Besides a reduction of the search space, such a limitation offers further benefits to be addressed in section 3. Despite the reduction, the search space remains enormous and hence intractable with simple search methods (e.g., hill-climbing or random search). Therefore, using a *Genetic Algorithm* (GA, [9], [11]) seems appropriate, because the GA has the potential to cope with intricate search spaces in the absence of any knowledge about their structure. Furthermore, a GA is less prone to getting trapped in a local optimum. Both properties are highly valuable for our purpose (cp. [12]). In the sequel, we describe the basics of the GA in the light of our application, implemented by the experimental program 'GIGA'.

A GA maintains a set of (sub-optimal) solutions, i.e., several points in the search space. In this context, a solution is preferably called an *individual*, and the whole set is referred to as a *population* or *generation*. Usually, the population size is fixed. For exploring the search space, the GA applies so-called *genetic operators* to (a subset of the) individuals of its current population. This way, new individuals can be created and hence new points in the search space can be reached. In order to keep the population size fixed, it must be determined which individuals are to be eliminated to make room for the new ones. For this purpose a so-called *fitness measure* is employed which rates the fitness (i.e., the ability to solve the problem at hand) of each individual of the current population. The genetic operators are applied to the most fit individuals producing "offspring" which then replaces the least fit individuals (*"survival of the fittest"*).

So, the GA basically proceeds as follows: Starting with a randomly generated initial population, the GA repeats the cycle comprising the rating of all individuals using the fitness measure, applying the genetic operators to (a selection) of the best individuals, and replacing the worst individuals with offspring of the best, until some termination condition is satisfied (e.g., an individual with a satisfactory fitness level has been created).

In our case an **individual** $\mathcal{I}$ corresponds to a concept description, i.e., a (finite) set of instances. The **fitness** of an individual is measured in terms of its classification accuracy regarding a given set T of training instances. To this end we apply the k-NN rule with $k = 1$. That is, for each instance $I \in T$ the nearest neighbor $I' \in \mathcal{I}$ is computed according to the Euclidean distance measure. A correct classification is registered if the classes associated with I and I' agree.

The classification accuracy of $\mathcal{I}$ is the percentage of correctly classified instances of T. If two individuals have the same classification accuracy, we prefer the one which uses fewer instances as concept description.

The **genetic operators** are subdivided into *reproducing* and *mutating* operators. Reproducing operators produce offspring, while mutating operators alter this offspring. GIGA employs two reproduction operators, namely *crossover* and *cloning*. The **crossover operator** randomly selects two distinct parents from the pool of $r\%$ best (surviving) individuals. A subset of the instances of each parent individual is chosen at random, and the union of these two subsets yields the "child" individual. Thus, this operator complies with the basic idea of crossover, namely providing the ability to combine good partial solutions.

The **cloning operator** simply copies a randomly selected parent individual. Cloning only makes sense in connection with mutation operators to be described shortly. It is reasonable in particular if the top ranking individuals are very close to an optimum, and slight variations (mutations) of them have a higher chance to actually yield an optimal individual than (mutations preceded by) crossover. Whenever offspring is to be generated, either crossover or cloning are chosen at random according to a given probability distribution.

The **mutation operators** modify individuals stemming from crossover or cloning. An individual $\mathcal{I}$ is subject to mutation with probability P_{mut}. If an individual *is* selected for mutation, the following mutation operators are applied in the given order. (1) *Deletion: One* instance of $\mathcal{I}$ is chosen at random and discarded. This *deletion operator* is applied with probability P_{del}. It is useful to get rid of instances which do not improve classification accuracy and hence unnecessarily hinder finding concise concept descriptions. (2) *Mutate Instances*: Each instance I of $\mathcal{I}$ is subject to *random mutation* with probability P_{rnd}. That is, if $I \in \mathcal{I}$ *is* chosen for random mutation, then, with probability P_{comp}, each component a of I (i.e. a is an attribute-value pair) including the class associated with I may be replaced by a random value taken from the respective range. This kind of mutation realizes "pure" random influences and is hence helpful in introducing the necessary diversity at early stages of the genetic search. (3) *Addition*: A random number of $n \geq 1$ instances generated at random are added to $\mathcal{I}$. The *addition operator* is applied with probability P_{add}.

In summary, GIGA searches for a concept description which is both concise and accurate w.r.t. the given training set. Accuracy and conciseness are respectively the first and second objective GIGA pursues by virtue of the employed fitness measure. Note that the fitness measure is the only (indirect) connection between a concept description found by GIGA and the training set. The merely implicit dependence on the training set gives rise to interesting properties of our approach which the following section will explain and demonstrate.

3   Properties of Our Approach

Section 1 already mentioned properties of our approach which we shall now examine more closely. Please note that the experiments of this section in connection with artificial domains mainly are to illustrate the point that is being made.

3.1 Generating Typical Instances

Classification using the nearest neighbor rule entails—in its standard form—storing all training instances as concept description. Apart from possibly considerable storage requirements, storing all training instances also slows down the classification of an unknown test instance, since it must be compared with each and every training instance in order to determine its k nearest neighbors. Therefore, one attempts to store only a "sufficient" subset of all training instances which allows for classifying these training instances with an "acceptable" accuracy rate. Most efforts aiming at a reduction of storage requirements essentially center on discarding all those training instances that are correctly classified even when removed from the training set (e.g. [7]). Refinements of this approach are based on selecting instances from the training set that satisfy certain criteria such as being *typical* or *near-boundary* instances (cp. [24, 2]).

Reviewing our approach as implemented by GIGA, it becomes clear that GIGA is searching for typical instances without having an explicit notion of typicality. Due to the fitness measure, concept descriptions are sought which (a) contain as few instances as possible while (b) representing the concept as accurately as possible. Typical instances (which correspond in the case of approximately equal-sized instance clusters to cluster centers) allow for subdividing the instance space with the desired parsimony and accuracy in connection with the 1-NN rule. The striking advantage of generating instances is that we do not depend on the occurrence of typical instances in the training set. Even in the "worst case" when the training set contains only near-boundary instances, GIGA can still search for typical instances where other approaches solely relying on the training data face serious problems.

We shall illustrate this claim with an example taken from the n-of-m concept domain (see also [24]). In this domain there are m attributes with binary values from $\{0, 1\}$ and two classes $C0$ and $C1$. If n or more attribute values of an instance are 1, then this instance belongs to $C1$. Otherwise it belongs to $C0$.

In [24] the special case '5-of-10' was utilized to demonstrate the significant improvements the approach which selects typical instances from the training set (TIBL) can achieve compared to other instance-based approaches, w.r.t. both classification accuracy and the reduction of storage requirements. The results produced by this approach are shown in the last two columns of table 1. For this special case, the most typical instances I_{C0} and I_{C1} of the classes $C0$ and $C1$ are the instances with ten 0s and ten 1s as attribute values, respectively. As a matter of fact, a concept description $\mathcal{C} = \{I_{C1}, I_{C0}\}$ consisting of these two most typical instances (in that order)[3] together with the 1-NN rule allows for correctly

---

[3] It is assumed that $\mathcal{C}$ associates the instances with five 1s with the class $C1$, because I_{C1} occurs before I_{C0} in $\mathcal{C}$. This mechanism for resolving ambiguities concerning the distance measure is applied by GIGA's fitness measure. Therefore, $\mathcal{C}$ would receive a "perfect" fitness rating.

Table 1. Experimental results concerning the 5-of-10 concept

Training Set Size	GIGA				TIBL	
	avg. acc.	avg. #inst.	avg. #cycles	avg. run time	avg. acc.	avg. #inst.
100	100%	2	83.5	13.68 sec	85.6%	19.6
200	100%	2	56.4	21.91 sec	94.0%	15.1
300	100%	2	78.6	41.23 sec	98.8%	15.2
400	100%	2	59.8	40.14 sec	99.5%	10.8

classifying all 2^{10} instances. C is optimal in the sense that there is certainly no more accurate and more concise concept description.

The experimental environment set up in [24] was replicated for our experiments with GIGA. [4] Four different sizes of training sets were used. Training sets were generated at random. Each row of table 1 displays the results obtained in connection with the respective training set size averaged over ten trials. All 1024 instances of the 5-of-10 concept were used as test data. For both GIGA (columns two through five) and TIBL the columns labeled 'avg. acc.' and 'avg. #inst.' display the average accuracy (w.r.t. the test data) and the average number of instances stored in the resulting concept description, respectively.

Columns two and three of table 1 reveal that GIGA was *always* able to find the optimal concept description C regardless of (the size of) the training set. Columns four and five list the average number of cycles and the average run time (CPU time)—obtained on a SPARCstation 10—GIGA required to accomplish this. As for TIBL, the results in columns six and seven clearly exhibit the dependence on the size of the training set: Performance improves (higher accuracy, less stored instances) as the size of the training set increases, since larger training sets have a higher probability to contain I_{C0} or I_{C1}.

3.2 Near-Boundary Instances and Irrelevant Attributes

IBL approaches employing similarity measures based on spatial distance have serious difficulties when exposed to concepts involving irrelevant attributes. Irrelevant attributes do not convey any information concerning class membership. But in particular in connection with the k-NN rule, the spatial proximity of instances w.r.t. irrelevant attributes can have a distorting influence. As a consequence, classification accuracy can degrade significantly.

A similar problem arises when a training set mainly consists of near-boundary instances, i.e., instances which are (very) close to concept boundaries. Near-boundary instances located at opposite sides of the boundary of two distinct concepts can nevertheless be very close to each other. As a matter of fact, they might be closer to each other than to other instances of the respective concept. Consequently, they may be classified incorrectly.

---

[4] For this and all following experiments, please refer to [6] for parameter settings and run time behavior.

Table 2. Near-boundary instances and irrelevant attributes

Training Set Size	1-NN avg. acc. test	GIGA				
		avg. acc. test	avg. acc. training	avg. #inst.	avg. #cycles	avg. run time
40	58.74%	97.12%	99.75%	2.5	144	7.37 sec
60	60.75%	98.93%	100%	2.6	209.5	15.05 sec
80	63.53%	100%	100%	2	80.6	7.76 sec
100	68.02%	100%	100%	2	93.5	10.27 sec

Near-boundary instances and irrelevant attributes are two major causes for poor performance of common IBL approaches based on the k-NN rule. The main reason is the fixation on (a subset of) the training set which might not provide the instances necessary for an appropriate concept description. When generating instances, however, we have the chance to find apt concept descriptions involving instances that do not exist in the training set. The following simple example illustrates these aspects.

There are two classes C_1 and C_2, and three attributes x, y and z whose values range from 1 to 20. An instance belongs to class C_1 if its attribute value for attribute x is in $\{1, \ldots, 10\}$. Otherwise it belongs to C_2. Training and test instances are randomly generated along the boundary—a plane—separating C_1 and C_2. This means that the attribute value for x is 10 w.r.t. instances of C_1 and 11 w.r.t. instances of C_2. Values for y and z are randomly chosen from $\{1, \ldots, 20\}$. The attributes y and z are irrelevant since class membership can be decided with the help of x alone. This example hence combines near-boundary instances and irrelevant attributes.

Any concept description consisting of two instances I_1 and I_2 satisfying the following conditions is optimal both w.r.t. classification accuracy and parsimony: The attribute values for x are $10 - a$ and $11 + a$ ($a \in \{0, \ldots, 9\}$), respectively. For both I_1 and I_2, the attribute values for y and z are b and c ($b, c \in \{1, \ldots, 20\}$). Even under these simple conditions it is very unlikely that two such I_1 and I_2 are in a training set of reasonable size, let alone the difficulty to extract exactly these two from the training set should they be there. GIGA, however, essentially searches for a concept description consisting of two such individuals since it represents a global optimum.

Our experiments regarding this two-class concept are summarized by table 2. We employed training sets of four different sizes (cf. first column of table 2). Half of the instances of such a training set belonged to C_1, and the other half to C_2. The results presented by each row of table 2 are the average of ten trials during each of which a random training set of the respective size was presented to GIGA and the k-NN algorithm, and tested with respect to ten also randomly generated test sets. Each test set had 50 instances of each class.

The second column of table 2 shows that the k-NN algorithm performs rather poorly. (We only list the results obtained with $k = 1$, but choosing $k > 1$ does not improve performance significantly, mostly even causing it to deteriorate.) Classification accuracy naturally increases with the size of the training set. Under the present conditions, the performance of the k-NN algorithm can be improved by varying the Euclidean distance metric through the use of weighted attribute value differences. In case concept boundaries are not aligned with the attribute axes, rotations are necessary to fully profit from a weighted Euclidean distance measure. But determining rotation angles and weights also amounts to a search problem (cp. [13]). Note that our approach is independent of the orientation of concept boundaries w.r.t. attribute axes. To put it another way, the search problem remains the same whether concept regions are aligned with attribute axes or not. (The instances of an optimal concept description are rotated the same way as the whole concept.)

Columns three through seven list the results obtained with GIGA, namely the average accuracy on the test and training sets, number of instances constituting the found concept description, number of cycles and CPU time. The classification accuracies attained demonstrate that GIGA can cope with the present situation very well. In connection with training sets of the sizes 40 and 60, however, GIGA did not succeed in finding an optimal concept description in *one* of the ten trials.[5] This may be a coincidence, but it is also possible that smaller training sets entail search spaces with more deceptive local optima.

3.3 Dealing with Noise

Noise tolerance is a property of classification systems which is particularly important in real-world applications which almost never are free of noise. Although our approach does not provide an *explicit* mechanism for dealing with noise (in contrast to, e.g., [1]), it nevertheless has a certain ability to tolerate noise. It derives this implicit ability from the fact that the concept descriptions which are searched for can be limited w.r.t. their size (i.e., n_I) resp. complexity.

If data is noisy, then there typically are subspaces of the instance space whose elements are all supposed to belong to a certain class, but they are pervaded to a degree by instances associated with alien classes which represent noise. In order to single out these noisy instances—which entails "cutting up" the instance space more strongly—concept descriptions have to be more complex. So, if the complexity (size) of concept descriptions is limited appropriately, then GIGA will search for *coarser* concept descriptions which kind of "ignore" noisy instances: Due to the restricted ability to cut up the instance space, GIGA can recognize larger coherent areas of the instance space which are associated with a certain class although they are "polluted" and pervaded by noise. Naturally, if the percentage of noisy instances exceeds a certain degree, then they cause distortions that cannot be compensated for anymore. The subsequent example is to illustrate this property.

There are three classes C_1, C_2, C_3, and two attributes x and y whose values range from 1 to 18. An instance belongs to class C_1 (C_2, C_3) if the value of its

---

[5] Besides finding an optimal concept description, having been trapped in a local optimum for more than 500 cycles is a further termination criterion. The average number of cycles and the run time naturally increase if termination was triggered by the latter criterion.

attribute x is in $\{1, \ldots, 6\}$ ($\{7, \ldots, 12\}$, $\{13, \ldots, 18\}$). The value of the (irrelevant) attribute y is chosen at random. Training and test data are generated at random, containing 150 instances (50 instances of each class). The test data is free of noise, whereas noise is introduced into the training data. To this end, for a certain percentage of randomly chosen instances of each class, the correct class label is replaced with an incorrect one (also chosen at random).

Figure 1 summarizes our experiments conducted in this domain. The accuracy results are averaged over ten trials (ten test sets per trial).

We employed GIGA with two (maximal) sizes of concept descriptions, namely $n_I = 10$ and $n_I = 5$ (cp. figure 1a and 1b, respectively).[6] The remaining parameters were set as in the preceding subsection. Figure 1c displays the performance of the k-NN algorithm using $k = 3$.

Figure 1 shows that classification accuracy on the (noise-free) test data is significantly higher compared to 3-NN when using GIGA and forcing it to search for coarse concept descriptions. As a matter of fact, accuracy remains on a high level with as much as 30% noise in the training data. The accuracy of 3-NN drops almost linearly right from the start. Note that the "coarser" setting involving $n_I = 5$ yields a slightly better performance than the less coarse one ($n_I = 10$). The threshold for the amount of noise GIGA can satisfactorily cope with seems to lie between 30% and 40% for this experimental data. Exceeding this threshold causes the accuracy rate to drop sharply. Note that the accuracy on the training data (dotted lines) decreases in almost perfect correlation with the percentage of noise, which suggests that GIGA is able to in a way "sort out" (most of) the noisy instances as long as there is not too much noise. This effect can of course not be observed in connection with the 3-NN classifier.

4 Experimental Results

While in section 3 artificial datasets were used to demonstrate specific properties of our algorithm, we now examine some well-known benchmark datasets. For the sake of comparable and reproducable results we chose only publicly available datasets from the *Machine Learning Repository* at the University of California at Irvine [17]. We took datasets with well-documented results and used the StatLog Evaluation Assistant—a set of UNIX shell scripts and C routines for the test of classification algorithms and the production of standardized performance measures [16]. We also used the same test method (leave-one-out, k-fold cross-validation, etc.) as reported in the literature and compared our results with the best reported results. The following datasets were examined:

Diabetes (Pima Indians): diabetes diagnosis on the basis of physiological measurements and medical tests [20]; the best results are reported in [16]; 768 instances, 8 real-valued attributes, 2 classes. **Breast Cancer (Wisconsin):** cancer diagnosis from cytological information; the best result is reported in [23,

---

[6] Note that—similar to the example of subsection 3.2—there are concept descriptions consisting of three instances which achieve perfect classification accuracy (for noise-free data).

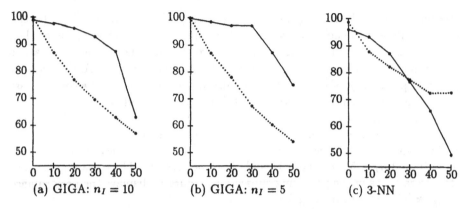

Fig. 1. Experiments with noisy data: The x axis displays the percentage of noise, and the y axis the (average) classification accuracy w.r.t. test data (straight lines) and training data (dotted lines).

24]; 699 instances, 10 integer-valued attributes, 2 classes. **Promoter sequences:** prediction of biological promoter activity for a sequence of nucleotides; past usage by [21]; 106 instances, 59 nominal attributes[7], 2 classes. **Heart Disease (Cleveland):** diagnosis of coronary artery disease; best result described by [8]; 303 instances, 14 integer-valued attributes, 2 classes. **Congressional voting:** determine party affiliation from congressional voting; introduced by [19]; 435 instances, 16 boolean attributes, 2 classes.

Results: Table 3 summarizes the classification accuracies obtained in this first experimental evaluation of GIGA. GIGA exceeded the best reported results in the diabetes and the breast cancer domain, and, after some experimentation concerning the appropriate value for n_I, also in the promoter sequence and the voting domain. Only for heart disease diagnosis, we were finally not able to produce an accuracy competitive with the best published results.

The experiments show that GIGA is able to find optimized concept descriptions also in noisy domains with imprecise concepts and thus can contribute to better solutions for practically relevant classification tasks. Optimal parameter adjustment seems to be the crucial point in some domains. Mostly, the value of n_I turns out to be the main problem. But this is less serious, since this value can iteratively be incremented until an optimal *"complexity fit"* [22] of the concept description is reached. Because most papers concentrate on test-set accuracy, we report only this result which is also likely to be the strongest point of GIGA. Nevertheless, comparisons of run time behavior, storage requirements and robustness in noisy and dynamic situations provide interesting work for the near future. Another point for further investigations is the thorough examination of the instances generated by GIGA, especially in comparison with TIBL or prototype-learners.

---

[7] Nominal values were replaced by integers according to their alphabetic order.

Table 3. Experimental results using real-world datasets

Dataset	test method	best reported algorithm	best reported acc.	GIGA acc.
Diabetes	12-fold cv	Logdisc	77.7%	80.5%
Breast Cancer	10-fold cv	Hyperplanes	95.9%	97.3%
Promoter	leave-one-out	KBANN	96.2%	98.1%
Heart Disease	10-fold cv	CLASSIT	78.9%	72.3%
Voting	train & test	STAGGER	90-95%	93.9%

5 Discussion

In this paper we presented GIGA, a novel approach to classification that employs a genetic search algorithm in order to approximate ideal concept descriptions to be used by a nearest-neighbor classifier.

Our algorithm follows the Pittsburgh approach to machine-learning oriented GAs [12, 10] in that each individual of the population encodes a complete solution of the classification problem. But in contrast to other systems that learn explicit abstractions from examples (e.g. decision trees), our instance-based concept description permits a *scalable* output-representation language with arbitrary granularity.[8] Experiments with ML benchmark datasets show that the system is able to find an appropriately fine-grained level to describe hard classification problems. This ability may be seen as another form of dynamically adjusting system bias (cp. [12]). But note that in our approach this adjustment is done implicitly, embedded in a rather elegant and easy to implement evolution cycle, whereas others need very sophisticated techniques.

Within the instance-based learning community, our approach consequently continues the idea of searching optimized concept descriptions as introduced by **IB3** [2] and **TIBL** [24]. The search for *"ideal"* instances seems to be unique in this community. However, the *Learning Vector Quantization* approach (LVQ, cp. for example [18]) in the area of neural networks essentially pursues a similar goal, but employing another search strategy. A more detailed comparison of GIGA and the LVQ approach belongs to the future work. The experiments with artificial datasets in section 3 illustrate conditions under which our approach of *not* relying on the given instances to construe a concept description becomes a striking advantage. The use of *few, typical* instances essentially amounts to an implicit generalization from examples that makes it easier to tolerate a remarkable level of noise as well as many near-boundary instances or irrelevant attributes in the training set. [13] propose an approach that does not construct new instances but transforms the given instances by rotations and attribute scalings which are optimized by a GA in order to support the k-NN classifier. This idea is somehow complementary to our approach. But it is not evaluated using real-world datasets, and it does finally not tackle the problem of bad input data

---

[8] Instance-based classifiers can piecewise-linearly approximate arbitrary concept boundaries.

(only the problem of bad input *representation*).

Mainly motivated by psychological studies [15], prototype learners (see e.g. [14, 5]) pursue a similar goal as we do in that they compute a concept prototype from attribute values and frequencies occurring in the training set. However, these systems are slightly more restricted to the given training instances as we are, since we can enforce an arbitrary level of generalization via the maximal number n_I of instances constituting a concept description. Furthermore, except for [5], prototype learners usually construct a *single* prototype instance per concept which is not always sufficient for an adequate concept representation. Of course, our flexibility is paid for by a high computational effort due to the genetic search. However, this search can still be improved through more sophisticated GA techniques and finally be performed in a highly-parallel way by multi-processor machines. Simple incremental improvements of classifiers in order to take into account new information, and the advantages of an any-time algorithm are further benefits.

Some limitations are naturally inherited from instance-based learning, for example the problem of finding appropriate distance metrics and the use of symbolic background knowledge. On the other hand, there are still promising future research directions, e.g. the co-evolution of the distance metric or the incorporation of individuals computed with Zhang's method or de la Maza's method into the first generation of the genetic algorithm.

To conclude we can say that GIGA represents an interesting complement for other learning approaches. In situations where instance-based learning seems appropriate, but is hindered by poor data quality, GIGA has the chance of considerably improving classification accuracy by spending large-scale computational power. This is the case in a number of practically relevant problems (see e.g. the breast cancer domain in section 4) where few reliable data and background knowledge is available, but classification improvements are highly valuable.

References

1. D.W. Aha and D. Kibler. Noise-tolerant instance-based learning algorithms. In *Proc. 11th IJCAI, Detroit, MI, USA*, pages 794–799, 1989.
2. D.W. Aha, D. Kibler, and M.K. Albert. Instance-based learning algorithms. *Machine Learning*, 6:37–66, 1991.
3. R. Bareiss, B. Porter, and R. Holte. Concept learning and heuristic classification in weak-theory domains. *Artificial Intelligence*, 45(1–2), 1990.
4. T.M. Cover and P.E. Hart. Nearest neighbor pattern classification. *IEEE Transactions on Information Theory*, 13:21–27, 1967.
5. P. Datta and D. Kibler. Learning prototypical concept descriptions. In A. Prieditis and S. Russell, editors, *Machine Learning: Proc. of the 12th Int. Conference ICML-95*. Morgan Kaufmann, San Francisco, CA, USA, 1995.
6. M. Fuchs and A. Abecker. Optimized nearest-neighbor classifiers using generated instances. Technical Report LSA-96-02E, University of Kaiserslautern, 1996.
7. G.W. Gates. The reduced nearest neighbor rule. *IEEE Transactions on Information Theory*, pages 431–433, May 1972.

8. J.H. Gennari, P. Langley, and D. Fisher. Models of incremental concept formation. *Artificial Intelligence*, 40:11–61, 1989.

9. J.H. Holland. *Adaptation in natural and artificial systems: An introductory analysis with applications to biology, control, and artificial intelligence.* Ann Arbor: Univ. of Michigan Press, 2nd edition, 1992.

10. C.Z. Janikow. A knowledge intensive genetic algorithm for supervised learning. *Machine Learning*, 13:198–228, 1993.

11. K. De Jong. Learning with genetic algorithms: An overview. *Machine Learning*, 3:121–138, 1988.

12. K.A. De Jong, W.M. Spears, and D.F. Gordon. Using genetic algorithms for concept learning. *Machine Learning*, 13:161–188, 1993.

13. J.D. Kelly and L. Davis. Hybridizing the genetic algorithm and the k nearest neighbors classification algorithm. In *Proc. 4th ICGA, San Diego, CA, USA*, 1991.

14. M. De La Maza. A prototype based symbolic concept learning system. In *Proc. of the 8th Int. Workshop on Machine Learning*. Morgan Kaufmann, 1991.

15. D.L. Medin and E.E. Smith. Concepts and concept formation. *Annual Review of Psychology*, (35):121–138, 1988.

16. D. Michie, D.J. Spiegelhalter, and C.C. Taylor. *Machine Learning, Neural and Statistical Classification*. Ellis Horwood, 1994.

17. P.M. Murphy and D.W. Aha. UCI Repository of machine learning databases [http://www.ics.uci.edu/~mlearn/MLRepository.html], Irvine, CA, University of California, Department of Information and Computer Science, 1994.

18. N.R. Pal, J.C. Bezdek, and E.C.-K. Tsao. Generalized clustering networks and Kohonen's self-organizing scheme. *IEEE Transactions on Neural Networks*, 4(4):549–557, 1993.

19. J.C. Schlimmer. *Concept acquisition through representational adjustment*. PhD thesis, University of California, Irvine, CA, 1987.

20. J.W. Smith, J.E. Everhart, W.C. Dickson, W.C. Knowler, and R.S Johannes. Using the ADAP learning algorithm to forecast the onset of diabetes mellitus. In *Proceedings of the Symposium on Computer Applications and Medical Care*. IEEE Computer Society Press, 1988.

21. G. Towell, J. Shavlik, and M. Noordewier. Refinement of approximate domain theories by knowledge-based artificial neural networks. In *Proceedings of the 8th National Conference on Artificial Intelligence (AAAI-90)*, 1990.

22. Sh.M. Weiss and C.A. Kulikowski. *Computer Systems That Learn – Classification and Prediction Methods from Statistics, Neural Nets, Machine Learning, and Expert Systems*. Morgan Kaufmann, 1991.

23. W.H. Wolberg and O.L. Mangasarin. Multisurface method of pattern separation for medical diagnosis applied to breast cytology. In *Proceedings of the National Academy of Sciences, USA*, volume 87, pages 9193–9196, December 1990.

24. J. Zhang. Selecting typical instances in instance-based learning. In *Proc. 9th ICML, Aberdeen, Scotland*, pages 470–479, 1992.

Towards a Totally
Distributed Meeting Scheduling System *

Leonardo Garrido-Luna[1] and Katia Sycara[2]

[1] Center for Artificial Intelligence, ITESM.
Sucursal de Correos "J". Monterrey, N.L. 64849 México
lgarrido@campus.mty.itesm.mx
[2] The Robotics Institute. Carnegie Mellon University.
Pittsburgh, PA 15213 USA
katia@cs.cmu.edu

Abstract. Meeting scheduling is an everyday task which is iterative, time-consuming, and tedious. Furthermore, it is a naturally distributed task where all attendees try to schedule a common meeting (their group goal) taking into account their individual preferences (their individual goals). In this paper, we present our preliminary work towards this direction; we view meeting scheduling as a distributed task where each agent knows its user's preferences and calendar availability in order to act on behalf of its user. Our experiments investigate how the calendar and preference privacy affect the process efficiency and the meeting joint quality under different experimental scenarios. The results show that the group performance is more stable and constant when agents try to keep their calendar and preference information private. We believe that these parameters play a key role in the non-centralized meeting scheduling task, specially if we are interested in building truly autonomous and independent agents.

1 Introduction

Meeting scheduling is a time-consuming, iterative, tedious, and naturally distributed task. It can take place only between two persons or among several persons. Sometimes, these people only try to schedule one meeting. However, most of the time people needs to schedule many meetings at the same time taking into account several constraints. In our daily life, meeting scheduling is a naturally distributed task which, many times, is performed by secretaries via telephone or, many other times, it is performed by ourselves via electronic mail.

Each potential attendee needs to take into account his/her own meeting preferences and calendar availability. Most of the time, each attendee has some uncertain and incomplete knowledge about the preferences and calendar of the other attendees; in fact, agents usually try to keep their calendar and preference

* This research has been sponsored in part by CONACYT under their scholarship program and by ITESM Campus Monterrey under their PCP program. Most of this work has been conducted at The Robotics Institute in Carnegie Mellon University.

information private. During the meeting scheduling process, all attendees should consider the main group goal (i.e. to schedule a meeting) but they also take into account individual goals (i.e. to satisfy their individual preferences).

There are several commercial products but they are just computational calendars with some special features (e.g. availability checkers, meeting reminders); in [16], a review of several of these products can be found. However, none of these products is a truly autonomous agent capable of communicating and negotiating with other agents in order to schedule meetings in a distributed way taking into account the user's preferences and calendar availability.

On the other hand, there have been much research work in meeting scheduling. Most of the earliest work reached interesting but limited success; see [4, 3, 5] for details.

We can found some interesting approahes in Artificial Intelligence such as [7] and [6]; these approaches focus in learning user preferences but they do not take to much attention to the social and distributed implications of the distributed meeting schedulling process.

We can find other research work in Decentralized Artificial Intelligence. Sen & Durfee's work [9, 10, 11, 12, 13] has been focused on solving the meeting scheduling problem using a centralized host agent capable of communicating with all other agents in order to schedule meetings using a negotiation based on contracts [14]; the main purpose of the host agent is to coordinate the search for a feasible schedule taking into consideration attendees' calendars. However, user preferences are not taken into account during the meeting scheduling process. They have focused their research on several search biases to get different density profiles in agents' calendars.

Other recent work in distributed meeting scheduling is due to Ephrati, Zlotkin and Rosenschein [1]. They presented an alternative approach which is economic in flavor. Using three centralized monetary-based meeting scheduling systems, they analyzed tradeoffs between the mechanism complexity and information preferences and they introduced the Clarke Tax Mechanism as a method for removing manipulability from them.

In [15], Sycara and Liu presented another approach based on modeling and communication of constraints and preferences among the agents. Here the agents are capable of negotiating and relaxing their constraints in order to find and reach agreement on schedules with high joint utility. Using this model, agents also can react and revise the schedule in response to dynamic changes.

In our work, we view meeting scheduling as a distributed task where each agent knows its user preferences and calendar availability in order to act on behalf of its user. Using Allegro CLOS, we implemented our system which consists of truly autonomous software agents running, as independent processes, on different computers. We have run several experiments in order to explore the tradeoffs between meeting quality and efficiency when varying some experimental parameters. We present, in this paper, some of our preliminary experimental results.

To begin with, we make a general description of our system in section 2 where we also present the general utility function we used to control and bias each individual agent search during negotiation. Manipulating the individual utility functions we set up some experiments which are described in section 3. Later, in section 4, we present our experimental results. Section 5 presents discussion and section 6 presents conclusions and future directions.

2 Multi-Agent Meeting Scheduling System

Our distributed meeting scheduling system does not have a centralized control. This means that there is not a specialized host agent and each agent is able to try to schedule a meeting via negotiation taking into account individual preferences and calendar availability.

Since we are primarily interested in investigating the behavior of truly autonomous and selfdriven agents, one of our main concerns is information privacy. In our system, each agent only knows its user meeting preferences and calendar information. However, agents can exchange information during negotiation.

A meeting has a date, start-time and duration and it is scheduled when all agents reach agreement on values for these attributes. Agents negotiate values for theses attributes taking into account three *time windows* given as input:

Date window. It indicates the range of days where the meeting can be scheduled.

Start-time window. It indicates the range of start-times to schedule the meeting.

Duration window. It indicates the range of durations where the meeting can be scheduled.

Each agent has a set of meeting preferences given as inputs for each particular meeting; this set represents its user's meeting preferences (i.e. the three meeting attributes values that are the most preferred by its user). The main goal is to schedule meetings considering the three time windows given as inputs. However, each agent has its own individual goal: to schedule the meeting maximizing its individual meeting preferences (i.e. the agents try to schedule the meeting in the calendar interval with the closest attributes to its user meeting preferences).

In order to schedule meetings, agents face two problems: one is that the agents can have different available calendar intervals and the other one is that they also can have different individual meeting preferences. Furthermore, the distributed environment and the information privacy are, of course, sources of other aspects that need to be taken into account. The agents are able to negotiate proposing and bidding values for the three meeting attributes (date, start-time and duration) according to their individual preferences and available time intervals. In our distributed system, agents can exchange their meeting preferences and calendar information according to some privacy policy which has been an adjustable parameter in our experiments. Basically, each agent is able to relax three different time constraints: date, start-time and duration. In addition to its preferences, each agent has weights (values between 0 and 1) that indicate how to relax each time constraint.

Our system exploits the coordination mechanism and communication protocol presented earlier in [15]. In our experiments, agents communicate and negotiate via message passsing. Each agent is able to relax its preferences when conflicts arise. The protocol we implemented is as follows:

- Agents exchange their calendar information (i.e. their available time intervals). As we will see later, this was one of the experimental parameters we varied in our experiments.
- The agent with the fewest available time intervals becomes the task coordinator who is responsible for sending the first proposal.
- Each agent that receives a proposal accepts or rejects it by replying the message. If the agent accepts it, it is able to share the priority value that it was assigned to that time interval by the agent. As we will see later, it was another experimental parameter we varied in our experiments.
- When the task coordinator receives all the replying messages and the proposal was accepted by all agents, the coordinator sums up the priorities to get the group utility measure for that meeting and send a final confirmation message to all agents sending the approval of the proposal and its group utility.
- However, when the proposal is rejected by at least one agent, the coordinator selects as a new task coordinator to the agent who opposes the current proposal. If there are more than one opposing agent, the agent with the fewest available time intervals is selected.
- The new task coordinator relaxes its time constraints and send a new proposal and the process is repeated.

The original coordination mechanism and communication protocol discussed in [15] takes into account multiple-meeting schedules and dynamic changes after a meeting have been approved (e.g. an agent can ask for further negotiation if it realizes that, due to dynamic local changes, it is possible to reschedule the meeting achieving higher utility).

During negotiation, agents look for free calendar intervals to be proposed. This search is biased using individual utility functions; the utility function gives a priority value to each available calendar interval according to the particular time windows, individual meeting preferences and relaxation weights. This gives us a search mechanism that can be biased by different relaxation heuristics.

Let us define a *calendar interval j* as a vector, $\mathbf{I}^j$, with three attributes: date, start-time and duration. Also, let us define the *preferences of the agent k* as a vector, $\mathbf{P}^k$, with the same three attributes. Furthermore, let us define the *relaxation weights of the agent k* (the weights assigned by agent k for relaxing each of the three time constraints) also as a vector, $\mathbf{W}^k$, with the same three attributes.

Now, we can define the *weighted distance (WDist)* between an *interval j* and the *preferences of the agent k*, taking into account its *relaxation weigths*, as:

$$WDist(\mathbf{I}^j, \mathbf{P}^k, \mathbf{W}^k) = \sum_{i=1}^{3}[\mathbf{W}_i^k \cdot Dist(\mathbf{I}_i^j, \mathbf{P}_i^k)]$$

Here, subscript i indicates the meeting attribute (1 is *date*, 2 is *start-time* and 3 is *duration*). $Dist(\mathbf{I}_i^j, \mathbf{P}_i^k)$ is the distance between $\mathbf{I}_i^j$ and $\mathbf{P}_i^k$ (i.e.the number of possible different instances of the attribute i between the attribute value of the interval j and the attribute value that is most prefered by the agent k).

Finally, we can present the *General Utility Function* we used in our experiments:

$$Priority_k(\mathbf{I}^j) = \frac{\sum_{i=1}^{3}[\mathbf{S}_i - 1] - WDist(\mathbf{I}^j, \mathbf{P}^k, \mathbf{W}^k)}{\sum_{i=1}^{3}[\mathbf{S}_i - 1]}$$

As we can see, this function is just the *normalized* weighted distance taking into account the *window sizes* which are seen as a vetor, $\mathbf{S}$, with the three time attributes. In other words, $\mathbf{S}_i$ is the window size of the meeting attribute i (i.e. the number of possible different instances of the attribute i in the time window given as input).

Each agent k can assign a priority value to each available time interval j. The maximum possible priority value is 1 and the minimum possible value is 0. The calendar interval with the highest value is the best option to propose. Using this general utility function with different relaxation weights and preferences, we can model different search biases during negotiation.

3 Experiments Description

In the experiments we present here, we consider the negotiation/scheduling process between three agents. We think that the results obtained with these three-agents experiments can be easy generalized to any n-agents meeting scheduling system. We have identified some experimental variables and we have been investigating the effect of each parameter in isolation from the other.

In order to avoid intractable combinatorics, we considered calendars of three days with three hours per day. Also, we used a *relaxation step* of 30 minutes (i.e. any possible calendar interval will have a duration and start-time multiple of 30 minutes).

So let us say that our calendar days are 1, 2, and 3. The start-times are 0, 30, 60, 90, 120, and 150. The possible durations are 30, 60, 90, 120, and 150. All these values define our three time windows discussed earlier: the *date window*, *start-time window*, and *duration window*.

The number of busy hours in a calendar may vary. Let us define the *calendar density* for a particular calendar as the number of busy hours in that calendar. In our experiments, we vary the calendar density from zero to six and we run each different experimental meeting scheduling scenario for each different possible calendar under each different calendar density.

We repeated each experimental scenario under every different calendar using each different calendar density with one agent while the rest of the agents had empty calendars. We calculated the average fastness and average joint quality when the last run of each calendar density is accomplished.

We measured the scheduling fastness in terms of the number of proposals and we measured the meeting quality as a joint quality, using the following formula:

$$JointQuality(\mathbf{I}^j) = \frac{\sum_{i=1}^{n} Priority_i(\mathbf{I}^j) \cdot 10}{n}$$

In this formula, the maximum possible value is 10 and the minimum one is 0. The variable n is the number of agents.

In this way, we obtained two graphs for each particular experimental scenario: the first one is an efficiency graph with the number of proposals and calendar density as axes; the second one is the meeting group quality graph with the joint quality and calendar density as axes.

As we said before, it is highly desirable to keep the agents' information private. Let us see how we varied the amount of information exchanged:

Calendar Information. Basically, we experimented with two kinds of calendar information exchanges: *total calendars* and *partial calendars*. In the former case, agents exchange all their available calendar intervals. In the latter case, agents exchange a portion of their available calendars. Furthermore, in this case we can have other cases varying the size of the exchanged calendars (e.g. proposing only two slots instead of four slots)

Preferences. We have here two other kinds of preference information exchanges: *public preferences* and *private preferences*. In the former case, agents inform the preference value of each calendar interval that they propose. In the latter case, agents inform their preference values after they have reach agreement on a time interval; this is done in order to measure the joint quality of the meeting. Later, any agent can propose another calendar interval, if it thinks that the joint quality can be improved.

It is interesting to note that if the agents are exchanging *public preferences* they can use the joint quality formula discussed previously instead of using their individual utility functions. Furthermore, it is also interesting to note that if they are exchanging *public preferences* and *total calendars*, it is possible to get an agreement with the highest possible joint quality in only one shot. This is possible because each agent knows all the information (i.e. there is no information privacy at all).

In the following paragraphs we present the experimental scenarios we set up:

Varying individual goals with *total calendars*. Here we varied the individual preference values and we plotted two curves. The first curve shows the process when all agents have the same preferences; let us call it *Common-Goals* curve. The second one, called *Disparate-Goals* curve, shows the process when each agent has different preferences.

Here agents exchange *total calendars* but they do not exchange *public preferences*. Therefore, they are using their individual utility functions to guide the search and they do not exchange their preferences until they reach an agreement. After this, each agent has the opportunity of proposing another time interval and this cycle ends until no agent has new proposals.

Varying individual goals with *partial calendars*. In this scenario, we varied the preference values again. As we said in the previous experimental scenario, the first curve, *Common-Goals*, shows the process when all agents have the same preference values. The second one, *Disparate-Goals*, shows the process when each agent has different preferences.

The difference between this scenario and the previous one is that this scenario was fixed to the exchange of *partial calendars* with only *private preferences* too. So that they also use their individual utility functions and not the joint utility formula to guide the search.

Varying individual goals with *public preferences*. Here we varied again the agents' individual goals, plotting two curves. The first one, called *Common-Goals*, shows the scheduling process when all agents have the same preferences. The second one, called *Disparate-Goals*, shows the process when each agent has different preferences.

Here, agents exchange *total calendars* and *public preferences*. Since they are working under the *public preferences* scheme they also use the joint utility formula, discussed earlier, instead of their individual utility functions.

Varying preference privacy with *total calendars*. As we discussed earlier, we have basically two kinds of preferences exchanges: *public preferences* and *private preferences*. We plotted one curve for each of them and we call them *Public-Goals* and *Private-Goals* respectively.

All agents exchange *total calendars* in this experimental scenario. The agents' utility functions were fixed to *Disparate-Goals*. That is, every agent has a different set of preferences.

Varying preference privacy with *partial calendars*. As in the previous experimental scenario, we plotted two curves: one called *Public-Goals* and the other one *Private-Goals*. Now, we fixed now the calendar exchange scheme to *partial calendars*.

As in the previous scenario, the agents' utility functions were fixed to *Disparate-Goals*.

4 Experimental Results and Analyses

Figure 1 displays the results we obtained varying individual goals with *total calendars*. As we expected, when all agents have the same preferences (*Common-Goals* curve) the scheduling fastness and meeting quality are, in general, better than when agents have different preferences (*Disparate-Goals* curve).

Also, we can see that the scheduling fastness of the *Common-Goals* curve is constant and the meeting quality is decreasing when the calendar density is

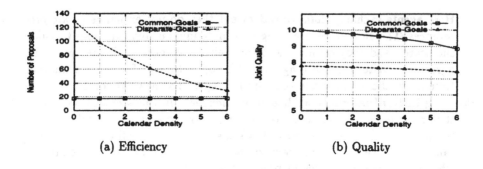

(a) Efficiency   (b) Quality

Fig. 1. Varying individual goals with *total calendars*

increasing. As we will see in the following graphs, this meeting quality is the best one that three agents can reach using our communication protocol.

On the other hand, the scheduling fastness of the *Disparate-Goals* curve is not constant, it decreases when the calendar density increases. However, this fastness always is slower than the *Common-Goals* fastness. The meeting quality of the *Disparate-Goals* is also decreasing but not as fast as the *Common-Goals*. However, the former always is lower than the latter.

Now, the results we obtained varying the individual preferences with *partial calendars* are shown in figure 2. Let us first note that, as in the previous case, the *Common-Goals* curve shows better results than the *Disparate-Goals* curve. We can also see that the meeting quality graph is very similar to the previous one. However, we can see a really different fastness graph now.

It is interesting to note the difference between this fastness graph and the previous one. Now, the scheduling fastness showed in figure 2 by the *Disparate-Goals* curve is improved when the calendar density is less or equal to 4. In fact, this scheduling fastness remains almost constant under every calendar density. As we saw in the previous graph, it was not the case with the the *Disparate-Goals*

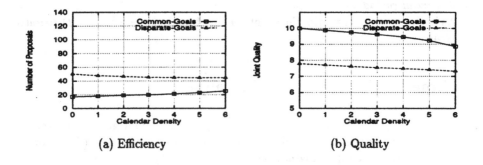

(a) Efficiency   (b) Quality

Fig. 2. Varying individual goals with *partial calendars*

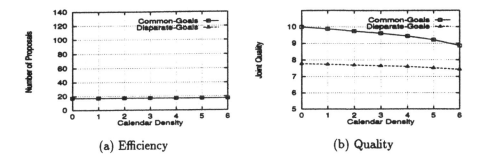

(a) Efficiency   (b) Quality

Fig. 3. Varying individual goals with *public preferences*

curve. On the other hand, the *Common-Goals* curve is increasing now, while it was constant in the previous graph. Fortunately, as we can see in figure 2, the increment is small and the curve does not raise very quickly.

We can explain these differences noting that, in general, agents explore less search space when they exchange *partial calendars* than when they exchange *total calendars*. However, sometimes they need to make more iterations because the *partial calendars* does not have a common intersection, as we saw earlier in the *Common-Goals* curve.

On the other hand, we can see that the joint quality in figure 1 is slightly better than that shown in figure 2. This can be explained noting that agents explore only *partial calendars* and they does not evaluate all the possible calendar intervals. So that it is possible to reach agreement on meetings with joint qualities lower than those qualities reached with *total calendars*.

Now, figure 3 shows the results obtained when we varied the individual goals with *public preferences* and also with *total calendars*. As we can see, both *Disparate-Goals* and *Common-Goals* curves show exactly the same low and constant fastness. Also, we can see that the meeting quality is the same as in the graph shown in figure 1.

This results are explained noting that in this experimental scenario there is not information privacy at all. Although agents have different individual goals the scheduling fastness is as fast as when they have common goals; this is because they are exchanging *public preferences* and they are able to use the joint quality formula to guide the search through the exchanged *total calendars*.

Now, let us look at figure 4; this figure displays the results varying preference privacy with *total calendars*. Remember that in this experimental scenario agents have different individual goals. As we can see, now we obtained a very similar fastness graph to that shown in figure 1. The difference is that we are now varying the preference privacy (remember that, in the experimental scenario shown in figure 1, agents exchanged *total calendars* and both curves showed the results when agents used different individual goals).

As we can see in the *Public-Goals* curve, when agents exchange *total calendars*

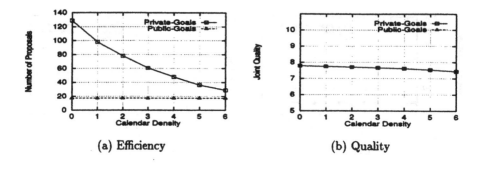

(a) Efficiency   (b) Quality

Fig. 4. Varying preference privacy with *total calendars*

they get low and constant scheduling fastness. This is because they are using the joint quality function to guide the search. However, if they exchange *private preferences* (look at *Private-Goals* curve), we can see that they spend more time because they use their individual utilities functions instead of the joint utility formula discussed earlier.

On the other hand, it is interesting to note that both curves have identical shape in the joint quality graph. This is because the agents have different goals and *total calendars* in both cases. Obviously, sooner or latter (depending on the preference privacy policy), they reach the same results. Of course, we are assuming that agents prefer to relax their constraints before failing to reach an agreement.

Figure 5 also shows our results when varying preference privacy but now with *partial calendars*. Again, both curves show agents with different individual goals. However, now they exchange *partial calendars*. As we expected, we obtained again identical meeting quality results for both curves.

However, we can see different results in the fastness graph. We see that we can obtain almost equal scheduling speeds with calendar densities greater or equal to

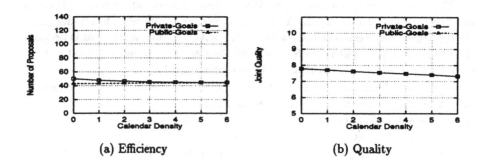

(a) Efficiency   (b) Quality

Fig. 5. Varying preference privacy with *partial calendars*

three. In fact, both curves are, in general, very similar. They are almost constant with similar values. It is interesting to contrast this graph with the previous fastness graph where both curves were very different. Meeting scheduling fastness remains more constant varying preference privacy with *partial calendars* than when varying it with *total calendars*.

5 Discussion

First of all, we need to note that our work has a primarily focus on social aspects of the meeting scheduling task. We are specially interested in aspects such as information privacy, negotiation, and group adaptation. However this does not mean that the inherent scheduling problem (which is known as an NP-complete problem [2]) does not have enough importance to be considered. We believe that in order to tackle realistic meeting scheduling scenarios we need to pay particular attention to social aspects involved in the distributed meeting scheduling process.

As we previously mentioned, there are other approaches (e.g. [7]) which focus on learning user preferences using induction trees and taking into consideration several meeting attributes. Eventually, our agents could have communication with one of these systems in order to get the set of user meeting preferences.

In general, our expectations were confirmed by the experimental results. However, we have discovered some interesting results that we would like to discuss here.

We can expect that the efficiency decreases when the difference between individual goals increases. This is particularly true when agents exchange *total calendars*. However, when they exchange only *partial calendars*, the performance is better (remember figure 1 and figure 2). The meeting quality is not affected when we move from the *total calendars* graph to the *partial calendars* graph. Furthermore, the scheduling fastness is more stable and slower, in average, when they exchange *partial calendars* than when they exchange *total calendars*. This result is interesting since we are primarily interested in scenarios where agents try to keep their calendar information private.

On the other hand, when agents are exchanging *public preferences*, they are able to look for an agreement using the joint utility formula reaching optimal meeting joint qualities with the fewest possible number of exchanged proposals (remember figure 3). However, we should remember that in our experiments we are working under the honesty assumption. This means that agents use preference information in order to really try to reach the meeting with the highest joint quality. However, this is not always true in real life.

It is interesting to note that varying preference privacy when agents exchange *partial calendars* does not affect the efficiency too much; we can see this in figure 5. This is interesting since in realistic scenarios we want to keep preference and calendar information private.

These experiments have shown that when agents schedule meetings trying to keep their information private, our multi-agent system behaves in a more stable way with better average fastness reaching the best possible meeting joint qualities. This is of particular interest to us because people always try to keep information private most of the time.

Our multi-agent system shows how we can provide automated support for the meeting scheduling task taking into account user preferences and keeping information private.

However, we have been working under some key assumptions: Our agents accept in advance the protocol and coordination policies. Our agents agree on meeting locations, since we have not model this parameter in our system yet. Our agents are honest; that is, they does not try to take advantage of the exchanged information in order to manipulate the outcome of the negotiation. They always try to reach the optimal joint meeting quality and, as human beings, first relax their preferences before failing to reach an agreement, as it has been discussed in [8].

6 Conclusions and Future Directions

We have presented some of the preliminary results we obtained through experimentation with our multi-agent meeting scheduling system. This system is based on the communication protocol presented earlier in [15]. The experiments presented in this paper show some of the relationships between different experimental variables, such as calendar and preference privacy. We believe that these variables play a key role in the distributed meeting scheduling task, specially if we are interested in building distributed systems with truly autonomous and independent agents where there is not a specific centralized host agent.

The results obtained through experimentation have confirmed some interesting points. Some of these results are of particular interest because they show some aspects of realistic scenarios where agents try to satisfy their own preferences keeping their information private.

However, as we stated earlier we have still kept some key assumptions. We intend to continue our research towards more realistic scenarios relaxing some of our assumptions discussed in the last section. We intend to let agents learn and infer other agents' mental attitutes and behaviors in order to model more complex and realistic scenarios where agents need to adapt to the whole group in totally distributed (descentralized) environments.

References

1. E. Ephrati, G. Zlotkin, and J. S. Rosenschein. A non-manipulable meeting scheduling system. In *13th International Workshop on Distributed Artificial Intelligence*, 1994.
2. M. R. Garey and D. S. Johnson. *Computers and Intractability: A Guide to the Theory of NP-Completeness.* Freeman and Co., 1979.
3. I. Greif. Pcal: A personal calendar. Technical Report TR-213, MIT Laboratory for Computer Science, Cambridge, Mass, 1982.

4. C. Kelley, J. F. and A. Chapanis. How professional persons keep their calendars: Implications for computarization. *Journal of Occupanional Psychology*, 55:141–156, January 1982.

5. C. Kincaid, P. Dupont, and A. Kaye. Electronic calendars in the office: An assessment of user needs and current technology. *ACM Transactions on Office Information Systems*, 3(1), January 1985.

6. P. Maes. Agents that reduce work and information overload. *Communications of the ACM*, 37(7):30–40, July 1994.

7. T. Mitchell, R. Caruana, D. Freitag, J. McDermott, and D. Zabowski. Experience with a learning personal assistant. *Communications of the ACM*, 37(7):80–91, July 1994.

8. H. Raiffa. *The Art and Science of Negotiation*. Harvard University Press, Cambridge, Mass., 1982.

9. S. Sen and E. H. Durfee. A formal study of distributed meeting scheduling: Preliminary results. In *ACM Conference on Organizational Computing Systems*, 1991.

10. S. Sen and E. H. Durfee. A formal analysis of communication and commitment. In *11th International Workshop on Distributed Artificial Intelligence*, 1992.

11. S. Sen and E. H. Durfee. The effects of search bias on flexibility in distributed scheduling. In *12th International Workshop on Distributed Artificial Intelligence*, 1993.

12. S. Sen and E. H. Durfee. Adaptive surrogate agents. In *13th International Workshop on Distributed Artificial Intelligence*, 1994.

13. S. Sen and E. H. Durfee. Unsupervised surrogate agents and search bias change in flexible distributed scheduling. In *First International Conference on Multi-Agents Systems*, 1995.

14. R. Smith. The contract net protocol: High-level communication and control in distributed problem solver. *IEEE Transactions on Computers*, 29(12):1104–1113, December 1980.

15. K. Sycara and J. Liu. Distributed meeting scheduling. In *Sixteenth Annual Conference of the Cognitive Society*, 1994.

16. E. Taub. Sharing schedules. *Mac User*, pages 155–162, July 1993.

Representations as Basis of Cognitive Processes

Christopher Habel
University of Hamburg
Computer Science Department & Doctoral Program in Cognitive Science
Vogt-Kölln-Str. 30, D-22527 Hamburg
habel @informatik.uni-hamburg.de

It is a widely-held view in Cognitive Science that investigating and explaining cognition should be based on the theoretical concepts of *computation* and *representation*. In agreement with the *Physical Symbol System Hypothesis* (Newell & Simon 1976), "A physical symbol system has the necessary and sufficient means for general intelligent action.", cognition can be seen as *computation* , i.e. cognition is based on constructing and transforming representations. Thus the behavior of the cognitive, computational system depends on the internal representations which it, in turn, effects. The properties of the representation influence the computation (and vice versa) as well as the demands of the processes that determine the underlying and resulting representations. Therefore, in studying cognitive processes the system of mutual constraints between representations and processes has to be taken into account.

Although the importance of clarifying the idea of *representation* is obvious from the theoretical side of cognitive science, especially from the philosophical and logical perspective, most empirically oriented researchers in cognitive science and artificial intelligence seem to use the concept of representation without explication. The scientific community of cognitive science and artificial intelligence seems to follow a principle of *division of labor*, namely, either to clarify or to use the notion of *representation*.

In the present paper I address some basic problems and phenomena with respect to the fundamental concept of *representation*, both from a theoretical and an empirical perspective. Especially, I focus on constellations, in which more than one representation is involved. The problems of *complex representation constellations* have hardly ever been investigated up to now (but, see Barwise & Etchemendy, 1995).

Fundamental Questions of Representation Theories

I start with some core questions in traditional – sign-theory oriented – representation theory (see von Eckhardt, 1993), which are limitied to *single-representation constellations* . Any theory of *representation* has to clarify what the conditions and properties of *A-represents-B* constellations are. In other words, we have to specify the correspondence (relation of representation) between two entities for which "A represents B" holds. To get a clearer understanding of the nature of representation it is necessary to distinguish between the fundamental aspects of the concept *representation*; on the one hand it refers to the representing entity *A*, on the other hand it concerns the act of representing and thus the complete constellation of *A representing B*. For the characterization of representational constellations we have to consider – at least – four aspects:

- *the represented entities*: The standard case, which assumes concrete objects in the external world as the represented entities, is too limited: not only objects – in the strict sense – have to be represented but also properties of and relations among objects, events, temporal and spatial entities, etc.

- *the representing entities:* Peirce's theory of signs distinguishes among three kinds of signs, namely *icons*, *indexes* and *symbols*. The dichotomy "icon vs. symbol", corresponding to the long-standing controversy on pictorial and/or propositional representations, is based on different ways of grounding the corresponcence between represented and representing entities. Whereas icons are assumed to be "similar to the represented object", symbols are abstract entities without resemblance to the external objects.

- *the representational correspondence:* Any theory of representation has to specify what is meant by "correspondence between represented and representing entities". A specific aspect of the grounding problem refers to the question of partiality (in contrast to totality, in a formal sense) of *domain and range* of the correspondence. Under normal circumstances, neither on the side of "external objects", i.e. the reality, which is represented, nor on the side of the potential representation bearers, i.e. the entities of the medium of representation, do all candidates participate in a representational constellation.

- *the function of the representation:* Representing is not an end in itself; representations are used to reach goals, especially to solve problems. In other words, representations *function as representations* in goal-directed processes. This is, for example, the central idea of Johnson-Laird's (1989) concept of a *Mental Model*. Mental models are a specific form of mental representations for situations of the world, i.e., they are - first and foremost - our internal representations of the external, the real world.

Cognitive Representations: Structural Isomorphism Approach

Following Palmer (1978, pp. 263ff.), *representation constellations* can be characterized by the represented (W_1) and the representing world (W_2), their internal structures, which can be seen as relational systems in the sense of formal model theory, and a partial mapping, ρ from W_1 to W_2, which is called the representational mapping.

$$\rho: \qquad W_1 \quad \rightarrow \quad W_2$$

representational mapping   represented world   representing world

Applying this general representation scheme to mental representations leads to a more complex representation constellation (Fig. 1), in which four worlds and three representational mappings are involved. According to the representational theory of mind, an essential module of any cognitive system is a mental model (W_2) of the real world (W_0). Cognitive Science investigates also second-level representations, namely representations (W_3) of mental representations (W_2). Note that W_2 is representation as well as representandum. On the other hand, in sciences (partial) mathematical models of the real world (W_1) are investigated. [Paivio's (1986, pp. 18ff.) discussion of Palmer's analysis of cognitive representations contains three levels of representation, namely W_0, W_2 and W_3 of Fig. 1; "non-cognitive" representations, W_1, (e.g. those of physics) are not discussed by Paivio.]

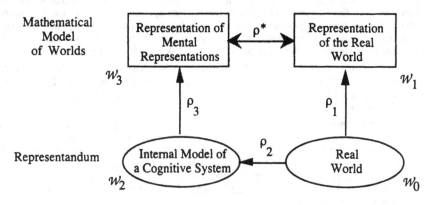

Fig. 1: The representation constellation for "mental representations"

Formats of Representations & Complex Representational Constellations

During the last two decades, research on imagery and mental rotation has given overwhelming evidence for analog representations of spatial configurations, i.e. representations with intrinsic spatial properties (cf. Kosslyn 1980, 1994; Palmer 1978). Such non-propositional representations are induced by both perceptual and linguistic inputs and are used successfully in reasoning tasks. This leads to a *principle of hybrid representation and processing*, which may be expressed as follows (Habel, Pribbenow & Simmons, 1995):

> A cognitive system that reasons successfully in a general (non-restricted) real world environment is based on a hybrid architecture, which combines propositional and pictorial representations and processes.

The assumption of a hybrid representation system which combines propositional and pictorial representations is also supported by evidence from research on comprehension and production of language. Thus the properties of and the constraints on both pictorial representations and the components processing them are determined by the modules for reasoning, visual perception and language processing (Landau & Jackendoff 1993).

But the property of hybridicity is not sufficient to guarantee successful and efficient reasoning processes. The main obstacle is that - in many cases - large amounts of information and detail lead to inefficiency up to intractability. Hobbs' (1985) solution to this problem is to view the world at different levels of granularity; following this idea, we postulate the *granular system principle* (Habel, Pribbenow & Simmons, 1995):

> A cognitive system reasoning successfully in a general (non-restricted) real world environment uses representations at different levels of detail (granularity). The reasoning processes primarily access information at a minimal granularity level, i.e. a level that is only as detailed as required.

Both hybrid and granular representation systems can be seen as specific cases of systems which have to handle complex representational constellations.

References

Barwise, Jon & Etchemendy, John (1995). Heterogeneous logic. In: J. Glasgow, H. Narayanan & B. Chandrasekaran (eds.): *Diagrammatic Reasoning: Cognitive and Computational Perspectives*. (pp. 211–234).Cambridge, MA: MIT-Press.

Habel, Christopher; Pribbenow, Simone & Simmons, Geoffrey (1995). Partonomies and Depictions: A Hybrid Approach. In: J. Glasgow, H. Narayanan & B. Chandrasekaran (eds.): *Diagrammatic Reasoning: Cognitive and Computational Perspectives*. (pp. 627–653). Cambridge, MA: MIT-Press.

Hobbs, J. R. (1985). Granularity. *Proceedings of 9th IJCAI*, 432-435.

Johnson-Laird, Philip N. (1989). Mental Models. In Posner, Michael I. (ed.). *Foundations of cognitive science*. (pp. 469–499). Cambridge, MA: MIT-Press.

Kosslyn, Stephen M. (1980). *Image and Mind*. Cambridge, MA.: Harvard UP.

Kosslyn, Stephen M. (1994). *Image and Brain*. Cambridge, MA.: MIT-Press.

Landau, Barbara & Jackendoff, Ray (1993). "What" and "where" in spatial language and spatial cognition. *Behavioral and Brain Sciences, 16*. 217-238, 255-266.

Newell, Allen & Simon, Herbert A. (1976) Computer science as empirical inquiry. *Communications of the ACM, 19*, 113–126.

Paivio, Allan (1986). *Mental Representation: A dual coding approach*. New York: Oxford University Press.

Palmer, Stephen E. (1978). Fundamental aspects of cognitive representations. In E. Rosch & B. Lloyd (Eds.), *Cognition and categorization* (pp. 259–303). Hillsdale, NJ.: Erlbaum.

Von Eckhardt, Barbara (1993). *What is Cognitive Science?* Cambridge, MA: MIT Press.

Improving the Functionality of a Text-to-Speech System by Adding Morphological Knowledge

Diane Hirschfeld [1], Heinz-Dieter Maas [2]

[1] Institut für Technische Akustik, Technische Universität Dresden,
email: diane@eakss1.et.tu-dresden.de

[2] Institut für Angewandte Informationsforschung e.V. (IAI) an der Universität des Saarlandes,
Saarbrücken, email: dieter@iai.uni-sb.de

Abstract. The quality-improvement of a speech synthesis system is tightly linked with the generation of natural sounding prosody. Reliable accentuation and structuring of the text based on syntactic knowledge are prerequisites for this goal. After the implementation of the morphological analysis system mpro, developed at IAI Saarbruecken, these functions are available in the text-to-speech system of the Dresden University of Technology.

Keywords: Text-to-speech (TTS), morphological knowledge base, prosody

1 Introduction

Speech synthesis as a part of modern information service systems is especially suitable for applications, where a frequent information change occurs and unrestricted vocabulary is required. As acoustic quality of speech synthesis is increasing due to time domain processing and the use of naturally spoken units, the requirements on procedures for linguistic processing are growing as well. Naturally sounding prosody may improve intelligibility and comfort of synthetic speech and is of central importance for the positive evaluation of the complete system.

The following article presents an experimentation software package of a text-to-speech system. Particular interest will be put on the description of knowledge representation in the linguistic part as well as on the improvement of the system's functionality due to the implementation of morphological knowledge and strategies.

2 Text-to-Speech Concepts

When generating fluent speech from written text, detailed linguistic processing is required. Deriving textual, syntactical and semantical structure is important for the presentation of the text in a perceptual adequate acoustic form.

Today's TTS-systems either consist of a set of modules, processing text in a strictly sequentially way [AL87] - where the output of every module becomes input to the following one - or are working in quasi-parallel on a central multi-level data structure ([LEU91], [BOE93]). Because of timing and memory-restrictions the latter approach seems to be nearer to the human speech generation process [LEV89].

3 The Dresden Text-to-Speech System

3.1 Design

Initially designed for serial processing, the Dresden TTS system consisted of a minimum number of modules necessary for the production of intelligible speech. The requirements for ease of understanding and comfort of synthetic speech caused the system to be expanded by modules for prosodic processing. The necessity of reliable accent setting arose beside the requirement for correct phonetic transcription. Some aspects of multilingual speech generation forced the further modularization and separation of language dependend (data based) and language independent (procedural) knowledge.

Interface standardisation and strict allocation of duties resulted in a system, where each module can be considered as an expert for a special task, containing the procedural knowledge about handling its proper data base.

Following the processing strategy the original text is enriched by additional information until graphemic information is not longer needed. Depending on the existance of additional information parallel processing and reprocessing of modules is enabled for experimental purposes. By meeting the interface requirements, switching between alternatives for special modules (i.e. prosodic processing) as well as adding of submodules from research partners is possible.

3.2 Linguistic Processing

During the first stage of text processing, the input character stream is formatted. The execution of character conversion, word and sentence boundary detection and number formatting (date, time, measure and currency expressions) takes place. Abbreviations are converted into their full form. Finally, function words are marked and converted into their phonetic form by the use of a lexicon with about 150 entries. Afterwards, grapheme-to-phoneme conversion is executed in the two following steps: In the full form lexicon, each exception word is assigned to its phonemic expression. For the unsolved tokens the phonetic rule base is sequentially executed from the most specialised to the most general. In case of correspondence of rule body and left and right context in rule and character sequence, the input is replaced by the phoneme string of the rule. Even for unknown words (as names, foreign words, etc.) rule based conversion provides a result.

According to accentuation and contextual information (position and number of syllables in the word, in the phrase, phoneme class, etc.) for each phoneme a segment duration is calculated [SOB95], using an adaptation of KLATT's durational model [KLA76] to the German language. Phrase boundaries are marked by pauses.

The intonation model [SCH94] superposes phrase and accent components, that are calculated using phrase boundary and phrase type information and co-ordinating syllable boundary, segment duration and accent position information. The form of pitch movements may be adjusted according to personal preferences of the user.

The generation of the control sequence finally projects the abstract phonetic segments and categories as well as the calculated values of the prosody-parameter-contour onto a sequence of synthesis units (diphones in our case).

3.3 Unsolved Problems

In German, word formation and sense modification are frequently achieved by composition and the use of affixes. Since both full-form exception lexicon and phonetic rule base are optimised for simple German words, our algorithm for grapheme-to-phoneme-transcription soon reaches its limits.

The subdivision of longer clauses or sentences into phrases based on knowledge about their syntactic structure may provide variety in the resulting speech. Other important contributions to the generation of prosody will be a reliable setting of lexical accent, the finding of a phrase accent and finally the weighting of lexical accents depending on their syntactic/semantic function in the phrase.

All listed functions are not yet available or work unsatisfactory in the Dresden TTS system. The morphological analysis system mpro provided solutions to most of the named problems.

4 MPRO - A System for Word Structure Analysis

The input text is analysed according to the rules of word formation of German by mpro. Besides, word class and inflection specific information result like case, number and gender or tense, mode, person and number, respectively. For the modification of pronunciation or determination of phrase boundaries or accent levels a rough syntactic analysis (partial parsing) takes place.

The system is built up of two main components:
· a morpheme-lexicon of about 27000 entries
· rules for word formation and phonetic transcription

Each entry in the lexicon contains knowledge about the features of an allomorph according to derivation, composition, possible use of prefixes and flectional properties and partly a phonemic representation that may be completed by details about syllabic structure and accentuation.

The whole analysis procedure is divided into the following steps:

The text reading component determines sentence, clause and word boundaries from the input text. By the help of a word form lexicon of about 4500 entries, containing function words, abbreviations and phrases, about 55% of the tokens of a text is identified.

Each unsolved word will be subject of a detailed morphological analysis. By taking all fitting substrings of the lexicon a directed graph is built up. Taking care of not entering senseless variants, lexical properties are added to each edge. A cyclic synthesis process applies word formation rules to the resulting structure, combines morphemes to new words, adds features of the new words to the graph, and so on. Final analysis result should be placed on an edge going from the beginning node to the end of the graph and might have the categories nomen, verb, adverb or adjective. Finally, ambiguities in membership to different word classes are reduced taking the word's context into consideration.

During syntactic analysis, different types of sentences, clauses, nominal and prepositional phrases are identified using a grammar of about 200 rules. Grammatical descriptions are added to the clauses and so the bases for accent weighting and phrasal structuring of the synthesis text is given. If the analysis is not unambiguous but results in a sequence of variants, the correctness should be proved by the acceptability of the resulting intonation contour.

Co-ordination and weighting of accents, consideration of boundary conditions and determination of allophonic variants of several phonemes, determination of syllable boundaries and elimination of special signs are to be done by the final module.

5 Results and Future Outlook

Working in parallel to the Dresden TTS system (Fig. 1.), mpro establishes a new expert, specialised in the word formation domain. Grapheme-to-phoneme transcription of words unknown to mpro is done by the old algorithm.

Informal perceptual tests showed significant improvement in speech quality as well as in acceptability and naturalness of speech melody and rhythm.

In order to provide an impression about the power of morphological analysis, a business text of 24000 words was analysed. Mpro failed in 134 cases, mostly printing errors, proper names and unusual compositions. Further completion of the morphological knowledge base, particularly of phonemic and accentuation data, as well as the expansion of prosody models for effective processing of offered additional information are future tasks.

At the moment, the system is implemented as Windows personal voice application in multimedia- and internet-services.

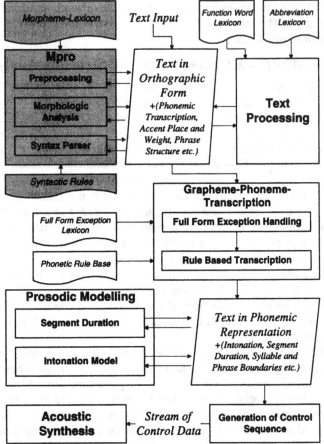

Fig. 1. Synthesis System after implementing mpro.

6 References

[SCH94] Schnelle, F.: „Einsatz eines prosodischen Modells für einen eingeschränkten Diskursbereich zur Verbesserung der Sprachqualität des Synthetisators VOICE", Diplomarbeit, TU Dresden, 1994. unpublished.

[SOB95] Sobe, J.: „Lautdauersteuerung für ein Sprachsynthesesystem auf Diphonbasis", Diplomarbeit, TU Dresden, 1995. unpublished.

[AL87] Allen, J., Hunnicut, M.S., Klatt, D.: „From Text to Speech: The MITalk System", Cambridge, 1987.

[BOE93] Boehm, A.: „Maschinelle Sprachausgabe deutschen und englischen Textes.", Aachen: Shaker, 1993, (Reihe Elektrotechnik)

[KLA76] Klatt, D.H.: „Linguistic Uses of Segmental Duration in English - Acoustic and Perceptual Evidence.", J. Acoust. Soc. Am. 59, 1976, pp. 1208-1221.

[LEU91] van Leeuwen, H.C., te Lindert, E.: „Speech Maker: Text-to-Speech Conversion Based on a Multi-Level, Synchronized Data Structure.", Proc. of 2nd European Conference on Speech Communication and Technology, vol.3, Genova, 1991, pp.1231-1234.

[LEV89] Levelt, W. J. M.: „Speaking - From Intention to Articulation.", ACL-MIT Press Series in Natural Language Processing, Cambridge, 1989.

Solving Hard Combinatorial Problems with GSAT – A Case Study

Holger H. Hoos

Technische Hochschule Darmstadt, Fachgebiet Intellektik,
D-64289 Darmstadt, Germany
email: hoos@intellektik.informatik.th-darmstadt.de

Abstract. In this paper, we investigate whether hard combinatorial problems such as the Hamiltonian circuit problem HCP (an $\mathcal{NP}$-complete problem from graph theory) can be practically solved by transformation to the propositional satisfiability problem (SAT) and application of fast universal SAT-algorithms like GSAT to the transformed problem instances. By using the efficient transformation method proposed by Iwama and Miyazaki in 1994, one obtains a class of SAT-problems which are especially hard for SAT-algorithms based on local search such as GSAT. We identify structural properties of these problems which are responsible for GSAT's poor performance on this problem class. An empirical analysis indicates that several methods which have been designed to improve GSAT on structured problems are not effective for SAT-transformed HCP-instances.

1 Introduction

One of the basic paradigms of AI states that many problems from different domains can be formulated as logical problems and therefore general methods for solving logical problems can be used for their solution. Actually, this idea provides strong motivation for developping and studying algorithms for general logical problems like the satisfiability problem in propositional logic (SAT). This general approach seems particularly interesting for computationally hard (i.e. $\mathcal{NP}$-hard) problems for which no specialized, efficient algorithms are available.

In this paper, we examine whether GSAT, an incomplete, model-generating algorithm for SAT, can be practically used to solve hard instances of the *Hamiltonian circuit problem (HCP)*, a combinatorial problem from graph theory. For a given graph G, the HCP is the task of finding a cyclic tour (Hamiltonian circuit) in G that visits every vertex exactly once. This problem is $\mathcal{NP}$-complete (like SAT) and therefore, unless $\mathcal{P} = \mathcal{NP}$, not solvable by polynomial-time algorithms [10]. Any instance G of HCP can be transformed into a propositional CNF-formula α in such a way that the satisfiabilty of α is equivalent to the existence of a solution to the HCP, and the models of α correspond directly to the Hamiltonian circuits in G. Thus it is principally possible to use model-generating SAT-algorithms (like GSAT) for finding Hamiltonian circuits in graphs [7].

To practically realize this approach, one has to assure that the size of the original problem is not growing too much as a result of the SAT-transformation.

Furtheron, the time complexity of the transformation must be small wrt. the time complexity of the problem itself. Transformations satisfying these conditions shall be called "efficient transformations" in the sequel [7]. Efficient SAT-transformations are currently available for several graph problems, including HCP [7]. Principally the SAT-problems generated by these methods show an order of magnitude which seems to be managable by powerful SAT-algorithms like GSAT. Thus it makes sense to examine the idea of solving HCP-instances by the means of algorithms for the general SAT-problem in more detail.

The remainder of this paper is structured in the following way: In the next section we will present an efficient SAT-transformation for HCP due to Iwama and Miyazaki [7]. Furtheron we describe the GSAT algorithm [14] and some of its variants which have been successfully applied to various classes of SAT-problems. In Sect.3 we consider the application of GSAT to the HCP; in particular, we show that due to certain structural properties of the SAT-transformed HCP-instances these problems can be expected to be rather difficult for GSAT despite the efficient transformation method beeing used. The results of an experimental study of GSAT's performance on SAT-transformed HCP-instances presented in Sect.4 confirm this conjecture and show, which extensions of the basic GSAT algorithm can be used to improve its performance on the given problem class. Finally, in Sect.5 we sum up our results and discuss their implications on the underlying, general approach.

2 Preliminaries

In this section we first describe, how HCP-instances can be efficiently transformed into SAT-instances. Then we present the GSAT algorithm, a powerful, model-generating algorithm for the SAT-problem which has been applied successfully to many classes of SAT-problems.

2.1 Efficient SAT-Transformation for HCP

In 1994, efficient SAT-reductions of several graph problems including HCP were proposed by Iwama and Miyazaki [7]. The basic idea for transforming instances of HCP into CNF formulae is to focus on permutations of the given graph's vertices. This is done by assigning an integer value to each vertex, which defines its position in the permutation. The function which assigns such a *vertex position* to each vertex of the graph is called a *vertex assignment*. A vertex assignment encodes a permutation of the vertices, iff the following conditions hold:

- every vertex position is *valid* (i.e. no position is greater than the total number of vertices in the graph),
- the vertex positions are pairwise different (i.e. identical positions are never assigned to different vertices).

A vertex assignment codes for a Hamiltonian circuit of the given graph, iff

- it codes for a permutation of the vertices,

- nodes with successive positions in this permutation are always connected by an edge,
- there is an edge connecting the first vertex of the permutation to the last one.

This characterization can be used to transform any given instance of HCP into a constraint satisfaction problem (CSP) on integers (i.e. vertex positions). But now there is a straightforward SAT-transformation at hand: one simply has to code every vertex position by a number of propositional variables using the binary representation of integers. Thereby, every contraint on vertex positions can be translated into a CNF-clause which finally transforms the integer CSP into a SAT problem.

To give the formal description of the transformation algorithm, we first need some definitions: Let $G = (V, E)$ be a graph with n vertices, vertex set $V = \{v_0, \ldots, v_{n-1}\}$ and edge relation $E \subseteq V \times V$. To every vertex v_i $(0 \le i \le n-2)$ a set of $k = \lceil \log_2(n-1) \rceil$ propositional variables is assigned, which are denoted by $v_{i,1}, \ldots, v_{i,k}$. Since using this approach, Hamiltonian circuits are represented by cyclic permutations of the vertices, the position of vertex v_{n-1} can be fixed to $n-1$ (with 0 being the first position) without loss of generality. Furtheron we define $C(i, l)$ as the CNF-clause containing propositional variables $v_{i,1}, \ldots, v_{i,k}$ in such a way, that $C(i, l)$ evaluates to false iff position l is assigned to vertex i. The conjunction of two clauses c_1, c_2 is denoted by $c_1 \cup c_2$.

Efficient SAT-Reduction of HCP (Iwama and Miyazaki, 1994)

Step 1: For every vertex v_i $(0 \le i \le n-2)$ and every integer l $(n-1 \le l \le 2^k - 1)$ generate the clause $C(i, l)$. (The set of these clauses is satisfied iff a valid position is assigned to each vertex.)

Step 2: For every pair of vertices v_i, v_j $(0 \le i, j \le n-2)$ and every integer l $(0 \le l \le n-2)$ generate the clause $C(i, l) \cup C(j, l)$. (This set of clauses is satisfied iff all valid vertex positions are pairwise different.)

Step 3: For every pair of vertices v_i, v_j $(0 \le i, j \le n-2)$ with $(v_i, v_j) \notin E$ and every integer l $(0 \le l \le n-2)$ generate the clause $C(i, l-1) \cup C(j, l)$. (This set of clauses is satisfied iff any pair of vertices with successive positions are connected by an edge).

Step 4.1: For every vertex v_i $(0 \le i \le n-2)$ with $(v_i, v_{n-1}) \notin E$ generate the clause $C(i, n-2)$.

Step 4.2: For every vertex v_i $(0 \le i \le n-2)$ with $(v_{n-1}, v_i) \notin E$ generate the clause $C(i, 0)$. (Steps 4.1 and 4.2 are special cases of Step 3 for vertex v_{n-1}, to which implicitly always the position $n-1$ is assigned; cf. above).

For any given graph G with n vertices this algorithm generates a CNF-formula α with $(n-1)\lceil \log_2(n-1) \rceil$ propositional variables which is satisfiable iff G contains a Hamiltonian circuit. Furtheron the models of α directly correspond to the solutions of the HCP. The algorithm has polynomial time complexity (wrt. n) and can be applied to both directed and undirected graphs. Thus we get:

Result 1. *For the HCP, an efficient SAT-transformation is given by the Iwama-Miyazaki algorithm.*

A simple argument shows, that one cannot expect to find SAT-transformations of HCP using significantly fewer propositional variables (see [7] for details). The CNF-formulae which are obtained from HCP-instances using this algorithm will be referred to as *HC-formulae* in the sequel.

2.2 GSAT – a Fast, Incomplete SAT-Algorithm

GSAT is a heuristic SAT-algorithm proposed in 1992 by Selman, Levesque and Mitchell [14] which is based essentially on local search in the space of all variable assignments of the input CNF-formula. Starting with a randomly chosen assignment A, in every step of the procedure the value of one propositional variable is flipped, i.e. changed from true to false or vice versa. The selection of the variable to be flipped is based on the difference in the number of currently satisfied clauses the flip would cause. This value, which is positive for those flips that cause an increase in the number of satisfied clauses, is called the *score* of a variable. In every step, a variable with maximal score is flipped; if there are several variables with maximal score, one of these is randomly selected.

Thus, GSAT basically performs a kind of local hillclimbing on the number of satisfied clauses, which can be viewed as the global optimization of an objective function. Of course, the models of the input fomula are exactly those assignments satisfying all clauses simultanously. When such an assignment is reached, the GSAT algorithm terminates. If after a given number maxSteps of flips no solution is found, the algorithm restarts its local search by randomly choosing a new variable assignment. If after a given number maxTries of these tries still no model is found, GSAT terminates. The standard GSAT procedure can be formalized as follows:

```
procedure GSAT(α)
  for i := 1 to maxTries do
    A := randomly chosen assignment of the variables appearing in α;
    for j := 1 to maxSteps do
      if A satisfies α then return(B);
      else
        x := randomly chosen variable of α with maximal score
             under the current assignment A;
        flip value of x in A;
        end if;
      end for;
    end for;
  return (''no model found!'');
  end GSAT;
```

Note, that due to the random choices for the initial assignment and between equally good flips, GSAT is a non-deterministic algorithm. Another important property of GSAT is its incompleteness: However the parameters maxTries and maxSteps are chosen, if the input formula is satisfiable, there is no guaranty that GSAT finds a model. So in contrast to complete SAT-algorithms like the Davis-Putnam procedure (DP), GSAT can never determine the *unsatisfiability* of a given formula. However, it has been shown, that variants of the GSAT algorithm can outperform complete systematic search methods like DP on large classes of SAT-problems.

Another difficulty with local search methods like GSAT is that they can get "stuck" in local optima of the objective function which do not represent solutions. To cope with that, several techniques have been proposed, the most basic of these being the restart mechanism, which is realized in the basic algorithm as stated above.

An important extension of the basic algorithm is the "random walk" strategy [13]. Here, with a fixed probability walkProb-instead of a standard hillclimbing-step a so-called "walk-step" is performed; this is done by randomly selecting one of the variables appearing in currently unsatisfied clauses. Therefore, by each walk-step at least one formerly unsatisfied clause becomes satisfied. In contrast to ordinary hillclimb-steps, a walk-step may cause a decrease in the total number of satisfied clauses even if improving flips would have been possible. In consequence, by using random walk the local search becomes somewhat less directed; therefore the chances of escaping from local optima of the objective function are better than in the case of basic GSAT. Experimental analysis has shown, that for most problem classes the random-walk strategy significantly improves GSAT's performance [13].

Another GSAT variant called "clause weighting" is based on the idea of modifying the objective function in such a way that local optima are "levelled" [12]. This is done by assigning an integer value (weight) to each clause. When starting GSAT, all weights are initialized to the same value. Whenever an unsuccessful try is aborted, the weights of all currently unsatisfied clauses are increased by a constant value. The evaluation of the variable scores is modified such that a clause with weight w is treated like a set of w identical unweighted clauses in standard GSAT. This mechanism ensures that clauses which frequently have been found to be unsatisfied at the end of an unsuccessful try get a higher priority in succeeding tries. It has been shown that particularly for classes of structured problems (like SAT-encoded planning problems) this method causes significant improvement of GSAT's performance [11].

3   Applying GSAT to the HCP

From a theoretical point of view, the situation looks quite promising: By the Iwama-Miyazaki algorithm one can transform HCP-instances with n nodes into SAT problems with $n \log_2 n$ propositional variables. The GSAT algorithm has shown to be capable of solving SAT problems up to 500 variables in reasonable time, so one could expect to practically solve HCP-instances with approximately 50 variables by applying GSAT to the transformed problem instances. However, for several reasons this conjecture does not hold; as we will see, the transformed HCP-instances yield a class of SAT-problems which are very hard for local search algorithms like GSAT.

Since it is a well-known fact that the performance of SAT algorithms can depend heavily on the structure of a given class of problems, a careful characterization of the SAT-tranformed HCP-instances should be a good starting point. As we already know, the Iwama-Miyazaki method transforms any HCP-instance with n nodes into a CNF-formula with $(n-1)\lceil \log_2(n-1)\rceil$ propositional variables. But what about the number of clauses? Examination of the transformation algorithm shows that in steps 1, 4.1 and 4.2 at least $\Theta(n)$ and at most $\Theta(n^2)$ clauses with length $k = \lceil \log_2(n-1)\rceil$ are generated. Out of steps 2 and 3 one gets $\Theta(n^3)$ clauses of length $2k$, where the exact number of clauses depends on the number of vertices n and the edge-relation E of the given graph G.

Several authors claim that in general, a large ratio of clauses/variables might even improve GSAT's performance on a given class of formulae [3, 4]. Thus the situation doesn't look too bad for the HC-formulae under consideration. But in practice, the cubic length of the formula (wrt. n) may cause storage problems even for HCP-instances of modest size. This point is stressed by a simple example: Transforming a specific HCP-instance with 50 vertices by the given algorithm, one obtains a CNF-formula of 2,023,578 literals containing 294 variables and 169,047 clauses. Therefore, since the corresponding graph has a vertex degree of 1 (actually being one single, big Hamiltonian circuit) and seen under a practical point of view, we observe an almost dramatic increase in problem size caused by the transformation. As we will see, the situation is even worse, since in addition to this cubic blowup in problem size, the single steps of the GSAT-algorithm are slowed down significantly by another structural property of the HC-formulae.

To see why this happens, we have to look at the evaluation of variable scores in GSAT in more detail. For many problem classes (like Random-k-SAT [4]), a flip of one variable usually does *not* affect the scores of *all* other variables. On these problems the performance of GSAT can be significantly improved by using the following method of scoring (similar to the one described in [2]), which we will call "score-by-need": At the begin of each try, after selecting the initial assignment, the scores for all flips are evaluated and memorized. After each step of the algorithm (i.e. after each flip) now only the scores of those variables have to be updated, which share any clause with the flipped one [15]. Here a number of propositional variables is said to *share a clause* c, iff all of them appear in c. Variables which share at least one clause are said to *depend* on each other. So the actual number of scores which have to be evaluated in each step is determined by the variable-dependencies of the given formula.

Using this method, the average-case time complexity of each GSAT-step can be reduced from $O(n^2)$ to $O(1)$ for Random-3-CNF-formulae with constant clauses/variable-ratio [1]. Unfortunately, the score-by-need method is not effective for HC-formulae, because these show a property we call *complete variable-dependency*: in these formulae any variable depends on all other variables. In consequence, using the score-by-need method for problems with complete variable-dependency, after each flip one essentially has to evaluate the scores of all variables anew. Thus, as in contrast to problems with *sparse* variable-dependency, as Random-3-CNF with constant clause/variables-ratio [4], the score-by-need method cannot be used to improve the time efficiency of GSAT-steps for problem classes displaying this property.

Another structural property of HC-formulae is given by the fact, that any two variables assigned to the same vertex share much more clauses than variables belonging to different vertices. (Note, that all clauses encode constraints on vertex positions and therefore contain all the variables belonging to the respective vertices.) Consequently, when applying GSAT to this problem class, one should expect to obtain improved performance by using extensions of the basic algorithm which have been shown to be particularly effective for classes of structured problems (such as clause weights, [11]).

Several subclasses of the HCP greatly differ with regard to their time complexity. One important parameter is the vertex degree of the given graph (i.e. the number of edges entering resp. leaving each vertex). Since in the experimental part of this work, the HCP on directed graphs (digraphs) has been examined, we concentrate on the vertex out-degree here. Obviously, for digraphs with out-degree 1 the HCP has linear time complexity. To see this, consider the following algorithm: Start at an arbitrary vertex and repeatedly follow the single edge leaving the vertex you have visited last. Remember all the vertices you have visited; when you arrive at any vertex you have already visited, your tour is a Hamiltonian circuit iff it contains all vertices of the given graph.

However, for out-degree 2 the HCP is already $\mathcal{NP}$-complete.[1] So the vertex out-degree is an important parameter of the HCP in digraphs. Anyway, after transforming a given HCP-instance to SAT using the Iwama-Miyazaki method, the information about the digraph's vertex-out degree is no longer represented explicitly. On the contrary, there is no obvious difference between CNF-formulae corresponding to HCP-instances with out-degree 1 and 2. So one should be doubtful whether the simplicity of HCP-instances with out-degree 1 is conserved by the SAT-transformation. Indeed it would be staightforward to assume, that the performance of a SAT-algorithm on a class of transformed problem instances depends strongly on the transformation method used.

Considering application of GSAT or similar local search methods, there is one more important aspect about the structure of intances taken from these problem classes: the avarage number of solutions per instance. Many researchers agree, that problems having very few solutions are typically very hard for local search algorithms like GSAT (see for instance [3]). Obviously, for HCP-instances with vertex out-degree 1 there exists either one solution or no solution at all. Solvable instances with out-degree 2 may have several solutions, but as our experiments have shown, these typically also have only one solution. However, instances of both problem classes have usually a large number of near-solutions (i.e. assignments satisfying *almost* all conditions encoded by the clauses). This observation leads to the conjecture that the HC-formulae corresponding to the mentioned subclasses of the general HCP should be particularly difficult for GSAT-like SAT-algorithms, whereas SAT-transformed HCP instances with larger vertex out-degree, which usually have a greater number of solutions, should be solved more efficiently. Summing up, we get:

---

[1] This follows immidiatly from the standard prove for $\mathcal{NP}$-completeness of the general HCP, as can be found in [10].

Result 2. *HC-formulae should be expected to be very difficult for GSAT for several reasons: The large number of clauses can easily cause storage problems; due to complete variable-dependency the score-by-need method for efficient score evaluation is not effective; the inherent easiness of HCP-instances with vertex out-degree 1 might get lost by the transformation process; and problem instances with small vertex out-degree have only very few solutions but a large number of near-solutions.*

4 Experimental Results

In this section, we present and discuss the results of our experimental work, in which we applied variants of the GSAT algorithm to several sets of SAT-transformed HCP-instances. We use an empirical approach based on a method which is frequently applied in the analysis of SAT-algorithms (see [6, 1]). Since no suitable benchmark problems were available, we first generated several sets of solvable instances.[2] On these test-sets we evaluated the performance of several variants of the GSAT-algorithm (implemented as portable C-programs). As performance criteria we used the success rate $sr = st/tt$ (where st denotes the number of successful tries and tt the total number of tries for a specific experiment) and the average number of steps (i.e. flips) per successful try denoted by ss.[3] Measuring relative instead of absolute execution time (i.e. steps of the algorithm instead of CPU-time) has the great advantage of abstracting from specific properties of the implementation and the runtime environment and thus allows to concentrate on the behaviour of the algorithm itself. To capture these aspects, we introduce τ_s, defined as the average CPU-time needed to execute one single step of GSAT. Typical values for τ_s^{-1} (steps per second) measured for $HC_1(n)$-Problems using our GSAT implementation on a DEC Alpha 5/250 machine range from 500 for $n = 10$ to 4.29 for $n = 50$.[4]

Because of the reasons stated above, the following subclasses of HCP were being considered for experimental analysis:

$HC_1(n)$: solvable instances with n vertices and out-degree 1
$HC_2(n)$: solvable instances with n vertices and out-degree 2

As pointed out before, one should expect that these classes are different wrt. their difficulty for GSAT-like algorithms. For various problem sizes n between 10 and 30, test-sets for these classes were randomly generated by constructing first a Hamiltonian circuit of the given size and afterwards adding randomly selected edges, until every vertex had exactly the specified out-degree. To abstract from random differences between the $HC_2(n)$ instances, the test-sets for these classes consisted each of 100 problem instances.

---

[2] Since GSAT is an incomplete algorithm, it doesn't make much sense to apply it to potentially unsolvable problem instances for evaluation purposes.

[3] We consider only successful tries, because in unsuccessful tries always exactly maxSteps steps are performed.

[4] One should be able to improve the performance of our implementation by further optimizing the program code.

4.1 GSAT with Random Walk

From the experimental work of other authors we know that GSAT's performace can be significantly increased on a large number of problem classes with different structural properties by using the random walk strategy [13]. Since early in our experimental work it became clear, that this also holds for the HC-formulae, we decided to study the influence of the walkProb-parameter on the performance of GSAT in more detail. Note, that basic GSAT (without random walk) is equivalent to the extended algorithm with walkProb=0, whereas walkProb=1 yields a variant which does *only* walk-steps.

For these experiments the test-sets for $HC_1(10)$ (one instance) and $HC_2(10)$ (100 instances) were used. For each instance maxTries=100 tries were being performed; the maxSteps-parameter was experimentally adjusted to 2000 to ensure maximal success rates between 50% and 100%. The diagrams in Fig.1 show the success rates sr resp. solution costs ss as a function of the walk-probability walkProb (denoted as wp).

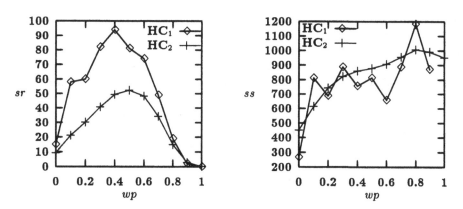

Fig. 1. Influence of random walk on GSAT's performance

Both sr-curves display a distinct, single maximum at walkProb=0.4 for HC_1 and walkProb=0.5 for HC_2.[5] Note further that for both problem classes, increasing walkProb beyond this optimal value causes rapid decreases in success rates. Other than basic GSAT (walkProb=0), the pure random walk strategy (walkProb=1) finds no solutions at all. The different locations of the maximum for HC_1 and HC_2 indicate that the problems with vertex out-degree 1 require a slightly more directed search (and therefore less walk-steps) than the much more difficult problems with out-degree 2. The reason for this may be that the objective function for HC_2-problems shows a greater number of local optima (at least for these problems there exist much more vertex permutations which use *almost* only edges of the given graph; the corresponding variable assignments therefore satisfy almost all clauses of the given formula).

---

[5] The optimal value of walkProb=0.5 is frequently used in other empirical studies and is often cited as a recommendation of Bart Selman.

There is one more interesting observation about these results: Although beyond the optimal walk-probability the number of solutions found by GSAT decreases steeply, the solution costs keep increasing for a while. As the problem instances usually have only one solution, this clearly indicates that for these walkProb-settings, walk-steps more and more impede the local search.

Summing up these observations, we get the following result: GSAT's performance on both problem classes HC_1 and HC_2 can be signficantly improved by using the random walk strategy. For fixed maxSteps-values, optimal settings of walkProb=0.4 for HC_1 and walkProb=0.5 for HC_2-instances could be indentified. As a consequence, these walkProb-settings were used for all other experimental series.

4.2 GSAT with Clause Weights

As mentioned before, the method of clause weighting has been found to improve GSAT's performance on several classes of structured problems [11, 3]. Therefore, one should expect that this extension of basic GSAT might also cause an increase in performance for the SAT-transformed HCP-instances which show a distinct structure as discussed in Sect.3. To check this hypothesis, we applied GSAT *with* and *without* clause weighting (denoted as GSAT+clw resp. GSAT−clw) to an identical test-set of 100 $HC_2(10)$-problems. All clause weights were initialized to 1 at the beginning of each experiment, and eventually increased by 1 for the clauses left unsatisfied at the end of unsuccessful tries (cf. Sect.2.2). For each problem instance, 100 tries were being performed with a walk-probability of 0.5, the value found to be optimal in another experimental series (see above). The performance values determined by these experiments are shown in Table 1 (where ms denotes the value of the maxSteps-parameter, sr the success rate and ss the average number of steps per solution).

Table 1. Influence of clause weighting on GSAT's performance on $HC_2(10)$-problems

	maxSteps	success rate sr	steps/solution ss
GSAT−clw	1000	32.31%	484.31
	2000	52.41%	876.11
GSAT+clw	1000	36.76%	479.33
	2000	57.29%	872.09

Whereas the solution costs ss are merely different for both variants, there is a slight increase in the success rate for GSAT+clw. Due to the great variance in the performance values for the single experiments this is not a statistically significant result in our opinion. Nevertheless, compared with the performance increases which have been reported to be achieved by using clause weights on other problem classes [11, 3], our results clearly indicate that for the given HC-formulae, clause weighting is not a very efficient method to improve GSAT's performance. We believe that this observation is independent of the problem size which is supported by analogous results on the test-set for $HC_2(8)$. Thus we conclude:

Result 3. *Using clause weighting has no significant influence on the performance of GSAT on Iwama-Miyazaki-transformed HC_2-instances.*

4.3 RBR-Extension of HC-Formulae

Another approach to cope with structured problems being very difficult for the GSAT algorithm (like the hierarchical structured cross-word-puzzle problems [9]), has been recently proposed by Kask and Dechter [8]. This method is called *restriced bound resolution (RBR)* and consists basically of adding resolvents of the original clauses to the given CNF-formula. To avoid creating too many new clauses, there is a restriction on the length of the added resolvents. RBR-resolution is usually realized as a prepocessing step for GSAT or other SAT-algorithms. The idea behind this procedure is to make the structure of the problem more explicit by adding resolvents of the original clauses.

Without going into the technical details of RBR-resolution here, we now report our results on HC-formulae. To see whether GSAT's performance can be improved by RBR-extending the problem instances, we first evaluated two different RBR-extensions of the formulae from our standard test-set for $HC_2(10)$ (100 instances) using bounds of 4 resp. 8 for the length of resolvents.[6] The resulting sets of extended instances shall be denoted as RBR_4 resp. RBR_8.

To these test-sets we applied GSAT with random walk (walkProb was set to the optimal value of 0.5). Despite the result of Sect.4.2, we also used clause weights, because a priori it is not clear, whether this method shows the same behaviour on RBR-extended formulae.[7] For every problem instance, 10 tries were performed. Table 2 shows the results obtained from experiments together with the results for GSAT on the original test-set (same parameter values).

Table 2. Influence of RBR-resolution on GSAT's performance on $HC_2(10)$-problems

	maxSteps	success rate sr	steps/solution ss
no RBR	1000	36.76%	479.33
	5000	84.04%	1742.35
RBR_4	1000	30.70%	491.04
	5000	81.00%	1787.14
RBR_8	1000	29.30%	456.55
	5000	81.60%	1670.26

---

[6] The choice of these bounds was motivated by the fact that the original clauses of $HC_2(10)$-problems are always of length 4 or 8.

[7] However, it is not to be expected that this way the results might become worse.

Considering the structure of the HC-formulae, one might have expected an improved performance of GSAT on the RBR-extended problems. But quite on the contrary, the results show slightly lower success rates and comparable solution costs for the extended test-sets. So we might conclude:

Result 4. *GSAT's performance on Iwama-Miyazaki-transformed HC_2-instances is not improved by application of RBR-extension; considering its time complexity, this kind of preconditioning does not seem to be profitable here.*[8]

5 Conclusion

Summing up the results presented in the previous sections, we have shown that HC-formulae (i.e. HCP-instances, transformed into SAT-problems by the Iwama-Miyazaki method) form a problem class which is very difficult for GSAT-like SAT-algorithms. Because of complete variable-dependency, a structural property which distinguishes these formulae from other classes of SAT-problems (as Random-k-SAT with constant clauses/variables ratio), the score-by-need strategy for efficient update of variable scores is rather useless in the case of HC-formulae.

Furtheron, our experimental results indicate that for solvable HCP-instances with vertex out-degree 2 transformed by the Iwama-Miyazaki method, standard mechanisms for improving GSAT's performance (RBR-extension and clause weighting) are apparently not effective. However, by using random walk (another standard extension of GSAT), a significant improvement can be achieved. Apparently, these formulae are structured in a way that makes them difficult not only for GSAT, but also for various extensions of the basic algorithm developped especially for improving its performance on structured problems. Thus, our results suggest that the class of HC_2-formulae can be used as a benchmark for evaluating the performance of SAT-algorithms based on local search.

The question whether systematic, complete SAT-algorithms (like efficient variants of the Davis Putnam procedure) might outperform GSAT-like local search methods on the problem class under consideration is still to be answered.[9] We also don't know yet, what specific structural aspects of HC-formulae make them so difficult for GSAT and cause both RBR-extension and clause weighting to fail. But we are convinced that further examination of these issues might lead to important insights concerning both SAT-transformations of problem instances from other domains and universal SAT-algorithms.

With respect to SAT-transformation, our results show clearly that for practical purposes other criteria than just the number of propositional variables have to be considered. As we have seen, for the application of GSAT to SAT-transformed problems, at least variable-dependency plays an important role. Thus we are convinced that the identification of these criteria and the development of more

---

[8] However, it cannot be ruled out that for different walk-probabilities (esp. walkProb=0), RBR-extension might be more effective.

[9] Actually, there is reason to believe, that the kind of forward checking realized by DP-algorithms may prove to be very effective for suitably coded HCP-instances.

efficient SAT-algorithms are closely related issues. The general approach of transforming specific instances of application problems into a logical domain (like SAT)
and practically solving these transformed problems in an adequate way using
general-purpose algorithms is of great importance to the field of AI. Therefore
we strongly believe that further investigation of this approach, based on concrete
applications, is a rewarding subject of AI-research.

References

1. A. Beringer, G. Aschemann, H.H. Hoos, M. Metzger, and A. Weiß. GSAT versus
   Simulated Annealing. In A. G. Cohn, editor, *Proceedings of the European Conference on Artificial Intelligence*, pages 130–134. John Wiley & Sons, 1994.
2. N. Boissin and J.-L. Lutton. A parallel simulated annealing algorithm. *Parallel
   Computing*, 19:859–872, 1993.
3. Byungki Cha and Kazuo Iwama. Performance test of local search algorithms using
   new types of random CNF formulas. In *Proceedings of the International Joint
   Conference on Artificial Intelligence*, pages 304–310, 1995.
4. J.M. Crawford and L.D. Auton. Experimental results on the crossover point in satisfiability problems. In *Proceedings of the AAAI National Conference on Artificial
   Intelligence*, pages 21–27. MIT press, 1993.
5. Ian P. Gent and Toby Walsh. An empirical analysis of search in gsat. *(Electronic)
   Journal of Artificial Intelligence Research*, 1:47–59, 1993.
6. Ian P. Gent and Toby Walsh. Towards an understanding of hill–climbing procedures
   for SAT. In *Proceedings of the AAAI National Conference on Artificial Intelligence*,
   pages 28–33. MIT press, 1993.
7. Kazuo Iwama and Shuichi Miyazaki. SAT-variable complexity of hard combinatorial problems. In *Proceedings of the World Computer Congress of the IFIP*, pages
   253–258 (Volume 1). Elsevier Science B.V., North Holland, 1994.
8. Kalev Kask and Rina Dechter. SAT and local consistency. In *Proceedings of the
   International Joint Conference on Artificial Intelligence*, pages 612–622, 1995.
9. Kurt Konolige. Easy to be hard: difficult problems for greedy algorithms. In *Proceedings of the International Conference on Principles of Knowlege Representation
   and Reasoning*, pages 374–378, 1994.
10. Karl Rüdiger Reischuk. *Einführung in die Komplexitätstheorie*. Teubner Verlag,
    Stuttgart, 1990.
11. Bart Selman and Henry A. Kautz. Domain-independent extensions to GSAT: Solv-
    ing large structured satisfiability problems. In R. Bajcsy, editor, *Proceedings of the
    International Joint Conference on Artificial Intelligence*, volume 1, pages 290–295.
    Morgan Kaufmann Publishers Inc., 1993.
12. Bart Selman and Henry A. Kautz. An empirical study of greedy local search for
    satisfiability testing. In *Proceedings of the AAAI National Conference on Artificial
    Intelligence*, pages 46–51. MIT press, 1993.
13. Bart Selman, Henry A. Kautz, and B. Cohen. Local search strategies for satisfia-
    biliy testing. Technical report, AT&T Bell Laboratories, Murray Hill, NJ, 1993.
14. Bart Selman, H. Levesque, and D. Mitchell. A new method for solving hard sat-
    isfiability problems. In *Proceedings of the AAAI National Conference on Artificial
    Intelligence*, pages 440–446. MIT press, 1992.
15. W.M. Spears. Simulated Annealing for hard satisfiability problems. Technical
    report, Naval Research Laboratory, Washington D.C., 1993.

Using Rippling for Equational Reasoning

Dieter Hutter

German Research Center for Artificial Intelligence (DFKI GmbH),
Stuhlsatzenhausweg 3, D-66123 Saarbrücken, Germany,
hutter@dfki.uni-sb.de, Tel. -49-681-302-5317

Abstract. This paper presents techniques to guide equational reasoning in a goal directed way. Suggested by rippling methods developed in the field of inductive theorem proving we use annotated terms to represent syntactical differences of formulas. Based on these annotations and on hierarchies of function symbols we define different abstractions of formulas which are used for planning of proofs. Rippling techniques are used to refine single planning steps, e.g. the application of a bridge lemma, on a next planning level.

1 Introduction

Heuristics for judging similarities between formulas and subsequently reducing differences have been applied to automated deduction since the 1950s, when Newell, Shaw, and Simon built their first "logic machine" [NSS63]. Since the later 60s, a similar theme of difference identification and reduction appears in the field of resolution theorem proving [Mor69], [Dig85], [BS88]. Partial unification results in a special kind of (E or RUE-) resolution step which introduces - in case of failure to unify - new inequalities that represents the differences of terms. This results in a top-down approach for equality reasoning where paramodulation is used only when needed.

In the field of inductive theorem proving syntactical differences between the induction hypothesis and induction conclusion are used in order to guide the proof [BvHS91, Hut90, Hut]. This method to guide induction proofs is called rippling / coloring terms and a large amount of papers have been published which report its success on practical examples. For equality reasoning we use these annotated terms to represent syntactical differences of formulas. Based on these annotations and on hierarchies of function symbols we define different abstractions of formulas which are used for a hierarchical planning of proofs. Also rippling techniques are used to refine single planning steps, e.g. the application of a bridge lemma, on a next planning level.

We summarize the notions and the underlying ideas of rippling with the help of an inductive proof and give also a sketch of our approach. Consider proving the following property about $\times$ and $+$

$$x \times s(y) = x + x \times y \qquad (1)$$

using the following equations, which define these functions.

$$0 + X = X \qquad\qquad 0 \times X = 0$$
$$s(X) + Y = s(X + Y) \qquad\qquad s(X) \times Y = Y + X \times Y$$

As a lemma we use the following property about $+$:

$$X + (Y + Z) = Y + (X + Z) \qquad (2)$$

Simple heuristics employed by most inductive provers suggest induction on x. The base-case $0 \times s(y) = 0 + 0 \times y$ is immediately solved by simplification with the base-cases of the definitions of $+$ and $\times$. In the step case we must prove

$$s(x) \times s(y) = s(x) + s(x) \times y \qquad (3)$$

where (1) serves as the induction hypothesis. Using rippling techniques the syntactical differences between the induction conclusion and the induction hypothesis are marked. Thus, newly introduced constructor symbols are shaded:

$$\boxed{s(}x\boxed{)} \times s(y) = \boxed{s(}x\boxed{)} + \boxed{s(}x\boxed{)} \times y \qquad (4)$$

This shading is represented with the help of annotated terms resp. C-terms ([Hut90, Hut, BW95]). Informally, we obtain the annotated formula (4) if we attach an information to each occurrence of a symbol in (3) whether it is shaded or not. The non-shaded parts of the formula represent the *skeleton* while the shaded parts constitute the *context* (resp. wave-fronts in [BvHS91]).

The idea of rippling is to restrict possible modifications of annotated formulas in such a way that the skeleton stays fixed during the deduction. Thus, each deduction step will only change the shaded parts of the formula while the non-shaded parts remain unaffected. Therefore, rippling will use annotated equations derived from equations of the given axiomatization. Corresponding to the recursive definitions for plus and times there are the following annotated equations.

$$\boxed{s(}X\boxed{)} + Y = \boxed{s(}X + Y\boxed{)} \quad (5) \qquad \boxed{s(}X\boxed{)} \times Y = \boxed{Y+}X \times Y \quad (6)$$

The lemma (2) about plus can be annotated in two ways:

$$\boxed{X+}(Y + Z) = Y + \boxed{(X+}Z\boxed{)} \quad (7) \qquad X + \boxed{(Y+}Z\boxed{)} = \boxed{Y+}(X + Z) \quad (8)$$

Since the shaded areas in one-hand side of the annotated equation must match those in the term being rewritten we may classify the colored equations according to their impacts to shaded areas in case of application. E.g. using (6), (5), or (8) from left to right will move shaded areas upwards wrt. the skeleton.

Now, in order to enable the use of the induction hypothesis, its left-hand (resp. right-hand) side has to occur in the modified conclusion. We can describe this goal only in terms of shaded and non-shaded areas. In case one side of the conclusion has the form $\boxed{}...\boxed{}$ we are finished. Thus, a very abstract plan of enabling the use of the induction is to rewrite $...(\boxed{}...\boxed{})...$ to $\boxed{}...(...)\boxed{}$.

This plan is refined by the following deduction. Applying (5) on the right and (6) on the left hand side yields:

$$\boxed{s(y)+}(x \times s(y)) = \boxed{s(}x\boxed{)} + \boxed{(y+}(x \times y)\boxed{)} .$$

Further rippling with (5) on the right yields:

$$\boxed{s(y)+}(x \times s(y)) = \boxed{s(}x + \boxed{(y+}(x \times y)\boxed{)}\boxed{)} .$$

Finally, we ripple with (8) on the right hand side and obtain

$$\boxed{s(y)+}(x \times s(y)) = \boxed{s(y+}(x + (x \times y))\boxed{)} .$$

The result is that the contexts on both sides of the equality have been moved to the outermost position on each side. Hence, the induction hypothesis is applicable and we can continue the proof by rewriting the left hand side with (1) which yields

$$\boxed{s(y)+}(x + (x \times y)) = \boxed{s(y+}(x + (x \times y))\boxed{)}$$

We are left with a first order equality problem there the skeleton of both sides coincide and all remaining differences between both sides are located inside the contexts. The general idea is alternately to modify the context in order to adapt the set of occurring symbols and to enlarge the skeleton by common occurrences of symbols on both sides. In our example we enlarge the skeleton to

$$\boxed{s}y\boxed{} + (x + (x \times y)) = \boxed{s}y + (x + (x \times y))\boxed{}$$

Again we try to move the contexts on both sides to the outermost position on each side. Applying (5) on the left side yields

$$\boxed{s}y + (x + (x \times y))\boxed{} = \boxed{s}y + (x + (x \times y))\boxed{}$$

The contexts on both sides coincide. Enlarging again the skeleton results in the final equation: $s(y + (x + (x \times y))) = s(y + (x + (x \times y)))$

2 Rippling

In many calculi the proof of a formula is reduced to the problem of manipulating its different parts. In order to prove an equation, for example, both sides of the equation have to be transformed until they finally coincide. Alternatively, with resolution based provers the resolution rule can only be applied if there are two complementary literals with unifiable termlists. Again, using paramodulation, the task of equalizing terms occurs in order to enable the resolution rule. Thus, proving the equality of terms or equivalences of formulas by identifying their syntactical structure is a main goal during the proof of formulas. According to the paradigm of difference reduction, the syntactical differences guide the process of modification in our approach.

2.1 Representation of Differences

The notion of annotated terms enables an explicit representation of differences between terms. Annotations are attached to the occurrences of each symbol indicating whether this occurrence belongs to the common part of both formulas or whether it is part of their differences.

Thus in contrast to describing differences by identifying minimal subterms which contain them (as in the RUE-approach), the notion of annotated terms allows one to represent the differences explicitly and therefore, seems to be a more adequate representation for implementing difference reduction techniques. Also, the explicit representation of differences is an important requirement in computing a measure of how far two terms or formulas differ which is a central aid in guiding (parts of) the proof search.

Once annotation has been computed describing the differences between two terms, both annotated terms share the same skeleton. Thus, the differences (or contexts) can be localized relative to that skeleton. In our example in section (1), all annotations are initially located in front of the induction variables. To enable the use of the hypothesis we moved the annotations into the outermost positions on both sides of the equality. Thus the positions of the annotations reflect the progress of the proof in our example: the closer the contexts are to the outermost positions, the further the proof has progressed.

In general, measures computing the size of the differences may take into account several properties: the size of the skeleton, the positions of the contexts relative to the skeleton, the size of the contexts, the ordering on the symbols occurring in the contexts, etc. In our example in section 1, after applying the induction hypothesis the residual contexts of both sides are located at outermost positions but the proof is still not finished. Thus, measures guiding the proof are refinements of a lexicographical ordering on the size of the common skeleton and the positions of the contexts.

2.2 Constrains Given by the Skeleton

According to our methodology, two annotated terms have to be modified in order to enlarge their common skeleton. Hence, we are only interested in deduction steps which do not weaken the common skeleton. On the contrary we have to find appropriate steps which enlarge the skeleton as in section 1.

The constraint to preserve the given skeleton reduces the search space of the deduction. Deduction steps have to respect the common skeleton and only the contexts can be modified. Applying an annotated equation E to a subterm t requires that first, the left hand side of E matches (resp. unifies) the subterm t and second, that the skeleton of the left hand side of E matches the skeleton of t. As a consequence, the contexts of the left hand side of E match the contexts of t. From an operational point of view, the application of the equation E will remove the contexts and create instances of the contexts on the right hand side of E in t. The positions of the contexts in the modified t will correspond to the positions of the contexts on the right hand side of E.

Consider the right hand side of the modified conclusion: $s(x) + (y + (x \times y))$ If we ignore the annotations, then the lemma (2) would be applicable obtaining a term $y + (x + (x \times y))$. But given the annotations, neither lemma (7) nor lemma (8) are applicable since in both cases parts of the skeleton of the conclusion would match the contexts of the annotated equation. In contrast, applying (5) to the term yields a term $(x + (y + (x \times y)))$ such that the skeleton is preserved. Comparing the original term and the result of the application only the context s has changed its position relative to the skeleton.

Annotating terms is also used to focus the attention of the deduction process to specific subterms of a formula. Since the skeleton remains invariant, admissible deduction steps will only change the context parts of the annotated term. Thus, declaring parts of a term to be part of the skeleton prevents them from being modified. In contrast to other approaches (e.g. RUE) this notion is not restricted to contexts which are proper subterms or superterms of the formula. We are able to treat arbitrary contexts regardless whether they are intertwined with skeletons or not. For instance in the example above the equation was applied to a subterm $(x) + ((x \times y))$ which contains both, context and skeleton.

2.3 Handling Existential Quantifiers

In terms of inductive theorem proving existentially quantified variables denote so-called *sink positions*. Let, for instance, x be a existentially quantified variable, then in order to prove an equation $s(a + b) = x + y$ the system may use the corresponding skeleton position of x on the left hand side as a sink position (i.e. as a target position for context to be removed). Once it succeed, we obtain for instance an equation $s(a) + b = x + y$ which can be solved by instantiating x and y appropriately.

In case the variable occurs more than once, we have to take care that each occurrence of this variable corresponds to the same sink term. Thus, the problem occurs of coordinating different sink positions of the same variable. E.g. $s(s(s(s(a + a)))) = x + x$ has to be modified to: $s(s(a)) + s(s(a)) = x + x$.

In our system these sink positions are adjusted in the following way. Once a context has been propagated to a sink position yielding a term $f(t)$, all other sink positions of the same variable are checked whether their corresponding term is a subterm of $f(t)$. In this case $f(t)$ can be obtained by moving additional context to that sink position. In order to determine which part of the context at top-level has to be moved to which sink position we do backward reasoning. We add the missing context at the other sink positions and move these parts towards the top-level. In case the context at top level coincide to the given context we are finished. Reversing each step will move the contexts to corresponding sink positions.

3 Planning Based on Differences

Given two annotated formulas which have to be identified, the goal of the difference reduction is to equate the corresponding contexts in both formulas. Once, we succeed in identifying common parts within corresponding contexts (i.e. contexts at the same positions wrt. the skeleton) we add them to the common skeleton and continue the modification until no context remains in either term. Thus, step by step, the common skeleton increases and the contexts are reduced during the modification process. In order to adapt the context we use different abstractions on annotated terms:

3.1 Abstraction to Position of Contexts

In order to enlarge the skeleton first, we have to localize the contexts in both terms at same positions (with respect to the common skeleton) and to identify the corresponding contexts. Once parts of corresponding contexts have been added to the skeleton these parts are split into contexts and skeleton giving rise to a next iteration of adapting the position of the contexts wrt. the skeleton.

Consider again the example in section 1. After the use of the induction hypothesis the skeleton was enlarged by an occurrence of $+$ which caused that the remaining contexts were located at different skeleton positions. Thus, the context of the left hand side was moved to the corresponding position of the right hand context which finished the proof since the contexts could be trivially identified.

Thus, a major goal of the modification process is the movement of contexts into appropriate positions. If we abstract from the shape of contexts, the application of annotated equation will simply move contexts with respect to the skeleton. In this sense the consequences of applying an equation (or in general a rule) is predictable before the result of application is calculated. Rules can be classified according to the direction in which they will move contexts. Ignoring the shape of the contexts results in an abstraction of (annotated) terms which allows one to plan parts of the deduction process. E.g. we may specify in which directions contexts have to be moved during the application as it is done within induction proofs. A planner may use such a knowledge in order to compute a way through the skeleton that the context must be moved along. E.g. applying the annotated equation (5) from left to right will always move context of the first argument of $+$ in front of $+$.

3.2 Abstraction to Maximal Symbols

Common parts of the context may be added to the skeleton in order to restrict further the possible manipulation of the context. The crucial point of enlarging the skeleton is the selection of appropriate common parts since in general we may enlarge the skeleton in several ways. We have to take care which common parts of the contexts we select to enlarge the skeleton. As a result of many examples it turned out to use the definition hierarchy of the symbols occurring in the contexts to determine possible candidates for the skeleton. For example, since s and $+$ are used to define $\times$ it is awkward to enlarge the skeleton by occurrences of s or $+$ while $\times$ still occurs in some context. Consider a context like ▇▇▇▇▇▇. If we add the first occurrence of $s(x)$ to the skeleton (obtaining $s(x)$▇▇▇▇), unfolding the definition of $\times$ gets impossible due to the skeleton restrictions such that such a step would hamper rather than facilitate a proof.

Hence, we define the following definition hierarchy: given two symbols f and g, $f < g$ holds if f occurs in the definition of g. $<^*$ is defined as the transitive closure of $<$. A symbol f occurring in some context c of an annotated term is called a *maximal* symbol of c iff there is no symbol g in c with $f <^* g$. Also, specific formulas constitute a $<$-relation, like $\forall x, y. f(x, y) = g(h(x), k(y))$ implies $g < f$ and $h < f$. In the context of program verification there is a notion of a theory (collection of datatypes and operations on them) and a USING-relation on theories. E.g. a theory `list of natural numbers` uses a theory `number`. In some cases this USING-relation also constitutes a $<$-relation between functions specified in different theories.

Thus, in order to equalize contexts, the system first concentrate on the maximal symbols of both sides which is another abstraction of annotated terms in order to get an inspiration how to guide the proof search. The first subgoal of equalizing the contexts is to equalize the sets of maximal symbols on both sides.

3.3 Enlarging the Skeleton

In case the sets of maximal symbols agree on both sides we try to enlarge the skeleton. We choose an occurrence (usually the topmost occurrence) of a maximal symbol f on each side and relate them. Suppose, $f(q_1, ..., q_n)$ and $f(r_1, .., r_n)$ are the corresponding occurrences of f. In order to obtain a common skeleton for both they have to be manipulated until they share a common subterm $f(t_1, ..., t_n)$, i.e. we obtain annotated terms of the form ▓$f(t_1, ..., t_n)$▓. In order to achieve this goal we first manipulate both terms to satisfy the pattern $f(▓t_1▓, ..., ▓t_n▓)$. Once we have reached this subgoal, the original goal can be obtained by using rippling out techniques. We are left with the same problem of creating a common skeleton for the corresponding arguments (i.e. $q_1, ..., q_n$ and $r_1, .., r_n$) of the related occurrences of f. Hence, we iterate the procedure and equalize the maximal symbols of the corresponding arguments of f and enlarge their skeletons in order to obtain a term like $f(▓t_1▓, ..., ▓t_n▓)$.

3.4 Summary

Planning intermediate steps with the help of these abstractions allows one to construct proofs in a hierarchical way. In a first step we have to compute a common skeleton. Next, the contexts denoting the syntactical differences have to be moved into corresponding positions (wrt. the common skeleton) and finally the "shape" of the context has to be identified in order to enlarge the common skeleton. We use so-called maximal symbols to split existing goals of equalizing formulas into smaller subgoals. In case of maximal symbols occurring only on one hand side the subgoals describe the deletion of the occurrences of those symbols. In case both sides share the same set of maximal symbols some of their occurrences are related between both sides and the subgoal is created to equalize the related subterms. In case a maximal symbol occurs several times on either side heuristics guide the selection of the "appropriated" once. These heuristics take into account the set of variables and the nested structure of maximal symbols occurring in their arguments. This procedure will be iterated until all contexts have been identified and added to the skeleton.

Refining an abstract step into a more concrete deduction will usually require a sequence of additional deduction steps in order to enable either the predicted rule or to guarantee its preconditions. These additional steps form a subproof which is "only" useful in case the application of the rule can be enabled. Hence, in a natural way this methodology results in a hierarchical structuring of proof search. Each deduction step is done in order to achieve a specific goal which itself may be again part of a superior goal. Also this approach will recursively invoke new equality problems: Heuristics may select appropriate lemmata which should be used in order to achieve the asserted goal. Since in general a lemma may not immediately be applicable some modifications have to be done to the formula (resp. to the lemma) in order to enable its use. A subgoal arises requiring the matching of the appropriate subterm with the corresponding side of the lemma. After solving this subgoal, the lemma is applied and the proof attempt continues with its previous goal.

4 The Practice

In this chapter we present some examples to illustrate the use of this approach and give some empirical results. Essentially the heuristics described above guide the decomposition of a given goal into "smaller" subgoals until we are left with trivial tasks. They guide the selection and usage of so-called bridge lemmas and they determine subterms of the goals which have to be equalized in order to facilitate the overall proof. Technically they guide the selection of an appropriate skeleton, the generation of subgoals in order to assimilate the contexts and the way the skeleton is enlarged.

In the following we describe these heuristics as they are implemented in the INKA-system [HS96]. In two examples we use the proofs and especially the way the system automatically guided these proofs to illustrate the goal directed behavior of these strategies and also the pruning of the large search tree.

The first example will be a non-inductive part of an inductive proof. Assuming the definitions of $+$ and $\times$ in section 1 we define $\sum_{i=1}^{n} i$ and $\sum_{i=1}^{n} i^3$ by

$$sum(0) = 0 \qquad sum(s(X)) = (s(X) + sum(X))$$
$$sum3(0) = 0 \qquad sum3(s(X)) = (s(X) \times s(X)) \times s(X) + sum3(X)$$

Assume further, the associativity and commutativity law of $+$ and $\times$, and the distributivity law of $\times$ over $+$ is given as additional lemmas and we know that

$$sum(X) + sum(X) = s(X) \times X \qquad\qquad (9)$$

holds. Suppose now, we want to prove

$$sum3(x) = sum(x) \times sum(x)$$

by induction on x. Similar to the previous example the system enables the use of the induction hypotheses in the induction step and after applying the induction hypothesis there remains the following equality problem:

$$\mathbf{(s(x) \times s(x)) \times s(x)} + sum(x) \times sum(x)$$
$$= \mathbf{(} sum(x) \times sum(x) \mathbf{) + sum(x) \times s(x)) + (s(x) + sum(x)) \times s(x)}$$

Using the induction hypothesis, the right hand side of the induction hypothesis (which forms a part of the skeleton in the previous part of the proof) occurs on both hand sides and forms the initial common skeleton of both sides.

Since the context occurs on both sides at the same position wrt. the skeleton, in a next step it has to be equalized on both sides. In order to equalize the maximal symbols of both sides, we have either to remove the occurrences of sum on the right hand side or to create some occurrences of sum on the left hand side. In general the system first try to remove a one hand side symbol. For this reason the database is searched for an appropriate equation which allows one to remove some occurrences of sum (in favor to symbols already occurring in the problem). Except for the base case of the definition of sum the only suitable equation is (9).

Thus, a new subgoal is created to enable the use of (9) on the right hand side. In order to get an "inspiration" where a possible application of this equation could be, the system uses difference matching of the left-hand side of the equation and the right-hand side of the theorem which yields the following annotated right hand side of the theorem:

$$(sum(x) \times sum(x) + sum(x)) \times s(x)) + ((s(x) + sum(x)) \times s(x)) \qquad (10)$$

For this purpose the skeleton of (10) is an instance of the left-hand side of (9) and standard rippling techniques are applied to move the contexts outside until the skeleton occurs as a subterm $sum(x) + sum(x)$ in the modified right hand side of the theorem. Additionally one has to take care of the annotations of the original goal of equalizing both sides of the theorem:

$$(sum(x) \times sum(x) + sum(x) \times s(x)) + (s(x) + sum(x)) \times s(x)$$

In order to prevent loops, manipulations made in order to achieve the subgoal, must not violate the skeleton of the original goal. Both, the skeleton of the goal and the skeleton of the subgoal have to be preserved. We indicate the skeleton of the original goal by a light grey and obtain a recolored version of (10):

$$(sum(x) \times sum(x) + sum(x) \times s(x)) + ((s(x) + sum(x)) \times s(x))$$

Using standard rippling techniques the context inside the skeleton of the right hand side is moved outside with the help of appropriate rippling-out equations (based on the associativity and distributivity law). Without any search the system obtains the following deduction:

$$sum(x) \times sum(x) + (sum(x) \times s(x)) + (s(x) + sum(x)) \times s(x))$$
$$=_{distr.} sum(x) \times sum(x) + (sum(x) + (s(x) + sum(x)) \times s(x))$$
$$=_{assoc.} sum(x) \times sum(x) + ((sum(x) + sum(x)) + s(x) \times s(x)$$

At this stage the subgoal of enabling the use of (9) is achieved. After its application the system returns to the original goal of equalizing left and right hand side of the theorem

$$(s(x) \times s(x)) \times s(x) + sum(x) \times sum(x)$$
$$= sum(x) \times sum(x) + (x \times s(x) + s(x)) \times s(x)$$

In this case the sets of maximal symbols agree on both sides and in order to enlarge the skeleton we choose an occurrence of a maximal symbol on each side. In our example $\times$ is the only maximal symbol. Thus, we choose the topmost occurrences of $\times$ on both sides: $(s(x) \times s(x)) \times s(x)$ and $(x \times s(x) + s(x)) \times s(x)$. Analyzing the maximal symbols of both results in a link between the two occurrences of $\times$. Comparing the corresponding parameters of both occurrences of $\times$ the procedure enters its base case since in each case one of the two terms denotes a common skeleton. After relating corresponding symbols and adding them to the skeleton we are left with the following situation:

$$(s(x) \times s(x)) \times s(x) + sum(x) \times sum(x)$$
$$= sum(x) \times sum(x) + (x \times s(x) + s(x)) \times s(x)$$

In addition to the above representation, the relations between skeleton symbols on left and right hand side are also available to the system and maintained during the manipulation of the formula by the use of different skeleton-colors.

In a next step the annotated terms are equalized in a bottom-up procedure. We start with some innermost link between related symbols the arguments of which contain contexts, e.g. $s(x) \times s(x)$ and $x \times s(x)$. The task is to remove all contexts within the arguments of $\times$ which is — in this case — done by rippling out techniques which yield

$$(s(x) + x \times s(x)) \times s(x) + sum(x) \times sum(x)$$
$$= sum(x) \times sum(x) + (x \times s(x) + s(x)) \times s(x)$$

Next consider the related terms

$$\text{■}x \times s(x)\text{■} \times s(x) \text{ and } \text{■}x \times s(x)\text{■}\text{■} \times s(x).$$

Again we have to get rid of the contexts within the arguments of $\times$. In this case there are two possible ways. The first solution is to use rippling out and apply the distributivity law to ripple the contexts out. The second solution is to use the procedure described above to enlarge the skeleton of the arguments. In doing this we obtain a link between the two occurrences of the maximal symbol $+$. In contrast to previous cases we are not free to determine the skeleton of the arguments arbitrarily but any solution has to obey the existing link between the occurrences of $\times$ in the skeleton. Since on the left hand side $\times$ occurs in the second argument of $+$ while on the right hand side in the first argument, the subgoal is created to reformulate one of these terms in such a way that both occurrences of $\times$ occur in the same argument position. Hence, applying the commutativity law yields:

$$\text{■}x \times s(x)\text{■}\text{■} \times s(x)\text{■}sum(x) \times sum(x)$$
$$= sum(x) \times sum(x)\text{■}\text{■}x \times s(x)\text{■}\text{■} \times s(x)$$

Now, the procedure succeeds in enlarging the skeleton and we obtain:

$$x \times s(x) + s(x)) \times s(x)\text{■}sum(x) \times sum(x)$$
$$= sum(x) \times sum(x)\text{■}(x \times s(x) + s(x)) \times s(x)$$

We are left with the topmost contexts which again share $+$ as a maximal symbol. Relating both occurrences the links between their arguments forces again the application of the commutativity law which yields

$$x \times s(x) + s(x)) \times s(x)\text{■}sum(x) \times sum(x)$$
$$= (x \times s(x) + s(x)) \times s(x)\text{■}sum(x) \times sum(x)$$

Enlarging the skeleton again finishes the proof.

Another Example We will illustrate our approach by another example of SAM's lemma [GOBS69] which is still a challenge equality problem although it has also been solved by some resolution provers without paramodulation.

Given two associative, commutative, and idempotent functions f and g and additionally, the following set of axioms:

$$f(X, g(X, Y)) = X \quad (11) \qquad f(0, X) = 0 \quad (13) \qquad g(0, X) = X \quad (15)$$
$$g(X, f(X, Y)) = X \quad (12) \qquad f(1, X) = X \quad (14) \qquad g(1, X) = 1 \quad (16)$$
$$f(X, Z) = X \rightarrow f(g(X, Y), Z) = g(X, f(Y, Z)) \qquad (17)$$

the task is to prove the following formula:

$$f(f(y, u), v) = 0 \wedge f(x, g(u, v)) = 0 \rightarrow f(g(x, f(y, u)), g(x, f(y, v))) = x$$

Starting with an empty skeleton, we compare the maximal symbols of both sides. Since there are no function hierarchies f and g are considered as maximal symbols. Both symbols occur only on the left hand side. Hence, we are looking for an appropriate equation which would remove occurrences of f or g. From all possible equations only the left hand side of (11) and the left hand side of the first premises difference-match against the left hand side of the conclusion. Using a set-of-support heuristic the system prefers the first premise and tries to enable its application within the left hand side of the conclusion. Hence, we

obtain the following annotated left hand side in order to solve this subgoal:
$$f(\boxed{g(x}f(y,u)\boxed{)}, \boxed{x \Leftarrow f(y,v)})$$
Again rippling techniques apply to move the contexts out of the skeleton and thus, to enable the use of the first premise. Using the conditional C-equation of (17):
$$f(X,Z) = X \rightarrow f(\boxed{g(x,}Y\boxed{)}, z) = \boxed{g(x,}f(Y,Z)\boxed{)}.$$
we are able to manipulate the left hand side to
$$\boxed{g(x,}f(f(y,u), \boxed{x \Leftarrow f(y,v)})\boxed{)} \tag{18}$$
since the instantiated condition $f(x, g(x, f(y, v))) = x$ of (17) holds trivially due to axiom (11). The problem remains to move the second context outside. Again, the left-hand side of the conditional equation matches the appropriate subterm under the given theory but in this case the prover fails to establish the instantiated condition $f(x, f(y, u)) = x$ which now prevents the use of the equation. Also, the application of the context-deleting C-equation (15) fails due to a clash inside the unification. Thus the rippling process gets stuck.

In order to get the process back on its feet, unblocking strategies are used to overcome the unification clash. (15) would be applicable if 0 occurs instead of x as the first argument of g. Considering the second premise $f(x, g(u, v)) = 0$, we reformulate this problem as a rippling problem: we have to create an appropriate context around the occurrence of x inside the first argument of g in order to obtain a term
$$\boxed{g(x,}f(f(y,u), \boxed{g(f(x, g(u,v)), f(y,v))})\boxed{)}$$
Alternating backward and forward reasoning this problem is reduced to the task of removing the context within
$$g(x, f(f(y,u), g(\boxed{f(x,}g(u,v)\boxed{)}, f(y,v))))$$
which is also done by rippling techniques using (17), the associativity of f, and (11). Thus, the left hand side (18) is reformulated to
$$\boxed{g(x,}f(f(y,u), \boxed{g(f(x, g(u,v)), f(y,v))})\boxed{)}$$
and using the second premises and (15) yields the following result
$$\boxed{g(x,}f(f(y,u), \boxed{f(y,v)})\boxed{)}$$
Applying associativity and commutativity law of f finally yields
$$\boxed{g(x, f(}f(f(y,u),v)\boxed{)}$$
and the first premises is applicable and we are left with the trivial problem of solving
$$\boxed{g(x, f(0,y))} = x$$
which is solved with the help of (13), (15), and the commutativity of g.

5 Empirical Results and Related Work

The strategies presented in this paper are implemented and successfully tested within the INKA-system and are the basis of the equality reasoning part of this system. Both examples given in this section (and many others) are fully automatically proven by the system in the described way (In the first example INKA needs about 0.6 seconds to find the proof while Sam's lemma is proven in less than 7 seconds).

In order to examine the quality of the heuristics described above we monitored the systems behavior. Estimating the quality of the decomposition of the equality goal into a set of different equality subgoals we compared the number of suggested partitions with those partitions finally used in the proof. As it turned out only about 10% of the speculated decompositions had to be backtracked during both proof examples. Second, we examined the role of suggesting bridge lemmata. We counted the number of suggested bridge lemmata versus the number of bridge lemmata used in the final proof. As it turned out, the heuristics (e.g. heuristics to remove one side, maximal symbols) suggest a large number of candidates during the proof attempt (in case of $sum3$ about 80 equations and in case of SAM's lemma about 200 equations). Difference matching — used as a filter to restrict the amount of suggested bridge lemmata — rules out about 90% of these suggestions. About 50% of these candidates passing the difference matching test were used for the resulting proof.

In general, the INKA-System is itself integrated into a tool called VSE [VSE96] for the formal development of software. Within this tool several large industrial case studies have been performed and up to now more than 20,000 lines of code have been verified which causes that thousands of first order proof obligations were tackled automatically or with some user interaction by the INKA-system.

6 Final Remarks

Equating terms by difference reduction results in goal-directed strategies. Deduction steps are only done in order to achieve a specific well-defined goal which results in a monotonic behavior of the system: adding additional lemmata to a database will facilitate rather than hamper a proof. Also it enables the user to interact with the deduction system on a strategic level. On one hand the system is able to communicate its aims and the way it tries to achieve goals. This helps the user to detect potential gaps in the axiomatization and gives rise to speculate additional lemmata. On the other hand the user may explicitly change the goals of the system in order to change the system's behavior. For instance, one may either speculate a bridge lemmata and the system has to enable its application, or focus the attention of the system on subterms of the theorem which have to be identified.

Based on our experience in program verification several remarks can be made: The presented approach is well-suited in the area of program verification: Deduction problems in program verification are characterized by a very large (and structured) set of axioms. The formulas to be proven are often unwieldy while the proofs can be often guided by their syntactical structure. In contrast to theorems, say in group theory, they do not require a sophisticated blow-up of terms in order to prove the theorem. Hence, in many cases the syntactic structure of the theorems contain sufficient informations to guide the proof.

Despite the high automation of guiding proofs there are many proof obligations which require human interaction. Conventional fully automated theorem proving systems that carry out an exhaustive search following some complete (and therefore problem independent) strategy also turned out to be inadequate for our kind of applications. One reason for this is the limited possibility for user interaction where the activities of the user are restricted to certain preparations (formatting the input, choosing the search strategy and additional parameters) *before* the system is run.

Our strategies based upon it do not form a complete theorem prover for its own but have to be supplemented by other strategies concerning mainly how to equalize the context. As mentioned above this technique is open ended. Since its strategies especially decompose a given goal each of these obtained subgoals may also be tackled by other methods. Domain specific knowledge or strategies of other approaches can be easily incorporated to guide the modification of contexts. In the INKA-system, special procedures are implemented to handle contexts concerning the datatypes INTEGER and SETS and built-in knowledge on these types is used to identify the contexts.

References

[BS88] K. Hans Bläsius and J.H. Siekmann. Partial unification for graph based equational reasoning. In *9th CADE*, Springer, LNCS, 1988

[BSvH+93] A. Bundy, A. Stevens, F. van Harmelen, A. Ireland, and A. Smaill. Rippling: A heuristic for guiding inductive proofs. *Artificial Intelligence*, 62, pp. 185–253, 1993.

[BvHS91] A. Bundy, F. van Harmelen, J. Hesketh, and A. Smaill. Experiments with proof plans for induction. *Journal of Automated Reasoning*, 7, 1991.

[BW93] D. Basin and T. Walsh. Difference unification. In *13th IJCAI*, Morgan Kaufmann, 1993.

[BW95] D. Basin and T. Walsh. A Calculus for and Termination of Rippling. To appear in the *Journal of Automated Reasoning*, 1995.

[CH94] J. Cleve and D. Hutter. A methodology for equational reasoning. In Hawaii International Conference on System Sciences 27, Eds : Jay F. Nunamaker, jr. and Ralph H. Sprague, jr., IEEE Computer Society Press, 1994

[Dig85] V.J. Digricoli. The management of heuristic search in boolean experiments with RUE resolution. In *9th IJCAI*, pp. 1154 – 1161, Los Angeles, California, 1985.

[GOBS69] J. Guard, and F. Oglesby, and J. Bennett, and L. Settle. Semi-automated mathematics. In *Journal of the ACM*, pp. 49-62, Vol. 16, 1969

[Hut] D. Hutter. Colouring terms to control equational reasoning. Journal of Automated Reasoning, forthcoming

[Hut90] D. Hutter. Guiding inductive proofs. In M.E. Stickel, editor, *10th CADE*, Springer, LNAI 449, 1990

[HS96] D. Hutter, and C. Sengler INKA - The Next Generation In J. Slaney, M.McRobbie, editor, *13th CADE*, Springer, LNAI, 1996

[Mor69] J. Morris. E-resolution: an extension of resolution to include the equality relation. In *IJCAI-69*, 1969.

[NSS63] A. Newell, J.C. Shaw, and H.A. Simon. The logic theory machine. In Feigenbaum and Feldman, editors, *Computers and Thought*, pp. 61-79. McGraw-Hill, 1963.

[VSE96] D. Hutter, B. Langenstein, C. Sengler, J. Siekmann, W. Stephan, A. Wolpers Deduction in the Verification Support Environment. In *FME-96*, Oxford, Springer, LNCS, 1996

Reasoning about Action and Change: Defeasible Observations and Actions with Abnormal Effects *

Janusz Jabłonowski, Witold Łukaszewicz, Ewa Madalińska-Bugaj

Institute of Informatics, Warsaw University
Banacha 2, 02-097 Warsaw, POLAND
emails: (janusz, witlu, ewama)@mimuw.edu.pl

Abstract. We provide a very general framework to reason about action and change. Our approach generalizes existing formalisms aimed at this type of inference in three respects. Firstly, we admit actions with abnormal effects, i.e. actions that may behave abnormally with respect to their intended specifications. Secondly, we admit defeasible observations, i.e. observations that are subject to invalidation. Thirdly, we admit arbitrary priorities between abnormalities, what allows us to prefer some actions and/or observations while resolving conflicts.

To represent actions, we use Dijkstra's methodology, originally developed for reasoning about programs. To deal with abnormalities, Dijkstra's approach is combined with Reiter's version of default logic with priorities.

1 Introduction

In our recent paper [9], we have provided a general framework to deal with actions that may exhibit abnormal behaviour. More precisely, with each action A we have proposed to associate a pair of specifications, S_1 and S_2, corresponding respectively to a normal and an abnormal execution of A. The intention is that A behaves according to S_1 unless the contrary follows from observations. Consider, for instance, an action *shoot*. We may define its normal behaviour as making a gun unloaded and a turkey dead, provided that the gun is loaded, and the abnormal one as making the gun unloaded. Now, if all we know is that the action starts in a state where the gun is loaded, we conclude that after the action the turkey is dead. However, if we observe that the turkey is alive after executing the action, we have to withdraw the previous conclusion and to assume that the action behaved abnormally.

In this paper, we generalize our previous work in two respects.

- Firstly, we admit defeasible observations, i.e. observations that are subject to invalidation. This brings us closer to real applications, where observations, especially those made by a robot, are often incorrect.
- Secondly, we admit arbitrary priorities between various abnormalities. This allows us to prefer some actions and/or observations while resolving conflicts. In consequence, we obtain a very general framework to reason about action and change.

---

* This research was supported by KBN grant 8 T11C 040 10.

To represent actions, we use Dijkstra's formalism originally developed to reason about programs [3, 4]. The major advantage of Dijkstra's methodology for reasoning about action and change, when compared with purely logical approaches such as Situation Calculus [10, 5] or Features and Fluents [12], is its simplicity. We have shown this in our other papers, [7, 8], where Dijkstra's methodology is employed to model more conventional forms of reasoning about action and change. To distinguish between normal and abnormal behaviour of actions and between correct and incorrect observations, Dijkstra's formalism is combined here with Reiter's [11] default logic with priorities.

The paper is organized as follows. We begin with a brief introduction to Dijkstra's semantics for a simple programming language. Next, we provide a version of Reiter's default logic with priorities. In section 4, we show how to define action languages using Dijkstra's approach. Section 5 specifies a kind of reasoning we are interested in, whereas section 6 provides a simple method realizing this type of inference. Section 7 contains a number of illustrating examples. Finally, in section 8, we provide concluding remarks.

2 Introduction to Dijkstra's semantics

In [4] we are provided with a simple programming language whose semantics is specified in terms of formula transformers. More specifically, with each command S there are associated two formula transformers, called the *weakest liberal precondition* and the *strongest postcondition*, denoted by wlp and sp, respectively. Before providing the meaning of these transformers we introduce some terminology.[2]

First of all, we assume here that the programming language under consideration contains one type of variables only, namely Boolean variables. This assumption may seem overly restrictive, but as a matter of fact no other variables will be needed for our purpose.

Let V be a set of Boolean variables. A *state over* V is any function σ from the members of V into the truth-values $\{0, 1\}$. A state σ is said to be a *model* of a formula α iff α is true in σ.

An *assertion language* over a set V of Boolean variables, denoted by $\mathcal{L}(\mathcal{V})$, is the set of all formulae constructable in the usual way from members of V, sentential connectives ($\neg, \Rightarrow, \wedge, \vee, \equiv$) and truth-constants T (true) and F (false). In what follows, the term 'formula' refers always to a formula of some fixed assertion language. If $\beta, \alpha_1, \ldots, \alpha_n$ are formulae and $x_1, \ldots, x_n$ are Boolean variables, then we write $\beta[x_1 \leftarrow \alpha_1, \ldots, x_n \leftarrow \alpha_n]$ to denote the formula which obtains from β by simultaneously replacing all occurrences of $x_1, \ldots, x_n$ by $\alpha_1, \ldots, \alpha_n$, respectively. If x is a (Boolean) variable and α is a formula, then we write $\exists x \alpha$ as an abbreviation for $\alpha[x \leftarrow T] \vee \alpha[x \leftarrow F]$.

The formula transformers mentioned above are to be understood as follows. For each command S and each formula α:

---

[2] We ignore the *weakest precondition* transformer which plays a prominent role in reasoning about programs. The reason is that this transformer will not be used in the sequel.

- $wlp(S, \alpha)$ is the formula whose models are precisely all states such that whenever execution of S starts in any one of them and terminates, the output state satisfies α.
- $sp(S, \alpha)$ is the formula whose models are precisely all states such that each of them can be reached by starting execution of S in some state satisfying α.

A formal description of Dijkstra's semantics can be found in [1].

2.1 List of commands

The considered language consists of *skip* command, *assignment* to simple variables, *alternative* command and *sequential composition* of commands[3]. Semantics of these commands is specified in terms of formula transformers explained above.

1. **The *skip* command.** This is the "empty" command in that its execution does not change the computation state. The semantics of *skip* is thus given by

   $$wlp(skip, \alpha) = sp(skip, \alpha) = \alpha.$$

2. **The *assignment* command.** This command is of the form $x := e$, where x is a (Boolean) variable and e is a (propositional) formula. The effect of the command is to replace the value of x by the value of e. Its semantics is given by

   $$wlp(x := e, \ \alpha) = \alpha[x \leftarrow e].$$

   $$sp(x := e, \alpha) = \exists y.((x \equiv e[x \leftarrow y]) \wedge \alpha[x \leftarrow y]). \tag{1}$$

   If the variable x does not occur in the expression e, the equation (1) can be simplified. In this case

   $$sp(x := e, \alpha) = (x \equiv e) \wedge \exists x \alpha$$

   or equivalently

   $$sp(x := e, \alpha) = (x \equiv e) \wedge (\alpha[x \leftarrow T] \vee \alpha[x \leftarrow F]). \tag{2}$$

   In the sequel we shall often deal with assignment commands, $x := e$, where e is T or F. In this case the equation (2) can be replaced by

   $$sp(x := e, \alpha) = \begin{cases} x \wedge (\alpha[x \leftarrow T] \vee \alpha[x \leftarrow F]) & \text{if } e \text{ is } T \\ \neg x \wedge (\alpha[x \leftarrow T] \vee \alpha[x \leftarrow F]) & \text{if } e \text{ is } F \end{cases} \tag{3}$$

3. **The *sequential composition* command.** This command is of the form $S_1; S_2$, where S_1 and S_2 are any commands. It is executed by first executing S_1 and then executing S_2. Its semantics is given by

   $$wlp(S_1; S_2, \alpha) = wlp(S_1, wlp(S_2, \alpha));$$
   $$sp(S_1; S_2, \alpha) = sp(S_2, sp(S_1, \alpha)).$$

---

[3] The original Dijkstra's language contains *abort* command and *iterative* commands as well, but they are not needed for our purpose.

4. **The** *alternative* **command.** This command is of the form

$$\textbf{if } B_1 \rightarrow S_1 \parallel B_2 \rightarrow S_2 \parallel \cdots \parallel B_n \rightarrow S_n \textbf{ fi} \tag{4}$$

where $B_1, \ldots, B_n$ are formulae and $S_1, \ldots, S_n$ are commands. $B_1, \ldots, B_n$ are called *guards* and expressions of the form $B_i \rightarrow S_i$ are called *guarded commands*. In the sequel, we refer to the general command (4) as IF. The command is executed as follows. If none of the guards is true, then the execution aborts. Otherwise, one guarded command $B_i \rightarrow S_i$ with true B_i is *randomly* selected and S_i is executed.[4] The semantics of IF is given by

$$wlp(\text{IF}, \alpha) = \bigwedge_{i=1}^{n}(B_i \Rightarrow wlp(S_i, \alpha))$$

$$sp(\text{IF}, \alpha) = \bigvee_{i=1}^{n}(sp(S_i, B_i \wedge \alpha)).$$

3 Prioritized default logic for abnormality theories

In this section, we provide a prioritized version of Reiter's default logic [11] for a specific class of default theories, referred to as *abnormality theories*.[5] We assume the reader's familiarity with Reiter's original formalism.[6] An *abnormality theory* is a default theory $\langle A, \Delta \rangle$, where A is a set of propositional formulae and

$$\Delta = \left\{ \frac{: \neg ab_i}{\neg ab_i} \ : \ i = 0, \ldots, n \right\} \quad (n > 0). \tag{5}$$

In the sequel, the proposition symbols $ab_0, \ldots, ab_n$ will be called *abnormality symbols*. The default $: \neg ab_i / \neg ab_i$ will be said to *correspond to* the symbol ab_i.

An extension, in the sense of Reiter, of an abnormality theory T will be referred to as an *R-extension* of T. Note that abnormality theories belong to the class of normal default theories. Accordingly, each abnormality theory has at least one R-extension.

To obtain a prioritized version of default logic, one proceeds as follows.

Let $T = \langle A, \Delta \rangle$ be an abnormality theory with Δ specified by (5). We start by breaking the set $\{ab_0, \ldots, ab_n\}$ into disjoint sublists $AB_1, \ldots, AB_k$. The intention is that the defaults corresponding to the members of AB_1 are to be given the highest priority, those corresponding to the members of AB_2 the second priority, etc. We express this by writing $AB_1 > \cdots > AB_k$. If $k = 1$, then the priorities $AB_1 > \cdots > AB_k$ will be written $AB_1 > \{\}$.

Let $T = \langle A, \Delta \rangle$ be an abnormality theory with Δ specified by (5) and suppose that E is an R-extension of T. Consider priorities $AB_1 > \cdots > AB_k$. For each

---

[4] Note that when more than one guard is true, the selection of a guarded command is nondeterministic.

[5] We restrict ourselves to abnormality theories here because they are all we need in this paper.

[6] Prioritized versions of Reiter's default logic have been given some attention in the AI literature. The earliest proposal goes back to Brewka [2]. Here we specify a very simple prioritized default logic that is sufficient for our purpose.

$1 \leq l \leq k$, we write $E[l]$ to denote the set of those elements of AB_l whose negations are members of E. More formally,

$$E[l] = \{ab_i : ab_i \in AB_l \land \neg ab_i \in E\}.$$

If E and E' are R-extensions of T, then we say that E is *less than* E' wrt $AB_1 > \cdots > AB_k$, written $E <^{AB_1 > \cdots > AB_k} E'$, iff there exists l $(1 \leq l \leq k)$ such that for each $j < l$, $E[j] = E'[j]$ and $E'[l] \subset E[l]$.

Definition 1 Let T and $AB_1 > \cdots > AB_k$ be as before. A set of formulae E is said to be an extension of T wrt $AB_1 > AB_2 > \cdots > AB_k$ iff E is an R-extension of T which is minimal wrt $<^{AB_1 > \cdots > AB_k}$. A formula α is said to be a consequence of T wrt $AB_1 > \cdots > AB_k$ iff α is a member of all extensions wrt $AB_1 > \cdots > AB_k$. ∎

Since each abnormality theory has at least one R-extension and since each abnormality theory has a finite set of defaults, we immediately have

Theorem 1 Let T be an abnormality theory. For any priorities $AB_1 > \cdots > AB_k$, there exists at least one extension of T wrt $AB_1 > \cdots > AB_k$. ∎

Example 1 Consider the theory $T = \langle A, \Delta \rangle$, where $A = \{ab_1 \lor ab_2\}$ and $\Delta = \{: \neg ab_1/\neg ab_1, : \neg ab_2/\neg ab_2\}$. T has two R-extensions: $E_1 = Th(\{ab_2, \neg ab_1\})$ and $E_2 = Th(\{ab_1, \neg ab_2\})$. E_1 is the unique extension of T wrt $\{ab_1\} > \{ab_2\}$. E_2 is the unique extension of T wrt $\{ab_2\} > \{ab_1\}$. Both E_1 and E_2 are extensions of T wrt $\{ab_1, ab_2\} > \{\}$. ∎

4 Action languages

To define an action language, one starts with an alphabet consisting of primitive symbols from the following pairwise disjoint classes: (1) A finite set of Boolean variables, called *fluents* (these serve to describe the application domain under consideration); (2) A denumerable set of *abnormality symbols*: $ab_0, ab_1, \ldots$; (3) A finite set of *action symbols*; (4) Two truth-constants: T and F; (5) Usual sentential connectives.

The classes (2), (4)-(5) are fixed, whereas the classes (1) and (3) varies from an alphabet into an alphabet. Accordingly, each alphabet is uniquely determined by its fluents and action symbols.

A *formula* is a Boolean combination of fluents, abnormality symbols and truth-constants. A formula containing no abnormality symbols is said to be an *observation*. The set of *observation expressions* is the smallest set of formulae satisfying:

(1) An observation is an observation expression;
(2) If α is an observation and ab_i is an abnormality symbol, then $\neg ab_i \Rightarrow \alpha$ is an observation expression.
(3) if α is an observation and β is an observation expression, then $\alpha \land \beta$, $\alpha \lor \beta$, $\alpha \Rightarrow \beta$, $\alpha \equiv \beta$ are observation expressions.

Remark 1 Clause (3) deserves special attention. It allows us to construct observation expressions combining defeasible observations with certain ones. In particular, the same observation can be viewed as defeasible or certain, depending on the context. Assume, for instance, that there are two fluents s and a, standing for *smoke* and *alive* (a turkey), respectively. Suppose further that a robot observed that the turkey is alive. We may wish to view this observation as certain if no smoke is present, but as defeasible otherwise. To represent this, we can use the observation expression $(\neg s \Rightarrow a) \wedge (s \Rightarrow (\neg ab_i \Rightarrow a))$.

Two observation expressions are said to be *disjoint* if they do not contain the same abnormality symbol.

The objects we shall be primarily interested in are (*action*) *scenarios*. These are expressions of the form

$$SC = \langle \alpha_0 \rangle \, A_1; \langle \alpha_1 \rangle \, A_2; \ldots; \langle \alpha_{n-1} \rangle \, A_n \, \langle \alpha_n \rangle \tag{6}$$

where $A_1, \ldots, A_n$ are action symbols and $\alpha_0, \ldots, \alpha_n$ are pairwise disjoint observation expressions. The scenario has the following intuitive interpretation: α_0 holds in the initial state, then the actions $A_1, \ldots, A_n$ are sequentially performed, and α_i, for $0 < i \leq n$, holds after performing the action A_i.

In intermediate states, if no observation is made, i.e. $\alpha_i \equiv T$, we omit this element in the scenario.

As we remarked earlier, our approach is based on the assumption that to each action symbol A, there are assigned two specifications, describing normal and abnormal performance of A.

The crucial point in using Dijkstra's methodology is to interpret action symbols occurring in a scenario as commands of the programming language defined in the previous section. The construction of such a command is a two step process. Firstly, with each action symbol A we associate two commands, denoted $S_1(A)$ and $S_2(A)$, describing respectively normal and abnormal performance of A.[7] It should be stressed that neither $S_1(A)$ nor $S_2(A)$ may contain abnormality symbols. These are auxiliary symbols serving to distinguish between normal and abnormal performances of actions. Given $S_1(A)$ and $S_2(A)$, we define a *command schema* corresponding to A, written $S(A)$, by

$$\textbf{if } \neg ab \to S_1(A) \; [\!] \; ab \to S_2(A) \textbf{ fi} \tag{7}$$

where ab is a parameter which will be replaced by some abnormality symbol from $\{ab_0, ab_1, \ldots\}$. Having the above command schema, the chosen action symbol can be provided with Dijkstra-style semantics.

An action A is said to be *rigid* if $S_1(A) \equiv S_2(A)$. Intuitively, rigid actions are those where no distinction is made between their normal and abnormal executions. In other words, rigid actions always behave in the same way. Obviously, the command schema, $S(A)$, corresponding to a rigid action A can be simplified to $S_1(A)$ (or $S_2(A)$).

---

[7] The ability to represent the effects (normal and abnormal) of chosen action symbols as commands of the programming language is the necessary condition to use Dijkstra's approach to reasoning about action and change. We do not claim here that this is always possible. However, most of the actions that have been considered in the AI literature enjoy this property.

Let $S(A)$ be a command schema of the form (7). An *instance* of $S(A)$ is the result of replacing the parameter ab by some abnormality symbol from $\{ab_0, ab_1, \ldots\}$. If $S(A)$ is a simplified command schema corresponding to a rigid action A, i.e. $S(A)$ contains no ab parameter, then $S(A)$ is its own instance.

5 Action scenarios as classes of computations

In our earlier paper [9], we considered a class of computations, denoted by $[S_1; \ldots; S_n](\alpha_0, \ldots, \alpha_n)$, where $S_1, \ldots, S_n$ are commands and $\alpha_0, \ldots, \alpha_n$ are formulae. This class represents the class of all computations under control of $S_1; \ldots; S_n$ that start in a state satisfying α_0, terminate in a state satisfying α_n and, in addition, any state of any computation from this class that can be reached after executing $S_1; \ldots; S_i$ ($0 < i < n$) satisfies α_i.

Let SC be an action scenario given by (6). We write $\mathcal{C}(SC)$ to denote the class of computations

$$[S^I(A_1); \ldots; S^I(A_n)](\alpha_0, \ldots, \alpha_n) \tag{8}$$

where $S^I(A_i)$ is an instance of $S(A_i)$. It is assumed that different instances, including different instances of the same action, contain different abnormality symbols. Also, the introduced abnormality symbols must be different from abnormality symbols occurring in $\alpha_0, \ldots \alpha_n$.[8]

We would like to identify the scenario SC with the class of computations $\mathcal{C}(SC)$. Unfortunately, $\mathcal{C}(SC)$ is too large to properly represent the scenario SC. The reason is that replacing an action symbol A by the command of the form **if** $\neg ab_i \rightarrow S_1(A) \; [\!] \; ab_i \rightarrow S_2(A)$ **fi** we make no distinction between normal and abnormal performance of the action represented by A[9]. We also do not distinguish between correct and incorrect observations. On the other hand, our approach is based on the implicite assumption that normal performances of actions are to be preferred over abnormal ones and that correct observations are to be preferred over incorrect ones. Also, if there are conflicts among various abnormalities, they should be resolved according to the chosen priorities $AB_1 > \cdots > AB_m$. In the rest of this section, we specify a subclass of $\mathcal{C}(SC)$ that captures this intuition.

We start with some preliminary terminology.

Let c be a computation from the class $\mathcal{C}(SC)$. We say that an action A_i is *realized normally in a computation* c iff the abnormality symbol occuring in A_i is assigned the value 0 in all states of c. We say that an observation described by an observation expression α_i is *correct in a computation* c iff the abnormality symbol occurring in α_i is assigned the value 0 in all states of c.[10]

---

[8] It should be stressed that normality/abnormality does not concern an action, but rather its execution. Accordingly, we should use different abnormality symbols not only for different action symbols, but also for different occurrences of the same action symbol (and for observation expressions).

[9] In the sequel we shall not distinguish between an action symbol and the action it represents.

[10] Note that abnormality symbols are inaffected by actions, i.e. no action can change their values. Accordingly, abnormality symbols have constant values in all states of c.

Let $\{ab_0, \ldots, ab_r\}$ be the set of all abnormality symbols occurring in a scenario SC of the form (6). Assume that this set is divided into sublists $AB_1, \ldots, AB_m$ with priorities $AB_1 > \ldots > AB_m$. Let c be a computation from the class $\mathcal{C}(SC)$. We write $AB_i(c)$ to denote the set of those members of AB_i which are assigned the value 1 in all states from c.

Let c and c' be members of $\mathcal{C}(SC)$. We write $c <^{AB_1 > \cdots > AB_m} c'$ iff there exists l, $1 \leq l \leq m$, such that for each $j < l$, $AB_j(c) = AB_j(c')$ and $AB_l(c) \subset AB_l(c')$. We say that c is $<^{AB_1 > \cdots > AB_m}$-minimal in the class $\mathcal{C}(SC)$ iff there does not exist c' such that $c' <^{AB_1 > \cdots > AB_m} c$.

Clearly, the intended computations wrt priorities $AB_1 > \ldots > AB_m$ are those which are $<^{AB_1 > \cdots > AB_m}$-minimal in the class $\mathcal{C}(SC)$.

Definition 2 Let SC be an action scenario given by (6). The *intended class of computations wrt priorities* $AB_1 > \ldots > AB_m$ *corresponding to* SC, written $\mathcal{IC}^{AB_1 > \cdots > AB_m}(SC)$, is the class of all $<^{AB_1 > \cdots > AB_m}$-minimal elements from $\mathcal{C}(SC)$. ∎

We shall need the following notion.

Let SC be an action scenario of the form (6). The set of $k-states$ $(0 \leq k \leq n)$ of the class of computations $\mathcal{C}(SC)$ (resp. $\mathcal{IC}^{AB_1 > \cdots > AB_m}(SC)$) is the set of all states such that each state from this set can be reached by some computation $c \in \mathcal{C}(SC)$ (resp. $c \in \mathcal{IC}^{AB_1 > \cdots > AB_m}(SC)$) after executing $A_1; \ldots; A_k$.

6 Reasoning about scenarios

In this section, we provide a method to reason about action scenarios.

We shall be interested in the following reasoning task: "Given an action scenario $SC = \langle \alpha_0 \rangle A_1; \langle \alpha_1 \rangle A_2; \ldots; \langle \alpha_{n-1} \rangle A_n \langle \alpha_n \rangle$, a formula γ, an integer k $(0 \leq k \leq n)$ and priorities $AB_1 > \ldots > AB_m$, determine whether γ holds in all k-states of $\mathcal{IC}^{AB_1 > \cdots > AB_m}(SC)$.[11]

Consider a scenario $SC = \langle \alpha_0 \rangle A_1; \langle \alpha_1 \rangle A_2; \ldots; \langle \alpha_{n-1} \rangle A_n \langle \alpha_n \rangle$ and the class of computations $\mathcal{C}(SC)$ given by (8). In view of Theorem 2 ([9]), we know that the set of all k-states of $\mathcal{C}(SC)$ is characterized by the formula

$$D_k(\mathcal{C}(SC)) = SP_k^{\mathcal{C}(SC)} \wedge \neg WLP_k^{\mathcal{C}(SC)} \tag{9}$$

where the formulae $SP_k^{\mathcal{C}(SC)}$ and $WLP_k^{\mathcal{C}(SC)}$ have been defined by the following induction:

$$SP_0^{\mathcal{C}(SC)} = \alpha_0; \quad WLP_n^{\mathcal{C}(SC)} = \neg \alpha_n$$

and for $0 < k \leq n$

$$SP_k^{\mathcal{C}(SC)} = \alpha_k \wedge sp(A_k, SP_{k-1}^{\mathcal{C}(SC)});$$
$$WLP_{n-k}^{\mathcal{C}(SC)} = \neg \alpha_{n-k} \vee wlp(A_{n-k+1}, WLP_{n-k+1}^{\mathcal{C}(SC)}).$$

---

[11] For $k = 0$, i.e. when we want to determine whether γ is true in the initial state, the above reasoning task is known as the *temporal postdiction problem*. For $k = n$, i.e. when we want to determine whether γ holds in the final state, the task is usually referred to as the *temporal prediction problem*.

To characterize the set of k-states of the class $\mathcal{IC}^{AB_1>\ldots>AB_m}(SC)$ we use the prioritized version of Reiter's default logic. More precisely, we define a default theory $\mathcal{T}_k(SC) = \langle A, \Delta \rangle$, where A (the set of axioms) consists of the formula $D_k(\mathcal{C}(SC))$ and Δ (the set of defaults) is specified by $\{: \neg ab_i / \neg ab_i | 0 \leq i \leq N\}$, where $\{ab_0, \ldots ab_N\}$ is the set of all abnormality symbols occurring in the scenario SC. The next theorem, whose proof will be given in the full version of this paper, shows that extensions of the theory $\mathcal{T}_k(SC)$ wrt $AB_1 > \ldots > AB_m$ provide a complete description of k-states of the class $\mathcal{IC}^{AB_1>\ldots>AB_m}(SC)$.

Theorem 2 Let $SC = \langle \alpha_0 \rangle A_1; \langle \alpha_1 \rangle A_2; \ldots; \langle \alpha_{n-1} \rangle A_n \langle \alpha_n \rangle$ be an action scenario. A formula γ holds in all $k - states$ of the class $\mathcal{IC}^{AB_1>\ldots>AB_m}(SC)$, $0 \leq k \leq n$, iff γ is the member of all extensions of the default theory $\mathcal{T}_k(SC)$ wrt $AB_1 > \ldots > AB_m$. ∎

∎

Corollary 1 Let SC be specified as before. A formula γ holds after performing the actions $A_1; \ldots; A_k$, $0 \leq k \leq n$, iff γ is the member of all extensions of the default theory $\mathcal{T}_k(SC)$ wrt $AB_1 > \ldots > AB_m$. ∎

Remark 2 A scenario $SC = \langle \alpha_0 \rangle A_1; \langle \alpha_1 \rangle A_2; \ldots; \langle \alpha_{n-1} \rangle A_n \langle \alpha_n \rangle$ gives rise to $n + 1$ different default theories: $\mathcal{T}_0(SC), \mathcal{T}_1(SC), \ldots \mathcal{T}_n(SC)$. It can be shown, however, that the extensions of all these theories are based on the same sets of generating defaults.[12] Accordingly, when sets of generating defaults for $\mathcal{T}_i(SC)$, $0 \leq i \leq n$, are computed, they can be used for all default theories corresponding to the scenario SC. ∎

7 Examples

In this section we present three examples illustrating our approach. The action language we use is based on five fluents: a, l, h, d and s, standing for *alive* (a turkey), *loaded* (a gun), *hidden* (a turkey), *deaf* (a turkey) and *smoke*.

Example 2 Let $SC = \langle \neg ab_0 \Rightarrow l \rangle$ load; shoot $\langle a \rangle$, where $S(load)$ is

if $\neg ab \rightarrow l := T$ ▯ $ab \rightarrow skip$ **fi**

and $S(shoot)$ is

if $\neg ab \rightarrow$ **if** $l \rightarrow a := F; l := F$ ▯ $\neg l \rightarrow skip$ **fi** ▯
$ab \rightarrow l := F$ **fi**.

We first provide Dijkstra-style semantics for the above command schemata. Performing routine calculations one easily obtains[13]:

- $sp(S(load), \alpha) = (\neg ab \wedge l \wedge (\alpha[l \leftarrow T] \vee \alpha[l \leftarrow F])) \vee (ab \wedge \alpha)$;
- $sp(S(shoot), \alpha) = \neg ab \wedge ((\neg a \wedge \neg l \wedge \alpha[a \leftarrow T, l \leftarrow T]) \vee (\neg a \wedge \neg l \wedge \alpha[a \leftarrow F, l \leftarrow T]) \vee (\neg l \wedge \alpha)) \vee ab \wedge \neg l \wedge (\alpha[l \leftarrow T] \vee \alpha[l \leftarrow F])$.

---

[12] See [11], for the definition of this notion.
[13] We ignore the transformer wlp here because it will not be needed.

We calculate $D_2(\mathcal{C}(SC))$, where $\mathcal{C}(SC) = [S^I(load); S^I(shoot)](\neg ab_0 \Rightarrow l, T, a)$.

$$D_2(\mathcal{C}(SC)) = SP_2^{\mathcal{C}(SC)} \wedge \neg WLP_2^{\mathcal{C}(SC)}$$
$$= a \wedge sp(S^I(shoot), sp(S^I(load), \neg ab_0 \Rightarrow l))$$
$$= a \wedge sp(S^I(shoot), \neg ab_1 \wedge l \vee ab_1 \wedge (\neg ab_0 \Rightarrow l))$$
$$= a \wedge (\neg ab_2 \wedge ((\neg a \wedge \neg l \wedge (\neg ab_1 \vee ab_1)) \vee (\neg a \wedge \neg l \wedge (\neg ab_1 \vee ab_1)) \vee (\neg l \wedge (\neg ab_1 \wedge l \vee ab_1 \wedge (\neg ab_0 \Rightarrow l))))) \vee ab_2 \wedge \neg l \wedge ((\neg ab_1 \vee ab_1) \vee (ab_1 \wedge ab_0))$$
$$\equiv a \wedge \neg l \wedge (\neg ab_2 \wedge ab_0 \wedge ab_1 \vee ab_2).$$

The default theory $T_2(SC) = \langle \{D_2(\mathcal{C}(SC))\}, \{: \neg ab_i/\neg ab_i \mid 0 \le i \le 2\}\rangle$ has two R-extensions: $E_1 = Th(\{a, \neg l, ab_0, ab_1, \neg ab_2\})$ and $E_2 = Th(\{a, \neg l, \neg ab_0, \neg ab_1, ab_2\})$. These extensions correspond to two possible courses of events: either the initial observation was incorrect, *load* was performed abnormally and *shoot* normally (E_1) or the initial observation was correct, *load* was performed normally and *shoot* abnormally (E_2). This alternative is all we can conclude if there is no preference among the abnormality symbols, i.e. if the priorities are $\{ab_0, ab_1, ab_2\} > \{\}$.

Assume now that the correctness of the initial observation is given the highest priority, whereas there is no preference between actions: $\{ab_0\} > \{ab_1, ab_2\}$. In this case we infer that the initial observation was correct, *load* was performed normally and *shoot* abnormally. (E_2 is the only extension of $T_2(SC)$ wrt $\{ab_0\} > \{ab_1, ab_2\}$.)

Suppose now that the normal performance of *shoot* is given the highest priority and there is no preference between the initial observation and *load*: $\{ab_2\} > \{ab_0, ab_1\}$. In this case, we conclude that the initial observation was incorrect, *load* was performed abnormally and *shoot* normally. (E_1 is the only extension of $T_2(SC)$ wrt $\{ab_2\} > \{ab_0, ab_1\}$.)

Finally, assume that the actions are given the highest priorities: $\{ab_1, ab_2\} > \{ab_0\}$. Again, we cannot say what went wrong: E_1 and E_2 are extensions of $T_2(SC)$ wrt $\{ab_1, ab_2\} > \{ab_0\}$. ∎

Example 3 Let $SC = \langle a \wedge \neg s \rangle$ *shoot* $\langle\langle (\neg s \Rightarrow \neg a) \wedge (s \Rightarrow (\neg ab_1 \Rightarrow \neg a))\rangle\rangle$,[14] where $S(shoot)$ is defined by

if $\neg ab \to$ **if** $l \to a := F; l := F; s := T \parallel \neg l \to skip$ **fi** $\parallel$
$ab \to$ **if** $l \to l := F; s := T \parallel \neg l \to skip$ **fi fi.**

A little reflexion should convince the reader that the intended conclusions are: (1) The gun was loaded in the initial situation. (2) There was smoke in the final situation.[15] The semantics of the action *shoot* is

---

[14] Note that the observation expression $(\neg s \Rightarrow \neg a) \wedge (s \Rightarrow (\neg ab_1 \Rightarrow \neg a))$ states that $\neg a$ is assumed to be a correct observation if there is no smoke and a defeasible observation otherwise.

[15] To see this, observe first that (2) follows from (1) in view of the definition of $S(shoot)$. To show (1), assume to the contrary that there is an initial state in which the gun is unloaded. Inspecting the specification of $S(shoot)$, we immediately see that starting the action *shoot* in this state, we reach the same state as the result of performing the action. In particular, $a \wedge \neg s$ must hold in this final state. A contradiction with $\neg s \Rightarrow \neg a$.

- $wlp(S(shoot), \alpha) = ((\neg ab \wedge l) \Rightarrow \alpha[l, s, a \leftarrow F, T, F]) \wedge ((ab \wedge l) \Rightarrow \alpha[l, s \leftarrow F, T]) \wedge \neg l \Rightarrow \alpha;$
- $sp(S(shoot), \alpha) = \neg l \wedge ((s \wedge \neg a \wedge \neg ab \wedge \alpha[l, s, a \leftarrow T, F, F] \vee \alpha[l, s, a \leftarrow T, F, T] \vee \alpha[l, s, a \leftarrow T, T, F] \vee \alpha[l, s, a \leftarrow T, T, T]) \vee \alpha \vee (s \wedge ab \wedge (\alpha[l, s \leftarrow T, F] \vee \alpha[l, s \leftarrow T, T])))$.

Note that $(\neg s \Rightarrow \neg a) \wedge (s \Rightarrow (\neg ab_1 \Rightarrow \neg a))$ is equivalent to $a \Rightarrow (s \wedge ab_1)$. In the sequel we will use the latter formula. We calculate $D_0(\mathcal{C}(SC))$, where $\mathcal{C}(SC) = [S^I(shoot)](a \wedge \neg s, a \Rightarrow (s \wedge ab_1))$.

$$
\begin{aligned}
D_0(\mathcal{C}(SC)) &= SP_0^{\mathcal{C}(SC)} \wedge \neg WLP_0^{\mathcal{C}(SC)} \\
&= a \wedge \neg s \wedge \neg wlp(S^I(shoot), \neg(a \Rightarrow (s \wedge ab_1))) \\
&= a \wedge \neg s \wedge ((\neg ab_0 \wedge l) \vee (ab_0 \wedge l \wedge (\neg a \vee ab_1)) \vee \\
&\quad (\neg l \wedge (\neg a \vee (s \wedge ab_1)))) \\
&\equiv l \wedge a \wedge \neg s \wedge (\neg ab_0 \vee ab_1).
\end{aligned}
$$

The default theory $\mathcal{T}_0(SC) = \langle \{D_0(\mathcal{C}(SC))\}, \{: \neg ab_0/\neg ab_0, : \neg ab_1/\neg ab_1\} \rangle$ has one R-extension $E = Th(\{D_0(\mathcal{C}(SC)), \neg ab_0, \neg ab_1\})$. Since $\mathcal{T}_0(SC)$ has one R-extension only, our conclusions do not depend on priority settings. Clearly, $l \in E$, so we infer that the gun was loaded in the initial situation. We now calculate $D_1(\mathcal{C}(SC))$.

$$
\begin{aligned}
D_1(\mathcal{C}(SC)) &= SP_1^{\mathcal{C}(SC)} \wedge \neg WLP_1^{\mathcal{C}(SC)} \\
&= (a \Rightarrow s \wedge ab_1) \wedge sp(S^I(shoot), a \wedge \neg s) \\
&= (a \Rightarrow s \wedge ab_1) \wedge \neg l \wedge ((s \wedge \neg a \wedge \neg ab_0) \vee (a \wedge \neg s) \vee (s \wedge ab_0 \wedge a)) \\
&\equiv \neg l \wedge s \wedge ((\neg a \wedge \neg ab_0) \vee (a \wedge ab_0 \wedge ab_1)).
\end{aligned}
$$

The default theory $\mathcal{T}_1(SC) = \langle \{D_1(\mathcal{C}(SC))\}, \{: \neg ab_0/\neg ab_0, : \neg ab_1/\neg ab_1\} \rangle$ has one R-extension, namely $E = Th(\{D_1(\mathcal{C}(SC)), \neg ab_0, \neg ab_1\})$. Since $s \in E$, we conclude that there was smoke in the final situation. Observe that $\neg a$ is also a member of E, so we additionally infer that the turkey was dead in the final situation. ∎

Example 4 Let $SC = \langle a \wedge \neg h \rangle \, load; \langle \neg ab_1 \Rightarrow h \rangle \, shoot \, \langle \neg ab_2 \Rightarrow \neg a \rangle$, where *load* is a rigid action specified by

if $\neg d \rightarrow l := T; \; h := T \; [\!] \; d \rightarrow l := T$ **fi**

and $S(shoot)$ is

if $\neg ab \rightarrow$ **if** $l \wedge \neg h \rightarrow a := F; l := F \; [\!] \; \neg l \vee h \rightarrow l := F$ **fi** $[\!]$
$\quad ab \rightarrow l := F$ **fi**.

Semantics for these actions is given by[16]

- $wlp(S(load), \alpha) = (\neg d \Rightarrow \alpha[l, h \leftarrow T, T]) \wedge (d \Rightarrow \alpha[l \leftarrow T]);$
- $wlp(S(shoot), \alpha) = ((\neg ab \wedge l \wedge \neg h) \Rightarrow \alpha[l, a \leftarrow F, F]) \wedge ((\neg ab \wedge (\neg l \vee h)) \Rightarrow \alpha[l \leftarrow F]) \wedge (ab \Rightarrow \alpha[l \leftarrow F]).$

---

[16] We ignore *sp* here because this transformer will not be needed.

We calculate $D_0(\mathcal{C}(SC))$, where $\mathcal{C}(SC) = [S^I(load); S^I(shoot)](a \wedge \neg h, \neg ab_1 \Rightarrow h, \neg ab_2 \Rightarrow \neg a)$.

$$
\begin{aligned}
D_0(\mathcal{C}(SC)) &= SP_0^{\mathcal{C}(SC)} \wedge \neg WLP_0^{\mathcal{C}(SC)} \\
&= a \wedge \neg h \wedge \neg wlp(S^I(load), \neg ab_1 \wedge \neg h \vee wlp(S^I(shoot), \neg ab_2 \wedge a)) \\
&= a \wedge \neg h \wedge \neg wlp(S^I(load), \neg ab_1 \wedge \neg h \vee ((\neg ab_0 \Rightarrow (\neg l \vee h)) \wedge \\
&\quad \neg ab_2 \wedge a)) \\
&= a \wedge \neg h \wedge \neg((\neg d \Rightarrow (\neg ab_2 \wedge a)) \wedge (d \Rightarrow ((\neg ab_1 \wedge \neg h) \vee \\
&\quad ((\neg ab_0 \Rightarrow h) \wedge \neg ab_2 \wedge a)))) \\
&\equiv a \wedge \neg h \wedge ((\neg d \wedge (ab_2 \vee \neg a)) \vee d \wedge ((ab_1 \vee h) \wedge ((\neg ab_0 \wedge \neg h) \vee \\
&\quad ab_2 \vee \neg a))) \\
&\equiv a \wedge \neg h \wedge ((\neg d \wedge ab_2) \vee (d \wedge ab_1 \wedge \neg ab_0) \vee (d \wedge ab_1 \wedge ab_2)).
\end{aligned}
$$

The default theory $T_0(SC) = \langle \{D_0(\mathcal{C}(SC))\}, \{: \neg ab_i/\neg ab_i \mid 0 \leq i \leq 2\} \rangle$ has two R-extensions, E_1 and E_2, given by $Th(\{D_0(\mathcal{C}(SC)), ab_1, \neg ab_0, \neg ab_2\})$ and $Th(\{D_0(\mathcal{C}(SC)), \neg ab_1, \neg ab_0, ab_2\})$, respectively. E_1 is the unique extension of T wrt $\{ab_2\} > \{ab_0, ab_1\}$. E_2 is the unique extension of T wrt $\{ab_1\} > \{ab_0, ab_2\}$. Finally both E_1 and E_2 are extensions of T wrt $\{ab_0, ab_1, ab_2\} > \{\}$. Since $d \in E_1$ and $\neg d \in E_2$, we conclude d if ab_2 has higher priority than ab_1, whereas we conclude $\neg d$ if ab_1 is given higher priority than ab_2. ∎

8 Conclusions

We have combined Dijkstra's semantics for programming languages with Reiter's default logic with priorities to formalize reasoning about action and change. Our approach generalizes existing formalisms aimed at this type of inference in three respects. Firstly, we admit actions with abnormal effects, i.e. actions that may behave abnormally with respect to their intended specifications. Secondly, we admit defeasible observations, i.e. observations that are subject to invalidation. Thirdly, we admit arbitrary priorities between abnormalities, what allows us to prefer some actions and/or observations while resolving conflicts.

References

1. Apt K., Olderog E. Verification of Sequential and Concurrent Programs. Springer-Verlag, New York 1991.
2. Brewka G. Preferred Subtheories – An Extended Logical Framework for Default Reasoning. In Proc. IJCAI-89, Detroit, 1989.
3. Dijkstra E. W. A Discipline of Programming. Prentice Hall, 1976.
4. Dijkstra E. W., Scholten C. S. Predicate Calculus and Program Semantics. Springer-Verlag, 1990.
5. Gelfond, M,. Lifschitz, V., Rabinov, A. What Are the Limitations of Situation Calculus? In: Proc. AAAI Symposium of Logical Formalization of Commonsense Reasoning, Stanford, 55-69, 1991.
6. Lifschitz, V. Formal Theories of Action. In: Readings in Nonmonotonic Reasoning, M. Ginsberg (ed.), Morgan Kaufmann Publishers, Palo Alto, 35-57, 1988.

7. Lukaszewicz,W., Madalińska-Bugaj, E. Program Verification Techniques as a Tool for Reasoning about Action and Change. In: *KI-94: Advances in Artificial Intelligence, Proceedings of 18th German Conference on Artificial Intelligence*, Springer-Verlag, Lecture Notes in Artificial Intelligence, **861**, 226-236, 1994.

8. Lukaszewicz,W., Madalińska-Bugaj, E. Reasoning about Action and Change Using Dijkstra's Semantics for Programming Languages: Preliminary Report. In: *Proc. IJCAI-95*, Montreal, Canada, 1950-1955, 195.

9. Lukaszewicz,W., Madalińska-Bugaj, E. Reasoning about Action and Change: Actions with Abnormal Effects. In: *KI-95: Advances in Artificial Intelligence, Proceedings of 19th German Conference on Artificial Intelligence*, Springer-Verlag, Lecture Notes in Artificial Intelligence, **981**, 209-220, 1995.

10. McCarthy, J., Hayes, P.J. Some Philosophical Problems from the Standpoint of Artificial Intelligence. In: B. Meltzer and D. Michie (eds.), *Machine Intelligence* 4, 1969, 463-502.

11. Reiter, R. A Logic for Default Reasoning. *Artificial Intelligence Journal*, **13**, 81-132, 1980.

12. Sandewall, E. *Features and Fluents: The Representation of Knowledge about Dynamical Systems*. Oxford Logic Guides, **30**, Oxford Science Publications, 1994.

FALLDATEN: Case-Based Reasoning for the Diagnosis of Technical Devices*

Gerd Kamp[1], Petra Pirk[2], Hans-Dieter Burkhard[2]

[1] Fachbereich Informatik, University of Hamburg Hamburg
[2] Fachbereich Informatik, Humboldt-University Berlin

Abstract. We investigate the suitability of case-based reasoning supporting experts during technical diagnosis. Diagnosis is not considered as a classification task, but as a process to be guided by computer assisted experience. This corresponds to a flexible "case completion" approach. Flexibility is also needed for the expert view with predominant interest in the unexpected, unpredictable cases. Integration of further knowledge sources (domain knowledge, common knowledge) is investigated in the project. Two different approaches based on semantic nets are investigated: FALLEXPERTE-D makes use of Case Retrieval Nets (CRN) that are based on spreading activation techniques. FALLDATEN-DL employs description logics enhanced by concrete domains.

1 Introduction

Diagnosis is a task which usually needs a lot of (human) experience. Hence it is considered as a domain, where CBR can be applied with great benefits. The following reasons are listed in [15]:

- Experiences play a major role in nearly every domain.
- By using available experiences (encoded as cases) directly, the famous knowledge acquisition bottleneck is avoided to some extent.
- In some domains it seems desperate trying to encode all the knowledge in rule- or model- based form.
- The inference process is transparent for people not involved in AI research.
- Applications are easier to build, and they rapidly demonstrate ongoing results.
- Applications can evolve: As new situations are observed they may be added as new cases and the system may thus extend its scope of expertise.

In our project, diagnosis support for technical devices is investigated from the view point of CBR, where documented misbehavior and solutions serve as a base (experience) for further decisions.

---

* This research was supported by the DFG.

2 CBR for second-level support of technical devices

2.1 Diagnosis as classification

Diagnosis is often considered as a classification problem. This view can be found e.g. in [20] where diagnosis is defined as a problem solving type where

1. the problem domain consists of two disjoint sets representing symptoms and diagnoses;
2. a problem is described by a set of symptoms;
3. the solution of a problem consists of one or more diagnoses;
4. further symptoms may be asked for to improve the result of problem solving.

This corresponds to the description of a *diagnostic case* as: *"case = problem + solution"* where the problem is given by a set (vector) of symptom values, and the solution is the diagnosis. The underlying hypothesis for the use of CBR is then expressed as: *"similar symptoms ⇒ similar (same) diagnosis."*

Hence the classification view to diagnosis seems to be very well related to CBR. CBR retrieval is then often considered as the task, to find the n most similar cases, and the diagnosis is computed by some voting procedure (e.g. in comparison with "n-nearest neighbor" procedures). This view is also the base for the most successful application area of CBR: Help-desks [23].

Help-Desks Help-desks are computer-based system that aid people in providing assistance over the phone. Users needing advice contact a help-desk operator. He listens to the user describing the problem, and then provides a recommendation based on his experience. Unfortunately, operators having this experiences are hard to find and expensive. The goal of a help-desk system is therefore to enable a less experienced person[3] to deal with standard, frequent questions and to free the experts[4] for the more complicated tasks.

Available help-desk systems fulfill this goal: Help-desk operators are normally semi-skilled workers, having only some special training on using the help-desk. They and more or less unexperienced. With this training they try to recognize certain patterns in the end users description and use these patterns as queries to the case base. Current help-desk systems normally use an attribute-value vector description and some numerical similarity function. This results in a system guiding the user in its search for the problem solution and is therefore especially suited for users that are unexperienced in the problem domain, e.g. first-level support persons such as help-desk operators.

2.2 Case Completion

If one wants to support technicians or other second-level support persons, diagnosis as classification is inappropriate for a number of reasons:

---

[3] Also referred to as a first-level support person

[4] or second-level support persons

Use in multiple situations The relevance of symptoms changes for different diagnostic situations, and it is not necessary to know all symptom values. Hence it is not useful to have a fixed set (vector) of symptoms for all cases. Instead, different (usually small) sets of symptoms are relevant for different problems. This leads to more complex case-representations than attribute-value vectors, i.e. object-oriented approaches. Furthermore the system has to support the technician in situations other than diagnosis e.g. preparation of visits etc. [10, 9].

Diagnosis as a process Starting with some known symptoms, further tests must be performed until enough knowledge about the problem is collected. A good diagnosis tool should guide this process.

No Problem/Solution Distinction Special facts in case descriptions (e.g. "engine defect") may be considered in some contexts as part of a problem description, while they may serve as the "solution" in other contexts.

Extensibility During the development and use of a system, new information and data might become useful and accessible: Again a flexible use of symptoms with the possibility of extension is necessary. The same applies for the treatment of unexpected cases (cases which are not expected when the diagnosis tool was implemented – but just such cases might be of special interest for the expert user).

User driven vs. system driven Because the user is an expert, he wants to be in control. A second-level service support system has to leave the initiative to the technician, it serves as a system that provides the information the technician wants to have in a particular situation. This is in contrast to the help-desk model where the initiative belongs to the system and the user is to provide the information which the system cannot deduce.

All this leads to a different model of CBR, that is significantly different from the "case = problem + solution" of the previous section and has to fulfill at least the following requirements:

1. No single, fixed set of attributes as case representation.
2. Possibility to extend the case descriptions.
3. Handling of partial information, e.g.missing values.
4. Flexible retrieval of cases.

CBR is therefore considered under the aspect of *Case Completion*. Given some (partial) information concerning the actual case, we look for *more information*: Which is the next test, which are the potential candidates for diagnosis, how do I proceed in order to repair something etc. The actual problem is solved if we have *"sufficient information"*[5]. Hence, the case retrieval must act in some sense like a data base system. A query formulated within some query language (e.g with some specified values of attributes) is answered by a set of objects (e.g. diagnostic cases) which match with the given values: Each tuple serves as

---

[5] This is in some sense the basic information retrieval approach, where the user has an information need, and uses the some system in order to gather more information.

a completion of the query. In contrast to existing data base systems, we have to look for all (complete) cases which match by similarity and not exactly[6].

2.3 Integration of knowledge

CBR should not substitute model knowledge and general domain knowledge when it is available. If we know some rules or functional dependencies for sure, we should use them rather than a set of cases which behave according to that rule[7]. Thus, CBR is not to be understood as an isolated approach but as an approach which needs the integration of the other AI-techniques. This is especially true, when one wants to support second-level support personnel. In particular, the following kinds of knowledge may be relevant, and it should be possible to include them in a second-level support system:

Knowledge about the devices: In our domain knowledge about the devices, machines, plants etc. that are to be supported is available. Especially there is at-least knowledge about the device types and the device structure. It should be possible to use that knowledge.

Knowledge about mechanics/electromechanics: In addition there is (at least to some extent) background knowledge about the behavior of the device. This knowledge (e.g., about the the kinematic structure) often refers to physical laws such as $M = F \times r$. One should be able to represent this laws and use them e.g., for the determination of missing values.

Knowledge about time and space: Often the description of faults as well as the repairing instructions requires means to describe spatio-temporal relations between parts.

2.4 Basic approach within the Project FALLDATEN

Within FALLDATEN we are tackling the issues mentioned in the above sections from different angles using two approaches, that both have their roots in semantic nets:

1. FALLEXPERTE-D developed at Humboldt-University employs *spreading activation* techniques within *case retrieval nets*.
2. FALLDATEN-DL realized at the University of Hamburg uses *description logics* enhanced by *concrete domains*.

The description logics are related to those parts of diagnosis which rely on taxonomies and classification techniques. The case retrieval nets are useful for connecting items from different taxonomies.

---

[6] But a number of data base vendors are working on systems that allow for so called "vague" retrieval, For an example of a research prototype see [18].

[7] There may be some cases where the use of a set of tables is better suited than a function, mainly due to complexity reasons. For a discussion of the use of case-bases vs. general knowledge see [22].

3   FALLEXPERTE-D

As a demonstration and research tool the case-based system FALLEXPERTE-D is being developed. The project investigates theoretical approaches concerning the structured representation of cases and inference using concept hierarchies. Generic knowledge bases for technical domains (e.g. computer networks) are developed and temporal and spatial inference methods for case-based diagnostic systems are explored.

In FALLEXPERTE-D descriptions of malfunctions and their rectification are collected using highly flexible problem descriptions. On the basis of these, abstract cases can be constructed by the system (with necessary confirmation by the expert). Such a case captures the experiences of all problem descriptions belonging to a particular situation, such as alternative suppositions, possible reasons, statistical knowledge etc. Both, the concrete and the abstract cases may be employed as a basis for diagnostic support in an application. The concept hierarchy (as part of the background knowledge) contains the domain-specific vocabulary known to the system; it forms the basis for formal representations, structured descriptions of components, and abstract formations of concepts. Using this concept hierarchy, domain specific similarities may be recognized, e.g. according to specialization and has-part relationships. FALLEXPERTE-D is being equipped with a core of domain-specific technical concepts and relationships; the concept hierarchy may be extended and modified at any time. Effect nets are an additional data structure in the FALLEXPERTE-D system to describe diagnostic knowledge. In these, known causalities between components of a technical device and their behavior are described in terms of "effect chains". Such local statements about the behavior of certain components form a complex effect net that may be utilized for diagnostic support.

Hence at present time the diagnosis knowledge of our system FALLEXPERTE-D is stored in three independent knowledge bases.

The case base comprises the descriptions of the concrete case facts, i.e. the descriptions of the concrete fault situations and their repair. These cases compose the primary diagnostic knowledge of the system. In a generic case base concrete cases will be summarized and stored to suitable, generalized cases.

The taxonomy defines basic technical vocabulary, i.e. the used notions of the diagnostic system and semantical relations between these notions. This taxonomy describes supplementary domain knowledge and represents system background knowledge.

The effect net describes effect relationships between the individual components of a technical unit. So familiar effect relationships of parts of a technical unit or physical laws can be represented within the net. The net describes the certain knowledge about the cause effect relationships of components of a technical unit, e.g. so-called textbook knowledge etc. Therefore the effect net is an additional possibility to input directly diagnostic knowledge into the system, besides the cases. The effect net represents system background knowledge too.

In FALLEXPERTE-D all descriptions of occurred fault situations and their diagnoses or solutions will be collected. Our system generates generic defect cases on the basis of this concrete knowledge. This step is controlled by a human expert. A generic defect case summarizes all experiences from concrete situations for a certain diagnosis, e.g. alternative assumptions, possible causes, statistical distributions etc. It is also possible to get those generic case descriptions directly from human experts. This is important for being able to handle former not protocolled data of the technical device. For the sake of efficiency and plausibility we use the generic case base as basis for a concrete defect diagnosis support.

The concrete defect descriptions will be introduced into the system by technical stuff working with that special technical device. This is done in a stepwise manner. These inputs will be strongly supported by the system. That means to minimize the set of inputs and to automatically find similar cases in order to guide the technician in the further diagnosis by suggesting the next step.

On one hand the language for concrete case descriptions shall be flexible. But on the other hand it should also support system tasks like case storage or similarity assessment. Therefore we see a defect description as a unrestricted list of observations, where an observation describes a certain symptom. Using this structure we can formalize case descriptions without a loss of flexibility. Each observation is a formalized information entity. So in FALLEXPERTE-D each defect situation is represented as a set of formalized observations. Each observation has the same formal structure [9, 19]:

> Where? (e.g. printer)
> How? (e.g. after the third page)
> What? (e.g. does not print correctly
> When? (e.g. always)

The use of the technical taxonomy within this structure does not too much restrict the user but it supports computational tasks and it even supports the user by providing a case description vocabulary. The user inputs into the different observation components (where,what,how,when) shall not be restricted, but application oriented and flexible.

Currently, applications are being developed for diagnosing a bicycle and computer networks (as an example for a really large application domain). Additional information can be found in [5] and internal technical reports [19], [12].

3.1 Case Retrieval Nets

Diagnostic cases are considered as the combination of different single events. Each event is described by an *information entity (IE)*, while a case is a chain of such information entities. An IE may be used to describe a special symptom value, a special parameter of a device, a hypothesis about a fault, a trial of repair etc. They idea of IEs is to have atomic constituents of cases which may be compared for different cases. Cases may overlap in their components, hence a case base is thought of as a net with IE-nodes and case nodes, which we call a *Case Retrieval Net* ([6, 16]).

Basic Ideas IE-nodes are connected by weighted "similarity-arcs": An activated IE-node can propagate activity via these arcs to other IE-nodes (denoting similar events). Thus, an initial activation of some IE-nodes (which are relevant for a query) can be propagated through the net to other IE-nodes. After this process, the IE-nodes have some activity which depends on their similarity to the initially activated IE nodes.

IE-nodes are connected to case-nodes by weighted "relevance arcs", just as the cases are considered as collections of IEs. Thus, the activations of the IE-nodes can be further propagated to the case nodes. The resulting activation of case nodes is the measure for their similarity to the actual problem (query). Thus, CRNs meet the requirements from Section 2.2:

1. Any (reasonable) set of IEs may constitute a case, hence there are no fixed sets of symptoms.
2. Partial information (missing values) do not cause any problems to retrieval.
3. The concept of information entities is flexible enough to allow additional, not predefined events in a case description by simply adding new nodes to the net.
4. There is no formal difference between "problem" and "solution", all are described by IEs, and each of them may be activated in a query.
5. Case completion can be realized for any set of initially activated IEs: The spreading activation process selects those cases which are the nearest ones to the initial query. Then all additional IEs from these cases can be used to complete information.

A diagnostic case is considered as a set of IEs, and any subset can be used to retrieve the whole case (including the remaining IEs). For example it is not only possible to infer a malfunction of a car but also to ask for symptoms usually associated with a particular malfunction. There is no predefined distinction between "problem" and "solution". During a diagnosis process, some IEs are already known and the task is to come to a sufficient completion (including e.g. the diagnosis or a successful repair strategy). Using the case base, proposals for completion are inferred like suggestions for further tests or repair experiments.

The integration of background knowledge by CRNs is still under investigation: A concept is given by a set of IEs as a "vertical" collection, e.g. a set of IEs specifying the same attribute with similar values (all IEs for the attribute **time** with values around 7 **a.m.** form the concept "in the morning"). In contrast: cases are "horizontal" collections of IEs usually specifying different attributes. Using "concept arcs" (similar to the relevance arcs), a "concept-node" might be activated from a related IE-node (and vice versa, a concept node might activate its corresponding IE-nodes).

Then, on the level of concept nodes, we can implement rules by arcs between concept nodes (the rule "temperature is low in the morning" is implemented as an arc between the **in-the-morning**-node and the **temperature-is-low**-node. Then an activation of the **in-the-morning**-node causes an activation of the **temperature-is-low**-node which again may lead to further activations (of case-nodes at the end).

4 FALLDATEN-DL

Description logics (DL) have a long tradition in organizing information with a powerful representation scheme and clearly defined semantics. This semantic greatly enhances the explainability of the systems. Furthermore cases can automatically be indexed and retrieved by the inference services of a terminological reasoner. Additionally, one of the main application areas of terminological reasoners are information systems [4], and they provide a flexible query language that can be used for the retrieval of relevant data [7].

All this suggests the use of description logics for the case completion approach presented in Section 2.2 and attracted us to propose the use of description logics for CBR in [11]. Similar considerations led to the investigation of DL for CBR in [1, 14] and Information Retrieval (IR) [17]. All this systems have in common that they are only operating on *abstract domain*. But in order to fulfill the requirements of Section 2.2 and to bridge the gap to object-oriented CBR systems one needs in addition *concrete domains*.

4.1 Description Logics

Description logics systems mainly consist of two parts a so called TBox[8] containing terminological knowledge and an ABox[9] containing assertional knowledge[10]:

TBox At the core of description logics is the notion of *concept terms*. Starting with primitive concept and role terms, new concepts terms can be constructed from others by a set of concept forming operators. There are mainly three categories of such operators [8]:

- *Boolean operators* (and C_1 ...), (or C_1 ...), (not C_1)), allowing for the combination of concepts without a reference to their internal structure.
- *Role Forming operators* that allow new roles to be defined, e.g. composition of roles (compose $r_1 \circ r_2$).
- *Operators on Role Fillers* that operate on the internal structure of the concept terms, e.g. provide quantification over role fillers (some r C).

Terminological axioms in the form (define-concept C C) associate a concept name C with a concept term C and are used to define the relevant concepts of an application. Finally a *TBox* ($\mathcal{T}$) is a finite set of terminological axioms.

ABox Cases and other concrete objects are realised as instances of concepts. New instances o can be introduced into the ABox via (define-distinct-individual o), and assertions α concerning the membership of an instance o to a concept

---

[8] Terminological Box.

[9] Assertional Box.

[10] We can not elaborate on the basics of description logics and refer the reader to [2] for a more detailed introduction.

C , or about existing relations (functions) between two objects o_1 and o_2 can be made through (state (instance o C)) resp. (state (related o_1 o_2)). The set of assertions finally constitutes the ABox $\mathcal{A}$.

Thus, it is clear that the requirements 1 and 2 from Section 2.2 are fulfilled: Case representations are just arbitrary concepts and new concepts can easily be added in order to adapt to the evolution of the case representations.

4.2 Similarity Assessment

What distinguishes a description logic approach to CBR from pure object-oriented ones, is that one is able to formally define a model-theoretic semantics by means of an interpretation function $(^\mathcal{I})$. This semantics allows for a formal definition of a number of powerful inferences. In our context the following inference services are of particular interest:

Classification Classification is the most prominent TBox inference service. This done by calculating the *subsumption* hierarchy, i.e. the subconcept-superconcept relationship between concepts. Technically a concept C_1 subsumes another concept C_2 if each model for C_2 is also a model for C_1 (i.e. $C_1^\mathcal{I} \supseteq C_2^\mathcal{I}$).

Realization Realization is an ABox inference service that determines, given an object o of the ABox, the set of most specific concepts $\{C_1, \ldots, C_n\}$ that this object belongs to.

Retrieval The retrieval problem is dual to the realization problem. Here the set of Abox objects (instances) $\{o_1, \ldots, o_m\}$ are returned that fulfill a given concept C.

All this inference services can be reduced to the *consistency* problem of an ABox, that is testing if an Abox has a model ($\mathcal{A}^\mathcal{I} \neq \emptyset$) (see e.g. [3] for details). Further it can be shown that there exist sound and complete algorithms for certain description languages, especially for the language $\mathcal{ALCF}$[11], which we have chosen for our system[12]. It is clear that these inference services enable us to fulfill the requirements 3 and 4 of Section 2.2:

1. On one hand the query language is identical to the concept language, as arbitrary partial information can be given as a concept term and the *retrieval* service is used to deliver the objects (cases) that match the query. Furthermore match itself is not an exact match but uses the full inferential power of the underlying logic. This procedure is especially useful if one is using the system only for information and retrieval purposes and no new information is added (no new assertions are made)

---

[11] again we cannot go into detail, for a description of $\mathcal{ALCF}$ see [8].

[12] This constitutes a major difference to the approaches presented in [1] and [17]. Whereas the first uses LOOM which has a very expressive and undecidable language and therefore only incomplete inferences the question of decidability of the language behind the second systems still remains open, but is supposed to be undecidable.

2. On the other hand, if one wants to use the system in a more traditional CBR way, i.e. a new case should be solved by looking for similar cases and the new case is added to the case base, realization is better suited. It can be used for dynamically indexing the ABox objects with respect to the TBox. Existing objects o_j are indexed by their respective most specific concepts $I(o_j) = \{C_{j1}, \ldots, C_{jm_j}\}$. When new assertions are made the affected objects are automatically re-realized and hence reindexed. Realization can then be used to find the most specific concepts $I(o_k) = \{C_{k1}, \ldots, C_{km_k}\}$ for the new case. A simple, pure relational similarity measure retrieves the objects that are indexed under the same set of concepts, $\{o_l \mid I(o_l) = I(o_k)\}$. Obvious extensions to this similarity measure that deliver some ranking procedure are then the number of common subsets $\{o_l \mid I(o_l) \subseteq I(o_k)\}$, $sim(o_l, o_k) = \mid I(o_l) \cap I(o_k) \mid$, or some tree distance within the concept hierarchy.

4.3 Concrete Domains

The previous section more or less gave the general framework for a CBR system based on description logics. But in order to it in technical domains more expressive description languages are needed. In addition to the *abstract domain*, several *concrete domains* such as numbers, strings and symbols must be added to the language and the inference services of the description logic[13]. These are needed in order to give parameter values, names etc. Current terminological systems such as LOOM, CLASSIC, KRIS and TAXON more or less only realize a single concrete domain over numerical values [13]. A scheme for the integration of *admissible* concrete domains developed by Baader and Hanschke [3, 8] and used within KRIS and TAXON, theoretically allows for much more expressive concrete domains that still preserves the decidability of the resulting concept language $\mathcal{ALCF}(\mathcal{D})$, and hence there exist sound and complete algorithms for the above inference services.

Based on TAXON we developed CTL [13], a system where concrete domains are realized through a well-defined interface to external algorithms . Constraint Logic Programming (CLP) systems allow us to easily realize a whole range of concrete domains, e.g. over sets of symbols and numbers. In particular, we are able to handle systems of arbitrary linear polynomials. In the following we give a minimal example how this can be used to implement a system that enables us to represent and use some of the knowledge mentioned in Section 2.3.

4.4 A simple example

Knowledge about devices Lets suppose one wants to support a second-level support person responsible for mechanisms consisting of wheels or gearwheels such as bike drivetrains or clockworks. Since such mechanisms can consist of an arbitrary number and constellation of wheels, a representation based on an attribute-value vector as in help-desk applications is not possible.

---

[13] This requirement arises in other domains too, but in technical domains it is vital.

The first thing to do is to formally describe the different possible types of elements of such an mechanism. The usual way to do so in kinematics are links[14] (see Fig.1 1.): Links have in common that they carry a force. Further there is a special kind of link, a rotational-link that has two additional "slots" for the radius of the link and the torque. The force and the torque are greater or equal zero, the radius is strictly greater zero. The natural way of describing the kinematic

```
1.
(define-primitive-attribute link.force Top)
(define-primitive-concept link
  (and Top (some link.force (minimum 0))))

(define-primitive-attribute rot.radius Top)
(define-primitive-attribute rot.torque Top)
(define-constraint x>0 (?x) (?x > 0))
(define-constraint x>=0 (?x) (?x >= 0))
(define-primitive-concept rotational-link
  (and link (constrain rot.radius x>0)
            (constrain rot.torque x>=0)))
```

```
2.
(define-primitive-attribute pair.link1 top)
(define-primitive-attribute pair.link2 top)
(define-primitive-concept kinematic-pair
  (and (all pair.link1 link)
       (all pair.link2 link)))

(define-concept rot-pair
  (and kinematic-pair
       (all pair.link1 rotational-link)
       (all pair.link2 rotational-link)))
```

Fig. 1. Links and Pairs

structure of a device is via so called kinematic pairs. Only a few different types of "simple" kinematic pairs[15] exist [21]. Kinematic pairs consist of two links, a rotational pair is a pair where both links a rotational links (see Fig.1 2.).

This suffices to describe the "core ontological" properties of wheel mechanisms. In addition much more concepts could be defined e.g., gearwheels, wheels that come from a certain manufacturer etc.

Knowledge about mechanics/electromechanics In addition to this knowledge about different types of parts and the structure of the device, there is background knowledge. First there is knowledge about physical laws e.g., that the torque of a rotational link is the product of the radius and the force. To our knowledge there are only a few CBR systems that allow for the representation of such knowledge, and most of them do this by defining rules that compute the value of a certain attribute from the values of some others, i.e. the propagation of values is directed.

In contrast to that we utilize a full featured constraint system, allowing for undirected propagation. That allows us to redefine the definition of rotational-link (see Fig.2 1.).

This ensures that whenever two of the three attributes of a rotational link in the ABox are given, the third is calculated and used in further inferences. Furthermore there maybe some knowledge about the normal behavior (Fig.2 2.) and different faults (Fig.2 3.) that can occur. In our case a rotational pair can be OK, it can be broken or it is slipping.

---

[14] In this and the following code fragments we are using KRSS, a standard machine readable notation for description logics, which we extended by define-constraint a construct to define concrete domain predicates.

[15] A simple kinematic pair is a pair where the two links have a contact surface rather than a contact line or a single contact-point.

```
1.
(define-constraint x*y=z (?x ?y ?z) (?x * ?y = ?z))
(define-primitive-concept rotational-link
   (and link (constrain rot.radius x>0)
             (constrain rot.torque x>=0)
         (constrain rot.radius link.force rot.torque
                    x*y=z)))
2.
(define-constraint x=y (?x ?y) (?x = ?y))
(define-concept ok-rot-pair
   (and rot-pair
      (constrain (compose pair.link1 rot.torque)
                 (compose pair.link2 rot.torque)
                 x=y)))
```

```
3.
(define-concept slipping-rot-pair
   (and rot-pair
      (constrain (compose pair.link1 rot.torque) x>0)
      (constrain (compose pair.link2 rot.torque) x>0)
      (or (constrain (compose pair.link1 rot.torque)
                     (compose pair.link2 rot.torque) x>y)
          (constrain (compose pair.link2 rot.torque)
                     (compose pair.link1 rot.torque) x>y))))
(define-constraint x=0 (?x) (?x = 0))
(define-concept broken-rot-pair
   (and rot-pair (or
      (and (constrain (compose pair.link2 rot.torque) x>0)
           (constrain (compose pair.link1 rot.torque) x=0))
      (and (constrain (compose pair.link1 rot.torque) x>0)
           (constrain (compose pair.link2 rot.torque) x=0)))))
```

Fig. 2. Adding knowledge

Realization This TBox should be sufficient to give an example how realization works. We first introduce a kinematic pair and two rotational links (Fig.3 1.) and connect them (Fig.3 2.). This information is sufficient for the system to

```
1.
(define-distinct-individual rot-pair1)
(define-distinct-individual link1.1)
(define-distinct-individual link1.2)
3.
(state (related link1.2 8 link.force))
(state (related link1.2 3 rot.radius))
(state (related link1.1 0 rot.torque))
```

```
2.
(state (and
   (instance rot-pair1 kinematic-pair)
   (instance link1.2 rotational-link)
   (instance link1.1 rotational-link)
   (related rot-pair1 link1.1 pair.link1)
   (related rot-pair1 link1.2 pair.link2)))
```

Fig. 3. Realization

deduce that `rot-pair1` is a rot, and it is automatically realized and indexed under `rot-pair`. Giving the values of some parameters (Fig.3 3.) firstly leads to the deduction that the torque of `link1.2` is equal to 24 and secondly, since the value of the torque of `link1.1` is zero `rot-pair1` is automatically classified as a `broken-rot-pair`. Hence, the use of additional knowledge not only enables us to calculate additional parameter values, it also provides some kind of consistency-based diagnosis.

5 Outlook

Currently, research is performed in several directions: Within FALLEXPERTE-D diagnosis protocols are investigated from a computer net domain. Descriptions of background knowledge (taxonomies) are developed for that domain and evaluated using the protocols. The use of CRNs for case retrieval and for implementing concepts/rules, generic cases and effect nets is studied. Within FALLDATEN-DL interfaces to other CLP and IR systems for the realization of further concrete domains are investigated from a theoretical point (i.e. their admissibility) as well as from a practical point (i.e. how to actually interface the systems).

References

1. K. D. Ashley and V. Aleven. Using Logic to Reason with Cases. In *Topics in Case-Based Reasoning*, Berlin, 1994. Springer Verlag.
2. F. Baader, H. Bürckert, B. Hollunder, A. Laux, and W. Nutt. Terminologische Logiken. *KI*, (3):23–33, 1992.

3. F. Baader and P. Hanschke. A Scheme for Integrating Concrete Domains into Concept Languages. Research Report, DFKI, Kaiserslautern, Germany, Apr. 1991.

4. R. Brachman, D. MacGuiness, P. Patel-Schneider, L. Resnick, and A. Borgida. Living with Classic: when and How to Use a KL-ONE-like Language. In *Principles of Semantic Networks*. Morgan Kaufmann, 1991.

5. H.-D. Burkhard, R. Kühnel, and P. Pirk. Case-based Diagnosis in a Technical Domain. In *Artificial Intelligence and Information-Control Systems of Robots*. World Scientific Publishing, 1994.

6. H.-D. Burkhard and M. Lenz. Case Retrieval Nets: Basic Ideas and Extensions. In *Proc. 4th German Workshop on Case-Based Reasoning*, 1996.

7. P. Devanbu, R. Brachman, P. Selfridge, and B. Ballard. LaSSIE: a Knowledge-based Software Information System. In *Domain Analysis and Software Systems Modeling*, pages 150–162. IEEE Computer Society Press, 1991.

8. P. Hanschke. *A Declarative Integration of Terminological, Constraint-Based, Data-driven, and Goal-directed Reasoning*. Dissertation, Universität Kaiserslautern, 1993.

9. G. Kamp. AMS - A Case-Based Service Support System. In *Proc. of the 7th IEA/AIE conference*, pages 677–683, Austin, TX, 1994. Gordon and Breach.

10. G. Kamp. Integrating Semantic Structure and Technical Documentation in Case-Based Service Support Systems. In *Topics in Case-Based Reasoning*, Berlin, 1994. Springer Verlag.

11. G. Kamp. On the use of CBR in Corporate Service and Support. In *Proc. EWCBR'94*, pages 175–184. Acknosoft Press, 1994.

12. G. Kamp, B. Neumann, P. Pirk, and H.-D. Burkhard. Fallbasierte Diagnose für technische Systeme. Zwischenbericht an die DFG, 1994.

13. G. Kamp and H. Wache. CTL – a description logic with expressive concrete domains. Technical report, LKI, 1996.

14. J. Koehler. An Application of Terminological Logics to Case-based Reasoning. In *Proc. of KR94*, Bonn, Germany, 1994.

15. M. Lenz, E. Auriol, H.-D. Burkhard, and M. Manago. CBR for Diagnosis and Decision Support. *KI*, (1), 1996.

16. M. Lenz and H.-D. Burkhard. Case retrieval nets: Foundations, properties, implementation and results. Technical report, Humboldt-Universität, 1996.

17. C. Meghini, F. Sebastiani, U. Straccia, and C. Thanos. A Model of Information Retrieval based on a Terminological Logic. In *SIGIR93*, pages 298–307, Pittsburgh, PA, 1993. ACM Press.

18. A. Motro. VAGUE: A User Interface to Relational Databases that Permits Vague Queries. *ACM TOIS*, 6(3):187–214, July 1988.

19. P. Pirk. Konzept für eine fallbasierte Expertensystemkomponente zur Diagnose-unterstützung im technischen Bereich. Forschungsbericht, Humboldt-Universität Berlin, 1993.

20. F. Puppe. *Einführung in Expertensysteme*. Springer, 1991.

21. F. Reuleaux. *The Kinematics of machinery - outlines of a theory of machines*. Macmillan & Co, New York, NY, 1876.

22. M. M. Richter. The Knowledge Contained in Similarity Measures. ICCBR95.

23. S. Weß. Intelligente Systeme für den Customer-Support. *Wirtschaftsinformatik*, 38(1):23–31, 1996.

Integration of Prosodic and Grammatical Information in the Analysis of Dialogs*

Walter Kasper and Hans-Ulrich Krieger

DFKI GmbH
Stuhlsatzenhausweg 3
D-66123 Saarbrücken, Germany
{kasper,krieger}@dfki.uni-sb.de

Abstract. The analysis of spoken dialogs requires the analysis of complete multi-sentence turns. Especially, the segmentation of turns in sentential or phrasal segments is a problem. In this paper we present a system for turn analysis. It is based on an extension of HPSG grammar for turns and takes into account extra-linguistic prosodic information. We show how this information can be integrated and represented in the grammar, and how it is used to reduce the search space in parsing.

1 Introduction

A fundamental concept of Head-Driven Phrase Structure Grammar (HPSG; cf. [6, 7]) is the notion of a SIGN. A SIGN is a structure integrating information from all levels of linguistic analysis such as phonology, syntax and semantics. This structure also specifies interactions between these levels by means of coreferences which indicate the sharing of information and how the levels constrain each other mutually. Such a concept of linguistic description is attractive for several reasons:

- it supports the use of common formalisms and data structures on all levels of linguistics
- it provides declarative and reversible interface specifications between the levels
- all information is available simultaneously
- no procedural interaction between linguistic modules needs to be set up

Though the concept of SIGN is very general grammars developed in this framework usually only deal with morphological, syntactic and perhaps semantic information. Also, they are confined to the description of phrases not beyond the level of single sentences.

On the other hand, the VERBMOBIL project (cf. [13, 3]) deals with the translation of spoken dialogs. The basic unit of natural language dialogs is not a

---

* This work was funded by the German Federal Ministry of Education, Science, Research and Technology (BMBF) in the framework of the Verbmobil Project under Grant *01 IV 101 K/1*. Also, we have to thank the reviewers for valuable comments. The responsibility for the contents of this study lies with the authors.

sentence but a *turn* representing the complete contribution of a participant. *Turns* usually consist of more than one segment as they would be described in a sentence-based grammar. One fundamental problem in analyzing dialog turns is to segment them correctly into such smaller units as described in a grammar. Correct segmentation is not only crucial for the correct semantic and pragmatic interpretation but also for the efficiency of the parsing process in order to reduce the search space. We will call this the *segmentation problem*. In the case of written text punctuation marks help in segmentation. In spoken language there are no punctuation marks, and audible breaks in spoken utterances often do not correspond to sensible linguistic phrase boundaries. Such breaks can be coughs or they are due, e.g., to breathing, hesitation or corrections. On the other hand there are prosodic, intonational clues to support the linguistic segmentation task. But this requires that the linguistic analysis process is sensitive to such grammar-external information. In this paper we describe the integration of grammatical and prosodic information from the representational as well as the computational point of view. The approach can serve as a model for integrating linguistic and other types of non-linguistic information as well.

In the following we first give a survey of the underlying system architecture and the types of prosodic information used (*focus* and utterance *mood*). After that, an extension of a HPSG grammar of German suitable for the analysis of dialog turns is discussed. Then the two kinds of interaction between grammatical analysis and prosody are described: on the one hand, the integration of prosodic information constrains the parsing process, on the other hand the representation of prosodic events constrains the possible distribution of such events. But prosodic information or its detection is not always reliable: it might be missing at expected positions or come in at wrong positions. Therefore a recovery procedure for prosodic errors is presented to make the parsing process robust.

2   Architecture

The architecture of the linguistic components of the dialog translation system is shown in Figure 1. The parsing process is distributed on two parsers running in tandem. The first one is the parser for the word lattices coming from speech recognition, the other one is the constraint solver which also builds the semantic representation.[2] The word-lattice parser [14] uses the full HPSG grammar offline (viz., for training). At run time, only the context-free skeleton of the grammar is used. Because this set of rules overgenerates w.r.t. the original grammar, certain rule application are in fact not valid. Such applications are ruled out by the second parser.

Semantics construction (the so-called SEM-parser) is fed with hypotheses from the word-lattice parser and uses them to reconstruct deterministically the chart on the basis of the full grammar. This is possible by associating every lexicon entry and every rule with an identifier added at compile time and shared by

---

[2] The approach to distributed parsing with HPSG grammars is described in [1]. A full description of the system is given in [2].

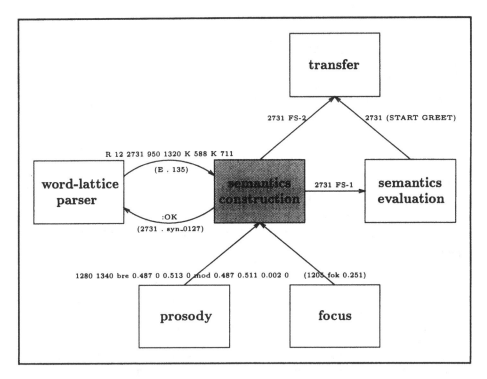

Fig. 1. *The overall architecture of our experiments. The semantics construction (SEM-parser) integrates different sources of information: (i) word/rule application hypotheses from the word-lattice parser, (ii) prosodic boundaries, and (iii) focus. Both prosodic boundaries and focus information are mapped onto word lattice hypotheses inside the SEM-parser as described in Section 5. Legal readings are further sent to semantics evaluation and transfer. The annotations at the arrows depict the different protocols between the components.*

both parsers. Because the search space is massively reduced by the word-lattice parser (approx. one order of magnitude less hypotheses), unification inside the SEM-parser is time-synchronous with the corresponding rule application inside the first parser.

This special architecture allows for efficient filtering of word hypotheses without giving up correctness of the analysis results which is guaranteed by the SEM-parser. Since lexicon entries and rules are identified by unique indexes, expensive communication via feature structures is avoided. In case that a rule application hypothesis fails under feature structure unification, a message is sent back to the word-lattice parser. This allows it to narrow down the set of emitted hypotheses.

The SEM-parser additionally receives hypotheses from two prosodic components. The one simply termed PROSODY is the detector for phrase boundaries and sentence mood as described in [12]. The other one is a detector for focus ([5]).

In VERBMOBIL three types of phrase boundaries are distinguished ([8]):

B2 "weak" phrase borders within intonational phrases
B3 "strong" intonational phrase border
B9 irregular phrase boundaries

Of these, the *B3* borders are the ones related to utterance mood and turn segmentation. Three types of moods are distinguished prosodically:

– progredient
– interrogative
– declarative (or rather "non-interrogative")

The PROSODY component transmits confidence values about the existence of a *B3* boundary together with confidence values about the mood. Similarly, the FOCUS components sends confidence values about focus events. Their use will be described in the following sections after a survey of the underlying HPSG grammar for turn analysis.

3 Codescriptive Grammars for Dialog Turns

The basic units of dialogs are not sentences but *turns*:

tut mir leid. am neunundzwanzigsten um drei habe ich schon eine Besprechung. am Dienstag den dreißigsten um drei, das ginge bei mir.
(I am sorry. On the 29th at 3 I already have a meeting. Thursday the 30th at 3, that would be fine)

Turns usually consist of more than one of what we call a *turn segment*. In the example the most likely segmentation is indicated by punctuation marks. Turn segments need not be complete sentences but can be sequences of nearly any kind of phrase:

also. am Montag. um wieviel Uhr denn dann?
(OK. On monday. At what time then?)

In spoken turns the punctuation marks of course are missing, and the fact that any kind of linguistic category can also be a turn segment, that is, a "complete" utterance in itself, makes segmentation on purely linguistic grounds a highly ambiguous task. A grammar provides only weak constraints on utterances such as

– subcategorization: verbs or prepositions require the presence of certain complements
– verb-end constructions in German (e.g., subordinate clauses) mark the end of a turn segment

On the other hand, a turn like *am montag kommt er* without any further clues can be understood as consisting of one declarative sentence but also as consisting of an elliptical prepositional phrase followed by an interrogative sentence.

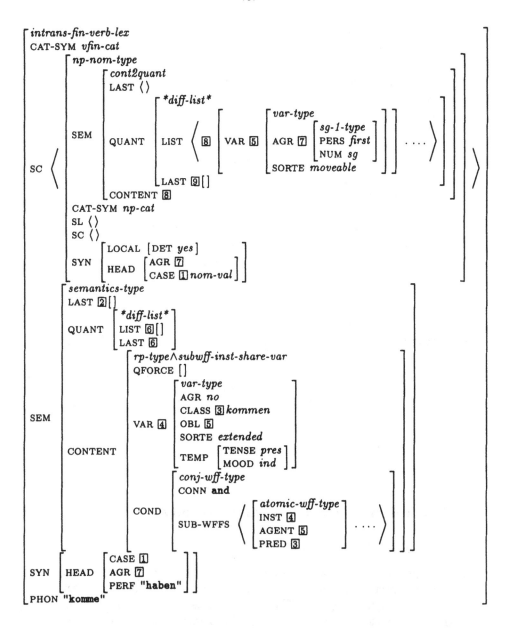

Fig. 2. *Lexical entry for the verb* komme *containing its syntactic and semantic properties simultaneously.*

In the VERBMOBIL project we use an HPSG grammar described in the typed feature formalism $\mathcal{TDL}$ (cf. [4]) for the analysis of dialog turns. It is a codescriptive grammar specifying simultaneously syntax and semantics. As an example, Figure 2 shows a lexicon entry of a verb with its syntactic subcategorization frame and predicate-argument-structure. In order to deal with turns consisting of several segments the HPSG approach had to be extended especially in order to deal with the semantic composition of the turn segments. Also non-linguistic events in a dialog turn, e.g. pauses and coughs required a treatment in the grammar. The additional rules for turns do not simply concatenate turn segments but impose an intermediate structure on turns between phrasal turn segments and complete turns in order to deal among other things with special properties of the *uptake* phase at the beginning of a turn, with interruptions, linguistic "garbage" and echo phrases. Semantically, turns are represented by a linear conjunction of the semantical representations of the turn segments which is passed to semantic evaluation for further processing, such as reference resolution and dialog act identification with respect to the dialog model.

Other extensions of the approach were required to capture information from prosody, especially information about the *mood* of an utterance and about focussed phrases.

The main problem for such a turn-based grammar is the problem of segmenting a turn into the correct turn segments. As indicated above, linguistic constraints are very weak and not sufficient. On the other hand, spoken language contains clues about segmentation. There is a significant prosodic difference when *on monday he will come* is uttered as one statement or a sequence of two segments each expressing a different speech act.

Taking into account such prosodic clues for turn segmentation is not only important for a correct grammatical analysis but also for the efficiency of the analysis process itself. Experiments showed that correct segmentation reduces the search space for the parser up to 70% by eliminating the segmentation ambiguities which give rise to different readings.

4   Integration of Grammar and Prosody

4.1   Typed Interfaces for Mood and Focus

Since the prosodic information especially about mood and focus is relevant for semantic interpretation it must be incorporated into the semantic representation built up in the parsing process. The use of a typed feature formalism allows an elegant and flexible solution to this task. We associate a type as shown below with each kind of prosodic event:

```
;;; types for representing prosodic mood

prosodic-decl-type := prosodic-b3-mood-type &
                        [ PRAG.PMOOD deklarativ-s ].


prosodic-frage-type := prosodic-b3-mood-type &
                        [ PRAG.PMOOD frage-s ].
```

```
;;; type for marking the focussed word

phon-focus-mark-type := [ PHON #focus,
                          SEM.CONTENT.VAR.FOCAL #focus ].
```

When a prosodic event occurs the associated type is unified with the feature structures for the word hypotheses which include the time of the prosodic event. This approach yields a typed interface between grammar and prosody with the following advantages:

- *Flexibility:* it is easy to modify the representation of mood since it is sufficient to change the type definition
- *Constraint Interaction:* it allows the grammar to use the prosodic information in a straightforward way as additional constraints which might interact with other constraints such as syntactic sentence mood. Constraints on prosodic events are discussed below (sections 4.2 and 4.3)
- *Reversibility:* the grammar can constrain the kind and loci of prosodic events. This is important in generating spoken language.

4.2 Constraining Prosodic Mood

The information about prosodic mood is first incorporated at the lexical level into the feature structure by unification. This means it fills the value of PMOOD (for *prosodic mood*) in the PRAGmatics substructure of the linguistic SIGN. Since the mood is not a property of the word but rather of the turn segment which is terminated by that word it is projected to the turn segment level along the right edge of the derivation tree for the segment. We call this the *prosodic-mood-principle* which is inherited by each rule schema:

```
prosodic-mood-principle := [ PRAG.PMOOD #pmood ]
                           -->
                           < ..., [ PRAG.PMOOD #pmood ] >.
```

The principle ensures that each turn segment can be marked for prosodic mood at most once. This predicts that between two *B3* hypotheses there must be a segment boundary.[3] In this way, the prosodic-mood-principle supports turn segmentation independently of the parser. It is important to note that the principle is not in conflict with the delay strategies the parser employs for reducing its search space on prosodic events (see section 5), especially not with its recover strategy: since the mood information is projected *only* along the right edge of the tree, the recognition of a prosodic boundary at a position which syntactically cannot be a segment boundary (e.g. between a preposition and its object) will do no harm as the prosodic information will be kept local in the word but will not be projected to higher phrasal levels.

---

[3] Of course, this presupposes the reliability of the detector.

4.3 Focus

Focus in spoken language serves to mark phrases by stress. Focus is not only important semantically as being associated with certain semantic operators ([10, 9]) but has also important discourse functions by highlighting on important parts of the utterance. Also, for translation from German to English the focus position can make all the difference as in the following example:

> Lassen Sie uns *noch* einen Termin ausmachen
> (= Let's arrange another appointment)
>
> Lassen Sie uns noch einen *Termin* ausmachen
> (= Let us arrange an appointment, too)

The hypotheses from focus detection are incorporated into the lexical structure of the word by unification with the **phon-focus-mark-type**. This type marks the focussed word on the semantic index (the **SEM.CONTENT.VAR** structure) of the complete phrase. This expresses a strong constraint on possible focus distribution because this semantic index is global for the maximal projection line. The constraint allows that a turn segment carries more than one focus (as actually happens). But, within a maximal phrase, though any word can be the focussed one there cannot be more than one, as illustrated in the following example:

- *this* small man
- this small *man*
- * *this* small *man*

The data from VERBMOBIL dialogs show no violation of these principles.

Figure 3 shows the results of integrating the prosodic information in the first segment of the turn

> das ist *schlecht* . wie wär's am Dienstag.
> (= That's bad. How about tuesday?)

where the word *schlecht* was focussed and also correctly recognized as segment boundary. This is marked in the representation of the verbal head's **INSTance** structure in the features **FOCAL** and **PRAG.PMOOD**. If the focus had been on *that* the focus marker would have occurred on the index-**VAR** of the first element on the **QUANTifier** list being the representation of *that*.

5 Rule Selection in the Parser

Information about utterance boundaries and focus is not only represented in the semantic analysis but also employed within the SEM-parser to reduce the space of possible rule applications. Mapping parsing hypotheses onto prosodic information is achieved by means of the signal time which is available to all modules. This is depicted in Figure 4. Information about *B3* boundaries is used inside the parser to rule out certain rule application. This is achieved by telling the

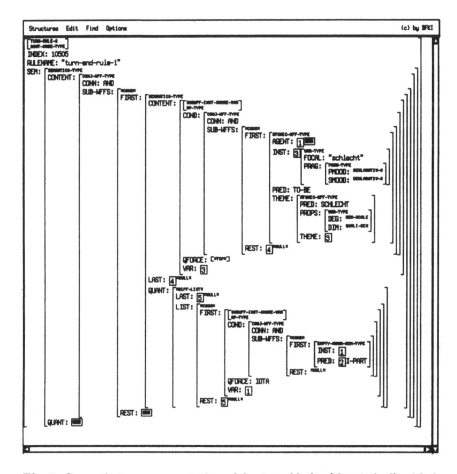

Fig. 3. *Semantic turn representation of* das ist schlecht *(that is bad) with focus on* schlecht *and mood information.*

parser which rules are segment-connecting and which are only segment-internal. Clearly, segment-connecting rules enforce a *B3* boundary between segments— actually between the last lexical chart edge of one segment and the first lexical edge of the following segment. The opposite case holds for the segment-internal rules: here, no *B3* boundary is allowed inside a chart edge which originates from such a rule application. As already mentioned, such constraints heavily reduce the number of possible readings of an utterance up to 70%. This increases parsing efficiency considerably (smaller chart, less unification/copying), but also non-valid readings are ruled out thereby.

6 Robustness

Unfortunately, the prosodic data are not as reliable as the selection mechanism described above presupposes. The recoginition rate for the boundaries is about

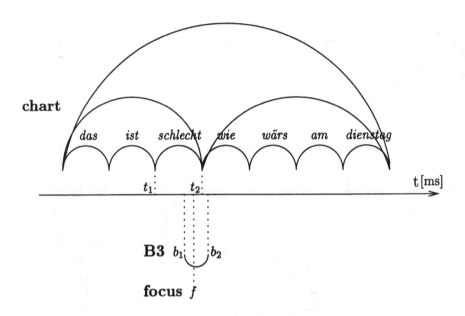

Fig. 4. *Mapping B3 and focus information onto lexical chart edges. B3 bound-aries are given in terms of time intervals which must satisfy the constraint $t_1 \leq b_1 \leq t_2$ with respect to the lexical item's time interval $[t_1, t_2]$. The fo-cus is specified via a time point for which the constraint $t_1 \leq f \leq t_2$ must hold. Both B3 and focus are associated with confidence values which must be above a threshold. In our case,* schlecht *both bears the segment boundary as well as the focus.*

86% ([11]). So, often segment boundaries are not detected and therefore missing and sometimes the position is excluded on syntactic grounds. Therefore, the system must be robust enough to handle such situations of missing or misplaced boundary information.

One mechanism for protecting the parser against wrong prosodic information is the use of thresholds. *B3* and focus information carry a confidence value be-tween 0 and 1, expressing the (un)certainty of the data. There are different values for the mood information, that is, for progredient, interrogative, and declarative mood. The SEM-parser accepts a *B3* boundary value only if the confidence is above a certain threshold (and not merely above 0.5, i.e., greater than non-*B3*). One can further refine the thresholds additionally for the separate moods. On-ly if both thresholds are surpassed, the mood information is included into the corresponding lexical edges. The same holds for the focus information.

But this mechanism alone cannot prevent that prosody postulates an utter-ance boundary at a wrong position. In such a situation, the selection mechanism for rules would not allow that segment-internal rules are applied here. Clearly, this might lead to unwanted readings or even make an analysis impossible.

In order to deal with such situations we designed a dynamic recovery mechanism which allows to reuse previously excluded hypotheses. Instead of removing them completely from the agenda, their application is only delayed. Delayed hypotheses originate in different situations:

1. *Lexical hypotheses.* For lexical items for which prosodic information exists a copy of the original edge is added to the set of delayed hypotheses.
2. *Rule hypotheses.* Segment-connecting/segment-internal rule hypotheses which are excluded on prosodic grounds are also added to that set of delayed hypotheses.
3. *Missing hypotheses.* Rule hypotheses which depend on delayed/excluded edges must also be delayed.

Delayed hypotheses are applied only when the agenda of "legal" edges is empty and has not led to an analysis.

7 Conclusion

The VERBMOBIL project deals with translation of spoken dialogs. This requires the linguistic analysis components to be capable to deal with complete turns in a dialog because there are no obvious sentence boundaries in spoken language as in written language. Also, they must be capable to take into account extra-linguistic information from the speech signal. In this paper we presented an approach to solve these problems. We suggested an extension of sentence grammars to the turn-level. We showed how in a typed feature formalism such as *TDL* extra-linguistic information from prosody can be integrated elegantly with linguistic information embodied in the HPSG grammar. We also showed how the grammar can exploit this information as additional constraints. Additionally, we described how the parser itself can exploit the extra-linguistic information to reduce its search space in a robust manner, and so improve the parsing efficiency. The methods developed have the potential for application in other areas as well.

References

1. Walter Kasper, Hans-Ulrich Krieger, and Abdel Kader Diagne. Distributed parsing with HPSG grammars. In *Proceedings of the 4th International Workshop on Parsing Technologies, IWPT-95*, pages 79–86, Prag, 1995.
2. Walter Kasper, Hans-Ulrich Krieger, Jörg Spilker, and Hans Weber. From word hypotheses to logical form: An efficient interleaved approach. In *Proceedings of KONVENS '96*, Bielefeld, 1996.
3. Martin Kay, Jean Mark Gawron, and Peter Norvig. *Verbmobil. A Translation System for Face-to-Face Dialog*, volume 33 of *CSLI Lecture Notes*. Chicago University Press, 1994.
4. Hans-Ulrich Krieger and Ulrich Schäfer. *TDL*—a type description language for constraint-based grammars. In *Proceedings of the 15th International Conference on Computational Linguistics, COLING-94, Kyoto, Japan*, pages 893–899, 1994.

5. Anja Petzold. Strategies for focal accent detection in spontanous speech. In *Proc. of the 13th ICPhS*, pages 672–675, 1995.

6. Carl Pollard and Ivan A. Sag. *Information-Based Syntax and Semantics*. Vol. 1: Fundamentals, volume 13 of *CSLI Lecture Notes*. Stanford: CSLI, 1987.

7. Carl Pollard and Ivan A. Sag. *Head-Driven Phrase Structure Grammar*. Chicago: University of Chicago Press, 1994.

8. Matthias Reyelt. Ein System zur prosodischen Etikettierung von Spontansprache. Verbmobil-Report 86, TU Braunschweig, 7 1995.

9. Mats Rooth. A theory of focus interpretations. *Natural Language Semantics*, 1:75–116, 1992.

10. Mats E. Rooth. *Association with Focus*. PhD thesis, University of Massachusetts, 1985.

11. Volker Strom. Die Prosodiekomponente in NTARC I.2: Satzmodusbestimmung aus der F0. Verbmobil:Technisches Dokument 6, IKP Universität Bonn, 1994.

12. Volker Strom. Detection of accents, phrase boundaries and sentence modality in German with prosodic features. In *Eurospeech 1995*, pages 2039–2041, 1995.

13. Wolfgang Wahlster. Verbmobil: Übersetzung von Verhandlungsdialogen. Verbmobil-Report 1, DFKI, Saarbrücken, 1993.

14. Hans Weber. *LR-inkrementelles, probabilistisches Chartparsing von Worthypothesenmengen mit Unifikationsgrammatiken: Eine enge Kopplung von Suche und Analyse*. PhD thesis, Universität Hamburg, Department of Computer Science, 1995.

Application of a Genetic Algorithm for Plausible Justification of Observations

M.A. Kłopotek, S.T. Wierzchoń, M. Michalewicz

Institute of Computer Science
Polish Academy of Sciences
01-237 Warszawa, ul Ordona 21, Poland
e-mail: klopotek,stw,michalew@ipipan.waw.pl

1 Introduction

The idea of graphical expert systems was initiated by Pearl [5]) and worked-out by Lauritzen and Spiegelhalter [2]. Its generalization to different uncertainty formalisms was proposed by Shafer, Shenoy and Mellouli [6] and refined to the form of so-called Valuation-Based Systems by Shenoy [7]. Under probabilistic context the knowledge about interrelationships among variables from a fixed set X* is represented on the qualitative level by a directed graph G = (X*,E*) and on the quantitative level by a set of conditional probabilities $p(x|Pa(x))$ where $Pa(x)$ stands for the set of parents of x in the graph G. Now, the joint probability distribution can be represented as the product of all the probabilities $p(x|Pa(x))$.

Finding the k Most Plausible Explanation (MPE) of a given evidence S_e in a Bayesian belief network means an optimization problem to identify a set of composite hypotheses H, which will yield the k largest $P(H|S_e)$ where a composite hypothesis is an instantiation of all the nodes in the network except the evidence nodes [9]. Partial ordering of the most probable composite hypotheses is important in several application domains like diagnosis, prognosis evaluation, assessment of certain design methodologies [9]. The problem of finding total order of composite hypotheses is NP-hard [4] as is the problem of finding several most probable hypotheses [1]. Previously two general approaches were proposed to handle the complexity of the task. One is to restrict the type of network to be dealt with such as single connected networks [9], or bipartite graph[10]. Another approach is to shift the complexity to spatial domain [8, 6]. Algorithms have been also elaborated for the special task of finding only the first one or two most probable explanation [5]. Methods developed for singly connected networks fail for multiply connected networks. One possible way out of this problem is to create compound variables (combine several variables into one) in order to obtain a singly connected graph [5]. However, the computational load of processing the compound variable is exponentially increased. One can also transform a Bayesian network into a hypertree, but this process has exponential time complexity. Hyperedges in a hypertree may behave similarly to compound variables.

This paper proposes still another, "genetic" solution method of this problem within the general framework of Valuation Based Systems of Shenoy [7]. A genetic algorithm has been elaborated for solving k-MPE problem working "inductively": After discovering a configuration solving the (k-1)-MPE-problem, the solutions for 1-, 2-, ..., $k-1$-MPE problems are blocked and the same algorithm finds the solution of $k - MPE$. Both the probabilistic case and case of Dempster-Shafer Theory of Evidence have been investigated.

2 Genetic Algorithm for Finding MPE.

Following e.g. [3] we define general genetic algorithm as a kind of a probabilistic algorithm which maintains a population of individuals $P(t) = \{x_1^t, x_2^t, ..., x_n^t\}$ for iteration t. Each individual represents a potential solution to the problem at hand, and, in any genetic program, is implemented as some data structure S. Each solution $x_i(t)$ is evaluated to give some measure of "fitness". Then, a new population - iteration $(t+1)$ - is formed by selecting the more fit individuals. Some members of the new population are recombined, i.e., transformed by means of two "genetic" operators to a new form. These operators are: (1) the unary mutation operator that create new individuals by a small changes in a single individual, and (2) the n-ary, where $n \geq 2$, crossover operator, which creates new individual by combining parts on the n individuals. After some number of iterations the program converges, and the best individual represents the optimum solution.

This idea quite interestingly translates into a program for finding most probable explanations both in probabilistic and generalized, Dempster-Shafer, case. Below we present details concerning the implementation.

2.1 Probabilistic Case

Here the situation is quite simple. The aim is to find such a configuration $\theta^* = \{\theta_1^*, \theta_2^*, ..., \theta_*\}$ that

$$p(x_1 = \theta_1^*, x_2 = \theta_2^*, ..., x_m = \theta_m^*) = \max_{\theta \in \Theta} \prod_{i=1}^{k} p(x_i = \theta_i | Pa(x_i) = \theta(Pa(x_i))$$

where $\theta(Pa(x_i)$ stands for the projection of the configuration θ onto the set of variables $Pa(x_i)$. Hence as an individual we take simply a vector $x = \theta$, where each member θ_i of θ takes its values from the domain of the variable x_i. Hence we depart from the "standard" binary representation of the individuals. This however fastens computations.

The mutation and crossover operators are implemented in almost standard way. There is a nuance, however. Frequently we ask for an MPE already knowing values of some variables. If C stands for the set of clamped variables, then, after the recombination phase the values at positions corresponding to the variables form the C must remain unchanged. There is a number of strategies to attain this goal. But in our implementation we used the next one. In case of mutation denote p_m the probability of mutation. Then for each element of the individual x and such that it does not correspond to a variable from the C we generate a random real number r from the unit interval. If $r < p_m$ we replace this element by another from the domain of the corresponding variable. The crossover is obvious also, that is we choose two parent individuals and the crossing point, and finally we replace the parents by a pair of their offsprings.

The fitness of each individual is computed by means of the maximized function $p(\cdot)$. The values of a conditional probability $P(x_i | Pa(x_i))$ are stored in the structure *universe* defined below

```
universe = record
variables: SetOfVariables; (*i.e. variables = {X_i ∪ Pa(X_i)}*)
```

```
card: byte; (*cardinality of the set variables *)
valuations: array [1..k] of real; end;
```

In our implementation we assume that the variables are numbered consecutively from 1 to *variables* (number of variables). Further the variables stored in the field *variables* are written in the next order: first is given he conditioned variable and next the conditioning variables.

Assuming that the domains of all the variables are stored in the table referred to as *domains* and that individuals are represented as arrays called *config* the value of the conditional probability $P(x_i|Pa(x_i))$ for a given individual x are computed by means of the next function

```
Function FindValuation(x: config; sp: universe): real;
var j,position,size: integer;
begin
    with sp do
    begin
        position := x[variables[card]];
        size := domains[variables[card]];
        for j:= card-1 downto 1 do
        begin
            position := position + size*(x[variables[j]]-1);
            size := size*domains[variables[j]];
        end;
        FindValuation := valuations[position];
    end;
end; {FindValuation}
```

The set of all universes is stored in the array referred to as *universes*. Now it is easy to write down the function that computes fitness of an individual x. Besides the already mentioned function FindValuation we need a boolean function Blocked. It is needed when we compute k-MPE. That is a solution to an i-MPE problem, $i < k$, is removed on a stack of blocked configurations. Now, looking for the k-th explanation we check is the individual x belongs to this stack. If so, we mark it as blocked and we search for another individual.

2.2   Case of Dempster-Shafer Calculus

Extension of this approach to Dempster-Shafer theory of evidence is not straightforward. Valuations are not defined exclusively for elements of Θ, but rather for elements of the power set of Θ. Observed variables do not need to be clamped to a single value, but they can represent a set of values. There is the problem which configuration evaluation function to optimize: mass, belief, plausibility or the commonality function. They represent various aspects of partial ignorance of reasoner's knowledge and impose differing complexity burdens. E.g. if $f(x) = (\bigoplus_i Bel_i)(x)$ should be target function, then in general f(x) is not a function of $Bel_1(x)$, $Bel_2(x)$, ... because of Dempster rule of evidence combination. One needs to decide how to understand a justifying configuration we are looking for: as a cross product of singleton values of all the variables, as a cross product of subsets of domains of all variables, or as a subset of the cross product of all the domains of all variables. Should we seek optimal non-singleton configurations while maximizing the commonality function then for every non-singleton configuration C, any configuration $C' \subset C$ is at least as optimal as C.

In our approach we made the following assumptions: First we decided that we want to find k most optimal singleton configurations. We just understand that the belief function represents an imprecise information on some singleton configurations. We assumed that we want to find most plausible configurations that is ones that cannot be rejected. Just we find an explanation good if it is hard to prove it wrong rather then being easy to be proved right. These two choices greatly simplified our task. One can prove that then the following target function gets its maximum at the configuration solving the k-MPE problem:

$$f(\underline{x}) = (\bigoplus_{i=1}^{n} Q_i)(\underline{x}) = \prod_{i=1}^{n} Q_i(\underline{x}^{\downarrow Space(Q_i)})$$

($Space(Q_i)$ - the set of variables for which Q_i is defined) subject to constraints that (1) the set of observed variables E has values restricted to the observed sets of values (2) when we are looking for ith most probable solution, we punish f() so that f($\underline{x}$)=0 whenever $\underline{x}$ is one of already found 1st,2nd, (i-1)st most probable configurations configurations.

The configurations are represented and evaluated essentially in the same way as in probabilistic case. The genetic algorithm differs in that mutation and crossover operators keep values of observed ("clamped") variables within the observed value sets (rather than restricting them to a single value). That is mutation is not forbidden at clamped variables but rather the scope of mutation is restricted to the subset of the values of the given variable.

Notice that in probabilistic case f() was in fact the sought ith most probable configuration probability itself, but in DST case f() is only proportional to the sought ith most plausible configuration plausibility.

References

1. G. Cooper: The computational complexity of probabilistic inference using Bayesian belief networks. *Artif.Intell.* **42**, 1990, 395-405
2. S.L. Lauritzen, D.J. Spiegelhalter: Local computation with probabilities on graphical structures and their application to expert systems. *J. Roy. Stat. Soc.*, 1988, B50: 157-244.
3. Z. Michalewicz: *Genetic Algorithm + Data Structure = Evolution Program* . Springer-Verlag, Berlin, 1994.
4. N.Pal, J.Bezdek, R.Hemanisha: Uncertainty measures for evidential reasoning I: a review. *Int. J.Approx. Reasoning* **7**(3/4), 1992, 162-183.
5. J. Pearl: *Reasoning in intelligent Systems: Networks of Plausible Inference*, Morgan Kaufmann Publishers, 1988.
6. G. Shafer, P.P. Shenoy, K. Mellouli: Propagating belief functions in qualitative Markov trees. *Int. J. of Approx. Reasoning* **1**, 1987 ,349-400
7. P.P. Shenoy: Conditional independence in valuation-based systems. *Int. J. of Approx. Reasoning*, **10**, 1994, 203-234.
8. S.E. Shimony, E. Charniak: A new algorithm for finding MAP assignments to belief networks. *Proc. Conference on Uncertainty in AI*, Cambridge, MA,, 1990 98-103.
9. B.K.Sy: A recurrence local computation approach towards ordering composite beliefs in Bayesian belief networks, *Internat. J. of Approx. Reasoning* **9**, 1993, 17-49
10. T.Wu: A problem decomposition method for efficient diagnosis and interpretation of multiple disorders, *Proc. 114th. Symp.Computer Appl. in Medical Care*, 1990, 86-92.

Managing Multiple Contexts Efficiently

Gerhard K. Kraetzschmar[1] and Josef Schneeberger[2]

[1] University of Ulm, Neural Information Processing Department,
Oberer Eselsberg, 89069 Ulm, Germany, Net: gkk@neuro.informatik.uni-ulm.de
[2] FORWISS, Knowledge Acquisition Research Group,
Am Weichselgarten 7, 91058 Erlangen, Germany, Net: jws@forwiss.uni-erlangen.de

Abstract. Assumption-based reasoning – using an ATMS – suffers from severe performance problems when the number of assumptions becomes very large. This is due to the exponential growth of ATMS labels. We suggest a new approach (FRMS) that avoids this problem by extending the RMS with context management functionality. This gives the problem solver explicit control over the contexts it actually needs.
Keywords: Reasoning. Planning. Agents and Multiagent Systems.
Type of Contribution: Poster.

1 Introduction

Assumption-based reasoning is required in many domains, such as planning, scheduling, and diagnosis. In planning, for example, we reason about the effects of actions, events, and future states of the world. The theory of action implemented by the planner imposes dependencies on events and world states. An example for assumption-based reasoning is then to determine the effects after executing a certain sequence of actions in a particular world state [BLS92, BKS94].

We consider propositional assumption-based reasoning problems [dK86]. A problem solving agent has to maintain a set of data (beliefs). A given domain theory defines dependencies (justifications) between beliefs. By making an assumption the problem solver assumes a proposition to hold without necessarily having a justification for it. Assumption-based reasoning is then the problem of determining the consequences of a particular set of assumptions (environment), i.e. to decide whether a proposition is the logical consequence of (or can be derived from) the assumptions. We call this problem the *consequence decision problem*. The other problem to be solved (*context determination problem*) is to determine the set of all such consequences, i.e. the *context* of the environment.

Assumption-based reasoning can be isolated in a separat utility (Fig. 1) called reason maintenance system (RMS). An RMS module has an internal state, which incorporates a representation of the assumption-based reasoning problem that has been supplied by the problem solver so far. The problem solver can efficiently retrieve information about the assumption-based reasoning problem by using functions from the RMSs logical query interface; in particular, the RMS can decide the consequence decision and context determination problems.

Although our concerns are multiagent systems requiring *distributed* reason maintenance [Kra96], we focus on *monotonic, multiple-context, assumption-based*

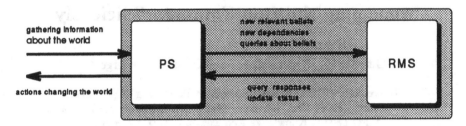

Fig. 1. Architecture of a RMS-based problem solving agent.

reason maintenance here. The ATMS [dK86] is the standard system for multiple-context reason maintenance. However, it suffers from severe performance problems, if the number of assumptions becomes very large [Gei94]. We present FRMS, a new system that provides the same basic functionality as the basic ATMS, but avoids its performance problems.

The ATMS uses a dependency net consisting of two kinds of nodes: propositions and justifications. The proposition nodes carry labels that are a compact representation of the derivability of the proposition. A label is a set of all minimal environments that allow to derive that proposition. The structure of the ATMS label is the reason for the performance problems. As the number of assumptions grows linearly, the number of possible environments can grow exponentially. For many standard applications the ATMS is *likely* to actually construct and represent a large number of environments, with dramatic effects on space and time. The problem to be solved here is how to manage efficiently multiple contexts for large numbers of assumptions, while retaining as much functionality from the ATMS as possible.

2 Solution Approach

Since the ATMS does not know which contexts the problem solver is interested in, it implicitly assumes *all* contexts interesting. Since our FRMS is capable to store and retrieve information about *relevant* contexts, it must perform context management. The FRMS can exploit the knowledge about interesting contexts to provide its services more efficiently. We use a simpler label data structure and a more efficient label propagation procedure. In particular, the effort needed for label propagation does no longer depend on the number of assumptions.

To the problem solver, the FRMS provides the same functionality as a basic ATMS. In addition, there are interface functions the problem solver can use to declare certain environments as interesting. Usually, this will be done by the problem solver automatically when its search procedure decides to investigate a particular partial solution. An answer will be provided very quickly, if an environment has previously been declared interesting. Note, that the FRMS can still answer *all* queries that an ATMS may answer; the problem solver only needs to declare an environment as relevant first. However, the total effort needed to store problem solver data and to answer its queries will be significantly less for

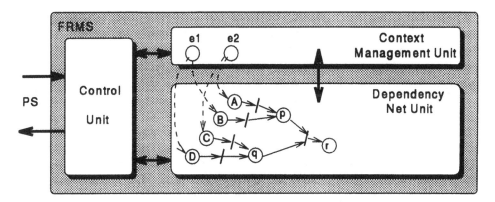

Fig. 2. Architecture of an FRMS module.

an FRMS than for an ATMS, unless the problem solver actually investigates a very large portion of all contexts.

The *specification of the FRMS*[3] consist of three parts: i) the definition of the logical state, ii) the state change (update) functions, and iii) the query functions. The state is a concise representation of the assumption-based reasoning problem provided by the problem solver. The update functions allow to modify the state, i.e. the problem solver can add propositions, assumptions, environments, and justifications. The logical query functions (holds-in, context) allow to access the partial representation of the derivability relation. holds-in checks whether a formula ϕ is consistently derivable in the environment e. context simply returns (for environment e) all relevant propositions ϕ which holds-in e.

An *FRMS module* (Fig. 2) consist of three units: i) The dependency net unit stores nodes (representing propositions) and justifications. ii) The context management unit provides the functionality to manage environments. iii) The control unit for communication with the problem solver. The FRMS uses various flags and labels for compact storage of information necessary to provide the FRMS services. In particulare, the label *Elab* of a proposition node p is just a subset of environments where p holds-in. In order to correctly represent the assumption-based reasoning problem specified by the problem solver, certain integrity constraints must hold for labels and flags [KS96].

As we claim the FRMS to be significantly more efficient than the ATMS, especially for large numbers of assumptions, a look at space and runtime complexity is in order. Let us look at space first. The overall space needed by the context management unit is limited by the upper bound $card(Environments) \times 2 \times card(Propositions)$. The total space required by the dependency net is bounded by $card(Propositions) \times ((2 \times card(Justifications)) + card(Environments))$. Hence, the *total space requirements grow at most polynomially with the number of relevant propositions, assumptions, justifications, and environments*. As the number of propositions increases, the number of *possible* environments grows

---

[3] A more detailled and formal specification is given in the long paper [KS96]

exponentially. Just as no practical problem solver will ever need to represent an exponential number of justifications, we also believe that it will never actually investigate an exponential number of environments. *The basic difference between the FRMS and the ATMS is that the FRMS makes this fact explicit and provides the necessary functionality to exploit it.*

Now let us look at runtime requirements. The function holds-in requires a simple element test with linear runtime and context can be done in constant time. The time required for the update functions is also neglectible except when *Elab* label propagation is involved (add-justification, add-environment). At the worst, all environments are added to the *Elab* labels of all proposition nodes. In general, the incremental label can only decrease in size and propagation stops as soon as the remaining increment is empty. Thus, the runtime of label propagation depends at most polynomially on the size of the FRMS state components.

3 Conclusions

The FRMS solves the problem of reasoning efficiently with multiple contexts and large numbers of assumptions. It achieves this efficieny by requiring the problem solver to explicitly specify the environments it is interested in. The additional information the FRMS possesses in comparison to an ATMS is the key for fast query and update functions, compact labels and efficient propagation procedures. The first author has extended the FRMS ideas to distributed reason maintenance problems [Kra96] and developed the system MXFRMS. We are currently most interested in applying this new family of reason maintenance systems to the domain of (multiagent and distributed) planning and scheduling; in particular, we are engaged in building flexible plan and schedule management systems using this technology.

References

[BKS94] C. Beckstein, G. K. Kraetzschmar, and J. Schneeberger. Distributed Plan Maintenance for Scheduling and Execution. In C. Bäckström and E. Sandewall, editors, *Current Trends in AI Planning*. IOS Press, 1994.

[BLS92] M. Beetz, M. Lindner, and J. Schneeberger. Temporal Projection for Hierarchical, Partial-Order Planning. In *Proc. of ISAI-92*. AAAI Press, 1992.

[dK86] J. de Kleer. An Assumption-based TMS. *Artificial Intelligence*, 28:127–224, 1986.

[Gei94] T. Geisler. Ein anwendungsunabhängiges Unterstützungssystem zum integrierten annahmenbasierten und temporalen Schließen. Master's thesis, University of Erlangen, February 1994.

[Kra96] G. K. Kraetzschmar. *Distributed Reason Maintenance*. PhD thesis, University of Erlangen, Erlangen, Germany, 1996.

[KS96] G. K. Kraetzschmar and J. Schneeberger. FRMS: A focus-based reason maintenance system. Available via http from: http://www.forwiss.uni-erlangen.de/~jws/papers/ki96-lv.ps, 1996.

Inductive Learning in Symbolic Domains Using Structure-Driven Recurrent Neural Networks*

Andreas Küchler[1] and Christoph Goller[2]

[1] Department of Neural Information Processing
Computer Science, University of Ulm, D-89069 Ulm, Germany
[2] Automated Reasoning Group
Computer Science Institute, TU Munich, D-80290, München, Germany

Abstract. While neural networks are widely applied as powerful tools for inductive learning of mappings in domains of fixed-length feature vectors, there are still expressed principled doubts whether the domain can be enlarged to structured objects of arbitrary shape (like trees or graphs). We present a connectionist architecture together with a novel supervised learning scheme which is capable of solving inductive inference tasks on complex symbolic structures of arbitrary size. Labeled directed acyclic graphs are the most general structures that can be handled. The processing in this architecture is driven by the inherent recursive nature of the given structures. Our approach can be viewed as a generalization of the well-known discrete-time, continuous-space recurrent neural networks and their corresponding training procedures. We give first results from experiments with inductive learning tasks consisting in the classification of logical terms. These range from the detection of a certain subterm to the satisfaction of complex matching constraints and also capture certain concepts of syntactical variables.

1 Introduction

In almost all fields of life people and systems assisting them have to deal with structured objects. Annotated graphs (trees, terms, diagrams) are a universal formalism for representing and modeling structural relations between objects (hierarchies, causal, temporal and spatial dependencies, explanations, etc.) and are successfully applied in fields like medical and technical diagnosis, molecular biology and chemistry, software engineering, geometrical reasoning, speech, language and text processing. Faced with the growing mass and the structural complexity of data there is an increasing need to have an automated tool which inductively "learns" to classify, recognize and evaluate structured objects or to discover regularities between them.

While neural networks are successfully applied as powerful inductive learning devices when dealing with numerical feature vectors of a fixed length, there are still expressed doubts [6] whether those numerical models in principle can be used

* This research was supported by the German Research Foundation (DFG) under grant No. Pa 268/10-1 and by the EC (ESPRIT BRP MIX-9119)

in a symbolic domain. Since the late eighties there have been several publications demonstrating that these limitations can be partially broken [11, 4, 2, 1, 13, 3, 8].

Recently a simple neural network architecture (the *folding architecture*) together with a novel supervised learning scheme, *backpropagation through structure* (BPTS) was presented which is capable of processing labeled directed acyclic graphs (LDAG) of arbitrary size [7]. Here we will extend this model, give a formal description and discuss whether and how it could be utilized for inductive learning tasks in symbolic domains. Our conjectures are supported by promising results from experiments on inductive classification tasks.

This paper is organized as follows. First the meaning of the terms *inductive learning* and *symbolic domain* have to be related to our context and fixed by some formal definitions. Section 3 gives an introduction to the folding architecture by separating statical from dynamical aspects. BPTS, a gradient-descent supervised learning procedure for the folding architecture, is derived by generalizing the well-known BPTT approach to DAG-processing in Section 4. First experiments and results in applying the proposed method to inductive classification tasks on logical terms are reported in Section 5. Section 6 relates our approach to some other numerical and symbolic models. We conclude with some remarks about the justification of having different coexistent models in the field of inductive learning in symbolic domains.

2 Preliminaries

2.1 The Intended Inductive Learning Tasks

The class of inductive learning tasks on symbolic domains (ILS) we consider here is defined as a tuple ILS $= (\varXi, \mathcal{P})$, where $\varXi$ is an unknown function of the type $\varXi : S \to I\!\!R^q$ with $q \in I\!\!N, S \subseteq \mathcal{S}$ and S is a (possibly infinite) subset of the general symbolic domain $\mathcal{S}$ (see Section 2.2). $\mathcal{P}$ is a large but finite set of examples partially describing $\varXi$, i.e. $\mathcal{P} = \{(s_1, t_1), (s_2, t_2), \ldots, (s_p, t_p)\}$ where $\varXi(s_i) = t_i, s_i \in S, t_i \in I\!\!R^q$ and $i, p, q \in I\!\!N, 1 \le i \le p$. The learning task is to infer an *approximation* $\varXi_A$ (as good as possible) to the unknown function $\varXi$ based on the given finite example set $\mathcal{P}$ only. An ILS is defined without any explicit theory or knowledge about the function $\varXi$.

A special case is the function $\varXi$ restricted to $\varXi : S \to \{c_1, c_2, \ldots, c_p\}$ with $p \in I\!\!N$. This is a description of inductive p-class *classification* tasks where the c_i ($i \in I\!\!N, 1 \le i \le p$) are the corresponding class labels. The objective here is to infer a classifier $\varXi_C$ with a high accuracy, i.e. with a high probability of correctly classifying a randomly selected instance $(s, \varXi(s)), s \in S$.

In this article we focus on ILS as explained above, but it is clear that in principle $\varXi$ could be extended to structure-structure mappings, i.e. $\varXi : S^1 \to S^2$ where $S^1, S^2 \subseteq \mathcal{S}$. However, special care has to be taken about an adequate definition of approximation in the context of a corresponding inductive learning task.

The next section will give a detailed specification of the symbolic domain $\mathcal{S}$.

2.2 The Symbolic Domain

Graphs have been proven as a universal formalism for representing and modeling different kinds of knowledge (hierarchies, causal, temporal and spatial dependencies, explanations, arbitrary relations between objects, etc.) and are applied in nearly all scientific fields.

In this work we deal with an important subclass of general graphs. A *labeled directed graph* G is a triple (V, E, λ), where V is a finite set, E is a binary relation on V and $\lambda : V \rightarrow \Sigma$ a labeling function with the range of a finite alphabet Σ. The set V is usually called the *vertex set* of G, and its elements are called *vertices* or *nodes*. The set E is called the *edge set* of G, and its elements are called *edges*. A *labeled directed acyclic graph* (LDAG) is a cycle-free labeled directed graph, i.e. there exists a topological sort of the nodes. The *outdegree* (*indegree*) of a node v is the number of outgoing (ingoing) edges, $|\{x \mid (v, x) \in E\}|$ ($|\{x \mid (x, v) \in E\}|$). The outdegree of G is given by the maximum outdegree of all nodes $v \in V$.

A *topological sort* of a DAG $G = (V, E)$ is a linear ordering of all its vertices such that if G contains an edge (u, v), then u appears before v in that ordering. Note that topological sorts can be performed in time complexity of $\Theta(V + E)$.

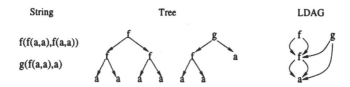

String	Tree	LDAG

f(f(a,a),f(a,a))

g(f(a,a),a)

Fig. 1. String, Tree and LDAG representation of a set of terms.

A *rooted* LDAG (RLDAG) is a DAG where there is exactly one node with indegree zero – the *root node*.[3] In our case the *symbolic domain* S is defined by the universe of all possible RLDAGs. For example *terms* over a given signature – the syntactical elements of every programming language – can be transformed into compact RLDAG representations. Each subterm of a term is represented by a vertex such that multiple occurrences of identical subterms are represented by exactly one vertex[4]. Edges are drawn from each term (subterm) representation to the representations of its argument terms (subterms). A *set of terms* can be packed into an augmented LDAG $G = (R, V, E, \lambda)$ by applying this procedure also to identical subterms occurring in different terms (see Figure 1) and maintaining a set R ($R \subseteq V$) of root nodes coming from each individual term RLDAG representation.

---

[3] Every LDAG can be uniquely completed to a RLDAG by introducing a new node r and inserting edges from r to all other nodes with indegree zero.

[4] This can lead to an exponential reduction of the number of vertices and edges, needed to represent the term. The whole transformation can be done in time $O(n \log(n))$ with respect to the original size of the term.

3   The Folding Architecture

The objective is to develop a neural architecture which can be utilized for solving a given ILS $= (\varXi, \mathcal{P})$ where $\varXi : S \to I\!\!R^q$, $q \in I\!\!N$, $|\mathcal{P}| = p$ and S is a given subset of the universe of RLDAGs. The principled idea is to combine a component for encoding elements of S into suitable connectionist distributed representations with a component to compute (approximation or classification) tasks on distributed representations.

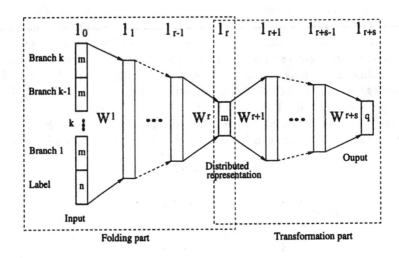

Fig. 2. The generic folding architecture

3.1   The Static View

Our generic *folding* architecture is layered and the static view is that of a specially scaled multilayer feedforward network (Figure 2). The first $r + 1$ layers $\{l_0, \ldots, l_r\}$ constitute the *folding* part, the next layers $\{l_r, \ldots, l_{r+s}\}$ including layer l_r the *transformation* part, where $s, r \geq 1$. All layers are fully-connected with real-valued weights in a feedforward manner and each unit in the layers is provided with a sigmoid transfer function.

The number $q \in I\!\!N$ of units (neurons) in the output layer l_{r+s} is task-specific as well as the maximum outdegree k which is defined by the domain S. The number of *hidden* layers and the number of neurons in each layer concerning the folding ($\{l_1, \ldots, l_{r-1}\}$) and transformation ($\{l_{r+1}, \ldots, l_{r+s-1}\}$) part is not predefined by the given ILS. Neither is m, the dimension of the representation layer l_r. The input layer l_0 is constituted by $n + k \cdot m$ units, n holding the representation for the vertex labels and k times m units provided for distributed representations of DAGs. The weight matrix corresponding to the layer l_j is denoted by W_j with $1 \leq j \leq r + s$, each unit is provided with an individual bias.

3.2 Processing Dynamics

There are no explicit feedback connections in the folding architecture. The recurrent processing is completely driven by the inherent recursive structure of the presented data from the symbolic domain. Informally speaking the folding part is used to "fold" a given structure $s \in S$ into a distributed representation (in $\mathbb{R}^m$). This is achieved by recursively setting the previously computed representations of the direct substructures together with the coding of the associated label at the input layer (Equation 3) and propagating them through the folding part (Equation 2). This process starts at the leaves (by using the label coding and k times the coding of the "empty structure") and ends up with a representation of the whole structure which is then pushed through the whole transformation part (Equation 1). An evaluation of the whole structure can be taken from the output layer.

We will now define the processing dynamics formally. For reasons of simplicity let $s \in S$ be a labeled tree, i.e. a RLDAG $G = (V, E, \lambda)$ where each node in V has an indegree of at most 1 (e.g. see Figure 1). Further let $t \in V$ be a node of s, C a coding function that maps symbolic labels to numeric codes ($C : \Sigma \rightarrow \mathbb{R}^n$) and $nil \in \mathbb{R}^m$ a special representation for the empty DAG. The output of neuron[5] i in layer l at recursion stage t is written as $o_i^{(l)}(t)$. $\theta_i^{(l)}$ denotes the bias associated with neuron i at layer l, $w_{ij}^{(l+1)}$ the weight of the connection between neuron i of the layer l and neuron j of layer $l+1$ and f is a (differentiable) sigmoid function. The continuous-space network dynamics are described by the following equations.

$$o_j^{(l+1)}(t) = f(net_j^{(l+1)}(t)) = f\left(\sum_i o_i^{(l)}(t)\, w_{ij}^{(l+1)} + \theta_j^{(l+1)}\right)$$

$$\text{for} \quad r \leq l < r+s, \quad t \text{ is a root node} \tag{1}$$

$$\text{for} \quad 0 \leq l < r, \quad \text{any } t \tag{2}$$

This means that the folding part for every node t is processed in a standard feedforward manner. However the transformation part is only involved for root nodes.

The outputs $o_i^{(0)}(t)$ are composed of the numeric codes for the labels and the previously computed representations of the dirct substructures. Let V_t be the set of direct successor nodes of t, i.e. $V_t = \{t_0, t_1, \ldots, t_{d-1}\} = \{v \mid (t, v) \in E\}$ and $0 \leq d \leq k$. The i-th component of a vector is denoted by $[\cdot]_i$. The outputs $o_i^{(r)}(t_x)$ produced by successor nodes t_x of t with $0 \leq x < d$ at layer r are fed back to layer 0.

$$o_i^{(0)}(t) = \begin{cases} [C(\lambda(t))]_i & : 0 \leq i < n \\ o_{(i-n)\bmod m}^{(r)}\left(t_{(i-n+m)\,\mathrm{div}\,m}\right) & : n \leq i < n+dm \\ [nil]_{(i-n)\bmod m} & : n+dm \leq i < n+km \end{cases} \tag{3}$$

---

[5] The first neuron will be indexed with 0.

4 Backpropagation Through Structure

The principled idea of using recursive backpropagation-like learning procedures for tree-processing has been mentioned first in [1], recently worked out and generalized to DAGs by [7]. We assume in the following the reader to be familiar with the standard backpropagation algorithm (BP) and its variant *backpropagation through time* (BPTT) [15]. For the sake of brevity we will only be able to give a sketch of the underlying principles of our approach called *backpropagation through structure* (BPTS).

4.1 Computing the Gradient Information

Given an ILS $= (\Xi, \mathcal{P})$ where $\Xi : S \to I\!\!R^q$, $q \in I\!\!N$, $\mathcal{P} = \{(s_1, t_1), \ldots, (s_p, t_p)\}$ and S consisting of trees only, let *root* denote the function mapping structures to their root nodes. In order to develop a supervised learning procedure an appropriate error measure[6] E in the space of parameters $W^1, \ldots, W^{r+s}$ w.r.t. the training set $\mathcal{P}$ has to be defined first.

$$E = \sum_{i=1}^{p} \sum_{j=0}^{q-1} \frac{1}{2} \left([t_i]_j - o_j^{(r+s)}(root(s_i)) \right)^2 \; ; \quad \Delta w_{ij}^{(l)} = -\eta \frac{\partial E}{\partial w_{ij}^{(l)}} \text{ for } 1 \le l \le r+s \quad (4)$$

Obviously, the folding architecture gives a good approximation to Ξ w.r.t the training examples if the mean squared error E (Equation 4, left) is minimized in the weight space. BPTS is a simple gradient-descent procedure following the weight update rule given in Equation 4 (right), where η is the learning rate[7].

The following metaphor helps us to explain the derivation and computation of the weight update rule. Imagine the folding part of the architecture is *virtually unfolded* (with copied weights) according to a given tree structure $s \in S$ (see Figure 3). The resulting feedforward network exhibits a computation process that is equivalent to the dynamics described in section 3.2. Thus, BPTS can be derived and formulated in analogy to the standard BP procedure. We keep the notations introduced (in Section 3.2) and define f' as the first derivative of f and $\delta_j^{(l)}(t)$ as the partial error (which is contributed by a node t) propagated back from the output layer to neuron j in layer l.

Equation 5 shows how the error for the output layer of root nodes is computed.

$$\delta_j^{(r+s)}(t) = f'(net_j^{(r+s)}(t)) \left([t_i]_j - o_j^{(r+s)}(t) \right) \; : \quad t = root(s_i), (s_i, t_i) \in \mathcal{P} \quad (5)$$

Equation 6 and 7 describe, how the error is propagated through the transformation and the folding layer. Again, the transformation layer is involved for root nodes only.

$$\delta_j^{(l)}(t) = f'(net_j^{(l)}(t)) \left(\sum_k \delta_k^{(l+1)}(t) \, w_{jk}^{(l+1)} \right)$$

$$\text{for} \quad r \le l < r+s, \quad t \text{ is a root node} \quad (6)$$

$$\text{for} \quad 0 \le l < r, \quad \text{any } t \quad (7)$$

---

[6] Note the only constraint that has to be obeyed is that E has to be differentiable.
[7] In our experiments we also added a momentum term μ.

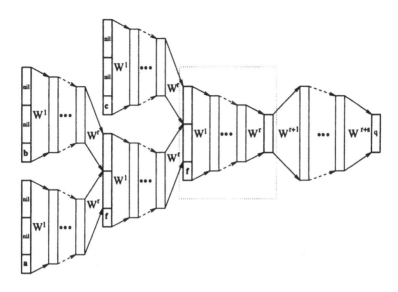

Fig. 3. Virtual unfolding, driven by the tree structure $f(f(a,b),c)$.

$\delta_j^{(0)}(t)$ has to be computed for $n \leq j < n+dm$ only, with d denoting the number of immediate successors nodes of t as in Section 3.2.

Equation 8 shows how an error term is recursively distributed among the direct successors of a node.

$$\delta_j^{(r)}(t) = \delta_{(n+xm+j)}^{(0)}(t') : \quad t \text{ is the } x\text{-th successor of } t'. \tag{8}$$

After a presentation of a set T of nodes occurring in structures of $\mathcal{P}$, all changes computed for each node $t \in T$ can be summed up according to the following equations.

$$\Delta w_{ij}^{(l)} = \eta \sum_{t \in T} o_i^{(l-1)}(t) \cdot \delta_j^{(l)}(t), \quad \Delta \theta_j^{(l)} = \eta \sum_{t \in T} \delta_j^{(l)}(t) \quad (\text{for } 1 \leq l \leq r+s) \tag{9}$$

4.2 Training Schedule for DAGs

We speak of BPTS applied in *batch* mode if a weight update (according to Equation 9) is done after the presentation of the whole training set $\mathcal{P}$. Let us assume that two substructures starting at the nodes t_a and t_b are identical. This means $\forall_{j,l} net_j^{(l)}(t_a) = net_j^{(l)}(t_b), o_j^{(l)}(t_a) = o_j^{(l)}(t_b)$. We notice (by Equation 9) that δ's stemming from different predecessors can be simply summed up

$$\Delta w_{ij}^{(l)} = \eta \sum_t o_i^{(l-1)}(t_a) \cdot \delta_j^{(l)}(t_a) + o_i^{(l-1)}(t_b) \cdot \delta_j^{(l)}(t_b) + \ldots = \eta \sum_t o_i^{(l-1)}(t_a) \cdot (\delta_j^{(l)}(t_a) + \delta_j^{(l)}(t_b)) + \ldots$$

and this sum can be propagated back into identical substructures (by Equations 7 and 8):

$$\delta_j^{(l)}(t_a) + \delta_j^{(l)}(t_b) = f'(net_j^{(l)}(t_a)) \sum_k \left(\delta_k^{(l+1)}(t_a) + \delta_k^{(l+1)}(t_b) \right) w_{jk}^{(l+1)} \tag{10}$$

This observation enables an efficient implementation of BPTS for DAGs. First, in a preprocessing step all structures $\{s \mid (s, \Xi(s)) \in \mathcal{P}\}$ (trees or DAGs) of the whole training set are packed into one single augmented DAG $G = (R, V, E, \lambda)$ (by representing each identical substructure as exactly one node, see Section 2.2). Let O_T be a topological ordering on the nodes V imposed by G.

A *training epoch* is defined by a *forward* (computing $o(t)$ according to the Equations 1–3), a *backward* phase (computing δ according to the Equations 5–8) and an *update* of the weights (according to the Equation 9). The forward phase starts with nodes having an outdegree of zero (leaves) and proceeds according to the reverse (O_T, descending) ordering – ensuring that distributed representations for identical substructures have to be computed only once. The backward phase follows the topological ordering O_T beginning at the root nodes of G. In this way δ's passed over different edges to a node t are summed up before t is processed. Thus, each node of G has to be processed only twice per epoch. The training stops after a predefined number of epochs, when the total error E is below a certain small threshold or when other performance criterions on data not used for training are satisfied.

The time complexity of one BPTS epoch in batch mode on $G = (R, V, E, \lambda)$ is characterized (a pessimistic estimation) by $O(|V| \cdot n_f^2 + |R| \cdot n_t^2)$, where n_f (n_t) is the total number of neurons in the folding (transformation) part of the architecture. The overall space complexity is epoch-independent and is expressed by $O(n_w + |V| \cdot n_f)$, where n_w is the total number of weights. Therefore, the compact DAG-representation for terms can lead to an exponential reduction of the overall space complexity and the time complexity of a BPTS epoch (see Section 2.2).

5 Experiments

5.1 Term Classification Tasks

For a first evaluation of the folding architecture and BPTS we used a set of 2-class[8] classification problems on logical terms. In most papers about ILS with connectionist methods (see e.g. [3, 4, 2]) linguistic applications have been chosen for tests and evaluation. We, however, identified some basic abstract problem classes and generated instances of these classes with different complexity for our experiments. These problem classes are no more than a first step towards a more detailed evaluation for ILS. It is clear, that many other interesting classes have to be investigated.

We consider only the representation and classification of *ground* terms, i.e. terms that do not involve variables. However, the classification tasks we propose involve the concept of logical variables (see below). Whenever we give example terms or pattern terms in the following, we will use Prolog notation, that is, lower case letters represent function symbols and constants, upper case letters represent all-quantified logical variables. We discriminate between four different

---

[8] We will always talk about the positive and negative class in this context.

problem classes named *label-occurrence*, *term-occurrence*, *instance* and *instance-occurrence*. For label-occurrence problems the difference between terms from the negative and the positive class concerns the occurrence of a special label (e.g. the constant c occurs in $f(t(a, i(b), j(i(c))))$, but not in $f(t(a, i(b), j(i(d)))))$. A term-occurrence problem is specified by a special pattern-term (e.g. $i(a)$) that has to occur as subterm in all positive examples, but never occurs in negative ones. For an instance problem all positive terms are instances of a special pattern-term containing all-quantified variables and negative examples mustn't have this property (e.g. $f(i(a), f(a, b))$ is an instance of the pattern term $f(X, f(a, Y))$, however $f(a, f(b, a))$ is not). If all terms from the positive class contain at least one instance of a special pattern term and all terms from the negative class do not, we speak of an instance-occurrence problem. In the context of instance and instance occurrence problems pattern-terms with multiple occurrences of variables demand special attention. A classifier for problems with such pattern-terms has to compare arbitrary subterms corresponding to different occurrences of variables, what may make these problems very difficult. Besides the four mentioned problem classes, we also considered disjunctive and conjunctive combinations, e.g. the occurrence of at least one out of a set of pattern terms (disjunctive) or the occurrence of all (conjunctive) of them as characteristic property for terms from the positive class.

The characteristics of each problem used for our experiments are summarized in Table 1. The first column of the table reports the name of the problem, the second one the signature (terms were composed of), and the third column shows the rule(s) used to generate the positive examples. The fourth column reports the number of terms in the training and test set respectively and the last column the maximum depth[9] of terms in the positive and negative class. For each problem about the same number of positive and negative examples was given. Both positive and negative examples have been generated randomly. Training and test sets are disjoint and have been generated by the same algorithm.

5.2 Results

Table 2 shows the best results we have obtained by experiments with the folding architecture and BPTS for each problem instance introduced in section 5.1, Table 1. The first column reports the problem name and the second one the topology of the network ($\Rightarrow n$, number units in the labels, $\Rightarrow m$, number of units for the representations). All problems were solved by a three-layer folding architecture with one single output unit ($r = 1, s = 1, q = 1$) with the exception of problem **termocc2** which was solved with an additional layer in the folding part ($r = 2$, and l_1 containing 6 units). The third column gives the training parameters ($\Rightarrow \eta$, learning parameter, $\Rightarrow \mu$, momentum) and the fourth column the steepness β of the sigmoid transfer function. Learning parameter, momentum and steepness were always identical for the whole network. The last three

---

[9] We define the depth of a term as the maximum number of edges between the root and leaf nodes in the term's LDAG-representation.

Problem	Symbols	Positive Examples.	#terms (train,test)	depth (pos.,neg.)
lbloccl long	f/2 i/1 a/0 b/0 c/0	no occurrence of label c	(259,141)	(5,5)
termoccl very long	f/2 i/1 a/0 b/0 c/0	the (sub)terms i(a) or f(b,c) occur somewhere	(280,120)	(6,6)
termocc2	t/3 f/2 g/2 i/1 j/1 a/0 b/0 c/0 d/0	the (sub)terms i(a) or f(b,c) occur somewhere	(400,200)	(7,7)
termocc4 me	t/3 f/2 g/2 i/1 j/1 a/0 b/0 c/0 d/0	the (sub)terms i(a) and f(b,c) occur somewhere	(500,500)	(5,5)
termocc4 me long	t/3 f/2 g/2 i/1 j/1 a/0 b/0 c/0 d/0	the (sub)terms i(a) and f(b,c) occur somewhere	(500,500)	(9,9)
termocc5 short	t/3 f/2 g/2 i/1 j/1 a/0 b/0 c/0 d/0	the (sub)terms j(i(g(a,b))) or f(j(b),i(c)) or t(b,i(c),d) occur somewhere	(1200,1200)	(5,5)
termocc5 me	t/3 f/2 g/2 i/1 j/1 a/0 b/0 c/0 d/0	the (sub)terms j(i(g(a,b))) or f(j(b),i(c)) or t(b,i(c),d) occur somewhere	(3000,3000)	(9,9)
inst1 long	f/2 a/0 b/0 c/0	instances of f(X,X)	(202,98)	(6,6)
inst4 long	f/2 a/0 b/0 c/0	instances of f(X,f(a,Y))	(290,110)	(7,6)
inst8	f/2 a/0 b/0 c/0	instances of f(X,f(a,X))	(300,300)	(7,7)
inst9	t/3 f/2 g/2 i/1 j/1 a/0 b/0 c/0 d/0	instances of t(i(X),g(Y,b),b)	(600,600)	(9,9)
inst9 sn	t/3 f/2 g/2 i/1 j/1 a/0 b/0 c/0 d/0	instances of t(i(X),g(Y,b),b)	(606,606)	(9,9)
inst7 sn	t/3 f/2 g/2 i/1 j/1 a/0 b/0 c/0 d/0	instances of t(i(X),g(X,b),b)	(600,600)	(9,9)
inst5	t/3 f/2 g/2 i/1 j/1 a/0 b/0 c/0 d/0	instances of t(a,i(X),f(b,Y)), g(i(f(b,X)),j(Y)) or g(i(X),i(f(b,Y)))	(268,132)	(7,6)
instocc2	t/3 f/2 g/2 i/1 j/1 a/0 b/0 c/0 d/0	an instance of t(i(X),g(Y,b),b) occurs somewhere	(500,500)	(9,9)

Table 1. A set of classification problems involving logical terms.

columns report the classification performance ($\Rightarrow$ %Tr./%Ts. the percentage of terms of the training/test set correctly classified) and the number of learning epochs needed to achieve these results. As sigmoid transfer function tanh was used. Network weights were initialized randomly with values from $]-1.0, 1.0[$. Since we have considered 2-class decision problems the output unit was taught with values $-1.0/1.0$ for negative/positive membership. The classification performance measure was computed by fixing the decision boundary at 0.

The simulations have been carried out with several restarts (no more than ten) for each problem to improve the performance by slightly varied parameters and changes in the network topology. It should be possible to further improve the results. We can only present very first results and the number of experiments does not allow to infer statistically relevant propositions, but the results indicate that inductive learning and generalization on a symbolic domain can be done with neural networks. To give an impression of the performance of the learning we want to note, that one epoch took from less than 1 to 20 seconds on a SUN SPARC 10 workstation depending on the network topology and the number of examples in the training set.

Problem	Topology		Learning Par.		Steepness	% Tr.	% Ts.	#epochs
	n	m	η	μ	β			
lblocc1 long	8	2	0.001	0.6	0.5	99.61	100	108
termocc1 very long	8	6	0.001	0.6	0.5	99.64	98.33	3522
termocc2	13	4	0.0003	0.2	1	98.25	99	2859
termocc4 me	10	5	0.0005	0.3	1	99	92.4	7100
termocc4 me long	10	5	0.0005	0.3	1	90.2	85.2	1136
termocc5 short	10	6	0.0003	0.2	1	98.083	93.5	8733
termocc5 me	10	6	0.0002	0.2	1	92.367	91.7	1073
inst1 long	6	3	0.005	0.6	0.5	95.56	92.86	4250
inst4 long	6	3	0.003	0.6	0.5	100	100	150
inst8	6	5	0.005	0.5	1	98	97.667	201
inst9	10	4	0.002	0.5	1	100	99.833	40
inst9 sn	10	5	0.001	0.5	1	98.185	99.175	1045
inst7 sn	10	6	0.001	0.5	1	99	95.167	1997
inst5	13	3	0.001	0.6	0.5	98.88	94.70	2155
instocc2	10	5	0.001	0.5	1	98	98	233

Table 2. The best results obtained for each classification problem.

Some interesting details should be mentioned: For termocc1 very long and termocc2 we nearly got the same classification performance. However for termocc2 an additional layer in the folding part was needed and it was impossible to get similar good results without it. Both problems are defined by the same pattern-terms, but the classification seems to become more difficult with the bigger signature of termocc2. However the problems termocc4 me, termocc4 me long, termocc5 short and termocc5 me are solvable without hidden layers in the folding part, though based on the same complex signature as termocc2. With the problem inst1 long we show, that a very simple case of multiple variable occurrence is solvable, however a perfect solution (100 % correct classification on the test set) was not possible. This is the case for inst8 too, while inst4 long without multiple occurrence of a variable is solved perfectly. For examples with many different symbols and complex patterns defining the positive class, randomly generating negative examples leads to terms not very similar to the positive ones. This may be the reason, why e.g. inst9 is learned so quickly. For inst9 sn we have generated special negative examples, differing from positive ones only slightly (e.g. by one or two symbols) and added them to the training and test set. This really had influence on the learning. One more unit for the representation layer and many more epochs of training were needed to achieve a classification performance comparable to that of inst9. The pattern-term defining inst7 sn is very similar to the one from inst9 sn and inst9. However the variable X occurs twice. Similar to inst9 sn we added negative examples, very similar to positive ones (e.g. instances of $t(i(X), g(Y, b), b$ with $X \neq Y$) to the negative class in the training and test set. No significant difference to inst9 sn can be noticed concerning the learning and classification performance.

6 Related Work

6.1 The (L)RAAM Model

The Labeling Recursive Autoassociative Memory (LRAAM) [13, 11] is a symmetrical three-layer feedforward network used to generate (unique) fixed-width distributed representations for labeled directed graphs. The architecture of the LRAAM can be imagined by mirroring the folding part $r = 1$ of our architecture at the representation layer l_r (Figure 2).

The objective of an (L)RAAM is to obtain a compressed representation (hidden layer activation) for a node by training (with the Backpropagation procedure) recursive autoassociations of the label coding together with representations of the direct successor nodes. There have been several attempts to solve inductive learning (classification) tasks on tree domains by using RAAM models. Distributed representations for trees are generated by the RAAM, "frozen" and then fed into other network components which are trained in a supervised way to solve the given task [3, 2]. Others combine the encoding task of the LRAAM with the inductive learning task of subsequent network modules by imposing a strong interaction on the corresponding training procedures [4, 8].

Our approach – the folding architecture trained in a supervised manner – takes a different point of view. The encoding of structures is melted with further transformations into one single process. The objective is not to generate unique representations for structures but to obtain representations that are exclusively tuned for the given ILS. First experimental comparisons give strong evidence that our method is really superior to the combined LRAAM model when dealing with inductive (classification) tasks [7].

6.2 Discrete-Time Continuous-Space Recurrent Neural Networks

Discrete-time continuous-space recurrent neural networks are successfully applied to robust inductive sequence processing, e.g. inductive grammatical inference, learning of dynamical systems behaviour, time series prediction [5]. There is a large variety of architectures (for a classification and experimental comparison see [9]). A common property among the members of this discrete-time recurrent network "zoo" is that neurons are allowed to receive directly (or indirectly, communicated by other neurons) feedback from their own activations with an arbitrary but a priori fixed time delay of discrete time steps.

Our approach – *structure-driven* continuous-space recurrent neural networks – may be viewed as a generalization of their time-discrete relations, since the delay of feedback is driven by the recursive nature of the presented data, i.e. activations can be delayed arbitrary time steps before being fed back.

We guess that many concepts developed for discrete-time recurrent networks (architectural variations like single-layer higher-order networks [9], learning procedures like RTRL, RBP [15], knowledge extraction and injection techniques [5], theoretical results regarding the computational power [12], etc.) can be lifted to structure-driven recurrent networks.

Recently, [14] proposed a framework for different architectures built of so-called *complex recursive neurons*. Neurons with direct feedback can be obtained as a special case of our folding architecture by setting the number of layers in the folding part to $r = 1$. Single-layer recurrent networks can be derived by setting $r = 1, s = 0$ and reserving some neurons from the representation layer l_1 as output units.

6.3 Evolving Transformation Systems

Recently a framework for inductive learning was given and lead to the provocative claim that neural networks cannot discover generalization in a symbolic environment [6]. The argumentation is based on a mainly symbolic model, the so-called *evolving transformation system* (ETS). An ETS has a *symbolic* and a *geometric* component. The former consists of a set of structured objects, a basic set of finite edit operations (to manipulate objects) and a finite set of operators to build new operations from that basic set. The geometric (or topological) component is defined by a family of distance functions measuring the distance between two structured objects. The edit operations are annotated with real-valued weights. The distance function is computed by taking the minimum sum of weights over all possible sequences of operations that can transform one object into the other. Solving an ILS (binary classification task) means to evolve the given set of operations and weights so that the distance between objects of different classes is maximized while the distance of objects within the same class is minimized.

It is argued that artificial neural network (ANN) models operate on an *algebraic* (matrix-vector operations in a finite-dimensional space) and a *geometric* component (metrics in that space). Further all metrics being consistent with the algebraic component are proven to be equivalent to the Euclidean metric. The ETS model is able to create an infinite family of (not equivalent) distance functions while ANNs have a uniquely defined geometric component. In [6] the authors draw the conclusion that ETS models are more powerful than ANNs and (together with some other arguments) ANNs cannot discover inductive generalization in a symbolic environment.

Here we want to express (at least) some scepticism about this generalized claim which seems to capture all thinkable neural network models. First, providing three layers, sigmoid transfer functions, an infinite number of units in the hidden layer and an infinite precision feedforward networks are proven to be universal approximators [10] and discrete-time continuous-space recurrent networks (Section 6.2) have the computational power of Turing-machines [12]. Obviously, structure-driven recurrent neural networks only rely on an unique *geometric* component (the Euclidean distance) but they are based on a mixed *algebraic-symbolic* component (the space of operations on structures constituted by the weights) which is evolved (directed to solve the given ILS) during the training process.

7 Conclusions

We proposed the folding architecture provided with the supervised gradient-based learning procedure BPTS, a model which may be viewed as only one instance of a whole class of possible structure-driven continuous-space recurrent neural networks. The processing of DAGs is entirely driven by their recursive symbolic nature. We have shown that inductive learning tasks in symbolic domains can be transformed into numerical optimization (supervised learning) problems. Although it is too early to judge the generalization properties of our model the reported experiments give strong evidence that a trained architecture yields a good approximative solution of the presented learning task. The weight set together with the architecture may be regarded as an adaptable operator (processing, combining and manipulating structures and substructures) which is evolved towards the solution.

Our approach requires a large set of training examples but does not need any explicit theory or knowledge about the learning task. This scenario justifies our model as a complement to symbolic approaches (like inductive logic programming). We are currently working on a hybrid (symbolic/connectionist) reasoning system, in which the folding architecture is applied to learn search control heuristics for an automated deduction system.

There are many open questions. Although there are some interesting theoretical results for feedfoward networks [10] and discrete-time continuous-space recurrent neural networks [12] it can only be speculated about the computational power of the folding architecture. Furthermore, as the folding architecture and BPTS is inferred from classical network models we also have to deal with well-known problems like model selection, convergence properties, local minima, resource consumption, etc.

One can observe the strict borders between symbolic and numeric computing begin to vanish. Both ETS (Section 6.3) and the model presented here are based on a mixed symbolic-numeric component. The hope is that an adequate combination will eliminate the disadvantages of the single components.

References

1. G. Berg, "Connectionist Parser with Recursive Sentence Structure and Lexical Disambiguation," in *Proceedings Tenth National Conference on Artificial Intelligence - AAAI-92*, pp. 32–37, AAAI, Menlo Park, California, USA, 1992.

2. D. Blank, L. Meeden, and J. Marshall, "Exploring the symbolic/subsymbolic continuum: A case study of raam," in *The Symbolic and Connectionist Paradigms: Closing the Gap*, (J. Dinsmore, ed.), LEA Publishers, 1992.

3. V. Cadoret, "Encoding Syntactical Trees with Labelling Recursive Auto-Associative Memory," in *Proceedings of the 11th Conference on Artificial Intelligence (ECAI 94)*, (A. Cohn, ed.), pp. 555–559, John Wiley & Sons, 1994.

4. L. Chrisman, "Learning Recursive Distributed Representations for Holistic Computation," *Connection Science*, no. 3, pp. 345–366, 1991.

5. C. L. Giles and C. W. Omlin, "Extraction, Insertion and Refinement of Symbolic Rules in Dynamically Driven Recurrent Networks," *Connection Science*, vol. 5, no. 3 & 4, pp. 307–337, 1993.
6. L. Goldfarb, J. Abela, V. C. Bhavsar, and V. N. Kamat, "Can a Vector Space Based Learning Model Discover Inductive Class Generalization in a Symbolic Environment?," *Pattern Recognition Letters*, no. 16, pp. 719–726, 1995.
7. C. Goller and A. Küchler, "Learning Task-Dependent Distributed Representations by Backpropagation Through Structure," in *Proceedings of the IEEE International Conference on Neural Networks (ICNN'96)*, 1996. to appear.
8. C. Goller, A. Sperduti, and A. Starita, "Learning Distributed Representations for the Classification of Terms," in *Proceedings of the 14th International Joint Conference on Artificial Intelligence (IJCAI-95)*, (C. S. Mellish, ed.), pp. 509–515, Morgan Kaufmann Publishers, August 1995.
9. B. Horne and C. Giles, "An Experimental Comparison of Recurrent Neural Networks," in *Advances in Neural Information Processing Systems (NIPS 7)*, (G. Tesauro, D. Touretzky, and T. Leen, eds.), pp. 697–, MIT Press, 1995.
10. K. Hornik, M. Stinchcombe, and H. White, "Multilayer Feedforward Network are Universal Approximators," *Neural Networks*, vol. 2, pp. 359–366, 1989.
11. J. B. Pollack, "Recursive Distributed Representations," *Artificial Intelligence*, no. 46, pp. 77–105, 1990.
12. H. T. Siegelmann and E. D. Sontag, "On the Computational Power of Neural Nets," *Journal of Computer and System Sciences*, vol. 50, pp. 132–150, 1995.
13. A. Sperduti, "Encoding of Labeled Graphs by Labeling RAAM," in *Advances in Neural Information Processing Systems (NIPS 6)*, (J. D. Cowan, G. Tesauro, and J. Alspector, eds.), pp. 1125–1132, 1994.
14. A. Sperduti and A. Starita, "Supervised Neural Networks for the Classification of Structures," Technical Report TR-16/95, University of Pisa, Dipartimento di Informatica, 1995.
15. R. J. Williams and D. Zipser, "Gradient-Based Learning Algorithms for Recurrent Networks and Their Computational Complexity," in *Backpropagation: Theory, Architectures and Applications*, (Y. Chauvin and D. E. Rummelhart, eds.), ch. 13, pp. 433–486, Hillsdale, NJ: Lawrence Erlbaum Associates, 1994.

Belief Revision in a Nonclassical Logic

Gerhard Lakemeyer and Wilfried Lang

Institute of Computer Science III
University of Bonn
Römerstr. 164
D-53117 Bonn, Germany
{gerhard,langw}@cs.uni-bonn.de

Abstract. The original theory of belief revision by Alchourrón, Gärdenfors, and Makinson (AGM theory) is based on classical logic. Properties like consistency and logical consequence play an important role in their postulates which define the different types of belief change. While these notions are suitable under the assumption of an ideal logical reasoner, they are not in the case of a reasoner with limited resources because of computational intractability.

The goal of this paper is to develop a theory of belief change based on tautological entailment, a fragment of relevance logic, which has been proposed as a more suitable model of limited deductive reasoning with attractive computational properties. Here we present two approaches. In the first we propose postulates for belief revision under tautological entailment which impose a notion of consistency slightly weaker than the classical one. However, it still turns out to be too strong for practical purposes. In the second approach, we define revision in terms of contraction and expansion, from which a weaker consistency requirement emerges with the benefit that the new belief change operations have efficient implementations.

1 Introduction

Most of the recent work on belief revision builds, one way or another, on the ground breaking ideas by Alchourrón, Gärdenfors, and Makinson (AGM), whose theory of belief revision states basic principles for rational changes of belief ([AGM85], [Gär88]). AGM assume that the epistemic state of an agent is represented by a set of sentences (called *belief set*), which is closed under a consequence operator at least of the power of classical propositional logic (see [Gär88] for details). The AGM theory describes three types of belief change:

- *Expansion* simply adds information to the current state whithout any concern for consistency.
- *Revision* incorporates new information as well, but makes sure that the new epistemic state is logically consistent.
- *Contraction* removes information from the current epistemic state.

While the AGM theory is concerned only with the logical properties of belief change in infinite belief sets, their work has been applied to finite knowledge bases (see, for example, [Neb89]). Since notions like logical consistency are central to the AGM theory, it is not surprising that revision, when applied to knowledge bases, is inherently intractable (see, e.g., [EG92] for a detailed analysis of the complexity of belief revision).

It seems that this bad computational behavior is inescapable as long as we insist on belief sets being closed under the consequence operator defined by AGM. Hence the purpose of this paper is to propose a theory of belief change which is based on a weaker form of logical consequence and which may offer us better computational properties. For that reason we have chosen tautological entailment, a fragment of relevance logic [AB75, Dun76], which is tractable for a large class of sentences [Lev84], as a new basis for belief change.

Once we leave the AGM logic, the meaning of consistency may change. Indeed, the semantics underlying tautological entailment is at the extreme end of things since it has no built-in concept of consistency, which gives us more freedom when designing a theory of belief change. In this paper we propose two theories, one based on a notion of consistency which is weaker than the classical one yet still too strong for practical purposes, and another which is weak enough to allow for efficient belief revision in knowledge bases.

The paper is organized as follows. In Section 2, we briefly review the AGM postulates. In Section 3, we do the same for tautological entailment. In Section 4, we introduce postulates for revision based on tautological entailment and a strong notion of consistency. Section 5 considers contraction, which gives rise to a tractable revision operator with a weak notion of consistency. We end the paper with a brief summary and outlook on future work.

Throughout the paper we assume a propositional language with a countably infinite set of atomic propositions. Sentences are formed in the usual way using the connectives $\neg$ and $\vee$.[1] A *clause* c is a disjunction of literals and a *literal* is either an atom or its negation. In the following K denotes a belief set and A, B, α, and β denote arbitrary sentences.

2 The AGM Theory

The belief change operators are viewed as functions from a belief set K and a sentence A into a new belief set, denoted as K_A^+, K_A^*, and K_A^- for expansion, revision, and contraction, respectively. These functions are defined implicitly through postulates, which themselves are justified on intuitive grounds.[2]

---

[1] We freely use the other operators $\wedge$, $\supset$, and $\equiv$ as the usual abbreviations.

[2] But see [KM90] for scenarios, where some of the postulates seem less intuitive.

Expansion is the simple case, since its postulates are uniquely satisfied by the straightforward inclusion of A into K, that is $K_A^+ = \{\gamma \mid K \cup A \models \gamma\}$, where $\models$ is the usual consequence relation of classical logic (see [Gär88] for the postulates and the representation). Revision and contraction, on the other hand, deserve our attention because their postulates give rise to many nontrivial realizations in classical logic and their adaptation to the nonclassical case is less clear.

Definition 1 AGM Revision.

A function $* : K \times A \to K_A^*$ is called an AGM revision, if the following postulates are satisfied:

(AGM^*1)	K_A^* is a belief set	(closure)
(AGM^*2)	$A \in K_A^*$	(success)
(AGM^*3)	$K_A^* \subseteq K_A^+$	(inclusion)
(AGM^*4)	if $\neg A \notin K$, then $K_A^* = K_A^+$	(vacuity)
(AGM^*5)	K_A^* is inconsistent iff A is inconsistent	(inconsistency)
(AGM^*6)	if $\models (A \equiv B)$, then $K_A^* = K_B^*$	(extensionality)
(AGM^*7)	$K_A^* \cap K_B^* \subseteq K_{A \vee B}^*$	(conjunction 1)
(AGM^*8)	if $\neg B \notin K_{A \vee B}^*$, then $K_{A \vee B}^* \subseteq K_B^*$	(conjunction 2)

Gärdenfors [Gär88] discusses in detail why these postulates are intuitively acceptable. Here we need to be brief. (AGM^*1) simply states that the result of a revision better be a legal epistemic state. (AGM^*2) requires that the new information is believed afterwards. On the other hand, no information beyond A may be added (AGM^*3). If no conflict arises, revision should reduce to expansion (AGM^*4). Otherwise, by the inconsistency postulate (AGM^*5), revision must make sure that the resulting belief set is consistent provided A itself is. (AGM^*6) tells us that the syntactic form of a new belief is irrelevant. Finally, (AGM^*7) and (AGM^*8) provide constraints on the relationship between the result of revising a belief set with a compound sentence and the result of revising it with its components.

Definition 2 AGM Contraction.

A function $- : K \times A \to K_A^-$ is called an AGM contraction, if the following postulates are satisfied:

(AGM^-1)	K_A^- is a belief set	(closure)
(AGM^-2)	if $\not\models A$, then $A \notin K_A^-$	(success)
(AGM^-3)	$K_A^- \subseteq K$	(inclusion)
(AGM^-4)	if $A \notin K$, then $K_A^- = K$	(vacuity)
(AGM^-5)	if $A \in K$, then $(K_A^-)_A^+ = K$	(recovery)
(AGM^-6)	if $\models (A \equiv B)$, then $K_A^- = K_B^-$	(extensionality)
(AGM^-7)	$K_A^- \cap K_B^- \subseteq K_{A \wedge B}^-$	(conjunction 1)
(AGM^-8)	if $B \notin K_{A \wedge B}^-$, then $K_{A \wedge B}^- \subseteq K_B^-$	(conjunction 2)

Most of the postulates of contraction are similar in spirit to the corresponding revision postulates. The recovery postulate (AGM^-5) is novel and requires that contraction should be done in a way that the old belief set can be recovered by a simple expansion of the resulting belief set.

Since we need it later, we remark that revision can be defined in terms of contraction and expansion, that is, revising K by A can be thought of as first retracting $\neg A$ from K and then expanding the result by A [Lev77]. Formally,

Definition 3 Levi identity. $K_A^* = (K_{\neg A}^-)_A^+$.

Revision functions satisfying the Levi identity equation also satisfy the AGM-postulates [AGM85].

3 Tautological Entailment

One way to weaken the notion of logical implication is to extend the class of underlying models. Intuitively, the more models there are which satisfy a given set of assumptions, the smaller the set of sentences gets which are true in all these models, that is, follow from the assumptions.

In classical propositional logic a model is simply a truth assignment to the atomic proposition. Let us denote the truth values by the singleton sets $\{t\}$ and $\{f\}$. We now introduce the notion of a *situation* which extends truth assignments by allowing two additional truth values $\{\}$ and $\{t, f\}$. Intuitively, a situation s assigns $\{\}$ to a proposition if s supports neither the truth nor the falsity of the proposition and $\{t, f\}$ if s supports both its truth and falsity. Formally,

Definition 4. Let $\mathcal{P}$ be the set of atomic proposition.
A situation is a function $s : \mathcal{P} \longrightarrow 2^{\{t,f\}}$.

Definition 5 Support Relation.

Let $\models_T$ and $\models_F$ be two relations between situations and sentences. $s \models_T \alpha$ should be read as "the situation s supports the truth of α" and $s \models_F \alpha$ as "s supports the falsity of α."

1. $s \models_T p$, iff p is atomic and $t \in s(p)$
   $s \models_F p$, iff p is atomic and $f \in s(p)$.

2. $s \models_T \neg\alpha$, iff $s \models_F \alpha$
   $s \models_F \neg\alpha$, iff $s \models_T \alpha$

3. $s \models_T (\alpha \vee \beta)$, iff $s \models_T \alpha$ or $s \models_T \beta$
   $s \models_F (\alpha \vee \beta)$, iff $s \models_F \alpha$ and $s \models_F \beta$

If we define validity as true support in all situations, one can easily see that there are no valid sentences in this logic. For example, the situation which assigns {} to all atomic propositions satisfies no sentence. Conversely, there is no notion of unsatisfiabilty/inconsistency either since the situation which assigns $\{t, f\}$ to all atoms satisfies all sentences.

Nevertheless, the semantics gives rise to an interesting form of logical consequence, called tautological entailment, a fragment of relevance logic [AB75]. The above 4-valued semantics is due to Dunn [Dun76] and was later adapted to a modal logic of explicit belief by Levesque [Lev84].

Definition 6 Tautological entailment.

$\alpha \to \beta$ iff for all situations s, if $s\models_T \alpha$, then $s\models_T \beta$.

Let K be a set of sentences. Then $K \to \alpha$ iff for all situations s, if $s\models_T \gamma$ for all $\gamma \in K$, then $s\models_T \alpha$. $Cn^{TE}(K) = \{\alpha \mid K \to \alpha\}$. $\alpha \leftrightarrow \beta$ is used as an abbreviation for $(\alpha \to \beta)$ and $(\beta \to \alpha)$.

Since the set of situations includes all classical truth assignments, tautological entailment is obviously sound with respect to classical logical consequence. On the other hand, tautological entailment is much weaker. Most importantly, modus ponens is no longer a valid inference rule, that is $p \wedge (p \supset q) \not\to q$. Levesque [Lev84] discovered that this weakness in inference power has a nice computational pay-off when we confine ourselves to sentences in conjunctive normal form (CNF).

Theorem 1 (Levesque) *Let $\alpha = \bigwedge \alpha_i$ and $\beta = \bigwedge \beta_j$ be sentences is CNF. Then $\alpha \to \beta$ iff for every clause β_j there is a clause α_i such that the literals in α_i form a subset of the literals in β_j.*
If α and β are in CNF, then $\alpha \to \beta$ can be computed in time $O(|\alpha| \times |\beta|)$.[3]

4 Revision Based on Explicit Consistency

If we want to consider belief change with respect to a weaker logic, we first of all need to redefine what we mean by belief sets. Obviously, in our case these should now be closed under tautological entailment rather than classical logical consequence. In reference to Levesque's model of explicit belief [Lev84], we call them explicit belief sets.

---

[3] Requiring both α and β to be in CNF is quite reasonable in practice. For one, conversion into CNF preserves equivalence under tautological entailment. For another, think of α as the knowledge base (KB) and β as the query. KB's are usually built up incrementally so that only a very small portion needs to be converted into CNF at any one time. Furthermore, if β is at most logarithmic in size of the KB, then the conversion of β into CNF is polynomial in the size of the KB.

Definition 7. A set of sentences K is an explicit belief set iff $K = Cn^{\mathrm{TE}}(K)$.

As long as there is no ambiguity we will continue to use the term belief set in addition to explicit belief set. Since consistency plays such an important role in AGM revision, we have a problem when we want to use our 4-valued logic as the new basis. Every sentence is satisfiable! So revision could simply be reduced to expansion, since inconsistencies in the sense of not being satisfiable by any situation cannot arise. Rather than trivialising the problem this way, we would like to impose at least some notion of consistency on our belief sets. On the other hand, we do not want to revert back to classical consistency because it is a computational mine field. The following definition attempts to fall between the extremes.

Definition 8. A set of sentences K is called explicitly consistent iff for all sentences A, if $A \in Cn^{\mathrm{TE}}(K)$ then $\neg A \notin Cn^{\mathrm{TE}}(K)$. K is explicitly inconsistent iff it is not explicitly consistent.

Example 1. The belief set $K = Cn^{\mathrm{TE}}(\{\neg A, (A \lor B), \neg B\})$ is explicitly inconsistent, since both $(A \lor B)$ and $\neg(A \lor B)$ are in $Cn^{\mathrm{TE}}(K)$. (Note that $\neg(A \lor B) \leftrightarrow (\neg A \land \neg B)$.) On the other hand, $Cn^{\mathrm{TE}}(\{(A \lor B), (A \lor \neg B), (\neg A \lor B), (\neg A \lor \neg B)\})$ is explicitly consistent even though it is classically inconsistent.

Given the above example and the fact that every explicitly inconsistent set is also classically inconsistent, explicit consistency is strictly weaker than its classical counterpart.

We will now introduce a set of revision postulates, which are guided by the desire to achieve explicitly consistent belief sets.

Definition 9 CONS Revisions.

A function *: $K \times A \rightarrow K_A^*$ is called a CONS revision, if the following postulates are satisfied:

$(CONS^*1)$	K_A^* is an explicit belief set	(closure)
$(CONS^*2)$	$A \in K_A^*$	(success)
$(CONS^*3)$	$K_A^* \subseteq K_A^+$	(inclusion)
$(CONS^*4)$	if K_A^+ is explicitly consistent, then $K_A^* = K_A^+$	(vacuity)
$(CONS^*5)$	K_A^* is expl. inconsist. iff A is expl. inconsist.	(inconsistency)
$(CONS^*6)$	if $(A \leftrightarrow B)$, then $K_A^* = K_B^*$	(extensionality)
$(CONS^*7)$	$K_A^* \cap K_B^* \subseteq K_{A \lor B}^*$	(conjunction 1)
$(CONS^*8)$	if $(K_{A \lor B}^*)_B^+$ is expl. consist., then $K_{A \lor B}^* \subseteq K_B^*$	(conjunction 2)

The changes compared to the original AGM postulates call for some explanations. $(CONS^*5)$, the analog of (AGM^*5), reflects the idea that revision should lead to an explicitly consistent belief set unless A itself is explicitly inconsistent. The original vacuity postulate (AGM^*4) has to be modified as well in order to be compatible with $(CONS^*5)$ as the following example demonstrates.

Example 2. Assume we use (AGM^*4) instead of $(CONS^*4)$ and let $K = Cn^{\text{TE}}(\{A, A \supset B\})$, which is to be revised by $\neg B$. Since $B \notin K$, by (AGM^*4), we obtain $K^*_{\neg B} = Cn^{\text{TE}}(\{A, (A \supset B), \neg B\})$. But $K^*_{\neg B}$ is explicitly inconsistent, since $(A \wedge \neg B) \in Cn^{\text{TE}}(K^*_{\neg B})$ and $(\neg A \vee B) \leftrightarrow (A \supset B) \in Cn^{\text{TE}}(K^*_{\neg B})$.

An argument very similar to the above shows that (AGM^*8) needs to be modified as well. Intuitively, only requiring that $\neg B \notin K^*_{A \vee B}$ as in (AGM^*8) is just not strong enough since it does not rule out that K^*_B is explicitly inconsistent forcing K^*_B to retract some information from K. At the same time $K^+_{A \vee B}$ may well be explicitly consistent so that $K^*_{A \vee B} \not\subseteq K^*_B$. An example is $K = \{C, C \supset \neg B\}$. On the other hand, requiring that $(K^*_{A \vee B})^+_B$ is explicitly consistent remedies the situation.

We remark that, while it is possible to use (AGM^*7) in its original form, this may not be advisable since it eliminates some natural forms of revision. We refer to the next section for a more detailed discussion of this issue.

The following function * shows that the CONS-postulates are indeed coherent.

$$K^*_A = \begin{cases} K^+_A & \text{if } K^+_A \text{ is explicitly consistent} \\ Cn^{\text{TE}}(A) & \text{otherwise} \end{cases}$$

Proposition 10. *The revision function* * *satisfies all eight CONS-postulates.*[4]

One of the advantages of tautological entailment is that deduction is easily provided when we confine ourselves to knowledge bases in CNF. Our original motivation for studying tautological entailment in connection with revision was the desire to obtain more tractable forms of revision than the original AGM-proposal allows.

Unfortunately, the CONS-postulates seem to fail us in this respect. The problem is that, no matter what actual revision function we choose on the basis of our postulates, $(CONS^*4)$ and $(CONS^*5)$ force us to determine whether a belief set is explicitly consistent.

Theorem 2 *Given a finite set of sentences Σ in CNF, determining whether Σ is explicitly consistent is NP hard.*

---

[4] Proofs of all results can be found in the full paper [LL96].

The proof is done by reducing the satisfiability problem of classical logic to this problem. In particular, for any Σ, Σ is satisfiable in propositional logic iff $\Sigma \cup \bigcup_{p \in \Sigma} (p \vee \neg p)$ is explicitly consistent, where p ranges over all the atoms occurring in Σ.

Theorem 2 tells us essentially that it is very unlikely to find a tractable revision function that satisfies the CONS-postulates. If we want better computational properties, we have to give up explicit consistency to some extent, an approach we take up in the next section.

5 The BASE System

It is not at all clear what the best way is to modify the CONS-postulates in order to gain tractability. Fortunately, the Levi-identity suggests another approach, namely by defining revision indirectly as a contraction followed by an expansion. Of course, for that we need to define what contraction and expansion mean under tautological entailment.

As in classical logic, expansion turns out to be straightforward. In fact the AGM-postulates for expansion carry over with the obvious minor changes and we omit them here for reasons of space and remark that they are uniquely satisfied by the equation $K_A^+ = Cn^{\text{TE}}(K \cup \{A\})$, which has a trivial implementation when applied to finite knowledge bases by adding A to the knowledge base.

Interestingly, contraction can be given postulates under tautological entailment that are very close to the original AGM-postulates as well. Moreover, as we will show, they do allow for an efficient implementation. In light of the Levi identity, we then obtain a tractable form of revision as well.

Definition 11 BASE Contraction.

A function $- : K \times A \rightarrow K_A^-$ is called a BASE contraction, if the following postulates are satisfied:

$(BASE^-1)$	K_A^- is an explicit belief set	(closure)
$(BASE^-2)$	$A \notin K_A^-$	(success)
$(BASE^-3)$	$K_A^- \subseteq K$	(inclusion)
$(BASE^-4)$	if $A \notin K$, then $K_A^- = K$	(vacuity)
$(BASE^-5)$	if $(A \leftrightarrow B)$, then $K_A^- = K_B^-$	(extensionality)
$(BASE^-6)$	$K_A^- \cap K_B^- \subseteq K_{A \wedge B}^-$	(conjunction 1)
$(BASE^-7)$	if $B \notin K_{A \wedge B}^-$, then $K_{A \wedge B}^- \subseteq K_B^-$	(conjunction 2)

Notice that there are only two places where we differ from AGM: a simpler version of the success postulate and the missing recovery postulate. $(BASE^-2)$

turns out to be simpler than (AGM^-2) simply because tautological entailment has no notion of validity to worry about. As far as recovery is concerned, Gärdenfors already argues at length that recovery may or may not be desirable even in classical logic [Gär88]. When it comes to tautological entailment, the verdict is clear. Recovery is impossible. For consider $K = Cn^{\text{TE}}(A)$ for some atom A. Clearly $A \notin K_{A \vee B}^-$ because of $(BASE^-2)$. However, it is easy to show that for any set of sentences X such that $X \not\vdash A$, $X \cup \{A \vee B\} \not\vdash A$. Therefore $(K_{A \vee B}^-)_{A \vee B}^+$ cannot contain A.

Theorem 3 *The recovery postulate is incompatible with the success postulate under tautological entailment.*

A contraction operator which satisfies our postulates and operates on finitely representable belief sets, that is, knowledge bases (KB's), can now be defined as follows. We assume that both the KB and the information A to be retracted are in clausal form, that is, they are finite sets of clauses. To retract A and in order to remove as little information as possible from KB, we only remove enough clauses from KB so that one of the remaining clauses in A no longer follows from KB. Given Theorem 1, it suffices to remove all those clauses from KB that subsume a clause c in A. As a simple minimality criterion, we consider a c for which the set of subsuming clauses in KB is minimal. For convenience and in order to obtain a deterministic algorithm, we assume that the set of finite sets of clauses is ordered according to some lexicographical scheme.

Function BASE-Contract(KB, A)

1. For each clause c in A determine the set Γ_c of clauses in KB which subsume c.
2. Let Γ_{min} be the smallest set among the Γ_c. (If there is there is more than one candidate, choose the least one according to the lexicographical ordering.)
3. **Return** KB$-\Gamma_{min}$.

We obtain the following properties for this operator. A belief set K is called finitely representable iff there is a finite set of clauses KB such that K $= Cn^{\text{TE}}(\text{KB})$.

Theorem 4

1. *BASE-Contract satisfies the postulates $(BASE^-1) - (BASE^-7)$ for finitely representable belief sets.*[5]

---

[5] Since the contraction postulates are defined for arbitrary sentences A, we implicitly assume a conversion from a sentence into clausal form before calling BASE-Contract.

2. *Given finite sets of clauses* KB *and* A, *BASE-Contract can be computed in time* $O(|\text{KB}| \times |A|)$.[6]

Revision is now defined as $K_A^* = (K_{\neg A}^-)_A^+$. The functions satisfying this equation are governed by the following postulates.

Definition 12 BASE Revision.

A function $* : K \times A \to K_A^*$ is called a BASE revision, if the following postulates are satisfied:

$(BASE^*1)$ K_A^* is an explicit belief set	(closure)
$(BASE^*2)$ A $\in K_A^*$	(success)
$(BASE^*3)$ $K_A^* \subseteq K_A^+$	(inclusion)
$(BASE^*4)$ if $\neg A \notin K$, then $K_A^* = K_A^+$	(vacuity)
$(BASE^*5)$ $\neg A \notin K_A^*$ provided A is explicitly consistent	(inconsistency)
$(BASE^*6)$ if (A $\leftrightarrow$ B), then $K_A^* = K_B^*$	(extensionality)
$(BASE^*7)$ $(K_A^-)_{A \vee B}^+ \cap (K_B^-)_{A \vee B}^+ \subseteq K_{A \vee B}^*$	(conjunction 1)
$(BASE^*8)$ if $\neg B \notin K_{A \vee B}^*$, then $K_{A \vee B}^* \subseteq K_B^*$	(conjunction 2)

Notice that, except for $(BASE^*5)$ and $(BASE^*7)$, the postulates look very similar to the AGM-postulates. The rationale behind $(BASE^*7)$ will become clear once we discuss an actual revision function that satisfies the Levi identity. As for $(BASE^*5)$, the following example shows that revising with an explicitly inconsistent A may result in $\neg A$ being a member of the revised belief set. Let $K = \{\}$ and $A = B \wedge \neg B$. Since $\neg A \notin K$, the revision reduces to an expansion with A, and it is easy to see that $K_A^* = Cn^{\text{TE}}(\{A\})$ tautologically entails $\neg A$, that is, $B \vee \neg B$. Finally, note that $(BASE^*5)$ gets away with requiring explicit consistency rather than the stronger classical consistency.

To define a revision function operating on finite knowledge bases, let KB and A be finite sets of clauses and let $\overline{A}$ be the set of clauses representing the negation of A, i.e. $\overline{A}$ corresponds to the conjunctive normal form of $\neg \bigwedge_{c \in A} c$. Let us assume we have a function BASE-Expand(KB,A), which implements $[Cn^{\text{TE}}(\text{KB})]_A^+$ in the obvious way by returning KB$\cup A$. Given BASE-Contract, we can then define BASE-Revise in a straightforward way.

Function BASE-Revise(KB,A)
    Return BASE-Expand(BASE-Contract(KB,$\overline{A}$),A)

Theorem 5 *BASE-Revise satisfies the postulates* $(BASE^*1) - (BASE^*8)$ *for finitely representable belief sets.*[7]

---

[6] Note our comments at the end of Section 3 about the cost of keeping both KB and A in clausal form.

[7] We could have easily defined BASE-Revise for arbitrary KB's including infinite ones resulting in a revision function satisfying the postulates for all belief sets. However, since our motivation was guided by computational concerns, we feel justified restricting ourselves to the finite case.

Given BASE-Revise, we can demonstrate why we have to settle for $(BASE^*7)$ instead of the stronger (AGM^*7).

Example 3. Assume $K= Cn^{TE}(\{\neg A, \neg B\})$ for atomic A and B. Revising K by A with BASE-Revise removes $\neg A$ and expands with A, so $K_A^* = Cn^{TE}(\{A, \neg B\})$. Similarly, a revision with B produce $K_B^* = Cn^{TE}(\{B, \neg A\})$. Then $K_A^* \cap K_B^* = Cn^{TE}(\{(A \lor B), (\neg A \lor \neg B), (\neg A \lor A), (\neg B \lor B)\})$. However, a revision with $(A \lor B)$ either equals $Cn^{TE}(\{\neg A, (A \lor B)\})$ or $Cn^{TE}(\{\neg B, (A \lor B)\})$ according to BASE-Revise. In either case, only one tautology is included in $K_{A \lor B}^*$, but both are included in the intersection of K_A^* and K_B^*. Hence (AGM^*7) does not hold.

While (AGM^*7) is too strong a requirement, the weaker and, admittedly, technical $(BASE^*7)$ holds in any case. The example also shows that our choice to leave (AGM^*7) as part of our CONS-postulates would exclude quite natural ways of revising a belief set. As it turns out, the problem really only has to do with dangling tautologies. In [Lan95] it is shown that belief sets which are closed under tautologies in addition to being closed under tautological entailment do not have this problem and (AGM^*7) is acceptable unconditionally.

While, according to $(BASE^*5)$, BASE-Revise(KB,A) is guaranteed not to contain $\overline{A}$ as long as A is explicitly consistent, other inconsistencies may creep in. In fact, the corresponding revised belief set may no longer be explicitly consistent as the following example demonstrates.

Example 4. Let KB=$\{A, (A \supset B), C\}$ for atomic A, B and C, and assume we want to revise with $\neg B$. Since BASE-Contract(KB, $\{B\}$) = KB (note: $\{B\}$ = $\overline{\{\neg B\}}$), KB$'$ = BASE-Revise(KB, $\{\neg B\}$) = $\{A, (A \supset B), \neg B, C\}$. It is easy to see that Cn^{TE}(KB$'$) contains both $(A \land \neg B)$ and $\neg(A \land \neg B)$. (Note that $\neg(A \land \neg B) \leftrightarrow (A \supset B)$).

While BASE-Revise cannot guarantee global consistency, it has the advantage of being efficiently computable in many cases, which follows easily from Theorem 4.

Theorem 6 *If A is at most logarithmic in the size of* KB, *then BASE-Revise can be computed in time* $O(|KB|^2)$.

The assumption that A is at most logarithmic in the size of KB is necessary because $\overline{A}$ can be exponential in the size of A. As such this restriction seems reasonable for most realistic KB's.

We end this section with a remark regarding the fact that BASE-Revise is not guaranteed to preserve the explicit consistency of a knowledge base. The nice computational properties of BASE-Revise suggest an off-line and incremental strategy to detect and eliminate explicit inconsistencies, thereby increasing a user's confidence in the coherence of the knowledge base:

Repeat generate a new query A in CNF.
　　If both KB $\longrightarrow A$ and KB $\longrightarrow \overline{A}$ then
　　　　BASE-Revise(KB, A) or BASE-Revise(KB, $\overline{A}$).
Until all queries are tested or interrupt.

Of course, the algorithm does not tell us which of A or $\overline{A}$ to remove. This would require either user intervention or a pre-specified entrenchment ordering. Note that each step of the loop is tractable as long as A remains of reasonable size (logarithmic in the size of the KB). Hence we have an any-time method to look for explicit inconsistencies, that is, the more time we spend on this the more confidence we have that there are at least no glaring contradictions.

6　Related Work

Recently, Restall and Slaney [RS95] independently considered revision based on tautological entailment. While their postulates for revision and contraction are similar, though not identical, to ours, the emphasis of their investigations seems in many ways complementary to ours. They are mainly concerned with establishing representation results similar to those obtained for AGM revision, in particular, epistemic entrenchment, partial meet contraction, and Grove's systems of spheres [Gro88]. Our efforts, on the other hand, have been driven entirely by computational concerns and the desire to retain as much of classical consistency of a knowledge base as possible.

7　Conclusion

In this paper we discussed a theory of belief change based on tautological entailment, which was previously shown to have attractive computational properties. We first considered postulates for revision, which offer a notion of consistency somewhat weaker than classical consistency. Unfortunately, it still turns out to be too strong from a computational point of view. In order to overcome this deficiency, we approach revision indirectly by considering contraction and expansion as the fundamental operations from which revision is defined through the Levi identity. The postulates for contraction turn out to be very close to the original AGM postulates except that recovery becomes untenable under tautological entailment. Finally, while the resulting revision functions no longer satisfy the consistency requirements of our first proposal, they do allow for efficient implementations.

Lang [Lan95] also considers the 3-valued variant of the underlying logic, where the truth value {} is omitted. Except for minor changes in the postulates, the results reported here all carry over to the 3-valued case. Lin [Lin94] proposes an interesting notion of consistent reasoning in the presence of inconsistencies. It would be interesting to consider belief change under this framework as well (see [Lan95] for some preliminary results). Of course, finding other nonclassical logics with interesting properties for revision remains an interesting challenge and, finally, other forms of belief change such as update in the sense of [KM90] should be investigated as well from the point of view of nonclassical logic.

References

[AB75]   Anderson, A. R., and Belnap, N. D., *Entailment, The Logic of Relevance and Necessity*, Princeton University Press, 1975.

[AGM85]   Alchourrón, C. E., Gärdenfors, P., and Makinson, D., On the Logic of Theory Change: Partiell Meet Contraction and Revision Functions, *Journal of Symbolic Logic*, **50**, 1985, pp.510-530.

[Dun76]   Dunn, J. M., Intuitive Semantics for First-Degree Entailments and Coupled Trees. *Philosophical Studies*, **29**, 1976, pp.149-168.

[EG92]   Eiter, Th. and Gottlob, G., On the Complexity of Propositional Knowledge Base Revision, Updates, and Counterfactuals. *Artificial Intelligence* **57**(2-3), 1992, pp. 227-270.

[Gär88]   Gärdenfors, P., *Knowledge in Flux: Modeling the Dynamics of Epistemic States*, Bradford Books, MIT Press, Cambridge, MA, 1988.

[Gro88]   Grove, A., Two modellings for theory change. *Journal of Philosophical Logic* **17**, pp. 157-170, 1988.

[KM90]   Katsuno, H., Mendelzon, A.O., *On the Difference Between Updating a Knowledge Database and Revising it*, Technical Report KRR-TR-90-6, Department of Computer Science, University of Toronto, 1990.

[LL96]   Lakemeyer, G. and Lang, W., *Belief Revision in a Nonclassical Logic*. Technical Report IAI-TR-96-4, Institute of Computer Science III, University of Bonn, 1996.

[Lan95]   Lang, W., *A Revision function for a nonclassical logic*, Master's Thesis (in German), Institute of Computer Science, University of Bonn, 1995.

[Lev84]   Levesque, H. J.,The Logic of Implicit and Explicit Belief, *Proc. of the National Conference on Artificial Intelligence (AAAI-84)*, 1984, pp. 198-202.

[Lev77]   Levi, I., Subjunctives, dispositions and chances, *Synthese*, **34**, 1977, pp. 423-455.

[Lin94]   Lin, J., Consistent Belief Reasoning in the Presence of Inconsistency: Preliminary version, *Proceedings of the Fifth Conference on Theoretical Aspects of Reasoning about Knowledge*, Pacific Grove, CA, 1994.

[Neb89]   Nebel, B., A Knowledge Level Analysis of Belief Revision, *Proc. of the 1st International Conference on Principles of Knowledge Representation and Reasoning*, Morgan Kaufmann, 1989, pp. 301-311.

[RS95]   Restall, G. and Slaney, J., *Realistic belief revision*, Technical Report TR-ARP-2-95, School of Information Sciences and Engineering, Australian National University, 1995.

Avoiding Combinatorial Explosion in Automatic Test Generation: Reasoning about Measurements is the Key

Harald Lange, Ralf Möller, Bernd Neumann[1]

University of Hamburg, Computer Science Department, Laboratory for Artificial Intelligence
Vogt-Kölln-Str. 30, 22527 Hamburg
{hlange,moeller,neumann}@informatik.uni-hamburg.de

Abstract: The main thesis of this paper is that reasoning about measurements can be used as a basic mechanism for generating test plans for analogical circuits. Motivated by an application scenario, reasoning about measurements incorporates domain knowledge about testing conditions, local behavior of circuit components (fault modes covered by measurements) and the topological structure of the circuit to be tested. With the test generation architecture introduced in this paper, a combinatorial explosion which is problematic in model-based test generation approaches can be avoided.

1   Introduction

The automatic generation of test plans for technical systems becomes more and more important, especially since the producer of a technical product can be made liable for any damage that is caused by the product. Test generation and quality control is not only important for new products. Systems that have been repaired or maintained must also be tested again. A test plan is a sequence of tests (or measurements) being used to indicate that the behavior of a system is correct w.r.t. a formal specification. The composition of tests must consider several criteria. First of all, the test plan must be complete in some sense, i.e. if there is a fault in a component, it should be detected by at least one test. In most cases, non-trivial assumptions must be made to guarantee completeness: the fault model completeness assumption [13], the single-fault assumption and the non-intermittency assumption [11]. Thus, at the current state of the art, completeness can be guaranteed only in a weaker sense (but see [3] for extensions to handle multiple faults). Second, tests or measurements are associated with costs and the goal of test plan generation is also to reduce these costs. Third, user interface concerns are also important, i.e. in some domains, tests must be composed in such a way that a human engineer (operator of the test machinery) is adequately supported.

Test plan generation is related to technical diagnosis. The theory about technical diagnosis can provide the basis for test generation because a sequence of measurements is used in a similar way to refute all possible fault models for circuit components. However, instead of determining a faulty component, with test generation systems the correct behavior of all components must be shown. In this paper, we focus on computing con-

1.   Work in this project has been done in collaboration with "DTK: Gesellschaft für Technische Kommunikation mbH", Hamburg. We would like to thank U. Haferstroh, A. Josub, M. Orligk and M. Schmidt. Many thanks also to our students A. Kaplunova and H. Paulsen who not only implemented large parts of the interface and the test generator but also contributed many good ideas for the PETS architecture. The project was supported by the Wirtschaftsbehörde of Hamburg.

firming test sets and do not consider test sets that identify the reason for a certain fault (tests for identification).

Because of the enormous commercial importance, the generation of tests for *digital* circuits has been considered in numerous publications. See e.g. the D-Algorithm of Roth [12] and the subsequent work of Fujiwara [5]. Distributed model-based test generation has been proposed for VHDL descriptions of digital circuits [7]. Even in simple circuits, there is always the danger of combinatorial explosion. The problem is that components can usually not be measured in isolation but must be tested in an aggregate which can be very complex.

Other approaches known in VLSI testing like graph-based algorithms for evaluating boolean functions introduced by Bryant (OBDDs: ordered binary decision diagrams, see e.g. [2]) exchange computational complexity with data structure size (exponential storage complexity in the worst case). The idea behind OBDDs is to combine the variables of models for basic components in a recursive bottom-up process until the complete circuit is modeled. The graph structure provides a fast way to determine the value of a single variable given the value of other variables. However, the data structures grow exponentially.

Much less work has been published for the generation of test plans for *analogical* circuits. Modeling the behavior of physical systems in general and qualitative modeling in particular (cf. Struss [15] [16] [17]) is necessary when tests for single constituents are to be generated from first principles. Though, in principle, it has been shown that model abstraction [16] and model-based test generation for single constituents can also be applied to aggregate testing [15], the computational complexity is NP-complete. Furthermore, as Struss emphasizes, the solution introduced in [15] "shifts the burden to the hard task of modeling".

Although the selection of models has been automated in some domains (e.g. [10], [13]), models are usually defined manually. Modeling also comes at a cost that must not be neglected in practical applications (see [8] for a discussion of different aspects and domain characteristics). In addition, in some domains, the limited observability of physical quantities must be taken into account. Thus, the application domain defines several constraints that should not be neglected for efficient test generation.

The real world application scenario discussed in this paper has the following characteristics and constraints:

- Analogical and digital components must be dealt with.
- Circuits are composed of a large amount of components (1000-5000 per assembly) with high interconnectivity.
- Components cannot be measured in isolation (approx. 10-20 terminals only).
- If components and their models must be adapted or extended, this must be done by domain experts, not experts of the test generation system, i.e. formal models for component behavior should be as simple as possible to reduce training time.
- The actual testing machinery is given in the industrial context, i.e. the set of possible measurements is restricted.
- The structure of the circuits and the derivation of measurements is influenced by the user interface for the operator of the testing machine (for details see below).

In collaboration with our project partner DTK whose employees are experienced in manual test plan generation we developed a new approach to automatic test plan generation for combined analogical and digital circuits. Manual test plan generation takes up to four person months per assembly, and because several hundreds of different assembly types have to be tested, automatic test plan generation saves an enormous amount of money. The system we developed is called PETS (in German: Prüfplan-Erstellung für Technische Systeme). It is now in operation at DTK.

The approach is to some extent coupled to the problems in the domain and is not as general as the work of Struss. In the group of Struss, some experiments on combining model-based test generation techniques with the OBDD approach of Bryant indicate that combinatorial explosion is likely to occur even in small circuits (see Inderst [6]). A first approach of Inderst uses some test data from PETS but, in reasonable time, his system can handle only half of the small circuit presented in Figure 1 (see below).

Our approach is different. The constraints imposed by the application domain provide a lot of insights into how complexity can be dealt with. Inspired by the actions taken by the domain experts, we *model test generation as reasoning about necessary and possible measurements* of circuit elements (and circuit element *aggregates*) rather than reasoning primarily about component behavior. The test generation algorithm directly works on the kind of possible measurements defined by the test environment. Reasoning about measurements can be seen as supplementary to reasoning about component behavior because it relates local component behavior and global system structure.

The paper is structured as follows. In the next section, we discuss the application domain and explain components and structure of the circuits to be tested. The discussion derives a set of optimization criteria for test plans. The third section introduces our approach to solve the test generation problem. After discussing the relations to model-based test generation in the fourth section, the paper concludes with a summary and an outlook.

2 PETS: The Application Scenario

Even today, most railroad systems are controlled by relay circuits because relays are quite reliable. After repair or maintenance, relay assemblies must be tested. An assemby consist of 10 to 40 relays, each of which controls up to fourteen contacts (switches). According to the relay type, contacts are either opened or closed when the relay is switched. Relays can influence each other (coupled relays). In addition, in assemblies there are many types of analogical components: resistors, lamps, relay coils, diodes, capacitors, transformers, etc. Besides source and ground terminals, a relay assembly consists of several other external terminals which can be used for tests and measurements.

2.1 The PETS interface

Circuits are described by drawings which are organized into several sheets (connected with "continuation elements" known from flow-charts). For test generation an internal (object-oriented) representation of circuit elements and circuit structure is required. Depending on the element class, every circuit element is characterized by a set of

216

attributes which are shown in the drawings. To support the creation of the internal circuit representation, a small circuit editor (in the spirit of a domain-specific CAD system) has been developed. The interface is also used to visualize test generation results. Figure 1 presents a small sample circuit (called SC for "switch control").

In the PETS interface, the usual icons of railroad signal technology are used. Contacts are represented by small bars. Contacts can be open (bar on one side of the wire) or closed (bars on both sides of the wire, think of a water pipe which is interrupted by a sheet metal plate). The relay type is indicated by different arrows which also indicate whether the contact is either open or closed when the relay is excited. The coil (or coils) of a relay are separated from the contacts and can possibly be found on different sheets. A complete relay is identified by several components spread throughout the circuit (the association of contacts and coils to relays is given by the numbers shown near the elements).

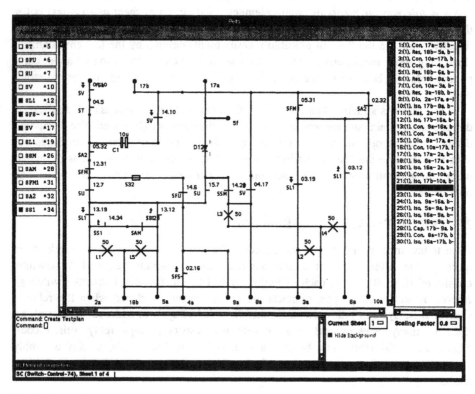

Fig. 1. Screenshot of the PETS interaction window. The main pane shows the circuit with lamps (crosses) and contacts (bars). In the left part the relays and their states are indicated by check-boxes. Relays can be interactively switched by clicking either on a check-box or on a contact in the main window. The right column presents the measurements paths generated by PETS. The second measurement (resistance measurement) is selected. In the main pane, the corresponding measurement path from terminal 17a to 5a is highlighted.

2.2 Characteristics of the Test Environment

The test environment for relay circuits to be used in the railroad maintenance workshop has already been developed and is not subject to change (see Figure 2). A relay assembly is attached to a test automaton. Two-point measurements are possible between any two terminals. Tests are carried out with test voltages applied to suitable terminals without operating voltage between the source and ground terminals. The measurement voltage will be small such that relays are not switched by their coils. An external mechanical system with pneumatic valves will be used to set the state of relays. This system is controlled by a small computer which also records the measurement values. A final test plan is treated as a "program" for this computer.

The test system supports five kinds of two-point measurements: conduction and non-conduction measurements (for contacts), resistance measurements (for resistors, lamps, coils), diode as well as capacity measurements. It should be noted that the small set of measurements is not extremely domain-dependent. Other computer-supported systems must also take their respective workshop environment into account. For instance,

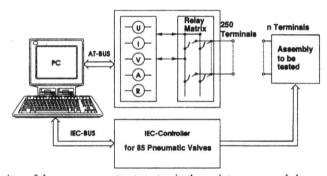

Fig. 2. Overview of the measurement automaton in the maintenance workshop.

in a car repair workshop, due to the available measurement equipment and training of personnel, only a limited set of measurements (limited w.r.t. to the physically possible measurements) can be carried out. The set of possible measurements covers several fault models for different components. Furthermore, the set of fault models for contacts (to be ruled out by refutation measurements [14]) is rather small (stuck-at-open, stuck-at-closed). These fault models directly correspond to a conduction and a non-conduction measurement, respectively. For analogical element types, there are specialized measurements, too (diode and capacity measurements). Thus, for each circuit element, there exists a set of necessary measurements. The final test plan should include all required measurements for each component that can be tested by external measurements. Every measurement is characterized by a specific relay position. For instance, in order to carry out a resistance measurement for a lamp, a path from two terminals at the outside of the assembly must be found. The path must not contain a shortcut around the elements to be tested. Note that it is not always possible to directly measure a single circuit element because, due to the connection topology, in some circuits every measurement path (in any kind of relay position) also contains other elements. Even worse, for some components, the connection topology of a circuit might not even allow an external measurement at all. For instance, in the lower left part of Figure 1 two contacts are arranged in parallel to two lamp elements, i.e. there is no way to do an external non-conduction measurement for the contacts because it is not possible to set the relays of the circuit in such a way that the shortcut of the contacts by the lamps can be avoided. All that PETS can do in situations like these is to report the circuit elements that cannot be tested.

2.3 Optimization Criteria for Test Plan Generation

In the PETS context, the initial relay position is defined by the test automaton (Figure 2). However, the subsequent test states of the circuit are subject to optimization because the number of relay switches should be minimized. Note that in other domains (e.g. vehicle diagnosis [8]), test generation is simplified drastically because the static test states of the system are prescribed.

In general, it is desirable to minimize the number of measurements. But since there might be several elements on a measurement path, a measurement does not necessarily directly reveal a broken element (nor the exact cause of the fault). In order to minimize search time for the electrical engineer, measurement paths should be rather short. Furthermore, for the engineer's user interface (see Figure 2), the sequencing of measurements must correspond to the organization of circuits into sheets. The complete circuit will be tested sheet by sheet and measurements should be local to a single sheet. Thus, in this scenario serveral conflicting optimization criteria are important:

- minimization of the number of relay switches,
- minimization of the length of measurement paths,
- minimization of the number of measurements,
- minimization of sheet crossings.

However, these criteria are no hard constraints.

2.4 Worst-Case Complexity Considerations

Every relay position results in a different circuit topology. Thus, since there are up to 40 relays in a circuit, in principle, 2^{40} different circuits have to be considered. Assuming that there are 10 to 20 terminals which are candidates for two-point measurements in each circuit, it becomes clear that a general model-based test generation system can be used only for small circuits (see the results of Inderst [6]).

Considering the test automaton, we focus on two-point measurements between terminals rather than on local definitions of component behavior. For each type of circuit element, a set of necessary measurements is defined. However, due to circuit topology, several circuit elements must be combined in order to find two-point measurements between terminals. The main idea behind the PETS approach is to reduce complexity by focussing on measurements rather than on component behavior. For example, for a serialization of ten contacts only eleven measurements are necessary (one conduction measurement with all contacts closed and ten non-conduction measurements with one contact open in each measurement). However, in the worst case, a behavioral model has to consider 2^{10} different states (either by simulation or encoded with OBDDs).

In the following chapter we will discuss how test plan generation can be modeled as reasoning about measurement combinations. We will see that the circuit topology itself imposes some sort of global constraints on the complete set of measurements combined in a test plan.

3   Reasoning about Measurements

In the PETS architecture, measurements are first-class objects which can be combined to new measurements according to a set of rules. The parameters of different measurements depend on the attributes of the elements being tested. Before the operations on measurements are described and necessary measurements are derived, we introduce several kinds of circuit transformations that are required to implement reasoning about measurements.

3.1   Circuit Transformations and Measurement Composition

Two-Pin Circuit Elements

The circuit might contain elements that have more than two pins (e.g. transformers). In a first step, these elements are replaced by two-pin elements. For instance, a transformer is replaced by two resistors representing the coils.[2]

Topological Connectors: Considering Possible Faults in Structure

The connection topology is another example for a circuit transformation. It should be noted that in the PETS scenario the model for the topology of a circuit is incomplete. The "wires" shown in the drawings are only logical connections. They do not directly

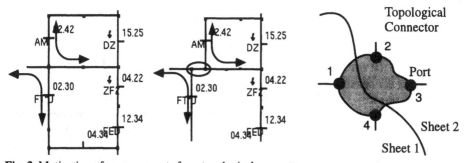

Fig. 3. Motivation of measurements for a topological connector.

correspond to physical wires but describe the connection topology between circuit elements only. In the left part of Figure 3, a small clipping of a circuit is shown. Let us assume, the four-point connector below the contact of the relay AM is "covered" by two measurements (indicated by arrows). It is easy to see that an additional measurement would be necessary to exclude broken wires if the actual physical wiring were defined as presented in the middle of Figure 3. Since models of the concrete physical wiring of circuit elements are definitely not available, the situation shown in Figure 3 cannot be ruled

---

2. There may also be a shortcut between the two substitute resistors as an additional fault model for a transformer. These situations are covered by a set of additional shortcut tests which are not discussed in this paper.

out and some kind of worst case reasoning must be applied to cope with *faults in structure* (see also [1]).

So-called *topological connectors* are abstractions from the "wires" between circuit elements. The circuit is transformed into another representation where topological connectors are abstract nodes between two-pin circuit elements. In order to correctly handle the worst case, (i) all ports must be covered by the set of measurements "crossing" the topological connector, and (ii) the cover must be connected. Thus, besides the two measurements in the left part of Figure 3, an additional measurement is required (for example from Port 1 to Port 3). Other combinations are also possible. A topological connector might cross the boundaries of sheets (see Figure 3 for an example). Sheet information is important because, in general, measurements across sheet boundaries should be avoided to support a more ergonomic interaction style for the operator interface. Thus, although the set of measurements {1-2, 2-4, 3-4} satisfies the "ports-must-be-connected" constraint, it is less optimal considering the above-mentioned optimization criteria. The final test plan must include enough measurements such that the ports of every topological connector are connected. Ports of a topological connector might be terminals and the "ports-must-be-connected" constraint ensures that all terminals are tested in the final test plan.

Serial-Parallel-Analysis

A reduction of circuit size can be achieved by the well-known serial-parallel analysis (sp-analysis) which has also been successfully applied to problems in qualitative diagnosis [8]. The compound elements (aggregates) derived step by step are also associated with measurements. However, not all combinations of measurements are allowed and some high-level combinations might rule out measurement candidates which were possible at lower level aggregates.

Table 1 and Table 2 define the serial and parallel combinations of measurements, respectively. Each entry in the table defines the type of the compound measurement and characterizes the basic circuit elements that can be marked as measured (row = only the elements of the row aggregate are measured, col = only the elements of the column aggregate are measured, bth = the elements of both indices, the row and and the column aggregate, can be measured, non = no element can be marked as measured in the compound circuit). For instance, when a conduction measurement (column) is combined with a non-conduction measurement (row) in a serial combination, the resulting measurement will be a non-conduction measurement but only the circuit elements of the row aggregate can be marked as measured. The measurement status "exp" means that currently, the parameters of measurements cannot be determined by PETS and have to be determined "experimentally" by model-based simulation (either quantitative or qualitative, see below).

Measurements are also associated with a direction. Combining, for example, diode measurements with different directions is not valid. The complete composition tables for the direction of aggregate measurements are given in Table 3 (serial combinations) and Table 4 (parallel combinations).

Table 1. Serial combination of measurement directions (b-e = begin-to-end, e-b = end-to-begin, b-n = both necessary, b-p = both-possible, exp = experimental, n-p = none-possible). Measurements with direction n-p will no longer be considered.

serial	b-e	e-b	b-n	b-p	n-p	exp
b-e	b-e	n-p	exp	b-e	n-p	exp
e-b	n-p	e-b	exp	e-b	n-p	exp
b-n	exp	exp	b-n	b-n	n-p	exp
b-p	b-e	e-b	b-n	b-p	n-p	exp
n-p	n-p	n-p	n-p	n-p	n-p	n-p
exp	exp	exp	exp	exp	n-p	exp

Table 2. Parallel combination of measurement directions.

par	b-e	e-b	b-n	b-p	n-p	exp
b-e	b-e	b-n	b-n	exp	b-e	exp
e-b	b-n	e-b	b-n	exp	e-b	exp
b-n	b-n	b-n	b-n	exp	b-n	exp
b-p	exp	exp	exp	b-p	b-p	exp
n-p	b-e	e-b	b-n	b-p	n-p	exp
exp	exp	exp	exp	exp	exp	exp

Table 3. Serial combination of measurements (con = conduction, nco = non-conduction, res = resistance, cap = capacity, dio = diode, exp = experimental measurement).

serial	con	nco	res	cap	dio	exp
con	con/bth	nco/col	res/bth	cap/bth	dio/bth	exp/bth
nco	nco/row	nco/non	nco/row	nco/row	nco/row	nco/row
res	res/bth	nco/col	res/bth	exp/bth	exp/bth	exp/bth
cap	cap/bth	nco/col	exp/bth	cap/bth	exp/bth	exp/bth
dio	dio/bth	nco/col	exp/bth	exp/bth	exp/bth	exp/bth
exp	exp/bth	nco/col	exp/bth	exp/bth	exp/bth	exp/bth

Table 4. Parallel combination of measurements.

par	con	nco	res	cap	dio	exp
con	con/non	con/row	con/row	con/row	con/row	con/row
nco	con/col	nco/bth	res/bth	cap/bth	dio/bth	exp/bth
res	con/col	res/bth	res/bth	exp/bth	exp/bth	exp/bth
cap	con/col	cap/bth	exp/bth	cap/bth	exp/bth	exp/bth
dio	con/col	dio/bth	exp/bth	exp/bth	exp/bth	exp/bth
exp	con/col	exp/bth	exp/bth	exp/bth	exp/bth	exp/bth

Sp-Analysis is also done for contact constellations. For instance, a parallel combination of contacts can be used for a non-conduction measurement (of both contacts, see Table 2). A conduction measurement cannot be performed on two parallel contacts. However, because sp-aggregation can proceed at a higher level, the resulting measurement will still be a conduction measurement but none of the contacts is marked as measured (see the corresponding entry in Table 2). Dual results can be found for serial combinations of non-conduction measurements (see Table 1).

After sp-analysis, more abstract compound circuit elements are defined. Each compound element defines a set of necessary and possible measurements (with attributes for directions and required relay positions). As has been mentioned before, a specific aggregate of ten serial contacts requires only eleven measurements to refute all fault models. Besides the derivation of possible and necessary measurements, the sp-analysis ensures that larger nets can be handled.

For each of the compound elements, *paths* from the external "pins" of a compound to terminals (in different topological connectors) must be found. In order to find these paths, the circuit is treated as a labyrinth.

3.2 Finding Measurement Paths: Traversing a Labyrinth

Starting from the initial state of the circuit (with all relays being in a predefined starting state), PETS defines a search space of possible relay switches to generate serial measurement paths. The current version of PETS does not search for relay states where parallel configurations of compound elements can be found (e.g. for non-conduction measurements).

Finding Half-Paths

Considering each compound element of the transformed circuit, paths to topological connectors with terminals must be found. For each outgoing pin of a compound element, PETS traverses the corresponding circuit graph of topological connectors and other compound elements and in a breadth-first manner because shorter paths should be generated first. The extension of a path is possible when the measurements associated with the new head (either a topological connector or a compound element) are compatible to the measurement of the path (serial compositon, see Table 1 and Table 3). PETS treats all possible combinations of measurements as different path candidates (so-called half-paths). All path candidates are expanded until a topological connector with a terminal is found. Sometimes, the extension of a path will only be possible when a contact is closed, i.e. a relay must be switched. However, the labyrinth is tricky and switching a relay is not possible in all situations because of the interdependencies of the contacts of a relay.

PETS must ensure that switching a relay for path extension does not open a contact on the path itself! Therefore, with every half-path candidate a relay position vector is associated. For each relay, the relay position vector defines the required state (either excited or non-excited) or contains a wildcard when both states are still possible. Note that in some circuits, switching a relay might also switch another relay because they can be coupled.

Combining Half-Paths and the Associated Measurements

After the half paths have been generated, they must be combined. Half-paths can be combined when the intersection of the elements is empty and the associated relay state vectors as well as the associated measurements are compatible. Relay state vectors are compatible when the states of the corresponding relays are either equal or at least one of the states is undefined (wildcard). Measurements are combined according to Table 1 and Table 3. Measurements are compatible when at least one basic circuit element can still be measured.

Avoiding Shortcuts: Blocking Cycles

The serial combination of half-paths is only a necessary condition for combining two half-paths. In addition, there must exist a relay position such that the circuit elements on the path are not shorted by side-paths connected to the main path. Thus, for generating a full path, the octopus arms starting from the "main" path (see Figure 2 for an example) must be followed and shortcuts must be detected. If there is a shortcut, a contact on the shortcut path must be opened, i.e. another relay must be switched and PETS must find a contact whose relay position is not yet bound by the relay state vector.[3]

A (full) measurement path is a sequence of topological connectors and compound elements. It starts and ends with a different topological connector. The space of measurement path candidates for compound elements (aggregates after sp-analysis) is generated by delayed evaluation programming techniques, i.e. only those candidates which are really needed are actually generated. In the next section, we will discuss how PETS combines the candidates to a complete test plan.

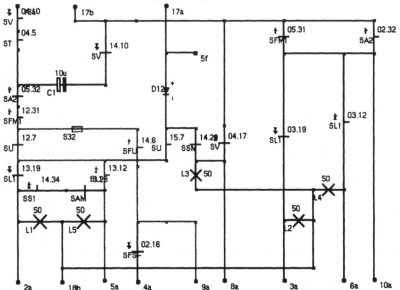

Fig. 4. Another measurement path for a non-conduction measurement (see also Figure 2).

---

3. The current implementation takes the first contact that is found while following a side-path and whose relay can be switched. This is not always the best solution because relay switches are not minimized. PETS sacrifices optimality for computation time in this respect.

3.3 Generating the Test Plan: A Two-Stage Approach

The task of PETS is to find a sequence of measurements (a test plan) such that all elements are tested (necessary measurements), all constraints are fulfilled (e.g. topological connector constraints) and the above-mentioned optimality criteria are satisfied. Test plan generation is realized by a two-stage process indicated by the following procedure:

```
procedure test-plan-generation(circuit)
    circuit-state := initial-circuit-state(circuit);
    while unmeasured-elements-existing(circuit)
            and measurements-possible(circuit) do
        measurements := applicable-measurements(circuit-state);
        while not(emptylist(measurements)) do
            m := first(sort(measurements, g1));
            measurements := rest(measurements);
            mark-elements-as-measured(elements(m), circuit);
            add-to-test-plan-of-circuit(circuit, m);
        end
        circuit-state := next-circuit-state(circuit, g2);
    end
end
```

The initial relay state (i.e. the corresponding circuit state) is defined by the measurement machinery. When there are still circuit elements for which measurements are required, the list of measurements that are applicable in the chosen circuit state are determined. Measurement candidates have been generated by the process described in the previous section. A measurement is applicable in a certain circuit state when the associated relay state vectors are compatible. i.e. when the associated relay state vector either requires the same relay state as found in the current circuit state or contains a wildcard. PETS orders the set of possible measurements with the cost function $g_1(m) = w_1$ elements(m) - $w_2 \, \Delta b(m)$ where elements(m) is the number of basic circuit elements that are tested with measurement m, and $\Delta b(m)$ is the number of new elements that can be tested with m. The idea is (i) to generate short measurement paths and (ii) to reduce the number of measurements.

The measurement with the lowest cost is added to the test plan. PETS continues with the previous step and computes a new ordering relation. When in a certain relay state no more measurements are available or no more elements can be tested by subsequent measurements, the next relay position is determined. PETS considers every possible successor state and takes the one that minimizes $g_2(s) = w_3 \, \Delta R(s) - w_4 \, \Delta B(s)$ where $\Delta R(s)$ returns the number of relay switches in comparison to the previous circuit state and $\Delta B(s)$ defines the number of new circuit elements that can be tested in the new relay state. The weights of the local optimization criteria can be changed by the PETS user (the interactive interface provides sliders to determine reasonable values). They allow a rough consideration of the optimality criteria. A global optimization (over all circuit states and two-point measurements) would be computationally much more expensive with only limited value in practice.

3.4 Evaluation and Performance Considerations

As discussed before, by switching relays PETS only generates serial measurements path. There is no attempt to look for circuit states where parallel configurations of compound elements are created. Parallel compounds are useful for non-conduction measurements. However, in all circuits that have been used as test circuits for PETS, the serial combination of compounds on a measurement path was sufficient to compute measurements for all components that can be tested with the prescribed test automaton.

Experiences with PETS have shown that in some rare cases, for aggregation not only the direction of measurements are important but also the attribute values of circuit elements. For instance, due to measurement inaccuracies, a serial combination of a 100 Ohm resistor R1 and a 10kOhm resistor R2 will hardly reveal resistance deviations of R1. In this case, the serial combination should be allowed for R2 (there might be no other way to measure it), but for R1 an additional measurement path should be found. The generation of a test plan for the small circuit in Figure 1 with 14 relays and 20 contacts generates 33 measurements and takes approximately 30 seconds on a SPARC 10. All elements are tested except two contacts parallel to two lamps (see the discussion above). Other nets with up to 40 relays and 500 contacts and other elements take up to one hour of computation time.

4 Conclusion

In this paper, we have introduced a methodology for generating test plans that avoids combinatorial explosion. The key idea is to generate a test plan by reasoning about measurements. For reasoning about measurements PETS represents knowledge about measurement combinations (see the measurement combination tables above) and knowledge about testing the topological circuit structure (see the treatment of topological connectors). The combinatorial complexity can be reduced because there are far less measurements possible than system states (defined by local models of component behavior). In order to derive the complete set of measurements for a test plan, only a fragment of the system states has to be considered. However, a shortcoming of the current version of PETS is that parameters for some measurements must still be manually derived (so-called experimental measurements). This is the place where traditional model-based testing techniques could be integrated. For local element constellations on a measurement path, a more elaborate reasoning strategy based on models about component behavior can indeed be tractable. Thus, both approaches can complement each other, and it would be very interesting to combine PETS with a model-based simulation component. New approaches to model-based diagnosis reduce computation cost by interleaving model-based inference phases with probing (or measurement) phases (de Kleer and Raiman [4]). The key idea is to gain new information about components at some state of model-based inferencing to reduce the set of diagnosis candidates. Thus, computation time is taken into account as an optimality criterion. However, in the PETS scenario, concrete results of measurements are not available during test plan computation.

At the end, it should be noted that multiple faults are no problem in the PETS scenario as long as they do not cancel each other out. When a measurement reveals that one element on a measurement path must be faulty, the engineer will manually look for the culprit and, after the repair, the whole assembly will be tested again. But, unfortunately, one can easily construct circuits where a fault will remain *undetected* by a test plan because of interfering multiple faults. Further work is required to extend test plans with additional measurements to rule out these multiple fault problems.

References

1. Böttcher, C., *No Faults in Structure? – How to Diagnose Hidden Interactions*, in: Proc. IJCAI'95, Morgan Kaufmann Publ., 1995, pp. 1728-1734.

2. Bryant, R.E., *On the Complexity of VLSI Implementations and Graph Representations of Boolean Functions with Application to Integer Multiplications*, in: IEEE Transactions on Computers, Vol. 40, No. 2, February 1991, pp. 205-213.

3. De Kleer, J., Williams, B.C., *Diagnosing Multiple Faults*, in: Readings in Model-Based Diagnosis, Hamscher, W., Console, L., De Kleer, J. (Eds.), Morgan Kaufmann Publ., 1992, pp. 100-117.

4. De Kleer, J., Raiman, O., *Trading off the costs of inference vs. probing in diagnosis*, in: Proc. IJCAI'95, Morgan Kaufmann Publ. 1995, pp. 1736-1741.

5. Fujiwara, H., Shimono, T., *On the Acceleration of Test Generation Algorithms*, in: Proc. IEEE Transactions on Computers, pp., 1137-1144, 1983.

6. Inderst, R., *Automatische Testgenerierung auf der Basis einer qualitativen Modellierung physikalischer Systeme*, in German, Diploma Thesis, University of Munich, Feb. 1995.

7. Khaani, F., Navabi, Z., *VHDL Structural Models for the Implementation of Path Sensitation Test Generation*, http://www.ece.neu.edu/info/vhdl/Postscript_papers/.

8. Mauss, J., Neumann, B., *Diagnosis by Algebraic Modeling and Fault-Tree Induction*, in: Proc. DX-95, 6th Int. Workshop on Principles of Diagnosis, Goslar, Germany, pp. 73-80, 1995.

9. Mauss, J., Neumann, B., *How to Guide Qualitative Reasoning about Electrical Circuits by Series-Parallel Trees*, in: Proc. QR'96, 10th Int. Workshop on Qualitative Reasoning, Stanford, CA, 1996.

10. Nayak, P.P., *Automated Modeling of Physical Systems*, Lecture Notes in Artificial Intelligence 1003, Springer 1995.

11. Raiman, O., de Kleer, J., Sarasvat, V., Shirley, M., *Characterizing Non-Intermittent Faults*, in: Proc. AAAI'91, Morgan Kaufmann Publ., 1991, pp. 849-854.

12. Roth, G.P. *Computer Logic, Testing, and Verification*, Computer Science Press, 1980.

13. Struss, P., *What's in SD? Towards a Theory of Modeling for Diagnosis*, in: Readings in Model-Based Diagnosis, Hamscher, W., Console, L., De Kleer, J. (Eds.), Morgan Kaufmann Publ., 1992, pp. 419-449.

14. Struss, P., Dressler, O., *Physical Negation - Integrating Fault Models into the General Diagnostic Engine*, in: Proc. IJCAI 89, Morgan Kaufmann Publ., 1989, pp. 1318-1323.

15. Struss, P., *Testing Physical Systems*, in: Proc. AAAI'94, Morgan Kaufmann Publ., pp. 251-256.

16. Struss, P., *Model Abstraction for Testing of Physical Systems*, in: Proc. QR'94, 8th Int. Workshop on Qualitative Reasoning, Nara, Japan, 1994.

17. Struss, P., Malik, A., Sachenbacher, M., *Qualitative Modeling is the Key*, in: Proc. DX-95, 6th Int. Workshop on Principles of Diagnosis, Goslar, Germany, pp. 73-80, 1995.

Case Retrieval Nets: Basic Ideas and Extensions

Mario Lenz and Hans-Dieter Burkhard

Dept. of Computer Science, Humboldt University Berlin, Axel-Springer-Str. 54a,
10117 Berlin, Germany, Email: {lenz,hdb}@informatik.hu-berlin.de

Abstract. An efficient retrieval of a relatively small number of relevant cases from a huge case base is a crucial subtask of Case-Based Reasoning. In this article, we present *Case Retrieval Nets* (CRNs), a memory model that has recently been developed for this task. The main idea is to apply a spreading activation process to a net–like case memory in order to retrieve cases being similar to a posed query case. We summarize the basic ideas of CRNs, suggest some useful extensions, and present some initial experimental results which suggest that CRNs can successfully handle case bases larger than considered usually in the CBR community.
Keywords: Case-based Reasoning, Case Retrieval, Spreading Activation

1 Introduction

Within the field of case-based reasoning, a major area of research in recent years has been the development of techniques allowing for an efficient and yet flexible retrieval of relevant cases. This has led to a number of sophisticated techniques for this subtask, as for example indexing techniques ([13]); *kd*–trees ([17, 18]); the heuristic *"Fish–and–Sink"* approach ([14]); the CRASH memory model ([3]); and *Knowledge-directed Spreading Activation* (KDSA, [19]).

As an alternative technique especially suitable for the design of decision support systems ([4, 8]), we developed the concept of *Case Retrieval Nets* (CRNs) as a memory structure supporting efficient but nevertheless flexible case retrieval. In contrast to ABS (an earlier model using *spreading activation*, cf. [9]), CRNs are more generally applicable and do rest on a sound formal framework which allows for the investigation of properties. Besides the theoretical investigations, we already performed a number of empirical tests with CRNs. The complete documentation of the results can be found in [7].

Before we go into the details about CRNs, we would like to outline what we consider as requirements for a case retrieval technique. Basically, there are three conditions to be met: efficiency, completeness, and flexibility (cf. also [3, 17]):

Efficiency concerns the effort required to access relevant cases. Access of these cases should avoid exhaustive search in memory.

Completeness assures that every sufficiently similar case in memory will be found during retrieval. (The corresponding problem of correctness is often solved as a secondary selection step over the retrieved cases.)

Flexibility expresses that there are no inherent restrictions concerning the circumstances under which a particular piece of knowledge can be recalled.

In general, these conditions express contradictory goals: Most techniques for pre-structuring the case memory increase efficiency but limit the flexibility.

2 Basic ideas of *Case Retrieval Nets*: An Example

The most fundamental item in the context of CRNs are so-called *Information Entities* (IEs). These may represent any basic knowledge item, such as a particular attribute-value-pair. A *case* then consists of a set of such IEs, and the *case base* is a net with nodes for the IEs observed in the domain and additional nodes denoting the particular cases. IE nodes may be connected by *similarity arcs*, and a case node is reachable from its constituting IE nodes via *relevance arcs*. Different degrees of similarity and relevancy may be expressed by varying arcs weights. Given this structure, case retrieval is performed by

- activating the IEs given in the query case,
- propagating this activation according to similarity through the net of IEs,
- and collecting the achieved activation in the associated case nodes.

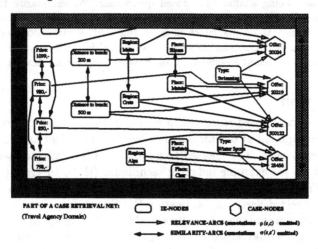

PART OF A CASE RETRIEVAL NET:
(Travel Agency Domain)

IE-NODES   CASE-NODES

RELEVANCE-ARCS (annotations $\rho(e,c)$ omitted)
SIMILARITY-ARCS (annotations $\sigma(e,e')$ omitted)

Fig. 1. Example of a CRN in the TRAVEL AGENCY domain.

The idea is illustrated for the TRAVEL AGENCY domain ([6]) in Figure 1: A case is a special travel offer, denoted by a case descriptor, e.g. <Offer 20219>. It consists of a set of corresponding IEs giving the specification of that offer, in case of <Offer 20219> the IE nodes <Type:Swimming>, <Price:980>, <Place:Matala>, <Region:Crete>, <Distance to beach:500 m> are associated to that case node. Asking for an offer in Crete for swimming and not too far from the beach, the IE nodes <Type:Swimming>, <Distance to beach:200 m> and <Region:Crete> are initially activated. By similarity, the IE nodes <Region:Malta> and <Distance to beach:500 m> will be activated in the next step, but the amount of activation depends on arc weights. Finally, the three offers <Offer 20024>, <Offer 20219>, <Offer 500122> will each get some activation depending on the incoming activations of IE nodes and their relevances. The highest activated cases may be proposed to the customer. A first list of proposals might include alternative solutions which are pruned after the customer decided for either of them.

This simple example already points out some features of the memory model:

- It can handle only *partially specified queries* without loss of efficiency (most case retrieval techniques have problems with partial descriptions).
- Case retrieval is seen as *case completion*, i.e. whatever part of a case is given as a description, the retrieval algorithm will deliver the remaining part and thus complete the case. In contrast to, for example, classification tasks there is no distinction between a *description* of a problem and a *solution*[1].
- It can be tuned to express different similarities/relevances at run time (by simply changing related arc weights), while most other techniques need a new compilation step.
- Cases can (but need not) be described by attribute vectors. Thereby, the cases may be related to different attributes (e.g., for Winter Sports, the <Distance to beach> is not relevant).
- Insertion of new cases (even with new attributes) can be performed incrementally by injecting related nodes and arcs.

3   A formal model of *Case Retrieval Nets*

In this section we will give a formal description of *Case Retrieval Nets* in a basic (*"flat"*) version allowing for a detailed investigation of the approach.

Definition 1 An *Information Entity* (IE) is an atomic knowledge item in the domain, i.e. an IE represents the lowest granularity of knowledge representation, such as a particular attribute-value-pair.   □

Definition 2 A *case* consists of a unique case descriptor and a set of IEs.   □

Definition 3 A *Basic Case Retrieval Net* (BCRN) is defined as a structure $N = [E, C, \sigma, \rho, \Pi]$ with

E is the finite set of IE nodes;
C is the finite set of case nodes;
σ is the *similarity function*

$$\sigma : E \times E \to \mathcal{R}$$

which describes the similarity $\sigma(e', e'')$ between IEs e', e'';
ρ is the *relevance function*

$$\rho : E \times C \to \mathcal{R}$$

which describes the relevance $\rho(e, c)$ of the IE e to the case node c;
Π is the set of *propagation functions*

$$\pi_n : \mathcal{R}^E \to \mathcal{R}.$$

for each node $n \in E \cup C$.   □

---

[1] This is in some sense similar to queries to a database where arbitrary parts of the database record may be specified to obtain other parts — however, there is nothing like a *primary key* to support efficiency.

The graphical description (cf. Figure 1) is given by a graph with nodes $E \cup C$ and directed arcs between them. The arc from $e' \in E$ to $e'' \in E$ is labeled by $\sigma(e', e'')$, the arc from $e \in E$ to $c \in C$ is labeled by $\rho(e, c)$ (arcs are omitted if they are labeled by zero). The functions π_n are annotations to the nodes n.

An IE e belongs to a case c (is *associated* to it) if $\rho(e, c) \neq 0$. Its relevance for case c is given by the value of $\rho(e, c)$ expressing the importance for re-finding e in a retrieved case c. Similarity between IEs e', e'' is measured by $\sigma(e', e'')$. The functions π_n are used to compute the new activation of node n depending on the incoming activations (a simple setting may use the sum of inputs as π_n).

Definition 4 An *activation* of a BCRN $N = [E, C, \sigma, \rho, \Pi]$ is a function $\alpha : E \cup C \to \mathcal{R}$ □

In the graphical notation, the activations $\alpha(n)$ are further annotations to the nodes $n \in E \cup C$. Informally, the activation $\alpha(e)$ of an IE e expresses the importance of that IE concerning the actual problem. The influence of an IE to case retrieval depends on that value and its relevances $\rho(e, c)$ for the cases c. Negative values can be used as an indicator for the rejection of cases containing that IE.

Formally, the propagation process for the basic model is given by:

Definition 5 Consider a BCRN $N = [E, C, \sigma, \rho, \Pi]$ with $E = \{e_1, ..., e_s\}$ and let be $\alpha_t : E \cup C \to \mathcal{R}$ the activation at time t. The activation of IE nodes $e \in E$ at time $t + 1$ is given by

$$\alpha_{t+1}(e) = \pi_e(\sigma(e_1, e) \cdot \alpha_t(e_1), ..., \sigma(e_s, e) \cdot \alpha_t(e_s)),$$

and the activation of case nodes $c \in C$ at time $t + 1$ is given by

$$\alpha_{t+1}(c) = \pi_c(\rho(e_1, c) \cdot \alpha_t(e_1), ..., \rho(e_s, c) \cdot \alpha_t(e_s)).$$ □

To pose a query, the activation of all IE nodes may start with

$$\alpha_0(e) = \begin{cases} 1 & : & \text{for the IE nodes } e \text{ describing the query case} \\ 0 & : & \text{else} \end{cases}$$

For more subtle queries, α_0 might assign different weights to special IE nodes, and some *context* may be set as initial activation for further nodes.

Given α_0 and Definition 5 it is well-defined how the activation of each node $n \in C \cup E$ has to be computed at any time. In particular, case retrieval by propagation of activations is a three-step process (as in the introduction):

Step 1 – Query : Given the query, α_0 is determined for all IE nodes.

Step 2 – Similarity : The activation α_0 is propagated to all IEs $e \in E$:

$$\alpha_1(e) = \pi_e(\sigma(e_1, e) \cdot \alpha_0(e_1), ..., \sigma(e_s, e) \cdot \alpha_0(e_s)),$$

Step 3 – Relevancy : The result of step 2 is propagated to the case nodes $c \in C$:

$$\alpha_2(c) = \pi_c(\rho(e_1, c) \cdot \alpha_1(e_1), ..., \rho(e_s, c) \cdot \alpha_1(e_s)).$$

Putting all the formulae together, we obtain the following result:

> Consider a BCRN $N = [E, C, \sigma, \rho, \Pi]$ with the activation function α_t as defined in Definitions 4 and 5. The result of the case retrieval for a given query activation α_0 is the *preference ordering* of cases according to decreasing activations $\alpha_2(c)$ of case nodes $c \in C$.

Case based systems with attribute vectors often use a similarity measure which is computed as the weighted sum of attribute similarities (*composite* similarities). These can easily be implemented by special BCRNs ([10]). As experiments show (cf. Section 5 and [7]), the implementation of case retrieval using CRNs is efficient. Moreover, (B)CRNs offer the possibilities of extensions in various ways, some of which will be given now.

4 Extensions of *Case Retrieval Nets*

While Section 3 presented a formal model of the most basic type of *Case Retrieval Nets*, this section focuses on some useful extensions to BCRNs. Due to the limited space, however, these extensions will only be described informally — formal descriptions can be found in [10].

4.1 Improving retrieval: Lazy Spreading Activation

A first improvement of BCRNs concerns the spreading activation scheme as proposed on page 4: Instead of propagating activation to the case nodes only after all IE nodes have been activated, a kind of *any–time* algorithm, called *Lazy Spreading Activation*, can be employed. The key idea is to subsequently extend the scope of IEs considered from more similar to less similar ones (cf. Figure 2). Each time before activation is propagated to less similar IEs, however, the case nodes associated to those IEs accessed so far are updated. Thus the propagation of activation to less similar IEs may be aborted if sufficiently similar cases have been accessed. A sound formalism (which in particular guarantees completeness and correctness) can be found in [11].

The advantage of *Lazy Spreading Activation* concerns such IE nodes e which are connected by similarity to many other IE nodes e' (but with different degrees of similarity $\sigma(e, e')$). If a query containing e is *close* to some cases in the case base, then we may find that only those IE nodes e' are really used which are close (similar) to e. In such cases it seems unreasonable to perform the propagation through the entire net of all IEs in step 2 of the scheme on page 4 before any case node is accessed. (Similar arguments hold for IE nodes which are connected to many cases, but with different degrees of relevance.)

4.2 Improving structuring: Microfeature CRNs

According to flat case representations, the simple model of BCRN has considered IEs as atomic entities. This implies that the similarity function σ needs to be fully specified, i.e. in BCRNs it is necessary that for each $e_i, e_j \in E$ the value of $\sigma(e_i, e_j)$ be specified. For practical applications, where a large number of possible

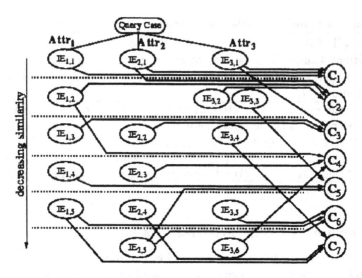

Fig. 2. Illustration of *Lazy Spreading Activation*. Similarity to the initially activated IEs decreases from top to bottom. The *lower levels* are accessed only if necessary, i.e. only if the number of cases associated to the more similar IEs is not sufficient.

values exists for each attribute, this may be impossible or at least uncomfortable. On the other hand, one often has the opportunity to organize the different attribute values (or IEs) in such a way that certain *concepts* can be utilized. This is the idea of *Microfeature CRNs* which employ a number of domain specific *microfeatures* to support similarity assessment between different IEs. When taking this approach, an IE is no longer necessarily an atomic, *non-decomposable* item, as described in Section 2, but rather represents the granularity chosen for describing cases. Each IE may, however, be a collection of further properties, concepts, or microfeatures. The major difference between microfeatures and concepts in the traditional sense is that microfeatures may be related to each other in terms of similarity, too. This is usually not applied to concepts.

As an example consider the TRAVEL AGENCY domain again: Here each particular destination is represented by an IE which, in turn, has a set of microfeatures, such as `location`, `climate`, `landscape` etc. (cf. Figure 3). The `locations` of two different IEs, for example, may then be compared; and the similarity concerning the various microfeatures, or *aspects*, is utilized to determine the similarity between two IEs. The combination of *sub-partial* similarities from the microfeature level to the partial similarities of IEs was implemented in our system based on the number of common microfeatures:

$$\sigma(e_i, e_j) = card(\{m \,|\, m \text{ is a microfeature of } e_i\} \cap \{m \,|\, m \text{ is a microfeature of } e_j\})$$

but more sophisticated computations might imitate the procedure from the upper level of cases e.g. by

$$\sigma(e_i, e_j) = \sum_{m_i \text{ of } e_i, m_j \text{ of } e_j} w_{e_i, m_i} \cdot sim_{MF}(m_i, m_j) \cdot w_{m_j, e_j}$$

where the $w_{...}$ determine the weights (importances) of particular microfeatures w.r.t. an IE, and sim_{MF} is a similarity function comparing two microfeatures. This approach to similarity assessment not only avoids the above mentioned completeness of σ, but also allows for a convenient way to incorporate a notion of *context* in similarity assessment: As in different situations different aspects are important, the influence of the various microfeatures will vary according to the weight $w_{...}$ — giving rise to a context-sensitive similarity measure.

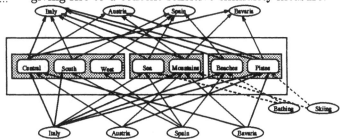

Fig. 3. Utilizing microfeatures (middle level) to determine similarity of IEs (upper level) in the TRAVEL AGENCY domain.

5 Empirical Results

In this section, we want to present some empirical results achieved from experiments with various case bases which seem to be very promising as far as the applicability of CRNs to large case bases is concerned. This research was motivated by the observation that (to our knowledge) all investigations have been performed using fairly small case bases: For example, in the INRECA research project ([1, 2]), the largest case base (the TRAVEL AGENCY data) contained nearly 1,500 cases with the other test benches being considerably smaller[2]. To be a successful technique for real applications, however, CBR has to be able to handle larger case bases, too.

5.1 The selected case bases

In order to confirm the applicability of *Case Retrieval Nets* to large case bases we selected the following data sets:

a) data from the TRAVEL AGENCY domain ([6]);
b) the CHESS database containing particular chess endgame positions;
c) the CONNECT-4 database describing positions in the game of connect-4;
d) the LETTER database of black-and-white rectangular pixel displays to be identified as letters.

The data sets b) to d) have been taken from the *Repository of Machine Learning and Domain Theories* ([12]) provided by the University of California. All four data sets vary concerning size, type of attributes used and other properties. No data set contained missing values. Some more details are given Table 1.

---

[2] Note that we only consider the number of cases here — not size and structure of cases, complexity of similarity assessment etc.

Table 1. Properties of the used data sets

Data set	No of cases	No of attributes	Type(s) of attributes	Type of similarity metric
TRAVEL AGENCY	1,471	8	symbolic & numeric	Weighted sum of feature similarities
CHESS	28,056	7	symbolic	Ratio of shared attributes
CONNECT-4	67,557	43	symbolic	Ratio of shared attributes
LETTER	20,000	17	numeric except class	Ratio of shared attributes

The TRAVEL AGENCY case base has been included in this report for two reasons: Firstly, it has been used for comparative analyses in a number of previous articles describing other retrieval techniques (e.g. [1]). Secondly, the employed similarity metric is more knowledge intensive than for the other data sets. Hence, there is a large number of similarity links as described in the CRN model.

5.2 Tests performed

To test whether CRNs are able to handle larger case bases, we performed a number of case retrievals and measured the time required. In particular, we

- randomly selected a number of queries to be posed to the system;
- varied the specifity (number of attributes specified in a query);
- measured the CPU time required for retrieving the relevant cases (using the basic 3-step scheme presented on page 4);
- averaged the time over all queries of the same specifity.

Concerning the first point we have not yet performed extensive statistical tests confirming the random selection of queries. However, we always averaged over a number of queries of the same specifity. The second point we expected to be an important parameter influencing the retrieval time required since the complexity of retrieval in the CRN model grows with the number of attributes specified.

To allow for a meaningful evaluation, we compared the retrieval time in CRNs with the CPU time required for linear search (for the TRAVEL AGENCY data) respectively for the database transactions[3] (for the UCI data sets).

The tests have been performed using the CABATA system ([6]) on a 90 MHz Pentium©-PC for the TRAVEL AGENCY data, respectively an implementation of CRNs on a SUN SPARC–20 workstation and comparison to a commercial SYBASE database for the UCI data. In the following we will present, and briefly discuss, the results obtained from the experiments described above. Instead of presenting huge tables containing the retrieval times we will, however, display only some figures summarizing the trends.

---

[3] In fact, that decision places a handicap on the CRN model as CRNs retrieve cases in accessible data structures while the pure database transaction time does only capture the CPU time required for accessing the cases in the internal structures but not their conversion to data structures accessible to the actual program. If, however, this is included than this *reading out* of data exceeds the transaction time by far.

5.3 Results for the TRAVEL AGENCY domain

Figure 4 displays the results from posing a number of different queries to the CABATA system. Firstly, CRNs are much faster (up to 10 times) than is linear search. Secondly, the time required in CRNs depends (as expected) on the specifity of the query whereas the time for linear search remains constant. Also, the speed-up compared to a flat linear search is much larger than reported for other techniques ([5]).

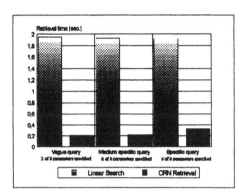

Fig. 4. Comparing linear search and CRN retrieval for the TRAVEL AGENCY domain.

5.4 Results for the UCI domains

The results in all three UCI domains were highly similar. Consequently, we will only show here the results obtained for one dataset, namely for the CONNECT-4 domain. Differences between the datasets will only be mentioned briefly in the text. For a more detailed discussion of these results cf. [7, 10].

Figure 5 displays the retrieval times required by the CRN approach for the data describing the CONNECT-4 domain. As expected, the time varied significantly depending on the specifity of the query. This is not only true for the actual retrieval time but also for the increase of time with larger case bases: While the increase is nearly linear for the fully specified queries, there is nearly no increase for the highly vague queries.

In Figure 6 (which compares CRN retrieval against database transaction times) this tendency can be observed, too: In general, the black lines illustrating CRN retrieval raise slower if less attributes are specified. While CRNs are slower than databases for the CONNECT-4 domain, the reverse ordering could be observed for the CHESS dataset. In the LETTER domain, finally, which method was faster, did depend on the specifity of the query. What is not displayed in any of these figures is that a drastic increase in retrieval time occurred if more than 35,000 cases were loaded. This is probably due to a shortage of memory which causes the system to spend a considerable amount of time with swapping data in order to allocate additional memory.

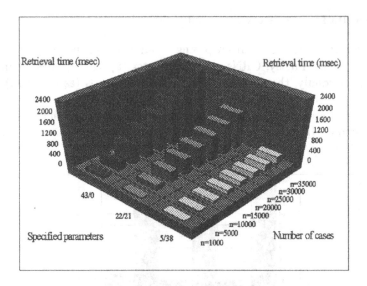

Fig. 5. Retrieval in CRNs depending on the size of the case base and the specifity of the query demonstrated for the CONNECT-4 domain.

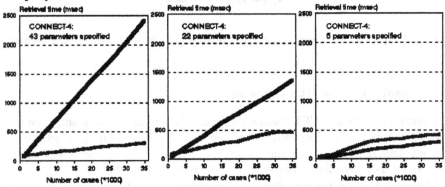

Fig. 6. CRNs (black) compared to database transactions (grey) for the CONNECT-4 domain for highly specific (left), medium specific (middle) and highly vague queries.

6 Related Work

Case Retrieval Nets inherit a number of techniques from other approaches to case retrieval and from completely different areas. A few of these will be mentioned here briefly:

The *similarity* and *propagation functions* of Definition 3 indicate that CRNs share some ideas with recurrent Neural Networks. In particular, the computations performed locally in each node support this comparison. When allowing activation to be propagated also after step 3, the behavior of CRNs comes even closer to Neural Networks. However, in CRNs each node represents a particular symbol (IE or case), and it is the activation of single nodes that matters — not entire patterns of activation.

kd–trees ([17, 18]) employ a pre-structuring of case memory into a decision tree like structure. Hence they limit flexibility of case retrieval. However, they have been designed particularly for diagnostic systems, here the loss of flexibility is probably not so severe. kd–trees utilize the so-called BWB- and BOB-Tests (cf.[17]) in order to determine which cases still need to be considered to guarantee completeness. In the *Lazy Spreading Activation* strategy of CRNs a similar technique is used, except that here each attribute is considered in isolation. This yields a more coarse estimation which is, however, easier to compute.

The *"Fish–and–Sink"* strategy ([14]) developed within the FABEL project also employs a net–like structuring of the case base. However, the nodes here directly correspond to cases which are connected via links representing their similarity concerning particular *aspects* of the domain. The IEs of CRNs do not have a counterpart. FISH–AND–SINK works by determining the utility of an arbitrary case and applying the obtained result to other cases *near* the original selected one. In order to assure completeness, one has, however, still to search the entire case base exhaustively.

The CRASH system ([3]) uses an activation passing scheme for case retrieval, too. The major difference to CRNs is that in step 2 of retrieval activation is propagated through a network of *world knowledge*. On the one hand, this allows for the integration of a deep background knowledge into the case retrieval system. On the other hand, it makes retrieval highly complex if this *world knowledge* is sufficiently broad. Also the acquisition of this knowledge may cause severe problems. In CRNs, on the contrary, the required memory structures automatically arise from the case descriptions in the form of IEs.

In the CONSYDERR system ([15]) a formal approach to combine rule-based and similarity-based reasoning utilizing microfeatures is described. Similarly, microfeatures may be employed in CRNs. However, the *Fuzzy Evidential Logic* developed for CONSYDERR is not applicable as there is no rule-based reasoning on the upper level representing IEs.

Knowledge-directed Spreading Activation (KDSA) ([20, 19]) is an improved variant of the basic spreading activation algorithms. In KDSA the spreading activation process is performed in several steps, too: Each time an analogue has been retrieved from memory, the quality of it is evaluated by a heuristic mapping component. Based on the degree of usefulness determined by this mapping component, some *"... search control module modifies the direction of subsequent spreads of activation into more promising areas of the knowledge base"* ([19]). KDSA has been designed mainly for cross-domain analogies where the goal is to retrieve *"... semantically distant analogies"*. This differs from our standpoint in so far as we assume that the goal of retrieval is to access previously encountered cases describing problem situations in the same domain. Given this assumption, the task of the heuristic mapping component of KDSA (namely to determine how close a retrieved case is to the query) can be fulfilled by simply assessing the similarity between the query and the retrieved case — that's exactly what *Case Retrieval Nets* do. What's more, if retrieval performed by *Lazy Propagation of Similarity* as described in Section 4.1), then retrieval in CRNs becomes similar to KDSA in so far as spread of activation is limited and hence blind and exhaustive search is avoided.

7 Summary

The main goal of this article was to present a formal description of *Basic Case Retrieval Nets*. Summarizing we can state that:

- CRNs support efficient case retrieval. This claim has been tested using the CABATA system and in tests with case bases of up to 35,000 cases ([7]).
- Retrieval using CRNs is based on a sound formalism, in particular it is complete as mentioned in Section 4.1.
- CRNs support flexible case retrieval as cases are considered as sets of IEs — hence each part of a case may be used to retrieve other parts and no *a priori* distinction between a *problem description* and a *solution* is necessary.
- Construction and maintenance (insertion, deletion of cases) is straightforward and computationally cheap.

A prerequisite for the applicability of CRNs is that a composite similarity measure is applied, i.e. that similarity of two cases is determined according to the similarity of the features describing the cases. In more detail, CRNs are useful if similarity between different values of certain attributes is taken into account — although Tversky's *Contrast Rule* ([16]) may be implemented, too: In this case, the similarity function σ is reduced to the identity checking function.

Concerning the test performed so far we may say that:

- CRNs are able to handle case bases of reasonable size. Most remarkably, the number of cases in the above tests goes far beyond the size of case bases in other systems.
- While a shortage of memory could be observed when storing about 40,000 cases of the CONNECT-4 domain, 35,000 cases of this data set and the complete data of the other test benches could be handled without difficulties.
- CRNs require considerably less retrieval time (about 10%) than linear search.
- CRNs are not always as fast as the corresponding transactions in commercial databases (see Footnote 3 for a remark on this). However, even in these situations retrieval in CRNs is slower only by a factor which remains small and seems acceptable.
- As expected, the retrieval time in CRNs depends on the specifity of the queries while this has basically no effect on the database transactions.

References

1. E. Auriol, K.-D. Althoff, S. Weß, and S. Dittrich. Integrating induction and case-based reasoning: Methodological approach and first evaluations. In J.-P. Haton, M. Keane, and M. Manago, editors, *Advances in Case-Based Reasoning (Proc. EWCBR-94)*, pages 18–32. Springer, LNAI 984, 1994.

2. E. Auriol, S. Weß, M. Manago, K.-D. Althoff, and R. Traphöner. INRECA: A seamlessly integrated system based on inductive inference and case-based reasoning. In M. M. Veloso and A. Aamodt, editors, *Case-Based Reasoning Research and Development (Proc. ICCBR-95)*, pages 371–380. Springer, LNAI 1010, 1995.

3. M. G. Brown. *A Memory Model for Case Retrieval by Activation Passing*. PhD thesis, University of Manchester, 1994.

4. H.-D. Burkhard and P. Pirk. Technical diagnosis: Fallexperte-D. *Proc. 4th German Workshop on CBR*, Berlin, 1996. Humboldt University.

5. K. Goos. Preselection strategies for case based classification. In B. Nebel and L. Dreschler-Fischer, editors, *KI-94: Advances in Artificial Intelligence*, pages 28–38. Springer, 1994.

6. M. Lenz. Case-based reasoning for holiday planning. In W. Schertler, B. Schmid, A. M. Tjoa, and H. Werthner, editors, *Information and Communications Technologies in Tourism*, pages 126–132. Springer, 1994.

7. M. Lenz. Case Retrieval Nets applied to large case bases. *Proc. 4th German Workshop on CBR*, Berlin, 1996. Humboldt University.

8. M. Lenz, E. Auriol, H.-D. Burkhard, M. Manago, and P. Pirk. CBR für Diagnose und Entscheidungsunterstützung. *Künstliche Intelligenz, Themenheft Fallbasiertes Schließen*, 10(1):16–21, 1996.

9. M. Lenz and H.-D. Burkhard. Retrieval ohne Suche? In B. Bartsch-Spörl, D. Janetzko, and S. Weß, editors, *Fallbasiertes Schließen - Grundlagen und Anwendungen, Proc. XPS-95 Workshop on CBR*, pages 1–10, Kaiserslautern, 1995.

10. M. Lenz and H.-D. Burkhard. Case Retrieval Nets: Foundations, properties, implementation, and results. Techn. Report, Humboldt University, Berlin, 1996.

11. M. Lenz and H.-D. Burkhard. Lazy propagation in Case Retrieval Nets. In W. Wahlster, editor, *Proc. ECAI-96*, pages 127–131, Los Angeles, 1996. John Wiley and Sons.

12. P. M. Murphy and D. W. Aha. *UCI Repository of Machine Learning Databases and Domain Theories*. University of California, Irvine, CA, 1992.

13. E. L. Rissland, D. B. Skalak, and M. T. Friedman. Case retrieval through multiple indexing and heuristic search. In *Proc. IJCAI-93*, pages 902–908, 1993.

14. J. W. Schaaf. "Fish and Sink": An anytime-algorithm to retrieve adequate cases. In M. M. Veloso and A. Aamodt, editors, *Case-Based Reasoning Research and Development (Proc. ICCBR-95)*, pages 371–380. Springer, LNAI 1010, 1995.

15. R. Sun. Robust reasoning: integrating rule-based and similarity-based reasoning. *Artificial Intelligence*, 75(2):241–295, 1995.

16. A. Tversky. Features of similarity. *Psychological Review*, 84:327–352, 1977.

17. S. Weß. *Fallbasiertes Problemlösen in wissensbasierten Systemen zur Entscheidungsunterstützung und Diagnostik*. PhD thesis, Universität Kaiserslautern, 1995.

18. S. Weß, K.-D. Althoff, and G. Derwand. Using kd-trees to improve the retrieval step in case-based reasoning. In S. Weß, K.-D. Althoff, and M. M. Richter, editors, *Topics in Case-Based Reasoning, Proc. EWCBR-93*, pages 167–181. Springer, 1994.

19. M. Wolverton. An investigation of marker-passing algorithms for analogue retrieval. In M. M. Veloso and A. Aamodt, editors, *Case-Based Reasoning Research and Development (Proc. ICCBR-95)*, pages 371–380. Springer, LNAI 1010, 1995.

20. M. Wolverton and B. Hayes-Roth. Retrieving semantically distant analogies with knowledge-directed spreading activation. In *Proc. AAAI-94*, 1994.

Putting Default Logics in Perspective

Thomas Linke[1], Torsten Schaub[2]

[1] Department of Mathematics and Computer Science, University of Bremen,
D-28359 Bremen, tlinke@wowbagger.pc-labor.uni-bremen.de
[2] Faculté de Sciences, Université d'Angers, 2 Boulevard Lavoisier,
F-49045 Angers Cedex 01, torsten.schaub@univ-angers.fr

Abstract. The evolution of Reiter's default logic has resulted in diverse variants sharing many interesting properties. This process however seems to be diverging because it has led to default logics that are difficult to compare due to different formal characterizations dealing sometimes even with different objects of discourse. This problem is addressed in this paper. That is, we elaborate on the relationships between different types of default logics. In particular, we show how two recently proposed variants, namely rational and CA-default logic, are related to each other and existing default logics.

1 Introduction

Default logic has become the prime candidate for formalizing consistency-based default reasoning since its introduction in [14]. Since then, several variants of default logic have been proposed in order to rectify either purportedly counter-intuitive or technical problems of the original approach. Among them, justified default logic[3] [8], cumulative default logic [1], J-default logic [2], constrained default logic [15], along with more recent proposals, such as CA- and Q-default logic [5] and rational default logic [11]. But even though this evolutionary process has resulted in diverse variants sharing many interesting properties, it seems to be diverging. This is not only due to the fact that the aforementioned variants use different objects of discourse (like ordinary or labeled formulas) but also that some of them employ different formal means (like explicit fixed-point operators or maximal set constructions) for characterizing sets of conclusions that render the resulting variants hardly comparable. This shortcoming is addressed in this paper.

We give results relating different types of default logics. In particular, we show how the more recent ones, namely rational- and CA-default logic, are related to each other and to previously proposed default logics. As a formal tool, we have chosen constrained default logic due to it's explicit distinction between a set of beliefs and its underlying consistency assumptions. This hybridness will serve us as a primary instrument for comparing and relating the respective approaches. In fact, we consider constrained default logic as presented in [3]. This variant essentially marries and extends the work found in [2] and [15]. As a

---

[3] Originally called *modified* default logic.

side-effect, we can thus rely on the already established relationships gathered around constrained default logic: While [16] and [2] fix its relationship to justified, cumulative and classical default logic, [12] relate it with rational default logic.

2 Default logic

This section introduces Reiter's classical default logic along with some important formal properties.

Default logic augments classical logic by *default rules* of the form[4] $\frac{\alpha:\beta}{\gamma}$. Such a rule is called *normal* if β is equivalent to γ; it is called *semi-normal* if β implies γ. We sometimes denote the *prerequisite* α of a default rule δ by $Pre(\delta)$, its *justification* β by $Just(\delta)$ and its *consequent* γ by $Cons(\delta)$. A set of default rules D and a set of formulas W form a *default theory* (D, W) that may induce a single or multiple *extensions* in the following way.

Definition 2.1 [14] *Let (D, W) be a default theory. For any set of formulas S, let $\Gamma(S)$ be the smallest set of formulas S' such that*

E1 $W \subseteq S'$,
E2 $Th(S') = S'$,
E1 *For any $\frac{\alpha:\beta}{\gamma} \in D$, if $\alpha \in S'$ and $S \cup \{\beta\}$ is consistent then $\gamma \in S'$.*

A set of formulas E is a classical extension of (D, W) iff $\Gamma(E) = E$.

Any such extension represents a possible set of beliefs about the world at hand.

In order to illustrate the above and the following definitions let us consider default theory

$$\left(\left\{ \frac{:b}{c}, \frac{:\neg b}{d}, \frac{:\neg c \wedge \neg d}{e} \right\}, \emptyset \right) . \tag{1}$$

This default theory combines several potential conflicts which provide an indication of how far a default logic commits to its consistency assumptions (given by the justifications of the given default rules).

The joint application of the first two default rules indicates whether a given system detects inconsistencies among the set of justifications during the formation of an extension. More formally, this tells us about the underlying type of *regularity*.[5] In fact, [4] distinguish between *weak* and *strong regularity*. A set of default rules D' is *weakly regular* wrt a set of facts W iff $W \cup Cons(D') \cup Just(\{\delta\})$ is consistent for each $\delta \in D'$; while D' is *strongly regular* wrt a set of facts W iff $W \cup Cons(D') \cup Just(D')$ is consistent. We call a default logic weakly or strongly

---

[4] Reiter [14] considers default rules having finite sets of justifications. [10] show that any such default rule can be transformed into a set of default rules having a single justifications. An even stronger property is enjoyed by the variants of Section 3, for which multiple justifications are equivalent to their conjunction, as a single justification.

[5] The notion of regularity is due to [6, 4].

regular according to its treatment of default rules, generating extensions. In fact, classical default logic enjoys weak regularity. To see this, observe that theory (1) yields one classical extension $Th(\{c, d\})$ generated by the first two default rules, whose justifications b and $\neg b$ are individually but not jointly consistent with $Th(\{c, d\})$.

The application of the third default rule (in the presence of one of the first two rules) indicates the property of *semi-monotonicity*, as introduced in [14]: A default logic is semi-monotonic iff for any default theory (D, W) and any set of default rules $D' \subseteq D$, we have that if E' is an extension of (D', W) then there is an extension E of (D, W) where $E' \subseteq E$. Note that semi-monotonicity implies the existence of extensions. Observe that classical default logic is not semi-monotonic. This is reflected by the fact that the third default rule does not contribute to any extension of theory (1); while it clearly contributes to the single extension of $(\{\frac{:\neg c \wedge \neg d}{e}\}, \emptyset)$.

Another property, namely cumulativity, is central to the variants discussed in Section 4 and so postponed to this point. A discussion of the ramifications of these properties is unfortunately beyond the scope of this paper; detailed discussions can be found in [13, 16, 1, 3].

3 Strongly regular default logics

Apart from classical, justified, and Q-default logic, all of the aforementioned variants enjoy strong regularity [4]. This section elaborates on the relationship between two such variants, namely constrained and rational default logic.

3.1 Constrained default logic

Our formal point of departure is given by constrained default logic [3]. As mentioned above, this is motivated by the fact that constrained default logic allows us to distinguish between an extension an its underlying consistency assumptions: An extension, E, comes with an underlying set of constraints, C, which is used for accumulating the set of justifications of the applied default rules:

Definition 3.1 [3] *Let (D, W) be a default theory. For any set of formulas T, let $\Upsilon(T)$ be the pair of smallest sets of formulas (S', T') such that*

CE1 $W \subseteq S' \subseteq T'$,
CE2 $S' = Th(S')$ *and* $T' = Th(T')$,
CE3 *For any $\frac{\alpha : \beta}{\gamma} \in D$, if $\alpha \in S'$ and $T \cup \{\beta\} \cup \{\gamma\}$ is consistent then $\gamma \in S'$ and $\beta \wedge \gamma \in T'$.*

A pair of sets of formulas (E, C) is a constrained extension of (D, W) iff $\Upsilon(C) = (E, C)$.

This variant enjoys strong regularity and semi-monotonicity (which implies the existence of extensions). This is reflected by default theory (1) that yields three constrained extensions:

$$(Th(\{c\}), Th(\{c, b\})),$$
$$(Th(\{d\}), Th(\{d, \neg b\})),$$
$$(Th(\{e\}), Th(\{e, \neg c \wedge \neg d\})).$$

(2)

In order to relate constrained and rational default logic, we give next a slight modification of Definition 3.1 providing another notion of an extension:

Definition 3.2 *Let* (D, W) *be a default theory. For any set of formulas* T *let* $\overline{T}(T)$ *be the pair of smallest sets of formulas* (S', T') *such that*

$\overline{\textbf{CE1}}$ $W \subseteq S' \subseteq T'$,
$\overline{\textbf{CE2}}$ $S' = Th(S')$ *and* $T' = Th(T')$,
$\overline{\textbf{CE3}}$ *For any* $\frac{\alpha : \beta}{\gamma} \in D$, *if* $\alpha \in S'$ *and* $T \cup \{\beta\}$ *is consistent then* $\gamma \in S'$ *and* $\beta \wedge \gamma \in T'$.

A pair of sets of formulas (E, C) *is a modified constrained extension of* (D, W) *iff* $\overline{T}(C) = (E, C)$.

This definition is obtained from Definition 3.1, by replacing the condition that $T \cup \{\beta\} \cup \{\gamma\}$ is consistent in **CE3** by the condition that its subset $T \cup \{\beta\}$ is consistent in $\overline{\textbf{CE3}}$.

Even though this modification plays merely on the integration of the consequent γ into the consistency check, it has an important effect on the formal properties. To see this, consider theory (1) from which we obtain two modified constrained extensions:

$$(Th(\{c\}), Th(\{c, b\})),$$
$$(Th(\{d\}), Th(\{d, \neg b\})).$$

(3)

Notably, there is no extension containing e. This reveals that our modification has led to the loss of semi-monotonicity, even though it has preserved strong regularity.

The notion of a modified constrained extension serves for two purposes. First, it will help us to clarify the relationship between constrained and rational default logic and second, it will help us to establish a relationship between rational and CA-default logic in Section 5.2.

3.2   Rational default logic

Before we elaborate on the relationship between constrained and rational default logic, we repeat here the original definition of a rational extension, taken from [12]: For a set of default rules D, define

$$Mon(D) = \left\{ \frac{Pre(\delta)}{Cons(\delta)} \;\middle|\; \delta \in D \right\}.$$

For a set of inference rules A, let $Th^A(\cdot)$ denote the consequence operator of the formal proof system obtained from propositional calculus and rules set A. A notion central to rational default logic is that of an active set of default rules:

Definition 3.3 [12] *A set A of default rules is active wrt sets of formulas W and S iff it satisfies the following conditions.*

AS1 $Just(A) = \emptyset$ or $Just(A) \cup S$ *is consistent,*
AS2 $Pre(A) \subseteq Th^{Mon(A)}(W)$.

The set of all subsets of a set of default rules D which are active wrt W and S is denoted by $\mathcal{A}(D, W, S)$.

Define $\mathcal{MA}(D, W, S)$ to be the set of all maximal elements in $\mathcal{A}(D, W, S)$. Then, a rational extension is defined as follows:

Definition 3.4 [12] *Let (D, W) be a default theory. A set of formulas S is a rational extension of (D, W) if $S = Th^{Mon(A)}(W)$ for some $A \in \mathcal{MA}(D, W, S)$.*

Note that $S = Th^{Mon(A)}(W)$ is indeed a fixed-point equation because A is defined in terms of S through condition $A \in \mathcal{MA}(D, W, S)$.

When looking at theory (1), we observe two rational extensions,

$$Th(\{c\}),$$
$$Th(\{d\}), \tag{4}$$

which correspond to the actual extensions given in (3) for modified constrained default logic. Observe furthermore that $Th(\{e\})$ is not a rational extension of (1) since $\{\frac{:\neg c \wedge \neg d}{e}\}$ is not *maximally* active wrt $W = \emptyset$ and $S = Th(\{e\})$. This is because $\{\frac{:\neg c \wedge \neg d}{e}, \frac{:b}{c}\}$ is active wrt $W = \emptyset$ and $S = Th(\{e\})$. This illustrates that rational default logic is strongly regular albeit it is not semi-monotonic.

3.3 Relationships between strongly regular default logics

At this point, the key question is clearly that on the relationship between rational and (modified) constrained default logic. In (4) we have just seen that rational default logic yields the same extensions as modified constrained default logic. In fact, both variants can be proven to be equivalent, as we demonstrate next. All proofs of theorems are given in [7].

The first half of the equivalence is given in the next theorem.[6]

Theorem 3.1 *Let E be a rational extension of default theory (D, W) and let $A \in \mathcal{MA}(D, W, E)$ be such that $E = Th^{Mon(A)}(W)$. If $C = Th(E \cup Just(A))$ then (E, C) is a modified constrained extension of (D, W).*

Define $GD_m(D, S, T) = \{\frac{\alpha : \beta}{\gamma} \in D \mid \alpha \in S \text{ and } T \cup \{\beta\} \text{ is consistent}\}$ for a default theory (D, W) and sets of formulas S and T. Then, the second half is the following one.

Theorem 3.2 *Let (E, C) be a modified constrained extension of default theory (D, W). Then, E is a rational extension of (D, W) and $GD_m(D, E, C) \in \mathcal{MA}(D, W, E)$.*

---

[6] Compare this half of the equivalence with Theorem 3.3, dealing with original constrained default logic.

In view of these theorems, the characterization of modified constrained extensions given in Definition 3.2 provides us with a specification of rational extensions by means of a traditional fixed-point operator, here $\overline{T}$.[7] This allows for a comparison of rational default logic with its relatives on equal grounds. Moreover, such a characterization supplies us with further insights into the structural properties of rational default logic. For instance, it shows that constrained and rational default logic are equivalent, if all default rules are semi-normal. For the semi-normal default rule $\frac{\alpha : \gamma \wedge \beta}{\gamma}$, the consistency conditions in **CE3** and $\overline{\text{CE3}}$, namely that $T \cup \{\gamma \wedge \beta\} \cup \{\gamma\}$ is consistent and that $T \cup \{\gamma \wedge \beta\}$ is consistent, respectively, are obviously equivalent. This observation was proved by other methods in [12].

To sum up, one obtains rational default logic by eliminating the consequent in the consistency condition of constrained default logic. In this way, rational default logic can be seen as a simple yet effect-full generalization of constrained default logic.

In fact, [12] show that each rational extension is also a constrained extension:

Theorem 3.3 *If E is a rational extension of (D, W) with $E = Th^{Mon(A)}(W)$ and $C = Th(E \cup Just(A))$ for a $A \in \mathcal{MA}(D, W, E)$ then (E, C) is a constrained extension of (D, W),*

In other words, the set of constrained extensions of a default theory forms a superset of its rational extensions.

4 Assertional default logics

Let us now turn to a family of default logics aiming at the property of *cumulativity*. This property stipulates that the addition of a conclusion to the premises should not change the entire set of conclusions (see [9]). In default logics, this is usually interpreted in the following way (cf. [1]): If a default theory (D, W) has an extension containing α, then E is an extension of (D, W) containing α iff E is an extension of $(D, W \cup \{\alpha\})$.

For example, default theory $(\{\frac{:a}{a}, \frac{a \vee b : \neg a}{\neg a}\}, \emptyset)$ has one classical extension, $Th(\{a\})$, containing $a \vee b$. Adding the latter conclusion to the set of facts yields $(\{\frac{:a}{a}, \frac{a \vee b : \neg a}{\neg a}\}, \{a \vee b\})$ whose classical extensions are $Th(\{a\})$ and $Th(\{\neg a, b\})$. This demonstrates the failure of cumulativity for classical default logic. The same applies for justified, constrained, and rational default logic.

As first observed by Brewka in [1], this phenomenon can be addressed by keeping track of consistency assumptions, whenever a default conclusion is added to the premises. For this purpose, he introduced so-called *assertions*, which are formulas labeled with a certain set of consistency assumptions.

Definition 4.1 [1] *Let $\alpha, \gamma_1, \ldots, \gamma_m$ be formulas. An assertion ξ is any expression of the form $\langle \alpha, \{\gamma_1, \ldots, \gamma_m\}\rangle$, where $\alpha = Form(\xi)$ is called the asserted*

---

[7] A pseudo-iterative definition of modified constrained extensions is given in [7].

formula and the set $\{\gamma_1, \ldots, \gamma_m\} = Supp(\xi)$ is called the support of α.[8]

Intuitively, assertions represent formulas together with the reasons for believing them.

For propagation of supports, one has to extend the standard inference relation in the following way.

Definition 4.2 [1] *Let S be a set of assertions and let $\widehat{Th}$ denote the assertional consequence operator. Then, $\widehat{Th}(S)$ is the smallest set of assertions such that*

1. $S \subseteq \widehat{Th}(S)$,
2. *if* $\xi_1, \ldots, \xi_n \in \widehat{Th}(S)$ *and* $Form(\xi_1), \ldots, Form(\xi_n) \vdash \gamma$, *then* $\langle \gamma, Supp(\xi_1) \cup \ldots \cup Supp(\xi_n) \rangle \in \widehat{Th}(S)$.

Finally, an *assertional default theory* is a pair (D, W), where D is a set of default rules and W is a set of assertions. These formalities are common to all variants discussed in this section.

4.1 Cumulative default logic

Actually, Brewka adds in [1] cumulativity *and* strong regularity to default logic.[9] Moreover, cumulative default logic is semi-monotonic and thus guarantees the existence of *assertional extensions*, which are defined in the following way.

Definition 4.3 [1] *Let (D, W) be an assertional default theory. For any set of assertions S, let $\Omega(S)$ be the smallest set of assertions S' such that*

AE1 $W \subseteq S'$,

AE2 $\widehat{Th}(S') = S'$,

AE3

For any $\frac{\alpha : \beta}{\gamma} \in D$, if $\langle \alpha, Supp(\alpha) \rangle \in S'$ and $Form(S) \cup Supp(S) \cup \{\beta\} \cup \{\gamma\}$ is consistent then $\langle \gamma, Supp(\alpha) \cup \{\beta\} \cup \{\gamma\} \rangle \in S'$.

A set of assertions $\mathcal{E}$ is an assertional extension for (D, W) iff $\Omega(\mathcal{E}) = \mathcal{E}$.

Let us illustrate the restoration of cumulativity by regarding the theory given at the start of this section: $(\{\frac{:a}{a}, \frac{a \lor b : \neg a}{\neg a}\}, \emptyset)$ has assertional extension $\widehat{Th}(\{\langle a, \{a\}\rangle\})$, including $\langle a \lor b, \{a\}\rangle$. Adding assertion $\langle a \lor b, \{a\}\rangle$ yields assertional default theory $(\{\frac{:a}{a}, \frac{a \lor b : \neg a}{\neg a}\}, \{\langle a \lor b, \{a\}\rangle\})$ which has the same assertional extension. This is because only the first default rule applies, while the second one is blocked since its justification $\neg a$ is inconsistent with the support of $\langle a \lor b, \{a\}\rangle$.

---

[8] The two projections extend to sets of assertions in the obvious way. For notational convenience, the projection *Supp* is also (ab)used to denote the support of an asserted formula, eg. $\langle \alpha, Supp(\alpha) \rangle$.

[9] Cumulative default logic was actually the first strongly regular default logic.

4.2   CA-default logic

In view of cumulative default logic's many properties, the question arises whether cumulativity is also obtainable in the absence of semi-monotonicity or strong regularity. This question is addressed in [5], where it is shown that neither of the two previous properties is required for cumulativity. To show this, [5] develop two other cumulative variants, namely CA- and Q-default logic. While neither of them is semi-monotonic, the former is strongly regular and the latter is weakly regular.

In what follows, we elaborate on CA-default logic and show how it is related to the strongly regular default logics described above. A *CA-extension* of an assertional default theory is defined as follows.

Definition 4.4 [5] *Let* (D, W) *be an assertional default theory. For any set of assertions* S, *let* $\overline{\Omega}(S)$ *be the smallest set of assertions* S' *such that*

CA1 $W \subseteq S'$,
CA2 $\widehat{Th}(S') = S'$,
CA3 *For any* $\frac{\alpha : \beta}{\gamma} \in D$, *if* $\langle \alpha, Supp(\alpha) \rangle \in S'$ *and* $Form(S) \cup Supp(S) \cup \{\beta\}$ *is consistent then* $\langle \gamma, Supp(\alpha) \cup \{\beta\} \rangle \in S'$.

A set of assertions $\mathcal{E}$ *is a CA-extension for* (D, W) *iff* $\overline{\Omega}(\mathcal{E}) = \mathcal{E}$.

In fact, CA-default logic yields the same assertional extensions as obtained in cumulative default logic from the theory given at the start of this section. The general relationship between both variants is detailed in the next section.

4.3   Relationships between assertional default logics

As already pointed out by [5], CA- and cumulative default logic are equivalent on semi-normal assertional default theories. This is so because Definition 4.3 and 4.4 turn out to be equivalent when restricted to semi-normal default rules, like those of the form $\frac{\alpha : \gamma \wedge \beta}{\gamma}$. In such a case, the consistency conditions in **AE3** and **CA3**, namely that $Form(S) \cup Supp(S) \cup \{\gamma \wedge \beta\} \cup \{\gamma\}$ is consistent and that $Form(S) \cup Supp(S) \cup \{\gamma \wedge \beta\}$ is consistent, respectively, are obviously equivalent. A similar relationship was given above between constrained default logic and its modified counterpart, which amounts to rational default logic.

In addition, we can demonstrate that in the general case, each CA-extension is also an extension in cumulative default logic:

Theorem 4.1 *Let* (D, W) *be an assertional default theory and* $\mathcal{E}$ *be a set of assertions. If* $\mathcal{E}$ *is a CA-extension of* (D, W) *then there is an assertional extension* $\mathcal{F}$ *of* (D, W), *with* $Form(\mathcal{E}) = Form(\mathcal{F})$ *and* $Supp(\mathcal{E}) \subseteq Supp(\mathcal{F})$.

In other words, the set of assertional extensions of an assertional default theory forms a superset of its CA-extensions. Again, a similar relationship was given in Section 3 between constrained and rational default logic.

5 Interrelationships

The ending of the previous section raises the question of the interrelationships between the previously described assertional default logics and the variants of default logic discussed in Section 3. This question is the central issue of the present section.

5.1 Constrained and cumulative default logic

The relationship between constrained and cumulative default logic was established in [16, 3]. When comparing the definition of assertional and constrained extensions, we observe that both require for the application of a default rule $\frac{\alpha : \beta}{\gamma}$ that its justification β and its consequent γ are jointly consistent with the set of justifications and consequents of all other applying default rules. In fact, one can show that there is a direct correspondence between the formulas in the actual extension of a constrained extension and the asserted formulas in an assertional extension:

Theorem 5.1 [3] *Let (D, W) be a default theory and $(D, \mathcal{W})$ the assertional default theory, where $\mathcal{W} = \{\langle \alpha, \emptyset \rangle \mid \alpha \in W\}$. Then, if (E, C) is a constrained extension of (D, W) then there is an assertional extension $\mathcal{E}$ of $(D, \mathcal{W})$ such that $E = Form(\mathcal{E})$ and $C = Th(Form(\mathcal{E}) \cup Supp(\mathcal{E}))$; and, conversely if $\mathcal{E}$ is an assertional extension of $(D, \mathcal{W})$ then $(Form(\mathcal{E}), Th(Form(\mathcal{E}) \cup Supp(\mathcal{E})))$ is a constrained extension of (D, W).*

Observe that we get a one-to-one correspondence between the actual extensions, namely $E = Form(\mathcal{E})$. However, the constraints of a constrained extension correspond to the deductive closure of the supports and the asserted formulas of the extension. Thus, we can map assertional extensions onto constrained extensions only modulo equivalent sets of supports.

For illustration, consider theory (1). This theory has three assertional extensions:

$$\widehat{Th}(\{\langle c, \{b, c\}\rangle\}),$$
$$\widehat{Th}(\{\langle d, \{\neg b, d\}\rangle\}), \tag{5}$$
$$\widehat{Th}(\{\langle e, \{\neg c \wedge \neg d, e\}\rangle\}).$$

We see that the asserted formulas in the respective extensions in (5) correspond to those in the actual extensions obtained in (2) for constrained default logic.

Notice that Theorem 5.1 deals with assertional default theories $(D, \mathcal{W})$ having a non-supported set of assertional facts, ie. $Supp(\mathcal{W}) = \emptyset$. A relationship in the case of supported sets of assertional facts is given in [17] by appeal to so-called pre-constrained default theories.

5.2 Rational and CA-default logic

The interesting question is now whether one can establish a similar relationship between rational and CA-default logic. In fact, a comparison of the definitions of CA- and modified constrained extensions reveals that both require for the application of a default rule $\frac{\alpha:\beta}{\gamma}$ that merely its justification β is jointly consistent with the set of justifications and consequents of all other applying default rules. That is, both variants drop the requirement on the consequent γ that was imposed in constrained and cumulative default logic.

Indeed, it turns out that CA- and modified constrained default logic (and thus also rational default logic) are equivalent modulo representational issues. We have the following result:

Theorem 5.2 *Let (D, W) be a default theory and $(D, \mathcal{W})$ the assertional default theory, where $\mathcal{W} = \{\langle \alpha, \emptyset \rangle \mid \alpha \in W\}$. Then, if (E, C) is a modified constrained extension of (D, W) then there is a CA-extension $\mathcal{E}$ of $(D, \mathcal{W})$ such that $E = Form(\mathcal{E})$ and $C = Th(Form(\mathcal{E}) \cup Supp(\mathcal{E}))$; and, conversely if $\mathcal{E}$ is a CA-extension of $(D, \mathcal{W})$ then $(Form(\mathcal{E}), Th(Form(\mathcal{E}) \cup Supp(\mathcal{E})))$ is a modified constrained extension of (D, W).*

Let us illustrate this by our everlasting example. Theory (1) results in two CA-extensions:

$$\widehat{Th}(\{\{\langle c, \{b, c\} \rangle\}\}),$$
$$\widehat{Th}(\{\{\langle d, \{\neg b, d\} \rangle\}\}).$$
(6)

In analogy to the previous section, we observe that the asserted formulas in the CA-extensions in (6) correspond to those in the actual extensions obtained in (3) for modified constrained default logic. Moreover, we see that the accumulated set of constraints are the same in both default logics.

Our next result is a corollary to Theorem 5.2 and the results on the equivalence between modified constrained and rational default logic. It gives a precise characterization of the equivalence of rational and CA-default logic:

Corollary 5.3 *Let (D, W) be a default theory and $(D, \mathcal{W})$ the assertional default theory, where $\mathcal{W} = \{\langle \alpha, \emptyset \rangle \mid \alpha \in W\}$. Then, if E is a rational extension of (D, W) with $E = Th^{Mon(A)}(W)$ and $C = Th(E \cup Just(A))$ for a $A \in \mathcal{MA}(D, W, E)$ then there is a CA-extension $\mathcal{E}$ of $(D, \mathcal{W})$ such that $E = Form(\mathcal{E})$ and $C = Th(Form(\mathcal{E}) \cup Supp(\mathcal{E}))$; and, conversely if $\mathcal{E}$ is a CA-extension of $(D, \mathcal{W})$ then $Form(\mathcal{E})$ is a rational extension of (D, W).*

For completeness, we report here that [5] have established a similar relationship between their Q-default logic and Reiter's classical default logic. We refer the reader for details to [5].

6 Conclusion

The aim of this work was to shed more light on the relationships between different types of default logics. On the one hand, we have investigated the relationship among strongly regular default logics using a conventional logical language. We have argued that rational default logic amounts to a straightforward yet effectfull generalization of constrained default logic. This has been accomplished by providing an alternative characterization of rational extensions in the traditional style of direct fixed-point definitions. A quasi-iterative definition can be found in [7]. On the other hand, we have elaborated on the relationship between strongly regular assertional default logics. We have shown that the relationship between cumulative and CA-default logic is similar to the one between constrained and rational (modified constrained) default logic. Notably, we have demonstrated that every extension in CA-default logic is also an extension in Brewka's cumulative default logic. Finally, we have related both families of default logics. In particular, we have shown that rational and CA-default logic are equivalent modulo representational issues. This result relies heavily on the presence of modified constrained default logic as a mediator. In this way, CA-default logic turns out to be the assertional counterpart of rational default logic. Similar results have been obtained by [16, 3] and [5] on the relationships between constrained and cumulative default logic, and classical and Q-default logic, respectively.

In all, our major contribution was to put rational and CA-default logic in perspective to each other and existing default logics. This task was insofar a difficult one because rational extensions were originally characterized in a different way.

References

1. G. Brewka. Cumulative default logic: In defense of nonmonotonic inference rules. *Artificial Intelligence*, 50(2):183–205, 1991.
2. J. Delgrande and W. Jackson. Default logic revisited. In J. Allen, R. Fikes, and E. Sandewall, editors, *Proceedings of the Second International Conference on the Principles of Knowledge Representation and Reasoning*, pages 118–127, San Mateo, CA, April 1991. Morgan Kaufmann Publishers.
3. J. Delgrande, T. Schaub, and W. Jackson. Alternative approaches to default logic. *Artificial Intelligence*, 70(1–2):167–237, 1994.
4. C. Froidevaux and J. Mengin. Default logic: A unified view. *Computational Intelligence*, 10(3):331–369, 1994.
5. L. Giordano and A. Martinelli. On cumulative default logics. *Artificial Intelligence*, 66(1):161–179, 1994.
6. F. Lévy. Computing extensions of default theories. In R. Kruse and P. Siegel, editors, *Proceedings of the European Conference on Symbolic and Quantitative Approaches for Uncertainty*, volume 548 of *Lecture Notes in Computer Science*, pages 219–226. Springer Verlag, 1991.
7. T. Linke and T. Schaub. Putting default logics in perspective. Technical report, 1996. Submitted for publication.
8. W. Lukaszewicz. Considerations on default logic — an alternative approach. *Computational Intelligence*, 4:1–16, 1988.
9. D. Makinson. General theory of cumulative inference. In M. Reinfrank, J. de Kleer, M. Ginsberg, and E. Sandewall, editors, *Proceedings of the Second International Workshop on Non–Monotonic Reasoning*, volume 346 of *Lecture Notes in Artificial Intelligence*, pages 1–18. Springer Verlag, 1989.
10. W. Marek and M. Truszczyński. Normal form results for default logics. In G. Brewka, K. Jantke, and P. Schmitt, editors, *Nonmonotonic and Inductive Logic*,

volume 659 of *Lecture Notes in Artificial Intelligence*, pages 153–174. Springer Verlag, 1993.

11. A. Mikitiuk and M. Truszczyński. Rational default logic and disjunctive logic programming. In A. Nerode and L. Pereira, editors, *Proceedings of the Second International Workshop on logic Programming and Non-monotonic Reasoning.*, pages 283–299. MIT Press, 1993.

12. A. Mikitiuk and M. Truszczyński. Rational versus constrained default logic. In C. Mellish, editor, *Proceedings of the International Joint Conference on Artificial Intelligence*, pages 1509–1515. Morgan Kaufmann Publishers, 1995.

13. D. Poole. What the lottery paradox tells us about default reasoning. In R. Brachman, H. Levesque, and R. Reiter, editors, *Proceedings of the First International Conference on the Principles of Knowledge Representation and Reasoning*, pages 333–340, Los Altos, CA, May 1989. Morgan Kaufmann Publishers.

14. R. Reiter. A logic for default reasoning. *Artificial Intelligence*, 13(1–2):81–132, 1980.

15. T. Schaub. On commitment and cumulativity in default logics. In R. Kruse and P. Siegel, editors, *Proceedings of European Conference on Symbolic and Quantitative Approaches to Uncertainty*, pages 304–309. Springer Verlag, 1991.

16. T. Schaub. On constrained default theories. In B. Neumann, editor, *Proceedings of the European Conference on Artificial Intelligence*, pages 304–308. John Wiley & sons, 1992.

17. T. Schaub. Variations of constrained default logic. In M. Clarke, R. Kruse, and S. Moral, editors, *Proceedings of European Conference on Symbolic and Quantitative Approaches to Reasoning and Uncertainty*, pages 312–317. Springer Verlag, 1993.

EULE2: A Prototypical Knowledge-Based Decision Support System for the Performance of Office Tasks

Andreas Margelisch, Bernd Novotny, Ulrich Reimer

Swiss Life
Information Systems Research Group
Postfach
CH-8022 Zürich, Switzerland

email: {margelisch, novotny, reimer}@swssai.uu.ch

Keywords: Hybrid Knowledge Representation, Knowledge Based Systems

1   What is EULE2 ?

In Swiss Life, as in many other companies, office workers for customer support are no longer specialists, each one dealing with a restricted number of office tasks only, but are becoming generalists who must deal with all kinds of tasks. Office tasks underlie organisational regulations and federal law which are quite often rather complex. Therefore a decision support system which knows about the regulations and the law and which can guide a user through an office task would considerably increase quality and quantity of the office work being done[1].

The knowledge-based decision support system EULE2 (cf. [RM95]) developped at Rentenanstalt/Swiss Life meets this goal. The system is still prototypical but is intended to become productive and to be used by about 150 office workers.

In Section 2 we describe how EULE2 is used to perform an office task. We will identify three different kinds of knowledge that is needed by EULE2. Section 3 deals with the formalisms chosen to represent this knowledge. We will concentrate on knowledge about action and change, and on the integration of the different formalisms leading to a hybrid knowledge representation system.

2   Performing an Office Task in EULE2

In EULE2 an office task is divided into subtasks which correspond to work steps of the office task. Within a subtask, the office worker manipulates the knowledge base by creating new objects or modifying existing objects. Figure 1 gives an example of the office task *application for a life insurance*. Its subtasks are represented by solid boxes (e.g. S_0: *fill in application form*). Some typical

---

[1] Since Rentenanstalt/Swiss Life is an insurance company we will concentrate on insurance tasks. Nevertheless EULE2 is not specifically designed for insurance tasks. Similar requirements will appear in many other fields.

object manipulations in subtask S_0 are: create a new application form object, create a new customer object, and enter the sum insured into the application form object.

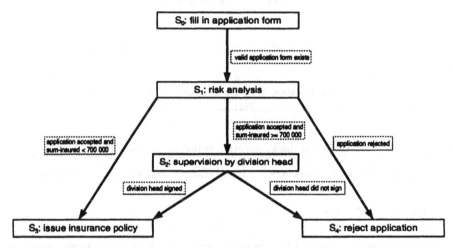

Figure 1: The office task: *application for a life insurance*

After each object manipulation EULE2 checks whether the knowledge base is still valid with respect to the underlying regulations and federal law. For example, if an application form exists that is signed by a minor and not by his guardian federal law is violated since the law requires the signature of an adult. If any violation occurs the object manipulation is rejected and an explanation is offered to the office worker.

After a valid object manipulation EULE2 checks for each subsequent subtask, whether its precondition is fulfilled. Certain subtask transitions may be illegal, certain others possible, while still others are yet undecidable because some facts are still missing. The office worker may decide to initiate one of the possible transitions or may inquire under what circumstances one of the still undecidable or illegal transitions would become permitted. When a transition is made EULE2 usually performs an action. For example, when the transition from S_1 to S_3 is made an insurance policy object is created.

In contrast to a workflow management system an office task in EULE2 is performed by one person. A synchronisation of parallel work steps is not needed.

The knowledge needed by EULE2 can be divided into three different kinds: concepts and objects, regulations, and actions. The following section deals with the representation of that knowledge.

3 Knowledge Representation in EULE2

The objects to be manipulated in EULE2 and the concepts they belong to require a terminological representation component. The terminological logic FRM serves this purpose (cf. [RLNR95]).

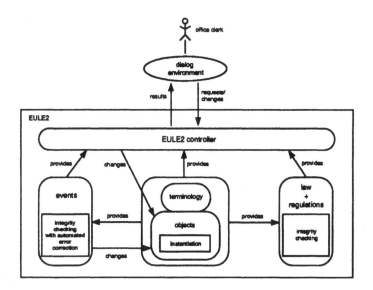

Figure 2: Architecture of EULE2

The organisational regulations and federal law that must be taken into account require a legal reasoning component[2]. For this purpose, a logic-based representation formalism is coupled with FRM. The legal knowledge is represented by deduction rules (to describe regulations as illustrated in Figure 3) and integrity constraints (to characterize invalid situations). Efficient algorithms for checking constraint satisfaction (to check if a knowledge base conforms to the legal knowledge) and constraint satisfiability (to check for inconsistencies in the legal knowledge itself) require deduction rules and integrity constraints to be range restricted (cf. [BDM88]).

$$swisslife\text{-}regulation(underwriting\text{-}reg, no\text{-}supervision\text{-}required, a, t_j, s) \Leftarrow$$
$$instance\text{-}of(a, application\text{-}form, \langle t_j, s \rangle) \wedge$$
$$property\text{-}of(a, sum\text{-}insured, n, \langle t_j, s \rangle) \wedge$$
$$n < 700'000$$

Figure 3: Definition of a company regulation

The interface between FRM and the logic-based representation formalism is based on a mapping of concept definitions and their instances to a small set of predefined predicates[3]. For example, the predicate $instance\text{-}of(i, c, \langle t_j, s \rangle)$ says that in subtask s of office-task t_j an object i being instance of the concept c exists. For reasons of efficiency each subtask has its own knowledge base. Using the predefined predicates all knowledge represented in FRM can be referred to deduction rules and integrity constraints.

---

[2] A general overview of legal knowledge representation is given in [BC91].
[3] For the integration of FRM and the logic-based formalism cf. [BMR94].

The actions, the transitions between subtasks they cause, and their preconditions require an event component capable of dealing with the representation of change. For representing actions, we employ the situation calculus (cf. [MH69]). We map this formalism to the representation formalism provided by the logic component by representing an action as an auto-correcting integrity constraint (cf. Figure 4).

$$
\begin{aligned}
&(1) \quad \forall t_j, s_1, s_2 \ : \ action(create\text{-}insurance\text{-}policy, t_j, s_1, s_2) \Rightarrow \\
&(2) \qquad\qquad \exists ip \ : \ instance\text{-}of(ip, insurance\text{-}policy, \langle t_j, s_2 \rangle) \wedge \\
&(3) \qquad\qquad ...\wedge \\
&(4) \qquad\qquad \forall i, c \ : \ instance\text{-}of(i, c, \langle t_j, s_1 \rangle) \Rightarrow instance\text{-}of(i, c, \langle t_j, s_2 \rangle) \wedge \\
&(5) \qquad\qquad \text{OTHER FRAME-AXIOMS}
\end{aligned}
$$

Figure 4: An auto-correcting integrity constraint for the action
"create-insurance-policy"

An auto-correcting integrity constraint describes which objects of the current subtask still exist and remain unmodified in the subsequent subtask and which additional objects have to exist. Execution of an action by the user means to add the corresponding action term to the knowledge base. As a result the associated auto-correcting integrity constraint becomes violated. To remove the violation a set of compensating facts (the correction) is deduced and added to the knowledge base. These additional facts represent the result of the initiated action.

An example will illustrate our approach:
Consider the office task given in Figure 1. Let *task-1* be the current task and S_1 the current subtask. The instance *af1* of the concept *application-form* shall exist. The transition from subtask S_1 to subtask S_3 coincides with the action "create-insurance-policy". Its execution leads to the additional action term *action(create-insurance-policy, task-1, S_1, S_3)* in the knowledge base. This causes a violation of the auto-correcting integrity constraint given in Figure 4, since in the new knowledge base of subtask S_3 neither an instance of the concept *insurance-policy* (see line 2 in Fig. 4) nor the instance *af1* (see line 4) exists. To compensate the violation the instances of the knowledge base of subtask S_1 are copied to the knowledge base of subtask S_3 (line 4 in Fig. 4) and an additional instance *ip1-task-1-S1-S3* of the concept *insurance-policy* is created (line 2 in Fig. 4).

The precondition of an action is either represented by a deduction rule (sufficient precondition) or by an integrity constraint (necessary precondition as shown in Figure 5).

$$
\begin{aligned}
\forall t_j \ : \ &instance\text{-}of(t_j, application\text{-}for\text{-}a\text{-}life\text{-}insurance) \wedge \\
&action(issue\text{-}insurance\text{-}policy, t_j, S_1, S_3) \Rightarrow \\
&\exists a \ : \ application\text{-}accepted(a, t_j, S_1) \wedge \\
&\quad swisslife\text{-}regulation(underwriting\text{-}reg, \\
&\qquad\qquad\qquad no\text{-}supervision\text{-}required, a, t_j, S_1)
\end{aligned}
$$

Figure 5: A necessary precondition represented by an integrity constraint

4 Future Work

A first prototype of EULE2 is implemented in Prolog and C on a Sun Sparc Station. EULE2 already allows to model and perform real office tasks, but to be used by office workers certain requirements still have to be satisfied. The two most important requirements are:

- **providing useful explanations:** Currently, EULE2 provides explanations about preconditions for transitions between subtasks merely as complex logical expressions.
  An explanation component is needed which provides the user with situation-specific information about legal (and illegal) actions and object manipulations, not in terms of the underlying representation language but in terms of generated natural language text.
- **providing tools for modelling and maintaining application domains:** For the still prototypical system only a few office tasks, laws and regulations are modelled. In a productive version of EULE2 the modelling is getting more complex, since nearly 80 office tasks must be modelled. To support building and maintaining such a model, a high level language will be developped.

References

[BC91]   T.J.M. Bench-Capon (ed): Knowledge-Based Systems and Legal Applications. Academic Press, 1991.

[BDM88]   F. Bry, H. Decker, R. Manthey: A Uniform Approach to Constraint Satisfaction and Constraint Satisfiability in Deductive Databases. In: J.W. Schmidt, S. Ceri, M. Missikof (eds): Advances in Database Technology - EDBT'88. Springer, 1988, pp. 488-505.

[BMR94]   U. Badertscher, R. Marti, U. Reimer: Integrating Terminological and Deductive Reasoning. In: Proc. 10. Workshop Logische Programmierung WLP 94, Zürich, 5.10. – 7.10.94.

[MH69]   J. McCarthy, P.J. Hayes: Some Philosophical Problems from the Standpoint of Artificial Intelligence. In: B. Meltzer and D. Michie (eds): Machine Intelligence 4, 1969, pp. 463–502.

[RLNR95] U. Reimer, P. Lippuner, M. Norrie, M. Rys: Terminological Reasoning by Query Evaluation: A Formal Mapping of a Terminological Logic to an Object Data Model. In: G. Ellis, R.A. Levinson, A. Fall, V. Dahl (eds): Proc. Int. KRUSE Symposium: Knowledge Retrieval, Use, and Storage for Efficiency. August 11–13, 1995, University of California at Santa Cruz, USA, pp.49–53.

[RM95]   U. Reimer, A. Margelisch: A Hybrid Knowledge Representation Approach to Reusability of Legal Knowledge Bases. In: Proc. of the Fifth International Conference on Artificial Intelligence and Law (ICAIL-95), College Park, Maryland, ACM Press, pp. 246 – 255.

When to Prove Theorems by Analogy?

Erica Melis*

Universität des Saarlandes, FB Informatik
D-66041 Saarbrücken, Germany
email:melis@cs.uni-sb.de

Abstract. In recent years several computational systems and techniques for theorem proving by analogy have been developed. The obvious practical question, however, as to whether and when to use analogy has been neglected badly in these developments. This paper addresses this question, identifies situations where analogy is useful, and discusses the merits of theorem proving by analogy in these situations. The results can be generalized to other domains.

1 Introduction

Theorem proving by analogy, as sketched in Figure 1, finds a proof for a target theorem guided by a proof or proof plan of a given source theorem which is similar to the target theorem. Several attempts to implement theorem proving

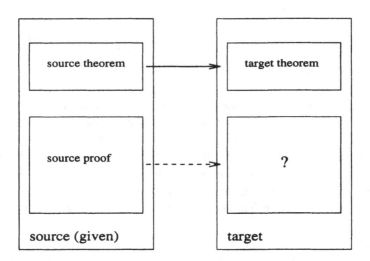

Fig. 1. Analogy in theorem proving

* The work was supported by the HC&M grant CHBICT930806 and by a grant in the SFB378

by analogy, e.g. [8, 18, 20, 9, 13], have been published. Most papers about analogy in theorem proving did refer to the well known use of analogy by mathematicians (e.g., [19]), but did not consider the actual tradeoff of automated theorem proving by analogy. On the contrary, for some approaches the storing, retrieval, and analogical replay take more time than regular theorem proving[2].

An analysis of the merits of using analogy is absolutely necessary in multi-strategy systems that are capable of both, theorem proving (without using analogy) and theorem proving by analogy. Therefore, we have to investigate how analogy pushes the problem solving horizon or improves the exploitation of the limited resources in order to evaluate the appropriateness of theorem proving by analogy. Such (limited) resources in computational theorem proving are

- Number of user interactions: Actually, user-interaction is a precious resource for interactive theorem provers that, more often than not, is used extensively.
- Run time and space: the main problem in automated theorem proving is the super-exponential search space that makes many problems intractable within limited time and space. Even some problems that appear to be easy to solve for humans who are able to structure a problem and to know good heuristics, cannot be proved automatically because of the size of the search space.
- Knowledge: Whereas too many given axioms, definitions, and lemmata blow up the search space immensely, missing axioms etc. prevent an automated theorem prover from finding a proof at all.

For problem solving in Newtonian physics, VanLehn and Jones [21] cognitively analyzed and characterized situations in which humans use analogy. They report different results for poor and good problem solvers. Similarly, we found that a distinction of different types of theorem proving systems is necessary in assessing the tradeoff in theorem proving by analogy.

Therefore, we discuss the advantages of augmenting three types of theorem provers with analogy. In the following, we investigate when to employ analogy in interactive theorem proving systems, in extensively searching automated systems, and in automated systems with little average search. We explain which advantages can be expected from the use of analogy in each type of system.

This is a paper about the experience with analogy facilities in different base systems that exhibits general principles. It is not a cognitive study, although the results resemble some findings of VanLehn and Jones as mentioned in the conclusion.

In this paper it is impossible to explain all details of these analogy facilities ANALOG, ABALONE, and internal analogy which are published in [13, 12, 15], respectively. We rather present examples of what these analogy facilities achieve.

---

[2] Personal communication with Christoph Walther who is an author of one of the approaches

2   Analogy in Interactive Theorem Provers: Omega

Current interactive theorem provers, e.g. Nqthm [1], require laborious user interactions. For instance, Shankar's proof of Gödel's theorem had 1741 lemmata that were formulated interactively for Nqthm. Augmenting an interactive system with an automated analogy facility naturally implies the advantage of reducing the number of user interactions and, thus, improve the efficient use of a limited resource. This applies in particular in long and complex proofs because they require many user interactions.

Take, for instance, the interactive Omega system [5], where automated theorem provers and tactics/methods can be invoked and Natural Deduction-rules can be applied. The analogy extension of its proof planner, as described in [13], works as a control strategy for the proof planner. The proof planner (interactively) produces a source plan that consists of methods, often supplied by the user.

Roughly, the analogy procedure works as follows: it higher-order matches the (parametrized) source and the target theorem and lemmata. The match triggers reformulations. Accordingly, the analogy procedure reformulates the source proof plan and suggests decisions for the choice of a (reformulated) method in the target proof plan, guided by the decisions in the source proof plan. It tests whether the reasons for this choice in the source hold in the target as well. If a target lemma is missing, lemma suggestion can yield certain reasons. Thereby it avoids the user interactions needed in order to provide the methods the target proof plan is constructed from, and to choose the right method.

In [14] we demonstrated how a user-supplied source proof plan for a Heine-Borel theorem HB1 can be transferred to a proof plan for another Heine-Borel theorem HB2, thus solving an open problem suggested by Bledsoe.

Theorem 1 Heine-Borel-1 (HB1). *If a closed interval $[a,b]$ of R^1 is covered by a family G of open sets (in R^1), then there is a finite subfamily H of G which covers $[a,b]$.*[3]

Theorem 2 Heine-Borel-2 (HB2). *If a closed rectangle $[a,b,c,d]$ of R^2 is covered by a family G of open sets (in R^2), then there is a finite subfamily H of G which covers $[a,b,c,d]$.*

In this example, the analogy procedure reduced the user interactions that provided subgoals to be proved by Natural Deduction inferences, by the automated theorem prover OTTER [11], or by a subplan from 32 to 1. Most of the HB1 proof plan was transferable by analogy as apparent from Figures 2 and 3. All reformulated source methods but `method-2'`, reformulated from `method-2`, are transferred. Only the submethod `method-21'` of the reformulated `method-2'` was transferable to the target. This left the minor target subgoal $g'5a$ to be proved by Omega.

---

[3] R^1 denotes the set of sets of real numbers and R^2 denotes the set of sets of ordered pairs (x,y) of real numbers x and y.

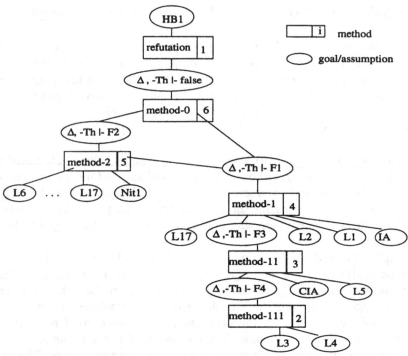

Fig. 2. The proof-plan of HB1

On the one hand, the analogical replay reduced the number of interactions. On the other hand, one additional interaction is required to provide the analogous source problem to the current analogy procedure. In case-based reasoning terms, so far the retrieval is performed by the user. This is natural though, if you remember that your maths professor told his students that they should prove some theorem B by analogy to a theorem A.

In systems that are designed as a proof assistance system, an additional argument in favor of analogy, is that an analogy facility can be a feature of human-like problem solving that contributes to the system's user acceptance.

3   Analogy in Systems with Little Average Search: *CIAM*

In this section, we record our experience with using analogy in the proof planner *CIAM*. *CIAM*, described in [3], has successfully been applied to inductive theorem proving.[4] As opposed to interactive systems, *CIAM* is an automated

---

[4] Induction is a generalization of Peano induction over the natural numbers that has the induction scheme $\frac{P(0), \forall k(P(k) \rightarrow P(k+1))}{\forall n(P(n))}$, where $P(0)$ is proved in the base case and $\forall k(P(k) \rightarrow P(k+1))$ is proved in a step case. $P(k)$ is called the induction hypothesis and $P(k+1)$ the induction conclusion. In this case, $(k+1)$ is the induction term. In the step case the induction conclusion is rewritten such that the induction hypothesis can be applied with a true result.

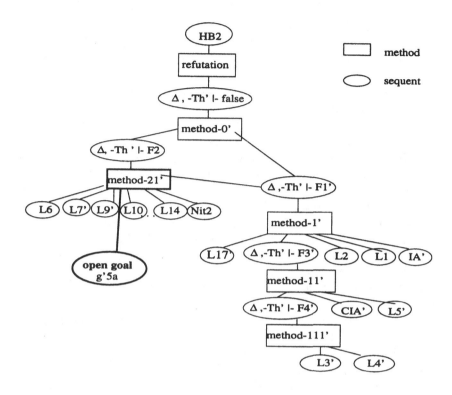

Fig. 3. The proof-plan of HB2

proof planner. It constructs proof plans that consist of methods. Some of these predefined methods are INDUCTION, WAVE, EVAL_DEF, NORMAL, and EQUAL. IN-DUCTION, e.g., chooses induction variables and an appropriate induction scheme and EVAL_DEF symbolically evaluates a term in the current planning goal by applying an equational definition of a function.

In $CIAM$ strong domain-specific search heuristics, such as *rippling* [6, 2], restrict the search for methods. Rippling systematically uses rewrites to remove differences between the induction hypothesis and the induction conclusion in a very goal-directed way so the former can be used in the proof. Because of the strong domain-specific control heuristics and because of the common plan patterns of inductive proofs[5], $CIAM$ is a proof planner that, opposed to most planners, typically performs *little search* for methods. For a comprehensive introduction to $CIAM$ see [3]. Given this behavior, usually $CIAM$ succeeds quickly if it masters a theorem at all.

Therefore, the derivational analogy[6] facility, ABALONE, is invoked only if *CIAM* does not succeed in a decent time limit (with the commonly loaded methods). Then the target planning process is guided by analogy to a source plan [12].

ABALONE's input is a source theorem, source rewrites, a source proof plan, a target theorem, and target rewrites. First, it incrementally produces second-mappings of the source and the target theorem and of the source and target rewrites as far as possible. These mappings of functions and relations preserve certain abstract representations of the source theorem and source rewrites that heuristically determine the proof pattern. The mappings are followed by an analogical replay of the source proof plan that includes certain reformulations of the proof plan and a check of the justifications (reasons) for the choice of the methods in the source. If a legal justification is violated in the target, no replay of the method takes place. The replay transfers a method if the failed justification is marked as "heuristic" rather than "legal". For a detailed description see [12] which is available via www. In case no given target rewrite matches some source rewrite S, the analogical mapping can suggest a target rewrite by applying the mappings to S.

The retrieval performance does not matter for the following advantages ABALONE provided because the improvements are in terms of problem solving capability rather than of speeding up. ABALONE did improve *CIAM*'s performance: in a situation where a lemma needed for the target proof is not given a priori, where a method not loaded by default is needed for planning a target theorem, or where other reasons e.g. the default control, prevent *CIAM* from finding a plan for the target theorem within reasonable time limits. In the following, we discuss these situations for theorem proving by analogy. The given examples are simple representatives for classes of problems that *CIAM* itself cannot prove but for which *CIAM* with ABALONE succeeds.

 – By overriding the control heuristics of the proof planner if justified by analogy, plans can be constructed which the proof planner would not find by itself. Example[7]:
   The source theorem div3: $\neg y = 0 \rightarrow div(plus(y, x), y) = s(div(x, y))$
   has the proof plan

```
NORMAL(...) then
   EVAL_DEF(div) then
      ELEMENTARY(...)
```

---

[6] Derivational analogy [4] guides the target solution by replaying decisions of the source problem solving *process*, and it uses information about reasons for the decisions (*justifications*)

[7] In the remainder of the paper s denotes the successor function, *div* division, *rev* denotes the reversion of lists, *length* the length of lists, and *app*, *cons* denote the append and cons list functions.

NORMAL places the antecedent ($\neg y = 0$) in the hypotheses list Hyp and then EVAL_DEF evaluates the definition of div. For the latter, a (heuristic) justification is that the antecedent C of the definition of div^8 is in Hyp (expressed by trivial(Hyp ==> C)). This means that EVAL_DEF(div) is applied if ($\neg y = 0$) is in Hyp only. ELEMENTARY recognizes the truth of the output of EVAL_DEF.

The target theorem:

$$\texttt{div3term}: \neg times(y,z) = 0 \to div(plus(y,x),y) = s(div(x,y))$$

cannot be planned by CL^AM. The reason is that EVAL_DEF(div)'s justification trivial(Hyp ==> $\neg y = 0$) is not satisfied after the application of NORMAL. because now $\neg times(y,z) = 0$ is in Hyp rather than $\neg y = 0$. div3term can, however, be planned by analogy to div3 that justifies to override the heuristic justification to proveable(Hyp ==> $\neg y = 0$). Then the (correct) target proof plan is obtained

```
NORMAL(...) then
  EVAL_DEF(div) then
    SUBPROOF(not(times(y,z)=0) => not(y = 0)) then
      ELEMENTARY(...)
```

– By suggesting the use of a method that is not commonly loaded, plans can be constructed which the proof planner would not find without user intervention. For instance, the method NORMAL is not loaded by default because it often misleads the planner.
Example: The source theorem zerotimes1: $x = 0 \to times(x,y) = 0$ has the proof plan

```
NORMAL(...) then
  EQUAL(...) then
    EVAL_DEF(...) then
      ELEMENTARY(...).
```

NORMAL first places the antecedent ($x = 0$) in the hypotheses list and then EQUAL replaces 0 for x in the term $times(x,y)$. This is followed by EVAL_DEF that evaluates $times(0,y)$ to 0 by the definition $times(0,X) = 0$ and by ELEMENTARY that recognizes the truth of (0=0).
Among others the analogical replay automatically transfers the NORMAL method and the resulting target proof plan is

```
NORMAL(...) then
  EQUAL(...) then
    EVAL_DEF(...) then
      ELEMENTARY(...).
```

---

[8] which is $\neg y = 0$

- Induced by the mapping constraints, analogy can find generalizations that make a success of $CI\!AM$ possible at all. An example is the generalization of the target theorem

$$plus(x, plus(x, x)) = plus(plus(x, x), x)$$

to the source theorem

$$plus(x, plus(y, z)) = plus(plus(x, y), z).$$

This type of generalization is called "generalizing variables apart" and belongs to those generalizations that are difficult to choose in inductive theorem proving and, therefore, are not included into $CI\!AM$.

- By suggesting lemmata that are needed for the target proof target theorems can be proved which $CI\!AM$ itself is not able to prove. Example: Given the source theorem:

$$length(app(a, b)) = length(app(b, a))$$

the proof of which uses the source rewrite

$$length(app(a, cons(v_0, b))) = s(length(app(a, b))).$$

While analogically replaying the source proof plan for the target theorem:

$$half(plus(a, b)) = half(plus(b, a))$$

the analogy facility suggests the target lemma:

$$half(plus(a, s(s(b)))) = s(half(plus(a, b)))$$

by applying the mappings established between the source and the target and other constraints.

4 Analogy in Systems with Extensively Searching Sub-routines: $CI\!AM3$

When working on analogy in $CI\!AM3$, we identified another situation where analogy did improve the system's performance. $CI\!AM3$ is a version of $CI\!AM$ that is extended by *critics* which are very search-intensive procedures that help to continue the proof planning when $CI\!AM$ itself gets stuck.

Critics [7] are an extension of proof planning that patch failed proof attempts. For instance, it can happen that INDUCTION selects an inappropriate induction scheme. Then planning using an incorrect scheme becomes blocked. The *induction revision critic* patches an incorrect choice of the induction scheme by introducing extra function variables into the induction term so that rippling can continue and gradually instantiates the function variables by higher-order matching with given rewrites. The instantiation requires to go back to the INDUCTION node and to suggest a revised induction term.

For instance, consider the conjecture

$$even(length(app(t, l))) = even(length(app(l, t)))\qquad(1)$$

INDUCTION originally suggests an induction on l because of the existence of a certain rewrite. This gives an induction conclusion of

$$even(length(app(t, cons(h, l)))) = even(length(app(cons(h, l), t)))$$

Applications of rewrites eventually yield the subgoal

$$even(s(length(app(t, l)))) = even(s(length(app(l, t))))$$

No further rewrite is applicable, so the planning process is blocked. The way the induction revision critic deals with this is to introduce function variables into the induction term the instantiation of which yields a revised induction term $cons(h_1, (cons(h_2, l)))$ with which the planning succeeds.

It can happen that within the same proof, the induction revision critic is called a number of times. The internal analogy avoids such waste of time. *Internal analogy* is a process that transfers experience from a completed (source) subgoal in the *same* problem to solve the current (target) subgoal. That is, internal analogy works on similar subproblems of a single problem.

For instance, the planning of the conjecture

$$even(length(app(x, y))) = even(length(app(y, x)))$$

includes four induction revisions from a one-step list induction to a two-step list induction. In this situation the internal analogy overrides the default control of $CIAM3$ at INDUCTION nodes in proof planning by overriding INDUCTION's default choice with an instantiation of the result of a prior application of the induction revision critic. Note that the internal analogy has been interleaved with regular proof planning.

On the one hand, the additional effort to store the relevant information is small for the particular internal analogy. The information that an induction revision took place, which subterm was affected by the critic application, and the previously revised induction scheme is stored in the respective INDUCTION nodes during the planning process. In addition, no or very simple mapping is necessary. The previous INDUCTION nodes have to be checked for critic applications in our procedure. On the other hand, by reducing the number of critic calls, search can be reduced in the following ways:

- In $CIAM3$, one of the most intensive sub-procedures is the search for the induction scheme. The internal analogy facility suggests an induction scheme so the search for these is eliminated.
- The effort needed to actually apply the induction revision critic again, in particular the expensive higher-order matching, is eliminated.
- The critic is not applied until $CIAM3$ has already chosen an incorrect induction rule and continued to the point where further planning is blocked. Internal analogy removes this backtracking altogether.

Hence, the savings by internal analogy outweigh the additional effort needed. The retrieval is included into the additional effort.

What about the additional effort in cases where no use can be made of analogy? In one kind of cases, different types of induction revision can occur in the same proof. If there is no map available from the stored justification, an incorrect induction revision is *not* imposed, and a second critic has to be applied as usual. Obviously, time is taken to look for a mapping from the stored justification to the current goal, which is redundant because the second revision has to be carried out anyway, but the computational cost is low.

The same happens in those cases where no critic is needed for a subsequent induction. Then no map from the stored justification will succeed, so the induction is not altered.

In a third kind of cases it happens that once a revision has taken place, a mapping from the justification to a future goal is successful, even though INDUCTION would correctly choose the induction scheme. So even though no critic application is avoided, the analogy can still be used to suggest an induction scheme. Even though analogy is not needed in this case, it is difficult to prevent analogy from being applied. This is not disadvantageous, however, since there is still a saving in time here, because the need to search for the induction variable and term is eliminated.

Some test results are given in Table 1. As expected, the costs associated

Conjecture	T1	T2
even(length(app(x,y)))=even(length(app(y,x)))	708	567
half(length(app(x,y)))=half(length(app(y,x)))	329	295
even((plus(x,y))=even(plus(y,x))	48	40
even(length(app(x,y)))=even(plus(length(y),length(x)))	107	96
half(plus(x,y))=half(plus(y,x))	48	45
even(length(x))=even(length(rev(x)))	141	122
even(half(plus(x,y)))=even(half(plus(y,x)))	2961	2650
half(length(x))=half(length(rev(x)))	55	53
even(plus(z,length(app(x,y))))=even(plus(z,length(app(y,x))))	3850	3502

T1 *is the time* C*IA*M 3 *needs to plan the given theorem without using internal analogy.* T2 *is the time it takes with internal analogy.*

Table 1. Some examples run by our system

with the internal analogy - storing the justification, comparing the justification with the subgoals at subsequent INDUCTION nodes, and suggesting the induction schemes - turned out to be less than those associated with the application of the induction revision critics. As a result, the time taken to prove the theorems given was reduced. As well as the gain in runtime, analogy makes the proof planning process clearer because the redundant part of the original proof caused by incorrect selection of induction schemes can be eliminated.

5 Conclusion

What can we learn from this experience? To make a long story *very* short,

- the use of analogy in interactive systems has several advantages;
- in systems that do little search, use analogy as a last resort to solve problems that cannot be solved otherwise;
- use analogy if it can replace a search-intensive subroutine at low cost;
- only if none of the preceeding criteria applies, then an empirical or theoretical analysis might reveal conditions for an efficient use of analogy for classes of problems.

In a little more detail and including related work, the story is summarized as follows:

1. For interactive systems
   (a) some user interaction can be replaced by an automated effort for the analogical transfer of a source proof or proof plan. With respect to the resource "human interaction", the bias is always in favor of analogy, in particular for long or complex solutions. This is independent of the complexity of the analogy procedure. Even if the retrieval is done interactively, user interaction is saved.
   Similarly, Reif and Stenzel [20] report substantial savings in software verification when a reuse facility is integrated into their system. This is because user interaction accounts for the lions share of formal software verification.
   (b) In assistance systems, analogy can be a feature of human-like problem solving that contributes to the system's user acceptance. Again, this argument in favor of analogy is orthogonal to any complexity argument.
2. For automated systems with extensive search, time is a resource that can be saved.
   (a) Analogy can save search by analogically replaying a source proof or proof plan. Here, the time taken for retrieval has to be taken as part of the (time) effort needed for analogy and the savings have to outweight the additional effort. Veloso [22] compares run times of regular problem solving vs. problem solving by analogy for domains or problems for which the problem solving involves a lot of search. Presumably, these results naturally transfer to theorem proving by analogy although no empirical tests have been conducted so far. For practical purposes, a worst case complexity analysis as in [17] will not do the job.
   This situation compares to the empirical results of VanLehn and Jones about poor physics problem solvers who display many episodes of analogical problem solving and use analogy instead of regular problem solving even when this is not most effective.
   (b) For specific search-intensive procedures internal analogy can save search at low costs, as explained in section 4. In case the internal analogy does not hold, the additional costs are low.

3. For automated systems with little average search, an analogy procedure is invoked when the base system is stuck (cannot prove the theorem from the given assumptions in a decent time limit). This means that analogy pushes the problem solving horizon of the base system. This fact amounts to a bias in favor of analogy independently of any complexity analysis including the retrieval. A system augmented by derivational analogy can solve more problems than the base system itself

   (a) by overriding the default control of the base system for the particular target or by replaying an uncommon system configuration. Again, this "learning" of control knowledge compares to the empirical results of VanLehn and Jones for good problem solvers (who have little average search) who learn search control by analogy.

   (b) by providing originally missing knowledge (lemmata) needed to solve the target problem. This also compares to empirical results of VanLehn and Jones for good physics learners who use analogy to fill knowledge gaps. Apart from analogy, other learning techniques such as EBL [16] and chunking [10] can provide control knowledge. We do not discuss them here.

6   Acknowledgment

I would like to thank Alan Bundy who influenced my struggle with $CIAM$ considerably by asking 'what does analogy buy?'. Thanks to Jörg Siekmann and Wolf Schaarschmidt for reading drafts of this paper.

References

1. R.S. Boyer and J.S. Moore. *A Computational Logic Handbook*. Academic Press, San Diego, 1988.

2. A. Bundy, Stevens A, F. Van Harmelen, A. Ireland, and A. Smaill. A heuristic for guiding inductive proofs. *Artificial Intelligence*, 63:185–253, 1993.

3. A. Bundy, F. van Harmelen, J. Hesketh, and A. Smaill. Experiments with proof plans for induction. *Journal of Automated Reasoning*, 7:303–324, 1991.

4. J.G. Carbonell. Derivational analogy: A theory of reconstructive problem solving and expertise acquisition. In R.S. Michalsky, J.G. Carbonell, and T.M. Mitchell, editors, *Machine Learning: An Artificial Intelligence Approach*, pages 371–392. Morgan Kaufmann Publ., Los Altos, 1986.

5. X. Huang, M. Kerber, M. Kohlhase, E. Melis, D. Nesmith, J. Richts, and J. Siekmann. Omega-MKRP: A Proof Development Environment. In *Proc. 12th International Conference on Automated Deduction (CADE)*, Nancy, 1994.

6. D. Hutter. Guiding inductive proofs. In M.E. Stickel, editor, *Proc. of 10th International Conference on Automated Deduction (CADE)*, volume Lecture Notes in Artificial Intelligence 449. Springer, 1990.

7. A. Ireland and A. Bundy. Productive use of failure in inductive proof. Technical report, Department of AI Edinburgh, 1994. Available from Edinburgh as DAI Research Paper 716.

8. R.E. Kling. A paradigm for reasoning by analogy. *Artificial Intelligence*, 2:147–178, 1971.
9. Th. Kolbe and Ch. Walther. Reusing proofs. In *Proceedings of ECAI-94*, Amsterdam, 1994.
10. J Laird, A. Newell, and P. Rosenbloom. SOAR:an architecture for general intelligence. *Artificial Intelligence*, 33(1):1–64, 1987.
11. W.W. McCune. Otter 2.0 users guide. Technical Report ANL-90/9, Argonne National Laboratory, Maths and CS Division, Argonne, Illinois, 1990.
12. E. Melis. Analogy in CLAM. Technical Report DAI Research Paper No 766, University of Edinburgh, AI Dept, Dept. of Artificial Intelligence, Edinburgh, 1995. available from http://jswww.cs.uni-sb.de/ melis/.
13. E. Melis. A model of analogy-driven proof-plan construction. In *Proceedings of the 14th International Joint Conference on Artificial Intelligence*, pages 182–189, Montreal, 1995.
14. E. Melis. Theorem proving by analogy – a compelling example. In C.Pinto-Ferreira and N.J. Mamede, editors, *Progress in Artificial Intelligence, 7th Portuguese Conference on Artificial Intelligence, EPIA '95*, Lecture Notes in Artificial Intelligence, 990, pages 261–272, Madeira, 1995. Springer.
15. E. Melis and J. Whittle. Internal analogy in inductive theorem proving. In *Proceedings of the 13th Conference on Automated Deduction (CADE-96)*, LNAI, Berlin, New York, 1996. Springer. also published as DAI Research Paper 803.
16. T.M. Mitchell, R.M. Keller, and S.T. Kedar-Cabelli. Explanation-based generalization: A unifying view. *Machine Learning*, 1:47–80, 1986.
17. B. Nebel and J. Koehler. Plan reuse versus plan generation. a theoretical and empirical analysis. *Artificial Intelligence*, 1995. Special Issue on Planning and Scheduling.
18. S. Owen. *Analogy for Automated Reasoning*. Academic Press, 1990.
19. G. Polya. *How to Solve it*. 2nd ed. Doubleday, New York, 1957.
20. W. Reif and K. Stenzel. Reuse of proofs in software verification. In R.K. Shyamasundar, editor, *Proc. 13th Conference on Foundations of Software Technology and Theoretical Computer Science*, volume 761 of *LNCS*. Springer, 1993.
21. K. VanLehn and R.M. Jones. Better learners use analogical problem solving sparingly. In *Proceedings of the Tenth International Conference on Machine Learning*, pages 338–345, Amherst, MA, 1993. Morgan Kaufmann.
22. M.M. Veloso. *Planning and Learning by Analogical Reasoning*. Springer, Berlin, New York, 1994.

Probabilistic Knowledge Representation and Reasoning at Maximum Entropy by SPIRIT

Carl-Heinz Meyer, Wilhelm Rödder
FernUniversität Hagen

Abstract: Current probabilistic expert systems assume complete knowledge of the joint distribution. To specify this distribution one has to construct a directed acyclic graph attached by a lot of tables filled with conditional probabilities. Often these probabilities are unknown and the quantification is more or less arbitrary. SPIRIT is an expert system shell for probabilistic knowledge bases which uses the principle of maximum entropy to avoid these lacks. Knowledge acquisition is performed by specifying probabilistic facts and rules on discrete variables in an extended propositional logic syntax. The shell generates the unique probability distribution which respects all facts and rules and maximizes entropy. After creating this distribution the shell is ready for answering simple and complex queries. The process of knowledge acquisition, knowledge processing and answering queries is revealed in detail on a nontrivial example.

Keywords: Expert System, Uncertain Reasoning, Maximum Entropy

1. Introduction

Probabilistic reasoning and knowledge representation are a powerful mathematical tool able to reflect uncertainty in human thinking. Within the last decade a growing number of scientists have agreed that a joint distribution P on a set V of discrete variables with finite domains is a good means to represent complex dependency and independence relations amongst them. So consequently it is a perfect knowledge base cf. [11], [14].

In this environment reasoning is understood as the calculation of conditional probabilities for event-conclusions given event-premises. Since for real world applications the number of elementary events in the probability space counts in billions a significant effort had to be made for an efficient storage of the distribution and a fast calculation of all probabilities. Conditional independence assumptions allow a decomposition of P and break it down to a considerably reduced number of (un-)conditional probabilities. Nevertheless for a high dimensional P the dependency and independence relations must be well organized to be consistent and yet determine a unique distribution. Graphs on V formalize the „skeleton" which together with (un-)conditional probabilities fixes the global P. Bayes-Networks, special Directed Acyclic Graphs (DAGs), are the most accepted and already standardized skeleton. Undirected and mixed graphs allow a richer structure than DAGs, but at the moment they are not standard [19].

To make these factorized distributions P admissible to local computations, they must be enriched by further conditional probabilities; the resulting graphical structure is a hypertree (cf. [7],[4]).

Yet for high dimensional distributions the construction of a Bayes-Net is not trivial at all and requires thousands of (conditional) probabilities. Often high-handed independence assumptions are necessary to form a manageable graph. These lacks might deter inclined users from the application of such a probabilistic knowledge based system.

SPIRIT is an Expert System Shell for building and applying knowledge bases on sets of discrete variables which differs significantly from conventional systems:

- Knowledge acquisition in SPIRIT is performed by processing facts and rules. Facts and rules are (un-) conditioned propositional sentences with a rich syntax and their respective desired probabilities.
- No explicit independence structure must be specified, avoiding the troublesome construction of a Bayes-Net or similar frames.
- Any query about possible conclusions from hypothetical premises allows an equally rich syntax as for knowledge acquisition.

This paper's objective is the presentation of the shell SPIRIT and its way of working with uncertain knowledge. So only a brief introduction to the history and theory of maxent-reasoning is given in chapter 2 and 3. The shell's features are detailed in chapter 4. We pass the steps Knowledge Acquisition (4.1), Knowledge Processing (4.2), Knowledge Representation (4.3), Queries and Response (4.4) in succession. All items are enriched by examples.

Finally we report on some medium sized applications of SPIRIT in chapter 5. Conclusions.

2. Historical Background on Maxent-Reasoning in Expert Systems

The application of reasoning at maximum entropy in expert systems goes back to the early eighties, where first attempts were made to generalise the Bayesian paradigm of inference:

- In 1982 Lemmer and Barth [10] and in 1983 Lemmer [9] apply the Lagrange multiplier method to calculate a revised distribution at minimum relative entropy with respect to a set of marginal distributions. Unfortunately their method is restricted to a fixed tree of cliques (they call them: Local Event Groups) which is used to store marginal distributions of a joint distribution.
- In 1983 Cheeseman [1] proposes maximum entropy to generate a joint distribution given some linear constraints similar to our approach. He uses the Lagrange multiplier method to calculate the unknown parameters and derives a factorisation of the distribution which can be efficiently handled by grouping summations into smaller subsummations. In fact this grouping is equivalent to a decomposition of the joint into small marginal distributions.

- In 1984 Shore and Johnson [16] give an axiomatic foundation for the use of maximum entropy as a general inference method. In 1986 Shore [15] suggests the application of this method in expert systems.
- In 1986 Nilsson [12] describes a probabilistic logic which leads to a set of distributions restricted by linear equations. He suggests to choose the one with maximum entropy but he fails to calculate this distribution efficiently for 'great' systems. Our approach is an extension of this work in a sense which is best described as *probabilistic conditional logic*.
- In 1989 Wen [18] reveals an iterative procedure to calculate the distribution with maximum entropy given linear constraints generated by prescribed marginal and conditional probabilities. This work is very similar to our approach but Wen uses a very restricted language (Belief Network Description Language) in his Probabilistic Expert System Shell PESS.
- In 1991 Kane [5] extends Nilssons probabilistic logic to the probabilistic conditonal logic mentioned above. The fundamental idea is good but the derivations of the formulas for calculating the Maxent-distribution have some flaws. Also it is not clear if Kane has developed an expert system based on his theoretical work.
- In 1992 Hajek, Havranek and Jirousek suggest in their monography [3] a Maxent-distribution as a knowledge base for probabilistic expert systems. They present a space saving implementation of the well known Iterative Proportional Fitting Procedure to calculate this distribution given a set of full marginal distributions. It is not clear how this procedure can be applied to a set of single (un-) conditional probabilities.

3. Knowledge Processing in SPIRIT

To describe briefly the theoretical background of SPIRIT we need the following mathematical prerequisites:

The knowledge base consists of a finite set of variables $V=\{V_1,...,V_n\}$ with finite domains and a probability distribution P on the field of all events on V. Events are identified with propositional sentences on literals $V_i=v_i$ (where v_i is a realization of V_i) built by negation, conjunction and disjunction.
If S is such a sentence, its probability is $P(S)=\sum_{v\subset S} P(v)$, where v runs through all complete conjunctions v in the canonical disjunctive normal form of S.

To generate a distribution P for representing knowledge, we first assign desired probabilities x_f or x_r to facts or rules. Here a fact F is a propositional sentence as defined above and a rule is an expression $F_2|F_1$ with F_1,F_2 being facts. The assignments are understood as an imperative: find a P for which $P(F)=x_f$ or $P(F_2|F_1)=x_r$; they are considered to be (un-) conditional probabilities.

Consequently, the first step of knowledge acquisition in SPIRIT consists of the formulation of a set of such facts and rules as well as the assignment of consistent desired probabilities:

$$P(F_{2i}|F_{1i}) = x_i \, , \ i = 1,...m \tag{1}$$

(Since F_{1i} might be tautological, (1) includes both facts and rules).

Of course, in general (1) does not determine a unique P but rather a set of distributions. This is true because the number of rules in (1) is rather small and in most cases, the set of rules will be insufficient to define a skeleton like a Bayes-Net. The concept of entropy and relative entropy will help to remove this lack.

For two distributions P and P_0 on V the relative entropy of P with respect to P_0 is defined as

$$R(P,P_0) = \sum_v P(v)\, ld\left(\frac{P(v)}{P_0(v)}\right), \tag{2}$$

with ld denoting the binary logarithm. If P_0 is the uniform distribution, $R(P,P_0)$ becomes up to a constant equal to $-H(P)$, where :

$$H(P) = -\sum_v P(v)ldP(v) \tag{3}$$

and is called (absolute) entropy of P.
A distribution $P=P^*$ which minimizes (2) subject to (1) has desirable properties, such as:

- it preserves the dependency structure of P_0 as much as possible when forced to satisfy (1), see [13].
- it minimizes additional information in P_0 beyond that already existing in P_0, cf. [3],[16].

We take the convincing arguments in the referred papers as a good reason to solve the following problem when acquiring knowledge additional to P_0 by facts and rules:

$$\text{Min } \sum_v P(v)ld\left(\frac{P(v)}{P_0(v)}\right)$$

s.t. $\tag{4}$

$$P(F_{2i}|F_{1i}) = x_i \, , \ i = 1,...,m.$$

In SPIRIT we solve (4) iteratively applying only one restriction at a time, thus generating a sequence of distributions $P_0, P_1, ..., P_{k-1}, P_k, ...$ for which each P_k has minimal relative entropy with respect to P_{k-1}. It is well known that this procedure converges towards P^* [2]. The application of a single restriction on P_{k-1} to get P_k is an immediate consequence of the Kuhn-Tucker theorem. In short:

If $P(F_{2i}|F_{1i}) = x_i$, $(i = k \bmod m)$ is the next rule to be applied, the Langrange multiplier method yields:

$$P_k(v) = \begin{cases} P_{k-1}(v)\alpha, & \forall v \subset \overline{F_1} \\ P_{k-1}(v)\alpha\beta^{-x}, & \forall v \subset F_1\overline{F_2} \\ P_{k-1}(v)\alpha\beta^{1-x}, & \forall v \subset F_1 F_2 \end{cases}$$

with $\beta = \dfrac{x}{1-x} \dfrac{P_{k-1}(F_1\overline{F_2})}{P_{k-1}(F_1 F_2)}$ and α is a normalizing constant.

Here barring indicates negation and we write $F_1 F_2$ for $F_1 \wedge F_2$.

Up to now we developed how entropy substitutes in an ideal way the Bayes-Net as skeleton. It remains to show how local computability is guaranteed in SPIRIT.

Each rule (or fact) involves a certain group of variables and very likely implies dependency relations among them. So each such set of variables forms in a natural way a cluster for which the marginal distribution should be fully stored. The set of all clusters constitutes a hypergraph on V, in general a cyclic one. SPIRIT therefore seeks for an acyclic hypergraph -a hypertree- in such a way that each of the above clusters as a whole is contained in a hyperedge. The corresponding algorithms are similar to those for triangulating a graph [6] [17]. For these hyperedges the marginal distributions are fully stored. So global computations are reduced to local computations: modifications in a hyperedge can be 'propagated' throughout the hypertree.

The compact presentation of mathematical prerequisites was necessary to understand the different devices to be shown in the next chapter.

4. The Shell and its Features in Detail

4.1 Knowledge Acquisition

One of the best ways to explain the process of knowledge acquisition is perhaps „learning by example". The following example performs a very simple car diagnosis (car diagnosis is sometimes used to demonstrate the abilities of Bayes- Nets, cf. [20]):

Example 1: The working of a car engine depends on the correct status of the fuel system and the electrical system. The electrical system depends on spark timing and spark quality. Though the timing depends on the correct phase of the distributor while the spark quality is influenced by the sparking plugs and the voltage at plug. The fuel system is okay if the fuel pump works and the carburetor is not soiled and the tank is full of course. The battery voltage is weak or dead if the alternator is faulty or the fan belt is broken. A broken fan belt or no oil pressure often causes very hot temperature which can damage the engine (cf. Fig. 1 and Fig. 3).

After declaring the types and the values of 18 variables (shown on the right side in Fig. 1) it is possible to specify some probabilistic facts and rules according to the verbal description above:

Fig. 1: Facts and rules of the car diagnosis example

The facts are propositional sentences and the rules link two such sentences by „$\Rightarrow$ ". Facts and rules have to meet certain syntax demands, see Fig. 2.

```
< Rule >  ::= < Fact > ⇒ < Fact >

< Fact >  ::= {¬} < Atom >|(< Fact >) {∧|∨ < Atom >|(< Fact >) }

< Atom >  ::= < Variable > {=|≠|<¹|>¹|∈|∉ < Value >|< Valuelist > ²}     1:Ordinal 2:Non–Boolean

< Valuelist >  ::= < Value > {,< Value >}
```

Fig. 2: Syntax of probabilistic facts and rules

The propagation of a rule can follow either the philosophy 'float' or 'ground'. A floating rule in SPIRIT is handled as in (4), see chapter 2. In this version the user does not impose any restriction upon the probability of the premise - it might float. If he grounds it, he wants the probability of the premise to remain unchanged.

Example 2: The probability distribution P^* which represents the rule $P(B|A)=1$ for boolean variables A, B is shown for 'float' and 'ground' in the following table (e.g. ff stands for $A = f \wedge B = f$).

ff	ft	tf	tt	
0.25	0.25	0.25	0.25	uniform P_0
0..333..	0..333..	0.00	0..333..	'float' P^*
0.25	0.25	0.00	0.5	'ground' P^*

Observe that both philosophies respect the desired rule probability, but only 'ground' maintains $P^*(A=t)=P_0(A=t)=0.5$. In SPIRIT the more natural application of rules is that of type 'float', but if the user wants to preserve the condition structure in the premise he should use the option 'ground'.

Example 3: The probability distribution P^* which represents the rule $P(C|A \wedge B)=0.9$ is shown for 'float' and 'ground' in the following table (e.g. fff stands for $A = f \wedge B = f \wedge C = f$).

fff	fft	ftf	ftt	tff	tft	ttf	ttt	
0.1250	0.1250	0.1250	0.1250	0.1250	0.1250	0.1250	0.1250	'uniform'
0.1354	0.1354	0.1354	0.1354	0.1354	0.1354	0.0187	0.1687	'float'
0.1250	0.1250	0.1250	0.1250	0.1250	0.1250	0.0250	0.2250	'ground'

Both philosophies respect the desired rule probability, yet 'float' introduces a slight dependence between A and B (e.g. $P(B|A) = 0.4090 \neq 0.5$), whereas 'ground' does not. This dependence was sometimes criticized (cf. [14], p. 464). We do not follow this argumentation since an additional independence requirement also implies additional information. This should be avoided if not explicitly wanted.

A nice side effect of 'ground' consists in the ability of creating and importing Bayesian Networks in SPIRIT.

Once all variables and rules are specified, the shell is ready for the computation of the knowledge base.

4.2 Knowledge Processing

The proper knowledge processing consists of the construction of the hypertree, mentioned in chapter 2, as well as the iterative calculation of the joint distribution.

To construct the hypertree, SPIRIT offers optional algorithms [6], [17]. Their efficiency might vary for different knowledge bases. Once the hypertree is determined the shell starts an iterative process of applying all facts and rules to the actual distribution. The user is informed about the number of full iterations (all rules) and the

actual rule applied. Further information concerns entropy: the relative entropy between the distributions after and before the rule application (c.f. chapter 2), the absolute entropy of the uniform distribution minus the sum of all processed relative entropies, and the actual absolute entropy of the joint distribution.
SPIRIT detects whether

- the knowledge base is ready   or
- inconsistent rules have been supplied by the user. In this case the shell supports the revision of inconsistencies.

„Alpha-Learning" allows inductive learning from an arbitrarily-sized sample of realizations of all variables by the knowledge base. In each hyperedge every cell in the contingency-table is actualized by the formula $p_{new}=(1-\alpha)p_{old}+\alpha f$, where p_{old} is the probability before alpha-learning and f the frequency in the sample. $0 \leq \alpha \leq 1$ is a weight which must be suitably chosen by the user. The knowledge base then applies p_{new} to a set of previously defined rules and goes through the learning process again. The idea behind Alpha-learning is to adjust subjective by „objective" probabilities.

The reverse process is also possible, namely to draw a sample which follows the joint distribution.

Once the knowledge base is completed -either by rules and their specified probabilities or by rules 'filled' with frequencies from a sample- it is ready for queries and responses. Before explaining that feature we will show how the shell SPIRIT informs the user about the acquired knowledge.

4.3   Knowledge Representation

SPIRIT has two main features to represent the acquired information: an undirected Dependency-Graph and a mixed graph to visualize the structure of the rules. The Dependency-Graph is an undirected graph constructed as follows:

- for each variable generate a vertex
- two vertices are linked by an edge, if the variables appear in the same rule.

The graph has the Local Markov Property [14]. Bar-charts displayed in the vertices show the actual marginal distribution of the variable.
It is possible to switch to a mixed graph constructed as follows:

- for each variable generate a vertex
- link V_1 and V_2 by an arrow, if V_1 is in the premise and V_2 in the conclusion of the same rule
- link vertices V_1, V_2 by an edge if they appear both in the conclusion of the same rule.

The mixed graph can be interpreted as a Bayesian-Network, if all rules are 'grounded' and the quantification is according to the probability tables in bayesian networks.

The following Figure 3 shows the dependence graph and the respective mixed form for example 1. Confirm that the rules in Figure 1 do not generate undirected edges.

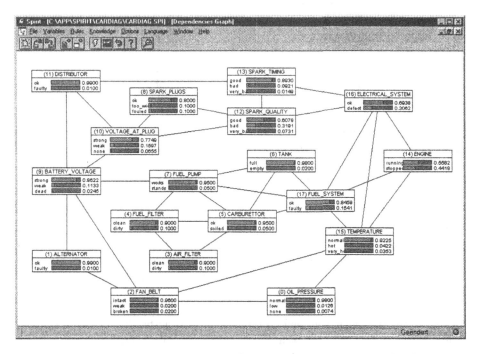

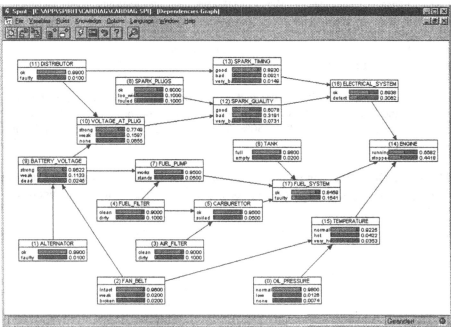

Fig. 3: Dependence and mixed graph of car diagnosis example

In this section we revealed properties of the dependence graph as it serves for visualization of the knowledge base. The graph might be used for consultations, too. This aspect and complex queries in SPIRIT are developed in the next chapter.

4.4 Queries and Responses

SPIRIT provides two forms of consulting: simple questions and complex queries. Simple questions are available in any conventional probabilistic knowledge base, complex queries are a sophisticated option in SPIRIT which will be developed below.

Simple questions are performed in the Dependency-Graph. They occur by instantiation of one or more variables' values and of propagation of this temporary modification through the whole knowledge base. Since this kind of query is common to any probabilistic knowledge base we omit an example and further discussion.

Complex queries are frequently necessary when consulting a (probabilistic) knowledge base. In SPIRIT a set of hypothetical temporary facts and/or rules can be formulated and then — given these circumstances — further „imperative" facts or rules might be evaluated. Both, hypothetical and imperative facts and rules allow the same rich syntax as during knowledge acquisition. We continue the example 1 of section 3.1:

Example 1 (continued): The spouse excitedly calls her husband: 'I can see a warning light blinking at the dashboard, what should I do ?' To make a telephone diagnosis the husband asks: 'Which one ?' After a discussion about the meaning of the controls at the dashboard, which we politely do not develop here, they make an agreement that the warning light indicates probably the oil pressure or the temperature control. Now the husband consults his wonderful new car diagnosis expert system and starts the query shown in figure 4.

To answer this query, SPIRIT calculates the conditional probability given virtual evidence and finds the result in figure 4. Note, that the probability of a broken fan belt increased significantly from 2% to 50%. The lady should call a garage and ask for a new fan belt.

Mathematically, SPIRIT in such a query calculates a distribution of minimal relative entropy with respect to the original one, given the hypothetical – temporary – restrictions.

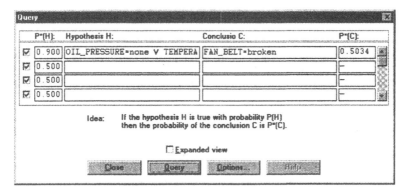

Fig. 4: A typical complex query in SPIRIT

4.5 Facts and Features of SPIRIT

The system SPIRIT consists of two parts: the kernel and the Graphical User Interface (GUI). The kernel is programmed in Standard-C++ with an interface for application-programmers. It should run under any operating system with a suitable C-Compiler. The GUI is developed for WINDOWS 95™ and supports at the moment three languages: German, English and Portuguese. There are also Import-Filters available for some of the common Belief-Network-Description Languages, e.g. Microsoft™ DSC-Format and HUGIN™ NET-Format. You may find a restricted Demo-Version on WWW under the following URL:

<http://www.fernuni-hagen.de/BWLOR/sp_demo.htm>.

5. Conclusion

Many applications of SPIRIT are on the way:

A medium sized example is BAGANG which allows medical diagnoses by Chinese medicine. It actually involves 200 rules and 50 variables.

SPIRIT is used to train efficiently personnel in a Brazilian management simulation game and a small-sized knowledge base supports decisions of a German bank concerning credit-worthiness.

A lot of Bayes-Net-type structured data-sets available by Internet (cf. [20]) were tested in SPIRIT. In the case of the very famous probabilistic model 'blue baby' [8] the rich syntax of SPIRIT allowed a considerable reduction from the original 341 conditioned and unconditioned probabilities to 164 facts and rules.

References

[1] P. Cheeseman (1983). A method of computing generalized Bayesian probability values for expert systems. Proc., 6.th Intl. Joint Conf. on AI (IJCAI-83), Karlsruhe, Germany, 198-202.

[2] Csiszár, I.; I-divergence Geometry of Probability Distributions and Minimization Problems, Ann. Prob. 3, S. 146-158, 1975.

[3] Hájek, P.; Havránek, T.; Jiroušek, R.; Uncertain Information Processing in Expert Systems, CRC-Press, Boca Raton, Florida, 1992.

[4] Jensen, F.V.; Jensen, F.; Optimal junction trees, in: Proceedings of the Tenth conference on Uncertainty in Artificial Intelligence, Ramon Lopez de Maturas, David Poole (eds.) Morgan Kaufmann Inc., 360-366, 1994.

[5] Kane, T.B.; Reasoning with Maximum Entropy in Expert Systems, W.T. Grandy, Jr. and L.H. Schick (eds.), Maximum Entropy and Bayesian Methods, 201-203, 1991

[6] Kjaerulff, U.; Triangulation of graphs — algorithms giving small total state space, Technical Report R90-09, Dept. of Mathematics and Computer Science, Aalborg University, 1990.

[7] Lauritzen, S.L.; Spiegelhalter, D.J.; Local Computations with probabilities on graphical structures and their application to expert systems, J. Roy. Stat. Soc. Ser. B, 50, 157-224 (with discussion), 1988.

[8] Lauritzen, S.L.; Thiesson, B.; Spiegelhalter, D.J.; Diagnostic systems by model selection: a case study, in: Selecting Models from Data, Lecture Notes in Statistics 89, P. Cheeseman and R.W. Oldford (eds.), Springer, 143-152, 1994.

[9] Lemmer, J.F.; Generalized bayesian updating of incompletely specified distributions, Large Scale Systems, 5, 1983

[10] Lemmer, J.F.; Barth, S.W.; Efficient minimum information updating for bayesian inferencing, in: Proc. Nation. Conf. on Artificial Intelligence AAAI, Pittsburgh, 1983

[11] Neapolitan, R.E.; Probabilistic Reasoning in Expert Systems — Theory and Algorithms, John Wiley & Sons, New York, 1990.

[12] Nilsson; N.J.; Probabilistic Logic, Artificial Intelligence 28 (no.1): 71 - 87. 1986

[13] Paris, J.B.; Vencovská, A.; A Note on the Inevitability of Maximum Entropy, Int. J. Approximate. Reasoning, 4, 183-223, 1990.

[14] Pearl, J.; Probabilistic Reasoning in Intelligent Systems, Morgan Kaufmann, San Mateo, California, 1988

[15] Shore, J.E.; Relative Entropy, Probabilistic Inference, and AI, in: Uncertainty in Artificial Intelligence, ed. L.N. Kanal and J.F. Lemmer, North-Holland, 1986

[16] Shore, J.E.; Johnson, R.W.; Axiomatic Derivation of the Principle of Maximum Entropy and the Principle of Minimum Cross Entropy, IEEE Trans. Inform. Theory IT- 26,1,26-37, (see also: comments and corrections..., in IEEE Trans. Inform. Theory IT-29, 1983), 1980

[17] Tarjan, R.E.; Yannakakis, M.; Simple linear-time algorithms to test chordality of graphs, test acyclicity of hypergraphs and selectively reduce acyclic hypergraphs, SIAM J. Comp.,13, 566-579, 1984.

[18] Wen, W.X.; Minimum Cross Entropy Reasoning in Recursive Causal Networks, in: Uncertainty in Artificial Intelligence 4, ed. R.D. Shachter, T.S. Levitt, L.N. Kanal, J.F. Lemmer, North-Holland, 1990

[19] Whittaker, J.; Graphical Models in Applied Multivariate Statistics, John Wiley & Sons, New York, 1990.

[20] Norsys Software Corp.; Library of Bayesian - Networks, available at the WWW under URL: http://www.norsys.com/networklibrary.html

Knowledge Based Image Understanding by Iterative Optimization

H. Niemann[a,b], V. Fischer[a,c], D. Paulus[a], J. Fischer[a]

[a]Lehrstuhl für Mustererkennung (Informatik 5)
Universität Erlangen-Nürnberg
Martensstraße 3, 91058 Erlangen, Germany;
[b]Forschungsgruppe Wissensverarbeitung
Bayerisches Forschungszentrum für Wissensbasierte Systeme
Am Weichselgarten 7, 91058 Erlangen, Germany
[c]IBM Deutschland GmbH, Institut für Logik und Linguistik,
Vangerowstraße 18, 69115 Heidelberg, Germany

Abstract In this paper knowledge based image interpretation is formulated and solved as an optimization problem which takes into account the observed image data, the available task specific knowledge, and the requirements of an application. Knowledge is represented by a semantic network consisting of concepts (nodes) and links (edges). Concepts are further defined by attributes, relations, and a judgment function. The interface between the symbolic knowledge base and the results of image (or signal) processing and initial segmentation is specified via primitive concepts.

We present a recently developed approach to optimal interpretation that is based on the automatic conversion of the concept oriented semantic network to an attribute centered representation and the use of iterative optimization procedures, like e.g. simulated annealing or genetic algorithms. We show that this is a feasible approach which provides 'any–time' capability and allows parallel processing. It provides a well–defined combination of signal and symbol oriented processing by optimizing a heuristic judgment function.

The general ideas have been applied to various problems of image and speech understanding. As an example we describe the recognition of streets from TV image sequences to demonstrate the efficiency of iterative optimization.

Key Words: semantic network, iterative optimization, knowledge based image analysis

1   Introduction

The general goal of automatic image interpretation is to extract from an image or image sequence the information relevant to perform a well–defined task in an *optimal* manner. It is not necessary to extract *all* information contained in the images but to provide the *relevant* information in a format which suites the subsequent usage, either by man or by machine. Usually, information is required in some symbolic and condensed form, not as arrays or subarrays of pixels.

---

[1] This work was funded partially by the German Research Foundation (DFG) under grant number SFB 182. Only the authors are responsible for the contents.

[2] The related work on *speech* understanding using iterative optimization was supported by the Real World Computing Partnership (RWCP).

Interpretation of sensory inputs can only be done with respect to an internal model of the environment, where in principle the observations may in turn modify the internal model. Hence, all interpretation is model–based or knowledge–based.

In this paper we present an approach to represent a model of the task domain or the a priori knowledge about it in a semantic network and to compute an interpretation which is optimal with respect to a given judgment function. From among the different approaches to optimization we describe combinatorial optimization techniques. We point out how knowledge based processing interfaces to data driven segmentation and preprocessing, but techniques for this are not the topic. Finally, we demonstrate the feasibility and efficiency of our approach by application.

Related work on applications of image interpretation is covered, for example, in [1, 2], some general books on image interpretation are, for example, [3, 4], and some books on knowledge representation and use are, for example, [5, 6].

2 Overview

The general goal of image understanding is the computation of a symbolic description B of an image f or image sequence f_τ which

- optimally fits to the observed data (or pixels),
- is maximally consistent with internally represented task–specific knowledge,
- and best suits the demands of a user as defined by an explicit model of the task–domain.

Hence, it is an *optimization problem* and should be formulated (see Section 3) and solved (see Section 4) as such.

Two main phases of processing are assumed: an initial phase of mainly data–driven processing and a phase of mainly model–driven processing. However, it is not assumed in general that these two phases are strictly sequential in the sense that the first phase must be finished before the second may start. Rather it is assumed that the timing of the phases, the data used by them, and the order of switching between phases is determined by a control strategy implemented by a control module or control algorithm.

The data–driven phase of processing consists of *preprocessing* and *initial segmentation*. The goal of preprocessing is to improve the image quality in order to obtain better results during subsequent processing. In general it transforms an image f into another image h. The goal of initial segmentation is to decompose the image into *segmentation objects* O like lines or regions and to obtain their attributes and relationships. We assume that no explicitly represented task–specific knowledge is used, but only general knowledge valid for (almost) all images, for example, about color, geometry, or image formation.

The main topic of this paper is an approach to knowledge representation in the concepts C of a semantic network as well as its use for image understanding, and the formulation of image understanding as the computation of a best scored instance $I^*(C_g)$ of a goal concept C_g.

3 Framework for Knowledge Based Processing

Initial Description According to the above processing model, data driven image processing and initial segmentation is viewed as a sequence of operations, that transforms an image f into an *initial description* $\mathcal{A}$ which in general is a network $\langle O \rangle$ of *segmentation objects* O. In our applications we mainly use straight and circular lines for segmentation. The initial (symbolic) description defines the *interface* to knowledge based processing.

In general, a segmentation object has a *type* T_O, for example, indicating that it is a straight line, or a circle and it has a *name* identifying the object, for example, the number of a straight line. In addition, it may have attributes, parts, structural relations among its attributes and parts, and it should have a judgment **G** which in general is a vector of real numbers. An *attribute* A has a type T_A, a value which may be a real number or a symbol from a finite terminal alphabet, and a judgment which is a real number. Examples of attributes are the length of a line, the angle between a line and the x-axis, or the area of a region. A *part* P of a segmentation object is itself a segmentation object and provides a decomposition into simpler components. For example, the 'right angle' has as parts two lines. A *structural relation* S expresses a constraint between attributes on objects (A_O), parts (A_P), and concretes $(A_K$, see below), of a segmentation object, for example, in a right angle the angles between each of the two lines and the x-axis are constrained. It is useful to consider fuzzy relations having an associated real number which measures the degree of fulfilment of the relation. Briefly, a segmentation object is a structure

$$
\begin{aligned}
O = [\,&D : T_O, && //\ \texttt{name}\,, \\
&(A : (T_A,\ \mathbb{R} \cup V_T))^*, && //\ \texttt{attribute}\,, \\
&(P : O)^*, && //\ \texttt{part}\,, \\
&(S(A_O, A_P, A_K) : \mathbb{R})^*, && //\ \texttt{relation}\,, \\
&\mathbf{G} : \mathbb{R}^n\,] && //\ \texttt{judgment}\,.
\end{aligned}
\tag{3.1}
$$

The notation $(A : \ldots)^*$ indicates that there may be an arbitrary number (including zero) of attributes in an object. The initial description of an image is a network of segmentation objects $\mathcal{A} = \langle O \rangle$.

Concept For knowledge representation we employ a suitably defined version of a semantic network [7] because it allows well–structured representation, efficient utilization, different types of optimization procedures, explanation tools, and was shown to provide excellent results in various applications.

Basically, a formalism for knowledge representation in an image analysis system should allow one to represent in the computer a certain *conception* denoting an entity in the real (physical) world, for example, a 'highway', a 'car', an 'accident on a highway', and so on. We represent a conception by a recursive structure

C and call this internal representation a *concept*

$$
\begin{aligned}
C = (&D : T_C, &&\text{// name}\\
&(P_{ci} : C)^*, &&\text{// context-indep. part}\\
&(P_{cd} : C)^*, &&\text{// context-dep. part}\\
&(K : C)^*, &&\text{// concrete}\\
&(V : C)^*, &&\text{// specialization} &&(3.2)\\
&(L : I)^*, &&\text{// instance}\\
&(A : (T_A \mapsto F))^*, &&\text{// attribute, computed by } F\\
&(S(A_C, A_P, A_K) \mapsto F)^*, &&\text{// relation, computed by } F\\
&(G \mapsto F)) &&\text{// judgment, computed by } F
\end{aligned}
$$

A detailed description of a concept in this sense is given in [7] and related work is found, for example, in [8, 6]. Some basic properties are illustrated in Figure 1.

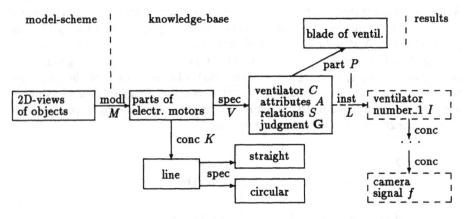

Figure 1. Examples of concepts linked to other concepts and modeling industrial parts.

The main defining components of a concept are its context–*independent* and context–*dependent parts* P_{ci}, P_{cd} and *concretes* K. The distinction between parts and concretes allows one to represent relations between different *levels of abstraction* or different conceptual systems. For example, in Figure 1 the 'parts of electric motors' are determined from 'lines' which are in a different conceptual system (or closer to the level of pixels); they are therefore related by a concrete–link. We omit the model scheme (Figure 1) from further discussion here and refer to [9, 10].

The distinction between context–independent and –dependent parts allows one to handle context–dependent relations between objects and their parts. With respect to the usage of a knowledge base this means that a context–independent part may be detected or infered *without* having the superior concept, whereas a context–dependent part can only be infered *after* having the superior concept.

In order to have compact knowledge bases and to define hierarchies of conceptions it is possible to introduce a concept as the *specialization V* of some other (more general) concept.

According to the above definition a concept C has a set of *attributes* (or features, properties) A each one referencing a function F which can compute the value of the corresponding attribute.

There may be *structural relations S* between the attributes A_C of a concept or of attributes A_P and A_K of its parts and concretes. Since in image processing noise and processing errors are inevitable, relations usually can only be established with limited precision. Therefore, each relation references a function F computing a measure of the degree of fulfilment of this relation, for example, in the sense of a fuzzy relation.

In the same class of objects there may be quite different types of objects. For example, there are chairs with three and with four legs, and a chair may have an armrest or not. One possibility is to define separate concepts for each type, but in order to have compact knowledge bases it is convenient to introduce a more flexible definition of a concept. Therefore a concept is allowed to have different so called sets of modalities H_i with the implication that each individual set may define the concept. Furthermore, obligatory and optional parts are introduced.

Instance and Modified Concept The occurrence of a specific object in an image is represented by an *instance $I(C)$* of the corresponding concept C. The relation between the concept and its instance is represented by a link L from C to $I(C)$. An instance is represented by a structure identical to (3.2) except that references to functions are replaced by the actual values computed by those functions from the image.

There may be the situation that some instances have been computed and allow the restriction of attribute values of a concept C which cannot yet be instantiated. In this case a so called *modified concept $Q(C)$* is created which allows the propagation of constraints both in a bottom–up and top–down manner. For example, the detection of one 'wheel' of a 'car' constrains both the location of the car (bottom–up) and of the other wheels (top–down). This way *constraints* are propagated bottom–up and top–down.

A *judgment* **G** of an instance or a modified concept is a vector of numbers computed by F, measuring the degree of confidence in the actual occurrence of the instance and its expected contribution to the success of analysis.

Knowledge–Based Processing The available task-specific knowledge is represented in a *model $\mathcal{M}$* which is a network of concepts $\mathcal{M} = \langle C \rangle$. Hence, knowledge about objects, events, tasks, actions, and so on is represented homogeneously by concepts related to each other by the various links.

In particular we assume that the goal of image analysis is itself represented by one or more concepts which we denote as the *goal concepts C_{g_i}*. The description of an image then is represented by an instance $I(C_g)$ of the goal concept. Since every concept has an attached judgment **G**, there is also a judgment $\mathbf{G}(I(C_g))$ of the goal concept. Now it is natural to request the computation of an *optimal* *instance* $I^*(C_g)$ of a goal concept and define knowledge based processing as the optimization problem

$$I^*(C_g) = \max_{\{I(C_g)\}} \{\mathbf{G}(I(C_g)|\mathcal{M}, \mathcal{A})\}, \tag{3.3}$$

$$\mathcal{B}(\boldsymbol{f}) = I^*(C_g). \tag{3.4}$$

The essential assumptions are that it is possible to

- compute a sufficiently reliable initial segmentation $\mathcal{A}$,
- acquire the relevant task-specific knowledge in the model $\mathcal{M}$,
- specify judgments $\mathbf{G}$ which are adequate for the task domain.

It has been demonstrated in several applications that this can be done, see for example, [11, 12].

Facing both the large amount of data and the limited processing time in most image understanding tasks, the exploitation of parallelism provides a promising way to compute an optimal instance $I^*(C_g)$ just in time with the sensory input. Whereas parallel algorithms for preprocessing and segmentation have nearly become a state of the art and may be found in various textbooks [13], parallel knowledge based processing is much less investigated. While the former algorithms often make use of the local nature of pixel–oriented computations, and therefore allow the use of simple data partitioning techniques, the parallelization of knowledge based processing is more difficult, since usually it requires the identification of inferences that may be executed simultaneously.

Most parallel semantic network systems employ an isomorphic mapping between the processors of a parallel hardware and the nodes and links of a knowledge base, which turned out to be a feasible approach if both concepts and inferences are simple [14]. However, since in our formalism a concept may have an arbitrary number of attributes and structural relations, complex concepts may become a bottleneck in parallel instantiation. Therfore, we employ an attribute centered representation of a semantic network, where each computation needed during instantiation is represented by a node of a directed acyclic graph [15, 16] that may be mapped to a multiprocessor system for purposes of parallel processing.

The automatic construction of the graph from the concept centered definition given by equation (3.2) is an important prerequisite to preserve the advantages of the well–structured knowledge representation by semantic networks. In our formalism this is possible, since the use of knowledge during instantiation only relies on the syntax of the network language, and not on the content of the knowledge base or intermediate results of analysis.

Since a concept usually is stored exactly once in the knowledge base, but it may be necessary to create several instances for one concept during analysis (as an example consider the wheels of a car), transformation of the network starts with the computation of the number of instances needed for instantiation of a goal concept C_g. This is achieved by a top–down expansion of the goal concept. Then, the expanded network is refined by the determination of dependencies between subconceptual entities. These are obtained from an examination of the interface to the procedural knowledge F, where a list of arguments is specified for each procedure. For each attribute, structural relation, and judgment of the expanded network a node v_k is created, and the name of the structure is attached to v_k as well as the corresponding procedures for the computation of a value or a judgment. If a node v_l is referenced via its name in the argument list of the procedures attached to v_k, a directed link $e_{lk} = (v_l, v_k)$ is created, expressing the fact that the computation of v_l must finish before the computation of v_k may start. Nodes without predecessors represent attributes that provide an interface to the initial segmentation, and nodes without successors usually represent the judgments of goal concepts.

4 Optimal Instantiation

As a prerequisite for goal–directed processing, we assume that a heuristic judgment function is available, which allows the quantitative treatment of alternative, uncertain, or imprecise results, that may arise during segmentation as well as during knowledge based processing (cf. Section 3). Results of initial segmentation in our applications are either scored heuristically or forwarded to knowledge based processing without a judgment of quality.

During knowledge based processing we have to distinguish between the judgment of an instance $I(C)$ of a concept C and the judgment of a state of analysis. The score of an instance in principle is always based on the quality of the match between data and model or on the quality of fulfilment of fuzzy inference rules. The score of a state of analysis is always based on the current estimate of the quality of a solution provided by a goal concept, see eq. (4.4) for combinatorial optimization. Therefore, instantiation is always directed towards optimal instantiation of a goal concept as requested in (3.3).

The attribute centered representation of a semantic network presented originally was developed to speed up analysis by the parallel computation of instances. Besides instantiation on the *network level* there is a *control level* (e.g. a search tree) that deals with the problem of finding an optimal interpretation, and in face of the required processing rates it seems reasonable to employ parallel processing on this level, too.

Parallel graph search algorithms, which are treated, for example, in [17], provide an obvious solution and are widely used in solving standard problems from artificial intelligence, like e.g. the Traveling–Salesman–Problem. However, since in our application state space search demands the collection of instances and modified concepts into nodes of the search graph, the control algorithm given above requires a large amount of communication between processors if the search space is explored in parallel. We therefore developed an *iterative optimization algorithm* which facilitates an efficient realization on a parallel hardware. In addition it provides an approximate interpretation at every iteration and therefore supports the fast computation of suboptimal interpretations, which may be used by other processing modules if less processing time is available (any–time property). For purposes of explanation, the algorithm may be divided into two stages:

- During bottom-up instantiation, values and judgments are computed for each attribute, structural relation, link or concept of the attribute network. Initially this will lead to many competing interpretations having low values of judgment.
- Interpretations obtained from bottom-up instantiation are iteratively improved by applying a combinatorial optimization procedure. Ideally, this will lead to a unique interpretation having a high value of judgment.

Bottom-up instantiation starts with the computation of attributes that provide an interface to the initial segmentation, and finishes with the judgment of goal concepts. Parallel bottom–up instantiation maps each node of the attribute network onto a processor and computes simultaneously those nodes, whose predecessors have already finished execution. We thereby obtain instances for the goal concepts, each provided with a judgment $G(I(C_g))$. From the best scored instances we create a vector

$$g = (G(I^*(C_{g_1})), \ldots, G(I^*(C_{g_n})) \tag{4.1}$$

representing the final result of a single iteration step.

Since results from inital segmentation are usually erroneous and due to the presence of ambiguities in the knowledge base (e.g. sets of modalities), there is a need for an efficient processing of competing hypotheses that are created during instantiation. Because the simultaneous treatment of competing hypotheses would result in both a large amount of communication between processors and a combinatorial explosion of intermediate results on the higher levels of the network, an iterative processing is employed.

The computation of instances (Figure 2) and their judgment is completely determined by assigning to each interface (attribute) node A_i a (possibly empty) subset $\{O_j^{(i)}\}$ of segmentation objects and selecting for each concept node C_k a unique modality $H_l^{(k)}$ (cf. Section 3). This allows us to characterize the *current state of analysis* by a vector

$$r_c = \left[(A_i, \{O_j^{(i)}\}) \mid i = 1, \ldots, m \; ; \; (C_k, H_l^{(k)}) \mid k = 1, \ldots, n\right], \tag{4.2}$$

where m is the number of interface nodes and n the number of concepts having more than one modality. Hence, we also may rewrite (4.1) as a function of the current state r_c by

$$g(r_c) = (G(I^*(C_{g_1})), \ldots, G(I^*(C_{g_n})|r_c) \tag{4.3}$$

and compute an optimal state of analysis by treating r_c as the current state z_c of a combinatorial optimization problem.

Figure 3 gives a general algorithm for solving the problem of optimal instanti-

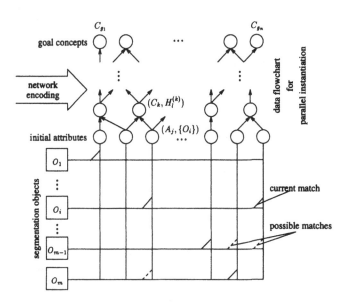

goal concepts

C_{g_1} C_{g_n}

network encoding

$(C_k, H_l^{(k)})$

initial attributes

$(A_j, \{O_i\})$

data flowchart for parallel instantiation

segmentation objects

O_1

O_i

O_{m-1}

O_m

current match

possible matches

Figure 2. The principle of bottom–up instantiation. Hypotheses resulting from actual matches between initial attributes and segmentation objects are propagated through the data flowchart, resulting in a judgment of goal concepts.

ation (3.3–3.4) by combinatorial optimization. The parts printed sans serif have to be adapted for optimal instantiation.

For the design of the required cost function ϕ, we assume that an error–free segmentation would support a single interpretation, and therefore results in an ideal judgment $G(I^*(C_{g_i})) = 1.0$ for the correct goal concept. On the other hand, at the same time this segmentation would give no evidence to any other goal concept, i.e. $G(I^*(C_{g_j})) = 0.0$. We would thus obtain the i-th unit vector e_i as an ideal result of instantiation, if the i-th goal concept provides the desired symbolic description.

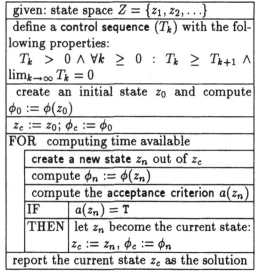

given: state space $Z = \{z_1, z_2, \ldots\}$

define a **control sequence** (T_k) with the following properties:

$T_k > 0 \wedge \forall k \geq 0 : T_k \geq T_{k+1} \wedge \lim_{k \to \infty} T_k = 0$

create an initial state z_0 and compute $\phi_0 := \phi(z_0)$

$z_c := z_0; \phi_c := \phi_0$

FOR computing time available

   create a **new state** z_n out of z_c

   compute $\phi_n := \phi(z_n)$

   compute the **acceptance criterion** $a(z_n)$

IF	$a(z_n) = T$
THEN	let z_n become the current state: $z_c := z_n, \phi_c := \phi_n$

report the current state z_c as the solution

Figure 3.: Algorithm for the minimization of a cost function by combinatorial optimization.

We approximate this behaviour and define

$$\phi(r_c) = \min_{1 \leq i \leq n} \{(e_i - \tilde{g}(r_c))^2\}, \qquad\qquad \tilde{g}(r_c) = \frac{g(r_c)}{\|g(r_c)\|} \qquad (4.4)$$

as a cost function, that computes the minimum distance from $g(r_c)$ to the unit vectors e_i. Note that this function provides a problem independent measure of costs, since no assumptions on the contents of the knowledge base are made.

Monte-Carlo-Methods The creation of a new state r_n and the choice of an acceptance criterion are motivated by the analogy between the annealing of a solid in condensed matter physics and the optimization of a system with many independent variables (cf. "simulated annealing algorithm" [18]).

In combinatorial optimization the temperature of a solid corresponds to the value T_k of a control sequence, and the cooling is achieved by a monotone decrease of T_k. The creation of a new state is performed by applying a small random perturbation to the current state r_c. A new state r_n is generated from the current state r_c by first selecting a tuple from among $(A_i, \{O_j^{(i)}\})$ or $(C_k, H_l^{(k)})$ in (4.2) with equal probability, and then exchanging the term $\{O_j^{(i)}\}$ or $H_l^{(k)}$ by a possible alternative, again with equal probability for each alternative.

If the new state generated this way has *lower* cost than the current state, it is accepted. In addition, a new state with *higher* cost may also be accepted. The acceptance of new states with *higher* costs is necessary as well to allow the escape from local minima of the cost function. However, accepting *all* states would prevent the algorithm from convergence, and therefore an acceptance criterion $a(r_n)$ is needed to decide which new state should be accepted or rejected. The general algorithm given in Figure 3 is specialized to different optimization procedures according to the different criteria

$$a(r_n) = \begin{cases} T : q \leq \exp(-1/T_k \cdot (\phi_n - \phi_c)) & \text{simulated annealing ,} \\ T : (\phi_n - \phi_c) \leq T_k & \text{threshold acceptance ,} \\ T : \phi_n \leq T_k & \text{great deluge ,} \\ T : \phi_n \leq \phi_c & \text{stochastic relaxation ,} \\ F : \text{else .} \end{cases} \qquad (4.5)$$

Whereas stochastic relaxation does not allow to escape from local minima, and therefore may be appropriate for certain cost functions only, the other algorithms derived from equation (4.5) can guarantee convergence into a global minimum, provided the decrease of the control parameter is sufficiently slow. Since this usually results in a large number of iterations and a large amount of computing time, there is a strong interest to speed up the optimization by a parallel exploration of the search space.

Genetic Algorithms Different from the optimization techniques introduced in the previous section, genetic algorithms perform a parallel exploration of the search space by the use of a set of current states or current solutions of the image interpretation problem. The set of solutions is called a *population*, the members of a population are referred to as *organisms*, and the population used in the k–th iteration of the algorithm is called the k–th *generation* [19]. Adopting the notation of (4.2) we denote the set of current states, that is, the current population, by

$$R_c = \{r_{c,1}, \ldots, r_{c,\mu}, \ldots, r_{c,p}\} \quad , \tag{4.6}$$

and an organism of this population by

$$r_{c,\mu} = \left[(A_i, \{O_j^{(i)}\})_\mu \mid i = 1, \ldots, m \; ; \; (C_k, H_l^{(k)})_\mu \mid k = 1, \ldots, n\right] \quad . \tag{4.7}$$

Costs have to be assigned to each newly created organism. In our application this demands the bottom–up instantiation of the data flowchart for each newly created organism; they constitute the temporary population R_t. Therefore, especially in the presence of a large knowledge base, it is desirable to keep $|R_t|$ small to perform as many iterations as possible. Thus, we decided to create only *one* new organism in each step of iteration ($|R_t| = 1$), and to employ a multi-point crossover operator to make use of the full size of the current population R_c, instead of a pair of organisms as provided by a single application of the operator. Hence, genetic otpimization in our case is performed by the following three steps: First, a new organism is created by multipoint crossover; this selects from among the tuples $(A_i, \{O_j^{(i)}\})_\mu$, $\mu = 1, \ldots, p$ one tuple with a probability proportional to the fitness of that organism and makes this tuple an element of the new organism in R_t; this is repeated for all tuples $(A_i, \{O_j^{(i)}\})_\mu$, $i = 1, \ldots, m$ and all tuples $(C_k, H_l^{(k)})_\mu, k = 1, \ldots, n$. Second, each tuple of the new organism is mutated by a small probability (we use $p_m = 5\%$). Third, the new population R_n is obtained from the best organisms in $R_c \cup R_t$.

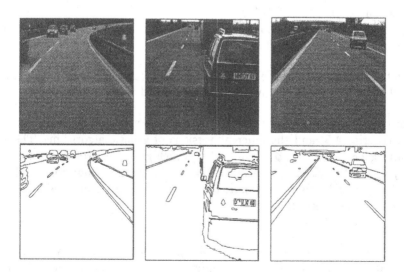

Figure 4. Gray–level images (top) and segmentation (bottom) from three different traffic scenes.

5 An Application

In this section we consider the problem of recognizing streets from TV image sequences recorded on a moving car. In the experiments described here, we used three image sequences, each consisting of 30 gray–level images, taken at video rate from a camera fixed in a moving car, see Figure 4 for an example from each sequence.

The goal of analysis was to obtain a description of the road and its markers, not to compute a complete interpretation in terms of cars, trucks, and traffic signs present in the scenes. Task–specific knowledge was developed in [20] and is represented in the semantic network formalism described in Section refA0301. An overview of the knowledge base is depicted in Figure 5. Encoding of the network into the attribute centered representation described results in a data flowchart consisting of 120 nodes, eleven of them representing initial attributes. On top

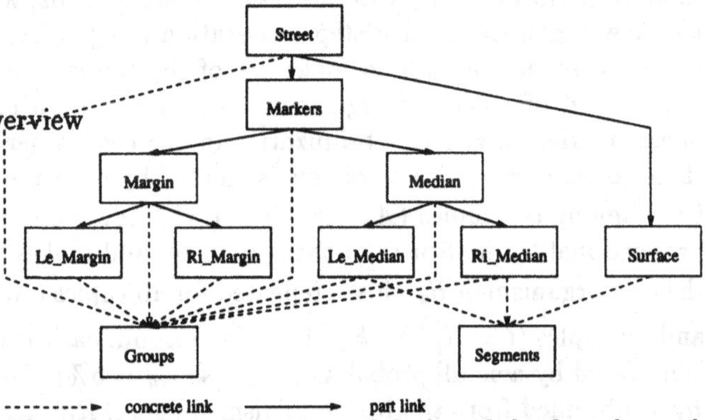

Figure 5.: Overall structure of the knowledge base for road detection.

of the flowchart, there is a single node for the computation of a judgment of the goal concept (in this case: "Street").

Data driven processing yields segmentation objects of regions for the roadway as well as for groups of regions that are considered as road markers.

In [16] we examined the various Monte–Carlo–methods given by the acceptance criteria (4.5) and the different versions of genetic algorithms. The speed of convergence $\nu(n) = P\{\phi_n - \phi_{min} \leq \varepsilon\}$, which gives the probability to reach a nearly optimal solution in n iterations was used for the evaluation of all methods. For the results shown in Figure 6, the size of the population was $|Z_c| = 16$, and $|Z_t| = 1$, see Section 4.

The threshold acceptance and great deluge algorithm perform worse than stochastic relaxation and are therefore omitted in the discussion. However, it was observable that all deterministic acceptance criteria perform significantly better than simulated annealing, which is in accordance to the results reported in [21, 22] for other optimization problems.

The computing time measured on a 1–master/p–slave configuration of coupled workstations (HP 735) using PVM is shown in Figure 7. The final result (computed from segmentation results in Figure 4) is given in Figure 8, which again shows one image out of each of the three image sequences. The grey value coding of the street markers and of the street surface show that those regions were interpreted correctly.

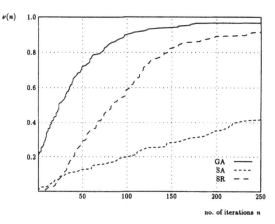

Figure 6.: Probability of convergence $\nu(n)$ after n iterations for the simulated annealing algorithm (SA), the stochastic relaxation algorithm (SR), and the multi point genetic algorithm (GA).

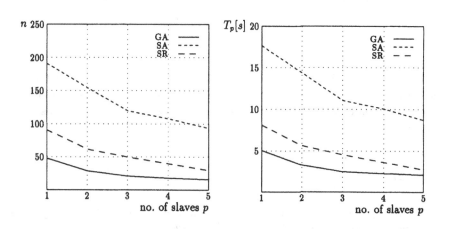

Figure 7. Number n of iterations (left) and computer time T_p (right) on a master/slave configuration of workstations.

In [23] the approach presented here for image understanding has also been successfully applied to *speech* analysis; this shows that the approach is useful for knowledge based pattern analysis in general.

Figure 8. Result of interpretation by iterative optimization.

6   Conclusion and Outlook

We defined knowledge based image interpretation as the problem to compute an optimal instance of a goal concept. The two main processing steps are the data–driven computation of an initial segmentation and the model–driven interpretation by instantiation of the goal concept. We presented an approach to knowledge representation which started form a concept based representation in a semantic network and proceeded to an attribute based representation.

For further work we will consider the implementation of an active vision task by concepts of a knowledge base of the type introduced in Section 3. This requires a careful, precise, and explicit modeling of the goal of active vision. As an example we plan to consider the closed loop of sensing and acting (camera and robot arm) in order to find and grasp a specified object which may be invisible from the current camera position.

The above mentioned task requires consideration of another point for future work, that is real time performance. The parallel implementation as well as the any–time capability of iterative optimization seem to be useful steps in this direction.

References

1. T. Matsuyama and V. Hwang. *SIGMA: A Knowledge–based Aerial Image Understanding System.* Plenum Press, New York, 1990.
2. I. Masaki, editor. *Vision–Based Vehicle Guidance.* Springer, Berlin, 1992.
3. O. Faugeras. *Three–Dimensional Computer Vision.* Artificial Intelligence Series. The MIT Press, Cambridge, MA, 1993.
4. H. Niemann. *Pattern Analysis and Understanding.* Springer Series in Information Sciences 4. Springer, Berlin, 2. edition, 1990.
5. P. Krause and D. Clark. *Representing Uncertain Knowledge.* Intellect Books, Oxford, 1993.
6. J.F. Sowa, editor. *Principles of Semantic Networks.* Morgan Kaufmann, San Mateo, Calif., 1991.

7. H. Niemann, G. Sagerer, S. Schröder, and F. Kummert. ERNEST: A semantic network system for pattern understanding. *IEEE Trans. on Pattern Analysis and Machine Intelligence*, 9:883–905, 1990.

8. A. Kobsa. The SB-ONE knowledge representation workbench. SFB 314 (XTRA), Memo Nr. 31, Univ. des Saarlandes, FB 10, Saarbrücken, F. R. of Germany, 1989.

9. D. Paulus, A. Winzen, and H. Niemann. Knowlege based object recognition and model generation. In *Proc. Europto 93, Computer Vision for Industry*, pages 382–393, München, 1994. SPIE Proc. No. 1989–47.

10. A. Winzen. Automatische Erzeugung dreidimensionaler Modelle für Bildanalysesysteme. Dissertation, Technische Fakultät, Universität Erlangen–Nürnberg, Erlangen, (1994).

11. H. Niemann, H. Bunke, I. Hofmann, G. Sagerer, F. Wolf, and H. Feistel. A knowledge based system for analysis of gated blood pool studies. *IEEE Trans. Pattern Analysis and Machine Intelligence*, 7:246–259, 1985.

12. H. Niemann, H. Brünig, R. Salzbrunn, and S. Schröder. A knowledge-based vision system for industrial applications. *Machine Vision and Applications*, 3:201–229, 1990.

13. H. Burkhardt, Y. Neuvo, and J. Simon, editors. *From Pixels to Features II. Parallelism in Image Processing*. North–Holland, Amsterdam, 1991.

14. L. Shastri. *Semantic Networks: An Evidential Formalization and its Connectionist Realization*. Research Notes in Artificial Intelligence. Pitman and Morgan Kaufmann Publishers, Inc., London and San Mateo, Calif., 1988.

15. V. Fischer and H. Niemann. Parallelism in a semantic network for image understanding. In A. Bode and M. Dal Cin, editors, *Parallel Computer Architectures. Theory, Hardware, Software, Applications*, volume 732 of *Lecture Notes in Computer Science*, pages 203–218. Springer-Verlag, Berlin, 1993.

16. V. Fischer. Parallelverarbeitung in einem semantischen Netzwerk für die wissensbasierte Musteranalyse. Dissertation, Technische Fakultät, Universität Erlangen–Nürnberg, Erlangen, 1995.

17. B.W. Wah, G. Li, and C. Yu. Multiprocessing of combinatorial search problems. In [24], pages 103–145. 1990.

18. N. Metropolis, A. Rosenbluth, M. Rosenbluth, A. Teller, and E. Teller. Equation of state calculations for fast computing machines. *Journal of Chemical Physics*, 21(6):1087–1092, 1953.

19. L. Booker, D. Goldberg, and J. Holland. Classifier systems and genetic algorithms. *Artificial Intelligence*, 40(1–3):235–282, 1989.

20. S. Steuer. Erstellung eines ersten Modells in ERNESTzur Identifikation der Straße und der Position des Kamerafahrzeugs im statischen Bild. Technical Report 3.2.B1 Projekt MOVIE, Bayerisches Forschungszentrum für Wissensbasierte Systeme (FORWISS) und Bayerische Motorenwerke AG (BMW AG), München, 1991.

21. G. Dueck and T. Scheuer. Threshold accepting: A general purpose optimization algorithm appearing superior to simulated annealing. *Journal of Computational Physics*, 90(1):161–175, 1990.

22. G. Dueck. New optimization heuristics: The great deluge algorithm and the record-to-record-travel. *Journal of Computational Physics*, 104(1):86–92, 1993.

23. V. Fischer, J. Fischer, and H. Niemann. An algorithm for any-time speech understanding. In *German Slovenian Workshop on Image and Speech Understanding*, to appear, Ljubljana, 1996.

24. V. Kumar, P. Gopalakrishnan, and L. Kumar, editors. *Parallel Algorithms for Machine Intelligence and Vision*. Springer-Verlag, New York, 1990.

Knowledge Organization Using the Development System FAENSY *

Wolfgang Oertel

Technical University of Dresden,
Department of Artificial Intelligence,
Dresden D-01062, Germany

Abstract. FAENSY is a generic development system for building dynamic knowledge-based application systems in practically relevant domains. Its knowledge model is based on a structural approach that uses predefined relations between complex objects and allows to define behaviours like analysis, synthesis, deduction, analogy, and induction over them.

1 Introduction

The development of applied knowledge representation and processing in the last years can be characterized by three kinds of systems. Traditional rule-based systems use acquired generic knowledge for solving specific problems in a deductive manner. The second type involves case-based systems that try to use former handled specific problems to solve actual specific problems by analogical reasoning. And at last, concepts and systems have been created, that support the acquisition and automatic learning of generic knowledge by inductive reasoning.

The practical work has shown, however, that not a single one of these approaches is suited to meet the needs of real domain modeling. Only a combination of the different methods can guarantee the success of systems to be developed in practically relevant domains. With FAENSY [2], a development system has been built to support the integration of the three approaches. The basis is a knowledge model that serves as a global organization mechanism.

2 Knowledge Organization

The knowledge organization of FAENSY combines the advantages of two technologies: the object orientation and the hybrid knowledge representation. The result is a model that is able to map states, processes, and regularities of a universe of discourse and to change this mapping during the permanent interaction between system and its environment.

* This research was supported by the Federal Ministry of Education, Science, Research and Technology (BMBF) within the joint project FABEL under contract no. 01IW104. Project partners in FABEL are GMD – German National Research Center for Information Technology, Sankt Augustin, BSR Consulting GmbH, München, Technical University of Dresden, HTWK Leipzig, University of Freiburg, and University of Karlsruhe.

The knowledge model KM is a formalism that defines a mapping by providing explicit knowledge EK, implicit knowledge IK, inference methods IM, and knowledge operations OP: $KM = (EK, IK, IM, OP)$.

The explicit knowledge EK can be regarded as a direct description of the universe of discourse. It consists of objects OB and relations RE between them. Objects and relations build a mathematical structure: $EK = (OB, RE)$. The implicit knowledge IK describes the reality indirectly by a set of structure transformation rules also called behaviours BE: $IK = BE$.

Inference Methods IM determine how the structure transformation rules are used to transform an explicit structure EK_1 into another explicit structure EK_2. The transformation process can be direct (using one transformation rule) or indirect (using a set of transformation rules in a sequence of direct transformations). All structures derivable by rules from explicit structures are called implicit structures. The knowledge operations OP give the possibility to query and update explicit and implicit knowledge structures.

2.1 Objects

With OB, a set of complex objects is given: $OB = \{o_1, o_2, o_3, ...\}$. The inside of each object is defined by a set of static or dynamic elements. These elements form the local structure of a knowledge base. Typically, they are knowledge elements. Depending on the set of available interpreters, various pure knowledge representations are possible here. So, there are logic formulas, production rules, constraints but also relations, networks or functions. Though, in principle, these elements are defined locally within the objects, they can refer to other objects, too. A low-level interface allows such an access.

Some composite objects stand for typical traditional knowledge units like cases, schemes, concepts, or similarities.

2.2 Relations

The objects are linked with each other by a set of predefined relations RE that form the global structure of a knowledge base: $RE = (I, G, C, A)$. The single relations have the following meanings:

- I - Idealization (R - Realization),
- G - Generalization (S - Specialization),
- C - Composition (P - Partialization),
- A - Association.

The idealization connects realistic objects with idealistic objects (objects that have different distances from its mapped original object, e. g. spatial/temporal and conceptual representations). The generalization links specific objects with generic objects (objects of different generality, e. g. episodic situations and generic regularities). And the composition connects partial objects with composite ones (objects of different grain size, e. g. elements and aggregates). The relations in the brackets stand for the inverse relations, respectively. With the association, objects belonging to each other in a way not determined more precisely can be linked (e.g. similar objects).

The defined relations between the knowledge objects are useful not only for getting an adequate representation of the universe of discourse and performing reasoning processes, but also for technical purposes like storing, changing, efficiency, and management.

2.3 Behaviours

The global dynamic behaviour is defined by a set of structure transformation rules: $BE = \{STR_1, STR_2, STR_3, ...\}$. A structure transformation rule STR contains two related structures: $STR = (S_1 \Longrightarrow S_2)$. The most important rules can be divided into the following classes:

- Analysis and Synthesis,
- Deduction and Induction,
- Analogy.

The effects of these rules can be described using the introduced relations. So, analysis rules takes realistic objects to produce idealistic objects. The opposite direction is supported by synthesis rules. Deductive rules generate specific objects using generic ones, and inductive rules generate generic objects using specific objects. Finally, analogical rules can be used to find or produce objects similar to given objects of the same idealization and generalization level.

So, the behaviours define the meaning of the global structure of a knowledge base. Elementary behaviours can be composed to composite behaviour structures. Some of them stand for typical reasoning approaches like case-based, scheme-based, concept-based, or learning methods. The meaning of the local structure of a knowledge base is given by predefined interpreters.

3 System Architecture

The development system FAENSY is organized as a knowledge base system on conceptual level. That means it contains a set of knowledge structures and a set of interpreters to interpret them. Both, knowledge structures and interpreters, are handled by a fixed management system supporting inference and administration tasks. Because knowledge structures and interpreters can be added, changed, and deleted, a high degree of flexibility is reached within the system. Fig. 1 shows the system structure in a graphical manner.

The interpreter base contains interpreters for logical clauses, production rules, constraints, similarity functions, and adaptation rules. They can be used for doing deductive, analogical, or inductive reasoning. In some cases, additional interfaces between them are necessary. The knowledge base, on the other hand, provides containers for all structures involved in the interpretation process, including objects, relations, and behaviours.

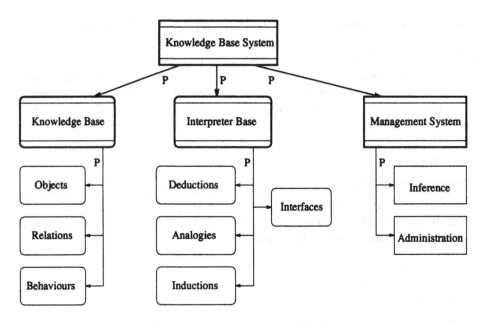

Fig. 1. Conceptual System Structure

From the software-technological point of view, the system has a three-level-architecture. Besides the central conceptual level, there is the internal level where operations for data and co-ordination structures (relations, networks, files, objects, processes) are available. The external level is made by operations allowing the presentation of all structures and operations of the other levels in the form of texts and graphics as well as the access to them by menus. The kernel of the system has been implemented in Allegro Common Lisp, the user interface utilizes the language Tcl/Tk. The whole system runs on Unix workstations.

4 Conclusion

The introduced system FAENSY and its knowledge model have provided the integrative implementational and conceptual basis for the development of knowledge-based application systems in the fields of public traffic [2], building architectures [1], forestry, and mechanical engineering. The common feature of the created systems is their high degree of practical acceptance in the respective domains.

References

1. S. Bakhtari, B. Bartsch-Spörl, W. Oertel: DOM-ARCADE: Assistance services for construction, evaluation, and adaptation of design layouts. In: J. S. Gero, F. Sudweeks: AI in Design'96. Kluwer Academic Publishers, Dordrecht, Standford, 1996.
2. W. Oertel: FAENSY: Fabel Development System. FABEL Report Nr. 27, GMD, Sankt Augustin, 1994

A Uniform Proof Procedure for Classical and Non-Classical Logics

Jens Otten*   Christoph Kreitz

Fachgebiet Intellektik, Fachbereich Informatik
Technische Hochschule Darmstadt
Alexanderstr. 10, 64283 Darmstadt, Germany
{jeotten,kreitz}@intellektik.informatik.th-darmstadt.de

Abstract. We present a proof procedure for classical and non-classical logics. The proof search is based on the matrix-characterization of validity where an emphasis on paths and connections avoids redundancies occurring in sequent or tableaux calculi. Our uniform path-checking algorithm operates on arbitrary (non-normal form) formulae and generalizes Bibel's connection method for classical logic and formulae in clause-form. It can be applied to intuitionistic and modal logics by modifying the component for testing complementarity of connected atoms. Besides a short and elegant path-checking procedure we present a specialized string-unification algorithm which is necessary for dealing with non-classical logics.

1 Introduction

Non-classical logics are used extensively in various branches of AI and Computer Science as logics of knowledge and belief, logics of programs, and for the specification of distributed and concurrent systems. In many of these applications there is a need for automated proof search. For *classical* predicate logic theorem provers based on resolution [14, 17], the connection method [4, 5, 8, 3], or the tableaux calculus [2, 1] have demonstrated that formal reasoning can be automated well.

Recently Wallen [15, 16] and Ohlbach [10] have extended the classical characterizations of logical validity on which the above proof methods are based into characterizations of logical validity for intuitionistic and various modal logics. These characterizations avoid the notational redundancies contained in natural deduction or sequent calculi for these logics and thus provide a theoretical foundation for developing proof procedures for a rich variety of non-classical logics.

In this paper we present a proof procedure which allows a *uniform* treatment of classical, intuitionistic, and modal logics. It is based on a unified representation of Wallen's matrix characterizations and generalizes Bibel's connection method [4, 5] for classical predicate logic accordingly. In order to keep the general methodology of the latter – following *connections* when investigating *paths* through a given formula – unchanged we had to take into account a considerable extension of the notion of *complementarity* which strongly depends on the logic under consideration. Whereas in the classical case two atomic formulae are complementary if they have different polarity but can be unified by some term-substitution, for non-classical logics also the *prefixes* of the two atomic formulae (i.e. descriptions of their position in the formula tree) have to be unifiable. Thus in addition to the usual term-unification our method requires a special *string-unification* for making two prefixes identical. The absence of normal-forms for most non-classical logics also makes it necessary to deal with a nested matrix instead of a clause-form. For

---

* Supported by the Adolf Messer Stiftung

this purpose we had to extend the notions of *actual clauses* and *active paths* which guide the search for a classical matrix-proof in normal-form.

The resulting proof procedure is based on ideas originally developed for a generalized connection based proof method for intuitionistic logic [11]. It consists of a connection driven algorithm which checks the complementarity of all paths through a given formula and uses a component for testing complementarity. The latter depends on the underlying logic and is based on the string-unification procedure developed in [12]. This modular design allows us to treat a rich variety of logics in a uniform and simple way.

Our paper is organized as follows. In section 2 we resume fundamental concepts and provide uniform matrix characterizations of logical validity for classical, intuitionistic and various modal logics. In section 3 we introduce the concepts which are used for guiding the proof search and present our uniform procedure. In section 4 we discuss explicit methods for testing complementarity in various logics, particularly the specialized string-unification algorithm. We conclude with a few remarks on possible extensions.

2 Matrix Characterizations of Logical Validity

After describing some basic notations we shall present a matrix-characterization of validity for classical logic pioneered by Bibel [5] and explain the modifications which are necessary for extending this characterization to intuitionistic and various modal logics. We refer to [16] for detailed explanations.

2.1 Preliminaries

We assume the reader to be familiar with the language of classical and modal first-order logic. To get a uniform notation we firstly define formula trees, polarities, types, and multiplicities.

Definition 1 (Formula Tree, Positions, Labels). A *formula tree* is the representation of a formula as a tree. Each node is marked with a unique name, its *position* (denoted by $a_0, a_1, \ldots$). By Pos we denote the set of all positions in the formula tree. The mapping $\mathrm{lab}(u)$ assigns to each position $u \in Pos$ in the tree its *label*. A position labeled with an atom is called an *atomic position*. The *tree ordering* $< \subseteq Pos \times Pos$ is the (partial) ordering on the positions in the formula tree, i.e. $a_i < a_j$ if (and only if) the position a_i is shown below a_j in the formula tree.

Example 1. Figure 1 shows the formula tree for $F_1 \equiv \forall x P x \Rightarrow P a \wedge P b$. It is, e.g., $\mathrm{lab}(a_0) = {}'\Rightarrow{}'$, $\mathrm{lab}(a_4) = {}'P a{}'$, $a_1 < a_2$ and $a_0 < a_4$.

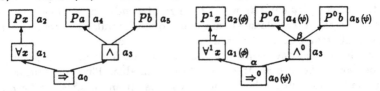

Fig. 1. Formula tree for F_1 (in the right tree nodes are marked with polarity/types)

Remark. Note that each subformula of a given formula corresponds to exactly one position in its formula tree, e.g. $\forall x P x$ corresponds to the position a_1.

Definition 2 (Polarity, Types).
1. The *polarity* of a position is determined by the label and polarity of its (direct) predecessor in the formula tree. The root-position has polarity 0.
2. The *principal type* of a position is determined by its label and polarity. Atomic positions have no principal type.
3. The *intuitionistic type* of a position is determined by its label and polarity. Only certain positions (atoms, $\Rightarrow$, $\neg$, $\forall$) have an intuitionistic type.

Polarities and types of positions are defined in table 1. For example, a position labeled with $\Rightarrow$ and polarity 1 has principal type β and intuitionistic type ϕ. Its successor positions have polarity 0 and 1, respectively.

principal type α	$(A \wedge B)^1$	$(A \vee B)^0$	$(A{\Rightarrow}B)^0$	$(\neg A)^1$	$(\neg A)^0$
sucessor polarity	A^1, B^1	A^0, B^0	A^1, B^0	A^0	A^1
principal type β	$(A \wedge B)^0$	$(A \vee B)^1$	$(A{\Rightarrow}B)^1$		
sucessor polarity	A^0, B^0	A^1, B^1	A^0, B^1		

principal type γ	$(\forall x A)^1$	$(\exists x A)^0$	principal type δ	$(\forall x A)^0$	$(\exists x A)^1$
sucessor polarity	A^1	A^0	sucessor polarity	A^0	A^1
principal type ν	$(\Box A)^1$	$(\Diamond A)^0$	principal type π	$(\Box A)^0$	$(\Diamond A)^1$
sucessor polarity	A^1	A^0	sucessor polarity	A^0	A^1

intuitionistic type ϕ	$(\neg A)^1$	$(A{\Rightarrow}B)^1$	$(\forall x A)^1$	P^1 (P is atomic)
intuitionistic type ψ	$(\neg A)^0$	$(A{\Rightarrow}B)^0$	$(\forall x A)^0$	P^0 (P is atomic)

Table 1. Polarity, principal type and intuitionistic type of positions

Example 2. The formula tree for F_1 where each position is marked with its polarity and principal type is given in figure 1. The positions a_1 and a_2 have intuitionistic type ϕ, positions a_0, a_4 and a_5 have intuitionistic type ψ.

Remark. For a given formula we denote the sets of positions of type α, β, γ, δ, ν, π, ϕ, and ψ by α, β , Γ, Δ, ν, Π, Φ, and Ψ.

A multiplicity encodes the number of distinct instances of subformulae to be considered during the proof search.

Definition 3 (Multiplicities).
1. The *first-order multiplicity* $\mu_Q : \Gamma \to I\!N$,
2. the *intuitionistic multiplicity* $\mu_J : \Phi \to I\!N$, and
3. the *modal multiplicity* $\mu_M : \nu \to I\!N$
assigns each position of type γ, ϕ and ν, respectively, a natural number.

Remark. By F^μ we denote an *indexed formula*, i.e. a formula and its multiplicity. We consider multiple instances of subformulae according to the multiplicity of its corresponding position in the formula tree and extend the notion of tree ordering accordingly. The new nodes in the formula tree get new positions but inherit the polarity and types from their source positions.

Example 3. The formula tree for F_1 with $\mu_Q(a_1)=2$ is shown in figure 2.[2]

Remark. For technical reasons we replace free variables in atomic formulae by their quantifier positions. Thus γ- and δ-positions appear in atomic formulae.

---

[2] Adopting Bibel's notion of multiplicity (instead of Wallen's) we copy the positions of type γ, ϕ or ν instead of their successors.

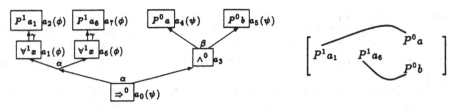

Fig. 2. Formula tree and matrix for F_1^μ and $\mu_Q(a_1)=2$

2.2 Classical Logic

To resume the characterization for classical logic [4, 5] we introduce the concepts of paths and connections. For the first-order (classical) logic it is further necessary to define the notion of a first-order substitution and the reduction ordering.

Definition 4 (Matrix,Path,Connection).
1. In the *matrix(-representation)* of a formula F we place the components of sub-formulae of principal type α side by side whereas components of subformulae of principal type β are placed one upon the other. Furthermore we omit all connectives and quantifiers.
2. A *path* through a formula F is a subset of the atomic positions of its formula tree; it is a horizontal path through the matrix representation of F.
3. A *connection* is a pair of atomic positions labeled with the same predicate symbol but with different polarities.

Example 4. The matrix for $F_1 \equiv \forall x\, Px \Rightarrow Pa \wedge Pb$ is given in figure 2. There are two paths through F_1, namely $\{a_2, a_7, a_4\}$ and $\{a_2, a_7, a_5\}$ ($\{Pa_1, Pa_6, Pa\}$ and $\{Pa_1, Pa_6, Pb\}$ in the notation of labels). The paths contain the connections $\{a_2, a_4\}$, $\{a_7, a_4\}$ and $\{a_2, a_5\}$, $\{a_7, a_5\}$, respectively.

Definition 5 (First-order Substitution, Reduction Ordering).
1. A *first-oder substitution* $\sigma_Q : \Gamma \to T$ assigns to each position of type γ a term $t \in T$ (the set of all terms) where again variables in t are replaced by positions of type γ and δ.[3] A connection $\{u, v\}$ is said to be σ_Q-complementary iff $\sigma_Q(\mathrm{lab}(u)) = \sigma_Q(\mathrm{lab}(v))$. σ_Q induces a relation $\sqsubset_Q \subseteq \Delta \times \Gamma$ in the following way: if $\sigma_Q(u) = t$, then $v \sqsubset_Q u$ for all $v \in \Delta$ occuring in t.
2. A *reduction ordering* $\lhd := (< \cup \sqsubset_Q)^+$ is the transitive closure of the tree ordering $<$ and the relation $\sqsubset_Q$. A first order substitution σ_Q is said to be *admissible* iff the reduction ordering $\lhd$ is irreflexive.

Example 5. $\sigma_Q = \{a_1 \backslash a, a_6 \backslash b\}$ is a first-order substitution for F_1. The induced reduction ordering is the tree ordering and irreflexive. Therefore σ_Q is admissible.

Theorem 6 (Characterization for Classical Logic [5]).
A (first-order) formula F is classically valid, iff there is a multiplicity $\mu := \mu_Q$, an admissible first-order substitution $\sigma := \sigma_Q$ and a set of σ-complementary connections such that every path through F^μ contains a connection from this set.

Example 6. Let μ_Q be the multiplicity of example 3 and $\sigma_Q = \{a_1 \backslash a, a_6 \backslash b\}$ be a first-order substitution. Then $\{\{a_2, a_4\}, \{a_6, a_5\}\}$ is a σ_Q-complementary set of connections and every path through F_1^μ contains a connection from this set. Therefore F_1 is classically valid.

---

[3] We consider substitutions to be *idempotent*, i.e. $\sigma(\sigma) = \sigma$ for a substitution σ.

2.3 Intuitionistic Logic

We shall now explain the extensions which are necessary to make the above characterization of validity applicable to intuitionistic logic. We define J-prefixes, intuitionistic substitutions and J-admissibility.

Definition 7 (J-Prefix). Let $u_1 < u_2 < \ldots < u_n = u$ be the elements of $\Psi \cup \Phi$ that dominate the atomic position u in the formula tree. The *J-prefix* $\text{pre}_J(u)$ of u is defined as $\text{pre}_J(u) := u_1 u_2 \ldots u_n$.

Example 7. For the formula F_1^μ we obtain $\text{pre}_J(a_2) = a_0 A_1 A_2$, $\text{pre}_J(a_7) = a_0 A_6 A_7$, $\text{pre}_J(a_4) = a_0 a_4$ and $\text{pre}_J(a_5) = a_0 a_5$.[4]

Definition 8 (Intuitionistic/Combined Substitution, J-Admissibility).
1. An *intuitionistic substitution* $\sigma_J : \Phi \to (\Phi \cup \Psi)^*$ assigns to each position of type ϕ a string over the alphabet $(\Phi \cup \Psi)$.
   An intuitionistic substitution σ_J induces a relation $\sqsubset_J \subseteq (\Phi \cup \Psi) \times \Phi$ in the following way: if $\sigma_J(u) = p$, then $v \sqsubset_J u$ for all characters v occuring in p.
2. A *combined substitution* $\sigma := (\sigma_Q, \sigma_J)$ consists of a first-order substitution σ_Q and an intuitionistic substitution σ_J. A connection $\{u, v\}$ is σ-*complementary* iff $\sigma_Q(\text{lab}(u)) = \sigma_Q(\text{lab}(v))$ and $\sigma_J(\text{pre}_J(u)) = \sigma_J(\text{pre}_J(v))$. The *reduction ordering* $\lhd := (< \cup \sqsubset_Q \cup \sqsubset_J)^+$ is the transitive closure of $<$, $\sqsubset_Q$ and $\sqsubset_J$.
3. A combined substitution $\sigma = (\sigma_Q, \sigma_J)$ is said to be *J-admissible* iff the reduction ordering $\lhd$ is irreflexive and the following condition holds for all $u \in \Gamma$ and all $v \in \Delta$ occuring in $\sigma_Q(u)$: $\sigma_J(\text{pre}_J(u)) = \sigma_J(\text{pre}_J(v)) q^*$ for some $q^* \in (\Phi \cup \Psi)^*$.

Example 8. For the formula F_1^μ the combined substitution $\sigma = (\sigma_Q, \sigma_J)$ where $\sigma_Q = \{a_1 \backslash a, a_6 \backslash b\}$ and $\sigma_J = \{A_1 \backslash \varepsilon, A_2 \backslash a_4, A_6 \backslash \varepsilon, A_7 \backslash a_5\}$ is J-admissible.[5] Then $\{\{a_2, a_4\}, \{a_6, a_5\}\}$ is a set of σ-complementary connections.

Theorem 9 (Characterization for Intuitionistic Logic [16]).
A formula F is intuitionistically valid, iff there is a multiplicity $\mu := (\mu_Q, \mu_J)$, a J-admissible combined substitution $\sigma = (\sigma_Q, \sigma_J)$, and a set of σ-complementary connections such that every path through F^μ contains a connection from this set.

Example 9. For F_1 let $\mu = (\mu_Q, \mu_J)$ be a multiplicity, where $\mu_Q(a_1) = 2$ and $\mu_J(a_1) = \mu_J(a_2) = 1$, and σ the combined substitution of example 8. Concerning example 8 the formula F_1 is intuitionistically valid.

2.4 Modal Logics

We shall now describe the extensions which are necessary to make the characterization of validity applicable to the modal logics D, D4, S4, S5 and T. We will define M-prefixes, modal substitutions and $\mathcal{L}$-admissibility.

Definition 10 (M-Prefix). Let $u_1 < u_2 < \ldots < u_n < u$ be the elements of $\nu \cup \Pi$ that dominate the atomic position u in the formula tree. The *M-prefix* $\text{pre}_M(u)$ of u is defined as $\text{pre}_M(u) := u_1 u_2 \ldots u_n$ for the modal logics D, D4, S4 and T, and as $\text{pre}_M(u) := u_n$ for S5 ($\text{pre}_M(u) := \varepsilon$, if $n = 0$ for D, D4, S4, S5, and T).

Example 10. Consider $F_2 \equiv \Box \forall x P x \Rightarrow \Box \forall y \Diamond P y$ and its formula tree in figure 3. As M-prefixes we get $\text{pre}_M(a_3) = A_1$ and $\text{pre}_M(a_7) = a_4 A_6$ ($\text{pre}_M(a_7) = A_6$ for S5).

---

[4] Positions of type ϕ (and ν) play the role of variables and are written in capital letters.
[5] By ε we denote the empty string.

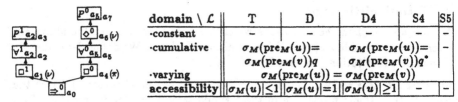

domain \ $\mathcal{L}$	T	D	D4	S4	S5
·constant	–	–	–	–	–
·cumulative	$\sigma_M(\mathrm{pre}_M(u))=$ $\sigma_M(\mathrm{pre}_M(v))q$		$\sigma_M(\mathrm{pre}_M(u))=$ $\sigma_M(\mathrm{pre}_M(v))q^*$		–
·varying	$\sigma_M(\mathrm{pre}_M(u)) = \sigma_M(\mathrm{pre}_M(v))$				
accessibility	$|\sigma_M(u)|\leq 1$	$|\sigma_M(u)|=1$	$|\sigma_M(u)|\geq 1$	–	–

Fig. 3. Formula tree for F_2 **Table 2.** Domain/accessibility conditions for modal logics

Definition 11 (Modal/Combined Substitution, $\mathcal{L}$-Admissibility).

1. A *modal substitution* $\sigma_M : \nu \to (\nu \cup \Pi)^*$ induces a relation $\sqsubseteq_M \subseteq (\nu \cup \Pi) \times \nu$ as follows: if $\sigma_M(u)=p$, then $v\sqsubseteq_M u$ for all characters v occuring in p.
2. A connection $\{u,v\}$ is σ-complementary, where $\sigma:=(\sigma_Q,\sigma_M)$ is a *combined substitution*, iff $\sigma_Q(\mathrm{lab}(u))=\sigma_Q(\mathrm{lab}(v))$ and $\sigma_M(\mathrm{pre}_M(u))=\sigma_M(\mathrm{pre}_M(v))$. The *reduction ordering* $\lhd$ is defined as $\lhd := (< \cup \sqsubseteq_Q \cup \sqsubseteq_M)^+$.
3. Let $\mathcal{L}$ be a modal logic such as D, D4, S4, S5 or T. A combined substitution $\sigma = (\sigma_Q, \sigma_M)$ is said to be $\mathcal{L}$-admissible iff the reduction ordering $\lhd$ is irreflexive, for all $u \in \Gamma$ the *domain condition* (for all $v \in \Gamma \cup \Delta$ occuring in $\sigma_Q(u)$, for some $q \in \nu \cup \Pi \cup \{\varepsilon\}$, $q^* \in (\nu \cup \Pi)^*$) and the *accessibility condition* holds (see table 2).

Example 11. Let $\sigma_i=(\sigma_Q,\sigma_{Mi})$ for $i=1,2,3$ where $\sigma_Q=\{a_2\backslash a_5\}$, $\sigma_{M1}=\{A_1\backslash a_4 A_6\}$, $\sigma_{M2}=\{A_1\backslash a_4, A_6\backslash\varepsilon\}$ and $\sigma_{M3}=\{A_1\backslash a_4, A_6\backslash a_4\}$. The only path through F_2 consists of the connection $\{a_3, a_7\}$. This connection is σ_i-complementary in D, D4, S4, T (for $i=1,2$) and S5 (for $i=3$). σ_1 is D4- and S4-admissible for constant and cumulative domains, σ_2 is S4- and T-admissible for constant, cumulative and varying domains, σ_3 is S5-admissible for constant, cumulative and varying domains.

Theorem 12 (Characterization for Modal Logics [16]).

Let $\mathcal{L}$ be one of the modal logics D, D4, S4, S5 or T. A formula F is valid in the modal logic $\mathcal{L}$, iff there is a multiplicity $\mu := (\mu_Q, \mu_M)$, a $\mathcal{L}$-admissible combined substitution $\sigma = (\sigma_Q, \sigma_M)$, and a set of σ-complementary connections such that every path through F^μ contains a connection from this set.

Example 12. For F_2 let $\mu = (\mu_Q, \mu_M)$, where $\mu_Q(a_2)=\mu_M(a_1)=\mu_M(a_6)=1$, and σ_i (for $i=1,2,3$) the combined substitutions as defined in example 11. The formula F_2 is valid in D4, S4, S5 and T for the constant and cumulative domain and valid in S4, S5 and T for the varying domain.

3   A Uniform Proof Search Procedure

According to the above matrix characterization the validity of a formula F can be proven by showing that all paths through the matrix representation of F contain a complementary connection. In this section we describe a general path checking algorithm which is driven by connections instead of the logical connectives. Once a complementary connection has been identified all paths containing this connection are deleted. This is similar to Bibel's connection method for classical logic [5] but without necessity for transforming the formula into any normal form. The algorithm avoids the notational redundancies occurring in sequent or analytic tableaux based proof procedures. Our technique can also be used for proof search in various non-classical logics where no normal form exists. Based on the matrix characterization we only have to modify the notion of complementarity while leaving the path checking algorithm unchanged.

3.1 Definitions and Notation

Before introducing the algorithm we specify some basic definitions and notations which allow a very short, elegant, and uniform presentation. We define α-/β-related positions, active goals, active paths, proven subgoals and provable subgoals.

Definition 13 (α-related, β-related).
1. Two positions u and v are α-related, denoted $u\sim_\alpha v$, iff $u\neq v$ and the greatest common ancestor of u and v, wrt. the tree ordering $<$, is of principal type α.
2. Two positions u and v are β-related, denoted $u\sim_\beta v$, iff $u\neq v$ and the greatest common ancestor of u and v, wrt. the tree ordering $<$, is of principal type β.

Remark. If two atoms are α-related they appear side by side in the matrix of a formula, whereas they appear one upon the other if they are β-related.

Example 13. Let $F_3 \equiv S \wedge (\neg(T\Rightarrow R)\Rightarrow P)\Rightarrow(\neg((P\Rightarrow Q)\wedge(T\Rightarrow R))\Rightarrow\neg\neg P\wedge S)$ with the matrix of F_3 in figure 4.[6] Then, e.g., $S^1\sim_\alpha T^0$, $R^1\sim_\alpha T^1$, $P^1\sim_\beta T^0$ or $T^1\sim_\beta Q^0$.

$$\left[\begin{array}{cccc} S^1 & \begin{bmatrix} T^0 \\ R^1 \\ P^1 \end{bmatrix} & \begin{bmatrix} [\,\tilde{P}^1 & Q^0\,] \\ [\,T^1 & R^0\,] \end{bmatrix} & \begin{bmatrix} S^0 \\ P^0 \end{bmatrix} \end{array}\right]$$

Fig. 4. Matrix of the formula F_3

Definition 14 (α-/β-related for a Set of Positions).
1. A position u and a set of positions S are α-related $(u\sim_\alpha S)$ if $u\sim_\alpha v$ for all $v\epsilon S$.
2. A position u and a set of positions S are β-related $(u\sim_\beta S)$ if $u\sim_\beta v$ for all $v\epsilon S$.

Example 14. For the F_3 we obtain, e.g., $T^1\sim_\alpha\{R^0,S^1,R^1\}$ and $T^0\sim_\beta\{R^1,P^1\}$.

The following definitions and lemmas always hold for a given (possibly indexed) formula F. By $\mathcal{A}$ we denote the set of all atomic positions in the formula F.

Definition 15 (Subpath, Subgoal).
1. A *subpath* $\mathcal{P}\subseteq\mathcal{A}$ is a set of atomic positions with $u\sim_\alpha(\mathcal{P}\backslash\{u\})$ for all $u\epsilon\mathcal{P}$.
2. A *subgoal* $C\subseteq\mathcal{A}$ is a set of atomic positions with $u\sim_\beta(C\backslash\{u\})$ for all $u\epsilon C$.

Remark. A subpath is a, possible uncompleted, "horizontal path" through a matrix; a subgoal is a, possible uncompleted, "vertical path" through a matrix.

Example 15. For F_3, e.g., $\mathcal{P}_1=\{S^1,T^1,P^0\}$, $\mathcal{P}_2=\{S^1,R^1,S^0\}$ and $\mathcal{P}_3=\{T^0,T^1,R^0\}$ are subpaths, $C_1=\{T^0\}$, $C_2=\{Q^0,T^1\}$ and $C_3=\{S^1\}$ are subgoals.

For a valid formula F every path through F has to contain a complementary connection (i.e. every path has to be complementary). The proof procedure described afterwards are based on the notion of "active path" and "proven subgoal".

Definition 16 (Active Goal, Active Path, Proven Subgoal).
An *active goal* is a tuple $(\mathcal{P},C)$ consisting of a subpath $\mathcal{P}$ and a subgoal C with $u\sim_\alpha\mathcal{P}$ for all $u\epsilon C$. We call $\mathcal{P}$ an *active path* and C a *proven subgoal*.

---

[6] In the following we use the labels instead of the (atomic) positions themselves. To distinguish the two atoms P^1 one atom is marked with a tilde ($\tilde{\ }$).

During proof search the active path will specify those paths which are just being investigated for complementarity. All paths which contain the active path $\mathcal{P}$ and additionally one element u of the proven subgoal will already have been proven complementary, since it has been shown that they contain a complementary connection (which may have occured within an extension of $\mathcal{P} \cup \{u\}$).

Example 16. For the formula F_3, e.g., $(\mathcal{P}_1, C_1)$, $(\mathcal{P}_2, C_2)$ and $(\mathcal{P}_3, C_3)$ are active goals. $\mathcal{P}_1$, $\mathcal{P}_2$ and $\mathcal{P}_3$ are active paths, C_1, C_2 and C_3 are proven subgoals.

Definition 17 (Open Subgoal). An *open subgoal* $C' \subseteq \mathcal{A}$ with respect to an active goal $(\mathcal{P}, C)$ is a set of atomic positions, such that $u \sim_\alpha \mathcal{P}$ and $u \sim_\beta C$ for all $u \in C'$ and there is no $v \in \mathcal{A}$ with $v \notin C'$, $v \sim_\alpha \mathcal{P}$ and $v \sim_\beta C$.

An open subgoal together with the active path specifies paths which include the active path but still have to be tested for complementarity. If all paths including the active path and one element of the open subgoal are proved successfully for complementarity then all paths containing the active path are complementary. Note that there may be more than one open subgoal for a given active goal.

Example 17. For F_3 the set $\{R^1, P^1\}$ is an open subgoal wrt. the active goal $(\mathcal{P}_1, C_1)$ (example 16); the empty set $\emptyset$ is the only subgoal wrt. $(\mathcal{P}_2, C_2)$ or $(\mathcal{P}_3, C_3)$.

Lemma 18 (Paths). *A subpath $\mathcal{P} \subseteq \mathcal{A}$ is a path iff there is no $u \in \mathcal{A}$ with $u \sim_\alpha \mathcal{P}$.*

Proof of the lemma. A path is a "complete horizontal path" through a matrix. □

Definition 19 (Provable Goal). An active goal $(\mathcal{P}, C)$ is called *provable* with respect to a formula F, iff there is an open subgoal C' wrt. $(\mathcal{P}, C)$, such that for all $u \in C'$ all paths $\mathcal{P}'$ through F with $\mathcal{P} \cup \{u\} \subseteq \mathcal{P}'$ are complementary.

Lemma 20 (Empty Open Subgoal). *Let $(\mathcal{P}, C)$ an active goal such that there is no $u \in \mathcal{A}$ with $u \sim_\alpha \mathcal{P}$ and $u \sim_\beta C$. Then $(\mathcal{P}, C)$ is provable.*

Proof of the lemma. If there is no $u \in \mathcal{A}$ so that $u \sim_\alpha \mathcal{P}$ and $u \sim_\beta C$, then $C' = \emptyset$ is the only open subgoal wrt. $(\mathcal{P}, C)$ (definition 17). Since the open subgoal C' wrt. $(\mathcal{P}, C)$ is empty, the active goal $(\mathcal{P}, C)$ is provable (definition 19). □

Proposition 21 (Provable Goal). *Let $(\mathcal{P}, C)$ be an active goal and there is an open subgoal C' wrt. $(\mathcal{P}, C)$ with $C' \neq \emptyset$. $(\mathcal{P}, C)$ is provable, iff there is a complementary connection $\{A, \bar{A}\}$ with $A \sim_\alpha \mathcal{P}$ and $A \sim_\beta C$, such that*
1. $\bar{A} \in \mathcal{P}$ or
2. $\bar{A} \sim_\alpha (\mathcal{P} \cup \{A\})$ and the active goal $(\mathcal{P} \cup \{A\}, \{\bar{A}\})$ is provable
and the active goal $(\mathcal{P}, C \cup \{A\})$ is provable.

Lemma 22 (Provability of $(\emptyset, \emptyset)$). *Let F be a formula. The active goal $(\emptyset, \emptyset)$ wrt. F is provable, iff every path through F is complementary.*

Proof of the lemma. $(\emptyset, \emptyset)$ is provable iff there is an open subgoal $C' \neq \emptyset$ such that every path $\mathcal{P}'$ with $\{u\} \subseteq \mathcal{P}'$ and $u \in C'$ is complementary. Since every path through F contains an $u \in C'$ (lemma 18, definition 17) they are all complementary. □

Theorem 23 (Validity of a Formula).
A formula F is valid in classical logic (intuitionistic logic/modal logic $\mathcal{L}$) iff there is a multiplicity μ and an admissible ($\mathcal{J}$-admissible/$\mathcal{L}$-admissible combined) substitution σ such that the active goal $(\emptyset, \emptyset)$ wrt. F^μ is provable.

Proof of the theorem. Follows from lemma 22 and the characterizations of validity for classical, intuitionistic, and modal logics (theorems 6,9, and 12). □

3.2 The Algorithm

We now represent the proof procedure for classical $(\mathcal{C})$, intuitionistic $(\mathcal{J})$ and the modal logics D, D4, S4, S5 and T. It consists of the uniform path-checking algorithm and a complementarity test which will be described in the next section.

Let F be a (first-order) formula, μ a multiplicity, σ a substitution, and F^μ an indexed formula. Furthermore let $\mathcal{A}^\mu$ be the set of atomic positions in the formula tree for F^μ and $\sim_\alpha$ and $\sim_\beta$ the relations α- and β-related.

The main function $\text{PROOF}_{\mathcal{L}}(F)$ in figure 5 gets an additional parameter $\mathcal{L}$ where $\mathcal{L} \in \{\mathcal{C}, \mathcal{J}, D, D4, S4, S5, T\}$ specifies the logic $\mathcal{L}$ under consideration. It returns *true* iff the formula F is valid in the corresponding logic.

```
Function PROOF_L(F)
    Input:     first-order formula F
    Output:    true, if, and only if, F is valid in the L-logic

    begin PROOF_L;
        m := 0;
        repeat
            m := m+1;  INITIALIZE_L^(m)(μ,σ);
            valid := SUBPROOF_L(F^μ,∅,∅);
        until valid=true;
        return true;
    end PROOF_L.
```

Fig. 5. Function $\text{PROOF}_{\mathcal{L}}(F)$

The function $\text{PROOF}_{\mathcal{L}}(F)$ first initializes the multiplicity μ and the (combined) substitution σ according to table 3. After that the function $\text{SUBPROOF}_{\mathcal{L}}$ is invoked on the initial subgoal $(\emptyset,\emptyset)$. If it returns *false* the multiplicity is increased stepwisely, until the function Subproof returns *true*.[7]

$\mathcal{L}$	$\mathcal{C}$	$\mathcal{J}$	D, D4, S4, S5, T
multiplicity μ	$\mu(u):=m, \ \forall u \in \Gamma$	$\mu(u):=m, \ \forall u \in \Gamma \cup \Phi$	$\mu(u):=m, \ \forall u \in \Gamma \cup \nu$
substitution σ	$\sigma:=\emptyset$	$\sigma:=(\emptyset,\emptyset)$	$\sigma:=(\emptyset,\emptyset)$

Table 3. $\text{INITIALIZE}_{\mathcal{L}}^{(m)}(\mu,\sigma)$

The function $\text{SUBPROOF}_{\mathcal{L}}(F^\mu,\mathcal{P},C)$ in figure 6 implements the test wether the active goal $(\mathcal{P},C)$ is provable with respect to F^μ. Note that all variables except for the set of atomic positions $\mathcal{A}^\mu$ and the (combined) substitution σ are local.

Within $\text{SUBPROOF}_{\mathcal{L}}$ a function $\text{COMPLEMENTARY}_{\mathcal{L}}(F^\mu,A,\bar{A},\sigma',\sigma)$ is used, which returns true iff the connection $\{A,\bar{A}\}$ in the (indexed) formula F^μ is complementary under a (combined) substitution σ in the logic $\mathcal{L}$ taking into account the substitution σ' computed so far. In this case the substitution σ is returned. $\text{COMPLEMENTARY}_{\mathcal{L}}$ depends on the peculiarities of each logic (see section 4).

Lemma 24 (Correctness and Completeness of $\text{SUBPROOF}_{\mathcal{L}}$).
The function $\text{SUBPROOF}_{\mathcal{L}}(F^\mu,\mathcal{P},C)$ returns true *if the active goal $(\mathcal{P},C)$ is provable with respect to F^μ; otherwise it returns* false.

Proof of the lemma. The function $\text{SUBPROOF}_{\mathcal{L}}$ uses the statements for a provable goal made in lemma 20 and proposition 21. □

---

[7] This technique of stepwise increasing the multiplicity is obviously not very efficient. In an efficient implementation the multiplicity for each suitable position is determined individually *during* the path-checking process (as in the usual connection method).

```
Function SUBPROOF_L(F^μ, P, C)
    Input:      indexed formula F^μ, active path P⊆A^μ, proven subgoals C⊆A^μ
    Output:     true, if (P, C) wrt. F^μ is provable; false, otherwise

begin SUBPROOF_L;
    if there is no A∈A^μ where A~_αP and A~_βC then return true;
    E := ∅;  σ' := σ;
    repeat
        select A∈A^μ where A~_α(P∪E) and A~_βC;
        if there is no such A then return false;
        E := E∪{A};  D := ∅;  valid := false;  noconnect := false;
        repeat
            select Ã∈A^μ where Ã∉D and |COMPLEMENTARY_L(F^μ, A, Ã, σ', σ)|
            and (1.) Ã∈P or (2.) Ã~_α(P∪{A});
            if there is no such Ã
                then noconnect := true
                else D := D∪{Ã}
                    if Ã∈P then valid := true
                        else valid := SUBPROOF_L(F^μ, P∪{A}, {Ã});
                    if valid=true then valid := SUBPROOF_L(F^μ, P, C∪{A});
        until valid=true or noconnect=true;
    until valid=true;
    return true;
end SUBPROOF_L.
```

Fig. 6. Function SUBPROOF_L($F^μ, P, C$)

Theorem 25 (Correctness and Completeness of PROOF_L).
The function PROOF_L(F) *returns* true, *iff the formula* F *is* L-*valid*.

Proof of the theorem. PROOF_L uses the relation between the validity of F wrt. logic L and the provability of the active goal $(∅, ∅)$ wrt. $F^μ$ (theorem 23) and searches for a suitable multiplicity $μ$. The theorem thus follows from lemma 24. □

Remark. Our algorithm is *not a decision procedure*, i.e. for an invalid formula it will not terminate. Note that the propositional part of each logic under consideration is decidable whereas in the first-order case there are no decision procedures.

4   Complementarity in Classical and Non-Classical Logics

Matrix characterizations of validity are based on the existence of admissible (combined) substitutions that render a set of simultaneously complementary connections such that every path contains a connection from this set. In our path-checking algorithm we have to ensure that after adding a connection to the current set there still is an admissible substitution under which *all* connections are complementary. For this purpose we invoke COMPLEMENTARY_L which implements a complementarity test for two atoms and depends on the particular logic. Whereas in the classical logic term-unification and a test for irreflexivity of the reduction ordering suffices to compute an admissible substitution, we need an additional string-unification algorithm to unify prefixes in the case of intuitionistic and modal logic.

After explaining the complementarity test for classical logic we extend it to intuitionistic logic and present details of the string-unification algorithm. We then deal with D, D4, S4, S5 and T which can be treated in a uniform way.

4.1 Classical Logic $\mathcal{C}$

In $\mathcal{C}$ two atoms are complementary if they can be unified under a term-substitution and the induced reduction ordering is irreflexive. For the former well-known unification algorithms [14, 9] compute a most general unifier which leads to the first-order substitution. For the latter efficient algorithms testing the acyclicity of a directed graph can be used. COMPLEMENTARY$_\mathcal{C}$ succeeds and returns σ_Q iff the two conditions in table 4 hold (term_unify(s,t) expresses term unification of s and t and results together with σ_Q' in the substitution σ_Q).

	$\mathcal{C}$
term unification	term_unify($\sigma_Q'(\text{lab}(A)), \sigma_Q'(\text{lab}(\bar{A}))) \rightsquigarrow \sigma_Q$
reduction ordering	$\lhd := (< \sqcup \sqsubseteq_Q)^+$ is irreflexive

Table 4. Function COMPLEMENTARY$_\mathcal{C}(F^\mu, A, \bar{A}, \sigma_Q', \sigma_Q)$

4.2 Intuitionistic Logic $\mathcal{J}$

For intuitionistic logic the complementarity test additionally requires that the prefixes of two connected atoms can be unified. For this purpose we use a specialized string unification (T-String-Unification) T_string_unify$_\mathcal{J}(p, q)$, described below, which succeeds if the prefixes p and q can be unified and leads altogether the substitution $\sigma_\mathcal{J}$. To guarantee admissibility the extended reduction ordering has to be irreflexive and an 'additional condition' has to be fulfilled. If all the properties of table 5 hold the function COMPLEMENTARY$_\mathcal{J}$ succeeds and returns $(\sigma_Q, \sigma_\mathcal{J})$.

	$\mathcal{J}$
term unification	term_unify($\sigma_Q'(\text{lab}(A)), \sigma_Q'(\text{lab}(\bar{A}))) \rightsquigarrow \sigma_Q$
string unification	T_string_unify$_\mathcal{J}(\sigma_\mathcal{J}'(\text{pre}_\mathcal{J}(A)), \sigma_\mathcal{J}'(\text{pre}_\mathcal{J}(\bar{A}))) \rightsquigarrow \sigma_\mathcal{J}$
additional condition*	$|\sigma_\mathcal{J}(\text{pre}_\mathcal{J}(v))| \le |\sigma_\mathcal{J}(\text{pre}_\mathcal{J}(u))|$
reduction ordering	$\lhd := (< \sqcup \sqsubseteq_Q \sqcup \sqsubseteq_\mathcal{J})^+$ is irreflexive ($\sqsubseteq_\mathcal{J}$ induced by $\sigma_\epsilon^{(\mathcal{J})} \circ \sigma_\mathcal{J}$)

$\sigma_\epsilon^{(\mathcal{J})}(w) := \epsilon$ for all $w \in \mathcal{F}$, $\circ$ is the composition of substitutions;
* must hold for all $u \in \Gamma$ and all $v \in \Delta$ occuring in $\sigma_Q(u)$.

Table 5. Function COMPLEMENTARY$_\mathcal{J}(F^\mu, A, \bar{A}, (\sigma_Q', \sigma_\mathcal{J}'), (\sigma_Q, \sigma_\mathcal{J}))$

T-String-Unification To unify the prefixes of two connected atoms we use a specialized string unification which respects the restrictions on the prefix strings p and q: no character is repeated either in p nor in q and equal characters only occur within a common substring at the beginning of p and q. This restriction allows us to give an efficient algorithm computing a minimal set of most general unifiers. Similar to the ideas of Martelli and Montanari [9] rather than by giving a recursive procedure we consider the process of unification as a sequence of transformations of an equation.

We start with a given equation $\Gamma = \{p{=}q\}$ and an empty substitution $\sigma = \emptyset$ and stop with an empty set $\Gamma = \emptyset$ and a substitution σ representing an idempotent most general unifier. Each transformation step replaces a tuple Γ, σ by a modified tuple Γ', σ'. The algorithm is described by transformation rules which can be applied nondeterministically. The set of most general unifiers consists of the results of all successfully finished transformations. For technical reasons we divide the right part q of the equation into two parts $q_1|q_2$, i.e. we start with $\{p = q_1|q_2\}, \{\}$.

Definition 26 (Transformation Rules for $\mathcal{J}$).
Let $\mathcal{V}$ be a set of variables, $\mathcal{C}$ a set of constants, and $\mathcal{V}'$ a set of *auxiliary variables* with $\mathcal{V} \cap \mathcal{V}' = \emptyset$. The set of *transformation rules* for $\mathcal{J}$ is defined in table 6.

R1.	$\{\epsilon = \epsilon|\epsilon\}, \sigma \quad\rightarrow\quad \{\}, \sigma$
R2.	$\{\epsilon = \epsilon|t^+\}, \sigma \quad\rightarrow\quad \{t^+ = \epsilon|\epsilon\}, \sigma$
R3.	$\{Xs = \epsilon|Xt\}, \sigma \quad\rightarrow\quad \{s = \epsilon|t\}, \sigma$
R4.	$\{Cs = \epsilon|Vt\}, \sigma \quad\rightarrow\quad \{Vt = \epsilon|Cs\}, \sigma$
R5.	$\{Vs = z|\epsilon\}, \sigma \quad\rightarrow\quad \{s = \epsilon|\epsilon\}, \{V\backslash z\}\cup\sigma$
R6.	$\{Vs = \epsilon|C_1t\}, \sigma \quad\rightarrow\quad \{s = \epsilon|C_1t\}, \{V\backslash\epsilon\}\cup\sigma$
R7.	$\{Vs = z|C_1C_2t\}, \sigma \quad\rightarrow\quad \{s = \epsilon|C_2t\}, \{V\backslash zC_1\}\cup\sigma$
R8.	$\{Vs^+ = \epsilon|V_1t\}, \sigma \quad\rightarrow\quad \{V_1t = V|s^+\}, \sigma$
R9.	$\{Vs^+ = z^+|V_1t\}, \sigma \quad\rightarrow\quad \{V_1t = V'|s^+\}, \{V\backslash z^+V'\}\cup\sigma$
R10.	$\{Vs = z|Xt\}, \sigma \quad\rightarrow\quad \{Vs = zX|t\}, \sigma \quad (V\neq X, \text{ and } s=\epsilon \text{ or } t\neq\epsilon \text{ or } X\in C)$

s, t and z denote (arbitrary) strings and s^+, t^+, z^+ a non-empty string. X, V, V_1, C, C_1 and C_2 denote single characters with $X \in \mathcal{V}\cup C\cup\mathcal{V}'$, $V, V_1 \in \mathcal{V}\cup\mathcal{V}'$ (with $V\neq V_1$), and $C, C_1, C_2 \in C$. $V' \in \mathcal{V}'$ is a new variable which does not occur in the substitution σ computed so far.

Table 6. Transformation Rules for Intuitionistic Logic (and Modal Logic S4)

By modifying the set of transformation rules we are also able to treat the modal logics D, D4, S5 and T (see [12] for details). Our algorithm is much simpler and considerably more efficient than other string unification algorithms developed so far. Ohlbach's algorithm [10], e.g., does not compute a minimal set of unifiers. In general the number of most general unifiers is finite but may grow exponentially with respect to the length of the unified strings.

4.3 Modal Logics

The modal logics also require T-string-unification. We have developed such procedures in [12] by considering the accessibility condition for each particular logic $\mathcal{L}$.[8] T_string_unify$_\mathcal{L}(p, q)$ computes the most general unifier for p and q with respect to the accessibility condition for $\mathcal{L}$. This leads to the substitution σ_M. For the cumulative and varying domain variants also the domain condition has to be taken into account. In table 7 we have summarized all conditions that have to be tested. COMPLEMENTARY$_\mathcal{L}$ succeeds, if all conditions in the row for $\mathcal{L}$ hold.

$\mathcal{L}$	D	D4	S4	S5	T
term unification	term_unify(σ_Q'(lab(A)), σ_Q'(lab($\bar{A}$))) $\rightsquigarrow \sigma_Q$				
string unification	T_string_unify$_\mathcal{L}$(σ_M'(pre$_M$(A)), σ_M'(pre$_M$($\bar{A}$))) $\rightsquigarrow \sigma_M$				
domain condition					
· constant	–	×[9]	–	–	–
· cumulative*	$|V|\leq|U|\leq|V|+1$	$|V|\leq|U|$	$|V|\leq|U|$	–	$|V|\leq|U|\leq|V|+1$
· varying*	$|U'|=|V'|$	$|U|=|V|$	$|U'|=|V'|$	uni$_{S5} \rightsquigarrow \sigma_M$	$|U'|=|V'|$
reduction ordering	$\lhd := (< \cup\sqsubseteq_Q\sqsubseteq_M)^+$ is irreflexive ($\sqsubseteq_M$ induced by σ_M')				

$U := \sigma_M(\text{pre}_M(u))$, $V := \sigma_M(\text{pre}_M(v))$, $U' := \sigma_\epsilon^{(M)} \circ \sigma_M(\text{pre}_M(u))$, $V' := \sigma_\epsilon^{(M)} \circ \sigma_M(\text{pre}_M(v))$, $\sigma_\epsilon^{(M)}(w) := \epsilon$ for all $w \in \mathcal{V}$; * must hold for all $v \in \Pi$ ($v \in \mathcal{V}\cup\Pi$ for varying domains) occuring in $\sigma_Q(u)$; uni$_{S5} \cong$ T_string_unify$_{S5}$($\sigma_M(\text{pre}_M(u)), \sigma_M(\text{pre}_M(v))$); $\sigma_M^* := \sigma_\epsilon^{(M)}\circ\sigma_M$ for D,S4,S5,T / σ_M for D4.

Table 7. Function COMPLEMENTARY$_\mathcal{L}(F^\mu, A, \bar{A}, (\sigma_Q', \sigma_M'), (\sigma_Q, \sigma_M))$

---

[8] For S4 the algorithm for intuitionistic logic (T_string_unify$_J$) suffices.

[9] We do *not* deal with the constant domain of D4 since there is need for additional search when computing the modal substitution σ_M.

5 Conclusion

We have presented a uniform proof procedure for classical and some non-classical logics which is based on a unified representation of matrix characterizations of logical validity for these logics. It consists of a connection-driven general path-checking algorithm for arbitrary formulae and a component for checking the complementarity of two atomic formulae according to the peculiarities of a particular logic. By presenting appropriate components for classical logic, intuitionistic logic, and the modal logics D, D4, S4, S5, and T we have demonstrated that our procedure is suited to deal with a rich variety of logics in a simple and efficient way.

The algorithm has been implemented in Prolog in order to allow practical experiments. In the future we intend to elaborate optimizations like a decision procedure for the propositional case, efficiency improvements like a dynamic increase of the multiplicities instead of a global one, and to provide a C-implementatuion to allow realistic comparisons. Furthermore we intend to investigate extensions of our procedure to additional logics such as (fragments of) linear logic and other non-classical logics for which a matrix characterization can be developed.

References

1. B. BECKERT AND J. POSEGGA. lean$T^{A}P$: lean, tableau-based theorem proving. *Proc. CADE-12*, LNAI 814, 1994.
2. E. W. BETH. *The foundations of mathematics*. North–Holland, 1959.
3. W. BIBEL, S. BRÜNING, U. EGLY, T. RATH. Komet. *Proc. CADE-12*, LNAI 814, pp. 783–787. 1994.
4. W. BIBEL. On matrices with connections. *Jour. of the ACM*, 28, p. 633–645, 1981.
5. W. BIBEL. *Automated Theorem Proving*. Vieweg, 1987.
6. M. C. FITTING. *Intuitionistic logic, model theory and forcing*. North–Holland, 1969.
7. G. GENTZEN. Untersuchungen über das logische Schließen. *Mathematische Zeitschrift*, 39:176–210, 405–431, 1935.
8. R. LETZ, J. SCHUMANN, S. BAYERL, W. BIBEL. SETHEO: A high-performance theorem prover. *Journal of Automated Reasoning*, 8:183–212, 1992.
9. A. MARTELLI AND UGO MONTANARI. An efficient unification algorithm. *ACM TOPLAS*, 4:258–282, 1982.
10. H. J. OHLBACH. A resolution calculus for modal logics. Ph.D. Thesis, Universität Kaiserslautern, 1988.
11. J. OTTEN, C. KREITZ. A connection based proof method for intuitionistic logic. *Proc. 4th TABLEAUX Workshop*, LNAI 918, pp. 122–137, 1995.
12. J. OTTEN, C. KREITZ. T-String-Unification: Unifying Prefixes in Non-Classical Proof Methods. *Proc. 5th TABLEAUX Workshop*, LNAI 1071, pp. 244–260, 1996.
13. J. OTTEN. Ein konnektionenorientiertes Beweisverfahren für intuitionistische Logik. Master's thesis, TH Darmstadt, 1995.
14. J. A. ROBINSON. A machine-oriented logic based on the resolution principle. *Jour. of the ACM*, 12(1):23–41, 1965.
15. L. WALLEN. Matrix proof methods for modal logics. *IJCAI-87*, p. 917–923. 1987.
16. L. WALLEN. *Automated deduction in nonclassical logic*. MIT Press, 1990.
17. L. WOS ET. AL. Automated reasoning contributes to mathematics and logic. *Proc. CADE-10*, LNCS 449, pp. 485–499, 1990.

Qualitative Reasoning under Uncertainty with Symbolic Probabilities

Daniel Pacholczyk[1] and Gilles Hunault[2]

[1] pacho@univ-angers.fr, LERIA - Faculté des Sciences, Université d'Angers
[2] gilles.hunault@univ-angers.fr, LERIA - Faculté des Sciences, Université d'Angers,
2 Boulevard Lavoisier, 49045 ANGERS CEDEX

1. Introduction

We present here the results obtained by using a *Symbolic Probability Theory* as a model of qualitative reasoning under uncertain information. The semantic model is based upon a many-valued predicate logic initially defined to deal with imprecise statements ([4]). We use two scales of degrees to manage both vagueness and uncertainty. The used many-valued predicate logic has been enriched with a particuliar predicate that takes into account the satisfaction of the concept of Certainty. Our symbolic operators and the theorems presented in § 2 are the counterparts of the classical operations and theorems of numerical probability theory. An example written in Natural Language is treated in § 3. We show in § 4 that it is possible to modify the size of the graduation scales in a way such that the results remain coherent.

2. The Model

For the chosen predicate logics [4] the connectors are $\cap, \cup, \supset$ and $\neg$. One interpretation $\mathcal{A}$ of this logics is done in a totally ordered set $\mathcal{U}_M$ of *Truth degrees* noted u_α such as {*false, very-little-true, ..., true*}. In $\mathcal{U}_M$, we have defined the operators $\wedge$("*and*"), $\vee$("*or*"), $\rightarrow$ ("*implies*"), $\sim$ ("*not*", a decreasing involution) as follows: $u_\alpha \wedge u_\beta = u_{min(\alpha,\beta)}$, $u_\alpha \vee u_\beta = u_{max(\alpha,\beta)}$, $u_\alpha \rightarrow u_\beta = u_M \, if \, \alpha \leq \beta \, else \, u_{M-\alpha+\beta}$ (known as Lukasiewicz's implication), $\sim u_\alpha = u_{M+1-\alpha}$. Finally, for any formula A, $A\models_\alpha A$ means that A is u_α-*true* (in $\mathcal{A}$) where $u_\alpha \in \mathcal{U}_M$. All the formal definitions, axioms, demonstrations and results can be found in [5].

Let $\mathcal{C}$ denote the set of formulas A such that for any interpretation $\mathcal{A}$ and for any valuation x of the variables, $A(x)$ is either *true* or *false* but we can not resolve the alternative *true/false*. We then use a totally ordered graduation scale $\mathcal{L}_M$ of M symbolic values noted v_α called *Certainty degrees*. For example, with $M = 7$, a linguistic translation of these degrees is v_1=impossible, v_2=very-little-probable, ..., v_7=certain. To manage this uncertainty, we define a function of $\mathcal{C}$ into $\mathcal{L}_M$, denoted by Prob. So, the statement "A is v_α-probable" is then translated into Prob(A) = v_α. Next, we introduce a symbolic additive operator $\mathcal{S}$ in $\mathcal{L}_M$ analogous to the "probabilistic addition". $\mathcal{S}$ must have the following properties: absorbing element, commutativity, associativity, increasing property. We have choosen for $\mathcal{S}$ the T-conorm $\mathcal{S}(v_\alpha, v_\beta) = v_M$ if $\alpha + \beta \geq M + 1$ else $v_{\alpha+\beta-1}$.

Moreover, we use an operator n in $\mathcal{L}_M$ defining the symbolic Complement as follows: $n(v_\alpha) = v_{M+1-\alpha}$ and we postulate that $Prob(\neg A) = n(Prob(A))$. We shall impose an adequation of this predicate to reality. Actually, if a statement is *true* (resp. *false*), the certainty degree associated to it is certain (resp. impossible). We also postulate that the Certainty of two equivalent statements degrees are equal. Finally, if the intersection of two elements is empty, the certainty of their union is the symbolic "sum" of their uncertainties. Postulates of Prob:

(1) If A and B are *semantically equivalent* then $Prob(A) = Prob(B)$
(2,3) If A is *true* (resp.*false*) then $Prob(A) = v_M =$ certain (resp.$v_1 =$ impossible).
(4) $Prob(\neg A) = n(Prob(A))$
(5) If $A \cap B$ is *false* then $Prob(A \cup B) = \mathcal{S}(Prob(A),Prob(B))$.

This Certainty predicate finds its real meaning only if it can be itself linked to this basis. It leads to a division operator, noted here C (Conditioning Criterion), or, in an equivalent way, to an multiplication operator noted here I (Independence Criterion) to which we impose some properties similar to those of the probabilistic multiplication: commutativity, absorbing element neutral element, increasing property, associativity, idempotent element. The conditioning criterion C is then defined by $C(v_\alpha,v_\lambda)=\{v_\beta|I(v_\alpha,v_\beta)=v_\lambda\}$ or equivalently by $v_\beta \in C(v_\alpha,v_\lambda) \Leftrightarrow v_\lambda=I(v_\alpha,v_\beta)$. Given I, there is a unique C that corresponds to I. For $M=7$, a possible choice for I and its corresponding C can be:

I	v_1	v_2	v_3	v_4	v_5	v_6	v_7
v_1	v_1	v_1	v_1	v_1	v_1	v_1	v_1
v_2	v_1	v_2	v_2	v_2	v_2	v_2	v_2
v_3	v_1	v_2	v_2	v_2	v_2	v_2	v_3
v_4	v_1	v_2	v_2	v_2	v_2	v_3	v_4
v_5	v_1	v_2	v_2	v_2	v_3	v_4	v_5
v_6	v_1	v_2	v_2	v_3	v_4	v_5	v_6
v_7	v_1	v_2	v_3	v_4	v_5	v_6	v_7

C	v_1	v_2	v_3	v_4	v_5	v_6	v_7
v_1	$[v_1,v_7]$	$\emptyset$	$\emptyset$	$\emptyset$	$\emptyset$	$\emptyset$	$\emptyset$
v_2	$\{v_1\}$	$[v_2,v_7]$	$\emptyset$	$\emptyset$	$\emptyset$	$\emptyset$	$\emptyset$
v_3	$\{v_1\}$	$[v_2,v_6]$	$\{v_7\}$	$\emptyset$	$\emptyset$	$\emptyset$	$\emptyset$
v_4	$\{v_1\}$	$[v_2,v_5]$	$\{v_6\}$	$\{v_7\}$	$\emptyset$	$\emptyset$	$\emptyset$
v_5	$\{v_1\}$	$[v_2,v_4]$	$\{v_5\}$	$\{v_6\}$	$\{v_7\}$	$\emptyset$	$\emptyset$
v_6	$\{v_1\}$	$[v_2,v_3]$	$\{v_4\}$	$\{v_5\}$	$\{v_6\}$	$\{v_7\}$	$\emptyset$
v_7	$\{v_1\}$	$\{v_2\}$	$\{v_3\}$	$\{v_4\}$	$\{v_5\}$	$\{v_6\}$	$\{v_7\}$

We then set, as in way classical probability: *the Conditional Certainty of B given A denoted* $Prob(B|A)$ *is such that* $Prob(B|A) \in C(Prob(A),Prob(A\cap B))$. We have proved the following theorems.

- *Theorem 2.6.1: Generalised Modus Ponens Rule*
    If $Prob(A)=v_\alpha$ and $Prob(A \supset B)= v_\delta$, then $Prob(B) \in [T(v_\alpha,v_\delta),v_\delta]$ where T is the T-norm associated with the previous T-conorm $\mathcal{S}$.
- *Theorem 2.6.2:*
    Put $Prob(A)=v_\alpha$ and $Prob(B)=v_\beta$. Then $Prob(A\cap B)=v_\gamma \in [T(v_\alpha,v_\beta), v_\alpha \wedge v_\beta]$ and $Prob(A\cup B)=v_\delta \in [v_\alpha \vee v_\beta, \mathcal{S}(v_\alpha,v_\beta)]$. Moreover, if $A \supset B$ is *true* then $v_\alpha \leq v_\beta$.
- *Theorem 2.6.3: C-conditional Detachment Rule*
    Put $Prob(A)=v_\alpha$ and $Prob(B|A)=v_\mu$. Then $Prob(B) \in [v_\lambda, v_\alpha \rightarrow v_\lambda]$ for $v_\lambda=I(v_\alpha,v_\mu)$.
- *Theorem 2.6.4: Compound Certainties Formula*
    If $Prob(A)= v_\alpha$ and $Prob(B|A)=v_\mu$ then $Prob(A\cap B)=I(v_\alpha,v_\mu)$.
- *Theorem 2.6.5: Uncertainty Propagation Rule*
    Let $Prob(A)=v_\alpha$, $Prob(B|A)=v_{\mu_1}$ and $Prob(C|B)=v_{\mu_2}$.

Then Prob(C) $\in[I(I(v_\alpha,v_{\mu_1}), v_{\mu_2}), I(v_\alpha,v_{\mu_1}) \to I(v_\alpha \to I(v_\alpha,v_{\mu_1}),v_{\mu_2})]$.

- *Theorem 2.6.6: Total Certainty Formula*

   Let $A_1,...,A_n$ be such that (i) Prob($\cup A_i$)=v_M, (ii) for all i and j of $\{1,...,n\}$ with $i \neq j$, Prob($A_i \cap A_j$)=v_1, (iii) for every i of $\{1,...,n\}$, Prob(A_i)=v_{α_i} and Prob($B|A_i$)=v_{μ_i}. Then, setting v_{γ_1}=$I(v_{\alpha_1},v_{\mu_1})$ and for all k=2,...,n, v_{γ_k}=$S(v_{\gamma_{k-1}},I(v_{\alpha_k},v_{\mu_k}))$, we get: Prob(B) = v_{γ_n}.

- *Theorem 2.6.7: Symbolic Generalised Bayes' Formula*

   With the same partition of A_i as above, Prob($A_i|B$)$\in$ $C(v_{\gamma_n},I(v_{\alpha_i},v_{\mu_i}))$.

   Remark:

The intuitive properties of our concept of Certainty lead to properties that are similar to those of Coherent State of Belief (axioms A0-A4) postulated by Darwiche & Ginsberg [3]. However, in contrast with their model, we can, at the same time, represent and manage the Imprecision and the Uncertainty. Note also that, in their theory, no link is established between their summation operator and the implication and that no inferential Process of deductive type is proposed. The axiomatics of I leads to a particular structure of Aleliunas' Probability Algebra [1, 7], finite and totally ordered but there are some differences: we have added to the theory a notion of Independence closely linked to the Conditional Certainty, a link has been made with the implication, and the deductive process has been enriched by a generalization of the Generalised Modus Ponens' rule. Our axiomatics of the Concept of Certainty does not give (in the propositional case) an Aleliunas' Probabilistic Logic [2]. Spohn has proposed a theory allowing to treat uncertain information [6]. He approaches the concept of Certainty (degree of strength of the Belief in his theory) in an ordinal way. He especially introduced the concept of ordinal degree of conditional Certainty. So, the theory used here presents a similarity with that of Spohn. In both cases, we are looking for a non probabilistic (in the classical sense) model of the concepts of certainty and of conditional certainty, even if the objectives are different. Spohn's approach being ordinal, the operators used are that defined in N, that is min + and -. It is clear that they differ basically from the operators S, I and n that we have built in the scale of certainty. The scale of Graduation in his theory is infinitely denumerable whereas ours, by definition, is finite.

3. An example in $\mathcal{L}_9$: the presidential election

Mr. Frenchy, a French man in the street, has troubles with the forecasts of the (French) institutes for opinion poll for the presidential election. He would like to know the Certainty he may have about the chances of the candidate A (his secret favourite), this depending of course on the quality of the estimation of these institutes. So he considers four situations: "candidate A leads" (A_1), "candidate B leads" (A_2), "candidate C leads" (A_3) and "neither A nor B nor C leads" (A_4). Depending on his personal knowledge and on the political programs of the candidates in the campaign, he esteems that it is frankly-improbable that A leads so Prob(A_1) =v_2 that is, it is really-improbable that B leads, probable that C leads and frankly-improbable that "neither A nor B nor C leads". Listening every

day to the evaluations of the poll institutes, he then esteems that their forecasts
are pretty good especially for the candidate A, rather good for the candidate B
but rather bad for the other candidates. In other words, considering the event
B : "the estimation of the institutes are correct", he esteems that it is probable
that these estimations are correct when A leads, that it is really-probable that
these estimations are correct when B leads, that they are frankly-probable when
C leads and at last that it is probable that these estimations are correct when
none leads. Knowing that, he can then deduce the certainty he can have about
the chances of the candidate A given that the estimations of the institutes are
correct. Using the *Symbolic Generalised Bayes' Formula* (*Th.* 2.6.7), he knows
that it is between frankly-improbable and little-probable that the candidate A
leads when the estimations are correct. So he is rather pessimistic about the
chances of his favourite candidate.

4. About the graduation scales

There is no objective way to decide, independently from the given problem,
which size M of the uncertainty graduation scale is the best. We may choose any
linguistic qualifiers though the derivation of qualifiers from one M to another
may not be explicit. But it is possible to make a correspondance between the
degrees of these different scales as shown by the following figure.

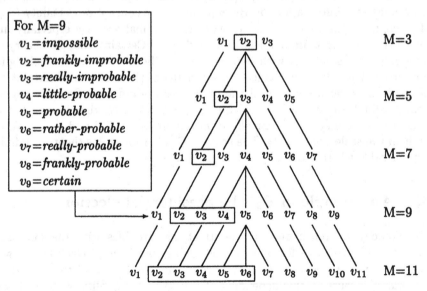

With this correspondance, a comparison has be done as follows: for the previous
example and for each scale, we have computed the certainty degree of the same
event. The results are represented by the boxes in the same figure. One has to
be careful: $[v_2, v_4]$ for M = 7 and $[v_2, v_4]$ for M = 9 does not mean the same
thing. Also, some choices have been made: v_4 for M = 7 may be taken as v_4, v_5
or v_6 for M = 9.

With this example all for all the other examples we have testes, the results are coherent: the intervals overlap or belong to the others, but we have never disjoint intervals or isolated values. But, it has to be noted that for a same value of M, the results are more or less satisfying for different problems. And also, for a same problem, there seems to be a better value of M, that is a value giving a smaller interval which in turn, gives a stricter approximation. So it is not possible to fix and use a unique value of M for all problems, neither to increase the number to give a more precise value of the intervals for all cases.

5. Conclusion

We have presented a model of Qualitative Reasoning under uncertain information based upon a *Symbolic Probability Theory*. We have illustrated the fact that, in situations where the classical Probabilities are ill adapted, our model works simply and gives results that conform to the human intuition. We also gave evidence that the results remain coherent when the size of the graduation scales varies.

References

1. Aleliunas R.: *A new normative theory of probabilistic logic.* Proc. of the Canadian A.I. Conf. M. Kaufmann Pubs., San Mateo. (1988) 67–74
2. Aleliunas R.: *A summary of New Normative Theory of Probabilistic Logic.* in Uncertainty in A.I. 4 (R.D. Schachter, T.S. Lewitt, L.N. Kanal, J.F. Lemmer Eds.). Els. Sc.Pubs. (1990) 199–206
3. Darwiche A., Ginsberg M.: *A symbolic generalization of probability theory.* in proceedings of the American Association for A.I.. San Jose, California. (1992) 622–627
4. Pacholczyk D.: *A New Approach to Vagueness and Uncertainty.* in C.C.-A.I. **9** Nu. 4. (1992) 395–435
5. Pacholczyk D.: *A Logico-symbolic Probability Theory for the Management of Uncertainty.* in C.C.-A.I. **11** Nu. 4. (1994) 417–484
6. Spohn W.: *A General Non-probabilistic Theory of Inductive Reasoning in Uncertainty.* in A.I. 4 Els. sc. Pubs. North Holland (1990) 149–158
7. Xiang Y., Beddoes M.P., Poole D.: *Can Uncertainty Management be realized in a finite totally ordered Probability Algebra.* in Uncertainty in Artificial Intelligence **5** Elsevier Science Pubs. (1990) 41–57

Narratives with Concurrent Actions: The Mutual Exclusion Problem

(Extended Abstract)[*]

Anna Radzikowska

Institute of Mathematics, Warsaw University of Technology,
Plac Politechniki 1, 00-661 Warsaw, Poland.
Email: annrad@im.pw.edu.pl

Action description languages, such as the well-known language $\mathcal{A}$ (see [3]), are formal models used to represent, in a natural way, various kinds of events occurring in dynamic systems. As it has been pointed out ([4]), they are useful to improve our understanding of different aspects of reasoning about actions.

We define an action description language $\mathcal{ALC}_0$[1] as a dialect of the language $\mathcal{A}$. Our language allows representing narratives with simple forms of concurrency, so its semantics essentially differs from that of $\mathcal{A}$. We center upon the notion of a *compound action* which intuitively means a set of *atomic* actions performed concurrently which start and stop cotemporaneously. $\mathcal{ALC}_0$ enables to represent a broad class of domains that permits partial/complete specification at any state of a system, descriptions of atomic/compound actions, actions with nondeterministic effects and causal chains of actions.

We focus on the mutual exclusion problem and the frame problem to guarantee that no conflicting actions are executed simultaneously and no spurious changes occur. While involving cases where specific conditions preclude execution of some actions, we deal with the qualification problem.

Domains of Actions

Traditionally ([5], [1], [2]), actions are viewed as conflicting if they led to contradictory results (the notion of a conflict was related to effects of actions). In contrast, we suggest the approach commonly accepted in the theory of concurrency ([7]): *actions are conflicting if sets of fluents affected by them are not disjoint* – no matter how they actually influence these fluents. Accordingly, we relate the notion of a conflict to accessibility to fluents.

As usual, we assume that a compound action *normally* inherits results of its subactions. However, this policy, when applied to nondeterministic actions, leads sometimes to unintuitive results. To cope with this problem, we suggest distinguishing *elementary* actions, that is actions which have their own specification in a domain. These actions are viewed as indivisible units (similarly to atomic actions) and do not inherit results of their subactions.[2] Any compound action A is then viewed as a composition of its *maximal* elementary components

---

[*] This work was supported by the KBN Grant 3 P406 019 06.

[1] In fact, $\mathcal{ALC}_0$ is an extension of our language $\mathcal{AL}$ introduced in [6].

[2] It may be viewed as an analogy to the following observation: chemical compounds make distinct substances usually characterized by different behaviour than elements they are composed of.

(relative to set inclusion). Performance of A is treated as a parallel execution of all its unconflicting maximal elementary subactions that can be performed and any joint result of these subactions is the effect of performing A. The remaining subactions are thought of as "forsaken" and are not performed. Hence, we restrict the inheritance policy to non-elementary actions only.

In the case of conflict we deal with an implicit form of nondeterminism – effects of conflicting actions depend on which actions are actually executed.

When a specific situation precludes the execution of an action, we deal with some kind of qualifications of actions. We treat an elementary action as an integral whole in the sense that its execution is possible in a situation which precludes neither the action itself nor any of its subactions.

When two unconflicting actions occur simultaneously and each one of them can be performed at this moment, we assume that they can be executed simultaneously if the situation does not preclude the execution of any action $C \subseteq A \cup B$.

We restrict to actions executed in a single unit of time and omit temporal characteristics of their performances.

The Action Language $\mathcal{ALC}_0$

$\mathcal{ALC}_0$ is a family of languages, each one of them is characterized by three nonempty sets: a set $\mathcal{F}$ of *fluents*, a set $\mathcal{A}$ of *atomic actions* and a set $\mathcal{T}$ of *timepoints* (here identified with $\mathbb{N}$).

A *compound action* is any finite set $\{a_1, \ldots, a_k\}$ of atomic actions.[3] A *formula* is a propositional combination of fluents.

A *domain description* is a set of statements of the following types:

1. A *value statement* is of the form

$$\alpha \text{ at } t \tag{1}$$

which means that a formula α is true at time t. If $t = 0$ then we write **initially** α.

2. An *action statement* is of the form

$$A \text{ occurs at } t \tag{2}$$

which intuitively says that an action A occurs at time t.

Value statements and action statements will be referred to as *propositions*.

3. An *effect statement* is of the form

$$A \text{ causes } \alpha \text{ if } \pi \tag{3}$$

which informally means that an action A makes a formula α true if a precondition π holds when A begins. If $\alpha \equiv \bot$ then we write **impossible** A **if** π saying that whenever π holds, A cannot be performed.

4. A *release statement* is of the form

$$A \text{ releases } f \text{ if } \pi \tag{4}$$

which informally states that a fluent f is exempt from the inertia law when an action A is performed if a precondition π holds at the beginning of A.

---

[3] We will often identify an atomic action a with the compound one $\{a\}$ and use the term "action" relative to a compound action.

5. A *trigger statement* is of the form

$$\pi \textbf{ triggers } A \tag{5}$$

which informally means that any state satisfying π immediately causes an occurrence of an action A.

6. An *invoke statement* is of the form

$$A \textbf{ invokes } B \textbf{ after } t \textbf{ if } \pi \tag{6}$$

with the intuitive meaning that executing an action A causes an occurrence of an action B t units of time later if π holds when A starts.

Example (Producer-Consumer Problem) A producer generates items and puts them into the buffer whenever it is empty. Two consumers remove an item from the buffer after the producer has put it there. Initially the buffer is empty.

> **initially** *Empty*;
> *Put* **causes** ¬*Empty*;　　*Put* **invokes** *GetA*;
> *GetA* **causes** *Empty*;　　*Put* **invokes** *GetB*;
> *GetB* **causes** *Empty*;　　*Empty* **triggers** *Put*.

Given a domain description D, we say that A is an *elementary action in D* iff there is an effect statement (3) (where $\alpha \not\equiv \bot$) or a release statement (4) in D describing A. The set of all elementary actions in D will be denoted by $\mathcal{E}_D$.

Every finite action A may be decomposed into the set of elementary actions $\{A_1, \ldots, A_n\}$ such that **(a)** for every $i = 1, \ldots, n$, $A_i \subseteq A$; **(b)** $\bigcup_{i=1}^n A_i = A$ and **(c)** for every $i = 1, \ldots, n$, there is no $B \in \mathcal{E}_D$ such that $A_i \subset B \subseteq A$. The set of such actions is called a *decomposition of A in D* and denoted by $DC_D(A)$.

A *history function* is a truth-valued function defined on the set of fluents $\mathcal{F}$ and the set of timepoints $\mathbb{N}$. This function can be easily extended for the set of all formulae according to the truth tables in propositional logic.

Given a history function H, a formula α holds at time t iff $H(\alpha, t) = 1$.

We say that executing an action $A \in \mathcal{E}_D$ at time t *affects* a fluent f iff there is an effect statement "A **causes** α **if** π" in D ($\alpha \not\equiv \bot$) such that π holds at time t and $f \in fl(\alpha)$[4], or there is a release statement "A **releases** f **if** π" in D such that π holds at time t.

Distinct actions $A, B \in \mathcal{E}_D$ are *conflicting at time t* iff there is a fluent f such that executions of A and B at time t affect f.

Actions $A, B \in \mathcal{E}_D$ are *possibly concurrently executable* at time t iff A and B are not conflicting at time t and for every action $C \subseteq A \cup B$ there is no statement "**impossible** B **if** π" such that π holds at time t.

A *structure* is a tuple $\Sigma = (H, O, E, I)$, where

- $H : \mathcal{F} \times \mathbb{N} \to \{0, 1\}$ is a history function;
- $O : \mathbb{N} \to \wp(\mathcal{A})$ is an *occurrence function* such that for any timepoint t, $O(t)$ yields a set of atomic actions occurring at time t;
- $E : \mathbb{N} \to \wp(\wp(\mathcal{A}))$ is an *executability function* such that for any timepoint t, $E(t)$ yields a set of actions executed at time t;
- $I : \wp(\mathcal{A}) \times \mathbb{N} \to \wp(\mathcal{F})$ is an *influence function* such that for any action $A \subseteq \mathcal{A}$ and any timepoint t, $I(A, t)$ yields the set of fluents influenced by a performance of A at time t.

---

[4] $fl(\alpha)$ denotes the set of all fluents occurring in α.

Given a domain description D, a structure $\Sigma = (H, O, E, I)$ is *well-founded with respect to* D iff for every timepoint t, $E(t) \subseteq DC_D(O(t))$ is maximal set of possibly concurrently executable actions at time t.

For a structure $\Sigma = (H, O, E, I)$ and a statement s, we define that Σ is a *structure for* s, written $\Sigma \bowtie s$, as follows:

- $\Sigma \bowtie \alpha$ **at** t iff $H(\alpha, t) = 1$
- $\Sigma \bowtie A$ **occurs at** t iff $A \subseteq O(t)$
- $\Sigma \bowtie A$ **causes** α **if** π iff $\forall t \in \mathbb{N}\, [\, H(\pi, t) = 1 \,\&\, A \in E(t)$
$$\Rightarrow H(\alpha, t+1) = 1 \,\&\, fl(\alpha) \subseteq I(A, t)\,]$$
- $\Sigma \bowtie A$ **releases** f **if** π iff $\forall t \in \mathbb{N}\, [\, H(\pi, t) = 1 \,\&\, A \in E(t) \Rightarrow f \in I(A, t)\,]$
- $\Sigma \bowtie A$ **invokes** B **after** t **if** π iff $\forall t' \in \mathbb{N}\, [\, H(\pi, t') = 1 \,\&$
$$(\exists C \subseteq A.\, C \in E(t')) \Rightarrow B \subseteq O(t'+t)\,]$$
- $\Sigma \bowtie \pi$ **triggers** A iff $\forall t \in \mathbb{N}\, [\, H(\pi, t) = 1 \Rightarrow A \subseteq O(t)\,]$.

We say that Σ is a *structure for* D iff Σ is a structure for every statement in D and it is well-founded with respect to D.

A structure $\Sigma = (H, O, E, I)$ for D may indicate occurrences of some actions unexplained by the domain and fluents actually not affected by actions. Then, for any action A and any timepoint t, sets $I(A, t)$ and $O(t)$ should be minimal. We say that a structure $\Sigma = (H, O, E, I)$ for D is a *frame for* D iff there is no structure $\Sigma' = (H', O', E', I')$ for D such that $H = H'$, $O' \prec O$ and $I' \prec I$.[5]

To preserve the inertia law, we require that all changes must result from executions of actions only. We say that a frame Σ for a domain description D is a *model of* D iff for every $t \in \mathbb{N}$, $\{f \in \mathcal{F} : H(f, t) \neq H(f, t+1)\} \subseteq \bigcup_{A \in E(t)} I(A, t)$.

A domain description D *entails* a proposition φ, written $D \models \varphi$, iff every model of D is a structure for φ.

Example (continued) For a domain description D, it is easy to check that for all even $t \in \mathbb{N}$, $D \models Empty$ **at** t and $D \models Put$ **occurs at** t; for all odd $t \in \mathbb{N}$, $D \models \neg Empty$ **at** t.

References

1. C. Baral, M. Gelfond: Representing Concurrent Actions in Extended Logic Programming, in *Proc. IJCAI-93*, pp. 866–871.
2. S. E. Bornscheuer, M. Thielscher: Representing Concurrent Actions and Solving Conflicts, in *Proc. of KI-94*, pp. 16–27.
3. M. Gelfond, V. Lifschitz: Representing Action and Change by Logic Programs, *The Journal of Logic Programming*, (17), 1993, pp. 301–322.
4. V. Lifschitz: Two Components of An Action Language, in *Proc. of 3rd Symposium of Logical Formalization of Commonsense Reasoning*, Stanford University, 1996.
5. F. Lin, Y. Shoham: Concurrent Actions in the Situation Calculus, in *Proc. of AAAI-92*, pp. 590–595.
6. A. Radzikowska: Formalization of Reasoning about Default Action (Preliminary Report), in *Proc. of FAPR-96*, pp. 540–554.
7. W. Resig: *Petri Nets: An Introduction*, Springer-Verlag, 1985.

---

[5] For two functions $\Phi, \Psi : X \to \wp(Y)$, $\Phi \prec \Psi$ denotes that for all $x \in X$, $\Phi(x) \subseteq \Psi(x)$ and $\Phi(x') \subset \Psi(x')$ for some $x' \in X$.

Tools for Autonomous Agents

Stuart Russell

Computer Science Division University of California, Berkeley, USA

The nature of the task environment in which an intelligent agent must operate has a profound effect on its design. It can be argued that AI has only recently begun to take seriously the problem of partial observability of the environment, despite the fact that this is perhaps the primary reason why intelligent agents need memory and internal representations.

In complex environments, partial observability goes hand in hand with uncertainty, and necessitates the development of new tools for representation, inference, decision making, and learning. I will describe work in progress on a suite of such tools centered around dynamic probabilistic networks, with application to the problem of driving in unrestricted highway traffic.

A Concept Language Extended with Different Kinds of Transitive Roles

Ulrike Sattler*

RWTH Aachen, uli@cantor.informatik.rwth-aachen.de

Abstract. Motivated by applications that demand for the adequate representation of part-whole relations, different possibilities of representing transitive relations in terminological knowledge representation systems are investigated. A well-known concept language, $\mathcal{ALC}$, is extended by three different kinds of transitive roles. It turns out that these extensions differ largely in expressiveness and computational complexity, hence this investigation gives insight into the diverse alternatives for the representation of transitive relations such as part-whole relations, family relations or partial orders in general.

1 Introduction

Terminological knowledge representation systems (TKR-systems) are powerful means to represent the unambiguous, well-defined terminological knowledge in technical and other domains. Mainly, TKR-systems consist of two parts: A knowledge base, which contains the explicit concept definitions given in a so-called concept language, and an inference engine which is able to infer implicit properties of the defined concepts such as satisfiability or subclass/superclass relations among these concepts. A concept language is characterized by a set of operators that can be used to define complex concepts (which are interpreted as subsets of an interpretation universe) and roles (which are interpreted as binary relations on an interpretation universe) from primitive concepts and roles.

Looking for a concept language with sufficient expressive power to be used for the representation of complex objects, one observes that part-whole relations are indispensable in the description of these objects. The following concept, for example, describes devices having at least one part that is a battery: device ⊓ (∃ has_part.battery).

Since part-whole relations have special properties used for reasoning about complex objects, they are subject to a great variety of investigations [ACG+94; Pri95; Sim87; Fra94]. A point of view supported by most of them is that there are different part-whole relations (such as component–aggregate and ingredient–object) with different properties, and that there is a general transitive part-whole relation. Hence part-whole relations deserve special attention and cannot be represented by simple binary relations.

---

* The author is sponsored by the Deutsche Forschungsgemeinschaft under Grant No. Sp 230\ 6–6

Even if a concrete decomposition of a given object may seem object inherent and natural, it is rather arbitrary in most cases. This can be seen by comparing decompositions of the same object made by different persons or made with different intentions. Hence, given an object, it is rarely possible to associate an exact level of decomposition to each of its parts. In one decomposition, two parts may be found in the same level whereas in another decomposition, these parts are at different levels. Thus, if we want to address a part of an object, it might be necessary to address various levels of decomposition. Furthermore, it might be necessary to refer to *all* levels of decomposition or to *all* parts of an object. If the maximum depth of decomposition is known in advance, this can be achieved by using a concept language that allows for disjunction of concepts, as for example in the following concept that describes devices having a carcinogenic part at some level of decomposition:

```
device ⊓ ((∃has_part.carcinogenic) ⊔
          (∃has_part.(∃has_part.carcinogenic)) ⊔
          (∃has_part.(∃has_part.(∃has_part.carcinogenic))) ⊔ ...)
```

If this maximum depth is not known in advance, other, more expressive means have to be used to refer to these parts[2]. A first approach is to represent the part-whole relation by a transitive role has_some_part that is interpreted as a transitive relation. Using this role, we are now able to represent dangerous devices as given above by device ⊓ (∃has_some_part.carcinogenic). On the other hand, there are cases where we want to distinguish between a *direct* part and a part of a part of ..., for example, this might be the case if an object is decomposed into components and we want to distinguish between a device equipped with a battery and a device having—at some level of decomposition—a part that has a battery. A concept language having the expressive power to formulate this difference is one where, beside primitive roles, one is allowed to use the *transitive closure* R^+ of a role R. The above examples can then be described by

$$device ⊓ (∃has\_part.battery) \quad \text{and}$$
$$device ⊓ (∃has\_part^+.(∃has\_part.battery)).$$

Unfortunately, extending the well-known concept language $\mathcal{ALC}$ [SS91] by the transitive closure of roles severely increases the computational complexity of the according inference problems such as subsumption or satisfiability. Even if this increase in complexity can be justified by the simultaneous growth in expressive power, one might not be willing to accept this complexity, and look for an alternative to the transitive closure of roles. Using results from Modal Logic [Lad77; HM92], it can be shown that the use of transitive roles is in general less expensive in terms of complexity than the use of the transitive closure of roles. In fact, it is the interaction between a role and its transitive closure which is responsible for the high computational complexity.

---

[2] As pointed out in [LB87], an important aspect of expressiveness is, however, "what can be left unsaid" in a representation.

The natural question arising here is whether there exists an alternative for the representation of transitive relations: One that is more expressive than transitive roles, and which has less dramatic effects on the computational complexity than the transitive closure of roles. Since the transitive closure of a relation $\mathcal{R}$ is the *smallest* transitive relation containing $\mathcal{R}$, a natural candidate for this alternative is *some* transitive relation containing $\mathcal{R}$.

In this paper, we present three extensions of the concept language $\mathcal{ALC}$ by different kinds of transitive roles:

- In $\mathcal{ALC}_+$, the operator $^+$ can be applied to role names. The role R^+ is then interpreted as the smallest transitive relation containing R.
- In $\mathcal{ALC}_{R+}$, certain roles have to be interpreted as transitive roles without the possibility to relate them to a generating role as in the first extension.
- In $\mathcal{ALC}_\oplus$, the operator $^\oplus$ can be applied to role names. The role $R^\oplus$ is then interpreted as some (not necessarily the smallest) transitive relation containing R.

As a consequence of the results given in [FL79], the basic inference problems for $\mathcal{ALC}$ extended by the transitive closure of roles, $\mathcal{ALC}_+$, are EXPTIME-complete, whereas these problems are PSPACE-complete for $\mathcal{ALC}$. Using results from modal logic [Lad77; HM92], we show that these problems remain PSPACE-complete for $\mathcal{ALC}_{R+}$. Finally, it turns out that for $\mathcal{ALC}_\oplus$, these problems are as hard as for $\mathcal{ALC}_+$, namely EXPTIME-complete.

2 Preliminaries

The concept language underlying this investigation is $\mathcal{ALC}$, a well-known concept language introduced by [SS91] and investigated, for example, in [HNS90; DLNN91; DLNN95].

Definition 1. Let N_C be a set of *concept names* and let N_R be a set of *role names*. The set of $\mathcal{ALC}$-concepts is the smallest set such that

1. every concept name is a concept and
2. if C and D are concepts and R is a role name, then $(C \sqcap D)$, $(C \sqcup D)$, $(\neg C)$, $(\forall R.C)$, $(\exists R.C)$ are concepts.

An *interpretation* $\mathcal{I} = (\Delta^\mathcal{I}, \cdot^\mathcal{I})$ consists of a set $\Delta^\mathcal{I}$, called the *domain* of $\mathcal{I}$, and a function $\cdot^\mathcal{I}$ which maps every concept to a subset of $\Delta^\mathcal{I}$ and every role to a subset of $\Delta^\mathcal{I} \times \Delta^\mathcal{I}$ such that

$$(C \sqcap D)^\mathcal{I} = C^\mathcal{I} \cap D^\mathcal{I}$$
$$(C \sqcup D)^\mathcal{I} = C^\mathcal{I} \cup D^\mathcal{I}$$
$$\neg C^\mathcal{I} = \Delta^\mathcal{I} \setminus C^\mathcal{I}$$
$$(\exists R.C)^\mathcal{I} = \{d \in \Delta^\mathcal{I} \mid \text{There exists some } e \in \Delta^\mathcal{I} \text{ with } (d, e) \in R^\mathcal{I} \text{ and } e \in C^\mathcal{I}\}$$
$$(\forall R.C)^\mathcal{I} = \{d \in \Delta^\mathcal{I} \mid \text{For all } e \in \Delta^\mathcal{I}, \text{ if } (d, e) \in R^\mathcal{I}, \text{ then } e \in C^\mathcal{I}\}$$

A concept C is called *satisfiable* iff there is some interpretation $\mathcal{I}$ such that $C^{\mathcal{I}} \neq \emptyset$. Such an interpretation is called a *model of* C. A concept D *subsumes* a concept C (written $C \sqsubseteq D$) iff $C^{\mathcal{I}} \subseteq D^{\mathcal{I}}$ holds for each interpretation $\mathcal{I}$. For an interpretation $\mathcal{I}$, an individual $x \in \Delta^{\mathcal{I}}$ is called an *instance* of a concept C iff $x \in C^{\mathcal{I}}$.

One can observe that extending $\mathcal{ALC}$ by composition or disjunction of roles does not change the expressive power of $\mathcal{ALC}$ because of the following equivalences:

$$\exists(R \circ S).C \equiv \exists R.(\exists S.C) \quad \text{and} \quad \exists(R \sqcup S).C \equiv (\exists R.C) \sqcup (\exists S.C).$$

In contrast, extending $\mathcal{ALC}$ by the transitive closure of roles really increases its expressive power (see [Baa91]).

3 $\mathcal{ALC}$ Extended by the Transitive Closure of Roles

Definition 2. $\mathcal{ALC}_+$ is the extension of $\mathcal{ALC}$ obtained by allowing, for each role $R \in N_R$, the use of its transitive closure R^+ inside concepts. Interpretations have to satisfy additionally:

$$(d, e) \in (R^+)^{\mathcal{I}}$$
$$\text{iff}$$

for $k \geq 1$ exists $d_0 = d, d_1, \ldots, d_k = e$ such that $(d_i, d_{i+1}) \in R^{\mathcal{I}}$ for all $i < k$.

On one hand, the effect of this extension on the expressive power can be seen by noting that $\mathcal{ALC}_+$ can no longer be viewed as a subclass of first order logic. This is due to the fact that the transitive closure of a relation cannot be expressed in first order logic, in contrast to transitivity.

On the other hand, $\mathcal{ALC}$ loses the *finite tree model property*[3] when extended by the transitive closure of roles. For example, the following concept describes instances of A having some R-successor in A and where each individual reachable over some R-path has itself some R-successor in A:

$$A \sqcap (\exists R.A) \sqcap (\forall R^+.(\exists R.A))$$

This concepts is satisfiable, but each of its models has either an infinite R-chain or it contains some R-cycle.

As a consequence of this fact, algorithms (like tableau-based algorithms) that try to construct a model of a concept containing the transitive closure of roles need special "cycle detection mechanisms" [Baa91]: They have to distinguish between cases where constraints on individuals propagated along some (possibly infinite) role chain are simply regenerated but satisfied and cases where their satisfaction is postponed in each step. This could happen for example while trying to construct a model of

$$A \sqcap (\exists R^+.\neg A) \sqcap (\forall R^+.A).$$

---

[3] A concept language has the finite tree model property if each satisfiable concept has a finite tree model.

This cycle detection demands for the storage of a high amount of information and cannot be accomplished using polynomial space: As stated in Theorem 3.1. and Theorem 4.4. of [FL79], satisfiability of $\mathcal{ALC}_+$-concepts is EXPTIME-complete. A translation of this result from dynamic logic to the vocabulary of concept languages can be found in [Sch91].

4 $\mathcal{ALC}$ Extended by Transitive Roles

Recently, results from the field of modal logic gave new insight into problems concerning concept languages: It is well-known [Sch91] that $\mathcal{ALC}$ is a notational variant of propositional multi-modal logic $\mathbf{K}_n$. In the present work, results for the modal logic $\mathbf{K4}_n$, which is a multi modal logic with n so-called agents extending propositional logic, gave the impetus to look closer at transitive roles. If $\mathcal{ALC}$-interpretations are restricted to those where all role names are interpreted as transitive relations, then there is a $1-1$ correspondance between $\mathbf{K4}_n$-formulae and $\mathcal{ALC}$-concepts in such a way that a formula ϕ is satisfiable iff its translation is satisfiable with respect to the restricted semantics. Since it is shown in [HM92] that satisfiability of $\mathbf{K4}_n$ formulae is PSPACE-complete, it is not surprising that we can even show that satisfiability of $\mathcal{ALC}$ extended by transitive roles (beside ordinary roles) is also PSPACE-complete.

Definition 3. $\mathcal{ALC}_{R+}$ is an extension of $\mathcal{ALC}$ obtained by allowing the use of transitive roles inside concepts. The set of role names N_R is a disjoint union of role names $N_P = \{P_1, P_2, \ldots\}$ and role names $N_+ = \{R_1, R_2, \ldots\}$. An interpretation $\mathcal{I} = (\Delta^\mathcal{I}, \cdot^\mathcal{I})$ has to satisfy additionally

$$\text{if } (d, e) \in R_i^\mathcal{I} \text{ and } (e, f) \in R_i^\mathcal{I}, \text{ then } (d, f) \in R_i^\mathcal{I}$$

for each role $R_i \in N_+$.

In this section, a tableau based algorithm is presented that tests for the satisfiability of $\mathcal{ALC}_{R+}$-concepts. The algorithm extends and combines those presented in [HM92] for multi modal logics in order to deal with the simultaneous use of both ordinary and transitive roles. It will be shown that this algorithm uses space polynomial in the length of the concept.

For simplicity, all concepts are supposed to be in *negation normal form*. This means that negation is applied to concept names only. A concept can be transformed into an equivalent one in negation normal form by pushing negation into concepts, for example $\neg(C \sqcup D) \equiv \neg C \sqcap \neg D$ and $\neg(\exists R.C) \equiv (\forall R.\neg C)$.

The tableau algorithm given below constructs a tree whose nodes represent individuals. Each node is labelled with a set of $\mathcal{ALC}_{R+}$-concepts. When started with an $\mathcal{ALC}_{R+}$-concept D in negation normal form, these sets can be restricted to subconcepts $\text{sub}(D)$ of D. It is easy to see that the number of subconcepts of D is linear in the length of D. Soundness and completeness of the tableau algorithm will be proved by showing that it creates a so-called tableau:

Definition 4. Let D be a $\mathcal{ALC}_{R+}$-concept and let $\{P_1, \ldots P_n, R_1, \ldots R_m\}$ be the set of role names occuring in D. A *tableau* $T = (S, L, \mathcal{P}_1, \ldots, \mathcal{P}_n, \mathcal{R}_1, \ldots \mathcal{R}_m)$ for D is defined as follows: S is a set of individuals, $\mathcal{P}_i, \mathcal{R}_i \subseteq S \times S$, and $L : S \to 2^{\text{sub}(D)}$ matches each individual to a set of subconcepts of D such that:

1. for some $s_0 \in S$ we have $D \in L(s_0)$, and for all $s \in S$ it holds that:
2. if $C \in L(s)$, then $\neg C \notin L(s)$,
3. if $C_1 \sqcap C_2 \in L(s)$, then $C_1 \in L(s)$ and $C_2 \in L(s)$,
4. if $C_1 \sqcup C_2 \in L(s)$, then $C_1 \in L(s)$ or $C_2 \in L(s)$,
5. if $(\forall P_i.C) \in L(s)$ and $(s, t) \in \mathcal{P}_i$, then $C \in L(t)$,
6. if $(\exists P_i.C) \in L(s)$, then there is some $t \in S$ with $(s, t) \in \mathcal{P}_i$ and $C \in L(t)$,
7. if $(\forall R_i.C) \in L(s)$ and $(s, t) \in \mathcal{R}_i$, then $C \in L(t)$ and $(\forall R_i.C) \in L(t)$,
8. if $(\exists R_i.C) \in L(s)$, then there is some $t \in S$ with $(s, t) \in \mathcal{R}_i$ and $C \in L(t)$.

Lemma 5. *An $\mathcal{ALC}_{R+}$-concept D is consistent iff there exists a tableau for D.*

Sketch of the proof: Let $T = (S, L, \mathcal{P}_1, \ldots, \mathcal{P}_n, \mathcal{R}_1, \ldots \mathcal{R}_m)$ be a tableau for D, define $\mathcal{I} = (\Delta^{\mathcal{I}}, \cdot^{\mathcal{I}})$ as follows:

$$\Delta^{\mathcal{I}} := S,$$
for all $C \in \text{sub}(D)$ define $s \in C^{\mathcal{I}}$ iff $C \in L(s)$,
$$P_i^{\mathcal{I}} := \mathcal{P}_i,$$
$$R_i^{\mathcal{I}} := \mathcal{R}_i^+ \text{ where } \mathcal{R}_i^+ \text{ denotes the transitive closure of } \mathcal{R}_i.$$

By induction on the structure of concepts, it can be shown that $\mathcal{I}$ is well-defined and that $D^{\mathcal{I}} \neq \emptyset$. For concepts of the form $(C_1 \sqcap C_2), \neg C_1, (\exists P_i.C), (\forall P_i.C)$ and $(\exists R_i.C)$ it follows immediately that they are correctly interpreted. If we have $(\forall R_i.C) \in L(s)$, $(s, t) \in \mathcal{R}_i$ and $(t, u) \in \mathcal{R}_i$, then $(\forall R_i.C) \in L(t)$ and $C \in L(u)$. Hence $s \in (\forall R_i.C)^{\mathcal{I}}$ holds and concepts of the form $(\forall R_i.C)$ are also correctly interpreted.

For the converse, let $\mathcal{I} = (\Delta^{\mathcal{I}}, \cdot^{\mathcal{I}})$ be a model of D. Define $T = (S, L, \mathcal{P}_1, \ldots, \mathcal{P}_n, \mathcal{R}_1, \ldots, \mathcal{R}_m)$ with:

$$S := \Delta^{\mathcal{I}},$$
$$\mathcal{P}_i := P_i^{\mathcal{I}} \text{ for } P_i \in N_P,$$
$$\mathcal{R}_i := R_i^{\mathcal{I}} \text{ for } R_i \in N_+,$$
$$L(s) := \{C \in \text{sub}(D) \mid s \in C^{\mathcal{I}}\}.$$

It follows by construction that T is a tableau for D. ∎

Using Lemma 5, an algorithm which constructs a tableau for an $\mathcal{ALC}_{R+}$-concept D can be used as a decision algorithm for satisfiability of D. The algorithm given here builds a tree starting with a single node and expanding it by either expanding labels of its leafs or by adding new nodes. Nodes of this tree are labelled with sets of subconcepts of D and are possibly marked "satisfiable".

Edges are either unlabelled or they are labelled with j or j^+ for role names P_j, R_j occuring in D (unlabelled edges are generated when testing whether an individual satisfies a disjunction because it satisfies the first or the second

R1 Construct a tree $\mathcal{T}$ consisting of a node x_0 labelled with $L(x_0) = \{D\}$.

R2 Repeat (a) to (d) and possibly expand $\mathcal{T}$ until none of them applies:

(a) (Pre-tableau) If x_i is a leaf of $\mathcal{T}$, $L(x_i)$ is clash-free, $L(x_i)$ is not a pre-tableau and C is the least witness to this fact, then

if $C = C_0 \sqcap C_1$, then $L(x_i) := L(x_i) \cup \{C_0, C_1\}$.

if $C = C_0 \sqcup C_1$, then create two successors x_{i0}, x_{i1} of x_i with
$$L(x_{ij}) := L(x_i) \cup \{C_j\}.$$

(b) (Successors) For x_i a leaf of $\mathcal{T}$, $L(x_i)$ a clash-free pre-tableau, do:
For each $(\exists P_j.C) \in L(x_i)$ create a j-successor x_{ij} with
$L(x_{ij}) := \{C\} \cup L(x_i)/P_j$.
For each $(\exists R_j.C) \in L(x_i)$, let
$\ell(x_i, (\exists R_j.C)) := \{C\} \cup L(x_i)/R_j \cup \{(\forall R_j.E) \mid (\forall R_j.E) \in L(x_i)\}$.
If for some ancestor w of x_i: $L(w) \supseteq \ell(x_i, (\exists R_j.C))$,
then create a j^+-successor x_{ij+} with $L(x_{ij+}) := \emptyset$,
else create a j^+-successor x_{ij+} with $L(x_{ij+}) := \ell(x_i, (\exists R_j.C))$.

(c) Mark a node x "satisfiable" iff

- $L(x)$ is not a pre-tableau and some successor of x is marked "satisfiable".
- $L(x)$ is a clash-free pre-tableau which does not contain a concept of the form $(\exists R_j.C)$ or $(\exists P_j.C)$.
- $L(x)$ is a pre-tableau, x has successors, and all of them are marked "satisfiable".

R3 If the root is marked "satisfiable", return "D is satisfiable" else "D is unsatisfiable".

Fig. 1. Tableau construction for a $\mathcal{ALC}_{R+}$-concept D

disjunct). A node y which is a successor of a node x is called a j- (resp. j^+-) successor of x if the edge between them is labelled with j (resp. j^+). A node x' is called a pre-successor of x if there is an unlabelled path from x to x'. A node x is called an ancestor of a node y if there is a path from x to y regardless of the labels of its edges. Concerning the labels of the nodes, the following abbreviations are introduced.

Let M be a set of concepts. We call M a *pre-tableau* iff M satisfies conditions 2–4 of Definition 4 with M in place of $L(s)$. We say that M *contains a clash* iff there is a concept C with $\{C, \neg C\} \subseteq M$. For a role name $R \in N_P \cup N_+$, let $M/R := \{C \mid (\forall R.C) \in M\}$. The maximum role depth of M, depth(M), is the maximum of nested $(\exists R.C), (\forall R.C)$ concepts of all concepts in M.

For the construction, we assume that concepts (in sub(D)) are linearly ordered and that $\{P_1, \ldots, P_n, R_1, \ldots, R_m\}$ is the set of role names occuring in D. The algorithm is given in Figure 1, and two examples of the tableau construc-

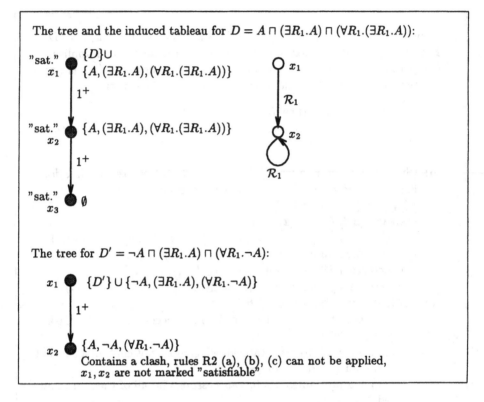

The tree and the induced tableau for $D = A \sqcap (\exists R_1.A) \sqcap (\forall R_1.(\exists R_1.A))$:

"sat." x_1 $\{D\} \cup$ $\{A, (\exists R_1.A), (\forall R_1.(\exists R_1.A))\}$ x_1

1^+ R_1

"sat." x_2 $\{A, (\exists R_1.A), (\forall R_1.(\exists R_1.A))\}$ x_2

1^+ R_1

"sat." x_3 $\emptyset$

The tree for $D' = \neg A \sqcap (\exists R_1.A) \sqcap (\forall R_1.\neg A)$:

x_1 $\{D'\} \cup \{\neg A, (\exists R_1.A), (\forall R_1.\neg A)\}$

1^+

x_2 $\{A, \neg A, (\forall R_1.\neg A)\}$
Contains a clash, rules R2 (a), (b), (c) can not be applied, x_1, x_2 are not marked "satisfiable"

Fig. 2. Two examples for tableau construction

tions can be found in Figure 2. Please note that the empty set is a clash-free pre-tableau.

Lemma 6. *For each $\mathcal{ALC}_{R^+}$-concept D, the tableau construction terminates.*

Proof: Let $|\mathrm{sub}(D)| = m$. We have $\mathrm{depth}(L(x)) \leq m$ for all nodes x. Since nodes are labelled with subsets of $\mathrm{sub}(D)$, $|L(x)| \leq m$ for all nodes x. Furthermore, if $C \in L(x)$, then $C \in L(x')$ for all pre-successors x' of x.

Besides showing termination, we want to give also an upper bound for the space needed by the algorithm, hence we investigate the depth of the tree constructed more closely.

Fact 1: Rule R2 (a) can be applied at most m times along an unlabelled path until it creates a node x such that $L(x)$ contains a clash.

Fact 2: If y is a j-successor of x, then $\mathrm{depth}(L(y)) < \mathrm{depth}(L(x))$. If y is a j^+-successor of x, $C \in L(y)$ and C is not of the form $(\forall R_j^+.C_1)$, then $\mathrm{depth}(\{C\}) < \mathrm{depth}(L(x))$.

Fact 3: If z is a j- or a j^+-successor of y, y is a k- or a k^+-successor of x and $j \neq k$, then $\mathrm{depth}(L(z)) < \mathrm{depth}(L(x))$.

Fact 4: The only way that the depth of the labels does not decrease is along some mixed j^+- and pre-path. Let $x_0, \ldots, x_k$ be nodes on such a path labelled with clash-free pre-tableaux $L(x_i)$ such that each x_i is a j^+-predecessor of $\tilde{x}_i$ and a pre-successor of $\tilde{x}_{i-1}$. Then each $L(\tilde{x}_i)$ can be divided into two parts $L1_i, L2_i$: The first consists of concepts of the form $\{(\forall R_j.E) \mid (\forall R_j.E) \in L(x_i)\} \cup L(x_i)/R_j$ and by construction we have $L1_i \subset L1_{i+1}$. The second is $L2_i = \{C\}$ where $(\exists R_j.C)$ led to the creation of $\tilde{x}_i$. Since for all ancestors w of $\tilde{x}$, we have $L(\tilde{x}_i) \not\subseteq L(w)$ or $L(\tilde{x}_i) = \emptyset$ by construction, there are at most m choices for $L2_i$ and at most m different choices for $L1_i$. Hence we have $k \leq m^2$.

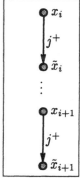

Collecting these facts, we have that the tree built by the tableau construction algorithm has depth at most m^4 and it is of bounded out-degree. Hence its construction terminates. ∎

Lemma 7. *A $\mathcal{ALC}_{R^+}$-concept D is satisfiable iff the tableau construction for D returns "D is satisfiable".*

Proof: Let $\mathcal{T}$ be the tree constructed by the tableau construction algorithm for D. Define a tableau $T = (S, L, \mathcal{P}_1, \ldots, \mathcal{P}_n, \mathcal{R}_1, \ldots \mathcal{R}_m)$ with
$$S = \{x \mid x \text{ is a node in } \mathcal{T}, x \text{ is marked satisfiable,}$$
$$\text{and } L(x) \text{ is a non-empty, clash-free pre-tableau}\},$$
$(x, y) \in \mathcal{P}_j$ iff y is a pre-successor of a j-successor of x,
$(x, y) \in \mathcal{R}_j$ iff y is a pre-successor of a j^+-successor of x and $L(y) \neq \emptyset$ or x has a j^+-successor z with $L(z) = \emptyset$, y is an ancestor of x and $L(y) \supseteq \ell(x, (\exists R_j.C))$

It is easy to see that T is a tableau for D: First, $D \in L(x)$ for all pre-successors x of the root x_0 of $\mathcal{T}$. Leafs of this subtree are either labelled with clash-free pre-tableaus or their labels contain a clash. If x_0 is marked "satisfiable", at least one of these leafs is marked "satisfiable", hence $D \in L(s)$ for some $s \in S$.

T satisfies properties 2–4 of Definition 4 because each $x \in S$ is labelled with a clash-free pre-tableau. R2 (c) creates for each $(\exists P_j.C) \in L(x_i)$ (resp. for those $(\exists R_j.C) \in L(x_i)$ where it is necessary) a j-successor (resp. j^+-successor) x_{ij} such that $C \in L(x_{ij})$, hence properties 6 and 8 are satisfied. Property 5 is satisfied because $L(x_i)/P_j \subseteq L(x_{ij})$ holds for all j-successors of x_i. Finally, property 7 holds because $L(x_i)/R_j \cup \{(\forall R_j.E) \mid (\forall R_j.E) \in L(x_i)\} \subseteq L(y)$ holds for all y with $(x_i, y) \in \mathcal{R}_j$.

For the converse, we show by induction on $h(x)$, the height of the subtree below x that, if x is not marked "satisfiable", then $X := \sqcap_{C \in L(x)} C$ is not satisfiable.

Let $h(x) = 0$, hence x is a leaf. If x is not marked satisfiable, it contains a clash and X is clearly unsatisfiable. Now let $h(x) = \ell + 1$. If $L(x)$ is not a pre-tableau and x is not marked satisfiable, then none of its successors is marked satisfiable. Hence we have $C_1 \sqcup C_2 \in L(x)$ and neither x_1 with $L(x_1) = L(x) \cup \{C_1\}$ nor x_2

with $L(x_2) = L(x) \cup \{C_2\}$ is marked satisfiable. It follows by induction that X is not satisfiable. If $L(x)$ is a pre-tableau and x is not marked satisfiable, then there is either some j- or j^+-successor of x which is not marked satisfiable or $L(x)$ does not contain any subconcept of the form $(\exists R.C)$ but contains a clash. In both cases, it follows by induction that X is not satisfiable. ∎

Theorem 8. *Satisfiability of $\mathcal{ALC}_{R^+}$-concepts can be decided using polynomial space.*

Proof: As stated in the proof of Lemma 6, the tree $\mathcal{T}$ constructed by the tableau construction algorithm for D is of depth at most m^4 where $|\text{sub}(D)| \leq m$. Once this algorithm has marked a node satisfiable, it can forget about the subtree below this node and reuse the space where it was memorized. Since each $L(x)$ is a subset of $\text{sub}(D)$, each $L(x)$ can be stored in m bits. Since there are less than m concepts of the form $(\exists R.C)$ in $\text{sub}(D)$, there are less than m subtrees directly below a node x, and we can memorize which of them still have to be investigated in m bits.

Hence at each moment the algorithm is running, it has to store the following information for its actual node x at depth h: $L(x)$; which of the subtrees below x still have to be investigated, and these two pieces of information for each of its h ancestors. This can be stored in $m + m + h(m + m) = (1 + h)2m$ bits. Since $h \leq m^4$, the tableau construction algorithm needs at most $c + 2m + 2m^5$ bits of storage for some constant c. ∎

Theorem 9. *Satisfiability of $\mathcal{ALC}_{R^+}$-concepts is PSPACE-complete.*

As $\mathcal{ALC}$ is a sublanguage of $\mathcal{ALC}_{R^+}$, PSPACE-hardness of satisfiability of $\mathcal{ALC}_{R^+}$-concepts follows immediately from PSPACE-completeness of satisfiability of $\mathcal{ALC}$-concepts (see [SS91]). PSPACE-completeness is then implied by Theorem 8. ∎

As we have seen, worst-case complexity of $\mathcal{ALC}_{R^+}$ is lower than those of $\mathcal{ALC}_+$. The price in expressive power one has to pay for this lower complexity is illustrated by the following example: Let a queen be defined as a women whose children are princes or princesses and whose descendants are nobles:

$$\text{queen} = \text{women} \sqcap (\forall \text{child}.(\text{prince} \sqcup \text{princess})) \sqcap (\forall \text{child}^+.\text{noble}). \quad (1)$$

This cannot be expressed if only a transitive role **descendants** can be used without the possibility to refer to successors of a subrole **child**: In 1, we express that all individuals p for which the longest **child**-path from an instance q of queen to p is of length 1 are instances of (**prince** $\sqcup$ **princess**) and that all individuals reachable over *some* **child**-path from q are instances of **noble**. If only transitive roles are available as in $\mathcal{ALC}_{R^+}$, we can not distinguish between those "close" role successors and those reachable over some longer **child**-path.

5 ACC Extended by Transitive Orbits of Roles

The investigation of $\mathcal{ACC}$ extended by transitive orbits, $\mathcal{ACC}_\oplus$, was motivated by the gap between $\mathcal{ACC}_{R^+}$ and $\mathcal{ACC}_+$ in both computational complexity and expressive power. $\mathcal{ACC}_\oplus$ is the natural candidate for a compromise between $\mathcal{ACC}_{R^+}$ and $\mathcal{ACC}_+$ because, on one hand, it allows to relate a relation with a transitive superrelation and, on the other hand, there is a chance that its handling could be algorithmically easier.

Definition 10. $\mathcal{ACC}_\oplus$ is an extension of $\mathcal{ACC}$ obtained by allowing the use of *transitive orbits* of roles inside concepts. The transitive orbit of a role R is denoted $R^\oplus$ and interpreted as a transitive role containing $R^\mathcal{I}$, i.e., we have

$$\text{if there exist } d = d_0, d_1, \ldots, d_k = e \text{ with } (d_i, d_{i+1}) \in R^\mathcal{I} \text{ for all } i < k$$
$$\text{then } (d, e) \in (R^\oplus)^\mathcal{I}.$$

A small example is given to highlight the difference between $\mathcal{ACC}_+$ and $\mathcal{ACC}_\oplus$ concepts. Let $* \in \{+, \oplus\}$, and let

$$\texttt{device} \sqcap (\exists \texttt{has\_part}^*.\texttt{carcinogenic}) \tag{2}$$

Let $* = \oplus$, let $\mathcal{I}$ be an interpretation of 2 and let d be an instance of 2. Then $\mathcal{I}$ is a correct interpretation even if there is no $\texttt{has\_part}^\mathcal{I}$ chain from d to some $c \in \texttt{carcinogenic}^\mathcal{I}$: For d being an instance of 2, it is sufficient that there is some $c \in \texttt{carcinogenic}^\mathcal{I}$ with $(d, c) \in (\texttt{has\_part}^\oplus)^\mathcal{I}$.

In general, each model of an $\mathcal{ACC}_+$-concept D is also a model of its $\mathcal{ACC}_\oplus$-counterpart which is obtained by replacing each R^+ in D by $R^\oplus$. If $C' \sqsubseteq D'$ holds for two $\mathcal{ACC}_\oplus$ concepts C', D', then clearly $C \sqsubseteq D$ holds for their $\mathcal{ACC}_+$-counterparts C, D. The converse does not hold:

$$(\forall R.(A \sqcap \neg A)) \sqsubseteq (\forall R^*.(A \sqcap \neg A))$$

holds for $* = +$ (if x has no $R^\mathcal{I}$-successors, then it has clearly no $R^{+\mathcal{I}}$-successors), but it does not hold for $* = \oplus$ (x can have an $R^{\oplus\mathcal{I}}$-successor without having an $R^\mathcal{I}$-successor).

The tableau construction algorithm given in Section 4 can easily be modified to handle $\mathcal{ACC}_\oplus$-concepts: In rule R2 (b), roles $R_i^\oplus$ are handled in the same way as role names $R_i \in N_+$. For an ordinary role R_j, possible labels of j-successors of x_i are

$$\ell(x_i, (\exists R_j.C)) := \{C\} \cup L(x_i)/R_j \cup L(x_i)/R_j^\oplus \cup \{(\forall R_j^\oplus.E) \mid (\forall R_j^\oplus.E) \in L(x_i)\}$$

and the same test whether an ancestor of x_i is labelled by a superset of $\ell(x_i, (\exists R_j))$ has to be accomplished. In contrast to the trees constructed for $\mathcal{ACC}_{R^+}$-concepts, the depth of trees constructed by this modified algorithm can no longer be bounded polynomially in the length of the concept. For example, if $\tilde{A}_i$ is defined as given below, each model of the concept

$$D = (\exists R.(\neg A_1 \sqcap \neg A_2 \sqcap \ldots \neg A_n)) \sqcap$$
$$(\forall R^\oplus.((\exists R.\top) \sqcap (\tilde{A}_1 \sqcap \tilde{A}_2 \sqcap \ldots \sqcap \tilde{A}_n)))$$

can have paths of length 2^n: It can be viewed as the representation of the binary encoding of the numbers 0 to $2^n - 1$. The concepts $\tilde{A}_i$ have to be defined in such a way that for the $k+1$-th $R^{\mathcal{I}}$-successor y of $x \in D^{\mathcal{I}}$ we have $y \in A_i^{\mathcal{I}}$ iff the i-th bit in the binary encoding of k is equal to 1. More precisely,

$$\tilde{A}_0 = (A_0 \sqcap (\forall R. \neg A_0)) \sqcup (\neg A_0 \sqcap (\forall R. A_0))$$
$$\tilde{A}_i = (\sqcap_{0 \leq j < i} A_j \sqcap ((A_i \sqcap \forall R. \neg A_i) \sqcup (\neg A_i \sqcap \forall R. A_i))) \sqcup$$
$$(\neg \sqcap_{0 \leq j < i} A_j \sqcap ((A_i \sqcap \forall R. A_i) \sqcup (A_i \sqcap \forall R. \neg A_i))).$$

The length of D is then quadratic in n whereas each model $\mathcal{I}$ of D has an $R^{\mathcal{I}}$-path of length in $O(2^n)$.

Theorem 11. *Satisfiability of $\mathcal{ALC}_\oplus$-concepts is* EXPTIME-*complete.*

Proof: Satisfiability of $\mathcal{ALC}_\oplus$-concepts is in EXPTIME because it can be decided by the modified tableau construction algorithm. It is easy to see that for an $\mathcal{ALC}_\oplus$-concept D, this modified algorithm creates a tree whose depth is exponentially bounded by the length of D because of the tests performed whether an ancestor is labelled by a superset of the label of new nodes.

To show that satisfiability of $\mathcal{ALC}_\oplus$-concepts is indeed EXPTIME-hard, we can modify the proof of EXPTIME-hardness for satisfiability in PDL given in [FL79]. The proof gives, for an alternating Turing Machine M, a PDL formula $f_M(x)$ such that $f_M(x)$ is satisfiable iff x is accepted by a simplified trace of M. The translation of this proof to $\mathcal{ALC}_+$-concepts is straightforward and ends with a concept D using a single role R and its transitive closure R^+. This concept is of the form

$$D = C_1 \sqcap C_2 \sqcap (\forall R^+. C_2)$$

where R is the only role name occuring in C_1, C_2. Furthermore, R^+ occurs neither in C_1 nor in C_2. Because of its special form, D is satisfiable iff its $\mathcal{ALC}_\oplus$-counterpart $D' = C_1 \sqcap C_2 \sqcap (\forall R^\oplus. C_2)$ is satisfiable:

Each model of D is clearly a model of D'. Now let $\mathcal{I}'$ be a model of D' with $x \in D'^{\mathcal{I}'}$. Then $x \in C_1^{\mathcal{I}'} \sqcap C_2^{\mathcal{I}'}$ and for all y with $(x, y) \in R^{\oplus \mathcal{I}'}$ it holds that $y \in C_2^{\mathcal{I}'}$. Let $\mathcal{I}$ be an interpretation of D which is equal to $\mathcal{I}'$ for concept and role names in C_1, C_2 and where $R^{+\mathcal{I}}$ is the transitive closure of $R^{\mathcal{I}'}$. Hence we have that $(x, y) \in R^{+\mathcal{I}}$ implies $(x, y) \in R^{\oplus \mathcal{I}'}$ for all $x, y \in \Delta^{\mathcal{I}}$. It follows that $y \in C_2^{\mathcal{I}}$ for all $(x, y) \in R^{+\mathcal{I}}$, and finally we have $x \in D^{\mathcal{I}}$. Hence $\mathcal{I}$ is a model of D. ∎

6 Conclusion

Transitive roles per se, without referring to an underlying subrole, are algorithmically easier to handle than the transitive closure of roles, whereas substituting the transitive closure of a role by some transitive superrole does not seem to make reasoning easier. Hence, when using a description logic based knowledge representation system, one should really think about whether the transitive closure of roles is needed for this application or whether one can live with transitive roles. In the latter case, a terminological knowledge representation system based on $\mathcal{ALC}$ can be modified in such a way that it is able to handle transitive relations without severely increasing its computational complexity, but nevertheless increasing its expressive power: In the definition of concepts or description of individual objects, one can now refer to parts (ancestors, friends or relatives) at a level of decomposition (in a generation, at a degree of relationship) not known in advance. An interesting question arising from these observations is whether this holds for extensions of other concept languages as well.

Acknowledgement I would like to thank Franz Baader, Diego Calvanese and the anonymous referees for valuable suggestions and comments.

References

[ACG+94] A. Artale, F. Cesarini, E. Grazzini, F. Pippolini, and G. Soda. Modelling composition in a terminological language environment. In *Workshop Notes of the ECAI Workshop on Parts and Wholes: Conceptual Part-Whole Relations and Formal Mereology*, pages 93–101, Amsterdam, 1994.

[Baa91] F. Baader. Augmenting concept languages by transitive closure of roles: An alternative to terminological cycles. In *Proc. of IJCAI-91*, 1991.

[DLNN91] F. Donini, M. Lenzerini, D. Nardi, and W. Nutt. The complexity of concept languages. In *Proc. of KR-91*, Boston (USA), 1991.

[DLNN95] F. M. Donini, M. Lenzerini, D. Nardi, and W. Nutt. The complexity of concept languages. Technical Report RR-95-07, DFKI, Kaiserslautern, Deutschland, 1995.

[FL79] M. J. Fischer and R. E. Ladner. Propositional dynamic logic of regular programs. *J. of Computer and System Science*, 18:194–211, 1979.

[Fra94] E. Franconi. A treatment of plurals and plural quantifications based on a theory of collections. *Minds and Machines*, 3(4):453–474, November 1994.

[HM92] J. Y. Halpern and Y. Moses. A guide to completeness and complexity for modal logic of knowledge and belief. *Artificial Intelligence*, 54:319–379, 1992.

[HNS90] B. Hollunder, W. Nutt, and M. Schmidt-Schauss. Subsumption algorithms for concept description languages. In *ECAI-90*, Pitman Publishing, London, 1990.

[Lad77] R.E. Ladner. The computational complexity of provability in systems of modal propositional logic. *SIAM J. of Computing*, 6(3):467–480, 1977.

[LB87] H. Levesque and R. J. Brachman. Expressiveness and tractability in knowledge representation and reasoning. *Computational Intelligence*, 3:78–93, 1987.

[Pri95] S. Pribbenow. Modeling physical objects: Reasoning about (different kinds of) parts. In *Time, Space, and Movement Workshop 95*, Bonas, France, 1995.

[Sch91] K. Schild. A correspondence theory for terminological logics: Preliminary report. In *Proc. of IJCAI-91*, pages 466–471, Sydney, 1991.

[Sim87] P. M. Simons. *Parts. A study in Ontology*. Oxford: Clarendon, 1987.

[SS91] Manfred Schmidt-Schauß and Gert Smolka. Attributive concept descriptions with complements. *Artificial Intelligence*, 48(1):1–26, 1991.

Representation in Auditory Cortex

Henning Scheich

Federal Institute for Neurobiology (IIN), Magdeburg, Germany

The basic functional organization of gerbil auditory cortex was mapped with unit recording of best frequency and with the fluoro–2–deoxyglucose mapping (FDG) technique. Among at least seven subfields in this cortex the primary auditory cortex (AI) and the anterior auditory field (AAF) showed prominent tonotopic organization with parallel dorsoventral iso–frequency contours (electrophysiology) in correspondence to FDG labelling of frequency band laminae. In an approach to elucidate mechanisms of learning aversive tone conditioning paradigms were found to reshape frequency receptive fields of single units in AI and also produced spatial shifts of tone representation in the tonotopic maps of AI and AAF. Both results suggest that spectral features as well as aspects of behavioral meaning of sounds may be represented even in primary auditory cortex. General meaningfulness in terms of occurrence of novel and salient stimuli may be reflected by expression of immediate early genes. Mapping with an antibody against the immediate early gene product c–Fos identified the spatial distribution of neurons in auditory cortex which changed metabolism as a result of stimulation with auditory signals in a new environment. Spatial representation of sounds in auditory cortex has also an orderly dynamic component which could be shown by optical recording of intrinsic signals. It is suggested by these convergent results that the essence of orderly spatial activity in sensory maps of cortex is a strategy to combine in the same neuronal substrate and in a form readable by other brain systems aspects of stimulus identification and of behavioral stimulus interpretation. This behaviorally oriented aspect of stimulus processing seems to be pronounced in human auditory cortex as shown by functional magnetic resonance imaging (IMRI).

A Terminological Qualification Calculus for Preferential Reasoning under Uncertainty

Klemens Schnattinger & Udo Hahn

Universität Freiburg, ⒬ Text Knowledge Engineering Lab
Europaplatz 1, D-79085 Freiburg, Germany
{schnattinger,hahn}@coling.uni-freiburg.de

Abstract. We introduce a qualitative model of uncertain reasoning and illustrate its application in the framework of a natural language understanding task. Considering uncertain reasoning as a preferential choice problem between alternative hypotheses, the model we provide assigns quality labels to single evidences for or against a hypothesis, combines the generated labels in terms of the overall credibility of a single hypothesis, and, finally, computes a preference order on the entire set of competing hypotheses. This model of quality-based uncertain reasoning is entirely embedded in a terminological logic framework.

1   Introduction

In this paper, we develop a qualitative, preference-based model of uncertain reasoning. Decision-making under uncertainty is here considered as the choice between several alternatives (or hypotheses). The *qualification calculus* we introduce serves as a system of preference computations that treats the problem of choosing from among several alternatives as a *quality-based decision task* and decomposes it into three constituent parts: the continuous *generation* of quality labels for single hypotheses, the estimation of the overall *credibility* of single hypotheses, and the computation of a *preference order* for the entire set of competing hypotheses. The key notion of *quality labels* captures different types of evidences for or against single alternatives and their specific statuses, i.e., their significance, reliability or strength.

This approach and its complete embedding in a terminological reasoning framework are motivated by requirements which emerged from our work in the overlapping fields of natural language parsing [7, 16] and learning from texts [5]. In order to cope with lexical and conceptual underspecification of the relevant knowledge sources in a constructive way the parsing process is interwoven with concept learning tasks. The common basis for text understanding as well as concept learning from texts are terminological knowledge representation structures. Both tasks are also characterized by the common need to evaluate alternative representation structures, either reflecting parsing ambiguities or multiple concept hypotheses. In order to deal with the emerging indeterminacy, e.g., in the learning task, two types of evidences are considered. The first one reflects *structural linguistic* properties of phrasal patterns or discourse contexts unknown words occur in (assuming that the type of grammatical construction exercises a particular interpretative force on the lexical item to be learned). The second one relates to *conceptual properties* of particular concept hypotheses as they are generated and continuously refined by the ongoing text understanding process (e.g., consistency relative to already given knowledge, independent justification from several sources). Each of these grammatical, discourse or conceptual indicators is assigned a particular quality label. The application of quality macro operators, taken from the qualification calculus, to these atomic quality labels finally determines which out of several alternative hypotheses are actually preferred.

2 Formal Foundations

We consider the problem of uncertain reasoning from a new methodological perspective, *viz.* one based on metareasoning about statements expressed in a terminological representation language. Terminological assertions are reified, contexts are used for the encapsulation of qualifying reasoning processes on reified terminological assertions, and truth-preserving translation rules mediate between different contexts. Hence, we exploit the full classification power from standard terminological systems for metareasoning. A detailed discussion of the underlying architecture is given in [19].

Terminological Logics. We use a concept description language with a standard set-theoretic semantics (the interpretation function $\mathcal{I}$). It has several constructors combining *atomic* concepts, roles and individuals (see Tables 1 and 3). By means of *terminological axioms* a symbolic name can be defined for each concept and role term; concepts and roles are associated with concrete individuals by *assertional axioms* (see Tables 2 and 4). A survey of the major properties of terminological languages is given by [22].

Syntax	Semantics
C_{atom}	$\{d \in C_{atom}^{\mathcal{I}} \mid C_{atom} \text{ is atomic}\}$
$C \sqcap D$	$C^{\mathcal{I}} \cap D^{\mathcal{I}}$
$C \sqcup D$	$C^{\mathcal{I}} \cup D^{\mathcal{I}}$
$\neg C$	$\Delta^{\mathcal{I}} \setminus C^{\mathcal{I}}$
$\exists R.C$	$\{d \in \Delta^{\mathcal{I}} \mid R^{\mathcal{I}}(d) \cap C^{\mathcal{I}} \neq \emptyset\}$
$\forall R.C$	$\{d \in \Delta^{\mathcal{I}} \mid R^{\mathcal{I}}(d) \subseteq C^{\mathcal{I}}\}$

Table 1. Syntax/Semantics for Concept Constructors

Axiom	Semantics
Terminological Axioms	
$A \doteq C$	$A^{\mathcal{I}} = C^{\mathcal{I}}$
$A \sqsubseteq C$	$A^{\mathcal{I}} \subseteq C^{\mathcal{I}}$
Assertional Axioms	
$a : C$	$a^{\mathcal{I}} \in C^{\mathcal{I}}$

Table 2. Axioms for Concept Constructors

Syntax	Semantics
R_{atom}	$\{(d,e) \in R_{atom}^{\mathcal{I}} \mid R_{atom} \text{ is atomic}\}$
$R \sqcap S$	$R^{\mathcal{I}} \cap S^{\mathcal{I}}$
$c\vert R$	$\{(d,d') \in R^{\mathcal{I}} \mid d \in C^{\mathcal{I}}\}$
$R\vert c$	$\{(d,d') \in R^{\mathcal{I}} \mid d' \in C^{\mathcal{I}}\}$
R^{-1}	$\{(d,d') \in \Delta^{\mathcal{I}} \times \Delta^{\mathcal{I}} \mid (d',d) \in R^{\mathcal{I}}\}$
$C \times D$	$C^{\mathcal{I}} \times D^{\mathcal{I}}$
$(R_1,..,R_n)$	$R_1^{\mathcal{I}} \circ .. \circ R_n^{\mathcal{I}}$

Table 3. Syntax/Semantics for Role Constructors

Axiom	Semantics
Terminological Axioms	
$Q \doteq R$	$Q^{\mathcal{I}} = R^{\mathcal{I}}$
$Q \sqsubseteq R$	$Q^{\mathcal{I}} \subseteq R^{\mathcal{I}}$
Assertional Axioms	
$a \, R \, b$	$(a^{\mathcal{I}}, b^{\mathcal{I}}) \in R^{\mathcal{I}}$

Table 4. Axioms for Role Constructors

REIF	$\doteq$	∀BINARY-REL.ROLES ⊓ ∀DOMAIN.THINGS ⊓
		∀RANGE.THINGS ⊓ ∀HYPO-REL.HYPO
BINARY-REL ⊑ ROLES	DOMAIN ⊑ ROLES	RANGE ⊑ ROLES HYPO-REL ⊑ ROLES

Table 5. General Data Structure for Reification

$\Re(a : C)$	r : REIF ⊓ r BINARY-REL INST-OF ⊓ r DOMAIN a ⊓
	r RANGE C ⊓ r HYPO-REL h
$\Re(a\ R\ b)$	r : REIF ⊓ r BINARY-REL R ⊓ r DOMAIN a ⊓
	r RANGE b ⊓ r HYPO-REL h

Table 6. Reification Function $\Re$

Reification in Terminological Logics. We have chosen a particular "data structure", itself expressed in terminological logics to make the reification format explicit (see Table 5). It provides the common ground for expressing qualitative assertions about the plausibility or credibility of various alternatives (see the translation rule schema below). ROLES is the concept for all roles including the relations INST-OF and ISA, THINGS is the (meta)concept for all concepts and instances and HYPO is the concept denoting all hypothesis spaces. The symbol REIF denotes the concept for all *reificators*, i.e., the anchoring terms introduced by the reification, and BINARY-REL, DOMAIN, RANGE and HYPO-REL denote its associated roles. With these conventions, we are able to define the bijective reification function $\Re$: **Axiom** → **Rex**, where **Axiom** is the set of assertional axioms and **Rex** is the corresponding set of reified expressions (see Table 6)[1]. Hence, $\Re(axiom_h) = r.expr$, where $axiom_h \in$ **Axiom** is known to be true in hypothesis space h and $r.expr$ is its corresponding reified expression. Note that the reificator r can be determined by the function π (e.g., $\pi(\Re(a\ R\ b)) = r$).

Multiple Contexts and Terminological Logics. Our use of contexts and translation rules for the mediation between different contexts builds on the work by [15] and [1]. Applying their formal results to a terminological reasoning framework, a valid notion of mutual, truth-preserving translatability between different reasoning contexts can be defined. A detailed description of the application of the formalism to the translation between multiple contexts is given by [20]. For brevity, we here just state a single second-order translation rule schema indicating that one context (the *initial* context) is completely translatable to another one (the *meta*context); $ist(\kappa, \phi)$ denotes a predicate which is **true** whenever formula ϕ is true in context κ:

$$\forall R : R \in \text{ROLES} \rightarrow (\forall c, d\ \exists p, q : ist(initial,\ c\ R\ d) \leftrightarrow$$
$$ist(meta,\ \pi(\Re(c\ R\ d)) = p \sqcap p\ \text{QUALIFIED}\ q))$$

In our application, the *initial context* contains the original terminological knowledge base and the text knowledge base reflecting the knowledge acquired from the underlying text by the text parser. Knowledge in the initial context is represented without any explicit qualifications, attachments, provisos, etc. The *metacontext*, on the other hand, consists of the reified knowledge of the initial context. In addition, qualifications can be expressed by instantiating the special role QUALIFIED with respect to some reificator (for a definition, cf. Table 7).

---

[1] We here restrict ourselves to the reification of assertional axioms. The remaining constructors can be reified in a straightforward way (cf. also [20]).

QUALIFIED $\doteq$ REIF × QUALITY-LABEL	QUALITY-LABEL $\sqsubseteq$ THINGS

Table 7. Role and Concept Definitions for Qualifications

In a similar way, we may construct a translation scheme according to which the metacontext is (re)translatable to the initial context (cf. [20]). This scheme incorporates the quality of hypotheses, which must exceed a specific threshold (for details of this selection process, cf. Section 5.3, Table 14).

3 Quality Labels

The set of quality labels we here discuss is taken from our natural language text understanding and concept learning application (though any other application seems equally reasonable, but possibly requires its own set of application-specific quality labels). We distinguish two different sources of evidences, *viz.* linguistic and conceptual ones. *Linguistic* quality labels are based on the observation that syntactic constructions differ in their potential to limit the range of conceptual interpretations for an unknown lexical item. For example, an apposition like "the operating system OS/2" doubtlessly determines the superclass of "OS/2" (here considered as the unknown item) to be "operating system", while case frame assignments for the main verb as in "OS/2 is supplied by IBM" are guided by less selective sortal constraints and, in the example, at best allow to infer "OS/2" to be one of the products of IBM (e.g., a computer or a piece of software). From a quality point of view, appositions are a strong source of evidence, while case frame assignments are a much weaker one for constraining the meaning of an unknown item by structural linguistic clues. We may then stipulate that concept hypotheses derived from appositions are more reliable than those derived from case frame assignments only, independent of the conceptual properties they are associated with otherwise. Note that depending on the type of syntactic construction encountered and the conceptual constraints associated with the lexical items involved, alternative hypotheses can often be formed. In any case, the reasons for their emergence (here, their syntactic construction type as defined in Table 8) are encoded (after reification) in the corresponding QUALIFIED role by means of *syntactic* qualification rules (cf. [6] for a more detailed discussion), i.e., they relate the reificator to a qualifying instance of a particular syntactic quality label (cf. also Tables 10 and 11 for an illustration).

APPOSITION	$\sqsubseteq$	QUALITY-LABEL
CASE-FRAME	$\sqsubseteq$	QUALITY-LABEL

Table 8. Linguistic Quality Labels

Similarly, the emerging conceptual representations of the content of the text and associated hypotheses in the text knowledge base can be evaluated in terms of qualifying statements. We here introduce five types of quality labels that can be derived from *conceptual* qualification rules (for more details, cf. [5]):
i: The *very positive* quality label M-DEDUCTION is generated whenever the same role filler has been multiply derived in different hypothesis spaces.

ii: The conceptual proximity of role fillers of a (non-ACTION) concept, which share a common concept class, leads to the *positive* quality label SUPPORT.

iii: The inherent symmetry (cross support) between two instances mutually related via two quasi-inverse relations (figuring as "inverted" role fillers of each other) is expressed by the *positive* quality label C-SUPPORT.

iv: The negative assessment for any attempt to fill the same mandatory case role of an ACTION concept more than once by different role fillers is expressed by the *negative* quality label ADD-ROLE-FILLER.

v: The *very negative* quality label INCONSISTENT-HYPO is generated for contradictory assertions in the same hypothesis space.

These conceptual quality labels are formally defined in Table 9 (note that their deduction is already grounded in the availability of certain role fillers of qualifying roles and, hence, allow for a "richer" definition than the linguistic ones):

M-DEDUCTION	$\doteq$	QUALITY-LABEL $\sqcap$ $\forall$M-DEDUCED-BY.REIF
SUPPORT	$\doteq$	QUALITY-LABEL $\sqcap$ $\forall$SUPPORTED-BY.REIF
C-SUPPORT	$\doteq$	QUALITY-LABEL $\sqcap$ $\forall$C-SUPPORTED-BY.REIF
ADD-ROLE-FILLER	$\doteq$	QUALITY-LABEL $\sqcap$ $\forall$ADD-FILLED-BY.REIF
INCONSISTENT-HYPO	$\doteq$	QUALITY-LABEL $\sqcap$ $\forall$INCONSISTENT-WITH.REIF
M-DEDUCED-BY	$\sqsubseteq$	M-DEDUCTION $\times$ REIF
SUPPORTED-BY	$\sqsubseteq$	SUPPORT $\times$ REIF
C-SUPPORTED-BY	$\sqsubseteq$	C-SUPPORT $\times$ REIF
ADD-FILLED-BY	$\sqsubseteq$	ADD-ROLE-FILLER $\times$ REIF
INCONSISTENT-WITH	$\sqsubseteq$	INCONSISTENT-HYPO $\times$ REIF

Table 9. Conceptual Quality Labels

As with syntactic qualifications, a conceptual qualification relates a reificator via the role QUALIFIED to a *qualifying instance*. Unlike syntactic qualifications, however, the qualifying instance itself is related via a special qualifying role (e.g., M-DEDUCED-BY) to another reificator. Such *qualifying assertions* are the raw data for the computation of conceptual quality labels for the qualifying instances by the classifier (e.g., M-DEDUCTION). An example of these principles is supplied in the next section (cf. Tables 10 and 11).

4 A Scenario for Quality-Based Reasoning

Consider the phrase "IBM sells OS/2" where "OS/2" is the unknown lexical item (in Table 10 "OS/2" is indicated by x). As the parser [16] operates incrementally, the analysis of the first part of this phrase ("IBM sells") leads to the creation of an instance of a SELL action (viz. *sell*-01), its AGENT role being filled by *IBM* in the hypothesis space $hypo_0$ (cf. phase 1 in Table 10).

The subsequent syntactic analysis of the remainder of the sentence and the associated operations of the hypothesis generation rules (cf. phase 2 in Table 10; see also [5] and [6] for a detailed treatment) lead to two readings, *viz.* x being the PATIENT filler of *sell*-01 in one alternative, and x being the (second) AGENT filler of the *sell*-01 action in the other. These ambiguities are represented by two hypothesis spaces — $hypo_1$, a specialization of $hypo_0$, holds the conceptual

Result of the reification mechanism after reading the first two words:	Phase
$r_0 = \pi(\Re(sell\text{-}01 : \text{SELL}))$ $r_5 = \pi(\Re(sell\text{-}01 \ \text{AGENT} \ IBM))$ r_0 HYPO-REL $hypo_0$ r_5 HYPO-REL $hypo_0$	1

Result of the reification mechanism after reading the entire sentence:		Phase
in $hypo_1$:	in $hypo_2$:	
$r_1 = \pi(\Re(x : \text{PRODUCT}))$	$r_6 = \pi(\Re(x : \text{PRODUCER}))$	
$r_2 = \pi(\Re(x : \text{OBJECT}))$	$r_7 = \pi(\Re(x : \text{OBJECT}))$	
$r_3 = \pi(\Re(x : \text{TOP}))$	$r_8 = \pi(\Re(x : \text{TOP}))$	
$r_4 = \pi(\Re(sell\text{-}01 \ \text{PATIENT} \ x))$	$r_9 = \pi(\Re(sell\text{-}01 \ \text{AGENT} \ x))$	
r_0 HYPO-REL $hypo_1$	r_0 HYPO-REL $hypo_2$	2
r_5 HYPO-REL $hypo_1$	r_5 HYPO-REL $hypo_2$	
r_1 HYPO-REL $hypo_1$	r_6 HYPO-REL $hypo_2$	
r_2 HYPO-REL $hypo_1$	r_7 HYPO-REL $hypo_2$	
r_3 HYPO-REL $hypo_1$	r_8 HYPO-REL $hypo_2$	
r_4 HYPO-REL $hypo_1$	r_9 HYPO-REL $hypo_2$	

Translation rules yield:		Phase
r_0 QUALIFIED q_0	q_0 : QUALITY-LABEL	
r_5 QUALIFIED q_5	q_5 : QUALITY-LABEL	
r_1 QUALIFIED q_1	r_6 QUALIFIED q_6	
q_1 : QUALITY-LABEL	q_6 : QUALITY-LABEL	
r_2 QUALIFIED q_2	r_7 QUALIFIED q_7	
q_2 : QUALITY-LABEL	q_7 : QUALITY-LABEL	3
r_3 QUALIFIED q_3	r_8 QUALIFIED q_8	
q_3 : QUALITY-LABEL	q_8 : QUALITY-LABEL	
r_4 QUALIFIED q_4	r_9 QUALIFIED q_9	
q_4 : QUALITY-LABEL	q_9 : QUALITY-LABEL	

Table 10. A Sample Qualification Process

representation of the PATIENT reading, whereas $hypo_2$, an alternative specialization of $hypo_0$, holds that of the AGENT reading. We suppose that the fillers of the AGENT and PATIENT roles of the concept SELL are restricted to PRODUCER and PRODUCT, respectively, and that PRODUCER as well as PRODUCT are each subconcepts of OBJECT and TOP. The operation of the translation rules which map these hypotheses from the initial context to the metacontext leads to the augmentation by (still formal) qualification statements as depicted by phase 3 in Table 10 (left column refers to $hypo_1$, while the right one stands for $hypo_2$;

Conceptual and syntactic qualification rules generate:		Phase
	q_5 ADD-FILLED-BY r_9	
q_2 M-DEDUCED-BY r_7	q_7 M-DEDUCED-BY r_2	
q_3 M-DEDUCED-BY r_8	q_8 M-DEDUCED-BY r_3	4
q_4 : CASE-FRAME	q_9 : CASE-FRAME	
	q_9 ADD-FILLED-BY r_5	

Classifier deduces:		Phase
	q_5 : ADD-ROLE-FILLER	
q_2 : M-DEDUCTION	q_7 : M-DEDUCTION	5
q_3 : M-DEDUCTION	q_8 : M-DEDUCTION	
	q_9 : ADD-ROLE-FILLER	

Table 11. A Sample Qualification Process (cont.)

entries above the separating line hold for both hypothesis spaces). On these data, syntactic as well as conceptual qualification rules operate and yield the quality refinement recorded by phase 4 in Table 11. In short, both hypothesis spaces contain multiple deductions of (x : OBJECT) and (x : TOP) leading to the M-DEDUCED-BY qualifications for q_2, q_3 and q_7, q_8, respectively, both are derived from case frame assignments (q_4, q_9), while only in $hypo_2$ the same AGENT role is filled twice, hence the ADD-FILLED-BY qualification for q_5 and q_9. The conceptual qualification labels derived by the classifier on the basis of these role fillers are given by phase 5 in Table 11. We will discuss the evaluation and the selection of hypothesis spaces in the subsequent section.

5 The Qualification Calculus

Based on the theoretical framework of terminological logics, in this section we turn to the formalization of the qualification calculus. In Section 5.1 we determine all qualifying instances for a single hypothesis space, on the basis of which all qualifying assertions, and, consequently, corresponding quality labels can be computed (Section 5.2). These quality labels are evaluated for each hypothesis space (Section 5.3) in terms of a quality threshold. The evaluation is triggered by each update of any of the hypothesis spaces. For those hypothesis spaces that continously pass these criteria a final ranking in terms of credibility (Section 5.4) is determined at the end of the text understanding process.

5.1 Formalization of qualifying instances for hypothesis spaces

Each reificator r is related to exactly one qualifying instance q. In order to compute all qualifying instances for one hypothesis space we employ the classifier and introduce in Table 12 a new role called HYPO-QUALIFIED, the terminological composition (cf. Table 3) of the inverse of the role HYPO-REL and the role QUALIFIED (for definitions cf. Tables 5 and 7).

HYPO-QUALIFIED	$\doteq$	(HYPO-REL^{-1}, QUALIFIED) $\sqcap$ HYPO $\times$ QUALITY-LABEL

Table 12. Qualifying Instances of a Hypothesis Space

Considering the example from Tables 10 (phases 2 and 3) and 11 (phase 4), in the hypothesis space $hypo_1$ the classifier deduces the fillers $q_0, q_1, q_2, q_3, q_4, q_5$ for the role HYPO-QUALIFIED, while in $hypo_2$ the fillers $q_0, q_5, q_6, q_7, q_8, q_9$ are deduced. For ease of reference, Fig. 1 contains a graphical representation of the conceptual relations involved.

5.2 Formalization of qualifying assertions for hypothesis spaces

Each qualifying instance q carries all qualifying assertions for a corresponding reificator r. With these qualifying assertions the classifier is able to deduce the corresponding quality labels for that reificator. Therefore, we introduce in Table 13 complex roles as compositions of the role HYPO-QUALIFIED and roles indicating various special types of conceptual qualifications that may occur. With these

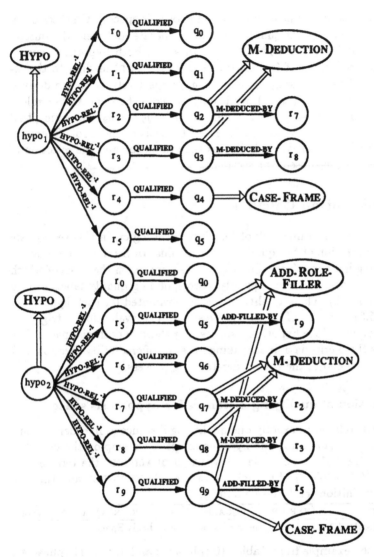

Fig. 1. Concept Graph Representation of the Underlying Qualification Relations

definitions the classifier relates each hypothesis space to qualifying assertions via their corresponding reificators.

Considering our example in Table 11 (phase 4), in the hypothesis space $hypo_1$ the classifier deduces r_7 and r_8 both to be fillers of the role H-M-DEDUCED-BY. Similarly, for $hypo_2$, r_2 and r_3 are fillers of the same role and, additionally, r_5 and r_9 are fillers of the role H-ADD-FILLED-BY. Given the definitions in Table 13, the classifier then deduces the quality label M-DEDUCTION twice in $hypo_1$ (for q_2 and q_3) and in $hypo_2$ (for q_7 and q_8), while only the latter hypothesis space also receives the quality label ADD-ROLE-FILLER twice (for q_5 and q_9, cf. Table 11, phase 5).

H-M-DEDUCED-BY	$\doteq$	(HYPO-QUALIFIED , M-DEDUCED-BY) $\sqcap$ HYPO $\times$ REIF
H-SUPPORTED-BY	$\doteq$	(HYPO-QUALIFIED , SUPPORTED-BY) $\sqcap$ HYPO $\times$ REIF
H-C-SUPPORTED-BY	$\doteq$	(HYPO-QUALIFIED , C-SUPPORTED-BY) $\sqcap$ HYPO $\times$ REIF
H-ADD-FILLED-BY	$\doteq$	(HYPO-QUALIFIED , ADD-FILLED-BY) $\sqcap$ HYPO $\times$ REIF
H-INCONSISTENT-WITH	$\doteq$	(HYPO-QUALIFIED , INCONSISTENT-WITH) $\sqcap$ HYPO $\times$ REIF

Table 13. Qualifying Assertions of a Hypothesis Space

5.3 Formalization of the ranked threshold criterion

The selection among hypothesis spaces is based on a ranked threshold criterion (defined in Table 14), which has evolved in a series of validation experiments. The first threshold level (denoted by THRESHOLD1) rejects inconsistent hypothesis spaces. Additionally, at least one APPOSITION label or the maximum number of verb interpretations (qualified as CASE-FRAME) is required. At the second level (denoted by THRESHOLD2), among the remaining hypothesis spaces, the one(s) with the least number of ADD-ROLE-FILLER labels is (are) chosen.

THRESHOLD1	$\doteq$	HYPO $\sqcap$ $\neg\exists$ H-INCONSISTENT-WITH.REIF $\sqcap$ ($\exists$ HYPO-QUALIFIED.APPOSITION $\sqcup$ MAX$_{\text{HYPO}}$|HYPO-QUALIFIED|$_{\text{CASE-FRAME}}$)
THRESHOLD2	$\doteq$	THRESHOLD1 $\sqcap$ MIN$_{\text{THRESHOLD1}}$|H-ADD-FILLED-BY

Table 14. Threshold Levels

Given this definition, we also need to define a new concept constructor intended to compute the minimal/maximal number of fillers of composed roles. First, we will define the concept constructor MAX[2] in Table 15, by which we may compute the instances with the maximal number of paths of a given composed role to its fillers. The constructor MIN is defined in a similar way.

Syntax	Semantics
$\text{MAX}(R_1,..,R_n)$	$\{d \in \Delta^{\mathcal{I}} \mid \forall e \in \Delta^{\mathcal{I}} : \mathbf{CRFC}((R_1,..,R_n)(d)) \geq \mathbf{CRFC}((R_1,..,R_n)(e))\}$
$\text{MIN}(R_1,..,R_n)$	$\{d \in \Delta^{\mathcal{I}} \mid \forall e \in \Delta^{\mathcal{I}} : \mathbf{CRFC}((R_1,..,R_n)(d)) \leq \mathbf{CRFC}((R_1,..,R_n)(e))\}$

Table 15. Concept Constructors MAX and MIN

$\mathbf{CRFC}(R(d))$ is a function (called *Composed Role Filler Count*) that counts all paths of the composed role R for a given instance d to the fillers of R:

$$\mathbf{CRFC}((R_1,\ldots,R_i)(d)) := \begin{cases} \|R_i(d)\| & \text{if } i=1 \\ \mathbf{CRFC}((R_1,\ldots,R_{i-1})(d)) + \sum_{e \in (R_1,\ldots,R_{i-1})(d)} (\|R_i(e)\| - 1) & \text{if } i > 1 \end{cases}$$

---

[2] To compute the numbers of role fillers properly, the so-called multiple path problem must be acounted for, which is related to the correct computation of cardinalities for different roles that share the same role fillers.

Considering Tables 10 and 11, the hypothesis space $hypo_1$ fulfills both threshold criteria as defined in Table 14, whereas $hypo_2$ only fulfills the first criterion. Both, $hypo_1$ and $hypo_2$, pass the first condition for the concept THRESHOLD1 as they are not related to a reificator via the role H-INCONSISTENT-WITH. Both hypothesis spaces also contain no APPOSITION label, while they share the maximum of qualifying instances which belong to the concept CASE-FRAME. This reasoning pattern is repeated below in more technical terms (cf. also Fig. 1 which depicts a graphical representation of the underlying qualification relations):

$$hypo_1 \in (\text{HYPO})^{\mathcal{I}} \qquad hypo_2 \in (\text{HYPO})^{\mathcal{I}}$$
$$(hypo_1, r_4) \in (\text{HYPO-REL}^{-1})^{\mathcal{I}} \qquad (hypo_2, r_9) \in (\text{HYPO-REL}^{-1})^{\mathcal{I}}$$
$$(r_4, q_4) \in (\text{QUALIFIED})^{\mathcal{I}} \qquad (r_9, q_9) \in (\text{QUALIFIED})^{\mathcal{I}}$$
$$(hypo_1, q_4) \in (\text{HYPO-QUALIFIED})^{\mathcal{I}} \quad (hypo_2, q_9) \in (\text{HYPO-QUALIFIED})^{\mathcal{I}}$$
$$hypo_1 \in (\neg\exists \text{ H-INCONSISTENT-WITH}.\text{REIF})^{\mathcal{I}}$$
$$hypo_2 \in (\neg\exists \text{ H-INCONSISTENT-WITH}.\text{REIF})^{\mathcal{I}}$$
$$hypo_1 \in (\text{MAX}(\text{HYPO}|\text{HYPO-QUALIFIED}|_{\text{CASE-FRAME}}))^{\mathcal{I}}$$
$$hypo_2 \in (\text{MAX}(\text{HYPO}|\text{HYPO-QUALIFIED}|_{\text{CASE-FRAME}}))^{\mathcal{I}}$$

The domain restriction HYPO of the role $\text{HYPO}|\text{HYPO-QUALIFIED}|_{\text{CASE-FRAME}}$ (cf. Table 3) turns out to be crucial for quality-based reasoning. Without any domain restriction the comparison of the composed roles, which starts with the instance d and all instances e, would be evaluated without constraining e to a specific concept type. In the general case, this leads to illegal results.

We may now continue our reasoning example with the evaluation of the MAX operator for $hypo_1$ (with respect to $hypo_2$ the same result is achieved for the selection of $e \in \{r_0, r_5, r_6, r_7, r_8, r_9\}$):

$$\text{CRFC}\left(\text{HYPO}|(\text{HYPO-REL}^{-1}, \text{QUALIFIED})|_{\text{CASE-FRAME}}(hypo_1)\right) =$$
$$\text{CRFC}\left(\text{HYPO}|(\text{HYPO-REL}^{-1})(hypo_1)\right) +$$
$$\sum_{e \in \{r_0, r_1, r_2, r_3, r_4, r_5\}} (\|\text{QUALIFIED}|_{\text{CASE-FRAME}}(e)\| - 1) =$$
$$\|\text{HYPO}|\text{HYPO-REL}^{-1}(hypo_1)\| - 5 =$$
$$6 - 5 = 1$$

The condition of THRESHOLD2, however, requiring the minimal number of qualifying instances which belong to the concept ADD-FILLED-BY under the domain restriction THRESHOLD1, is only satisfied by $hypo_1$. This can be shown by evaluating the MIN operator for the last two statements; the first one with respect to $hypo_1$:

$$\text{CRFC}\left(\text{THRESHOLD1}|(\text{HYPO-REL}^{-1}, \text{QUALIFIED}, \text{ADD-FILLED-BY})(hypo_1)\right) =$$
$$\text{CRFC}\left(\text{THRESHOLD1}|(\text{HYPO-REL}^{-1}, \text{QUALIFIED})(hypo_1)\right) +$$
$$\sum_{e \in \{q_0, q_1, q_2, q_3, q_4, q_5\}} (\|\text{ADD-FILLED-BY}(e)\| - 1) =$$
$$\text{CRFC}\left(\text{THRESHOLD1}|(\text{HYPO-REL}^{-1})(hypo_1)\right) +$$
$$\sum_{e \in \{r_0, r_1, r_2, r_3, r_4, r_5\}} (\|\text{QUALIFIED}(e)\| - 1) + (-6) =$$
$$\|\text{THRESHOLD1}|\text{HYPO-REL}^{-1}(hypo_1)\| + 0 - 6 =$$
$$6 - 6 = 0$$

and the second one for $hypo_2$, respectively:

$$\textbf{CRFC}\left({}_{\text{THRESHOLD1}}|(\text{HYPO-REL}^{-1},\text{QUALIFIED},\text{ADD-FILLED-BY})(hypo_2)\right) =$$

$$\textbf{CRFC}\left({}_{\text{THRESHOLD1}}|(\text{HYPO-REL}^{-1},\text{QUALIFIED})(hypo_2)\right) +$$

$$\sum_{e\in\{q_0,q_5,q_6,q_7,q_8,q_9\}}(\|\text{ADD-FILLED-BY}(e)\|-1) \qquad\qquad =$$

$$\textbf{CRFC}\left({}_{\text{THRESHOLD1}}|(\text{HYPO-REL}^{-1})(hypo_2)\right) +$$

$$\sum_{e\in\{r_0,r_5,r_6,r_7,r_8,r_9\}}(\|\text{QUALIFIED}(e)\|-1)+(-4) \qquad\qquad =$$

$$\|_{\text{THRESHOLD1}}|\text{HYPO-REL}^{-1}(hypo_2)\|+0-4 \qquad\qquad =$$

$$6-4 \qquad\qquad\qquad\qquad\qquad\qquad\qquad = \quad 2$$

5.4 Formalization of the ranked credibility criterion

Those hypothesis spaces that have repeatedly fulfilled the most restrictive threshold criterion in several evaluation cycles will be classified relative to three different credibility levels at the end of the analysis. At the first level of credibility all hypothesis spaces are selected with the maximum number of fillers of the composed role H-M-DEDUCED-BY. At the second level, among the remaining ones, if any, those are selected with the maximum number of fillers with respect to the role H-SUPPORTED-BY. Finally, at the third level of credibility, if any, those are selected among the remaining ones with the maximum number of fillers of the role H-C-SUPPORTED-BY. This ranking formally reflects the "goodness" of the quality labels already discussed in the description of Table 9.

The credibility ranking is reflected in the specialization hierarchy for different credibility concepts as defined in Table 16. CREDIBILITY1 is a specialization of THRESHOLD2, CREDIBILITY2 is a specialization of CREDIBILITY1, while CREDIBILITY3 specializes CREDIBILITY2. The classifier only tests the condition of a more specialized credibility concept, if the condition of the more general concept is fulfilled. The definitions of the credibility concepts are expressed using the terminological constructor MAX and the corresponding composed roles. Again, the domain restriction for the composed roles is crucial to restrict the domain instances of the composed role to the desired concept type.

CREDIBILITY1	$\doteq$	THRESHOLD2 $\sqcap$ MAX$_{\text{THRESHOLD2}}$	H-M-DEDUCED-BY
CREDIBILITY2	$\doteq$	CREDIBILITY1 $\sqcap$ MAX$_{\text{CREDIBILITY1}}$	H-SUPPORTED-BY
CREDIBILITY3	$\doteq$	CREDIBILITY2 $\sqcap$ MAX$_{\text{CREDIBILITY2}}$	H-C-SUPPORTED-BY

Table 16. Credibility Levels

In the example from above, the only remaining hypothesis space $hypo_1$ that belongs to concept THRESHOLD2 fulfills all credibility levels, because the maximum for $_{\text{THRESHOLD2}}$|H-M-DEDUCED-BY equals 2, and $hypo_1$ fulfills this condition. Hence, the classifier deduces that $hypo_1$ belongs to the concept CREDIBILITY1. Similarly, the classifier determines the membership of $hypo_1$ to the concepts CREDIBILITY2 and CREDIBILITY3, the maximum of each of these for (cross) support relations being 0.

6 Related Work

Any qualitative model of uncertain reasoning rivals with the quantitative mainstream. In numerical approaches (for a survey, cf. [21]), uncertainty is represented as a quantitative value (number or interval). Quantitative extensions of terminological logics (probabilistic ones [8, 11] and possibilistic ones [10]) follow the same methodological premises. The meaning of these values, however, is usually not evident at all and inference procedures manipulating them often lack perspicuity and evidence. Also, quantitative approaches neither account for the reasons which lead to a particular selection from a set of alternatives nor are they able to explicitly represent qualitative relations among propositions. These arguments have already led to qualitative reformulations of probabilistic logics (cf., e.g., [17]). In our approach, it is vital to use contradictory propositions and reasons for contradictions in order to initialize learning processes (such as versioning, constructive generalization; cf. [12]) and to select among alternative hypothesis spaces. Qualitative reasoning proceeds from several independent dimensions, e.g., incorporating linguistic or conceptual indicators, and arrives at a composite credibility judgment by combining the aggregated evidences from these different dimensions. Numerical approaches, however, tend to collapse these different dimensions by a direct mapping onto a single quantitative scale.

Our approach bears a closer relationship to the work of Cohen [2, 3], who aims at heuristic reasoning *about* uncertainty. The *endorsement theory* he proposes is based on the representation of explicit reasons for and against propositions (beliefs, disbeliefs). Similarly, we use quality labels to represent the positive or negative support with respect to a reificator (a reified proposition). Unlike the endorsement model, the quality labels are strictly formalized; furthermore, provisions are made to reason about several alternatives simultaneously.

Fox and Krause [4, 13] propose a decision-theoretic approach which is grounded in classical first-order logic and extended by *argumentations* in order to reason for and against decision options from generalized domain theories. In contrast to their use of classical FOL, we use more restrictive terminological logics. Among the advantages of the latter approach are the provision of an automatic classifier, which computes the necessary selections, and the extensibility in terms of the proposed meta-architecture. Within this framework, we are able to represent the reasons for and against propositions (using hypothesis spaces) in order to integrate reasoning and metareasoning in a common formal setting.

In the natural language understanding domain the selection from alternatives is usually referred to as a disambiguation task. In this sense, our approach to qualitative, preferential metareasoning bears some similarity with Hobbs *et al.*'s [9] abductive FOL-based reasoning approach, but we avoid the crucial problem of explicitly assigning particular (numerical) costs to single inference steps. As far as terminological reasoning models are concerned, our metareasoning scheme also constitutes an alternative to the preference ordering on defaults (also founded on a quantitative penalty model) as proposed by [18]. We diverge from any of these models insofar as we avoid taking refuge to quantitative criteria when qualitative considerations still seem computationally feasible.

7 Conclusion

We have introduced a qualitative, preference-based model for reasoning about uncertainty which is fully embedded in a terminological reasoning framework. Considering uncertain reasoning as a choice problem between different hypotheses, the model we provide assigns quality labels (indicating significance, reliability, strength) to single evidences for/against a hypothesis, combines the generated labels in terms of the overall credibility of a single hypothesis, and, finally, computes a preference order for the entire set of competing hypotheses.

The model has been developed and tested within a natural language application. This is clearly reflected by linguistic quality labels, while conceptual quality labels are less dependent on a particular application. The potential of the qualification calculus for more general applicability seems obvious, however. Given, for instance, the framework of a consultation, a robot or a vision system, linguistic quality labels have to be replaced, e.g., by quality labels for the credibility of human experts or the recognition accuracy of sensory devices.

The reasoning system, which is fully implemented in LOOM [14], is part of a large-scale text understanding and knowledge acquisition system [5, 6]. We are currently running experiments to extend and validate the collection of quality labels, formulate empirically plausible orderings among them, and thus try to formulate a coherent paradigm of qualitative reasoning under uncertainty.

Acknowledgments. This work was partially supported by a grant from DFG (Ha 2097/2-1). We like to thank the members of our group for fruitful discussions and the reviewers for helpful comments. We also gratefully acknowledge the provision of the LOOM system from USC/ISI.

References

1. S. Buvač, V. Buvač, and I. Mason. Metamathematics of contexts. *Fundamenta Informaticae*, 23(3), 1995.
2. P. Cohen. *Heuristic Reasoning about Uncertainty: An Artificial Intelligence Approach.* Los Altos/CA: Morgan Kaufmann, 1985.
3. P. Cohen. The control of reasoning under uncertainty: a discussion of some programs. In G. Shafer and J. Pearl, editors, *Readings in Uncertain Reasoning,* pages 177–197. San Mateo/CA: Morgan Kaufmann, 1990.
4. J. Fox and P. Krause. Symbolic decision theory and autonomous systems. In B. D'Ambrosio, P. Smets, and P. Bonissone, editors, *UAI'91 — Proc. 7th Conf. on Uncertainty in Artificial Intelligence*, pages 103–110. San Mateo/CA: Morgan Kaufmann, 1991.
5. U. Hahn, M. Klenner, and K. Schnattinger. Learning from texts - a terminological metareasoning perspective. In S. Wermter, E. Riloff, and G. Scheler, editors, *Connectionist, Statistical and Symbolic Approaches to Learning for Natural Language Processing*, pages 453–468. Berlin: Springer, 1996.
6. U. Hahn, M. Klenner, and K. Schnattinger. A quality-based terminological reasoning model for text knowledge acquisition. In N. Shadbolt, K. O'Hara, and G. Schreiber, editors, *EKAW'96 — Proc. 9th European Knowledge Acquisition Workshop*, pages 131–146. Berlin: Springer, 1996.

7. U. Hahn, S. Schacht, and N. Bröker.   Concurrent, object-oriented dependency parsing: the PARSETALK model. *International Journal of Human-Computer Studies*, 41(1-2):179–222, 1994.

8. B. Heinsohn.   Probabilistic description logics.   In R. Lopez de Mantaras and D. Poole, editors, *UAI'94 — Proc. 10th Conf. on Uncertainty in Artificial Intelligence*, pages 311–318. San Mateo/CA: Morgan Kaufmann, 1994.

9. J. Hobbs, M. Stickel, D. Appelt, and P. Martin. Interpretation as abduction. *Artificial Intelligence*, 63(1-2):69–142, 1993.

10. B. Hollunder. An alternative proof method for possibilistic logic and its application to terminological logics. In R. Lopez de Mantaras and D. Poole, editors, *UAI'94 — Proc. 10th Conf. on Uncertainty in Artificial Intelligence*, pages 327–335. San Mateo/CA: Morgan Kaufmann, 1994.

11. M. Jaeger. Probabilistic reasoning in terminological logics. In J. Doyle, E. Sandewall, and P. Torasso, editors, *KR'94 — Proc. 4th International Conf. on Principles of Knowledge Representation and Reasoning*, pages 305–316. San Mateo/CA: Morgan Kaufmann, 1994.

12. M. Klenner and U. Hahn. Concept versioning: a methodology for tracking evolutionary concept drift in dynamic concept systems. In A. Cohn, editor, *ECAI'94 — Proc. 11th European Conf. on Artificial Intelligence*, pages 473–477. Chichester: J. Wiley, 1994.

13. P. Krause, S. Ambler, M. Elvang-Goransson, and J. Fox. A logic of argumentation for reasoning under uncertainty. *Computational Intelligence*, 11:113–131, 1995.

14. R. MacGregor. A description classifier for the predicate calculus. In *AAAI'94 — Proc. 12th National Conf. on Artificial Intelligence. Vol. 1*, pages 213–220. Menlo Park: AAAI Press / M.I.T. Press, 1994.

15. J. McCarthy. Notes on formalizing context. In *IJCAI'93 — Proc. 13th International Joint Conf. on Artificial Intelligence. Vol. 1*, pages 555–560. San Mateo/CA: Morgan Kaufmann, 1993.

16. P. Neuhaus and U. Hahn. Trading off completeness for efficiency: the PARSETALK performance grammar approach to real-world text parsing. In *FLAIRS'96 — Proc. 9th Florida Artificial Intelligence Research Symposium*, pages 60–65. Florida AI Research Society, 1996.

17. D. Pacholczyk. Qualitative reasoning under uncertainty. In C. Pinto-Ferreira and N. Mamede, editors, *Progress in Artificial Intelligence. EPIA'95 — Proc. 7th Portuguese Conf. on Artificial Intelligence*, pages 297–309. Berlin: Springer, 1995.

18. J. Quantz. Interpretation as exception minimization. In *IJCAI'93 — Proc. 13th International Joint Conf. on Artificial Intelligence. Vol. 2*, pages 1310–1315. San Mateo/CA: Morgan Kaufmann, 1993.

19. K. Schnattinger, U. Hahn, and M. Klenner. Quality-based terminological reasoning for concept learning. In I. Wachsmuth, C.-R. Rollinger, and W. Brauer, editors, *Advances in Artificial Intelligence. KI'95 — Proc. 19th Annual German Conf. on Artificial Intelligence*, pages 113–124. Berlin: Springer, 1995.

20. K. Schnattinger, U. Hahn, and M. Klenner. Terminological meta-reasoning by reification and multiple contexts. In C. Pinto-Ferreira and N. Mamede, editors, *Progress in Artificial Intelligence. EPIA'95 — Proc. 7th Portuguese Conf. on Artificial Intelligence*, pages 1–16. Berlin: Springer, 1995.

21. G. Shafer and J. Pearl, editors. *Readings in Uncertain Reasoning*. San Mateo/CA: Morgan Kaufmann, 1990.

22. W. Woods and J. Schmolze. The KL-ONE family. *Computers & Mathematics with Applications*, 23(2-5):133–177, 1992.

Syntactic Disambiguation by Using Categorial Parsing in a DOOD Framework

Werner Winiwarter, Osami Kagawa, Yahiko Kambayashi

Department of Information Science, Kyoto University,
Sakyo, Kyoto 606-01, Japan

Abstract. We present a natural language interface for Japanese that relies on semantically driven parsing in that it applies syntactic analysis only if necessary for disambiguation. For this purpose we utilize a categorial parser which also analyzes incomplete or ungrammatical input efficiently. The complete linguistic analysis is performed by means of deductive object-oriented database (DOOD) technology so that we achieve an integrated framework with the target application. The interface has been applied successfully to the question support facilities of the VIENA Classroom hypermedia teaching system.

1 Introduction

In spite of the large amount of work on natural language interfaces, they are today still far away from widespread practical use (for a good recent survey see [1]). The reason for this are the many still existing limitations which are caused by two main factors: missing customization, resulting in unexpected restrictions, and missing integration, responsible for insufficient performance and wrong interpretation [10]. As concerns the former we stress the importance of empirically collecting the training and test data so that the system can be based on realistic input data to cover all relevant linguistic constructs. With regard to missing integration we adapt the Integrated Deductive Approach [15] by designing the natural language interface as component of a deductive object-oriented database system. Hereby we achieve a complete integration of the linguistic analysis with the target application which guarantees the consistent mapping of the user input to the corresponding semantic representation.

Another important reason why many previous attempts to build successful natural language interfaces failed is the fact that their characteristics in contrast to other applications of natural language processing were neglected: specific application domains with well-defined semantics, rather small delimited vocabularies, mappings to simple target representations, short input sentences without complex linguistic phenomena but including misspellings, ungrammatical or incomplete statements. There has been a remarkable recent change of attitude in research on natural language processing and computational linguistics away from the "toy problem syndrome" to building real-world end-user applications [6]. By following this argumentation, we developed a natural language interface for Japanese which has been applied successfully to the question support facilities of the VIENA Classroom system. VIENA Classroom is a distance education system in which the teaching material is prepared as hypermedia documents and presented to the students within a CSCW environment. The computed semantic representations are used for the retrieval of corresponding answers from a FAQ knowledge base or the collection of semantically equivalent new questions [16].

This paper focuses on the syntactic analysis in our interface which is only applied if necessary for disambiguation. For this purpose we utilize a robust categorial parser which also analyzes incomplete or ungrammatical input efficiently (see also [2, 9]). The rest of this paper is organized as follows. First, we provide a brief overview of the interface architecture before we deal in detail with the developed categorial grammar formalism. Finally, we give an insight into the parsing algorithm and its implementation as well as into the applied methods for syntactic disambiguation.

2 Interface Architecture

The interface architecture shown in Fig. 1 consists of three main modules: morphological and lexical analysis, unknown value list (UVL) analysis and spelling error correction as well as semantic, syntactic and pragmatic analysis.

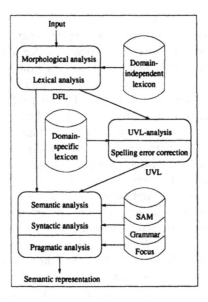

Fig. 1. Interface architecture

Morphological and lexical analysis operate directly on the Japanese questions which are entered by utilizing standard Japanese editor functionality, i.e. the students type the pronunciation of words after which the most probable choices for Kanji characters are presented for selection. Since Japanese script uses no spaces to separate individual words, tokenization is here no longer a trivial task.

By accessing a domain-independent lexicon, the input is transformed into a deep form list (DFL) which indicates for each token the surface form, category, subcategory and semantic deep form. For the creation of the domain-independent lexicon we adapt the lexical approach in that we store only canonical forms and assign to them all syntactic and semantic features. We also support a hierarchical structure of the lexicon by making use of the inheritance mechanisms of object-oriented database technology.

The second module includes UVL-analysis and spelling error correction. The former deals with domain-specific terms that are part of the input. By separating the analysis of domain-independent and domain-specific terminology, we guarantee an easy portation of the interface to other application domains. This also forms the basis for an efficient application of spelling error correction which is restricted to domain-specific terms because they are much more susceptible to the occurrence of spelling errors and also possess particular importance for the sentence meaning (for a more detailed description see [17]).

Semantic, syntactic and pragmatic analysis generate the semantic representation of the sentence by accessing the semantic application model (SAM). The latter provides activation rules for the selection of the correct semantic category on the basis of the DFL and UVL. If a semantic category is activated, the domain-specific terms of the UVL are used as arguments to fill the corresponding parameters of a semantic template resulting in the semantic representation. Syntactic analysis is only applied if it is necessary for disambiguation (see Sect. 5). Finally, pragmatic analysis deals with incomplete input by keeping track of the actual focus of the user session.

As implementation platform for the interface we use the deductive object-oriented database system ROCK & ROLL [4] which was developed at Heriot-Watt University. It solves the problem of updates in deductive databases by neatly separating the declarative logic query language ROLL from the imperative data manipulation language ROCK within the context of a common object-oriented data model. Another characteristic of ROCK & ROLL is that the data definition language makes a clean distinction between:

1. *type declarations:* describe the structural characteristics of a set of instance objects and the methods that can be applied to them,
2. *class definitions:* specify how the methods associated with a type are implemented.

3 Grammar

The categorial grammar formalism has a long history that reaches back to the early work of Bar-Hillel in the 1960s [3]. There exist many variations in notation and methodology such as Combinatory Categorial Grammar [12], Categorial Unification Grammar [14] or Lambek Categorial Grammar [8]. For recent extensions to the categorial grammar formalism see [5, 7].

The main common difference to other grammar formalisms is that all grammar rules are assigned to so-called *categories* which can be divided in:

1. *basic categories:* associated with the entries in the lexicon,
2. *complex categories:* derived through the application of grammar rules.

The original categorial theory consisted of only two combinatory rules for the formation of complex categories (the rules read as: if category A/B $(A\backslash B)$ is directly followed (preceded) by B, it can be transformed into A):

1. *forward functional application:*

$$A/B \ B \rightarrow A \ , \tag{1}$$

2. *backward functional application:*

$$B \ A\backslash B \rightarrow A \ . \tag{2}$$

One main shortcoming of the original notation of categorial grammar is that with a single application of a grammar rule only two adjacent categories can be applied to the derivation of a new category. To eliminate this deficiency we introduce several powerful extensions to the categorial grammar formalism which are not specifically designed for the particular use with Japanese input but in view of applications to a broad class of languages. As first basic step we change the notation for the two functional applications:

1. if category C is directly followed by B, then it can be transformed into A:

$$C: \ A \leftarrow /B \ , \tag{3}$$

2. if category C is directly preceded by B, then it can be transformed into A:

$$C: \ A \leftarrow \backslash B \ . \tag{4}$$

With this it is possible to permit the use of more than one category at the right side of the rule so that several functional applications can be applied in one step, e.g.:

$$C: \ D \leftarrow \backslash A \ \backslash B \ . \tag{5}$$

The right side of the rule can also be left empty which provides an easy way of specifying type raising [13]. Besides direct succession "/" and direct precedence "\" we provide the following additional *sequence conditions* to cover cases of free word order and long distance dependencies efficiently (see also [11]):

1. no condition on sequence of C and B:

$$C: \ A \leftarrow B \ , \tag{6}$$

2. indirect precedence, i.e. B must precede C but there can be several categories shifted between them:

$$C: \ A \leftarrow >B \ , \tag{7}$$

3. indirect succession:

$$C: \ A \leftarrow <B \ . \tag{8}$$

```
type application:                                  object type for single functional application
    properties:                                    attributes
        public:                                    visibility
            applied_category: category,            applied category
            sequence: string,                      sequence condition: "/", "\", " ", ">" or "<"
            occurrence: string;                    occurrence condition: "r" (required),
            ...                                        "o" (optional) or "*"
end-type

type applicationlist:                              list of functional applications
    public [application];
    ...
end-type

type rule:                                         grammar rule
    properties:
        public:
            derived_category: category,            new derived category
            rightside: applicationlist,            right side of grammar rule
            priority: int;                         priority of application of grammar rule
            ...
end-type

type ruleset:                                      set of grammar rules
    public {rule};
    ...
end-type

type category:                                     category
    properties:
        public:
            symbol: string,                        category symbol
            associated_rules: ruleset,             associated set of grammar rules
            complex_category: bool;                true if complex category, otherwise false
            ...
end-type

type mapping:                                      mapping rule for basic category
    properties:
        public:
            map_cat: string,                       category of token
            map_subcat: string,                    sub-category of token
            map_deepform: string;                  deep form of token
            ...
end-type

type mappingset:                                   set of mapping rules
    public {mapping};
    ...
end-type

type basic_category:                               basic category
    specialises: category;                         sub-type of category
    properties:
        public:
            associated_tokens: mappingset;         mapping rules for associated tokens
            ...
end-type
```

Fig. 2. ROCK & ROLL object type declarations for categorial grammar

Finally, we introduce the following *occurrence conditions* in addition to the default interpretation of a category as required in order to deal with optional and recursive constructs:

1. optional occurrence of category B:

$$C: \ A \leftarrow (B) \ , \tag{9}$$

2. occurrence of zero or more repetitions of category B:

$$C: \ A \leftarrow B^* \ . \tag{10}$$

This grammar formalism is mapped to the internal representation in ROCK & ROLL as shown in Fig. 2. The priority values are used to optimize the performance of the parser (see Sect. 4). For the correct mapping of the tokens contained in the DFL to the basic categories of the grammar we define *mapping rules* based on the category, sub-category, and deep form features of the individual tokens.

Basic categories with mapping rules for tokens in DFL:

basic category	category	sub-category	deep form
MOD	particle	modifier	
N	noun		
N	unknown		
OBJ	particle	object	
PER	punctuation	period	
PRO	pronoun		
QUE	particle	question	
SV	verb		do
TOP	particle	topic	
V	verb		

Complex categories:

DO	direct object	SAV	sahen verb
MP	modifying phrase	SUB	subject
NP	noun phrase	VP	verb phrase
Q	question		

Grammar rules:

category	grammar rule	priority
MOD:	MP $\leftarrow$ \NP	13
N:	NP $\leftarrow$ \MP*	11
OBJ:	DO $\leftarrow$ \NP	9
PRO:	NP $\leftarrow$	19
QUE:	Q $\leftarrow$ \VP (>SUB) (/PER)	3
SAV:	VP $\leftarrow$ (\DO)	5
SV:	SAV $\leftarrow$ \N	17
SV:	V $\leftarrow$	15
TOP:	SUB $\leftarrow$ \NP	7

Fig. 3. Example grammar

Figure 3 gives a small Japanese example grammar which we use throughout this paper. The dominance of the direct precedence sequence condition as well as the important role of particles as post-positional syntactic function words are characteristics of Japanese language. *Sahen verbs* are derived from nouns by adding the irregular verb *suru* (to do). As example for the internal representation, the instance objects for the question particle are displayed in Fig. 4.

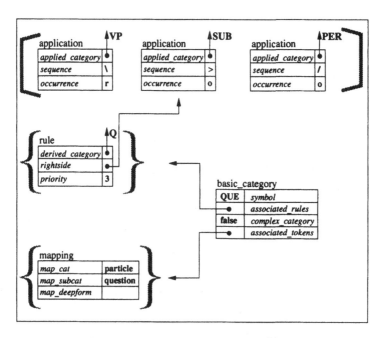

Fig. 4. Example of internal representation

4 Parser

The central object type for the parsing process is the *constituent* which is defined according to Fig. 5. As initializing step all tokens in the DFL are assigned to a linear list of constituents by associating them with the corresponding basic categories according to the mapping rules (see Fig. 6 for an example). If more than one basic category applies (e.g. V and SV in our example), the more specific one is selected. At the begin and at the end of the list an auxiliary start and end constituent is inserted as well as all references to child constituents are initialized with a nil constituent.

The actual parsing algorithm follows a bottom-up strategy. It avoids spurious ambiguity [18] by making use of the priority values assigned to each rule. Therefore, the deliberate choice of these priority values is of crucial importance to the efficiency of the parser. As basic heuristics the priority values decrease from the

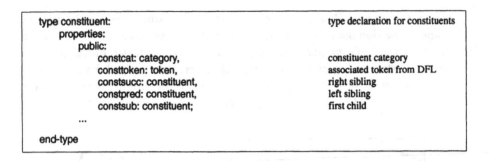

Fig. 5. ROCK & ROLL type declaration for constituents

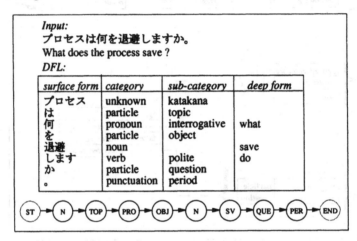

Fig. 6. Example of assignment of tokens to constituents

word to the sentence level and favor more complex constructs or exceptions (e.g. sahen verbs). The parsing algorithm consists of the following basic steps:

repeat

> *retrieve the set of candidate grammar rules associated with the current list of constituents;*
>
> **while** *set of grammar rules not empty and no successful derivation* **do**
>> *check applicability of rule with maximum priority value;*
>> **if** *applicable*
>>> **then** *derive new category and perform transformation of parsing tree*
>>> **else** *remove rule from set of candidates;*

until *no more successful derivation of new category.*

Figure 7 shows the object type declaration of *candidate*, which is used to store the set of candidate grammar rules, and the associated ROCK method for checking the applicability of a candidate rule.

```
type candidate:                                     type declaration for candidate rules
    properties:
        public:
            candconst: constituent,                 candidate constituent
            candrule: rule;                         candidate rule
        ROCK:                                       ROCK methods
            ...,
            applicable(cst: constituent, cend: constituent,   method for checking applicability of
                cnil: constituent): bool;           candidate rule and performing
end-type                                            transformation of parsing tree

class E.candidate                                   persistent class definition
    public:
        ...
    applicable(cst: constituent, cend: constituent,
            cnil: constituent): bool
    begin
        var appl: bool;                             applicability flag
        var cc: constituent;                        candidate constituent
        var cr: rule;                               candidate rule
        var rs: applicationlist;                    right side of candidate rule
        var newcat: category;                       derived category from candidate rule
        var clist: [constituent];                   list of new child constituents
        var c: constituent;                         current constituent
        var seq: string;                            sequence condition
        var occ: string;                            occurrence condition
        var applcat: category;                      applied category
        var continue: bool;                         control flag for repetitive applications
        var ccat: category;                         current category

        appl := true;                               initialize applicability flag
        cc := get_candconst@self;                   retrieve candidate constituent cc
        cr := get_candrule@self;                    retrieve candidate rule
        rs := get_rightside@cr;                     retrieve right side of candidate rule
        newcat := get_derived_category@cr;          retrieve derived category
        clist := [];                                initialize list of new child constituents
        c := cc;                                    assign cc to current constituent c
        foreach x in rs do                          for each application in right side do
        begin
            seq := get_sequence@x;                  retrieve sequence condition
            occ := get_occurrence@x;                retrieve occurrence condition
            applcat := get_applied_category@x;      retrieve applied category
            continue := true;                       initialize control flag
            if (seq = "\") then                     if sequence condition equals "\", then
                while (c <> cst) and (continue) do  while not arrived at start constituent
                begin                               and control flag is set
                    continue := false;              reset control flag
                    c := get_constpred@c;           retrieve left sibling of c
                    ccat := get_constcat@c;         retrieve current category ccat
                    if (ccat = applcat) then        if ccat equals applied category, then
                    begin
                        clist ++ c;                 insert c into clist
                        if (occ = "*") then         if occurrence condition equals "*", then
                            continue := true;       set control flag for repetition
                    end
                    else                            else ( ccat differs from applcat )
                        if (occ = "r") then         if occurrence condition equals "r", then
                            appl := false;          reset applicability flag
                end
            ...
        end
        if (appl) then                              if rule is applicable, then
            ...                                     (transformation of parsing tree)
        appl                                        return applicability flag
    end
end-class
```

Fig. 7. ROCK & ROLL code segment for test of applicability of grammar rule

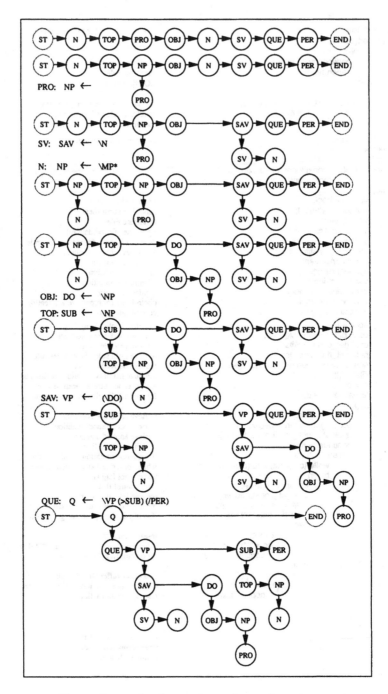

Fig. 8. Example of transformations of parsing tree

The transformation of the parsing tree is performed by the following steps:

1. create new constituent C_D for the derived category,
2. add candidate constituent C_C as first child to C_D,
3. remove all entries C in the list of new child constituents C_{CH} from parsing tree,
4. replace C_C by C_D in parsing tree,
5. add all $C \in C_{CH}$ as right siblings to C_C.

Figure 8 shows a detailed example of the transformations of the parsing tree during the syntactic analysis of the example sentence from Fig. 6.

5 Syntactic Disambiguation

In our architecture syntactic analysis is applied to disambiguating sentences which are semantically so closely related that the difference cannot be decided only on the basis of semantic information (see Fig. 9 for an example).

プロセスは何を退避しますか。
[what, save, X]
What does the process save ?

```
[(q, c, [
    (que, b, か),
    (vp, c, [
        (sav, c, [
            (sv, b, します),
            (n, b, 退避)
        ]),
        (do, c, [
            (obj, b, を),
            (np, c, [
                (pro, b, 何)
            ])
        ])
    ]),
    (sub, c, [
        (top, b, は),
        (np, c, [
            (n, b, プロセス)
        ])
    ]),
    (per, b, 。)
])]
```

何のプロセスを退避しますか。
[what_kind, X, save]
What kind of process do you save ?

```
[(q, c, [
    (que, b, か),
    (vp, c, [
        (sav, c, [
            (sv, b, します),
            (n, b, 退避)
        ]),
        (do, c, [
            (obj, b, を),
            (np, c, [
                (n, b, プロセス),
                (mp, c, [
                    (mod, b, の),
                    (np, c, [
                        (pro, b, 何)
                    ])
                ])
            ])
        ])
    ]),
    (per, b, 。)
])]
```

Fig. 9. Example of two ambiguous sentences

Now, syntactic disambiguation rules are used to distinguish between the two cases. As especially useful operator we defined *syntactic dominance* as follows (in contrast to the corresponding tree-theoretic concept). X *dominates* Y if the following conditions on the associated constituents C_X and C_Y are satisfied:

1. $C_X = C_Y$ or
2. C_R is the set of right siblings of C_X and $C_Y \in C_R$ or
3. C_Y is a descendent of C_X or
4. C_Y is a descendent of any $C, C \in C_R$.

For the example in Fig. 9 the rule X *dominates what.df* and its negation is applied, X signifies the domain-specific term "process" and *what.df* the value "what" for the deep form feature. Figure 10 gives the corresponding ROLL method, its invocation is formulated here as: *dominates("what", "df")@C_X*.

```
class E.constituent
    public:
        ...
        agree(string, string)                          method for test of agreement
        begin
            agree(S, "df") :- Cat == get_constcat@Self,     retrieve constituent category
                          get_complex_category@Cat == false,    fails if category is complex
                          Token == get_consttoken@Self,    retrieve associated token
                          get_tdeepform@Token == S;        test if deep form of token unifies with S
        ...
        end
        dominates(string, string)                      method for testing syntactic dominance
        begin
            dominates(S, T) :- agree(S, T)@Self;            test of agreement
            dominates(S, T) :- Succ == get_constsucc@Self,   retrieve right sibling
                          Cat == get_constcat@Succ,     retrieve constituent category
                          get_symbol@Cat =\= "nil",     fails if no right sibling
                          dominates(S, T)@Succ;         recursive call of method
            dominates(S, T) :- Sub == get_constsub@Self,    retrieve first child of constituent
                          Cat == get_constcat@Sub,      retrieve constituent category
                          get_symbol@Cat =\= "nil",     fails if no child
                          dominates(S, T)@Sub;          recursive call of method
        end
end-class
```

Fig. 10. ROCK & ROLL code segment for syntactic disambiguation

6 Conclusion

For quite some time AI approaches to syntactic analysis were dominated by the investigation of artificial, small-scale "toy problems". The understandable frustration in developers of real-world systems resulted often in the complete rejection of syntactic analysis, leading the way to oversimplified brute-force approaches. We think that we found a reasonable "compromise" in that we apply syntactic analysis only there where it is really necessary for disambiguation. By applying to this concept a powerful categorial grammar formalism, we developed an efficient parser within a deductive object-oriented framework.

A first successful test of the feasibility of this approach is the use of our interface architecture as component of the VIENA Classroom system. Future work will concentrate on a detailed evaluation study of the coverage and performance of the parser in practical use. In particular we want to analyze the consequences of the proposed extensions to the categorial formalism as well as the degree of generality of the syntactic disambiguation rules.

References

1. Androutsopoulos, I., Ritchie, G.D., Thanisch, P.: Natural Language Interfaces to Databases – an Introduction. Journal of Natural Language Eng. (1994)
2. Ballim, A., Russell, G.: LHIP: Extended DCGs for Configurable Robust Parsing. Proc. of the Intl. Conf. on Computational Linguistics (1994)
3. Bar-Hillel, Y.: On Categorial and Phrase Structure Grammars. Bar-Hillel, Y. (ed): Language and Information. Addison-Wesley, Reading (1964)
4. Barja, M.L. et al.: An Effective Deductive Object-Oriented Database Through Language Integration. Proc. of the Intl. Conf. on Very Large Data Bases (1994)
5. Bouma, G., Noord, G.: Constraint-Based Categorial Grammar. Proc. of the Annual Meeting of the ACL (1994)
6. Cunningham, H., Gaizauskas, R.J., Wilks, Y.: A General Architecture for Language Engineering (GATE). Techn. Rep. CS-95-21, University of Sheffield (1996)
7. Hoffman, B.: The Formal Consequences of Using Variables in CCG Categories. Proc. of the Annual Meeting of the ACL (1993)
8. Lambek, J.: The Mathematics of Sentence Structure. Buszkowski, W., Marciszewski, W., Benthem, J. (eds): Categorial Grammar. John Benjamins, Amsterdam (1988)
9. Lavie, A.: An Integrated Heuristic Scheme for Partial Parse Evaluation. Proc. of the Annual Meeting of the ACL (1994)
10. McFetridge, P., Groeneboer, C.: Novel Terms and Coordination in a Natural Language Interface. Rhamani, S., Chandrasekar, R., Anjaneyulu, K.S.R. (eds): Knowledge Based Computer Systems. Springer, Berlin (1990)
11. Morrill, G., Solias, T.: Tuples, Discontinuity, and Gapping in Categorial Grammar. Proc. of the Conf. of the European Chapter of the ACL (1993)
12. Steedman, M.: Dependency and Coordination in the Grammar of Dutch and English. Language, Vol. 61 (1985)
13. Steedman, M.: Type-Raising & Directionality in Combinatory Grammar. Proc. of the Annual Meeting of the ACL (1991)
14. Uszkoreit, H.: Categorial Unification Grammars. Proc. of the Intl. Conf. on Computational Linguistics (1986)
15. Winiwarter, W.: The Integrated Deductive Approach to Natural Language Interfaces. Diss., University of Vienna (1994)
16. Winiwarter, W. et al.: Collaborative Hypermedia Education with the VIENA Classroom System. Proc. of the Australasian Conf. on Computer Science Education (to appear)
17. Winiwarter, W., Kagawa, O., Kambayashi, Y.: Multimodal Natural Language Interfaces for Hypermedia Distance Education – the VIENA Classroom System. Proc. of the Intl. Congress on Terminology and Knowledge Eng. (to appear)
18. Wittenburg, K.: Natural Language Parsing with Combinatory Categorial Grammar in a Graph-Unification Based Formalism. Diss., University of Texas (1986)

Constructive Disjunction Revisited

Jörg Würtz[1] and Tobias Müller[2]

[1] German Research Center for Artificial Intelligence (DFKI), Stuhlsatzenhausweg 3,
D-66123 Saarbrücken, Germany, Email: wuertz@dfki.uni-sb.de
[2] Universität des Saarlandes, Stuhlsatzenhausweg 3, D-66123 Saarbrücken, Germany,
Email: tmueller@dfki.uni-sb.de

Abstract. Finite Domain Programming is a technique for solving combinatorial problems like planning, scheduling, configuration or timetabling. Inevitably, these problems employ disjunctive constraints. A rather new approach to model those constraints is constructive disjunction, whereby common information is lifted from the alternatives, aiming for stronger pruning of the search space. We show where constructive disjunction provides for stronger pruning and where it fails to do so. For several problems, including a real-world college timetabling application, benefits and limitations of constructive disjunction are exemplified. As an experimental platform we use the concurrent constraint language Oz.

1 Introduction

Constraint Logic Programming over finite domains, i.e., finite sets of natural numbers, has shown up to be able to handle real-life problems like planning, scheduling, configuration or timetabling (e.g. [5, 17, 7]). Constraints allow to prune the search space a priori. A constraint problem is solved by interleaving pruning by constraints and speculative assignment (choices).

Inevitably in most real-world applications are disjunctive constraints. Hence, it is natural that disjunctive constraints play a crucial role in artificial intelligence fields like planning, configuration, knowledge representation or expert systems. For example in timetabling there is the constraint that two lectures must not overlap in time while in computer hardware configuration we may have the constraint that two cards must not overlap in space.

Disjunctive constraints can be dealt with in several ways. They may be modelled as choice-points where constraints become active only after choosing one alternative [5] or by reasoning about the truth value of alternatives, without making choices, i.e., checking whether a clause of the disjunction is true or false (the so-called reified approach). A rather new approach is called constructive disjunction, which lifts common information from the alternatives. As an example consider the disjunction $A + 7 \leq B \lor B + 7 \leq A$ with $A, B \in \{1, \ldots, 10\}$. Its meaning might be that the task A with duration 7 must precede task B or, alternatively, that task B with duration 7 must precede task A, i.e., A and B must not overlap in time. In the left alternative, A can only take the value 1, 2 or 3, and B the value 8, 9 or 10, and vice versa for the right alternative. The reified approach only checks if an alternative becomes inconsistent, in which case the other alternative is installed. Hence, no further pruning arises in our example. But one can do better. We can derive that neither A nor B will take the value $4, 5, 6$ or 7. This information is lifted by constructive disjunction resulting in (possibly dramatic) pruning of the search space.

While there exist several papers on constructive disjunction [3, 8, 9, 17], there is not much published experience about the usefulness of constructive disjunction for practical applications. But this experience is crucial for considering constructive disjunction worthwile for one's own applications. The given examples in the literature are sometimes incorrect or misleading in that the problems could be better solved by other approaches or do not scale up expectedly. Some readers might feel this view this to be too negative, but to state cases where constructive disjunction does not pay off can prevent developers from getting stuck or to waste a lot of efforts. This is especially important for new techniques.

By comparing the different concepts of modelling disjunctive constraints in Section 3 we extract useful applications for constructive disjunction but state also cases (like scheduling) where more advanced constraint techniques are known which beat it by orders of magnitude. There are also occasions where constructive disjunction can be useful in principle (e.g. packing problems) but where examples in literature are better tackled by reified constraints. Experiences in [8] and our work on college timetabling [7] supports our thesis that constructive disjunction is a powerful and flexible means to improve search (speedup of an order of magnitude) in cases, where the problem is rather complex and one needs to find new heuristics for guiding the search.

As an experimental platform we use Oz [15, 16], which allows to evaluate the different concepts of modelling disjunctive constraints in a single system. Oz is a new language providing for concurrency and object-oriented programming, which makes it well-suited for applications in AI. But what makes Oz unique is its expressiveness and flexibility for problem-solving. By means of a user-accessible search combinator, search strategies can be individually programmed and problem-solving can be guided by inventing and exploring various heuristics. Moreover, a rich set of constraints allows to prune the search space in an efficient way.

2 Computation in Oz

2.1 Computation Model

The central notion in Oz is a computation space [14]. A computation space consists essentially of a constraint store and a set of associated tasks.

Constraints residing in the constraint store are equations between variables and/or values, as for instance atoms or integers, and constraints $x \in D$ where D is a finite domain, i.e., a finite set of nonnegative integers. Oz provides efficient algorithms to decide satisfiability and implication for the constraints in the constraint store.

Tasks inspect the constraint store and are reduced if the store contains sufficient information. On reduction a task may impose further constraints on the store or spawn new tasks. The computation space a task is spawned in is called its host space. A typical task is a disjunction like

```
or X::3#6 X::4#10
[] Y::1000#1050
end
```

which spawns local computation spaces, e.g. the local store of the first clause holds the constraint $X \in \{3,\ldots,6\} \cap \{4,\ldots,10\}$ (juxtaposition is read as conjunction and, e.g., $X::3\#6$ denotes the constraint $X \in \{3,\ldots,6\}$). If the store of the host space implies for example $Y \in \{0,\ldots,10\}$, the second clause fails and, thus, the constraint $X \in \{4,\ldots,6\}$ will be added to the host space. If one alternative is implied, e.g. $Y = 1020$ holds, the disjunctive task simply ceases to exist.

2.2 Propagators

For more expressive constraints, like $x + y = z$, deciding their satisfiability is not computationally tractable. Such constraints are not contained in the constraint store but are modelled by so-called propagators.

A propagator P can be thought of as a long-lived task which amplifies the constraint store S. The propagator can tell the store a constraint C whenever the conjunction $S \wedge P$ implies the constraint C. A propagator must remain in a computation space until it is implied by the constraint store. For instance, assume a store containing $X, Y, Z \in \{1,\ldots,10\}$. The propagator $X+Y<:Z$ amplifies the store to $X, Y \in \{1,\ldots,8\}$ and $Z \in \{3,\ldots,10\}$ (since the other values cannot satisfy the constraint).[3] Telling the constraint $Z=5$ causes the propagator to strengthen the store to $X, Y \in \{1,\ldots,3\}$. Imposing $X=3$ makes the propagator telling $Y=1$.

2.3 Disjunctive Constraints

In this section we discuss several ways to express disjunctive constraints in Oz for the example $|X - 1| = Y$ with $X \in \{1,\ldots,5\}$ and $Y \in \{0,1,5\}$. The constraint is equivalent to the disjunction $X - 1 = Y \vee 1 - X = Y$ and the Oz expressions $X::1\#5$ $Y::0|1|5|nil$.

Disjunctive Tasks. The example can be formulated as

```
or X - 1 =: Y
[] 1 - X =: Y
end
```

---

[3] An appended colon marks a finite domain propagator.

Since the global information on variables is visible in the local stores, the propagator in the first clause amplifies the first local store to X ∈ {1, 2} and Y ∈ {0, 1}. The store of the second clause contains the constraints X=1 and Y=0. Imposing the constraint X=2 makes the second clause fail. Thus, the remaining local computation space is lifted. The added propagator X-1=:Y imposes now the constraint Y=1.

Choice-Points. Oz provides also for disjunctive tasks, which can be used as choice-points (the keyword **or** is replaced by **dis**). The choice is delayed until no other computation (like constraint propagation) can take place, i.e., the computation space is stable (for details see [13]). The **dis**-task additionally prunes the search space by adopting the operational semantics of the **or**-task (distinguishing it from the choice-points as in CHIP [5]).

Reified Constraints. Reified constraints are propagators that reflect the validity of a constraint into a {0, 1}-valued variable. Because reified constraints avoid local computation spaces, they can be implemented more efficiently than disjunctive tasks.

Assume we want to reify a propagator P in a variable B (in Oz we write B=(P)). If B is constrained to 1 (resp. 0), then P (resp. its negation $\neg P$) is installed. Vice versa, if P is valid (resp. unsatisfiable), B is bound to 1 (resp. 0). Our example becomes:

```
R1 = (X - 1 =: Y)
R2 = (1 - X =: Y)
R1 + R2 >: 0
```

Since no propagator nor its negation is implied, the store is not changed. Telling the constraint X=2 is inconsistent with the propagator 1-X=:Y, which causes R2 to be constrained to 0. The inequality R1+R2>:0 amplifies the store by R1=1 which in turn causes the propagator X-1=:Y to be installed. This propagator tells immediately the constraint Y=1.

While constructive disjunction strengthens the pruning power of constraints, reified constraints add more expressivity to a system (like soft constraints or preferences in cost functions of branch & bound optimization). The cardinality combinator of [6], which states that the number of true constraints of a given set must be in a given interval of integers, can be modelled with reified constraints straightforwardly.

Constructive Disjunction. Assume a computation space containing a store S. A disjunctive combinator with n clauses spawns n local computation spaces, which consist of tasks $T_1, \ldots, T_n$ and constraint stores $S_1, \ldots, S_n$, respectively. For making the disjunction constructive we have to lift common information from the clauses. We merge each store S_i with the store S and call S'_i the resulting store after computation has terminated. Let L be the smallest set of constraints such that all S'_i imply L. We now lift L by adding it to S. For finite domains this means to compute the union of the domains of the occurring variables. In [8, 17] a more general form of constructive disjunction is proposed where also the tasks T_i are merged with the tasks T of the host space. In [3] it was shown that this general approach is very expensive but gains only a little compared to the variant we provide. Our approach is also justified by the performance results obtained in [10]).

Oz syntactically supports constructive disjunction (called CD in the sequel) by the keywords condis and end. The clauses can contain arbitrary finite domain propagators. Picking up our example, we obtain

```
condis X - 1 =: Y
[] 1 - X =: Y
end
```

But in contrast to the previous versions of disjunctions, X and Y are immediately constrained to $X \in \{1,2\}$ and $Y \in \{0,1\}$. This is the result of lifting common information from the clauses, i.e., $X \in \{1,2\}_{first} \cup \{1\}_{second}$ and $Y \in \{0,1\}_{first} \cup \{0\}_{second}$. Telling X=2 fails the second clause and promotes the first clause, which results in telling Y=1.

3 Applications

In this section we point out what kinds of constraints and problem solving techniques benefit from CD. Of course, we cannot examine all possible applications, but the chosen three problems allow to gain important insights for the use of different models for disjunctive constraints.

3.1 General Remarks

Due to its definition, CD prunes the search space only for those variables occurring in all alternatives of the disjunction. It may tighten the bounds of variables like Z in

```
condis X + XDur =<: Z
[] Y + YDur =<: Z
end
```

where X,Y might denote start times of tasks and XDur, YDur their respective durations, i.e., the task Z must be delayed until X and Y are finished.

Assume the distance of X and Y to be 4, i.e., the constraint $| X - Y | = 4$, and the domains $X, Y \in \{1, \ldots, 5\}$. CD leads to $X, Y \in \{1, 5\}$, i.e., holes are cut in the domains. But for the sake of efficiency many constraint languages reason mainly on the bounds of domains (for instance in Oz, we approximate $s=:t$ by $s=<:t$ $s>=:t$). Thus, CD may prune the search space, but other constraints may not profit from the occurring domain reduction. Only those constraints that reason on the whole domain benefit from these holes. As an example consider the constraint that at least one of X and Y must be 3. This constraint fails with the distance-constraint $| X - Y | = 4$, if $X, Y \in \{1, \ldots, 5\}$ holds.

Because constraint propagation is usually incomplete, choices must be made to assign values to variables (called labelling). Labelling strategies, which reason on the size of the domains, like first-fail (choose the variable with the smallest domain first), may benefit from CD's domain pruning: More information on variables is made available.

But in any case, one has to be aware that CD is computationally more expensive than reified constraints (see also the following sections). Hence, if the effects of CD cannot be exploited, it may slow down an application.

3.2 Square Packing

The problem is to pack a given set of squares into a master-rectangle such that all squares are used and no squares overlap [17]. The constraint that two squares at (XA, YA) and (XB, YB) with sizes SA and SB must not overlap (note that the coordinates are finite domains) employs CD:

```
condis XA + SA =<: XB    % X-clause
[]  XB + SB =<: XA       % X-clause
[]  YA + SA =<: YB       % Y-clause
[]  YB + SB =<: YA       % Y-clause
end
```

The X-clauses (resp. Y-clauses) express that squares do not overlap horizontally (resp. vertically). As soon as only the two X- or the two Y-clauses are left (because the others are failed), the domains may be reduced by CD. For example $XA + 8 \leq XB \lor XB + 8 \leq XA$ with $XA, XB \in \{1, \ldots, 10\}$ leads to pruning XA and XB to $\{1, 2, 9, 10\}$. As an additional constraint we have that for each X- (and Y-) coordinate P the sum of the square sizes S_i intersecting this coordinate must be less than the respective length L of the rectangle: $\sum B_i * S_i =<: L$, where $B_i = (X_i :: P - S_i + 1 \# P)$. The occurring holes by CD propagation can only fail the reified constraint, i.e., $B_i = 0$. Thus, CD does not lead to further pruning for this problem.

In [3] disjunctive constraints are modelled by CD and reified constraints. The authors claim that the constructive approach solves the problem with less choice-points for first-fail labelling, i.e., the occurring holes lead the search to a solution earlier. But this result is incorrect[4]; for one reported example both CD and reified constraints lead to the same number of choice-points, while for the other example, the reified approach needs half of the choice-points as needed by the constructive approach. If one uses naive labelling, the number of choice-points is the same for both approaches and examples. For this application, CD is not a good choice.

---

[4] We assume that this is due to a compiler error since replacing the suspicious code with semantical equivalent code allows us to reproduce in Agents [3] the same results as in Oz. For the first example we have rectangle length L=10 and the sizes are [6 4 4 4 2 2 2 2], and for the second we have L=20 and [9 8 8 7 5 4 4 4 4 3 3 3 2 2 1 1] for the sizes.

If one uses a special labelling strategy [17] (since first-fail does not scale up for larger problems), the number of choice-points are the same for all approaches. The following table gives the runtimes taken on a Sparc10 for two examples.

	CD	Reified	or	CD/Rei	CD/or
Expl. 1	780ms	670ms	770ms	1.16	1.01
Expl. 2	2190ms	1640ms	2970ms	1.34	0.74

While CD does not pay off for this application, more complex packing problems may benefit from it (e.g. if a minimum stock must be guaranteed, like $\sum B_i * S_i > : L$; see also 3.4).

3.3 Scheduling

The constraint that two tasks X and Y with durations XDur and YDur, respectively, must not overlap in time if they require the same resource, occurs often in scheduling:

```
condis X + XDur =<: Y
[] Y + YDur =<: X
end
```

As seen above, this constraint may cut holes in domains. In [8, 3], the bridge-problem is used as an example. The problem is to find the optimal schedule for building a bridge with limited resources and some additional time constraints. In [3] choice-points without active pruning, reified constraints and CD are compared for finding the first solution by first-fail labelling. The number of labelling steps grows from CD via choice-points to reified constraints. But this example is misleading because the optimal solution (in which one is interested for this problem) cannot be found after more than 10 million choices also with the CD-approach.

By the choice-point approach the optimal solution can be found, but reordering the choices leads to runtimes which are several magnitudes worse. Hence, this approach is not robust against different formulations of the problem

Therefore, in [8] the choice-points are extended by constraint lifting, according to CD. They obtain the optimal solution and the proof of optimality in 881 backtracking steps selecting the next choice-point by a strategy considering the involved variable domains in the disjunctions (being robust against reordering).

But modeling the disjunctive constraints by CD is too weak to solve really hard scheduling problems. There are constraint techniques inspired from Operations Research, which allow to solve hard scheduling problems [4, 2] (for example the proof of optimality for the notorious MT10 problem (see [11]) needs about 2000 choices in Oz). These techniques exploit domain specific knowledge. While for hard problems techniques like task intervals [4] or cumulative constraints [1] are used, the bridge problem can be solved by a rather naive labelling strategy and reified constraints needing only 176 backtracking steps. We choose the most demanded resource first and schedule it completely. For this resource we find the tasks which can be first on it, choose the one with the smallest possible start time and state constraints that the remaining tasks are scheduled after the chosen one. The disjunctions are modelled by reified constraints while the choices are made by the **dis**-task of Oz, i.e., we combine different ways of modelling disjunctive constraints.[5]

3.4 Real-world Applications

In [8] a more complex aircraft sequencing application is reported, where CD results in a speedup by a factor of 6.

At DFKI we have solved a real-life college timetabling problem [7] with several complex constraints (like a limited number of rooms or that teachers must teach at most three days a week). A frequently occuring constraint is that lectures must not overlap in time. This constraint was already seen above and CD is worthwile to be considered here. Further we need to express that a certain number of lectures may overlap. Therefore non-overlapping is reified in the variable B :

```
condis B=:1  X+XDur>:Y  Y+YDur>:X
[]  B=:0  X+XDur=<:Y
[]  B=:0  Y+YDur=<:X
end
```

If B=0 is known, CD pays off because the disjunction results in a simple non-overlapping constraint. Modelling these disjunctions constructively leads to stronger pruning because there occur reified constraints B=(X::D). Ocurring holes may constrain B to 0. Because the B's essentially occur in equations $\sum B_i =:L$ (like that the lectures of a teacher must be on L days), CD pays off for propagation.

As a labelling strategy we use a modified first-fail to select the variables, which benefits also from the more pruned domains. In comparison to reified constraints, the resulting speedup by using CD is about an order of magnitude (see also [7]). For this example we have a combination of more pruning and benefitting labelling heuristics.

4 Conclusion

We have compared constructive disjunction with other ways to model disjunctive constraints and have shown that constructive disjunction does not pay off for problems like scheduling where domain specific knowledge can be used in a constraint setting. But it is very useful for applications which are rather complex, where a special purpose strategy is unknown but flexibility is required. Here it can prune the search space and, thus, allows for better heuristics by providing more information on the problem variables. For real-world applications one needs also choice-points and reified constraints to evaluate the most efficient modelling of disjunctive constraints.

---

[5] If we model the disjunctions by CD and or-tasks,respectively, we obtain the runtime relations CD/Reified=1.8 and CD/or=0.6.

Remark and Acknowledgements

The research reported in this paper has been supported by the Bundesminister für Bildung, Wissenschaft, Forschung und Technologie (FTZ-ITW-9105), the Esprit Project ACCLAIM (PE 7195) and the Esprit Working Group CCL (EP 6028). We thank Joachim Niehren for valuable comments on this paper and Björn Carlson for making a prototype of Agents available for testing. The documentation of the DFKI Oz system is available from the programming systems lab of DFKI through anonymous ftp from **ps-ftp.dfki.uni-sb.de** or through WWW from **http://ps-www.dfki.uni-sb.de/oz/**.

References

1. A. Aggoun and N. Beldiceanu, 'Extending CHIP in order to solve complex scheduling and placement problems'. Mathl. Comput. Modelling, volume 17, number 7, pp. 57–73, (1993).
2. P. Baptiste and C. Le Pape, 'A theoretical and experimental comparison of constraint propagation techniques for disjunctive scheduling', in *IJCAI*, (1995).
3. B. Carlson and M. Carlsson, 'Compiling and executing disjuctions of finite domain constraints', in *ICLP*, pp. 117–131, (1995).
4. Y. Caseau and F. Laburthe, 'Improved clp scheduling with task intervals', in *ICLP*, (1994).
5. M. Dincbas, P. Van Hentenryck, H. Simonis, A. Aggoun, T. Graf, and F. Berthier, 'The constraint logic programming language CHIP', in *FGCS*, pp. 693–702, (1988).
6. P. Van Hentenryck and Y. Deville, 'The Cardinality Operator: A New Logical Connective for Constraint Logic Programming', in *ICLP*, pp. 745–759, (1991).
7. M. Henz and J. Würtz, 'Using Oz for college time tabling', in *International Conference on the Practice and Theory of Automated Time Tabling*, pp. 283–296, (1995).
8. J. Jourdan and T. Sola, 'The versatility of handling disjunctions as constraints', in *PLILP*, pp. 60–74, (1993).
9. T. le Provost and M. Wallace, 'Generalized constraint propagation over the CLP scheme', *Journal of Logic Programming*, **16**, 319–359, (1993).
10. T. Müller and J. Würtz, 'Constructive Disjunction in Oz', in *11. Workshop Logische Programmierung*, (1995).
11. J.F. Muth and G.L. Thompson, *Industrial Scheduling*, Prentice Hall, 1963.
12. T. Le Provost and M. Wallace, 'Generalized constraint propagation over the CLP scheme', *The Journal of Logic Programming*, **16**(3 & 4), 319–359, (1993).
13. C. Schulte and G. Smolka, 'Encapsulated search in higher-order concurrent constraint programming', in *ILPS*, pp. 505–520, (1994).
14. G. Smolka, 'The definition of Kernel Oz', DFKI Oz documentation series, Deutsches Forschungszentrum für Künstliche Intelligenz GmbH, Stuhlsatzenhausweg 3, D-66123 Saarbrücken, Germany, (1994).
15. G. Smolka, 'The Oz programming model', in *Computer Science Today*, Lecture Notes in Computer Science, vol. 1000, 324–343, Springer-Verlag, (1995).
16. *DFKI Oz Documentation Series*, eds., G. Smolka and R. Treinen, German Research Center for Artificial Intelligence (DFKI), Stuhlsatzenhausweg 3, D-66123 Saarbrücken, Germany, 1995.

17. P. Van Hentenryck, V. Saraswat, and Y. Deville, 'Design, implementation and evaluation of the constraint language cc(FD)', in *Constraints: Basics and Trends*, Lecture Notes in Computer Science, vol. 910, Springer Verlag, (1995).

Author Index

Springer-Verlag
and the Environment

We at Springer-Verlag firmly believe that an international science publisher has a special obligation to the environment, and our corporate policies consistently reflect this conviction.

We also expect our business partners – paper mills, printers, packaging manufacturers, etc. – to commit themselves to using environmentally friendly materials and production processes.

The paper in this book is made from low- or no-chlorine pulp and is acid free, in conformance with international standards for paper permanency.

Lecture Notes in Artificial Intelligence (LNAI)

Lecture Notes in Computer Science